THE SPANISH REPUBLIC
AT WAR 1936–1939

HELEN GRAHAM

CAMBRIDGE
UNIVERSITY PRESS

PUBLISHED BY THE PRESS SYNDICATE OF THE UNIVERSITY OF CAMBRIDGE
The Pitt Building, Trumpington Street, Cambridge, United Kingdom

CAMBRIDGE UNIVERSITY PRESS
The Edinburgh Building, Cambridge CB2 2RU, UK
40 West 20th Street, New York, NY 10011-4211, USA
477 Williamstown Road, Port Melbourne, VIC 3207, Australia
Ruiz de Alarcón 13, 28014 Madrid, Spain
Dock House, The Waterfront, Cape Town 8001, South Africa

http://www.cambridge.org

First published 2002

Printed in the United Kingdom at the University Press, Cambridge

Typeface Baskerville Monotype 11/12.5 pt   *System* LaTeX 2_ε [TB]

A catalogue record for this book is available from the British Library

ISBN 0 521 45314 3 hardback
ISBN 0 521 45932 x paperback

THE SPANISH REPUBLIC AT WAR
1936–1939

'. . . by some distance the best book I have read in any language on the Spanish Republic during the Civil War. The detailed – and thoroughly analytical – narrative of the politics of the Republic outshines anything that has been written before . . . A very major work by a mature historian writing at the height of her powers.'

Professor Paul Preston, London School of Economics and Political Science

This is a new and comprehensive analysis of the forces of the Spanish left – interpreted broadly – during the civil war of 1936–9, and the first of its kind for more than thirty years.

The book argues two crucial propositions. First, that the wartime responses (and limitations) of the Spanish left – republicans, socialists, communists and anarcho-syndicalists – can be understood only in relation to their pre-war experiences, world views, organisational structures and the wider Spanish context of acute uneven development which had moulded their organisations over previous decades. Second, that the overarching influence that shaped the evolution of the Republic between 1936 and 1939 was the war itself: the book explores the complex, cumulative effects of a civil war fought under the brutally destabilising conditions of an international arms embargo.

HELEN GRAHAM is Reader in Spanish History, Royal Holloway, University of London. Her book *Socialism and War: The Spanish Socialist Party in Power and Crisis, 1936–1939* was published by Cambridge University Press in 1991, and she has otherwise published widely on the political, social and cultural history of Spain in the 1930s and 1940s.

For Herbert Rutledge Southworth,
in memoriam 1908–1999

París, julio, tengo frío, mamá, tengo frío. Estaba llorando Rosell por Bonet, por Oviedo, por el frágil esqueleto del pajarillo de la Libertad, por sí mismo, y en la oscuridad crecía una bestia cúbica de mandíbula poderosa y labios despectivos sobre un fondo de marchas militares y gritos de rigor, rugidos invertebrados que expulsaban la música y la palabra.

Paris, July, I'm cold, Mamma, I'm so cold. Rosell was weeping for all of them, for Bonet, for Oviedo, for the fragile frame of the tiny bird that was Freedom, for himself, and out of the darkness there grew a monstrous massive-jawed, sneering beast, against a background of military marches and the obligatory shouting, incoherent roars drowning out music and words.

> Manuel Vázquez Montalbán, *El pianista* (Barcelona: Seix Barral, 1985), pp. 270–1

You who will emerge from the flood
In which we have gone under
Remember
When you speak of our failings
The dark time too
Which you have escaped

> Bertolt Brecht, 'To those born later'

Contents

Plates

Maps

Preface

This book is concerned with the Second Spanish Republic during the civil war of 1936–9 and the reasons for its defeat. Its central arguments can be encapsulated in two crucial propositions. The first is that the wartime responses (and limitations) of the Spanish left – republicans, socialists, communists and anarcho-syndicalists – can only be understood in relation to their pre-war experiences, worldviews, organisational structures and the wider Spanish national context of acute uneven development which had moulded their organisations over previous decades. The second is that the overarching influence that shaped the evolution of the Republic between 1936 and 1939 was *the war itself*.

It is remarkable the extent to which existing analyses have in practice relegated the war to background noise or narrative filler between chunks of political analysis that nevertheless remain largely dissociated from it. But the war had a complex and cumulative impact on every aspect of Republican polity and society. If we are to understand what happened and why, then we have to recreate its texture. More particularly because this was a civil war, and one fought under the devastating conditions of Non-Intervention imposed by Britain and France. This meant virtually total international isolation and a *de facto* economic embargo that placed the Republic – and only the Republic – at an enormous material disadvantage throughout.

Coverage of Non-Intervention to date has concentrated on its international diplomatic aspects and mainly on the first year of the war. But what destroyed the Republic was the long-term impact of Non-Intervention over nearly three gruelling years. It brought the daily erosion not only of the Republic's military capacity, but of its political legitimacy as well. For economic embargo prevented the Republic from sustaining the social and economic fabric of the home front and, in the end, from meeting even the minimal requirements of its population in terms of food and shelter. Vast too was the psychological cost of war under such conditions.

The international political diplomacy that produced and sustained Non-Intervention also repeatedly blocked all the Republic's political exits, making it impossible for it to negotiate an end to the conflict in 1938. In the last agonising months international mediation was still withheld, even though it was the only course that might have reduced the risk of massive violent reprisal against the defeated. In the end the Spanish Republic collapsed inwards under the huge, intolerable pressures born of the war. A war that others had forced the Republic to fight would end by consuming it utterly.

Acknowledgements

This book has been a long time in the making, and the volume of my debts is commensurate with the time scale. Sir Raymond Carr offered unfailing support as an academic referee. Along the way I enjoyed a Leverhulme Research Fellowship, which permitted a sustained period of archival research in Spain. Additional sabbatical leave from Royal Holloway allowed me to extend this further. I am grateful here to the College, but most especially to my departmental colleagues for covering teaching (and innumerable chores) in my absence. Enrique Moradiellos and Susana Botas offered me a warm welcome in Madrid, while Montserrat Delgado Moreno has put a roof over my head there more times than I can remember. In London Penny Green and Bill Spence helped me through the long haul. Historian friends and colleagues – in Britain and Spain, Hispanist and otherwise – offered me intellectual sustenance, leads, information, advice, encouragement and kindness in amazing quantity and variety. So my thanks here to: Michael Alpert, Julio Aróstegui, Richard Baxell, Jerry Blaney, Martin Blinkhorn, Kayvon Boyhan, Hilary Canavan, Jim Carmody, Julián Casanova, Andrew Dowling, Chris Ealham, Sheelagh Ellwood, Tim Fletcher, Jesus Garrido, María Jesus González-Hernández, Liz Harvey, Gerald Howson, Joel Isaac, Angela Jackson, Christoph Jahr, Tim Kirk, John Maher, Ricardo Miralles, Enrique Moradiellos, Rudolf Muhs, Gerard Oram, Pilar Ortuño, Hilari Raguer, Tim Rees, Nick Rider, Francisco Romero, Ismael Saz, Angelo Smith, Sandra Souto, Dan Stone, Angel Viñas and Mary Vincent. Santos Juliá and Borja de Riquer gave me valuable archival orientation and helped track down recalcitrant references. Sir Geoffrey Cox (*News Chronicle* correspondent in Madrid, October–December 1936) provided morale-boosting encouragement. My special thanks are due to Frank Schauff for generously sharing with me extensive material from his research in the Soviet archives. I am also grateful for the assistance of the Cañada Blanch Centre for Contemporary Spanish Studies (LSE), whose library proved an invaluable resource in the final preparation of the typescript. Tony Kushner, Manuel Vázquez Montalbán and Milton Wolff kindly agreed to the use of their words in my epigraphs. David Leach allowed me to include his photograph of the Serra de Pàndols memorial. The Republican poster on the book jacket is from the collection of Jordi Carulla and is reproduced with his kind permission. Bill Davies at Cambridge University Press has shown exemplary patience during the long gestation of this book. Francisco Romero read and commented on numerous draft chapters with his habitual incisiveness. Angela Cenarro has taught me a great deal about the Spanish Civil War, as well as offering much practical assistance. Paul Preston too has always been there to help. My debt to him goes a long way back – for his constant support and quite extraordinary generosity as a scholar over the many years of our friendship. This book is dedicated to Herbert Southworth, miner, librarian, bibliophile and pioneering historian of the Spanish Civil War – for his passionate belief in the transformative power of forensic history and for the monument to it which he has left us in his own work.

A fractured left: the impact of uneven development
(1898–1930)

The Spanish Civil War would begin with a military coup. Although there had been a long history of military intervention in Spanish political life, the coup of 17–18 July 1936 constituted an old instrument being used to a new end. It aimed to halt the process of mass political democracy kick started by the effects of the First World War and the Russian Revolution, and accelerated by the ensuing social, economic and cultural changes of the 1920s and 1930s. In this sense, the military coup against the democratic Second Republic in Spain was intended to have the same function as the fascist take-overs that followed the coming to power of Mussolini and Hitler in Italy and Germany. All these European 'civil wars' (because civil wars can take many forms) had their origins in the cumulative political, social and cultural anxieties provoked by a process of rapid, uneven and accelerating modernisation (that is, industrialisation and urbanisation) occurring across the continent. All those who supported Spain's military rebels in 1936 had in common a fear of where change was leading – whether their fears were of material or psychological loss (wealth, professional status, established social and political hierarchies, religious or sexual (i.e. gendered) certainties) or a mixture of these things.[1]

That the military should function in 1936 as the ultimate guardian of a certain kind of social and political order indicates not only the positive fact of its own (at least relative) ideological cohesion but also the extent of the fragmentation among other social and political groups. The historical protagonism of the Spanish army had its roots in the war-dominated nineteenth century. But its enduring twentieth-century political protagonism was a consequence of the lack of any minimally coherent bourgeois project for national development. The process of modern economic development in Spain occurred late and very unevenly – even judging

---

[1] For the wartime consequences of these fears, see chapter 2 below.

by the standards across Europe as a whole.[2] As a result, Spain's elites were highly regionally fragmented. This was exacerbated by the events of 1898 when Spain lost the remnants of its old overseas empire (principally Cuba and the Philippines). While elite groups and some sectors of Spain's middle classes were united in perceiving this as a political – even an existential – crisis, their responses to 'the disaster' were far from unified.[3] Most importantly, the economic consequences of imperial loss (in particular of protected markets) had galvanised the industrial plutocracy in Catalonia, the most economically and sociologically advanced region of Spain, to launch what would become a powerful middle-class movement for regional autonomy. As a result, the first two decades of the twentieth century saw a bitter and at times violent political struggle between the 'old' political centre in Madrid (representing the powerful landed elites) and the aspiring plutocratic autonomists of industrial Barcelona over the future direction of national economic policy. In essence this was a dispute over who would pay for infrastructural modernisation. Not only were Spain's elites unable to agree here, but in their continuing disagreement they would, by 1918, find themselves facing an actively mobilising labour force.

At the start of the twentieth century, however, Spain was still a rural sea out of which emerged a few urban, industrial 'islands'. These were confined predominantly to two areas. First, as we have seen, there was Catalonia (especially the industrial belt of Barcelona) on the north-east sea board which produced mainly textiles; and second, the north – the Basque Country (Vizcaya) and Asturias – was an area of heavy industry and mining. In a reduced number of other cities too (Madrid, Zaragoza, Valencia, Seville) the development of small industrial sectors was also gradually feeding urbanisation and the emergence of organised labour. Uneven development and the consequent lack of an integrated national

---

[2] J. Nadal, *El fracaso de la revolución industrial en España, 1814–1913* (Barcelona: Ariel, 1975); N. Sánchez Albornoz (ed.), *The Economic Modernisation of Spain 1830–1930* (New York: New York University Press, 1987); G. Tortela, *El desarrollo de la España contemporánea. Historia económica de los siglos XIX y XX* (Madrid: Alianza Universidad, 1994). A revisionist account in Leandro Prados de La Escosura, *De imperio a nación: crecimiento y atraso económico en España 1780–1930* (Madrid: Alianza, 1988). A résumé in A. Shubert, *A Social History of Modern Spain* (London: Unwin Hyman, 1990), pp. 9–56.

[3] S. Balfour, 'The Loss of Empire, Regenerationism and the Forging of a Myth of National Identity', in H. Graham and J. Labanyi (eds.), *Spanish Cultural Studies. An Introduction* (Oxford: Oxford University Press, 1995), pp. 25–31; S. Balfour, *The End of the Spanish Empire 1898–1923* (Oxford: Clarendon Press, 1997), pp. 64–91. The frenetic debate over 'regeneration' derived from anxieties similar to those that were provoking (ultimately social darwinist) discourses of 'degeneration' elsewhere in Europe at that time. Cf. also M. Richards, *A Time of Silence. Civil War and the Culture of Repression in Franco's Spain, 1936–1945* (Cambridge: Cambridge University Press, 1998), pp. 47–66.

market would in turn inhibit other sorts of exchange that might later have mitigated or modified the consolidation of antagonistic social constituencies and cultural perspectives or belief systems. None of these problems and symptoms was specific to Spain, of course. Acute urban–rural divisions along with emergent class tensions were the common by-products of modernising change in early-twentieth-century Europe. But our knowledge of hindsight, of the 'hot' civil war of 1936–9, inevitably leads us to ask what, if anything, was particular about the Spanish experience.

Until the First World War there were relatively low levels of demographic mobility (from countryside to city) in Spain. The rural majority was also highly atomised, living in villages and hamlets. Both these factors contributed to produce relative social stability. This did not mean the absence of social strife, but rather a situation where popular protest could be easily contained within a given locality. And for Spain's ruling elites – composed of its 'senior', landowning partner in uneasy alliance with the 'junior' urban-industrial component – the primary function of the state was to ensure this containment. While this could be ensured, and for as long as there was no orchestrated political or social challenge to elite hegemony, the fact of the elites' *own* fragmentation/regionalisation did not matter. Popular rebellion could go on being considered by both elites and the political authorities of the Restoration monarchy (1875–1923) as purely a matter of public order.

Until the mid twentieth century, for most of the Spanish population it was patterns of land ownership and agricultural exploitation that structured the political and social hierarchies they dwelt within and which shaped their cultural worldviews. These structures and cultural perspectives varied enormously, however, between the north, centre and south of Spain. The dominant form of land holding in the centre-south (New Castile downwards) was the *latifundio*. These were vast estates, run mainly by bailiffs in the absence of their aristocratic owners and farmed by virtual slave armies of landless day labourers. In the north and on the central tableland of Old Castile (the Meseta) the agrarian norm was the peasant smallholder or tenant farmer. Individual peasants and their families ranged from affluent to extremely poor depending on a variety of factors – inheritance law, tenure arrangements and geography/relief (that is, land quality and climate). But the fact of land ownership itself tended to produce more conservative social attitudes. In spite of the highly disparate levels of economic resource possessed by these rural lower-middle-class sectors, there was often a sense that they belonged to some commonality of landowners. This was more real than any sense of connection to their (rather more sparse) urban equivalents who increasingly had different values and aspirations. Moreover, within these rural worlds there were no integrative mechanisms operating that might have fostered a sense of national belonging – such as markets, or political/cultural options like a functioning system of national primary education or genuinely participatory forms of political representation. Nor could military service fulfil this function as it did, to some extent, in neighbouring France. The only wars in which Spain was involved (up to the civil war of 1936–9 itself) were old and new colonial ones – in Cuba and Morocco[4] respectively. But these failed signally to stimulate binding or sustained patriotic sentiment among any significant proportion of Spain's middling classes. Cuba was the last gasp of a dying empire, while Morocco was associated with the narrow economic interests of the crown and some aristocratic and clerical sectors who owned iron mines there.[5] In short, the colonial fervour exhibited elsewhere in Europe by the emergent middle classes was not replicated in Spain. Most remained indifferent, while the worker constituencies who bore the brunt of conscription were frankly hostile.[6] Spain's middling classes remained highly fragmented internally in a variety of economic, social and cultural ways – and, needless to say, the peasantry felt quite distinct from landless rural labourers (whether far away or nearby) even though their levels of subsistence may not always have differed greatly.

Apart from land ownership, the major force of cohesion across social classes in north and central Spain was religion. In the north and on the Meseta the worldview of virtually the entirety of rural dwellers – of whatever social extraction or status – was shaped by their Catholic faith (although this was not necessarily a homogeneous entity). Popular

---

[4] Under the terms of the Treaty of Cartagena (1907) the Great Powers had allotted Spain (which already controlled the enclaves of Ceuta and Melilla) the task of policing northern Morocco.

[5] Balfour, *The End of the Spanish Empire 1898–1923*; C. Serrano, *Final del Imperio. España 1895–1898* (Madrid: Siglo XXI, 1984). Morocco was a military protectorate – it was never settled by civilian colonists. For the later political importance of Spain's Moroccan policy, see P. La Porte, *La atracción del Imán: el desastre de Annual y sus repercusiones en la política europea 1921–23* (Madrid: Biblioteca Nueva, 2001). As La Porte indicates, it was only with the Annual catastrophe that the unpopular and underfunded Moroccan campaign was brought to the political fore in Spain.

[6] The best-known anti-militarist protest was the (also anti-clerical) Tragic Week of July 1909: see Joan Connelly Ullman, *The Tragic Week: A Study of Anticlericalism in Spain 1875—1912* (Cambridge, Mass.: Harvard University Press, 1968), esp. pp. 129–40; S. Balfour, *The End of the Spanish Empire 1898–1923*, pp. 114–31 and C. Serrano, *Le Tour du Peuple. Crise nationale, mouvements populaires et populisme en Espagne (1890–1910)* (Madrid: Casa de Velázquez, 1987). On popular anti-militarism see R. Núñez Florencio, *Militarismo y antimilitarismo en España 1888–1906* (Madrid:CSIC, 1990) and C. Gil Andrés, *Echarse a la calle. Amotinados, huelguistas y revolucionarios. La Rioja 1890–1936* (Zaragoza: Prensas Universitarias de Zaragoza, 2000).

attitudes towards Catholicism and the Church constituted a major defin-ing difference between north and south. In the centre/north the Church was popularly perceived as dignifying existence, providing humanity and meaning in a 'heartless world'. This perspective was sustained by the im-portant pastoral role performed by local priests who forged close links with their local communities. The Church also provided practical sup-port – often in the form of rural credit banks – which offered a life-saving resource to the small peasantry eking out a precarious and marginal economic existence, perpetually threatened by crop failure and fearful of falling prey to moneylenders.[7]

By contrast, the very different daily experiences of the labouring masses of centre-south Spain made them fiercely anti-clerical. There Church and priest were perceived as pillar and perpetuator of an op-pressive landed order. Given the vastness of the *latifundios* and the fact that monoculture was the norm in the rural centre-south, the landless labour-ers were usually dependent on a single source of employment which, even then, was only available for part of the year – at planting and harvesting times. In the absence of any public welfare provision or other forms of poor relief, this dependency created relations of social power which were neo-feudal. The reality of power in rural Spain made meaningless the for-mal existence of universal manhood suffrage since votes were implicitly at the disposition of the local landowner (as sole employer), via the offices of the local political boss or fixer (*cacique*), who in rural areas would quite of-ten be the estate steward or bailiff.[8] The latter's close relationship with the local priest symbolised for the rural workers of the south a microcosmic expression of the Church's legitimation-sanctification of the social and political order which enslaved them.[9] This in turn explains the abiding

---

[7] The residual influence of Carlist traditions was also important in northern Spain. On the later consequences of this, see J. Ugarte Tellería, *La nueva Covadonga insurgente. Orígenes sociales y culturales de la sublevación de 1936 en Navarra y el País Vasco* (Madrid: Biblioteca Nueva, 1998).

[8] The *cacique* controlled the levers of power in a given locality – land, employment, taxation, judges, magistrates etc. So in the north of Spain he might be a tax collector, lawyer or moneylender. Monarchist Spain (1875–1923) had a two-party system whereby the dynastic parties (Liberals and Conservatives) alternated in power (termed the *turno*). Each was guaranteed a 'turn' because majorities in the Cortes (Spanish parliament) were manufactured by means of electoral fraud. Candidates were imposed on constituencies according to previously agreed lists. The *caciques'* major function was thus to deliver the vote and ensure that the agreed 'result' materialised. This could be done either by means of a carrot (offering favours) or stick (coercion) depending on the region and whose vote it was.

[9] The rapprochement between the Church and the secular elites was the concomitant of a pro-cess of distancing between Church and people that had its roots in the disentailment process, W. J. Callahan, *Church, Politics and Society in Spain 1750–1874* (Cambridge, Mass.: Harvard University Press, 1984).

anti-clerical element in the popular protests against this brutal clientelism which were sparked from time to time by hunger and sheer desperation. The lack of any substantial rural middle class in the south – beyond those providing agricultural services for the *latifundistas* and thus bound by ties of custom and obligation within the neo-feudal social structure – made the nature of social oppression quite overt. At the same time, however, the sporadic, *ad hoc* nature of rural rebellion in late-nineteenth- and early-twentieth-century Spain and its atomised occurrence at the level of the village meant that it could be very easily quashed by the efforts of the rural police force, the Civil Guard. This functioned virtu-ally as a force of occupation in the countryside, thus constituting the third element in the rural poor's 'unholy trinity' (bailiff, priest and corporal of the Civil Guard). The fact that the Civil Guard was used primarily (in-deed almost exclusively) against the labouring classes reinforced in their eyes the idea of the state as a uniquely repressive force – in so far as it performed no countervailing 'positive' functions in areas such as public education or (even minimal) social welfare provision.

Given the picture of rural Spain just indicated, it is unsurprising that labour unions and worker organisations should have had little purchase therein prior to the disruption of the old networks of power that occurred with the coming of the Second Republic in 1931. The smallholding and tenant farmers of the centre and north were made either impervious or actively hostile to the left's message through a combination of their religious faith and the Catholic Church's provision of material assistance. But even in other areas of Spain where brutal social inequality was visible and unmediated – for example along the lower south-eastern sea board or, in particular, in the deep south of Andalusia and Extremadura – it is still difficult to speak of a rural 'proletariat' as such prior to the First World War. This is because it presupposes a level of articulation – in terms of culture, consciousness and organisation – that scarcely existed in the Spanish countryside before that time.

This did not mean, however, that the southern landless lacked political beliefs of their own. These they had found in anarchist millenarianism and direct action. During the second half of the nineteenth century and beyond, these offered the landless poor a far more functional – and in-deed *logical* – response to extant power relations and the perceived (im)possibility of incremental change than the state-reformism and grad-ualist tactics of the Spanish socialists. Social reformism, implicitly predi-cated on the bargaining power of labour, doubtless seemed as utopian or incredible to the unskilled and powerless of the saturated southern labour market in the 1910s as millenarian anarchism now seems to some western historians of the late twentieth and twenty-first centuries. It would only be in the 1930s, with the promise of state-led agrarian reform, that a socialist landworkers' union would begin to make rapid headway among the landless of Spain's deep south.

But to speak of any area of the rural south as organisationally 'anarchist' prior to 1931 can also lead to misconceptions. In Extremadura and Andalusia there was certainly a deep-rooted popular culture of collectivism that chimed with anarchist ideas. The poor south was also a milieu in which anarchist organisers circulated. But the level of stable organisational implantation of what would become in 1910 the CNT federation was – for a variety of practical, political and ideological reasons – never very great before the relatively more conducive political circumstances of the Second Republic. But by then, of course, the CNT would be competing hard for southern recruits with the socialist-led trade union, the UGT.

Beyond the rural south, the CNT was, like the UGT, predominantly an urban-based movement until the 1930s. (The CNT was stronger on the eastern seaboard, while the UGT had its strongholds in the industrial north and in the geographical (and political) centre of Spain in Castile.) This urban focus is also indicated by the pattern of later civil wartime collectivisation in Aragon or Valencia, for example, where the collectivist movement in the villages of the agrarian hinterland was initiated for the most part by anarchist cadres fanning out from the provincial towns or cities.[10] In the case of Aragon too, even the CNT's urban base only really developed in the years after the First World War.[11]

In urban Spain, the First World War acted, as it did elsewhere in Europe, as a catalyst and accelerator of social, economic, political and cultural change. It contributed enormously to undermining an order that had depended on the political demobilisation of the population. Spain had not participated in the war. But even if 'Spain did not enter the war . . . the war entered Spain'.[12] Because Spain was a neutral country able to sell to both sides, the war massively stimulated its economy. But while enormous profits were being made in war-related sectors, a crisis of domestic production arose because the industrial base was

---

[10] See chapter 4 below.

[11] J. Casanova, *Anarquismo y revolución en la sociedad rural aragonesa 1936–1938* (Madrid: Siglo XXI, 1985), pp. 32–9.

[12] F. Romero, 'Spain and the First World War: The Structural Crisis of the Liberal Monarchy', *European History Quarterly*, 25 (1995), 532.

insufficient to meet normal domestic demand as well as the extraordinary external demand. The result was massive internal inflation with deteriorating living standards and shortages of food and staple commodities for many sectors of the working classes – especially those not benefiting from the increased wages of war-related industry (although such increases still did not match inflation). War-induced distortions in the economy also produced severe sectoral unemployment that forced thousands to migrate – mainly to Bilbao or Barcelona – in search of work in flourishing war-related concerns. In response to the pressure of working-class protest at the subsistence crisis, the UGT and the CNT agreed a Labour Pact in July 1916 which was designed to pressure the monarchist government into action against cost of living hikes.

The fact of this union *rapprochement* indicates the severity of the crisis because, for it to have occurred, the UGT leadership had to overcome its enormous aversion to any alliance with the CNT, which it associated with confrontational tactics. Spain's socialist movement (PSOE/UGT) had evolved from an urban base of artisans and skilled workers – typified by Madrid itself, which, in spite of being the capital city, would retain into the 1930s a predominantly 'pre-industrial' labour structure.[13] And for all the UGT's extension to the industrial north (among the iron and steel foundry workers of the Basque Country and the coal miners of Asturias), its organisational ethos remained extremely cautious. Its leadership would never entirely cast off a certain guild approach to labour relations. Indeed, this was reinforced by the experience of the UGT-led urban general strike of August 1917, launched as one segment of a democratic political challenge to the exclusivist order of the monarchy. But when this bid failed, the socialists found themselves facing the onslaught of the victors' justice. The threat of confiscations (of union buildings, property and printing presses etc.) and the organisational dislocation that ensued traumatised the Madrid-based UGT leadership and subliminally reinforced its commitment to a gradualist strategy of reform which would avoid head-on challenges to the state or employers in the future.

As a result of 1917, then, the scene was set for subsequent dissension in the UGT between this cautious veteran leadership and those whose different experience of labour relations spoke to them of the need for more direct, confrontational tactics. The most important example of this would be the split between Madrid and the industrial north (Asturias and Bilbao (Vizcaya)). The intransigence of northern industrialists – of

---

[13] How this would change is a central theme of Santos Juliá's *Madrid 1931–1934. De la fiesta popular a la lucha de clases* (Madrid: Siglo XXI, 1984).

foundry and mine owners (intensified by the post-First World War slump in their fortunes) – and the angry expectations of the rank and file were edging UGT leaders in the north towards backing more radical, confrontational tactics. (These were precisely the kind of tactics being espoused with renewed vigour by the CNT, which had drawn from the experience of repression in 1917 conclusions diametrically opposed to those of the UGT leaders.) As a result, socialist union leaders in the north found themselves in a stand-off with a disapproving UGT national executive in Madrid. This conflict over union ideology and strategy would be a significant factor in the emergence of the Spanish Communist Party in 1921–2.[14] Its creation did not, however, resolve the internal debate over strategy in the socialist movement. Indeed, the existence of a separate party (even one as marginal as the pre-1936 Spanish Communist Party) created new organisational jealousies and animosities that would make the internal socialist debate even more fraught – as developments during the highly charged years of the Second Republic demonstrate. The years following 1917 would see a spate of isolated and uncoordinated acts of rural rebellion in Spain that are collectively known as the 'bolshevik three years' (*trienio bolchevique*). These rural outbursts helped stoke the fires of elite anxiety about social disorder. But for all their increased frequency and intensity, they were easily quelled by the Civil Guard. Rather it was in 'minority' urban Spain that the real challenge to the old order was growing.

This process had germinated with the colonial disaster of 1898. This injected new life into an urban middle-class republicanism that was highly critical of the old regime with its dominant clerical and military influences. In towns and cities, republican alliances began to erode the *caciques'* control in the decade leading up to the First World War. In the war's wake came further accelerating demographic change, as workers moved from countryside to town and city. Thus, just as the habitual mechanism of political control, the influence of the *cacique*, was foundering, so too the old techniques for guaranteeing public order were looking increasingly inadequate. Nowhere was this clearer than in Barcelona.

None of Spain's other urban centres cast even a pale reflection of the cultural, political and sociological complexity of Barcelona – Spain's

---

[14] G. Meaker, *The Revolutionary Left in Spain 1914–1923* (Stanford: Stanford University Press, 1974), pp. 346–84, esp. pp. 369, 371. The emergent Communist Party would have its strongest base in Bilbao, where for a time it controlled the *Casa del Pueblo*. On the radical strategy of the Basque socialists, see R. Miralles, 'La gran huelga minera de 1890. Los orígenes del movimiento obrero en el País Vasco', *Historia Contemporánea*, 3 (1990).

main industrial conurbation and its only real metropolis.[15] Anti-state sentiment and hostility to the socio-economic order of capitalism were to be found among organised workers and the poor elsewhere in Spain. But nowhere else could radical left minorities draw on any comparable tradition or structure of proletarian/popular political and cultural networks – from the popular *ateneus*, through alternative press and literary output, to forms of alternative sociability.[16] The pumping heart of all of these was the anarchist movement, whose creative energy offered a mirror image of Catalonia's unique bourgeois milieu of civic dynamism and its thriving traditions of cultural autonomy. Anarchist culture in twentieth-century Barcelona was also, of course, a political culture based on traditions of community self-help and direct action (for example popular requisition against food shortages and neighbourhood resistance to evictions).[17] Barcelona's anarchists were in semi-permanent mobilisation against the old order. Their protest was anti-clerical – against the Church's legitimation of that order – and anti-militarist, not least because the old regime's colonial wars were fought predominantly by the poor.[18]

But anti-clericalism was never the monopoly of Spain's anarchists.[19] Between 1901 and 1909 in Barcelona it was to be the principal mobilising mechanism of the Radical Republican Party, led by a shady demagogue and political opportunist called Alejandro Lerroux.[20] The fact that for

---

[15] Basque industrialisation in Vizcaya (focused on the city of Bilbao and the River Nervión) was also rapid. But there a ribbon of small industrial centres developed, with no comparable centre to Barcelona. The political division between indigenous workers and migrant Spanish labour was also far more extreme in the Basque Country than it was in Catalonia.

[16] B. Hofmann *et al.*, *Anarquismo español y sus tradiciones culturales* (Frankfurt-on-Main/Madrid: Vervuert-Iberoamericana, 1995); P. Solà i Gussinyer, *Educació i Moviment Libertari a Catalunya (1901–1939)* (Barcelona: Edicions 62, 1980); S. Tavera, 'La premsa anarco-sindicalista (1868–1931)', *Recerques*, 8 (1977), pp. 85–102; L. Litvak, *Musa Libertaria. Arte, literatura y vida cultural del anarquismo español (1880–1913)* (Barcelona: Antoni Bosch, 1981); T. Kaplan, *Red City, Blue Period. Social Movements in Picasso's Barcelona (1888–1937)* (Berkeley, Calif.: University of California Press, 1992).

[17] C. Ealham, 'Policing the Recession: Unemployment, Social Protest and Law-and-Order in Barcelona 1930–1936', unpublished Ph.D. thesis, University of London, 1995.

[18] J. Romero Maura, *'La Rosa del Fuego'. Republicanos y anarquistas: la política de los obreros barceloneses entre el desastre colonial y la Semana Trágica 1889–1909* (Barcelona: Grijalbo, 1989); X. Cuadrat, *Socialismo y anarquismo en Cataluña 1890–1911* (Madrid: Revista del Trabajo, 1976); J. M. Huertas Clavería, *Obrers a Catalunya* (Barcelona: Avenc, 1982); P. Gabriel, 'Sindicalismo en Cataluña 1888–1938', *Historia Social*, 8 (1990) and 'Población obrera catalana', *Estudios de Historia Social*, 32–3 (1985); A. Smith, 'Anarchism, the General Strike and the Barcelona Labour Movement 1899–1914', *European History Quarterly*, 27 (1) (1997). See also A. Balcells, *Trabajo industrial y organización obrera en la Cataluña contemporánea 1900–1936* (Barcelona: Ed. Laia, 1974) and Ullman, *The Tragic Week*. On popular anti-militarism, see also n. 6 above.

[19] On the social and cultural context of anti-clericalism, see F. Lannon, *Privilege, Persecution and Prophecy. The Catholic Church in Spain 1875–1975* (Oxford: Clarendon Press, 1987), pp. 9–35.

[20] J. Alvarez Junco, *El emperador del Paralelo. Lerroux y la demagogia populista* (Madrid: Alianza, 1990); J. R. Mosher, *The Birth of Mass Politics in Spain: Lerrouxismo in Barcelona 1901–1909* (New York:

a time he had considerable success in mobilising the Barcelona working class indicates one of the key specificities of the anarchist movement – its refusal to engage in the sphere of organised (i.e. parliamentary or municipal) politics. Given the absence from the Catalan frame of the PSOE – whose scarcely dissembled centralism would also come to antagonise such a strongly federalist region – this meant that the worker constituencies of Barcelona were, effectively until the 1930s, deprived of any real political voice for their interests.[21]

After the end of the First World War, conflict was escalating in the industrial heartland of Barcelona between the emergent influence of urban labour in the CNT, on the one hand, and employers' opposition to arbitration-based solutions on the other. This opposition stemmed in part from a particular political mentality. But that was itself heavily influenced by longstanding economic factors. The Catalan textile industry had always been ramshackle and undercapitalised. After the temporary reprieve granted by the exceptional circumstances of the 1914–18 war, it was plunged back into crisis because its products were not competitive on the international market. Employer intransigence (which included violent coercion) was an alternative to reduced profit margins. But it also promoted the ascendancy of the *exaltado* or extreme anarchist wing of the CNT over the more moderate syndicalists whose leaders were among the first to fall to the bullets of assassins hired by Catalan industrialists and business magnates. The result was spiralling violence on the streets of Barcelona between 1919 and 1923 as anarchist direct action squads fought it out with the yellow unions (*Sindicatos Libres*) and paramilitaries of shadowy provenance. With the connivance of General Martínez Anido, civil governor of Barcelona from October 1920, *Libres* gunmen were trained and armed in military barracks, and the notorious *Ley de Fugas* operated on a scale that verged on industrial. (This meant that CNT detainees were shot in cold blood, ostensibly 'while trying to

---

Garland, 1991); a summary in F. J. Romero, *Twentieth-Century Spain. Politics and Society 1898–1998* (Basingstoke: Macmillan, 1999), pp. 23, 25, 29. Lerroux's shadiness was compounded by the fact that he was funded by 'Madrid' in an attempt to block the progress of Catalan nationalism as a political force.

[21] It would be wrong to say, however, that the PSOE/UGT's early failure in Catalonia was simply the result of their centralist attitudes (after all, until the 1890s Catalonia was one of the UGT's major bases). In the 1902 general strike the UGT missed the opportunity to lead a radicalised labour movement in Barcelona because – even then – its leaders shied away from radical tactics. The resulting vacuum of leadership would be filled by syndicalists and anarchists, constituted from 1910 as the CNT. The mood of fierce anti-clericalism, fanned by Lerroux's demagogy, would also alienate the PSOE. From here, PSOE/UGT centralism – which itself intensified as a result of their lack of political purchase in Catalonia – became another grave source of tension within the left. For the emergence of a Catalanist political left, see chapter 1.

escape'.) Thousands of *cenetistas* were imprisoned or sent into internal exile – whither they were dispatched in chains and on foot. In effect, a low-intensity civil war was being fought.[22] It was a war not dissimilar in its causes and objectives to that occurring contemporaneously in Italy, where it would end with Mussolini and his Fascists being invited into power by the old elites.

Back in July 1909 the Catalan bourgeoisie had given thanks to God for delivery from the anti-militarist and anti-establishment rebellion known as the Tragic Week. They had built the Church of the Tibidabo in recognition of their salvation.[23] But in 1923 it was not prayers that the Catalan patronal offered up, but a military invocation. When General Miguel Primo de Rivera launched his coup in September 1923 he would have the full backing of a Catalan establishment that had until then claimed to be committed to the goal of regional autonomy within a new constitutional settlement.

It was precisely the perceived threat of urban mobilisation in the wake of the 1914–18 war, with revolutionary upheaval in Russia as a backdrop, that brought Catalonia's industrialists and business lobby to acquiesce in the killing of constitutional politics in Spain. In its place they accepted intervention by the ideologically ultra-centralist Spanish army because it could restore order on the streets of urban Catalonia, thus securing a form of social peace conducive to their own economic interests. The army (or more precisely its officer corps) increasingly saw itself as the patriotic guarantor of a certain conception of 'Spain' that was, according to the officers' lights, being repeatedly threatened – in 1909, 1917 and subsequently – by internal enemies and in particular by regionalists and organised labour.[24] Army officers were thus identifying as 'anti-national'

---

[22] F. Rey, *Propietarios y patronos. La política de las organizaciones económicas en la España de la Restauración, 1914–23* (Madrid: Ministerio de Trabajo y Seguridad Social, 1992) and 'Capitalismo catalán y golpe de Primo', *Hispania*, 168 (1988); E. González Calleja and F. Rey, *El Mauser y el sufragio. Orden público, subversión y violencia política en la crisis de la Restauración, 1917–31* (Madrid: CSIC, 1999); also articles by Rey and A. Balcells in *Estudios de Historia Social*, nos. 42–3 (1987); *L'Avenç*, no. 192 (May 1995) is a special issue on *pistolerismo*; S. Bengoechea, *Vuitanta-quatre dies de lock-out a Barcelona, 1919–20. Els precedents de la dictadura de Primo de Rivera* (Barcelona: Curial, 1998) and *Organització patronal i conflictivitat social a Catalunya. Tradició y corporativisme entre finals del segle i la dictadura de Primo de Rivera* (Barcelona: l'Abadia de Montserrat, 1994).

[23] This week of anti-clerical looting and street fighting was triggered by the call-up of conscripts for the Moroccan campaigns. Working-class Barcelona had been profoundly anti-militarist since the return of malaria-ridden 'walking dead' from the Cuban war. The Barcelona bourgeoisie took their cue from their French counterparts, who had constructed the Sacré Cœur after the defeat of the Paris Commune of 1870.

[24] The Spanish military's searching for a new role after 1898 was also, of course, in part driven by its desire to protect its own corporate interests: see G. Cardona, *El poder militar en la España*

those groups most closely bound up with and symbolising the deep social, political and cultural changes underway in Spain.

In spite of the Primo dictatorship's legal restrictions on labour organisation, however, the regime was not necessarily experienced by rural and urban workers as more oppressive than the preceding Restoration monarchist order under which associative freedoms and labour rights had, in practice, been absent. Primo was able to stabilise his dictatorship on a fairly low level of overt repression precisely because of the 1920s economic boom with which he coincided. But precisely because of the boom there was further large-scale population movement during the decade, as impoverished agricultural labourers headed from the misery of the rural south, with its quasi-feudal social relations of power, to the relatively freer, but equally economically exploitative, urban environments of Madrid and Barcelona – the latter the location of the international exposition of 1929. Indeed, the dictatorship's ambitious public works projects – underwritten by a system of special loans whose interest repayments would so cripple the Republic's reform project of the 1930s – were themselves a stimulus to the demographic shift of the 1920s. In the cities, the new arrivals worked in those sectors expanding under the boom conditions – above all as unskilled labour on vast building sites and public works projects constructing roads and the underground system.

With such a buoyant economic conjuncture Primo was able to indulge his own paternalistic notions of government. He called upon the UGT, which he saw as the 'responsible' face of labour, to collaborate in the founding of a state system of arbitration boards. These the socialist trade unionists would run as paid servants of the state from the labour ministry. Such an offer fitted well with the veteran UGT leadership's own aspirations to partnership with the state (British labour was very much the model here). As the cautious *ugestista* leaders saw it, fearful of the ghosts of 1917, entrenchment in the state bureaucracy would protect the organisational patrimony of the socialist movement. Their decision to collaborate with the dictator would, however, arm a crucial internal dispute with the parliamentary socialists who could not, under any circumstances, accept that it was legitimate to be involved with an anti-constitutional regime. But at the time this mattered far less to the leaders of the UGT than the opportunity which they saw collaboration

contemporánea hasta la guerra civil (Madrid: Siglo XXI, 1983) and C. Boyd, *Praetorian Politics in Liberal Spain* (Chapel Hill: University of North Carolina Press, 1979). Nor should we forget that the corporate interests of some military sectors would be one of the motives impelling the July 1936 coup.

with Primo as affording them permanently to overtake the CNT. In the years leading up to the military coup of 1923 the anarcho-syndicalist federation had been outstripping the UGT in recruitment and even making inroads into socialist strongholds.[25] But with the dictatorship the CNT had been declared illegal, as Primo saw this as the key to ending the running war on the streets of Barcelona.

But for all the prominence of the anarchist *exaltados* in this war, it is vital to remember that the CNT had other faces. Even if its Catalan branch would dominate the CNT numerically until 1931,[26] the organisation was a national one whose regional components each formulated a political ethic and practice in the light of the material circumstances of their particular memberships. In a country with such disparate levels of development as Spain's, this obviously also made for significant diversity *within* the organisations of the left. As well as the southern millenarians and Catalan and Aragonese street warriors, the CNT also included, for example, a Northern (Asturian) federation in which skilled workers and artisans predominated.[27] It was the presence of this syndicalist component that had reassured the UGT leaders sufficiently to make possible the historic Labour Pact of July 1916.[28] A year later, a group of self-proclaimed parliamentary syndicalists from Gijón even called for the formation of a political party to represent the CNT's interests.[29] Although this did not prosper, the very fact that it was mooted demonstrates the clear political affinities of some parts of the CNT with the UGT. In the north, cooperation between the two was also facilitated by their relative equilibrium of strength in the region and the similarity of the industrial disputes they were called upon to handle. At the same time, the fact that some *cenetistas* saw the value of elaborating a parliamentary political strategy highlights how the war-induced surge in labour mobilisation had crystallised important differences inside the CNT over ideology and practice – and in particular over how to deal with the state. Indeed, in Catalonia too

---

[25] B. Martin, *The Agony of Modernisation. Labor and Industrialisation in Spain* (Cornell University Press, 1990), p. 195 (for comparative figures).

[26] In 1919 the CNT's Catalan regional federation, with a membership of over 400,000, represented half of the total CNT membership for Spain, J. Peirats, *La CNT en la revolución española* (Madrid: Ruedo Ibérico, 1971), vol. I, pp. 27–8. During 1931–6 the Catalan federation would suffer a decline in membership. But the fact that it retained its formidable mobilising power in the streets and continued to provide the movement's most prominent leaders meant that it would retain its political dominance over the CNT nationally – see chapters 1, 4 and 5 below.

[27] P. Radcliff, *From Mobilisation to Civil War. The Politics of Polarisation in the Spanish City of Gijón 1900–1937* (Cambridge: Cambridge University Press, 1996), *passim*.

[28] P. Heywood, *Marxism and the Failure of Organised Socialism in Spain* (Cambridge: Cambridge University Press, 1990), pp. 41–2; A. Saborit, *Julián Besteiro* (Buenos Aires: Losada, 1967), pp. 87–8.

[29] Radcliff, *From Mobilisation to Civil War*, p. 128.

strong currents emerged in favour of modifying the CNT's strategy in a 'political' direction and of reviewing its interaction with the UGT.[30]

Between 1919 and 1923 syndicalist leaders (of whom the most famous was Salvador Seguí) who were fearful of the erosive effect that continued violent direct action would have on the CNT tried to steer the influential Catalan federation in the direction of organisational consolidation and a more nuanced syndical strategy.[31] Although a majority of syndicalists still resisted the idea of parliamentary politics, these organisational reforms were at root a response to the increasing complexity of industrial organisation and of industry's interaction with the state. But Seguí and his supporters met the determined opposition of the majority of the CNT – above all, in the Catalan and Andalusian federations.[32] Although the CNT's 1919 congress approved the conversion of its craft unions into modern, vertical industrial ones (the *Sindicatos Unicos*), it rejected their consolidation into national federations of industry.[33] But even progress towards the *Sindicatos Unicos* was slow and uneven.[34] Primo's collaboration with the UGT ensured that the internal debate in the CNT did not die.[35] But the dictatorship's criminalisation of the Confederation froze the possibility of any organisational revision at the same time as it gave radical, pro-direct action anarchists the upper hand once again in the political argument over what the CNT was for and how it should be organised. (Just as the use of establishment violence against the CNT in the post-First World War period had undermined the syndicalist reformers, so too the fact that Seguí was himself assassinated in 1923 boosted the credibility of more radical currents in the organisation.) Nevertheless, that the radicals felt it necessary to form a separate group, the Iberian Anarchist Federation (FAI), in 1927 in order to defend anarchist orthodoxy within the CNT indicates that the internal political differences remained unresolved.

[30] Their major focus was Angel Pestaña and his supporters in the *Solidaridad Obrera* editorial group (Joan Peiró *et al.*) as well as Salvador Segui, the Catalan CNT leader, C. Lorenzo, *Los anarquistas españoles y el poder* (Paris: Ruedo Ibérico, 1972), pp. 44–5.
[31] A. Pestaña, *Lo que aprendí en la vida* (Madrid, 1972), Part 1, pp. 88–9, 100–1; Part 2, p. 87.
[32] C. Lorenzo, *Los anarquistas españoles y el poder*, pp. 44–5.
[33] Ibid., pp. 36–7; Peirats, *La CNT en la revolución española*, vol. 1, p. 27; Radcliff, *From Mobilisation to Civil War*, pp. 179–80.
[34] The exception was in the already politically exceptional northern federation, Radcliff, *From Mobilisation to Civil War*, pp. 179–80.
[35] Lorenzo, *Los anarquistas españoles*, pp. 49–50; Pestaña, *Lo que aprendí en la vida*, Part 1, pp. 102–4. As Lorenzo indicates, some in the CNT, basing themselves on pure syndicalist ideas (i.e. ignoring the forms of the state) saw the way forward for the Confederation in emulating the UGT's role in the regime's labour tribunals (the *comités paritarios*).

Despite the FAI's injection of anarchist purism, the coming of the Second Republic in 1931 would see the acceleration of these internal CNT disputes over structure and strategy. (As we shall see in the next chapter, they would produce the so-called *treintista* schism that split both the CNT's Catalan and Valencian regional federations.) The resurgence of these debates probably had something to do with the numerical decline of the Catalan federation in relation to the national organisation as a whole. But more fundamentally (since the Catalan federation was also affected), these growing internal divisions were part and parcel of the larger process of social and economic change that had helped bring about the Second Republic itself. Improved communications and the beginnings of mass production, with more widely distributed printed political propaganda, were, by the 1920s, gradually transforming Spanish workers – including the as yet unorganised – into a new political constituency. With the Republic came a heightened sense of new possibilities for the left that would see a further acceleration of popular political mobilisation. In turn, some inside the CNT saw an enhanced opportunity for the organisation's partial political incorporation – at least sufficiently to defend its members and social constituencies through the newly available channels of municipal politics and state labour agencies.

It has been a historiographical commonplace to contrast the solid bureaucratic structures and practices of the UGT with the structural inchoateness and direct action of the CNT. From this analysis, however, we can conclude that to view the CNT and UGT as if they were structural and ideological polar opposites is neither useful nor accurate.[36] Rather each was a heterogeneous organisation containing divergent ideological perspectives and labour practices moulded by different kinds of (still predominantly urban) experience. Let us remember too that, just as the arguments raged inside the CNT in the 1930s, so would they in the socialist movement (PSOE/UGT) as the tensions that had provoked the communist schism of 1921–2 resurfaced. In short, the UGT and the CNT not infrequently resembled each other – and never more so than when they were struggling to maintain organisational cohesion in the face of the political and strategic dilemmas opened up by the Republic. It could scarcely have been otherwise given Spain's acute regional disparities economically, socially and culturally. If these factors had fragmented what were relatively far more powerful elite groups (as clearly they had), then how much more must uneven development have impacted on the

---

[36] This observation should also be of use in the increasingly vexed debate over how to explain the original pattern of anarchist and socialist organisational implantation in Spain.

organisational forms and political goals of the relatively far less powerful Spanish left. It is also important to remember that, apart from the brief experience of the First Republic in 1873, the left – even broadly construed to include all brands of republicanism – had not, prior to 1931, exercised national political power in Spain in the modern period.[37]

Only by understanding the multiple factors that had shaped the left – or, more accurately, lefts – prior to 1931 can we hope to understand properly what drove relations between them thereafter or what produced the schisms and conflicts within each. Nor can we otherwise make sense of what the Spanish left's component parts said and did during the civil war of 1936–9 – and, just as importantly, what they could not bring themselves to think or do.

However, understanding all of this is made even more difficult by the fact that after 1931 the organisations of the Spanish left – republicans, socialists, communists and anarcho-syndicalists – were also having to deal increasingly with other forms of political mobilisation, namely those affecting Spain's wide spectrum of middling classes. This process was also kick started under the Primo dictatorship and by the 1930s it would significantly have changed the political landscape, as these middling sectors sought political representation for their interests. Moreover, progessive sectors among the middling classes were joining not only specifically republican parties but also a range of socialist and communist organisations – including the USC and the BOC in Catalonia and, from spring–summer 1936, the united socialist–communist youth organisations.[38]

This mobilisation of Spain's middling classes was particularly evident where powerful regional nationalist sentiment existed, and above all in Catalonia. There the industrialist lobby's defection to Primo would (by 1931) see the autonomy movement politically reconfigured under the liberal-left leadership of the region's urban professional middle classes, but equally with support from middling rural sectors. Another key facet here was the mobilisation of middle-class youth in the context of a rising university population with equivalent rising expectations.[39] (The year 1927 would see the creation of the Federation of University Students (FUE) which was highly critical of the dictatorship.) This unprecedented mobilisation of youth would also exercise a profound

---

[37] Apart from 1873, the only other period since the French Revolution when the Spanish left could be said to have had some power was during the constitutional triennium of 1820–3.

[38] I refer to youth organisations in the plural because of the more complex situation in Catalonia: see R. Casterás, *Las JSUC ante la guerra* (Barcelona: Nova Terra, 1977), pp. 113–30. For more on this see chapter 1 below.

[39] Ibid., p. 45.

influence on the political life of the Second Republic, especially during the war.

More generally too the 1920s in Spain saw the acceleration of a process of cultural modernisation which affected middling constituencies in particular. The beginnings of mass production not only facilitated the wider distribution of printed political propaganda, but also, along with the radio, created a new leisure market which in turn consolidated a sense of identity among the new urban professional and commercial middling classes.[40] Also crucial to this process of cultural change was the reception of the Russian Revolution among these new middle classes. But this was not primarily a question of ideology.[41] Spain's new middle classes were not aspiring marxist-leninists. They were, however, 'aspiring' in other ways. Images of Soviet modernity in 1920s and 1930s Spain functioned in lieu of domestic ones (which were sparse). Their appeal tells us more about the social aspirations of these urban groups than their political ideas. The idea of the Soviet Union as an icon of modernity was something which particularly influenced lower-middle-class youth – that is, the kind of young men and women who would join the United Socialist and Communist Youth Organisation (JSU) in droves during the second half of 1936.[42]

Middle-class mobilisation in 1920s Spain also took the form of the burgeoning professional associations – of post office employees, rural doctors, clerks, teachers and the like – who through their adaptation to new, modern work methods came increasingly to have a sense of themselves as performing a broader public service.[43] To these groups the constitution was important because it held out the hope of a non-arbitrary form of power which could protect their own professional interests. Both as a movement of opinion and in organisational terms, these groups would be the most coherent oppositional sector of republicanism – indeed, this was so precisely because theirs was a practical republicanism tied to

---

[40] For example, commercial music and the *cuplé* played a key role in stimulating radio in urban middling-class homes: see S. Salaün, 'The *Cuplé*: Modernity and Mass Culture', in Graham and Labanyi, *Spanish Cultural Studies*, p. 93.

[41] R. Cruz, '¡Luzbel vuelve al mundo! Las imágenes de la Rusia y la acción colectiva en España', in R. Cruz and M. Pérez Ledesma (eds.), *Cultura y movilización en la España contemporánea* (Madrid: Alianza, 1997).

[42] Cf. 'Russia, together with other expressions of modernity such as "aviation, the radio, telephone" gave life great interest.' E. Montero, 'Reform Idealised: The Intellectual and Ideological Origins of the Second Republic', in Graham and Labanyi, *Spanish Cultural Studies*, p. 131.

[43] Ibid., pp. 129–30. Increasingly conscious of their own professional specialisation, these sectors put their 'faith' in technology and science – which was, of course, part of the perceived appeal of the Soviet Union – and saw their own social advancement as integrally linked to 'progress' writ large.

enlightened self-interest – and they played a crucial role in the collapse of monarchy in 1931.[44] Yet their potential usefulness thereafter was lost – both as a social support base and as a source of new state personnel for the modernising Republic. For republicanism in Spain was dominated by academics and lawyers with an excessively legalistic view of political change. Their conception of reform began and ended with the mechanics of a top-down state project, and they thus failed to link up organisationally with these professional groups. Given the undeniable fact that Spain's middling classes were politically, socially and culturally highly fragmented, and that their urban component was exiguous,[45] this failure to integrate the professional associations in the project of Republican reform would seriously threaten its viability, as we shall see.

By the end of the 1920s as the boom ended and dictatorial debts mounted, the Primo dictatorship entered terminal crisis. Its collapse followed shortly after that of the peseta. But the agrarian and industrial elites' disaffection from the dictatorship remained essentially a political one. For a start, members of the monarchist political class – men like Niceto Alcalá-Zamora, Miguel Maura and José Sánchez Guerra – were hostile because the Primo dictatorship had destroyed the old two-party system and thus rendered them politically obsolete at the same time as it cut them off from the sources of patronage afforded by the state.[46] More generally, there was mounting distaste among elite groups at the political 'novelty' of some of Primo's policies – in particular his policies of class co-option, such as the labour tribunals. The years of boom had blunted their fears of labour unrest. Both agrarian and industrial elites held fast to the naive belief that there could be a return in some shape or form to the safely 'traditional' – i.e. demobilised and exclusivist – order of the Restoration monarchy.

But existing levels of popular mobilisation had already made a return to such an order quite unrealistic. This was manifest in the explosion of anti-monarchist sentiment in the municipal elections of April 1931. Although the *caciques* managed to retain control of rural constituencies, urban Spain returned the 'voto-verdad' (authentic vote), revealing the extent of popular disaffection with the existing order. On the basis of

---

[44] E. Montero, 'The Forging of the Second Spanish Republic: New Liberalism, the Republican Movement and the Quest for Modernisation 1898–1931', unpublished Ph. D. thesis, University of London, 1989.

[45] The classic (pre-1931) republican experience of 'pocket' power – in a provincial city – is conveyed well in Radcliff, *From Mobilisation to Civil War*.

[46] Their disaffection also extended to the person of the monarch, Alfonso XIII, for his lengthy support of Primo.

this, a coalition of the liberal-left, representing those social constituencies excluded by the monarchist order, was able to press ahead and declare the Republic.[47] But what had really created the political space for it was not the strength or coherence of this coalition, but rather the political disarray of Spain's elites following the collapse of the dictatorship. In what amounted almost to a fit of absence of mind, they found themselves faced with the *fait accompli* of a Republic.[48]

Some still imagined that this might only amount to a change in the *form* of the regime and one, indeed, whose novelty could even benefit conservative Spain in the search for a means of relegitimising its own power. (This is likely to have figured in the political calculations of erstwhile monarchist politicians-turned republicans, such as Alcalá-Zamora, later Republican president, who were extracted from the same social world/families as the old elites.) But this ignored the fact that the collapse of the monarchist system was due precisely to its inflexibility, to the fact that it had proved incapable of assimilating new social constituencies. Thus in 1931 – in the context of a mounting international economic crisis which would soon impact on Spain – elite groups faced increasingly conscious and organised urban and rural working-class constituencies as well as politicised republican sectors of the urban (and some rural) middle classes. Moreover, they were facing these constituencies in a situation where political authority itself had, for the first time in the contemporary period in Spain, passed to a coalition of forces that unambiguously backed an agenda of social and economic reform. This coalition was now also about to be in formal control of the very instruments of public order – the police force and the army – to which Spain's agrarian and industrial elites had previously looked to avoid just such a political scenario.

But this state of affairs would prove less beneficial to the Spanish left than might at first appear. In June 1931 progressive forces would take control of national government in Madrid by dint of the authority invested in them by the ballot box. But old Spain had retained most of its economic power. (The Second Republic was not a socialist regime.) Moreover, the elites still had tremendous social power in the localities. The *cacique* system proper had been broken by Republican victory, but the networks of power and influence that underpinned it had not. The coming of the Republic would in fact institute a kind of 'stand-off'

[47] This coalition was based on the Pact of San Sebastián, signed in August 1930 by republicans and Catalan nationalists and soon supported by the PSOE. (In the Basque Country, the liberal nationalist minority, ANV, participated, but the more influential PNV did not.)

[48] S. Ben-Ami, *The Origins of the Second Republic in Spain* (Oxford: Oxford University Press, 1978).

between new and old Spain. While the new exercised formal executive political *authority*, the old still possessed formidable *power*.[49]

The scenes of jubilant Republican crowds in April 1931 appeared to suggest the realisation of the historic dream of Spanish republicanism – the unity of the awakened 'people' (*pueblo*) carrying all before it. But the experience of the subsequent five years would show that, ironically, the necessity for unity was a lesson more easily assimilated by the political right than by the left. Elite groups' past political experience combined with their sheer survival instinct saw them rapidly adapt to the new environment. Conservative forces would use the new political instruments at their disposal to block reform (for example by parliamentary obstruction) as well as deploying their formidable economic resources and local power bases to ensure that Republican laws remained inoperative even after they reached the statute book in Madrid. This concerted obstruction, as well as the political inexperience and strategic errors of the reformers, the lack of money (above all at a time of economic depression) and, to some extent, the instrinsic slowness of reform as a process – all these factors opened up fissures within the 'pueblo' and on the political left that further disabled change and advantaged conservative interests, as we shall see. Nevertheless, one should not exaggerate the failure of change after 1931. After all, those hostile to it would be sufficiently frightened by the prospect that the centre left's electoral victory of February 1936 might herald the re-emergence of a popular anti-hegemonic coalition bent upon reform, for them to resort to apocalyptic 'solutions' – namely a military coup. What would happen after the launch of the coup had not been foreseen by anyone. But looking back, we can see that the 'afterwards' of 'hot' civil war was also a means of resolving – albeit in a vastly more violent way – the uneasy balance or stand-off between class forces opened up in 1931, and, through that, the underlying question of which route Spain would take to modernisation – the democratic or the dictatorial.[50]

---

[49] This was what the Austrian socialist thinker Otto Bauer acutely defined as a 'transitional regime of class equilibrium'. Otto Bauer, 'Fascism', in T. Bottomore and P. Goode (eds.) *Austro Marxism* (Oxford, 1978) pp. 167–86. For a summary H. Graham and P. Preston (eds.) *The Popular Front in Europe* (Basingstoke: Macmillan, 1987), p. 10. Cf. also S. Juliá, 'Manuel Azaña: la razón, la palabra y el poder', in V. A. Serrano and J. M. San Luciano (eds.) *Azaña* (Madrid: Edascal, 1980).

[50] In the 1940s 'Francoism' itself would be constructed through the process by which the military dictatorship mediated between the different sectors of capital in order to weld together a new elite project – at the same time as it brokered power between the political 'families' and imposed social discipline on the defeated. A. Cazorla, *Las políticas de la victoria. La consolidación del Nuevo Estado franquista (1938–1953)* (Madrid: Marcial Pons, 2000); A. Cenarro, *Cruzados y camisas azules. Los orígenes del franquismo en Aragón, 1936–1945* (Zaragoza: Prensas Universitarias de Zaragoza, 1997); Richards, *A Time of Silence*.

CHAPTER I

The challenge of mass political mobilisation (1931–1936)

¡Vivan los hombres que nos traen la ley![1]

The coming of the Second Republic saw the emergence of a governing coalition of centre-left republican groups in alliance with the Spanish Socialist Party (PSOE). Its reforming agenda was driven by a progressive republican ideology borne by the liberal – but somewhat marginal – sectors of Spain's urban professional lower middle classes. Their numerical slightness made the support of the PSOE crucial. The PSOE's own solidity as a support was provided by the electoral muscle of its near million-strong trade union movement, the UGT.

The driving ethos of this 1931 coalition was to modernise Spain economically, to initiate democratising reforms and to Europeanise the country socially and culturally. These objectives were to be attained via a series of legislative measures comprising agrarian, labour and social reforms (including state provision of education). Land reform (predominantly of the vast southern estates) was intended to create a large class of smallholding peasants in the style of France in 1789 whose acquisition of land would make them a permanent support base for the regime. The Republic's other key reform was of the military. This had crucial political goals – namely to bring the institution fully under civilian constitutional authority and, in time, to republicanise it. By reducing the size of the notoriously 'top-heavy' officer corps it was also intended to release much-needed funds to finance the rest of the planned reform programme. Reform is always an expensive undertaking, but the Spanish republicans were embarking upon it at a time when the effects of European and world economic depression were just beginning to be felt.

---

[1] 'Long live the men who bring us the rule of law!' This was the greeting offered in one village to Republican campaigners shortly before the declaration of the Second Republic, cited in E. Montero, 'Reform Idealised', in Graham and Labanyi, *Spanish Cultural Studies*, p. 129.

'Reforming' the balance of socio-economic and political power in
Spain in this way was perceived by the republicans as a means of delivering the classic goals of political liberalism. Increasing rural income
levels – and especially those of the landless proletariat of the south – was
intended too to create a larger domestic market in order to stimulate industrial growth. While redistribution would also fulfil social democratic
requirements of social equity *per se*, republicans also looked to it to create
a more inclusive and thus more stable society and polity in which to
pursue the national economic growth they sought.

THE POLITICAL FAILURE OF 'HISTORIC' REPUBLICANISM (1931–3)

The republican agenda was without any doubt an extraordinarily ambitious and wide-ranging one. In part this reflected the stagnation of the
old regime and the long overdue need for basic modernising change to
bring Spain into line with its European neighbours. Conservative interests would lose no time in mobilising against change. But even more
ominous for the republicans would be the alienation over 1931–3 of
social groups whose support was crucial to the viability of the reform
project – such as urban and rural labour and sectors of the provincial
middle classes. The reasons why this alienation would occur were complex and the underlying problems were in considerable part connected
with the context of economic depression. But they were also the result
of strategic errors on the part of the republicans themselves.

The republicans had little sense of the need to build active political
alliances *bottom up* in society in order to ensure an adequate mass support base for the reforms they wished to make. This blind spot seems
ironic given both the accelerating political mobilisation underpinning the
Republic's birth and the new context of representative democracy that
it had ushered in. We could explain it in terms of the republicans' lack
of political experience. But while we should not minimise the impact of
this, or the obstacles faced by the reformers, this myopia is also indicative
of their particular understanding of politics. For the republicans, like the
conservatives who opposed them, belonged to an old political world that
was, at heart, uneasy with the idea of mass mobilisation. Spanish republicanism was progressive in that it favoured certain structural reforms
to redistribute socio-economic power in Spain. But it was also conservative in that modernising reform was envisaged as something to be
implemented *top down* by a political elite via the machinery of state.

Indeed, for Spain's republicans, 'the Republic' began and ended with the state. Reform was perceived predominantly as an abstract, intellectual problem – a view nowhere more clearly articulated than in the writings and parliamentary interventions of Spain's pre-eminent republican leader, Manuel Azaña, prime minister of the liberal biennium of 1931–3 and, from May 1936, president of the Republic.[2] Strongly influenced by regenerationist and Krausist thought, the republicans envisaged an idealised state with extended and renovated powers.[3] But the actually existing state in April 1931 was made up of institutions and personnel inherited from the monarchist regime. There would be a significant continuity in the personnel working within the state bureaucracy – *faute de mieux*, since the incoming coalition simply did not have sufficient numbers of experienced, politically conducive individuals at its disposal.[4] Again, this was in part the inevitable consequence of the long exclusion of the left (broadly construed) from power. But this lack of adequate personnel was also compounded by the republicans' blindspot around political mobilisation. As already mentioned, 'historic republicanism' – dominated by lawyers, professors and educationalists – had previously failed to link up with the relatively populous professional middle-class associations where republican sentiment had developed significantly during the 1920s. By failing to forge such links, the republican political class deprived itself of much-needed technical and managerial expertise as well as losing the opportunity to widen progressive republicanism's popular support base.[5] This would prove a costly failure. Political republicanism inside the state machine lacked the necessary technical expertise to implement and monitor the detail of reform on a daily basis. But nor, given the republican conception of politics, did they necessarily understand why this was important.

This conception also led the republicans to confuse the theoretical political authority of government with real political *power*. The Spanish republicans had a firm – if somewhat naive – belief in the power of the law

---

[2] The idea of the Republic being synonymous with state action was most clearly articulated by him: 'ser republicano era sólo una manera de entender el Estado y las reglas del juego político', J. Paniagua Fuentes, introduction to Azaña's *Discursos parlamentarios* (Madrid: CSIC, 1992). Also, J. Marichal, *El Intelectual y la política* (Madrid: CSIC, 1990), p. 78.

[3] E. Montero, 'Reform Idealized: The Intellectual and Ideological Origins of the Second Republic', in Graham and Labanyi, *Spanish Cultural Studies*, pp. 124–7. Krausism was a strongly ethical school of philosophy dominant among Spanish liberal reformers in the 1870s and 1880s, based on the work of the post-kantian German philosopher Krause, a contemporary of Hegel.

[4] On the difficulty of finding appropriate republican personnel, see M. Maura, *Así cayó Alfonso XIII* (Barcelona: Ariel, 1995), pp. 265–72.

[5] See the introduction above.

(*juricidad*). But while they had the authority to enact a new Constitution[6] and bring legislation to parliament in Madrid, the task of *implementing* these things would bring the reformers hard up against the reality of how social and economic power in the localities of Spain (above all in majority rural Spain) remained to a great extent in the hands of the old elites.

The images most associated with the Republic's birth – of masses of people in the streets, surging through the squares and open spaces of the capital, clambering over public buildings and monuments, toppling statues of the king – vividly depict the expectations raised by the new regime among socially and economically disenfranchised sectors of the population, something which would further accelerate mass mobilisation after 1931. But the republicans' own political culture and experience did not fit them to exploit its political potential. Indeed, they would soon be responding (for example around issues of public order) in ways that suggested a real fear of the uncontrollability of this process.

But this difficulty belonged not only to the republicans. Their coalition partners, the Spanish Socialists (PSOE), were also in various ways grounded in this statist, *top-down* understanding of political and social change. Those socialists who identified primarily with the parliamentary party rather than the union (UGT) shared much of the republicans' elitist regenerationist ethos, while it was, paradoxically, in the socialists' trade union wing that the republicans' disquiet over mass mobilisation would find its clearest echo. Influenced by their collaboration with the Primo de Rivera dictatorship in the 1920s, the UGT's veteran leaders had envisaged the inheriting of state power in 1931 as a means of squaring a crucial circle. It could ensure expanding membership and influence for the socialist movement while maintaining a high degree of control, thus not risking its organisational structures and patrimony – the traumatic memories of 1917 had left an indelible mark. But when the UGT's membership did begin rapidly to expand (and nowhere more than among the rural south's landless proletariat[7]), then the union leadership's attitude became decidedly ambivalent. For the PSOE/UGT, like most other European socialist movements of the time, had deeply ingrained views on what constituted the 'organisable' working classes. Fears were expressed about the likely effects of the mass influx of the politically uneducated on the fabric of the organisation (its 'historic profile') and on its political

[6] The Republican Constitution of October 1931 borrowed from previous radical republican experiments (Mexico, 1917 and (especially) Weimar Germany, 1919).

[7] The urban unskilled – for example on the building sites of Madrid – were another source of anxiety.

mission of reform.[8] The socialist leaders seemed to have no idea about what to do with the new members flooding in. Nor indeed were they ever really *utilised* as a political constituency – apart, that is, from their sterile deployment in the internecine war inside the socialist movement.[9]

The challenge facing republicans and socialists was twofold. First, they had to mobilise a viable support base for their own reforms. Second, they had to develop strategies to defuse or counter anti-reform movements of opinion that could foreseeably be mobilised against them within the emergent system of mass parliamentary democracy.

But it proved impossible to mobilise an adequate support base. For this to happen, republicans and socialists had to show that they could convert aims into implemented policies. The proposed reforms combined Azaña's 'statist' agenda with the social agenda of the PSOE. But this was far too ambitious a programme to be realisable. Either of the two agendas was, alone, guaranteed to provoke more opposition from powerful elite groups than the government could deal with. Moreover, both Azaña and the socialist union leader, Largo Caballero, overestimated the size of their electoral mandate for reform. Included within the votes sustaining the government coalition there were probably quite a proportion for Alejandro Lerroux's Radical Party and others whose commitment to a reforming agenda was, to say the least, ambiguous. To make matters worse, Azaña and the PSOE discounted the extent to which their mandate for reform was dependent on the support of the CNT's social constituencies who were, thereby, left disenfranchised. In sum, the internal tensions in the republican-socialist reform project would prevent it from ever mobilising a sufficient support base for itself. Nor could it prevent the opposition from counter-mobilising.

Ironically, it was to be precisely those forces hostile to reform that learned to adapt faster to the new political environment. The scale of mass Catholic mobilisation between 1933 and 1936 was perhaps less evidence of Spain's 'polarisation' *per se* than it was of the liberal left's failure to achieve its own prior mass mobilisation, most crucially of some of the lower-middle-class constituencies which then turned to the

---

[8] Urgent calls for the mass political education of the new and prospective membership were made at the PSOE's 1932 congress; see J. M. Macarro Vera, 'Causas de la radicalización socialista en la II República', *Revista de Historia Contemporánea* (Seville), 1 (Dec. 1982), p. 203. Similar fears would resurface after the Popular Front electoral victory of February 1936.

[9] P. Preston, *The Coming of the Spanish Civil War. Reform, Reaction and Revolution in the Second Republic* (henceforward *CSCW*), 2nd edn (London: Routledge, 1994); S. Juliá, *La izquierda del PSOE (1935–1936)* (Madrid: Siglo XXI, 1977) and H. Graham, *Socialism and War. The Spanish Socialist Party in Power and Crisis, 1936–1939* (Cambridge: Cambridge University Press, 1991).

populist right, with fatal consequences for the Republican project. For if it had not been for mass mobilised conservative opinion, it would have been difficult for the rebel officers to justify the – essentially Bonapartist – coup of July 1936, even in a country whose civil society was as relatively underdeveloped as Spain's. Although its leaders had been involved in anti-Republican conspiracies since the regime's beginning, it was only the presence of mobilised *civilian* opinion that allowed the military rebels to present their actions in 1936 as if they constituted a popular plebiscite.[10]

The stakes in this battle of counter-mobilisation were made clear from the start. From the formal declaration of the Republic in April 1931, powerful sectors of the hierarchy of the Catholic Church in Spain indicated their irreducible hostility to the political and cultural pluralism at the heart of the Republican project.[11] In his pastoral letter of 7 May, Cardinal Segura, the Spanish Primate, offered a provocative homage to the monarchy and in his collective letter of July he publicly declared the doctrine of popular sovereignty to be inimical to Catholic teaching. With these declarations, the contest was now on to form the opinion and achieve the support of 'Catholic Spain' (i.e. the provincial and rural middle classes). But we should be clear that this was about *constituting* a political force, not simply about giving voice to what already existed. For many, maybe most, in the ecclesiastical hierarchy the issues were immediately clear: the Republic was unacceptable *per se* precisely because it was pluralist. But attitudes were much less clear-cut at the outset among lay Catholics and many of the lesser/ordinary clergy. It was only as a result of the specific religious measures implemented by the Republic that these sectors came to be politically and culturally alienated from it more or less *en masse*.

In a country where religious loyalties and piety were as emotive and powerful a mobilising force in some regions as anti-clericalism was (predominantly among working-class constituencies) in others, the Republic simply could not afford to alienate the Catholic laity virtually in its entirety. In these terms, the high-profile anti-clericalism of the republicans' religious reforms was a strategic error of considerable proportions. The chamber elected in June 1931 to draft these reforms was driven by vehement republican hostility to the Catholic Church as an institution.

---

[10] Cf. the text of Franco's *Discurso del alzamiento* – the radio broadcast made from Tetuán on 17 July 1936 justifying the rebellion in terms of the conspirators' embodying the national will, F. Díaz-Plaja, *La guerra de España en sus documentos* (Barcelona: Plaza y Janés, 1969), pp. 11–13.

[11] Bishop Gomá (later Primate of Spain) wrote on 15 April that 'we have now entered into the vortex of the storm', quoted in Lannon, *Privilege, Persecution and Prophecy*, p. 179.

In a mirror image of the right's manichaeism, republicans proved entirely unable to distinguish between state secularisation measures – such as separation of Church and state, the provision of civil alternatives to Catholic marriage and burial, or the provision of non-religious state education – and measures which infringed the democratic rights and sense of identity of ordinary Catholics. In the latter category came legislating for the exclusion from teaching of the religious orders or instituting a plethora of municipal regulations which harassed Catholics daily: impositions on funeral processions, on the ringing of church bells, on the outdoor celebration of patronal feasts. Sometimes wayside shrines were removed, together with religious statues or plaques in village squares. The implications of a secular state would no doubt have been strange and initially unwelcome to many Catholics. But over time they would have been assimilable. At any rate, they were not the stuff of which counter-Republican mobilisation could have been made – unlike those measures which directly interfered with the daily culture and identity of Catholics and which were thus perceived as vindictive.

It may be that a further distinction needs making between republican repression of popular Catholic culture (the cults around local village saints, for example) and the question of educational policy. But even if one were to make a case for the political importance of restricting the teaching role of the religious orders, the fact remains that once again, the republicans failed to implement their policy successfully. Although the debarment of religious personnel was stipulated in the Constitution of 1931, the specific legislation (the Law of Congregations) only reached the statute books in May 1933 – barely five months before the disintegration of the republican-socialist coalition. In other words, little can have happened before the coming to power of a centre-right government that effectively froze the legislation. All the republicans had in fact achieved was the creation of aggrieved constituencies that were, thus, ripe for mobilisation by the enemies of reform. By the same token, the total removal of state financial support for the Church provoked the alienation of the lesser clergy – a sector whose initial position was one of guarded caution but certainly not open hostility to the Republic.

One must also be wary of using late-twentieth-century conceptions of civil rights (ethically compelling though these are) to assess republican religious policy. While we may wish that the republicans had been more liberal in this respect – thinking not least of the perennial philosophical-political debate over means and ends – their illiberalism was of its time. Moreover, they were also rather less illiberal and somewhat more

concerned about constitutional rights (if not yet civil/human rights properly speaking) than their opponents. (Conservative Catholics were outraged that their beliefs and practices were being subjected to restraints.
But they themselves entertained no concept of civil and cultural rights
within the Spanish state for freethinkers or atheists.) In the last analysis, we have to remember that no aspect relating to the Church in
1930s Spain could be divorced from high politics. For many republicans Catholic culture was, root and branch, a threat to the inculcation
of precisely the open, pluralist mentality needed to stabilise the democratic Republic in Spain. (We should remember too that the ecclesiastic
hierarchy was the most consistent and vociferous defender of the monarchy in the transitional period from the Primo dictatorship to Republic
(1929–31).) Moreover, there was also sometimes an important practical
dimension to the republicans' measures: saving on the stipend to clergy,
for example, was one way of garnering scarce resources (even scarcer
because of the recession) to fund the programme of state school building.

However, perhaps the main point to grasp here for our purposes is that
the republicans saw their commitment to secularisation as a matter of
fulfilling certain 'historic' republican ideals or ideological principles. Just
as with agrarian reform or anti-militarism, it was perceived as another
'cultural north' and borne as a crucial 'mark of identity'. But once again
the republicans had failed to think through the material consequences of
their policies in the new political environment. So the anti-clerical tendencies of 'historic' republicanism armed a counter-movement without
having in place any strategy for dealing with it.

Catholic Action – the organisational hub of what would become the
mass Catholic party CEDA (strictly speaking a confederation of various regionally based right-wing groups) – creatively elaborated a propaganda line suggesting that the Church's very existence was imperilled
by the atheistic material and spiritual depredations of the Republic. It
worked to good effect particularly among the intensely Catholic impoverished smallholders of central and north-central Spain. This process of mobilisation was greatly facilitated by the fact that the Church
had a well-established social-organisational infrastructure (i.e. Catholic
Action's own) embedded in the localities. The republicans had no comparable structures on which to build. Moreover, the fact that their agrarian
reform measures tended to neglect the specific problems of smallholders
and tenant farmers also hugely facilitated the mobilisation of such
groups by the CEDA – a party that received massive subsidies from the
large southern landowners who stood to lose most from the Republic's

agrarian law of September 1932.[12] Anti-clerical legislation alone did not provoke the Spanish oligarchy's campaign against the Republic, but in bringing about practical unity on the right, it massively facilitated the implementation of that campaign.

As a result, the provincial, commercial and rural smallholding classes of the agrarian interior (above all of Castile and Leon) were definitively conquered by resurgent conservatism. Via the CEDA or other conservative agrarian associations such as the CNCA (Confederación Nacional Católico-Agraria[13]) these sectors would effectively be recruited to the political project of agrarian counter-reform. In the process, 'Spanish' nationalism itself was definitively appropriated not only as a force of political conservatism (as had been clearly happening since the 1920s) but now of populist conservatism.

Elsewhere in Spain, on the peripheries – both urban and rural – the picture was less bleak for progressive republicanism. But here too political tension and fragmentation were still the order of the day. Nowhere was this more evident than in relations between the Madrid government and the highly Catholic and socially conservative Basque Country. The Basque Nationalist Party (PNV), which was emerging as a significant political force in the region, looked somewhat askance at 'anti-clerical Madrid' while it was also concerned to keep the PSOE's political influence at bay in Bilbao.[14] This was not only because the PSOE was a socialist party, but also because it was a centralist one. In fact neither side trusted the other. Although the republican-socialist coalition was open to the possibility of a Basque autonomy statute, it wanted to ensure that the devolved powers remained in the hands of Basque socialists and republicans. Following the PNV's – albeit relatively brief and abortive – alliance with the Carlists in 1931, republicans and socialists saw it as representing clerical conservatism and, especially given the anti-constitutional tenor of some of the PNV-Carlist proposals, as far from politically trustworthy.

[12] Preston, *CSCW*; E. Malefakis, *Agrarian Reform and Peasant Revolution in Spain* (New Haven/London: Yale University Press, 1970); A. Bosch, 'Nuevas perspectivas sobre la conflictividad rural en la Segunda República', *Historia Contemporánea*, 9 (1993), 141–66. A recent case study of the south is in F. Cobo Romero, 'El voto campesino contra la II República. La derechización de los pequeños propietarios y arrendatarios agrícolas jiennenses 1931–1936', *Historia Social*, 37 (2000), 119–42 and *Conflicto rural y violencia política* (Jaén: Universidad de Jaén/Universidad de Granada, 1998).

[13] The political organisation of Catholic smallholders in north and central Spain. Created in 1917, it was a forerunner of the CEDA and provided the core of its mass base.

[14] While the PNV was an influential force, the politically divided nature of the Basque region (i.e. with the strong influence of the traditionalist right (Carlists)) meant that it was not hegemonic. The PNV's influence was predominant in the province of Vizcaya. But in its capital, Bilbao, the PNV had to struggle against the PSOE. F. de Meer, *El Partido Nacionalista Vasco ante la guerra de España (1936–1937)* (Barañáin-Pamplona: EUNSA, 1992), p. 66.

But the PNV, under a new young leadership headed by José Antonio Aguirre, espoused an open and pragmatic conservatism rather than the closed integrist variety of Carlist Navarre. The PNV's political leadership was, moreover, significantly *less* conservative than its own lower-middle-class support base – especially those parts of it located in the rural interior. Accordingly, the pull of the Republican alliance would increase for Aguirre and his party in proportion to their disaffection from the integrist Catholic conservatism represented by the Carlists. (After it had rapidly become clear that an autonomy statute could not be used to bar Republican secularisation and social reform policies from the Basque Country, not only did the Carlists' interest in a statute wane, but they actively joined the monarchist right nationally in obstructing it.) Madrid began to use the prospect of an autonomy statute as a 'carrot' to attract the PNV into the Republican orbit. But the distrust between the two meant that negotiations were inevitably slower and more complex than those for the Catalan equivalent (promulgated in September 1932). There was disagreement particularly about the extent of devolved financial powers and over who should control the police and army in the region. An accord had still not been reached when the centre-right came to power in Madrid in November 1933 and the CEDA's outright hostility to autonomy blocked further progress. This hostility would result in the PNV's gradual, strategic rapprochement (though not entry) to what by the end of 1935 would be a re-emergent republican-socialist coalition. In this the efforts of the PSOE leader, Indalecio Prieto, were paramount. He had close personal ties with the Basque Country and was determined to strengthen the Republican coalition by bringing the PNV into its orbit.

Nevertheless, the basic republican thinking that social and educational reforms would, in the medium term, contribute to stability and development, allowing a new secular mentality to emerge as the basis for the 'Republican nation', remained problematic with regard to the Basque Country, as it did in other ways. However, the fact that a formal commitment to a Basque statute would feature in the electoral programme of the centre-left coalition in February 1936 ensured that the PNV strategically accepted the programme, even though it did not join the coalition. But the political and jurisdictional disputes that had constantly underlain the PNV's tortuous path to a *modus vivendi* with the Republic during 1931–6 meant that the statute would still not have been promulgated when the military rose in July 1936.[15] Once again, Republican Madrid

[15] Ibid., pp. 58, 67–72, 77.

would use the statute (which it eventually ceded in October 1936) to tie the industrial Basque Country to its war effort. Crucially, it would also accept PNV leadership of the new provisional Basque wartime government. But the fundamental disagreement over how much power it could deploy would immediately erupt with full force. This was so not least because the centrifugal impact of the military coup would by then already have conferred *de facto* 'powers' on the regions that far outstripped anything the central Republican government had ever intended to concede.[16]

A similar jurisdictional dispute would also develop between the central Republican government and Catalan nationalism – in spite of the fact that 1930s Catalanism was clearly on the left and substantively in agreement with the qualitative nature of republican reform, religious, social and agrarian. Catalan nationalism of the centre-left had been a fully subscribed member of the San Sebastián pact in 1930.[17] And when a coalition of political groups formed the Republican Left of Catalonia (ERC or Esquerra) in spring 1931, it had appeared the ideal interlocutor for the liberal reformers of Madrid, led as it was by the urban professional classes of Barcelona but with significant rural support in the region. In short, Catalonia, as the most socially variegated area in Spain, had the greatest potential for creating the counter-hegemonic alliance needed to shore up the reforming Republic.

But the Esquerra's relations with the republican-socialist government of 1931–3 were far from easy. In 1931 the Esquerra had initially declared for an independent Catalonia in a federal Spain. But it had agreed to forego this in return for Madrid ceding a statute of autonomy on generous terms. But these terms, as the Esquerra saw it, never materialised. In spite of the empathy over other sorts of structural reform and even though the Madrid republicans recognised the Catalans' claims as licit in principle, in the end their ingrained centralism was stronger. They sought to water down the powers granted under the statute of 1932 and, even then, delayed their transfer. That the Esquerra saw this as a promise broken explains Catalonia's enthusiastic assumption, in the wake of the July 1936 military coup, of *de facto* powers which, Republican president Azaña would complain bitterly, lay beyond the statute.[18]

---

[16] See chapter 4 below for an analysis of wartime relations between the PNV and the central Republican governments.
[17] The 1920s had seen the political leadership of Catalanism pass from the conservative Lliga to the centre-left; see the introduction above.
[18] For example, issuing currency and levying troops.

Nevertheless, right from 1931 the Esquerra was a powerful political force. It dominated in Catalonia in a way that the PNV never did in the Basque Country as a whole. The Esquerra's success here can be gauged by the fact that its identity would rapidly merge with that of the regional government (Generalitat) ceded under the terms of the 1932 autonomy statute. Moreover, in terms of agrarian reform, the Catalan republican left would, between 1934 and 1936, fight and eventually win the right to amend rural tenancies *en masse*. This had the effect of stabilising conditions and increasing security for the small tenant farmers (*rabassaires*) who were the most numerous sector in the Catalan countryside and a source of bedrock support for the Esquerra. The party fought this agrarian war first through legislative reform (the famous *ley de contratos de cultivo*[19]) and then in the courts. Finally it was the ballot box, in February 1936, which gave it victory. It would be this defeat that saw Catalonia's (minority) agrarian right – represented by the Institut Agrari de San Isidre – align itself with its counterparts elsewhere in Spain and ultimately, in July 1936, with the military rebels.[20]

But although the existence of strong regional nationalisms problematised the emergence of an overarching republican nationalism after 1931, it is also true that the Catalan government's dissatisfaction with Madrid was much exacerbated by the fact of economic recession. With greater budgetary resources the Generalitat could, for example, have funded its own schools and thus ensured the dissemination of Catalan language and culture. (Control of education remained beyond the autonomy statute and, while Madrid recognised Catalan as an official language, it required all school instruction to be undertaken in Spanish.) Financial stringency would be responsible for more than the political disappointment of Catalanists, however. For the commitment of the republicans – in Barcelona as much as Madrid – to orthodox, deflationary liberal economics at a time of international depression would make it impossible to provide a credible level of social welfare relief for the urban and rural dispossessed. Had it been possible to include them within a Republican 'new deal', then urban and rural labour (or at least some sectors of it) could have been mobilised as alternative support to compensate for the lack of a sufficiently broad base among middling sectors. But the difficulties here were enormous, as we shall see. It was the abiding distance between the reforming Republic and its potential working-class support base that

---

[19] The Law of Agricultural Contracts.
[20] Conservative Catalan nationalism, in the shape of the Lliga, made some electoral gains around 1933–4, but not enough to unseat the centre-left coalition in Catalonia.

made the price of its anti-clericalism too high. The combination of an uncompromising religious settlement with monetarist economics would deprive the republican-socialist coalition of any minimally sufficient social support base.

After initial high hopes of Republican reform, worker disaffection arrived quickly in metropolitan Spain – and most notably in the industrial heartland of Barcelona. For many workers, their daily experience was dominated by the *absence* of palliative reform (for the Republic had *promised* it[21]) alongside the brutality of what appeared to them to be a largely unreformed state apparatus in action. The underdeveloped Spanish state had long been defined in terms of its security forces. Under the old regime, the police and, *in extremis*, the army had functioned to defend the established social order and elite economic interest in a highly transparent fashion. While the coming of the Republic in principle meant the chance to develop other, integrative, state functions – such as education and welfare – in practice the options here were limited. Even before the worst effects of international depression kicked in, the Republic's scope for enacting social and labour reform or for increasing welfare spending was severely restricted. It was refused foreign loans while at the same time it faced a highly unpromising national economic situation, with a flight of capital as well as substantial debts inherited from the dictatorship – especially in the form of the loans taken out to fund Primo's public works.

The international depression would also take its toll. The underdevelopment of Spanish capitalism (and thus its lesser integration in the international system) meant that the repercussions of the 1930s crisis may have been relatively less in *macro-economic* terms (for example there was no sudden, new phenomenon of mass unemployment as there was in Germany). But we should not make the mistake of assuming that the impact of the crisis was therefore less severe for Spanish workers – who included large numbers of economic migrants obliged to return home. Moreover, Spain *already* had severe structural unemployment and highly casualised and sweated labour patterns which, under the impact of recession, and in the absence of even the most rudimentary public welfare net, pushed many sectors of the labouring classes to sub-subsistence levels. But as the republican-socialist coalition was never conceived as a revolutionary alliance, outright expropriation or other radically redistributive

---

[21] Echoing the republicans' own credo, there was a strong popular belief in the power of the *letter* of the law. Cf. the epigraph to this chapter and n. 1 above.

measures were not considered an option by either of the alliance's component parts.

Indeed, the only area in which the Spanish republicans were prepared to depart from strict fiscal 'rectitude' was education.[22] During 1931 they took out special loans to underwrite a target of 27,000 new schoolrooms (and teachers to staff them) in five years. In August 1931 a number of 'teaching missions' (*misiones pedagógicas*) were also established. In the form of literacy classes, mobile libraries, travelling theatre exhibitions and civic education, they brought 'culture and politics' to the villages of Spain. While the project has attracted criticism because of its undeniably paternalist overtones, it did reach people on a significant scale.[23] Indeed, the subsequent conservative administration was worried enough to slash the missions' budget in 1934–5. But the missions' main potential 'public' was labour, and to construct this as a social support base for the progressive Republic required rather more than the delivery of an abstract cultural message – conservative fears notwithstanding. What it demanded was a resolute, coherent and costed policy of practical social reform materially to underpin republican 'enlightenment'.[24] As one of the cultural missionaries memorably encapsulated the problem: '[the rural poor] needed bread and medicine, and we had only songs and poems in our bags'.[25] But apart from education, the republicans never even saw fit to produce a costing for the reform programme overall, within a formal budget.[26]

On the other hand, from the start the republicans demonstrated their strong line on law and order. A formative experience for urban labour came with the Barcelona rent strike that erupted in the summer of 1931. The city and its surrounding industrial belt had a uniquely high

---

[22] The ranks of political republicanism contained many teachers and educationalists who were greatly influenced by the ideas of the Institute of Independent Education. They believed that education was the key to modernising Spain.

[23] M. de Puelles Benítez, 'El sistema educativo republicano: un proyecto frustrado', *Historia Contemporánea*, 6 (1991), 159–71.

[24] One can argue that a greater awareness of this existed in Spanish socialist ranks – cf. the blueprint for social inclusion and nation building outlined in parliamentary socialist leader Indalecio Prieto's Cuenca speech (May 1936) demanding the 'interior conquest' of Spain. But the same abstraction can also be adduced to criticise parliamentary socialist discourses of popular mobilisation during the war; see chapter 4 below for a discussion of socialist premier Juan Negrín's wartime speeches.

[25] C. Cobb in Graham and Labanyi, *Spanish Cultural Studies*, pp. 136–7. The quotation, also cited by Cobb, is the playwright Alejandro Casona's.

[26] J. M. Macarro Vera, 'Social and Economic Policies of the Spanish Left in Theory and in Practice', in M. S. Alexander and H. Graham (eds.), *The French and Spanish Popular Fronts. Comparative Perspectives* (Cambridge: Cambridge University Press, 1989), pp. 171–84 and J. M. Macarro, 'Economía y política en el Frente Popular' in *Revista de Historia Contemporánea*, 7 (1996), 129–50. The PSOE's Indalecio Prieto left the treasury for public works in autumn 1931.

concentration of sweated factory labour and urban poor.[27] It was this social context of the extreme impoverishment of unskilled labour, plus a housing crisis within a deregulated housing market, which explain the strike.[28] It brought down the full force of Republican state discipline on tenants and their leaders.[29] They were subject to police harassment and 'preventive detention'. Their meetings were summarily banned, as were worker newspapers that publicised strike-related matters.[30] Associative rights were in practice being denied just as they had been under the monarchy. That it was, on this occasion, the Republic's newly formed Assault Guards who were called in to supervise evictions merely reinforced the sense of continuity. The new Republican regime, fearful of losing support among the urban (and especially the commercial) middle classes, justified these measures in the name of the 'authority principle'. It used the new Law for the Defence of the Republic (passed in October 1931) to declare the strike an 'illegal conspiracy' against the regime – thus permitting the intensification of police action.[31]

On numerous notorious occasions across Spain, Republican security forces would clash fatally head-on with protesting workers: at Castilblanco (December 1931), in Arnedo (Logroño) and Llobregat (Barcelona province), both in January 1932, and at Casas Viejas (Andalusia) in January 1933. But beneath these high-profile incidents there lay a daily experience of repression and exclusion.

In Barcelona especially, tensions increased as the republican authorities found themselves unable to deliver promised welfare measures within a severely restricted budget. (Nor of course did the establishment of an autonomous Catalan government in 1932 make much difference here.) The unemployed and others on the economic margins attempted to

[27] For an excellent analysis of the material world of unskilled sweated labour which 'made' the Barcelona working class, see Ealham, 'Policing the Recession', chapter 1, pp. 13–50.

[28] ILO figures indicate that Spanish workers were the lowest paid in Europe – with the exception of the Portuguese. Yet the Spanish food-price index was higher than in recession-hit Germany, where comparable wages were at least double. Ibid., pp. 142–3.

[29] This was before the promulgation of the Catalan statute, so the Madrid government was still in control of public order.

[30] The old monarchist eviction law was revised, reducing the period at which eviction could be enforced for rent arrears from 3 months to 8 days. Municipal byelaws were also pressed into service to label flats 'uninhabitable' in order to remove striking tenants. The flats would then be refilled with more pliable tenants, C. Ealham, 'Frustrated Hopes. The 1931 Rent Strike and the Republic' (unpublished article), pp. 13–14. On the rent strike see also N. Rider, 'The Practice of Direct Action: The Barcelona Rent Strike', in D. Goodway (ed.), *For Anarchism. History, Theory, Practice* (London: Routledge, 1989), pp. 79–105.

[31] As a result, the rent strike, as a mass action, wound down by the end of 1931. But the failure to resolve any of the desperate conditions that had sparked it meant that it would continue as a sporadic action throughout the life of the Republic: Ealham, 'Frustrated Hopes', pp. 23–4.

find their own solutions, for example by turning to itinerant street trade or setting up *ad hoc* outlets (such as informal street stalls) selling cheap food. But as these undercut established markets and shopkeepers, the authorities, heeding complaints from the Barcelona Chamber of Commerce, sent in the Civil Guard (many of whose agents had served under the monarchy) to arrest or dismantle the competition.[32] Pitched battles regularly ensued in the working-class neighbourhoods of Barcelona between the police and the poor – both sellers and customers. There could be no more graphic image of the social war waged between the Republic and its dispossessed.[33] Republican law, once heralded as offering these groups protection and redress, was, in the form of 'public order', increasingly becoming a weapon against them. Moreover, the interaction – calculated or otherwise – between public-order measures and the Republic's new labour legislation was systematically criminalising the most marginal groups of workers.

A key part of the labour legislation steered through under the auspices of the republicans' socialist coalition partners provided a national network of committees (*Jurados Mixtos*) to settle labour disputes. But such arbitration-based unionism, modelled on the practice of skilled sectors of the UGT, was of little use to Spain's army of unskilled, casualised and easily replaceable industrial and agrarian labourers. Their lack of bargaining power in the market place (above all in slump conditions) made the direct action tactics spearheaded by the anarcho-syndicalist CNT their only weapon.[34] But increasingly it was against these kinds of labour strategies and their implementors that the Republic's public-order legislation was targeted. The Law for the Defence of the Republic was in force throughout most of the period of republican-socialist government.[35] The Law of Employer and Worker Associations (April 1932)[36] was used to much the same end. Militants were detained and union

---

[32] The Republic created the Assault Guards as a new urban police force in 1931 and usually held the Civil Guard in reserve for emergencies. But in Barcelona the Civil Guard was retained as the normal policing body. The great continuity of police personnel (at least 'in the ranks' if not in positions of responsibility) ensured the perpetuation of authoritarian ideas and a culture of corruption. For policing in Barcelona and the failure of [Republican] professionalisation, see Ealham, 'Policing the Recession', pp. 117–22.

[33] Ibid., pp. 172, 192–3. This was a conflict which would continue unabated into the war years, exacerbated by ever-increasing shortages, inflation and the black market. See chapter 5 below.

[34] Although some CNT unions did accept the arbitration system – in spite of opposition from the CNT's national leadership. See the discussion of divisions in the CNT and CNT–UGT relations later in this chapter.

[35] In July 1933 it was replaced by the Public Order Act.

[36] Ley de Asociaciones Profesionales, Patronales y Obreras; see J. Casanova, *De la calle al frente. El anarcosindicalismo en España (1931–1939)* (Barcelona: Crítica, 1997), p. 55, p. 74, n. 13.

premises closed. In the summer of 1933 an anti-vagrancy law (*Ley de Vagos y Maleantes*) was also introduced.[37] This permitted the detention of those who could not prove that they had legal means of supporting themselves. It also outlawed the financial collections on which the CNT's organisation and strategies (especially spontaneous industrial action) depended, and it threatened collectors with internment.[38]

A test case under the Anti-Vagrancy Act was brought against a number of radical anarchist leaders from the FAI, including Buenaventura Durruti and Francisco Ascaso – neither of whom was unemployed – while they were on a speaking tour of Andalusia in 1933.[39] Such legislative harassment more or less obliged anarchist and communist activists – above all in Barcelona – to operate in clandestinity, particularly when they were organising the unemployed. Into this category came street sellers and itinerant workers of all kinds who could also be detained under the conditions of the anti-vagrancy law, in camps established for the purpose.[40] It was not lost on those so treated that the much-vaunted liberal freedom of association reached no further than skilled sectors of the UGT. Republican law and order was effectively branding non-social democratic constituencies of organised labour, plus anyone else forced for reasons of survival to operate beyond liberal economic nostrums, as 'enemies of the state'.[41]

The republicans would seem to have believed that the mere existence of 'the Republic' – or at least the *de jure* declaration of Republican liberties – would serve to pacify economically and politically marginalised sectors. Their constant evocation of 'the people' in parliamentary rhetoric

---

[37] This was used as a kind of 'judicial hoover' (Ealham,'Policing the Recession') to 'regularise' the detention of all those being held at that time for reasons of perceived 'undesirable' behaviour or lifestyle. The law was also retained after the re-election of the liberal left in the Popular Front elections of February 1936.

[38] The law specified financial collections by 'clandestine' organisations. This was a reference to the CNT's non-registration (prior to 1936) under the April 1932 law: Casanova, *De la calle al frente*, p. 141. The definition of 'collections' was also stretched to cover the meagre stipends paid to CNT activists, thus allowing the latter to be targeted also.

[39] Ealham, 'Policing the Recession', pp. 286–7.

[40] Some camps were specially established, but a lack of government resources meant that existing prisons (and in Barcelona prison ships) were used: Ealham, 'Policing the Recession', pp. 284–91. Most camps were in Barcelona with some in the south. But statistical information and details of camp regimes are sparse. A police report (Madrid interior ministry) refers to 107 individuals being detained in Seville in September 1933. I am grateful to Chris Ealham for this information and for his help with the material in this section.

[41] As discussed later in this chapter, Spanish socialist ethos (whether expressed by trade union leaders or parliamentary socialists) also underwrote the notion of organisable ('respectable') and unorganisable (disruptive/lumpen) elements of labour. One of the architects of the anti-vagrancy law was the lawyer and leading parliamentary socialist Luis Jiménez de Asúa.

contrasts with their growing horror during 1931–3 at the prospect of actively mobilising masses whom they had not the least idea how to cope with. As some of their middle-class constituencies expressed similarly derived fears over the perceived growth of crime and disorder, republican concern with the 'neutrality' of the street and public spaces increased.[42] These fears were probably a contributory factor in the republicans' failure to make effective public-order reform, and in particular, their signal failure to demilitarise the apparatus of public order. Republican attitudes here, of course, also betray their inability to relinquish an elite conception of politics rooted in the 'old demobilised world' of nineteenth-century liberalism.[43] But their heavy-handedness in the area of law and order certainly accelerated urban worker disaffection. Meanwhile, protests sparked by economic hardship were sharpened in the new political climate, which raised worker expectations of redress. But budgetary constraints meant that the Republic simply could not deliver the social 'salvation' demanded by mobilising worker constituencies.

Nowhere was the redemptive dimension of worker demands clearer than in the rural deep south of Spain. For it was there, of course, that the *de facto* power of the old elites remained most completely intact. Such paternalistic social reforms as had been attempted under monarchy and dictatorship were restricted to the urban arena, with the countryside remaining off limits. There the Civil Guard had long been enmeshed in clientelistic relations with the local landowning elites. As the underlying relations of socio-economic power remained basically unchanged across the political transition to a Republic, the Civil Guard continued to be used as an instrument to prevent, or at least slow up, the practical implementation of reform.[44] Slowness and obstruction affected the agrarian reform badly, compounded as the problems already were by technical, political and financial insufficiencies. By contrast, the raft of labour reforms[45] initiated by the socialist labour minister

---

[42] Casanova, *De la calle al frente*, p. 145 (inc. n. 12).

[43] For further discussion of this, see the analysis below of republican politics on the morrow of the February 1936 Popular Front elections.

[44] The 1930s still saw the Civil Guard used in time-honoured 'tradition' to keep the starving off uncultivated land and to prevent them poaching or scavenging for acorns and the like on estate property.

[45] Most importantly, a minimum wage and maximum working day; requiring landowners to hire through the labour exchanges and to contract workers on the basis of a strict rota; the role of the state-chaired arbitration boards (*Jurados Mixtos*) in both settling disputes and overseeing the fulfilment of the new labour norms.

Francisco Largo Caballero and overseen by the UGT's cadres, did start to make more of a material impact on both the political and socio-economic balance of power in the rural centre-south.[46] But while the rural elites understood the subverting potential of these norms (and would mobilise accordingly), for the rural dispossessed – focused on the icon of land reform – these changes seemed painfully slow and piecemeal.[47]

In terms of implemented policy, the socialist labour reforms probably achieved more than did republican land reform. But given the structural 'oversupply' of unskilled labour generated by the latifundia system of landholding, unemployment was a massive and endemic problem. The scale of welfare relief needed was way beyond anything that could have been contemplated within republican fiscal norms. The situation for destitute landless peasants was worsened by the international depression, which meant that state funds for public works relief were also modest. Indeed, the exhaustion of the public works budget before the particularly hard winter of 1932–3 explained much of the turmoil of that year.

Land reform too was bound by similar financial constraints. Indeed, these were exacerbated by one of the republicans' fundamental political principles – the inviolability of private property. For this meant that they were committed to indemnifying owners (in government bonds) at the full market value of the land acquired. Resettlement could thus occur only at a painfully slow rate. In such circumstances, no reform – however politically subversive in the medium term – could have been enough.[48] The implicit sense of *urgency* here was, of course, born of the new political perceptions among the rural poor, of the belief that the Second Republic would be synonymous with their own empowerment. Their faith could not long outlast the interaction of elite obstruction and republican limitations.

By mid 1933 the republican-socialist coalition was close to breaking point under the dual strain of the alienation of the disenfranchised and

[46] S. Juliá, 'La experiencia del poder: la izquierda republicana 1931–1933', in N. Townson (ed.), *El republicanismo en España (1830–1977)* (Madrid: Alianza, 1994), pp. 183–4.

[47] This impatience needs also to be seen in a brutal social context where the most reactionary of landowners and bailiffs taunted starving labourers to 'comed República' (literally 'eat the Republic', or 'let the Republic feed you').

[48] It is also unlikely that the republican model of settling plots of land on individuals would in any case have been economically feasible in the medium term – given the inhospitable conditions for agriculture in the south. But, once again, republican ideology had prevented the acceptance of the PSOE/UGT's preferred collectivist model of agrarian reform.

the mounting elite offensive. When the split came in September the de-cisive pressure was that applied to the republicans by an increasingly vociferous business lobby.[49] This was determined to detach the Socialist Party from government as the first step towards curtailing social re-form. But the tensions between republicans and socialists and within the socialist movement itself were also considerable by this stage. While parliamentary socialists might have wished for greater republican pol-icy consistency and application over reform, it was the socialist union leadership that felt most frustrated and exposed by the limits of republi-can economic strategy and political will. For these had exacerbated the effects of the right's obstruction of reform.

Throughout the life of the republican-socialist coalition government, Spain's employers' federation had waged a high-profile and intensely personal campaign against the labour minister, UGT general secre-tary Largo Caballero. This was aimed primarily at ending the executive power of the national labour arbitration committees.[50] At the same time, the socialist union leaders were also increasingly fearful that the UGT's presence in government risked making it seem responsible in the eyes of its members for the slowness of social welfare improvements and land reform. In particular they were worried about the effect on frustrated recent adherents to the socialist landworkers' federation (FNTT), which had expanded dramatically after April 1931 in the hope of government-led reform.[51] These anxieties were massively heightened by the context of violent clashes between urban and rural workers and Republican secu-rity forces. The UGT's leaders feared that their guilt by association with a regime that not only neglected workers' interests but also physically as-saulted them would lead to a haemorrhage of UGT members to the rival CNT. Given that the anarcho-syndicalist organisation had its own inter-nal problems, with hindsight this was perhaps an exaggerated fear, but it was nonetheless perceived as a real danger at the time. Nevertheless, socialist departure from power still seemed 'unthinkable' – precisely

---

[49] Socialist participation in government would split the Radical-Socialist Party, some of whose components would in 1933 also spearhead the internal republican campaign against agrarian and labour reform, N. Townson, *The Crisis of Democracy in Spain. Centrist Politics under the Second Republic 1931–1936* (Brighton/Portland: Sussex Academic Press, 2000), p. 170. Details of the multi-pronged attack on the PSOE as a party of government are in given Macarro Vera, 'Causas de la radicalización socialista en la II República', pp. 206–8. For the employers' lobby, see M. Cabrera, *La patronal ante la Segunda República* (Madrid, 1983).

[50] S. Juliá, 'La experiencia del poder: la izquierda republicana, 1931–1933', in Townson, *El repub-licanismo en España*, pp. 181–3.

[51] Preston, *CSCW*, pp. 30, 31, 78.

because no sector of the PSOE/UGT leadership had any political strategy but gradualist reform.[52]

As the tensions mounted inside republican ranks, the break with the socialists came in September 1933. In the event, it was the socialists who departed, under pressure from Largo Caballero. But his decision was doubtless hastened by the fear that internal republican differences would soon lead to the PSOE being asked to leave. With the left divided, and a Republican electoral law in force which actively favoured coalitions, the general elections of November 1933 saw the victory of a centre-right alliance whose electoral backbone came from the CEDA. The disintegration of the left coalition meant that the republicans were cut off not only from the socialists' electoral base but also from their organisational resources, which were the nearest thing the left had to a national political infrastructure. The lack of these assets would erode the political potential of progressive republicanism, separated as it was now from government resources, and with the mobilisation of a well-organised populist right accelerating apace. For the socialists too, exclusion from power would have no less seriously erosive effects. The trauma of departure would accelerate and embitter divisions within the movement during 1933–5. In turn these would fatally undermine attempts to resurrect a republican-socialist governmental alliance – although, in the end, this remained the *sine qua non* of social reform in Spain.

THE INTERNAL FRAGMENTATION OF SPANISH SOCIALISM (1933–6)

As conservative mass mobilisation consolidated around the CEDA, the left's social and political base became increasingly fragmented. While this fragmenting process reached beyond the socialist movement to anarchists, anarcho-syndicalists and communist groups, the most crucial fissure on the left was that running through the PSOE/UGT. Having blocked any resumption of republican-socialist alliance, Largo Caballero increasingly identified himself in the public eye with those sectors of the socialist movement which claimed that the reformist option had now demonstrably failed, that revolution was the inescapable conclusion and

---

[52] This point is excellently made in José Manuel Macarro Vera's subtle and suggestive article 'Causas de la radicalización socialista'. The author seems to assume, however, that evidence of CNT crisis *per se* means that the UGT cannot have feared losing members to it. But this assessment leaves out of account self-generating fears in a context of besieged social reform.

that the PSOE's organisation had to be 'bolshevised' in preparation for its role as the revolutionary vanguard party. (In approximate terms, these sectors constituted parts of the UGT, a majority of the socialist youth leadership[53] and minority sectors in the PSOE.) But no such process of bolshevisation occurred. Between 1934 and 1936 Largo spoke of a revolution that neither he nor anyone else in PSOE/UGT ranks was preparing. Some radicals among the socialist youth believed in it, assisted in their belief by the superficially theoretical discourse of left socialist intellectuals such as Luis Araquistain and Carlos de Baraibar. Their discourses were also used by Largo to bolster his own organisational position. Although no conscious bad faith was involved on Largo's part, this borrowing of a revolutionary language was not enough to make him a revolutionary. His revolutionism remained, throughout, purely the expression of a moral preference that Spanish socialism *should* change. 'That preference never put down roots in the structure or practice of the organisation.'[54] But it provoked fear among conservative groups whose access to firepower was, in the end, inevitably superior – in the shape of the army. Nor did Largo's supporters themselves make any contingency plans (such as the arming of defensive militia) to counter the potential recourse of conservative forces to 'catastrophist' solutions. When sectors of the officer corps rose against the Republic in July 1936, the socialist left's lack of any political strategy, let alone a revolutionary one, would become fully apparent.

In order to explain this apparently contradictory behaviour, it is important to disaggregate the political motives (conscious and unconscious) of Largo Caballero and the socialist left's trade union leadership from two other components.[55] First, the *context* of increasing discontent and some radicalisation of political intent among sectors of the socialist movement's grass roots, faced with the erosion of reform and working-class gains by a conservative government. Second, the separate agenda of the radicalised socialist youth leadership – which was not necessarily compatible with that of the UGT's veteran leadership.[56] In addition, socialist youth radicalism almost certainly had an important sociological – as opposed to

[53] But not necessarily of the socialist youth membership as a whole: R. Viñas, *La formación de las Juventudes Socialistas Unificadas (1934–1936)* (Madrid: Siglo XXI, 1978); H. Graham, 'The Socialist Youth in the JSU: The Experience of Organisational Unity, 1936–8', in M. Blinkhorn (ed.), *Spain in Conflict 1931–1939* (London: Sage, 1986), pp. 83–102.

[54] Macarro Vera, 'Causas de la radicalización socialista', p. 223.

[55] For an analysis of the socialist left, see H. Graham, 'The Eclipse of the Socialist Left: 1934–1937', in F. Lannon and P. Preston (eds.), *Elites and Power in Twentieth-Century Spain. Essays in Honour of Sir Raymond Carr* (Oxford: Clarendon Press, 1990), pp. 127–51.

[56] R. Vinyes, *La Catalunya Internacional. El frontpopulisme en l'exemple català* (Barcelona: Curial, 1983), p. 256; Graham, *Socialism and War*, pp. 69–73.

purely ideological – dimension. Although this is a relatively unexplored area to date, the 1930s in Spain also saw the eruption of youth as a major protagonist onto the political stage.

The political centre and stronghold of Caballerismo remained, nevertheless, the UGT executive – given both the numbers it controlled (especially in the massively expanded FNTT) and Largo Caballero's immense personal prestige in the PSOE/UGT as a whole. It is significant here that all Largo's justifications for breaking the alliance with the republicans hinged on the 'wrongs' of 1931–3: on the employers' campaign against reform (and himself), on police violence against workers and on the republican political class's outrageous lack of solidarity (as he saw it) with the PSOE in 1933. At no point did Largo ever justify socialist departure from government in terms of an alternative revolutionary strategy or any assessment of the future balance of political forces in Spain. He did not do so because no such calculation existed on the left. The UGT was far too valuable and hardwon an organisation for its substance and future to be risked in one revolutionary throw of the dice. For Largo Caballero and the veteran union leadership, whose formative experience had been that of the traumatic August 1917 general strike, the threat of state repression never seemed far away – even when one held ministerial office. For the UGT leaders, moreover, all strategy and policy had to fulfil a central objective: the defence, nurture and augmentation of the socialist organisation – identified, in a characteristically idiosyncratic reading, with the deepest interests of the *entire* Spanish working class.

But the organisational unity of the Spanish working class – however envisaged – was a goal whose practical possibilities seemed to be eroding precisely as the UGT's political rhetoric of proletarian unity became more insistent. The divisions and tensions both within and between the socialist and anarcho-syndicalist leaderships and their respective movements increased from April 1931 as the Republican environment stimulated mass political mobilisation.

Largo Caballero's objective in 1931 had been to use the leverage of state power – in particular the labour arbitration boards – to exclude the CNT from the frame. Unsurprisingly, this had further soured relations with anarcho-syndicalist leaders already distrustful of Largo after his collaboration with Primo in the 1920s. In fact, however, the UGT's tactics had rebounded. The slowness and obstruction of reform during 1931–3 turned the UGT's ministerial experience into a crisis of its own political identity. In a sense this was inevitable since the UGT as well as the CNT contained (after April 1931 just as before) both radical and reformist practices of labour resistance.[57] Moreover, the UGT was also acquiring a bigger following of unskilled, marginalised (often migrant) workers in the 1930s – that is, precisely those constituencies worst hit by unemployment and recession and for whom UGT arbitration-based unionism remained inaccessible.[58]

An absolutely fundamental fact to bear in mind here is that the grass roots of organised labour – whether in the UGT or the CNT – did not necessarily see parliamentary and direct action strategies[59] as mutually exclusive, or existing in some kind of rigid 'evolutionary' order. Many wanted access to both simultaneously. Nor did ordinary workers necessarily construct the UGT and the CNT as binary opposites in ideological terms. A certain amount of 'mixing and matching' went on. The richness of anarchism's political culture was undeniable, but the CNT's unpreparedness to engage with the Republican political system – in particular at the level of municipal politics – was a real weakness after 1931. It was this, for example, that gave the Spanish Communist Party (PCE) its opening in Seville in the early 1930s, where it began to build up a membership base.[60] (Just as the UGT's ambivalence to radical tactics had earlier given the Communist Party an entrée in the industrial north.) Moreover, it was probably this pragmatic and fluid political outlook among the grass roots of worker constituencies that explains the underlying appeal of the re-emergent strategy of centre-left electoral alliance, by spring 1936 known as the Popular Front. For many of those mobilised in the socialist, communist and anarcho-syndicalist movements, the Popular Front was a parliamentary strategy, but it was also *something more*.[61] Precisely for this reason the PCE would have a fairly easy ride politically when it made the transition from an exclusively worker front (*frente único*) to support the Popular Front.

Largo Caballero and his colleagues in the UGT leadership were themselves allergic to any kind of direct action. But they also realised that the feelings of their rank and file were not necessarily so clear-cut. The

[57] See the discussion in the introduction above.

[58] This is the situation which underlay, for example, many of the strikes in 1930s urban Madrid – including those of 1936 (construction and *hostelería* (cafés and catering)) when UGT strikers stayed out on strike with their CNT counterparts, disobeying their own leaders' calls for a return to work. Juliá, *La izquierda del PSOE*, pp. 253–64.

[59] For example, spontaneous industrial action or community-based initiatives such as rent strikes, housing occupations and campaigns against speculation (or food adulteration) by shopkeepers.

[60] J. M. Macarro Vera, *La utopía revolucionaria. Sevilla en la Segunda República* (Seville: Monte de Piedad y Caja de Ahorros de Sevilla, 1985), pp. 94–5.

[61] See further discussion later in the chapter.

revolutionary language that Largo began to adopt in his speeches, after the socialists had exited from government in 1933, was (consciously or otherwise) an attempt to contain radical currents in the socialist movement without, supposedly, incurring any organisational risk. In fact the risks would turn out to be great in more than one respect. For Largo and his executive would call for a national revolutionary strike, but then fail signally to lead it. When the strike erupted, in October 1934, its epicentre and leadership lay far from Madrid, in Asturias. As a result, Largo and his executive committee would come to be enveloped by the miners' rising there. The judicial fall-out, when the UGT leaders were brought to trial for rebellion against the state, activated all their worst memories of 1917. But even after the trial Largo would still carry on employing a vehement revolutionary rhetoric – now because, after October, he was also afraid of the UGT being outflanked on the left. But this was a highly irresponsible course because Largo still had no organisational blueprint for revolution. Moreover, the fact that the UGT was relatively more centralised than the CNT meant that this attempt to square the circle between radicalism and reformism would produce much greater internal tensions and would do so much rapidly.

The CNT, as a looser structure, with regional federations that, historically, had been virtually independent entities, had been able to live with political difference more easily. But socialism's governmental role between 1931 and 1933 had, nevertheless, opened up the internal fault lines in the anarcho-syndicalist organisation – for and against political participation. Syndicalists such as Angel Pestaña and Juan Peiró argued that it was now time to abandon anti-parliamentarianism in order to incorporate the CNT sufficiently to allow the defence of its militants and social constituencies through the newly available formal channels of municipal politics and state labour agencies.[62] The new Republican environment gave the CNT no choice but to compete in the political arena with the PSOE/UGT. Failure to renovate libertarian ideology and practice, they warned, would leave the CNT's rank and file exposed and would ultimately erode its base as members were attracted to the perceived benefits of its socialist rival as a union plugged into state power.[63] In the opinion of the reformers, by refusing to sanction

---

[62] Pestaña, like Peiró (the CNT's future industry minister in November 1936), had been part of the moderate group associated with *Solidaridad Obrera* that had acted as caretakers of the CNT in the 1920s, opposing the (often exiled) radical anarchists of Solidarios/Nosotros.

[63] For a forceful expression of this view, see Lorenzo, *Los anarquistas españoles y el poder*, p. 202.

the organisation's political engagement, the purist anarchists were not only assisting the UGT leadership in its bid to attract CNT members, but were also damaging the welfare and rights of the anarcho-syndicalist base. However, for the radical anarchists who, unlike large sectors of the CNT's own base, saw this question in binary terms, to propose political engagement of any sort amounted to a betrayal of the purpose and value of direct action and worker–state confrontations.

The reformers' arguments would seem to find an echo in the membership decline the CNT incurred during 1931–6. This would be steepest in the key Catalan regional federation (CRT), which dropped from 300,000 members in 1931 to around 136,000 by May 1936.[64] This did not necessarily impinge on the CNT's considerable informal mobilising power among radicalised and excluded social constituencies – particularly in Barcelona – but it did denote some kind of organisational 'crossroads'. Indeed, this was clearly defined for it by the *treintista* schism[65] of 1931 when unions in Catalonia and Valencia representing skilled workers in the most developed industrial sectors left the CNT. They judged their position to be untenable, yet saw no means of winning the argument over strategy against the radicals.[66] Some of the most powerful of these unions would never return. The fact that *treintismo* was so influential in Catalonia makes the point very clearly that this profound division in the CNT did not separate the organisation in the rest of Spain from the Catalan 'heartland' but rather that it ran straight through that libertarian heartland.

It is also worth noting that it was in areas where the *treintistas* were strong in Catalonia that the 1930s also saw breakthroughs for quasi-Catalanist political parties more left-inclined than the Esquerra. The main example here was the Catalan communist formation, the Bloc

---

[64] The CNT's major regional federations – Catalonia, the Levante and Andalusia/Extremadura – all experienced a decline during 1931–6. But the Catalan federation had dropped from its 1919 peak of 400,000 when it had represented half of the total CNT membership for Spain: J. Peirats, *La CNT en la revolución española* (3 vols., n.p.: Ruedo Ibérico, 1971), vol. 1, pp. 27–8. For the Catalan federation in the 1930s, see S. Tavera and E. Vega, 'La afiliació sindical a la CRT de Catalunya: entre l'eufòria revolucionària i l'ensulsiada confederal 1931–36', in (various authors) *Revolució i Socialisme*, vol. 2 (Barcelona, 1990), pp. 343–63, esp. pp. 350, 353. For the south, see Macarro Vera, *La utopía revolucionaria*, p. 62.

[65] So-called because of its origins in the thirty signatories to a reformist CNT manifesto in August 1931: Peirats, *La CNT en la revolución española*, vol. 1, pp. 59–63.

[66] They formed the Sindicatos de Oposición (FSL). J. Brademas, *Anarcosindicalismo y revolución en España 1930–1937* (Barcelona: Ariel, 1974), pp. 76–7, 91–2, 117–21; E. Vega, *El trentisme a Catalunya. Divergències ideològiques en la CNT* (Barcelona: Curial, 1980) and *Anarquistas y sindicalistas 1931–1936. La CNT y los Sindicatos de Oposición en el País Valenciano* (Valencia: Institució 'Alfons el Magnànim', 1987), pp. 225–6.

Obrer i Camperol (BOC[67]) – which in September 1935 would merge to become the core membership of the POUM.[68] This coincidence of *treintistas* with the BOC reinforces the point that the heart of the CNT's crisis was its continued rejection of parliamentary politics in a context of accelerating mass political mobilisation.[69] This was also likely to have been one reason why in a number of cities of historic CNT strength (Valencia, Seville and, to a lesser extent, Zaragoza) UGT membership was gradually rising during the period 1931–6.[70] It was also in the UGT that some of the *treintista* unions would eventually find a new home in 1936. For example, those in Sabadell and Manresa would join the Catalan UGT in the political exhilaration and mass enthusiasm over worker 'unity' following the Popular Front elections of February 1936.[71] Few syndicalists would go as far as Pestaña, who, in 1933, left the CNT to form the Partido Sindicalista.[72] But when he departed he left behind an escalating debate over ideology and organisational forms that would reverberate on and into the war period. Nor did this debate involve only the CNT. It also cut across the FAI, the anarchist federation created back in 1927.

The impulse to create the FAI had come from radicals concerned about the influence of syndicalist reformists in the CNT.[73] But the image of the FAI as a tight, cell-based organisation of the like-minded is somewhat misleading. The FAI was, by its own political definition, a loose network of individual anarchist groups across Spain.[74] This form meant that the FAI too reflected and transmitted the variations in anarcho-syndicalist political perspectives across the regions of Spain.[75] Its groups debated the same questions of ideological direction and organisational hierarchy/centralisation that the CNT did. And just as in the CNT, the

---

[67] Workers and Peasants Bloc.

[68] A. C. Durgan, *B.O.C. 1930–1936. El Bloque Obrero y Campesino* (Barcelona: Laertes, 1996), pp. 163–6. See also the analysis of left politics in Catalonia in 1931–6 below in this chapter.

[69] The CNT had acted decisively to prevent the BOC's entryism when it expelled BOC-led unions in 1932. This was when the BOC created its own trade union, the FOUS.

[70] Casanova, *De la calle al frente*, p. 59 (n. 32); Macarro Vera, *La utopía revolucionaria*, pp. 48–51.

[71] Balcells, *Trabajo industrial y organización obrera en la Cataluña contemporánea 1900–1936*, pp. 156–7.

[72] Peiró would also 'withdraw' *de facto* from the CNT when he saw the reformist route blocked. He would only return after the military rising of July 1936: Casanova, *De la calle al frente*, pp. 141–2 (n. 9).

[73] S. Christie, *We, the Anarchists! A Study of the Iberian Anarchist Federation (FAI) 1927–1937* (Hastings: The Meltzer Press/Jura Media, 2000), p. 21. See also the introduction above.

[74] S. Tavera and E. Ucelay-Da Cal, 'Grupos de afinidad, disciplina bélica y periodismo libertario 1936–1938', *Historia Contemporánea*, 9 (1993), 167–8.

[75] R. Fraser, *Blood of Spain. The Experience of Civil War 1936–1939* (Harmondsworth: Penguin, 1981), p. 548.

opinions expressed in those debates varied.[76] The FAI certainly numbered radical anarchists among its members – including some powerful and charismatic ones. But the FAI was not as politically homogeneous as it is usually portrayed – particularly not beyond Catalonia. It is important to bear this in mind when considering the political evolution of the FAI during the civil war.

The impact of the syndicalist reformers' arguments on the CNT-FAI as a whole during 1931–6 was diluted, however, by the way in which other CNT-identified social constituencies were experiencing the Republic 'on the ground'. The fact of slow or stalled reform, of the exclusion of unskilled and casualised labour from any 'new deal'; then, after November 1933, the centre-right administration's rolling back of even modest gains, all stymied the syndicalist reformers. As a result, organisational reform proceeded at a pace that was almost imperceptible.

As agreed by CNT congresses in 1918 and 1919, the craft union structure had been converted into industrial unions – the *sindicatos únicos*.[77] This meant bringing together in a single union (or branch) all the trades operating within a given industry – for example, the building or textile industry each constituted one industrial branch (among thirteen created overall).[78] In 1931 CNT congress agreed the next stage of consolidating these unions into *national* industrial federations – something that had been successfully opposed by anarchist radicals back in 1919. But there was little real progress here during 1931–6. Had the national federations of industry been created, they could have overcome the CNT's invertebrateness. The CNT's regional federations had always been virtually autonomous entities. The national leadership was elected to represent, but it had no power to enforce policy or organisational directives. In the course of strikes in the 1930s the CNT did not even have the organisational means to communicate with its own constituent unions – which seriously inhibited their efficacy.[79] In the absence of national federations, it was also difficult for the organisations of different industrial branches to communicate with each other. Indeed, little efficient communication – either top-down or laterally[80] – was possible beyond the regional level.

[76] Tavera and Ucelay-Da Cal, 'Grupos de afinidad, disciplina bélica y periodismo libertario 1936–1938', p. 173.
[77] The Sants congress of the Catalan region (CRT) in 1918 and the CNT national congress in 1919.
[78] On the CNT and industrial unionism see the summary in Fraser, *Blood of Spain*, p. 544 (n. 3).
[79] The national executive could neither advise nor adequately gather information: Brademas, *Anarcosindicalismo y revolución en España 1930–1937*, p. 73.
[80] The UGT was also defective here. The national executive in Madrid could, in normal circumstances, communicate relatively easily with all parts of the organisation. But in many areas internal regional and provincial articulation simply did not exist. J. M. Macarro Vera discusses

As a result, the CNT would have great difficulty coordinating modern urban industrial strikes during the Republican years.[81]

Although it has been little noted in the Anglo-American historiography, a major ideological and organisational crisis was looming in the CNT by 1936. In May, the CNT's famous Zaragoza congress would attempt to restore 'unity' by simply denying the cleavage. It endorsed the anti-parliamentary line 'by acclamation', while also agreeing to the reincorporation of some of the schismatic union federations that had left after the *treintista* split.[82] But in reality the congress resolved nothing. The conflict between syndicalist pragmatists and purist anarchists over the CNT-FAI's future structure would still be pending when the military rebelled in July 1936. After that point, the lack of national federations of industry would seriously hinder the coordination of resistance. Moreover, it would also mean, ironically, that radical anarchists would have no integrated organisational base from which to contest war policy with their political opponents in the Popular Front.

But the consequences of internal dissension between the CNT's leaders or of conflict with their UGT counterparts were not the only sources of left fragmentation during 1931–6. There were also bitter and violent disputes between some sectors of the two memberships. This conflict frequently stemmed from the daily impact of recession in a society where unemployment levels were high and few had access to any kind of public relief. As recent work has shown, this also led to a lot of new labour mobilisation at grass-roots level concerning specific local grievances.[83] This situation was further embittered by the fact that the CNT was also battling against the UGT's bid to control the labour market. Strike demands in 1932–3 – with over half of the strikes occurring in the agricultural and building sectors – reflected this climate: there should be no further reduction of the working day, a rota system should be implemented to ration work, and a quota established to ensure that the unemployed were hired.[84] There was virtual open warfare over control of the UGT-dominated labour arbitration machinery.

the Andalusian case, in S. Juliá (ed.), *El socialismo en las nacionalidades y regiones*, *Anales de Historia*, vol. 3 (Madrid: Fundación Pablo Iglesias, 1988), pp. 105, 118. The great difficulty of lateral communication between the different provincial and regional organisations of the UGT would be a severe impediment in wartime.

[81] Peirats, *La CNT en la revolución española*, vol. 1, pp. 53–7.

[82] CNT congresses tended to adopt decisions 'unanimously through acclamation/display'. See also Casanova, *De la calle al frente*, pp. 63–4, 87 for a resonant description of the dimensions of the CNT crisis.

[83] Cf. Gil Andrés, *Echarse a la calle. Amotinados, huelguistas y revolucionarios*.

[84] Juliá, 'La experiencia del poder: la izquierda republicana, 1931–1933', in Townson, *El republicanismo en España*, pp. 181, 185.

The CNT's September 1933 construction strike was primarily aimed at gaining union recognition and equal bargaining rights by breaking the UGT's monopoly on hiring at new construction sites. In the agricultural sector too there was constant conflict in 1931–3 between socialist and anarcho-syndicalist unions over the functioning of the arbitration boards.[85] Additionally, tensions were exacerbated by the operation of Republican public-order legislation, as we have seen. These antagonisms had much in common with those that occurred between the SPD and the KPD under the Weimar Republic. The KPD, like the CNT, increasingly identified with and mobilised those politically and economically excluded from the Republican order: the unskilled, the unemployed, migrants, the marginal.

On the Barcelona waterfront, the battle between the socialist and anarchist dockworkers' unions for members erupted once again into violence.[86] Members were important in their own right, but the particular violence of the 1930s dispute (and resulting fatalities) derived from the fact that work – as an increasingly scarce commodity – was allocated in the Republic's employment exchanges according to union size. There were some other specific sources of tension too. For example, in the 1930s the Catalan UGT became the new home for private security guards who had previously belonged to the Sindicatos Libres, the yellow unions of the 1920s that had collapsed with the fall of the Primo dictatorship. (*Ugetistas* in Catalonia were also sometimes used by employers to replace a striking CNT workforce, thus earning themselves a reputation for scabbing.) Elsewhere too there were other sorts of violent confrontation between the rank and file of the two 'sister' unions. In Seville the intra-organisational conflicts were made more fraught by the strong presence of communist

---

[85] For the agricultural sector, see M. Pérez Yruela, *La conflictividad campesina en la provincia de Córdoba 1931–1936* (Madrid: Ministerio de Agricultura, 1979), pp. 111, 119 ff., 228–9. For the construction strike, see S. Juliá, *Madrid 1931–1934. De la fiesta popular a la lucha de clases* (Madrid: Siglo XXI, 1984), pp. 229–58 and summary in S. Juliá, 'Economic Crisis, Social Conflict and the Popular Front: Madrid 1931–6', in P. Preston (ed.), *Revolution and War in Spain 1931–1939* (London: Methuen, 1984) pp. 137–58; S. Payne, *Spain's First Democracy. The Second Republic 1931–1936* (Madison: University of Wisconsin Press, 1993), p. 144. For Catalonia, see A. Balcells, 'El socialismo en Cataluña hasta la guerra civil', in S. Juliá (ed.), *El socialismo en las nacionalidades y regiones, Anales de Historia*, vol. 3 (Madrid: Fundación Pablo Iglesias, 1988), p. 34.

[86] These membership wars went back to 1916, when the CNT made an attempt to take over La Naval, a UGT dockers' union: F. Romero, *Spain 1914–1918. Between War and Revolution* (London: Routledge, 1999), p. 38. Then, during the Primo years, dockers in Barcelona, led by an ex-*cenetista*, had joined the UGT: Balcells, 'El socialismo en Cataluña hasta la guerra civil', p. 33. See also Gabriel Jackson, *The Spanish Republic and the Civil War 1931–1939* (Princeton, N.J.: Princeton University Press, 1965), p. 285; C. Ealham, 'Anarchism and Illegality in Barcelona 1931–37', *Contemporary European History* (July 1995); UGT executive committee minutes, Dec. 1936/Jan. 1937: see Graham, *Socialism and War*, p. 271, n. 51.

unions in direct opposition to the CNT's.[87] In Madrid new tensions emerged as the CNT moved into what had traditionally been a UGT stronghold.

The CNT was particularly strong among the large numbers of unskilled building labourers who, attracted by the boom in the industry in the 1920s, had flocked to Madrid to work on the big construction sites. Their situation had worsened as the industry, faced with the effects of recession, began to cut back. With no security or bargaining power, confrontational tactics and strike action were increasingly the only options available to these unskilled workers.[88] The UGT leadership, wary of the increasing number of CNT-backed strikes which it saw as a threat to its control in the capital, sought to reimpose the 1931–3 arbitration machinery of the Jurados Mixtos which it had run.[89] But this in fact only served to exacerbate the inter-union conflict. By spring 1936 the situation was explosive.

In April, the UGT's fears of loss of control seemed to be confirmed when, on the fifth anniversary of the Republic, many of its members, ignoring the opposition of both socialist and communist leaderships, joined the general strike declared by the CNT. The UGT press accused the CNT, tellingly, of fomenting 'rebellion against the state', while the CNT's responded by renewing its criticism of socialist collaborationism. Largo Caballero was the 'old corrupt collaborationist socialist', plugging into the state as he had in the 1920s during the Primo dictatorship and now advising republican ministers on how to 'handle' strikes in return for favoured status and renewed state privileges for the UGT. The inter-union conflict intensified with the Madrid construction strike that began in June 1936 and was still unresolved at the time of the military uprising. On 11 July the UGT (via its newspaper *Claridad*) called for a return to work, 'for the sake of the Popular Front, for the consolidation of victory over the bosses', which was met by another scathing attack from the CNT. More significantly a sizable percentage of the UGT base in the capital (24 per cent) was also hostile to a return to work and sided with the CNT.[90]

---

[87] Macarro Vera, *La utopía revolucionaria*, esp. pp. 214–42; 293–305; 313–43.

[88] Juliá, *Madrid 1931–1934*, pp. 147–220.

[89] The Jurados Mixtos in Madrid had broken down under grass-roots pressure in 1933.

[90] Juliá, *La izquierda del PSOE*, p. 260; '¿Feudo de la UGT o capital confederal? La última huelga de la construcción en el Madrid de la República', *Historia Contemporánea*, 6 (1991), 207–20. The political ramifications of the Madrid building strike would also reverberate during the war in the UGT leadership's reluctance to put Madrid building workers under military discipline (for example

This other kind of war – into which the July military coup and ensuing civil war erupted – brings home the extent to which the material effects of economic crisis had driven a wedge between the social constituencies of the left. The cumulative effect of such clashes in urban and rural Republican Spain created a legacy of distrust that eroded the political space for a substantive agreement between the UGT and the CNT during the war.[91]

But any feasible consolidation of forces to the left of the republican-socialist alliance had probably already been blocked for good by 1934 when, in different ways, both the CNT and the UGT effectively incapacitated the Workers' Alliance (Alianza Obrera). This was originally an initiative of the Catalan BOC, which wanted to use it as a launch pad for activism outside Catalonia.[92] But precisely because the Alliance was envisaged as an inter-organisational structure, it could, had it been realised, have offered a real opportunity for the left to consolidate and to coordinate its action. At the very least a functioning Workers' Alliance could have provided the crucial national coordination lacking on the left in the spring and early summer of 1936 when the military conspiracy was escalating.

However, the CNT refused point blank to participate in a 'political' initiative (although some *treintista* unions in Catalonia did ally themselves). Largo Caballero initially pledged socialist support. But in the course of 1934 it became clear that he was only interested in the Workers' Alliance as a means of extending the influence of the PSOE/UGT in areas where, traditionally, the socialist movement was weak – and primarily in Catalonia itself. But other components of the Workers' Alliance in Catalonia were wary of this – especially the Socialist Union of Catalonia (USC). This had split from the PSOE in 1923 precisely because of the party's lack of sympathy for nationalist issues. Nor had relations between the two improved under the Republic. The fact that, in the April 1931 municipal elections in Barcelona, the PSOE had allied with the notoriously anti-Catalanist Radical Party is indicative of its animosity towards the USC. Then in 1933 the PSOE's heavy-handed centralism killed off the USC's attempt to agree a measure of organisational

when building trenches and fortifications in autumn 1936) for fear of alienating them. See chapter 3 below.

[91] For examples of this ongoing conflict in wartime, see Graham, *Socialism and War*, pp. 64 (n. 45), 82 (n. 51).

[92] Payne, *Spain's First Democracy*, pp. 195–6.

devolution for Catalan socialism – even though this was in keeping with the spirit of the 1932 autonomy statute.[93]

The tensions within the socialist movement were not the only ones operating against the Workers' Alliance. Nor would the many underlying antagonisms at rank-and-file level that we have already discussed bode well for its future. But in the event, the Alliance never reached the starting line as a national entity. It was obstructed by the dead weight of Caballerista bureaucratism. In part this was a manifestation of the UGT's 'existential' fear that any initiative that did not emanate from itself was a threat to its control. In part too, however, it was a practical response to the well-grounded fear that the small, struggling PCE saw the Alliance as a way of attracting the socialist rank and file. But, whatever the case, without the near nationwide articulating capacity of the PSOE/UGT, the Workers' Alliance was simply not viable.

Inside Catalonia too the Alliance would be beset by problems. It initially integrated virtually all of the forces on the Catalan political left: the BOC, the USC, Rabassaires, Andreu Nin's tiny Communist Left Party (Izquierda Comunista) and (by December 1933) the small official Catalan section of the PSOE as well as its (more important) UGT section. But the Alliance's two core components were, first and foremost, the BOC and then the USC. The BOC, like the USC, had been born of a schism with a centralist parent party, in its case the PCE, which was, like the PSOE, unsympathetic to the political-cultural claims of nationalism.[94] But the consequences of the two schisms had been quite distinct. The USC was a small minority that had split off from a well-established parent socialist party with a considerable national presence in Spain. The BOC, however, had effectively taken over the cadres of the Catalan federation of the PCE which, when they ceded from the PCE at the end of the 1920s,[95]

---

93 Balcells, 'El socialismo en Cataluña hasta la guerra civil', pp. 35–6. In 1932 the PSOE accepted the Catalan statute as part of the general package of republican reforms. But this did not make it 'pro-statute'. Both the main leaders of the PSOE in 1930s Spain – Prieto and Largo Caballero – were hostile.

94 F. Morrow, *Revolution and Counter-Revolution* (1938; London: New Park Publications, 1976), p. 44; E. Ucelay da Cal, 'Socialistas y comunistas en Cataluña durante la guerra civil: un ensayo de interpretación', in *Socialismo y guerra civil*, *Anales de Historia*, vol. 2 (Madrid: Fundación Pablo Iglesias, 1987), p. 306.

95 The BOC was formed in November 1930 from the fusion of the Catalan federation of the PCE (FCCB) with Jordi Arquer's tiny dissident Partit Comunista Català (CC). The organisational independence of the BOC was confirmed in 1931 with the expulsion from the PCE of Joaquín Maurín, who would become the BOC's main political leader and strategist. See Durgan, *B.O.C. 1930–1936*; F. Bonamusa, *El Bloc Obrer i Camperol (1930–1932)* (Barcelona: Curial, 1974);

constituted most of the minuscule 'parent' Communist Party's *entire* national membership. In terms of political projects, the USC's socialism was closer to a pragmatic social democratic credo and immersed in a strong Catalanism, whereas the BOC leaders played down the nationalist question and offered a socialist programme expressed in radical, workerist language.[96]

But in spite of this difference of political emphasis, the BOC and the USC had been organisational rivals since the beginning of the Republic since they were competing for members amongt the same sectors of Catalan-speaking (and frequently Catalanist) urban lower-middle-class professionals and skilled workers.[97] The smaller USC, caught between the influence of the more powerful BOC and the CNT, had little choice but to exist in the political orbit of the Esquerra, with which it collaborated in the Generalitat.[98] Through this the USC achieved an institutional presence in Catalonia that it never could have aspired to on the basis of its own flimsy electoral showing.

The USC saw its participation in the Workers' Alliance in 1934 as a means of bolstering both itself as a political entity and a reforming agenda in Catalonia. The Alliance had brought together the political left in the region, including the UGT's Catalan section, access to which the USC had had vetoed only a year previously by the UGT's Madrid executive. Now the USC hoped that the Workers' Alliance could provide a valuable complement to its presence in the Generalitat. In other words, the Alliance would serve as an important source of popular pressure to maintain the rhythm of the Esquerra's social and political reform in parliament. In this USC aspiration we can glimpse something of the underlying rationale of the Popular Front alliance, as it would emerge

J. Estruch, *Historia del P.C.E.*, vol. 1 (Barcelona: El Viejo Topo, 1978), p. 60; Ucelay da Cal, 'Socialistas y comunistas en Cataluña durante la guerra civil', p. 308.

[96] Bonamusa, *El Bloc Obrer i Camperol 1930–1932*; Durgan, *B.O.C. 1930–1936*.

[97] For the BOC's urban base in Catalonia, see A. Durgan, 'Trotsky, the POUM and the Spanish Revolution', in *Journal of Trotsky Studies*, 2 (1994), 59 and also appendices 4–8 of Durgan, *B.O.C. 1930–1936*. For the BOC's rural support from 1931 see Durgan, *B.O.C 1930–1936*, pp. 140–1, 147–54 – although the Esquerra trounced both the BOC/POUM and the USC in rural Catalonia before the civil war.

[98] Balcells, 'El socialismo en Cataluña hasta la guerra civil', p. 34; Durgan, *B.O.C. 1930–1936*. Extrapolating back from figures for the BOC/POUM, the USC and the Catalan federation of the PSOE in July 1936 (for which see B. Bolloten, *The Spanish Civil War. Revolution and Counterrevolution* (Hemel Hempstead: Harvester/Wheatsheaf, 1991) (hereafter *SCW*), p. 397) it is likely that the USC would have had at least three times as many members as the official PSOE section, while the BOC was more than twice as big as the USC. In the pre-war period the Catalan UGT was also the smallest of the UGT's regional sections – although estimates vary quite considerably: see Bolloten, *SCW*, p. 862, n. 21.

later, in 1936, in Spain as a whole. (It is worth noting too that the USC would maintain its own electoral alliance with the Esquerra throughout the entire Republican period 1931–6, irrespective of the rupture of the republican-socialist coalition in 1933 across the rest of Spain.)

But it was precisely the USC's relations with Catalan republicanism, and especially its governmental collaboration, that constituted the bone of contention for the BOC. It saw Workers' Alliance membership as incompatible with participation in 'bourgeois government'. This would see both the Rabassaires and the USC depart. Thereafter, the Catalan Workers' Alliance struggled in vain against political marginalisation. The USC understood that reform in Catalonia (and even more in the rest of Spain) would always require – in the face of a determined right and a fragmented left – a broad coalition integrating both progressive middle-class republicanism and the organisations of the political left. But this crucial insight had not yet found its moment to be heard.

THE ASTURIAN OCTOBER (1934)

The one place that the Workers' Alliance did achieve its goal of unity – albeit in desperate and ultimately disastrous circumstances – was in Asturias. The historical collaboration of the UGT and the CNT in the north was crucial here. The region's heterogeneous mix of small centres of decentred (or 'ribbon') industrial production, smallholder agriculture, port activity (centring on Gijón) and artisan production had given rise to a great deal of overlap between the UGT and the CNT. Both unions represented those engaged in heavy industry and in artisan and service sectors. This created the basis for practical collaboration, especially as neither union was sufficiently dominant in the region to exclude the other. Pre-existing political sympathies were also bolstered during the early Republican years by the Northern CNT leaders' increasing hostility to radical anarchist currents. This animosity crystallised with the abortive general strike of December 1933 in Gijón, thus opening the way for the forging of the Asturian Workers' Alliance.[99]

Paradoxically, given the circumstances of its birth, the Workers' Alliance in Asturias soon found itself at the centre of growing political radicalisation as a result of economic tensions in the north. The recession had brought the chronic crisis of the Asturian coalmining industry to a head. Attempts to shore up the industry by savings that directly impinged on

---

[99] Radcliff, *From Mobilisation to Civil War*, p. 290.

the livelihoods or safety of the workforce had brought gravely deteriorating labour relations. Once again, the UGT leadership (both its national executive and that of its northern mining federation (SMA)) found itself in the familiar position of trying to control a radicalising rank and file.[100] June 1934 had already seen the frustration of rural labour spill out in a bitter and bloody FNTT strike. The spark that lit the fuse in October was provided by the CEDA. Its ministers entered the Madrid cabinet to claim, in a national climate of increasing protest and polarisation, the three most sensitive portfolios: Agriculture, Labour and Justice. The Spanish left, mindful of the German and Austrian precedents, saw this as fascism arriving by legal means. Its response was a general strike throughout Spain. This largely failed, as did the Esquerra's own, mainly symbolic, protest from the Generalitat. But Asturias exploded into armed rebellion – though many of those who took part saw what they were doing as a defence of Republican social reform. Again, the line between direct action and parliamentary action was seen as permeable – and not only by the newly politically mobilised.

The miners held out for two weeks. But their towns were bombed by the Spanish airforce, their coastal towns shelled by the navy and their valleys finally overrun by the Spanish army. A harsh and extensive repression ensued throughout Asturias in which General Franco, as *de facto* head of the war ministry, deployed both Moroccan troops and the Foreign Legion. Constitutional guarantees were suspended across Spain. The impact on the left was catastrophic. Thirty thousand people were imprisoned and many of them tortured.[101] Others went into exile – among them, Indalecio Prieto, the intelligent and energetic leader of the PSOE's parliamentary wing. Party and union premises were closed and the left's press silenced. Socialist town councils were overthrown, civil servants of liberal or left opinions were discriminated against, and everywhere employers and management took the opportunity to dismiss trade unionists and left activists *en masse*.

The damage wrought to the PSOE/UGT by the repression severely traumatised its leaders – none more so than the veterans of the UGT, for

---

[100] A. Shubert, *The Road to Revolution in Spain. The Coal Miners of Asturias 1860–1934* (Urbana/Chicago: University of Illinois Press, 1987), pp. 141–67 and see also pp. 121–40.

[101] Ibid., p. 163. For repression and prisoner numbers in Asturias specifically, see Radcliff, *From Mobilisation to Civil War*, p. 300 (n. 46). Between 3,000 and 4,000 received prison sentences of one year or more. The amnesty issue eclipsed all others in the Popular Front electoral campaign in Asturias, during which the CNT's northern federation officially called upon their members to vote: A. Shubert, 'A Reinterpretation of the Spanish Popular Front: The Case of Asturias', in Alexander and Graham, *The French and Spanish Popular Fronts*, pp. 222, 220.

whom the socialist movement's greatness was inscribed in its material patrimony. In fact, the UGT's Madrid-based executive had played no part in the Asturian events, nor had they been directly involved in the planning decisions taken by the Asturian Workers' Alliance. Indeed, given the total failure of the general strike in the Caballerista stronghold of Madrid, some inside the socialist movement would soon be asking if the noisy, self-proclaimed 'socialist left' had been actively involved anywhere. The PSOE executive was, nevertheless, called legally to account for the events. During his trial Largo Caballero, who was fearful of the punitive confiscation of the PSOE/UGT's assets, made his famous denial of responsibility for the Asturian movement. This would offer the Spanish Communist Party the opportunity it needed to come in from the political cold. Even though its role in October had been marginal, the PCE eagerly assumed responsibility for the events.[102] Initially the party projected it as a symbol of proletarian unity in the drive to achieve a communist-led 'united front' of workers. But we can also see in the aftermath of October the seeds of the PCE's subsequent inter-class strategy of Popular Front: for example in the party's incorporation of progressive republicans in the work of the PSOE's prisoners' aid committee. It was also after October that the PCE's Association of Anti-fascist Women (AMA) became active in recruiting across the boundaries of social and economic class.[103]

Until the shift to a Popular Front was endorsed in the summer of 1935 by the VII Congress of the Communist International (Comintern), the PCE was still formally committed to the policy of a purely worker front (*frente único*). However, as we have just seen, by late 1934 the national context in Spain, as elsewhere in Europe, was in practice pushing communist parties in the direction of what would soon become the new policy. This is scarcely surprising, of course. The growth on the ground of what in Spain was called 'the climate of unity' was everywhere a crucial formative influence on the emergent Comintern policy of Popular Front.[104]

Prior to the end of 1934 such inroads as the very small Spanish Communist Party had been able to make were the result of its being able to appeal to a more radical mood than the PSOE felt able to: for example in

---

[102] J. Díaz, 2 June 1935, the Monumental Cinema, Madrid, *Tres años de lucha* (3 vols., Barcelona: Laia, 1978), vol. 1, pp. 42–3.

[103] H. Graham, 'Women and Social Change', in Graham and Labanyi, *Spanish Cultural Studies*, pp. 108–9.

[104] Alexander and Graham, *The French and Spanish Popular Fronts*, one of whose unifying themes is that the Popular Front in Europe was a sociological phenomenon built from below as much as 'directed from above'.

Vizcaya and Asturias in the 1920s, as we have discussed in the introduction above. (It was no coincidence that the PCE union breakthrough in Asturias happened at the same time as the UGT's collaboration with the Primo dictatorship.[105]) Seville too became an important PCE base when the conclusion of Primo's extravagant works programmes in the 1920s left a mass of unemployed construction workers to whom the UGT's traditional arbitration-based unionism had neither use nor appeal.[106] In the early 1930s in Seville the PCE was able to benefit from the CNT's refusal to engage politically with the Republic. Indeed, in the late 1920s the PCE had acquired cadres and leaders (including future secretary general José Díaz) from a number of former CNT unions in Seville. The PCE also continued to benefit in Seville from the PSOE/UGT's caution and governmental compromise. This was the time when the PCE's then line of social fascism or 'class against class' appealed precisely because it fitted pre-existing tensions and conflicts between different working-class constituencies which were generated or exacerbated by economic depression.[107] As we have seen, the PSOE/UGT attempted to defend itself from PCE (and CNT) encroachment with its time-honoured tactic of combining a radical discourse with a moderate practice. But this was less credible now that the PSOE was itself within the circle of political power, rather than an outsider force as it had been through the years of the Restoration monarchy.

The PCE's continuing marginalisation in the 1920s and early 1930s has always been attributed to the Comintern's heavy-handed imposition of inappropriate and sectarian policies. This certainly occurred and had some devastating effects. For example, as already mentioned, it was largely responsible for the PCE losing the bulk of its membership when, on the eve of the Second Republic, the Catalan federation walked out of the party. But even apart from the Comintern effect, it is difficult to see what political space (or audience) on the left could have been available to the PCE prior to 1931. Its opportunity came precisely because of the political consequences of the Republic, the PSOE/UGT's involvement in it and the reluctance of both republicans and socialists to face up to the challenge of mass political mobilisation in a society like Spain's with quite low levels of general and political education. Consciously or otherwise, this was the challenge to which PCE secretary general José

---

[105] The anarchist-communist miners' union, SUM, was formed. But with the birth of the Republic in 1931 the UGT's Asturian miner's union (SMA) regained prominence.

[106] Preston, *CSCW*, p. 29; Macarro Vera, *La utopía revolucionaria, passim.*

[107] Cf. the German case in Graham and Preston (eds.), *The Popular Front in Europe*, pp. 5–6, 21–3.

Díaz was responding when in Madrid, in June 1935, he launched the campaign for a 'broad Popular Front'.[108]

The PCE's great strength by 1935 derived from the fact that it was striving for an inter-class political alliance that would mobilise 'the republican nation'. This meant both middle-class sectors and the existing organised labour movement, but it also meant reaching out to vast numbers among the middling classes and workers who were as yet unaffiliated to any political party or organisation. Of course, at one level this meant that the PCE was simply applying the Comintern line. And certainly, given that the party leadership was the 'disciplined' product of an earlier internal purge in 1932 and also devoid of any notably independent spirits or significant political theorists, it could not be argued that its adherence to the Popular Front consciously went beyond an obedience to iron party discipline and a very general belief in the political superiority of the Communist Party.[109] There was also the additional and highly specific problem of the personally overbearing Vittorio Codovilla, the Comintern delegate sent to Spain in 1932 to advise the party.[110] But, at another level, these issues are irrelevant because Popular Front as espoused by the Comintern and the PCE happened to be responding to an underlying structural and conjunctural necessity of the Spanish left (broadly understood) in the 1930s. First, there was the need to mobilise the population to help build the Republican state and second, the need to bring together the fragments of the counter-hegemonic project which had split into its component parts as a result of the stresses of the early Republican years of 1931–3. This cohesion was the essential precondition of the left's being minimally capable of mounting a successful challenge to the right – at the level of state cadres and political process as well as national symbols and values.[111] Nevertheless, the PCE was putting its shoulder to the wheel here in the inevitable hope that it could also nourish its own party by attracting sectors of the PSOE/UGT base. This would

---

[108] Díaz, *Tres años de lucha*, vol. 1, pp. 35–64.

[109] M. Azcárate, *Derrotas y esperanzas. La República, la guerra civil y la resistencia* (Barcelona: Tusquets Editores, 1994), p. 209. Dolores Ibárruri and Antonio Mije, among others, were obliged to perform self-criticisms in 1932 in order to remain.

[110] For more on Codovilla see chapter 3 below.

[111] H. Graham, 'Community, Nation and State in Republican Spain 1931–1938', in C. Mar-Molinero and A. Smith (eds.), *Nationalism and the Nation in the Iberian Peninsula* (Oxford: Berg, 1996), pp. 133–47.

produce increasing hostility and an accelerating organisational rivalry in 1935 between the communists and Largo Caballero's wing of the socialist movement. This was especially so because it was on the UGT that the PCE would concentrate its campaign.

PARLIAMENTARY SOCIALISM 1935–6: FROM FRAGMENTATION TO 'UNITY' – THE ROAD TO THE POPULAR FRONT

Meanwhile, within the broader socialist movement, the débâcle of the Asturian October and the tremendous cost to the left of the ensuing repression would rapidly conscript minds and hearts into action on two issues. First, the reconstitution of the republican-socialist alliance: this was crucial in the short term to win an election and release (via a political amnesty) the thousands of prisoners taken after October. In the medium term, it would ensure a return to a programme of progressive social and economic reform by parliamentary means. Second, it was imperative that the socialist left should not be allowed to disrupt this process – especially not as the other conclusion to be drawn from 'October' was that the party 'left' was in no meaningful sense revolutionary.[112] The view growing apace in the parliamentary socialist wing of the PSOE associated with Indalecio Prieto (but support for which also extended into sectors of the UGT and socialist youth) was that the 'left' was both ideologically bankrupt and organisationally disruptive. It had shown an abysmal failure of leadership initiative in October 1934. Nor, in spite of much radical rhetoric thereafter, had it produced a tangible policy line of its own, much less one capable of building the power structures necessary to orchestrate the anti-capitalist revolution whose imminence it proclaimed.[113]

For Largo and the UGT veterans, marooned without a policy since their departure from government in 1933, a revolutionary discourse seemed at some level to offer a 'solution' – the possibility of unblocking rightist obstruction in government while also preventing any other political group overtaking them on the left. To *speak* of revolution, moreover, entailed no risk to the socialist organisation. In fact, the UGT leaders would be proved wrong on all three counts. By 1935, the socialist

---

[112] Graham, *Socialism and War*, pp. 17–18.
[113] The consequences of this assessment for the civil war period are analysed in depth in Graham, *Socialism and War*. A resumé in Graham, 'The Eclipse of the Socialist Left 1934–1937', in Lannon and Preston, *Elites and Power in Twentieth-Century Spain*, pp. 127–51.

left itself – never a coherent force – was itself breaking up under the competitive onslaught from the PCE. In the union and party, but above all in the socialist youth, the attraction exerted by the Communist Party would increase through the year.

Prieto was, meanwhile, doing his utmost to resurrect the republican-socialist alliance. Notwithstanding his own ambivalent responses during the Asturian episode, the parliamentary PSOE had seen it come like an avalanche they were powerless to prevent and one whose wake had set back the fragile beginnings of republican-socialist negotiation (between Azaña and Prieto) made in the course of 1934. Paradoxically, however, October 1934 would assist the PSOE here in one crucial way. The hysterical campaign launched by the rightist press against Manuel Azaña, as the sinister author of a bloody revolution, would pluck him from the obscurity of the republicans' 'old-world politics' to what one might almost term modern political stardom.[114] After his release from prison, Azaña undertook across the spring and autumn of 1935 a massive publicity campaign to convince Spaniards, and particularly Spanish workers, of the urgent need to rebuild an electoral agreement on the left. Between May and October he toured major urban centres delivering his *discursos en campo abierto*, or open-air speeches. In Valencia he spoke before more than 100,000 people; in Bilbao the crowd was even bigger. On 15 October the campaign reached a crescendo at Comillas on the outskirts of Madrid when nearly half a million people turned up to hear Azaña make his appeal for unity on the left. Nor, given the prevailing political environment, was it a small matter for them to have come. In the words of the British journalist Henry Buckley, who witnessed the event:

This meeting had not been widely advertised. It was frowned on by the authorities and in some cases the Civil Guard turned back convoys of trucks carrying spectators. All vehicles bringing people from afar were stopped some miles outside Madrid, thus causing endless confusion and forcing weary men and women to trudge a long distance after a tiring ride. Admission was by payment. The front seats cost twelve shillings and sixpence and the cheaper ones ten shillings and half a crown. Standing room at the back cost sixpence. No one was forced to go to that meeting. Presence there, in fact, was much more likely to bring the displeasure of employer or landlord ... From the furthest points of Spain there were groups who had travelled in some cases six hundred miles in rainy cold weather in open motor lorries.[115]

[114] P. Preston, 'The Creation of the Popular Front in Spain', in Graham and Preston, *The Popular Front in Europe*, pp. 97–8.

[115] H. Buckley, *Life and Death of the Spanish Republic* (London: Hamish Hamilton, 1940), pp. 182–3.

An icon of the larger political process supervening, Comillas resonates still with the huge potential of that moment.

Prieto was able to use the tremendous popular response to the *discursos en campo abierto* to bring the socialist left back to supporting a renewed electoral alliance between the republicans and the PSOE/UGT. Largo Caballero was not easily persuaded. But he could not gainsay – and indeed was deeply impressed by – the strength of popular feeling, which, he realised, also infused the socialist grass roots. And here October 1934 would be the single most important factor in worker mobilisation behind the alliance whose electoral programme pledged an amnesty for all the political prisoners taken in the aftermath of the Asturian rising.

The PCE also worked hard to persuade Largo of the folly of insisting on a uniquely proletarian front – even sending in the veteran French union leader, Jacques Duclos, to argue the case. However, the communists were not the authors of Largo's 'conversion': it is clear that a veteran of Largo's standing could, in the end, do the political arithmetic for himself. Moreover, Largo – ever the wily veteran – also saw including the PCE as a way of controlling its political pretensions by tying it (albeit indirectly) into political responsibility for delivery of the electoral programme. Largo therefore made his own participation in the electoral alliance conditional on the PCE's inclusion. Prieto was not keen, in spite of the PCE's new Popular Front mode. Azaña and the republicans were even less happy. But in the end it was agreed that the PSOE/UGT would represent on the National Popular Front Committee all those forces to its left included in the electoral pact.[116] This made for a greater display of unity, but it also meant that the PSOE would have to pay for this in hard currency. For the allocation of the left's total number of candidates was taken not proportionally but from the PSOE/UGT's own share. But the biggest winners in this allocation of candidates were the republicans, who were significantly over-represented in relation to their numerical strength while the PSOE/UGT was under-represented.[117]

THE POPULAR FRONT

As far as republican over-representation was concerned, however, this was deliberate. Prieto understood, in a way that Largo Caballero did not, that a purely worker front would simply not be strong enough, taking

---

[116] The signatories were: the PSOE, UGT, PCE, POUM, Izquierda Republicana (Azaña), Unión Republicana (Martínez Barrio), Esquerra and Partido Sindicalista (Angel Pestaña).

[117] S. Juliá, *Orígenes del Frente Popular en España 1934–1936* (Madrid: Siglo XXI, 1979), p. 145.

the country as a whole. Given Spain's social and economic profile, the urban working class – even if backed up by very newly incorporated rural sectors – simply did not represent sufficiently broad strata to carry the weight of structural political change alone. A liberal centre-left political alliance like the Popular Front meant a guarantee of constitutional norms and social reform via parliamentary legislation. But it could not, by definition, be a programme of *socialist* reform. It could still, nevertheless, suppose radical structural change – such as Prieto would himself outline in May 1936 in his famous Cuenca speech, 'La conquista interior de España'.[118] Of course, what this implicitly meant was that Spanish workers were being asked to sacrifice some of their aspirations in order to keep on board middling constituencies who might otherwise be fished by the political right. But it had to be that or nothing. For only an inter-class front like Popular Front could unite enough of the fragmented 'lefts' – defined as all those middling and worker constituencies outside the power structures of old-regime Spain. Only together, as a counter-hegemonic coalition, could they withstand the force of the political elites whose power now linked up dangerously with that of the CEDA's mobilised popular conservative opinion. By 1936, then, the left in the rest of Spain had arrived at the political position occupied consistently since 1931 by a core of the Catalan left – republican and socialist.

In Catalonia, both the Esquerra and the USC had assumed the need for a broad coalition in 1931 and had never abandoned it. One major difference with the Popular Front in the rest of Spain, however, would be that in Catalonia the PCE itself remained as marginal in 1935–6 as it had been everywhere else prior to then. But if the PCE itself did not benefit in Catalonia from the fall-out after October 1934, then specifically Catalan communist and socialist formations would benefit. This did not happen at the expense of the PSOE, clearly, but instead at the expense of the, until then, politically unassailable Esquerra. Like the PSOE elsewhere, the Esquerra had suffered heavy repression in the wake of October precisely because of its organisational and institutional pre-eminence.[119]

---

[118] 'The interior conquest of Spain'. The allusion here was, evidently, to the need for domestic reform in 'post-imperial' Spain. I. Prieto, *Discursos fundamentales* (Madrid: Ediciones Turner, 1975), pp. 255–73.

[119] It is worth insisting on this comparison between the PSOE and the Esquerra given the similarity of their semi-eclipse after 18 July 1936. The two parties suffered a similar process of internal fracturing in spring and summer 1936 and both lost sustantial parts of their youth movements. On this process in the PSOE, see Graham, *Socialism and War*; on the Esquerra there is a resumé in Ucelay da Cal, 'Socialistas y comunistas en Cataluña durante la guerra civil', pp. 309–11.

The Catalan left was influenced, as its Spanish counterparts were, by the intensifying 'climate of unity' that had been growing since the events of October 1934. Negotiations began in the spring of 1935 to try to agree a basis for the organisational unification of the various socialist and communist parties in the region. Partly this was stimulated by the new opportunity to compete with the Esquerra. But the negotiations were also a response (emotional as well as intellectual) to the now clearly perceived need to overcome the structural fragmentation of pro-reform forces – an awareness that was infused with an even greater sense of urgency by the international situation. Equally, the discussions between the (socialist) Second International and (communist) Third International as well as the latter's new Popular Front policy increased the sense of propitiousness.

One singular feature of this process in Catalonia, however, was the remarkable fluidity of the potential alliances within the political (i.e. socialist and communist) left.[120] (It should be borne in mind too that a good number of the leaders of the political left in Catalonia had also begun in the CNT.) It even seemed possible that the proposed merger of socialists and communists might include both the BOC and the marginal Catalan section of the PCE (PCC) – something that, had it come to fruition, would have gone some considerable way to erasing the 'family' schism of the late 1920s. But the Catalan communists insisted on the exclusion from any putative merger of Andreu Nin's Communist Left because of his links with Trotsky.

At the core of the unity talks in Catalonia were the biggest groups, the BOC and the USC. Although they had been rivals since 1931, a merger would have produced a new player well on its way to holding its own as a partner in alliance with the Esquerra. But the outcome of the Workers' Alliance in 1934 did not augur well. And indeed, in the end, the attempt would fail because of basic disagreements between the two leaders over the political objectives and the geographical range of any new party. While the USC's Joan Comorera was as enthusiastic a supporter of a broad Popular Front-type alliance in 1935–6 as he had been in 1931, Joaquín Maurín of the BOC wanted this commitment to be strictly time limited to the election – that is, as a tactic to secure a political amnesty. And while the USC saw its desired role very clearly in terms of protagonising Catalan politics, Maurín wanted to play down

---

[120] Ucelay da Cal, 'Socialistas y comunistas en Cataluña durante la guerra civil', pp. 298–9, 305–7, 308, 318–19 and Balcells, *Trabajo industrial y organizacion obrera en la Cataluña contemporánea 1900–1936*, p. 143.

the BOC's Catalanism and (again as in 1934) to launch the new party on a political career throughout Spain.

This would see the BOC ally instead with Nin's Communist Left to form the POUM in September 1935 – in spite of Trotsky's own objections, vehemently made to Nin. But although Nin's group was politically sympathetic to Maurín's radical political and pan-Spanish aims and even keener to minimise the new party's Catalanism, it could add little by way of an extra-Catalan base on account of its own minuscule size. It had members in Madrid and Valencia, but so few that they counted as a groupuscule rather than a political party.[121] Many BOC members were uneasy about the merger. But most stayed in the new party because they felt that Maurín's political intelligence and strategic skill offered a sufficient guarantee for the future. A minority, however, left the BOC in protest at the merger and joined the Catalan Communists (PCC) instead.[122] The animosity between those who stayed and those who left was considerable, and this would feed into the Catalan left's war of political position after 18 July 1936. Nevertheless, the merger did make the POUM by the end of 1935 the largest socialist party in Catalonia by some margin.[123] Its core strength, however, derived from the Catalan – and Catalanist – members of the BOC in the region's other urban centres (for example Lleida, Girona and Tarragona). This might have been its strength. But it would in fact become a weakness during the war. In Maurín's absence (he was caught in the rebel zone) the contradictions would intensify between the POUM's own base – rooted in the Catalanist lower-middle classes – and the leadership's quasi anti-Popular Frontist strategy.[124]

THE EMERGENCE OF THE PSUC

The failure to agree terms for an alliance with the BOC would send the USC in search of other potential allies to bolster its political position. Comorera, for all that he was as moderate a social democrat as the USC contained, was of course influenced by the general sense of urgency on the left over the need to achieve strength through unity. But we should

---

[121] Nin's group was around 250–300 strong, while the BOC had several thousand members: V. Alba, *Dos revolucionarios: Joaquín Maurín, Andreu Nin* (Madrid: Seminarios y Ediciones, 1975), p. 389. See also P. Pagès, *El movimiento trotskista en España (1930–1935)* (Barcelona: Ediciones Península, 1975).

[122] Ucelay da Cal, 'Socialistas y comunistas en Cataluña durante la guerra civil', p. 311.

[123] Balcells, *Trabajo industrial y organización obrera en la Cataluña contemporánea 1900–1936*, p. 146. On the eve of the war the POUM had an estimated 6,000 members, though by December 1936 it claimed 30,000, F. Morrow, *Revolution and Counter-Revolution in Spain* (1938; London: New Park Publications, 1976), p. 45; Bolloten, *SCW*, p. 405.

[124] See chapter 4 below.

also remember that everything Comorera would agree to *en route* to the creation of a single socialist and communist party in Catalonia (the PSUC, formed in Barcelona in the summer of 1936) was driven by the USC's basic goal ever since it had properly begun to operate as a political party in 1931–2: *that it should form the ruling nucleus of a strong Catalanist social democratic party which would eventually displace the republican Esquerra.*[125] The PSUC offered a form of socialist unity in Catalonia that would allow the USC to lead. The larger POUM was excluded. At the same time, the merger in the PSUC of the various other fragments of the socialist and communist left in Catalonia would also provide crucial 'ballast' which would allow the new party to break out of the Esquerra's orbit and hold its own politically. The exclusion of the POUM also seemed to remove the threat of Catalan socialist unity becoming subordinate to a nationwide political strategy, such as the POUM had wanted and which, if successful, would once again have relegated the USC to a subordinate role – this time not to the PSOE, but to the POUM itself. Nor would the PSUC be subordinate to the PCE, for it was envisaged not as a section of the PCE, but as a separate and independent party (and as such the PSUC would be accepted by the Comintern[126]). PSUC unity permitted the reinforcement of the Catalan left against the Esquerra (to calm memories of 1931–3) but *without* breaking the Popular Front, as the POUM (and indeed the CNT) argued for, but to which the USC, as moderate social democrats, were absolutely opposed.

The prospect of PSUC unity also, crucially, freed the USC from the irksome influence of the PSOE. The intransigence of the highly centralist PSOE, which had resisted any concession to the Catalanism of the USC since its emergence in the 1920s, is a crucial factor in explaining the tactical preparedness of Comorera to do business with the Catalan Communists and the Comintern. In this respect it is highly significant that the decision taken in July 1935 to propose Comintern affiliation to the next USC congress was made by the USC executive without any prior talks having taken place with their Catalan Communist (PCC) counterparts. Indeed, in summer 1935 no apparatus yet existed for liaison of any kind between the USC and PCC.[127] Nor did the fact that freedom from the anti-Catalanist PSOE came at the price of Comintern

[125] Ucelay da Cal, 'Socialistas y comunistas en Cataluña durante la guerra civil', p. 305. Moreover, that Comorera did precisely this is evident in Comintern wartime criticisms of him. P. Togliatti, *Escritos sobre la guerra de España* (Barcelona: Crítica, 1980), pp. 247–8.
[126] See chapter 4 below.   [127] Balcells, 'El socialismo en Cataluña hasta la guerra civil', p. 38.

membership seem particularly risky. After all, as part of the new Popular Front line the Comintern had made its own a discourse that was highly sympathetic to nationalist claims. No doubt the Comintern's delegate to Catalonia, the Hungarian Ernö Gerö, who was involved in December 1935 in discussions to bring the USC and the PCC together, would have missed no opportunity to stress this. For the USC, as a party of the aspiring lower-middle classes, the image of the Soviet Union as an agent of social modernisation is also important in appreciating the appeal of the new policy.[128] Not least, the rank-and-file enthusiasm for unity on the left, which would reach a crescendo after the Popular Front election victory of February 1936, meant that the PSUC merger was an option that enjoyed significant *popular* support. In January 1936, the PCC would join in the unification discussions between the USC and the tiny Partit Català Proletari (PCP).[129]

This pre-history of the PSUC resolves the conundrum of Comorera's apparently contradictory attitudes both to unification itself and to Comintern affiliation.[130] In an ideal world Comorera would have preferred a Catalan social democratic party independent of ties with either the Spanish Socialist or Communist Parties, let alone with their respective Internationals. But in the real world, Comorera viewed everything strategically. The PSUC unification process was, anyway, gathering momentum across the spring and summer of 1936 as the constituent parties held meetings to ratify the unification. But the final, joint unification congress was only scheduled for late August, and the issue of the PSUC's relationship to the Comintern remained in a very real sense 'in the air' – even if positive noises were being made by the USC.[131] Comorera himself was probably less enthusiastic about Comintern affiliation than his favourable public pronouncements in March and June 1936 indicate. At the same time, however, he would certainly have felt far better disposed towards the Popular Frontist Catalan Communists and their International than towards the Catalan Socialists. After all, it was

[128] For more on this see the discussion in chapter 3 below.
[129] An offshoot of the radical nationalist Estat Català, the PCP (founded 1932) was of almost no political importance in itself. But by the end of 1934 it had come to control the powerful Barcelona shopworkers' association, the CADCI. Ucelay da Cal, 'Socialistas y comunistas en Cataluña durante la guerra civil', p. 309.
[130] A resumé of these is in Bolloten, *SCW*, pp. 397–8 (inc. nn. 10–13).
[131] From autumn 1935 through to spring 1936, USC leaders opposed to the new policy were displaced: Balcells, *Trabajo industrial y organización obrera en la Cataluña contemporánea 1900–1936*, p. 153; 'El socialismo en Cataluña hasta la guerra civil', p. 38.

the Caballerista-led Catalan PSOE federation in Barcelona which in
May 1936 sealed a long tradition of obstructionism by obliging Comorera to renounce USC support of the republicans in the Catalan government (and thus resign from his ministerial post in the Generalitat)
as the condition of PSOE entry to the PSUC unification discussions.[132]
Committed as Comorera was to supporting the Catalan government, he
had to accept the Caballeristas' ultimatum since, for his PSUC strategy
to work, he had to take the Catalan PSOE with him into the new party.
The Madrid PSOE would try to block this because of the Comintern
connection. But this time, in spring 1936, unlike in 1933, the Catalan federation of the PSOE and, more importantly, the Catalan UGT (which
the USC's own union, the UGSOC, had already joined) would break
away and back the PSUC.[133]

In Catalonia as elsewhere in Spain, the Popular Front elections
of February 1936 were stoking popular enthusiasm for political unity
on the left. In May 1936 the POUM's own trade union, the FOUS,
with approximately 6,000 members, also agreed to join the Catalan
UGT.[134] The latter was also strengthened by the influx of unions in
Sabadell and Manresa that brought around 14,000 and 3,300 members apiece. Their entry to the Catalan UGT was also highly symbolic.
Sabadell had been a key part of the CNT's support base in Catalonia
over the previous half-century. Manresa too was one of the *treintista* bases
that found a home in the CNT. Of the approximately forty thousand
members whose unions had left the CNT in 1931 and 1932, nearly half
would end up in the UGT.[135] In Catalonia too, the youth movements (of
both nationalism and the political left) were being increasingly drawn to
the vibrant, activist politics of the Popular Front.[136] The sphere of influence for what would soon be the PSUC was growing along with these
currents. But the nascent party's golden opportunity to compete with the
Esquerra would only come a few months later when the military coup
of July completely transformed the political terrain, by breaking the link
between electoral strength/institutional authority on the one hand and
political *power* on the other.[137]

---

[132] Balcells, 'El socialismo en Cataluña hasta la guerra civil', p. 39.

[133] For more on the PSUC and its wartime membership, see chapter 4 below.

[134] Bolloten, *SCW*, pp. 407–8. The extremely optimistic (not to say unrealistic) intention was to
radicalise the UGT in preparation for merger with the CNT.

[135] Figures from Balcells, *Trabajo industrial y organización obrera en la Cataluña contemporánea 1900–1936*,
pp. 156, 158–9.

[136] Ucelay da Cal, 'Socialistas y comunistas en Cataluña durante la guerra civil', pp. 310, 311.

[137] See chapter 4 below.

THE 'HOT' SPRING OF 1936

In the rest of Spain too the Popular Front elections had seen an explosion of popular political energy that showed no signs of abating. Everywhere the left's electoral victory had unleashed demands for the rapid reinstatement of workers who had been sacked after October 1934. There were calls too for urgent practical measures against unemployment and for the acceleration of social reform. In Asturias, local Popular Front committees – some newly created *after* the elections – showed their potential for becoming independent vehicles to press workers' demands.[138] The CNT was also vehemently critical of the restrictions on the political amnesty passed by the Popular Front on the morrow of its victory. The amnesty covered those convicted for political motives in the aftermath of October 1934. But it excluded those the CNT called 'social prisoners' – a category that included many CNT and FAI members detained under the anti-vagrancy legislation or in the insurrectionary attempts in the early years of the Republic (1931–2). This popular political pressure – in the streets, in public spaces, in town halls – ran counter to the preference of both republicans and the PSOE to 'contain' the Popular Front within parliamentary channels and to assert the authority of central government.[139] The PCE for its part sought to maintain extraparliamentary popular political mobilisation wherever it could. But, by the same token, its preference was for legal forms of protest.[140] But as we have noted before, many ordinary Spanish workers saw no necessary incompatibility between parliamentary action and direct action of more radical hue as a means of bringing change. Those who had joined the FNTT in the hope of state-led reform did not necessarily see this as debarring them from taking part in land seizures in March 1936.

[138] Shubert, 'A Reinterpretation of the Spanish Popular Front: The Case of Asturias', in Alexander and Graham, *The French and Spanish Popular Fronts*, pp. 213–25; Radcliff, *From Mobilisation to Civil War*, pp. 301–3 (on the 'two Republics' and the conflict of symbols between 14 April and 1 May celebrations in 1936 Gijón). The continued existence of local Popular Front Committees in Asturias after the February 1936 elections would provide a basis for local organisation after the 18 July coup.

[139] Prieto himself commented that the Popular Front as a mass movement had no reason to exist once the elections were over: J. S. Vidarte, *Todos fuimos culpables* (2 vols, Barcelona: Grijalbo, 1978), vol. 1, p. 99. On liberal republican anxieties and obsession with 'the neutrality of the street', see S. Juliá, *Manuel Azaña. Una biografía política* (Madrid: Alianza, 1990), pp. 459–69; Casanova, *De la calle al frente*, p. 145 (n. 12); H. Graham, 'Spain 1936. Resistance and Revolution: The Flaws in the Front', in T. Kirk and A. McElligott (eds.) *Opposing Fascism. Community, Authority and Resistance in Europe* (Cambridge: Cambridge University Press, 1999), p. 64.

[140] Cf. the similar moderating influence exerted by the PCF during the June strikes in France: D. A. L. Levy, 'The French Popular Front 1936–37', in Graham and Preston, *The Popular Front in Europe*, p. 69.

For the republicans in government after February, the fear of such popular action was out of all proportion to its extent and, moreover, to what
it signified.[141] The republicans certainly feared it more than they did the
military conspiracies against the Republic that had been rumoured ever
since the right's defeat at the polls. These anxieties ruled out any possibility of Azaña's government addressing the still pending issue of the
demilitarisation of public order. In this crucial question, as in so many
others, the republicans would, once again, reap the worst of all worlds.
In 1931 they had inflamed the feelings of many officers by pursuing with
vehement rhetoric the 'responsibilities' campaign against those alleged
to have committed crimes or to have been corrupt or incompetent under
the old regime.[142] But in reality few officers had been called to account.
So the republicans had alienated a powerful and dangerous sector in the
officer class, yet in practice failed to 'disarm' them.[143] The July rebellion
would be triggered by the military declaring a state of war – something
which (under the terms of the Republic's own 1933 public order Act)
still fell within their competence.[144] Had the republicans demilitarised
public order, not only would it have prevented the conspirators from
using legality as a cloak for their actions, but it would also have served
as an important consolidation of civilian constitutional authority on the
symbolic plane. For this too was an important component in the constitutional 'education' of the officer corps. In sum, the failure to demilitarise
public order stands as the example, *par excellence*, of the lethal nature of
Republican idealism.

To make matters worse, the government that issued from the February
1936 electoral victory was not in fact a 'Popular Front' government at all,
but an entirely republican one. Largo Caballero had made his support of
the electoral pact conditional on the assurance that the PSOE would not
participate in government thereafter. The Caballeristas – remembering
the experience of 1931–3 – argued instead for the formation of an exclusively workers' alliance. Simultaneously, they propounded the view –
largely constructed by Largo's political lieutenant, the party theorist Luis

---

[141] The republicans inherited the 'state of alarm' from the caretaker administration in charge
before the February Popular Front elections and they maintained it virtually uninterrupted
until the military coup in July 1936. M. Ballbé, *Orden público y militarismo en la España constitucional
(1812–1983)* (Madrid: Alianza, 1983), p. 387.

[142] Preston, *Franco. A Biography* (London: HarperCollins, 1993), pp. 76–7; C. P. Boyd,
' "Responsibilities" and the Second Republic, 1931–6' in M. Blinkhorn (ed.), *Spain in Conflict
1931–1939* (London: Sage, 1986), pp. 14–39.

[143] Ballbé, *Orden público y militarismo en la España constitucional*, pp. 391, 393.

[144] Ibid., pp. 13, 336.

Araquistain, that the republicans should be allowed to 'exhaust' themselves in government and then 'power' would drop like a ripe fruit into the hands of the socialists, who would then fulfil their historic mission and inherit the state. But this puerile 'theory' completely ignored the collateral effects of republican erosion: most particularly, that the weak all-republican cabinet was entirely incapable of dealing with the overriding challenge facing the Republic in the spring of 1936 – the military conspiracy escalating in the garrisons. Indeed, given the shape of republican demons, to many among them this would not even appear to be the overriding danger.

The parliamentary PSOE and Indalecio Prieto in particular (who had an impressive personal intelligence network) were far less sanguine about the situation in the garrisons. In May 1936, in an attempt to bolster the government by recreating the coalition of 1931–3, Prieto sought to replace Manuel Azaña as prime minister in a two-pronged strategy which saw Azaña appointed as Republican president. But the strategy failed because of opposition from Largo Caballero and his supporters, who threatened to split the PSOE if Prieto went into the cabinet. Party colleagues, including Prieto's close friend Juan Negrín, tried to persuade him to go ahead anyway and call Largo's bluff. But whether for fear of the damage that might be done to the PSOE or because he was not prepared to risk his own political reputation, Prieto refused.[145] As a result the Republic found itself in the worst of all possible positions. The government continued without the PSOE but also deprived of Azaña's stewardship. Azaña had agreed to be proposed as president only on condition that Prieto take over from him in the government. So Prieto was ill advised to have pursued his strategy at all if he was not prepared to brave the worst of the Caballeristas' threats. There can, of course, be no guarantee that with Prieto as premier the Republic could have defused the military time bomb. But the memory of his renunciation in May 1936, and what he saw as its consequences, would return to haunt Prieto during the war. For whatever the difficulty of attempting to prevent the rising, it paled into insignificance beside the enormous task of defending the Republic once the military rebellion was a fact. In the cupola of the PSOE, the realisation that a golden opportunity had been lost would weigh like a millstone after 18 July 1936. Ultimately it was the politics of May 1936 that would drive the actions of Prieto and his

---

[145] Graham, *Socialism and War*, pp. 35–6, 100. See P. Preston, *Comrades* (London: HarperCollins, 1999) for both Prieto's and Azaña's point of view, pp. 224–6, 260–1.

PSOE colleagues when they forced the famous cabinet crisis a year later in May 1937 which saw Largo Caballero resign as prime minister.[146] But even this could not neutralise the corrosive effect of the memory of May 1936 among leading socialists. The resulting paralysis of political will in the party hierarchy would be one important factor contributing to the deadly isolation of Juan Negrín as Republican prime minister after May 1937, as we shall see.

By May 1936 the socialist movement was effectively split into two, even though Prieto had chosen not to enter the government.[147] But although this made it appear as if the Caballerista wing was in control, in fact it was riven by internal contradictions and growing dissension.[148] Its crisis was both organisational and political. Politically, it had blocked Prieto's strategy, but it was difficult to discern what specific alternative it proposed. Certainly there is no evidence that Largo took any steps towards the practical implementation of a nationwide inter-organisational alliance such as the Alianza Obrera had had the potential to be in 1934.[149]

In fact a seismic shift was taking place which would dramatically alter the political landscape on the left. Crucial to this shift was the PCE. In Popular Front mode, it found itself to have more and more common ground with Prieto and the parliamentary PSOE. The PCE's great advantage over the socialists, however, was that it was campaigning wholeheartedly for an inter-class alliance, while the socialist movement was divided. But there was something else too. The PCE was the only political force in Spain arguing for an inter-class alliance based on mass mobilisation – necessary both as a resource to allow state building and also as the essential political legitimator of that state-building project itself. This crucial unifying and modernising dynamic at the heart of the PCE's Popular Frontism was encapsulated in the term 'pueblo laborioso' ('the productive nation') which the party coined and used from February 1936.[150]

---

[146] See chapter 5 below.　　[147] Graham, *Socialism and War*, pp. 27–8.

[148] Graham, 'The Eclipse of the Socialist Left 1934–1937', in Lannon and Preston, *Elites and Power in Twentieth-Century Spain*, p. 134.

[149] In September 1936 Largo Caballero would throw his weight behind the reconstitution of a left-liberal coalition government of precisely the sort he had consistently blocked between 1934 and 1936. See chapter 3 below.

[150] This built on José Diaz's call for a 'concentración popular antifascista' at the 2 June 1935 Madrid meeting, *Tres años de lucha*, vol. 1, pp. 47, 51, 61. Cf. the May 1935 Comintern manifesto (signed by Díaz, André Marty and Palmiro Togliatti), which referred to 'the socialist, communist, anarchist and syndicalist toilers of Spain', and also to 'the toilers of Catalonia, the Basque Country and

There was an aura of political vibrancy adhering to the PCE by the spring of 1936 – even though it was still quite a small political party.[151] It had made some headway in attracting support in the UGT since 1935. But it was in April 1936 that the PCE achieved its most startling success when the national leadership of the fifty thousand-strong socialist youth federation (FJS) agreed to merge with its much smaller communist counterpart.[152] In part this was the logical conclusion of the radicalisation of some sectors of the socialist youth organisation. But politics here has to be understood as rather more than a matter of abstract marxist-leninism. Many young Spaniards who were politically active on the left in spring 1936 simply saw the PCE as a more exciting and attractive option than the socialists, whose views on the proper role of a youth movement had changed little since the days of the founding fathers. It was thus the PCE that channelled the youth breakthrough to organised politics in 1930s Spain.

Although Largo Caballero had not been consulted about the youth merger, he spoke in its favour at the massive celebratory meeting held in the Ventas bullring, Madrid, on 5 April. Given the sheer numerical superiority of the FJS, Largo no doubt envisaged the unification as little more than the reabsorption of an errant minority by the 'historic' socialist movement. He also thought that it would give the socialist left a boost in its bid to thwart Prieto.[153] But quite the opposite would occur. For although Largo did not yet know it, the FJS leaders were in the

Morocco'. The PCF also referred to 'an alliance of all toiling people', *Humanité*, 5 June 1935. There was still a certain ambiguity (indeed tension) around whether 'toilers' defined primarily the working class or whether it also included middling-class sectors. This obliquely reflected the disagreements that still existed inside the Comintern over the advisability of moving from a homogeneously worker or united front to the inter-class Popular Front: E. H. Carr, *The Twilight of the Comintern* (London: Macmillan, 1982), pp. 148–50, 317.

[151] The PCE probably had in the region of 40,000 members, although it would claim over 100,000; Bolloten, *SCW*, p. 831; *Guerra y revolución en España 1936–39* (4 vols, Moscow: Editorial Progreso, 1966–77), vol. 1, p. 87. For some useful data on the comparative wartime growth of the PSOE, the PCE and the UGT, see M. Ortiz Heras, *Violencia política en la II República (Albacete 1936–1939)* (Madrid: Siglo XXI, 1996), p. 109, n. 43. This corroborates the speed of the PCE's growth, compared to a much more modest increase for the PSOE. But it was the UGT that grew fastest of all.

[152] The Communist Youth (UJC) had around 3,000 members. For the youth unification see Graham, *Socialism and War*, pp. 19, 22, 29–33 and 'The Socialist Youth in the JSU', in M. Blinkhorn (ed.), *Spain in Conflict 1931–1936* (London: Sage, 1986), pp. 83–102; Viñas, *La formación de las Juventudes Socialistas Unificadas (1934–1936)*. There was a precedent for this. In 1920 the Socialist Youth had departed the PSOE to form Spain's very first Communist Party.

[153] Both things are clear from Largo's speech, reproduced in various newspapers, including the PCE's *Mundo Obrero*, 6 April 1936.

process of shifting their affiliation to the PCE.[154] In the process they would bind the new united youth organisation to PCE and Comintern discipline. In effect, the whole of the FJS would be lost to the PSOE. But this would only become clear several months later, and the story of how it happened is inextricably bound up with the exceptional wartime conditions of autumn 1936, and in particular the siege of Madrid.[155] We have no way of knowing if the merger decision would have been ratified by FJS congress had normal peacetime life gone on. Certainly there was opposition inside the FJS to their own executive's decision. Many socialist youth sections simply refused to obey the April instructions. But the military coup exploded before any FJS congress could be held. The exceptional conditions of war would thus end by binding the majority of the socialist youth to membership of a united youth organisation, the JSU, which the PCE saw as the flagship of its Popular Front policy.

But increasingly prepared though Prieto's socialists and the communists were to reinvigorate the Republic's parliamentary project, the military rebellion took them almost equally unawares. The PCE had been training a militia, the MAOC (the Milicias Antifascistas Obreras y Campesinas), in the Casa de Campo scrubland adjacent to Madrid. But, like the party, it was fairly small. The Caballeristas were no better off, however. Their verbal revolutionism had never extended to the preparation of armed action. Indeed, their implicit definition of the revolution as a quasi-mystical event meant that it required no practical preparation (and thus involved no organisational risk for the UGT). In a sense, it was this mystical conception of how the revolution would occur (as a spontaneous rising should the military dare to oppose the popular will) which 'legitimised' the singular inaction of the socialist left/UGT national leadership – with deadly results. All militia organisation and training in the tense summer of 1936 was done *ad hoc* on the basis of local party and union cells. (The same was obviously true for the CNT.) There was no national coordination, even within the socialist movement, and, of course, none between the organisations of the left such as a Worker's Alliance might have provided. Absorbed by its own political balancing

---

[154] The FJS leaders informed Largo of this only in the autumn of 1936 – in December, according to one protagonist: see F. Claudín, *Santiago Carrillo. Crónica de un secretario general* (Barcelona: Planeta, 1983), p. 45. This inevitably caused a definitive break between Largo and the socialist youth leaders. Santiago Carrillo himself always dated his decision to join the PCE to the siege of Madrid in November 1936, but it seems likely that this was the culmination of a process that had begun back in the spring of 1936.

[155] See chapter 3 below.

act and mesmerised by republican crisis, the socialist left, with its eyes on state power, was caught virtually defenceless by the rebellion. For all of the Spanish left, 18 July 1936 was, in every sense, a cataclysm.[156]

CONCLUSION

Looking back, we can say that the reforming project of 1931 was eroded by the effects of economic crisis. Republican commitment to *laissez-faire* economics in conditions of depression made it impossible for the republican-socialist coalition to implement the kind of welfarist social and economic reform that could have integrated urban and rural labour (or substantial segments of it) in the Republic. The Republic could not broaden its support base to the left while it remained committed to orthodox liberal economics. The poor, unemployed and unskilled would look instead to those who articulated a radical critique of the existing order that directly addressed their plight.

But, ultimately, the stability of the Second Spanish Republic, like that of its Weimar counterpart of the 1920s in Germany, was never seriously threatened by those to its left. It could always control such disaffection through the use of the police. Quite a different matter was the destabilising impact of the right's political mobilisation of a mass conservative anti-reform movement. Liberal republicans' doctrinaire anti-clericalism had facilitated the mobilisation of Catholics across categories of socio-economic class. But the sequence of events examined here has also suggested that such a mobilisation might have been impeded if republicans and socialists had themselves been able to elaborate a strategy of mass mobilisation that would have allowed them to compete more successfully with the right for control of the middle ground. But, ironically for the left, republicans and socialists belonged to an old political world that feared rather than sought popular mobilisation. The failure to understand the need for this was to cost the Republic dear. The popular, or counter-hegemonic, alliance existing in potential in 1931 had fragmented. The Popular Front victory in the February 1936 elections offered the possibility of reversing that process to some extent. But political opponents were about to make sure that there would be no time for this. It was the existence of mass mobilised conservative opinion that made the military rebellion of July 'viable'. But it was the action of the coup itself that finally ripped apart the liberal project in Spain. For it removed from the

---

[156] Cf. M. Alpert, *El ejército republicano en la guerra civil*, 2nd edn (Madrid: Siglo XXI, 1989), p. 18.

Republican orbit a substantial sector of the social groups supporting forms of economic liberalism.[157] The wartime Republic still bore within it the cultural and political project of historically inclusive liberalism. But this would now have to be carried forward from a weaker social base. For not all the constituencies opposing the coup subscribed to that project.

[157] I have two things in mind. First, that some middling groups were lost outright because the military rising succeeded (for example in the Granadan *vega*). But there is a second and more important point here – that the coup's success also closed off further political evolutions. It seems likely that the threat of a military backlash in 1936 was going to allow the republicans to justify tougher public-order policies against the left. Likewise, the republicans' parliamentary programme of social and economic reform could also have justified tougher government measures against worker direct action, such as land seizures. (The Second Republic was not a socialist Republic – whatever the military rebels claimed.) This scenario might, in time, have permitted republicans, and even the PSOE, to make inroads into provincial middle-class support for the Radicals and CEDA. All this is counterfactual, of course. But the crucial point is not: the coup's success did more than simply freeze existing political choices – it wiped out other potentials for good.

CHAPTER 2

Against the state: military rebellion, political fragmentation, popular resistance and repression (18 July–4 September 1936)

Show me the words that will reorder the world.[1]

On 18 July 1936 the military rebellion[2] that had erupted the previous day in Melilla, Spanish North Africa, spread to garrisons on the mainland.[3] In symbolic terms it revealed the serious limits of Republican control over the state. In practical terms, in shattering both army and police[4] command structures the rebellion deprived the liberal republican government of the coercive force it needed to exercise centralised control of resistance measures. Without unified, coherent security forces – which in the 1930s remained the defining institution of the central state in Spain – the government's authority collapsed. The capital city of Madrid became, for a time, just another 'island' of conflict. Everywhere they could, the left's parties and unions declared a general strike as the first stage of mobilisation against the rebel military. (In Madrid this happened predominantly under PSOE and UGT direction, in Barcelona under the CNT's.) Proletarian protagonism obviously owed a great deal to workers' awareness that they had most to lose should the military rebellion succeed – an awareness that had been heightened over time by a string of bloody working-class defeats in 1920s and 1930s Europe

---

[1] Tony Kushner, *Angels in America* (London: Royal National Theatre/Nick Hern Books, 1994), Part 2: *Perestroika*, Act I, Scene 1, pp. 1–2.

[2] The ultra-reactionary rebel cabal drew its strength from the fact that it was backed by a junior officer class whose career prospects/professional aspirations had been curtailed by Republican budgetary restrictions. The bulk of senior army officers remained loyal to the Republic. See Cardona, *El poder militar en la España contemporánea hasta la guerra civil* and for Franco, Preston, *Franco*, pp. 69–143.

[3] On 18 July the rebels extended their control in Spanish North Africa to Ceuta, Tetuán and Larache.

[4] Here the Republic reaped the fatal consequences of its failure to demilitarise public order, M. Ballbé, *Orden público y militarismo en la España constitucional*, pp. 391, 393–5. If Civil and Assault Guards had been under civilian control, then their role could have been decisive in enough places to defeat it instantly. Sometimes Civil Guards were reluctant to oppose the Republic as the constituted authority. But their passivity was all the rebels needed.

(Italy 1922, Germany 1933, Austria 1934) as well as by the military repression following the Asturian miners' rising in northern Spain in October 1934.[5]

In Madrid at party and union headquarters members signed up to form militia forces. And some sympathetic Republican officers who were in a position to do so issued arms to them directly, in spite of republican government threats to have officers who did so shot.[6] The quantities of arms which could be provided in such ways, however, were too small to offer a serious or sustained defence against rebel military firepower. The left consequently called for the systematic arming of party and union cadres.

The centre-left republicans who constituted the Madrid government under the weak premiership of Santiago Casares Quiroga[7] were horrified by the thought that in order to defend liberal Republican legality they might have to arm the very proletarian cadres whose political agenda they feared and whose mobilisation they had, consequently, resisted since February 1936.[8] Whether for this reason, or for others, the government had consistently underrated the threat posed by conspirators in the military.[9] (This very much reflected the views of Azaña[10] – for Casares and the other ministers were the president's intimates.) Casares, with extremely little information to go on as a result of the fragmentation of communications consequent on the coup, played down the scale and significance of the garrison revolts in the desperate hope that they might indeed turn out to be a minor affair.[11] In lieu of material defence measures, a petrified Casares issued a number of decrees dissolving those

[5] See chapter 1 above.

[6] J. Zugazagoitia, *Guerra y vicisitudes de los españoles* (Buenos Aires, 1940; 3rd edn, Barcelona: Crítica, 1977), p. 58; Vidarte, *Todos fuimos culpables*, vol. 1, p. 238.

[7] Casares led the small Galician republican group, Organización Regional Gallega Autónoma (ORGA). (He was appointed prime minister when Azaña became president of the Republic in May 1936.) Zugazagoitia, *Guerra y vicisitudes*, pp. 39–46.

[8] See chapter 1 above.

[9] There is the famous story of Casares' outburst against Prieto's 'menopausal' tendencies when he tried to warn the premier against the military threat, I. Prieto, *Convulsiones de España. Pequeños detalles de grandes sucesos* (3 vols., Mexico: Ediciones Oasis 1967–9), vol. 1, p. 163; Zugazagoitia, *Guerra y vicisitudes*, pp. 39–41. For other vain attempts by Ignacio Hidalgo de Cisneros, Casares' aide-de-camp, see C. de la Mora, *In Place of Splendour* (New York, Harcourt, Brace & Co., 1939), pp. 209–10, 216–20. (Casares was both premier and war minister.) See also S. Carrillo, *Memorias* (Madrid:Planeta, 1993; 6th edn, 1994), p. 168 and Ballbé, *Orden público y militarismo en la España constitucional*, pp. 389–90.

[10] Juan Marichal suggests that even Azaña could not quite construct for himself the military threat in terms as vivid as those in which he posed the danger of an armed proletariat: see introduction to M. Azaña, *Obras completas* (4 vols., Madrid: Ediciones Giner, 1990), vol. 3, p. xxxii.

[11] A. Cordón, *Trayectoria* (Paris: Colección Ebro, 1971), p. 224.

military units involved in the rising and relieving troops of their duty of allegiance to rebel officers and the latter of their commands. Early in the evening of the 18th, the government broadcast claims on Madrid radio that the rebellion had been extinguished everywhere in Spain.[12] It was as if Casares were hoping – against all rationality – that such constitutional measures would be sufficient to alter the course of events, since he was not prepared to arm the unions.

The coup itself had in fact precipitated a full-scale crisis for historic republicanism as swathes of its natural constituents – smallholders and tenant farmers, traders, shopkeepers and small entrepreneurs – were definitively lost to it in rebel-conquered territory. Moreover, in the confusion of territorial dislocation, many middle-class republican functionaries and elected officials prevaricated or 'went missing', fleeing their public responsibilities. The judiciary collapsed.[13] From the ministries down to municipal and village councils, the state was ceasing to function either through a physical absence of personnel or through the vacillation of those still present. In the provinces, civil governors 'awaited instructions from Madrid', but neither the Madrid government nor the leadership of any other political party or organisation loyal to it had adequate means of acquiring an overview of what was happening across Spain. The Madrid government, for all it was in permanent emergency session,[14] had few resources, and to discover how the political geography on the peninsula was evolving it was reduced to a process of piecemeal canvassing (by telephone or telegraph). A response of '¡Arriba España!' ('Long live Spain!') inspired greater alarm since it signified rebel control. But republicans everywhere – leadership and cadres – feared for their lives and were uncertain where their political allegiance should lie in such a fluid situation. They were caught between their fear of the military's visceral anti-republicanism (in spite of the rebels' initial professions of 'good faith') and their awareness that the party and union militia providing the Republic's emergency defence represented a threat to their own preferred forms of social and political order.

In an attempt to heal the breach within republicanism, while also avoiding both the shedding of blood and the arming of the workers, in the early hours of the morning of 19 July Republican president Manuel

[12] Thereby also alerting much of the population to the alarming fact that the military rising had been nationwide.

[13] Fraser, *Blood of Spain*, p. 178.

[14] First in the war ministry (located in the Palacio Real (del Oriente) – called the Palacio Nacional during the Republican period) and then in the interior ministry in the Puerta del Sol.

Azaña appointed a new prime minister to head an emergency adminis-tration.[15] He was Diego Martínez Barrio, leader of Unión Republicana, president of the Cortes and the man who most symbolised republican-ism's social conservatism, pragmatism and compromise. His brief was to conduct telephone negotiations with the rebels' leader in the north, General Emilio Mola,[16] in order to achieve a truce. But within some three hours it was clear that the republicans' gamble had failed. The rebels were not interested in negotiating,[17] and the net result of Martínez Barrio's attempt was only to lose republicanism its last shreds of credibil-ity with the proletarian cadres who were facing down the military rebels in the streets of Madrid and in the Guadarrama sierra to the north of the capital. Martínez Barrio's efforts were seen as temporisation, which, in casting doubt on his supporters' commitment to resisting the coup, only accelerated the final eclipse of republicanism. By midday on 19 July he had no choice but to resign.[18]

Time was ever more of the essence. The republicans' indecision – epitomised by Casares' refusal to arm the workers' organisations – had already caused lives to be lost. President Azaña – not exempt from the epidemic of procrastination himself[19] – appointed the same day an-other all-republican cabinet under the premiership of chemistry profes-sor José Giral, Azaña's personal friend and close associate in Izquierda Republicana (Left Republicans).[20] Giral's tacit brief was to arm the mili-tia in order finally to quell the garrison revolts. It was hard for Azaña to find a republican politician prepared to accept leadership responsibility in this crisis situation, something which only emphasises the depth of the crisis which had struck republicanism. Giral was motivated in great part

[15] Although the suggestion of a 'moderate' (i.e. in fact a fairly conservative) republican cabinet to negotiate with the rebels came from the conservative republican lawyer and leader of the small National Republican Party, Felipe Sánchez Román. For the members of Martínez Barrio's cabinet, see J. M. Gómez Ortiz, *Los gobiernos republicanos. España 1936–1939* (Barcelona: Bruguera, 1977), p. 40 (originally listed in the *Gaceta de Madrid*, 19 July 1936).

[16] Mola was the 'director' of the military conspiracy. The intended general-in-chief of the rising, Sanjurjo, was killed when the plane bringing him from Lisbon to Burgos crashed soon after take-off on 20 July. H. Thomas, *The Spanish Civil War* (Harmondsworth: Penguin, 1977), p. 254.

[17] Mola explained this by reference to the irreconcilable values/objectives of the two sides. But obviously for the rebel chiefs there was also a personal imperative. For even if an amnesty had been negotiated as part of the truce, the leaders had effectively 'burned their boats' as far as professional advancement under a Republican regime was concerned.

[18] Azaña, *Obras completas*, vol. 4, pp. 714–16; D. Martínez Barrio, *Memorias* (Barcelona: Planeta, 1983), pp. 356–68; Zugazagoitia, *Guerra y vicisitudes*, pp. 63–5.

[19] Prieto expressed his exasperation at Azaña's 'abcesos de vacilación', A. Vélez, *Informaciones* (Madrid), 10 November 1977 (Vélez was the pseudonym of José María Aguirre, Largo Caballero's secretary).

[20] For a list of cabinet members see Bolloten, *SCW*, pp. 46–7.

by personal loyalty to Azaña. But his decision is also indicative of the reluctant acceptance by some republicans that, if the military would not negotiate, then the Republic's survival depended on the emergency popular defence forces with whom a *modus vivendi* would thus have to be reached.

Given the dislocation of army and police, these extremely eclectic local resistance movements provided important reinforcement for loyal elements in the security forces. Together they were all that stood between the Republic and defeat at rebel hands. Giral immediately petitioned the French Popular Front government for arms on 19 July. He simultaneously decreed the arming of party and union militia as well as the reopening of workers' centres and union headquarters closed by Casares.[21] CNT militants were also released from Madrid's Cárcel Modelo (Model Prison). Provincial civil governments were instructed by phone to distribute arms. (Although the instructions often came too late or else were simply not implemented.[22]) But we should not make the mistake of assuming that Giral controlled these forces his government was prepared to arm. Indeed, at this stage, the Madrid authorities were barely in control of what was happening in the capital itself.

There the militias' desperate search for arms and food supplies, especially in the early weeks, accelerated the process of state dislocation which the military rebellion had detonated. Both the Spanish Socialist and Communist Party leaderships intervened to support the quartermaster officers attempting to impose some sort of limits and discipline on the often excessive and always uncoordinated militia demands.[23] (Such was the mistrust of the professional military in the wake of the coup that when the small emergency staff of officers keeping things running at the War Ministry refused to meet militia requests, they instantly laid themselves open to the accusation that they were crypto-rebels.)

The Spanish Socialist Party (PSOE), which along with its trade union (UGT) was the most prominent organisational force in the capital at the start of the conflict, formed the Motorizada militia, which also fulfilled a public-order function in the city. Most of its membership was drawn from the minority of the Madrid socialist youth which had not left to join the united socialist-communist youth organisation (JSU) in April 1936.[24]

[21] On 14 July 1936 the government had closed monarchist, Carlist and anarchist centres, J. Lozano, *La Segunda República. Imágenes, cronología y documentos* (Barcelona: Ediciones Acervo, 1973), p. 224.

[22] Cordón, *Trayectoria*, p. 248.

[23] J. Martín Blázquez, *I Helped to Build an Army* (London: Secker & Warburg, 1939), pp. 125ff.

[24] Zugazagoitia, *Guerra y vicisitudes*, pp. 58–9, 130; Vidarte, *Todos fuimos culpables*, vol. I, p. 59; Graham, *Socialism and War*, p. 30. The PSOE and its youth militia replicated this public-order function in several cities: see, for example, Ortiz Heras, *Violencia política en la II República*, p. 106.

The JSU itself, rapidly expanding from among previously unaffiliated young people, organised a number of militias – Octubre, Largo Caballero, Joven Guardia and Pasionaria. The Spanish Communist Party (PCE), which was also rapidly recruiting new members in Madrid and the central zone from among unaffiliated youth and the ranks of the professional military, had its own militia, the Madrid-based MAOC (Milicias Antifascistas Obreras y Campesinas). Formed back in 1933, the MAOC also had a youthful profile. Since acquiring an effectively legal existence after the February 1936 Popular Front elections, it had functioned mainly to protect party meetings and premises. But it had also trained in the Casa de Campo with instructors who were often serving army officers. The MAOC would later become the nucleus of the PCE's Fifth Regiment (Quinto Regimiento), whose function in the initial training and shaping of the new Republican army was to be so crucial.[25]

But not only had the military coup fragmented the army. By inducing the collapse of Republican government at every level it also massively facilitated the upsurge in popular political violence which followed that collapse. This sudden explosion[26] was primed by rage at what was seen as the rebels' attempt to put the clock back to old-regime order by force, after their failure by electoral means. Although the intensity of this post-coup popular political violence varied across Republican territory, it was everywhere instigated by urban workers and landless labourers, who directed it overwhelmingly at the sources and bearers of the 'old power' – whether material (by destroying property records and land registries[27]) or human (the assassination or brutalisation of priests, Civil Guards,

[25] On the MAOC, see J. Modesto, *Soy del Quinto Regimiento* (Barcelona: Editorial Laia, 1978), pp. 47, 49–50, 61–2 and E. Líster, *Memorias de un luchador* (Madrid: G. del Toro, 1977), pp. 66–7; Alpert, *El ejército republicano*, p. 18. See also chapter 3 below.

[26] See Ortiz Heras, *Violencia política en la II República*, pp. 99–100; J. D. Simeón Riera, *Entre la rebelió y la tradició (Llíria durante La República y la Guerra Civil. 1931–1939)* (Valencia: Diputació de València, 1993), pp. 272–6 for a suggestive, if problematic, discussion of the 'pre-modern' dimension of this popular violence. Sometimes, however, the means of redress were other: see the case of rural labouring women in Pozoblanco (Cordoba) who demanded that the 'señoritas de derechas' ('conservative ladies') should be required to participate in the olive harvesting, G. García de Consuegra Muñoz, A. López López and F. López López, *La represión en Pozoblanco* (Cordoba: Francisco Baena, Editor, 1989), p. 74. As several authors note, *paseos* were often carried out by those from the surrounding area but not the same village as the victim(s). This could be attributed to the practical security offered by relative anonymity. It was also the pattern of pre-war anti-clerical violence (see Thomas, *Spanish Civil War*, p. 54) and probably owed something to community tabus. Ortiz Heras, *Violencia política en la II República*, p. 105; Simeón Riera, *Entre la rebelió y la tradició*, p. 208; C. Castilla del Pino, *Pretérito imperfecto. Autobiografía* (Barcelona: Tusquets Editores, 1997), pp. 186–8; Fraser, *Blood of Spain*, pp. 353, 358, 362.

[27] A. Bosch-Sánchez, *Ugetistas y libertarios. Guerra civil y revolución en el País Valenciano, 1936–1939* (Valencia: Institució Alfons el Magnànim, 1983), p. 32; Simeón Riera, *Entre la rebelió y la tradició*, pp. 205, 273 (n. 72).

police, estate bailiffs,[28] and shopkeepers associated with speculative pricing and other exploitative practices[29]). There is a clear link between post-coup popular violence and pre-war conflicts: for example over the blocking of land or labour reform legislation in certain localities or over worker dismissals after the general strikes of 1934 or over conflicts (again, over the implementation of social and labour reforms) in the aftermath of the February 1936 Popular Front elections. In the early months of the conflict, acts of terror perpetrated by the population at large would also be triggered by the news of mass shootings and other atrocities in rebel territory, as well as by the direct experience of enemy air attack, which saw assaults on imprisoned conservatives in a number of places.[30]

In the end, however, such acts of terror cannot be explained solely by reference to the conscious decision of individual (or collective) perpetrators. Violence as a popular response is always shaped by the dominant culture:[31] those who died embodied in the eyes of those who killed the privilege and property of a closed social, economic, political and juridical order that had daily done violence to them by excluding their most basic needs from its purview. It was the symbolic centrality of the Catholic Church as an institution to this exclusion that explains the notorious anticlerical dimension of the terror. The collapse of authority caused by the military coup ushered in a wave of killing of religious personnel unprecedented in the long and complex history of anti-clericalism in Spain.[32]

---

[28] Although *latifundistas* were habitually absentee landlords, landowners are listed among those killed in the south, García de Consuegra Muñoz, López López and López López, *La represión en Pozoblanco*, p. 69 (see also unpaginated appendix: 'Víctimas de la represión republicana').

[29] The inclusion of shopkeepers may seem an anomaly in an analysis of attitudes to the state. However, as discussed in chapter 4 in relation to Barcelona (but not exclusively to it), the Chamber of Commerce frequently called upon local government authorities to deploy police to 'resolve' disputes between shop owners and those engaged in alternative food procurement and sale for poor and marginal sectors of the population. For similar sorts of direct action, see Radcliff, *From Mobilisation to Civil War*, pp. 249–304.

[30] García de Consuegra Muñoz, López López and López López, *La represión en Pozoblanco*, pp. 55, 60; G. Cox, *The Defence of Madrid* (London: Victor Gollancz, 1937), p. 183; Ortiz Heras, *Violencia política en la II República*, pp. 106–8; G. Jackson, *The Spanish Republic and the Civil War*, p. 343; I. Gibson, *Paracuellos cómo fue* (Barcelona: Argos Vergara, 1983), pp. 178–9.

[31] For one formulation of this, see 'Del terror y la violencia', in F. Savater, *Para la anarquía y otros enfrentamientos* (Barcelona: Orbis, 1984), p. 68.

[32] On anti-clericalism in pre-war Spain, see especially: Ullman, *The Tragic Week*; also Romero Maura, '*La rosa del Fuego*'; Alvarez Junco, *El emperador del Paralelo. Lerroux y la demagogia populista*; D. Castro Alfín, 'Cultura, política y cultura política en la violencia anticlerical', in R. Cruz and M. Pérez-Ledesma (eds.), *Cultura y movilización en la España contemporánea* (Madrid: Alianza Editorial, 1997), pp. 69–97; J. de la Cueva Merino, 'El anticlericalismo en la Segunda República y la guerra civil', in E. la Parra and M. Suárez (eds.), *El anticlericalismo español contemporáneo* (Madrid: Biblioteca Nueva, 1998).

But we still have a relatively undifferentiated picture of wartime anti-clerical violence. The existing historical bibliography tends to chronicle rather than analyse.[33] Anthropological studies can open up fruitful avenues for the historian. But too great a concentration on the symbolic plane can also obscure the quite specific renegotiations of political power which anti-clerical violence signified in particular situations.[34] For these reasons we are in need of thorough local studies informed by interdisciplinary theoretical perspectives.[35] It is also important to remember that not all forms of popular terror against Catholics during the civil war were necessarily anti-clerical in origin. For example, the 'pillars' of Catholic associational life also frequently belonged to the local economic elites or were leaders of the political right (or sometimes both).[36] The killing of religious personnel was for many contemporary observers – in Spain and beyond – the most symbolically and ethically charged of all the forms of violence perpetrated during the civil war. For some commentators this remains the case today – even though its dimensions are dwarfed by other forms of killing carried out during the war (in both zones) against secular social constituencies.[37] Whatever one's assessment here, the fact remains that retaliatory popular terror – anti-clerical and otherwise – happened because it was perceived as offering the prospect of *tabula rasa*: a satisfyingly instantaneous dissolution of political oppression as well as reparation for accumulated social hurts.[38]

---

33 The standard works on anti-clerical killings during the civil war are Mgr Antonio Montero, *Historia de la persecución religiosa en España 1936–1939* (Madrid: BAC, 1961) and V. Cárcel Ortí, *La persecución religiosa en España durante la Segunda República (1931–1939)* (Madrid: Ediciones Rialp, 1990); see also J. Sánchez, *The Spanish Civil War as a Religious Tragedy* (Notre Dame, Ind.: University of Notre Dame Press, 1987).

34 Some useful exceptions in the work of B. Lincoln, 'Revolutionary Exhumations in Spain, July 1936', *Comparative Studies in Society and History*, 27 (2) (1985) and R. Maddox, 'Revolutionary Anti-Clericalism and Hegemonic Processes in an Andalusian Town. August 1936', *American Ethnologist*, 22 (1) (1995), pp. 125–43.

35 It would be useful if empirical work on a region like Aragon – such as the study currently under way on Barbastro (Huesca province) – could address the question of the qualitative differences in wartime anti-clericalism. (Aragon saw no church burning in 1931, and 'traditional' forms of anti-clerical demonstration had not included this previously.) Yet churches in Aragon (and Catalonia) were major foci of wartime anti-clerical violence in 1936.

36 J. Casanova, *Caspe 1936–1938. Conflictos políticos y transformaciones sociales durante la guerra civil* (Zaragoza: Institución Fernando el Católico, 1984), p. 45.

37 As the most important local studies make clear: see, for example, J. M. Solé i Sabaté and J. Villaroya i Font, *La repressió a la reraguarda de Catalunya (1936–1939)* (2 vols., Barcelona: Abadía de Montserrat, 1989–90); F. Moreno Gómez, *La guerra civil en Córdoba 1936–1939* (Madrid: Editorial Alpuerto, 1985). For an overview, see Santos Juliá *et al.* (eds.), *Víctimas de la guerra civil* (Madrid: Ediciones Temas de Hoy, 1999), pp. 117–57 (which also makes clear that the myth of the mass killing/rape of nuns was precisely that, pp. 140, 152–3).

38 'People were killed for pointless things – for example, because someone sang in church or was a bellringer.' But, as local historian J. D. Simeon Riera comments on this oral testimony, 'The motives might seem pointless to our way of thinking now, but for those who did the killing, the

Popular violence – urban and rural – occurred in the aftermath of a military rebellion which had disarticulated all of the Republic's pre-existing political and state structures. Therefore, it is not particularly useful to attach to it – as many historians and other commentators persist in doing – the prefixes of political movements or organisations: thus, for example, its frequent labelling as 'anarchist' terror – as if it were somehow the 'product' of CNT leadership directives.[39] In some places, local libertarian cadres identified with and channelled popular expressions of anger.[40] But the picture which emerges from local studies is clear: what happened in villages and neighbourhoods was very often not under the control even of the local committee, let alone of any political authority beyond that.[41] The uncertain correspondence between the left's political organisations and coercive action in the aftermath of the coup is epitomised by the vexed term 'the uncontrollables' (*incontrolables*). As the war went on, so its meanings would shift and expand.[42] But, originally, it was coined to describe the expropriationary terror and assassination implemented by anonymous groups or militia forces which often claimed, or had imputed to them, libertarian credentials.

The CNT faced an especial difficulty in refuting such accusations because libertarian organisational forms had always been quite loose. The FAI, in particular, had always consisted of tiny activist groups operating independently of all organisational controls – a situation that had already created friction inside the CNT before the war. After 18 July 1936 the boundaries of almost all the Republic's political organisations became more porous, and the CNT's more than most. Nor was there anything to prevent individuals or groups engaged in robbery or extortion from simply using libertarian symbols as a cover for their activities.

Church singer and the bellringer were part of a world that had to be annihilated', *Entre la rebelió y la tradició*, p. 273, n. 73. Such lay religious functions would no doubt also have invested those community members with a social power resented by others.

[39] There is a particularly exaggerated example of this in T. Mitchell, *Betrayal of the Innocents* (Philadelphia: University of Pennsylvania Press, 1998), pp. 86–8. This is part of a larger problem with certain accounts of 1930s Spain which see those who opted for the direct political action (often associated with the CNT) as 'ideological automata' – or, even more crudely, the 'dupes' – of radical political leaders in the CNT. An example of this is in Payne, *Spain's First Democracy*.

[40] Simeón Riera, *Entre la rebelió y la tradició*, pp. 203, 205, n. 37.

[41] J. M. Sabín, *Prisión y muerte en la España de la postguerra* (Barcelona: Anaya-Mario Muchnik, 1996), p. 16; Casanova, *Caspe 1936–1938*, p. 46. By the same token local committees were also usually laws unto themselves: there is a Valencian example in Simeon Riera, *Entre la rebelió y la tradició*, p. 194.

[42] Thus it was used to denounce more specifically inter- and intra-organisational political strife in the Republican zone, although again facilitated by weaknesses and gaps in state power – see chapter 5 below. The 'uncontrollables' was a term also used – loosely – to designate the activities of fifth columnists by the later stages of the war.

Conversely, a simplistic construction of 'the prisoner' as always and everywhere a fully fledged comrade-in-arms was still retained by some anarchist sectors – particularly in the FAI. In the aftermath of the 18 July coup, in areas where they were powerful enough so to do, libertarians released entire prison populations onto the streets in a *de facto* extension of the Popular Front's February 1936 amnesty for political prisoners.[43] Many of these prisoners also joined the libertarian militia. For example, the del Rosal column in Cuenca and the Valencia-based Iron Column (Columna de Hierro) both recruited (the latter heavily) from the ex-inmates of the San Miguel de los Reyes prison. The Iron Column would become notorious throughout the Valencia and Teruel areas during the latter half of 1936 for *ad hoc* expropriation, targeting both smallholders and the urban commercial middling sectors and, increasingly, for running battles with reconstructing local police forces.[44] Iron Column activities caused serious political friction *within* the libertarian organisation in Valencia and probably reinforced support for militarisation therein.[45] Even more threatening for the Republic as a whole was the growing alienation of the rural and urban middling classes of the Valencia region, who inevitably interpreted the Iron Column's activities as pure brigandage, thus deepening the social fissures exposed by rebellion. The pressure on the CNT's national leadership to curb its militants would increase as the escalating needs of wartime mobilisation put a premium on social unity. This would be one of the factors influencing the leadership's institution of mechanisms of centralised control in the CNT in the course of 1937.[46]

Nevertheless, even where the FAI is concerned, one must be careful not to identify it too readily with all the myriad forms of anonymous violence occurring in Republican territory after the collapse of the state. Lumpen activity occurred in many other permutations, while, conversely, the FAI was more than simply a sponge for political or other forms of desperado.[47] But whether or not those who inflicted death, terror and other forms of coercion had, or claimed, organisational affiliations to the CNT–FAI or other left political entities, the notion that they were somehow being 'directed' to carry out atrocities by specific national

---

[43] Ealham, 'Policing the Recession', p. 412.

[44] Bolloten, *SCW*, pp. 333–42. On del Rosal, see Zugazagoitia, *Guerra y vicisitudes*, p. 180; I. Prieto, *De mi vida*, vol. I (Mexico: Ediciones El Sitio, 1965), pp. 324–5.

[45] Casanova, *Anarquismo y revolución*, p. 113. The CNT's Juan Peiró publicly denounced the activities of uncontrollable elements: F. Jellinek, *The Civil War in Spain* (London: Victor Gollancz, 1938), p. 441.

[46] See chapter 5 below.   [47] Jellinek, *The Civil War in Spain*, pp. 331–2, 340–1.

or regional political leaderships bears scant relationship to how things occurred on the ground. Indeed, the entire mode of explanation which seeks to show how 'orders were given' seems to borrow rather too heavily from the conspiratorial mind-set (and publications) of the contemporary right, which went on to produce the (*post hoc* and justificatory) Francoist Causa General.[48] The forms of social and political violence which infested the Republican zone in the aftermath of the military coup were far too complex and chaotic to have been generated by conspiracy.

The history of post-coup popular violence in rural areas – anti-clerical, revolutionary and otherwise – may at first sight appear easier than its urban counterpart to elucidate, simply because the relation of power between the protagonists, as well as the socio-economic and political tensions in village communities, was relatively less complex and existed on a smaller scale. But beyond a certain point, this 'transparency' is deceptive. As Julián Casanova indicates in the case of Aragon, the historical evidence with which we operate is so fragmentary and ambiguous that it is difficult to ascertain how specifically local and personal feuding connected up with structural political conflict.[49] Nevertheless, in urban Spain the greater anonymity and fragmentation of life as well as the sheer concentration of population certainly make it more difficult to establish where anti-clerical and anti-capitalist motives ended and the settling of other – less overtly political – scores began.

In Madrid, as elsewhere, one of the most terror-inducing forms of popular violence was the *paseo*,[50] or execution at the margins of the judicial process, carried out by militia patrols acting on their own authority. A brutal form of settling political and class accounts, the *paseo* was at root a product of the deep social cleavages exposed by the military rebellion. But the anonymous, nocturnal form of the *paseo*, the ultimate unaccountability of the process, also made it a perfect cover for settling all manner of personal scores and for motives of sheer material acquisitiveness. Moreover, whether the motive was revolutionary justice, crypto-rebel provocation, material advantage or some mixture of these, the *paseos*

---

[48] A nationwide investigation into 'red wartime crimes', this effectively constituted the victorious Francoist state's lawsuit against the defeated.

[49] Casanova, *Anarquismo y revolución*, pp. 253, 254, 258. The same can be said of PSOE wartime factionalism. Correspondence from local organisations to the national executive (in the Archivo Histórico de Moscú, FPI) at times give a sense of how local disputes were being reclothed in the lexicon of factionalism.

[50] Literally 'a stroll', but one which always ended in death. While the *paseos* were not exclusively an urban phenomenon, they were a form whose 'potential' was obviously greater in cities and towns.

soon intensified the already high levels of social insecurity and distress from which no sector of the Republican population was immune.[51]

In these first weeks of the conflict when the initial shape of the rebel and Republican zones was being defined by force of arms, virtually the only articulation between the areas that would, from September, gradually be built up into the territory of the Republican state came from an *ad hoc* communications network provided largely by the transport unions of the UGT.[52] Information thus relayed to the UGT executive's headquarters in Madrid's Calle Fuencarral was passed on to the Giral cabinet, which was also being propped up by Indalecio Prieto and the Socialist Party executive committee in permanent/emergency advisorial session. Both Prieto and his fellow executive member Juan Negrín (later Republican finance minister and premier) also ran significant personal risks nightly by participating in informal patrols to curb the wave of *paseos* in the capital.[53] They were morally repelled by the *arbitrariness* of the *paseo*.[54] Indeed, a determination to end such abuses was what drove many socialists in their efforts to restore Republican state power.

However, neither the UGT nor the PSOE – as the other component(s) of the pre-war Popular Front axis – had themselves managed to avoid the negative effects of the centrifugal blast detonated by the military rebellion. This removed the control that the national leaderships of both union and party exercised over their respective organisations (already fragmented by the effects of the internal dispute), rendering them for a time as 'federal' as the anarcho-syndicalist CNT had in reality always been. Nor would this fragmentation prove easily or rapidly reparable. In various areas of Republican territory, local socialist sections unilaterally opted to merge either themselves or their local party and union newspapers with their PCE counterparts (where these existed).[55] In Malaga the socialists would consider merging with the CNT, complaining bitterly of

---

[51] On the repercussions for worker constituencies, see Ortiz Heras, *Violencia política en la II República*, p. 100. A related factor increasing working-class insecurity was the increased occurrence of violent internecine labour conflict, discussed below.

[52] Amaro del Rosal, *Historia de la UGT de España 1901–1939* (2 vols., Barcelona: Grijalbo, 1977), vol. 2, pp. 493–6; F. Largo Caballero, 'La UGT y la guerra', speech October 1937 (Valencia, 1937), p. 14; F. Largo Caballero, *Mis recuerdos*, 2nd edn (Mexico DF: Ediciones Unidas, 1976), p. 166; R. Llopis, 'Las etapas de la victoria', *Spartacus*, October 1937, p. 4.

[53] Marcelino Pascua in S. Alvarez, *Juan Negrín. Personalidad histórica*, vol. 2 (Madrid: Ediciones de la Torre, 1994), p. 280; (and for Valencia) M. Ansó, *Yo fui ministro de Negrín* (Barcelona: Planeta, 1976), pp. 165–6.

[54] The fate of a potential victim of repression could be very fluid. In a street situation, it depended often on whether someone else defended or attacked when the person was first accused. See M. Ortiz Heras, *Violencia política en la II República*, p. 105; Zugazagoitia, *Guerra y vicisitudes*, pp. 78–82.

[55] Graham, *Socialism and War*, pp. 75, 269 (n. 25).

being 'abandoned' by their own national leadership – a reaction which, again, derived from the fracturing of communication and organisational structures as well as from the acute shortage of arms (about which the socialist leadership in Madrid could do little).[56] At other times such initiatives of syndical unity grew out of the solidarity forged in the heat of militia defence, which was then transmuted into local 'unity' committees.

Conversely, the fragmentation of state and union power also allowed already acute tensions/conflicts between some sectors of the CNT and UGT rank and files to break into outright violence. In Barcelona, Aragon and Cartagena, property was ransacked and deaths and disappearances of *ugetistas* reported.[57] This intra-union antagonism was probably worst in Barcelona, where the clashes – especially between the dockworkers' unions – produced fatalities.[58]

What we can deduce from this contradictory simultaneity of inter-union conflict and collaboration is that the military rebellion – for all the singularity of the threat it posed to the Republic – did not erase the pre-war dynamic of intra-left relations with all their tensions, hostilities and contradictions. Indeed, what many accounts of the period tend to ignore is that while the coup fractured organisational structures, it left intact memories of conflict and deeper-rooted patterns of collective political behaviour and social identity. The underlying picture in Republican territory was thus complex and contradictory. The wartime political unity around which the left's entire discourse was constructed would, from the start, be up against serious obstacles. The fragmentation of the PSOE and UGT, moreover, combined with the virtual eclipse of republicanism, meant the effective dislocation of the Popular Front alliance.

In conditions of such unprecedented government crisis, the 'islands' of local or regional resistance were strengthened in their particularism. Local resistance to the military rising in the north, north-east, centre, Valencia region (comprising Valencia, Castellón and Alicante) and south was largely orchestrated by those parties and union organisations of the left[59] *in situ*, but, temporarily at least, was unconnected to any

[56] Letter to the PSOE national executive, 15 October 1936, in AH–23–16 (FPI); UGT executive minutes, 9 December 1936 (the UGT executive had learned of the proposed merger only incidentally via the Malaga press), Graham, *Socialism and War*, p. 185; Vidarte, *Todos fuimos culpables*, vol. 2, pp. 649–50.

[57] Graham, *Socialism and War*, pp. 64, 82, 86–7.

[58] For the pre-history of CNT–UGT conflict in Barcelona see chapter 1 above. For an analysis of the post-18 July situation in Barcelona/Catalonia, see chapters 4 and 5 below.

[59] The (Republican) Basque Country – i.e. predominantly industrial Vizcaya – is the exception here: the conservative Basque Nationalist party (PNV) retained political control. See chapters 4 and 5 below.

central (or even regional) leadership: anarchists and anarcho-syndicalists in Aragon; anarcho-syndicalists, anarchists and Catalanist communists (POUM) in Catalonia; the CNT and the UGT in the Valencia region; the PSOE and the UGT (backed up by the CNT and the PCE) in Madrid; anarchists, communist and UGT cadres in Malaga, UGT and CNT cadres in Jaen and Badajoz. These forces organised both the initial popular resistance and the committee structures which supported and supplied it.

The immediate key to Republican survival, however, lay in Barcelona and Madrid. In the former, the rising failed rapidly in the face of worker – and predominantly CNT – mobilisation, seconded by loyal Civil and Assault Guards. The municipal police were also loyal, being headed by Colonel Frederic Escofet, who, along with Major Pérez Farras,[60] had led the Catalan Guard in defence of the Generalitat in October 1934. The Catalan republican left reaped the dividend for having vetted the police service after its electoral victory in February 1936 to ensure that only those loyal to the Generalitat remained in positions of power. While Catalan premier Luis Companys had held out against calls to arm the workers on the evening of 18 July[61] – for fear of libertarian strength – the CNT had managed to storm several depots and some sympathetic officers had, as elsewhere, allowed them access to the arsenals. Thus resourced, they went out to meet the disparate rebel columns and picked them off, one by one, before they could converge to consolidate their strength in the city centre. General Goded, arriving from Majorca to take control of the rising, was instead taken prisoner. By the evening of 19 July only two barracks held out: San Andrés on the outskirts of the city and the Atarazanas near the port. Both would be stormed by CNT militia and Catalan security forces (Assault and Civil Guards), which thus ensured the complete suffocation of the rising in Spain's most radical and cosmopolitan city.[62] Goded's briefly worded recognition of defeat, in which he appealed to his followers to lay down their arms, was broadcast across Republican territory and gave the morale of Loyalist defenders a tremendous boost. Barcelona was a vital victory for the government,

[60] Pérez Farras would act as the anarchist leader Buenaventura Durruti's military adviser in Aragon: Thomas, *Spanish Civil War*, p. 316.

[61] He had similarly refused to arm the workers' organisations during the events of October 1934 in Barcelona.

[62] Accounts of the military rising and worker resistance in Barcelona can be found in J. Pérez Salas, *Guerra en España (1936–1939)* (Mexico, 1947); F. Escofet, *Al servei de Catalunya i la República* (Paris, 1973); Jellinek, *The Civil War in Spain*; D. Abad de Santillán, *Por qué perdimos la guerra* (Buenos Aires, 1940) and F. Borkenau, *The Spanish Cockpit* (1937; London, 1986). There is a summary in Thomas, *Spanish Civil War*, pp. 232–6.

for it ensured that all of Catalonia would remain loyal. But that victory would be the beginning of a long and intense struggle for political power between radical libertarians and the affluent urban and rural middle classes who constituted 'liberal Catalonia'.

In Madrid, meanwhile, the 18th had seen armed workers surround the Montaña barracks where General Fanjul was awaiting reinforcements from Getafe, Cuatro Vientos and Carabanchel. But the rebellion had in fact already been put down in these places. Fanjul was thus isolated and, without reinforcements, knew that he had insufficient forces to take the city centre. Early on 19 July the order came through from the Giral cabinet to arm the worker militias. Lorries were sent from the government arsenals to the headquarters of both the UGT and the CNT in the capital. But the bolts for the vast majority of the 65,000 rifles thus distributed were still inside the Montaña barracks, where those in charge refused to relinquish them in spite of orders from the war ministry to this effect. The militia siege of 19 July thus gave way to full and ultimately successful assault the following day, during which the bolts were duly acquired – if at a significant cost. For in spite of support from the Republican airforce which bombed the barracks, the death toll among the assaulting forces, mown down by insurgent machine guns mounted on the barracks windows, was extremely high. It was also high among the officers within (although Fanjul was himself taken prisoner). Some committed suicide while many more fell victim to militia anger – heightened as they came under fire on their approach to the barracks to accept the surrender which the white flag posted by the rebels ostensibly signified.

Once Madrid was safe for the Republic, the militia forces set off northwards to the Guadarrama sierra in order to stem the rebels' military advance on the capital. Mola's advance had been impeded by the necessary dissipation of the northern troops – some to be sent to San Sebastián and others to Aragon. The mixed columns advancing on Madrid (soldiers plus Carlist *Requetés* and Falangists) were halted at the Somosierra pass in the Guadarrama and at the Alto del León to the north-west. They were handicapped by a lack of arms and ammunition but also by stiff militia resistance where they had expected a 'walk-over'.

Militia action was an important component in the failure of the rebellion throughout most of populous, urban Spain and its hinterlands. Nevertheless, there were enough examples of urban labour movements being defeated in the July days for us to be wary of claiming that the militia alone were sufficient to guarantee Republican survival in the face of the garrison revolts. Madrid and Barcelona were very specific in terms of the sheer scale of proletarian organisation, and even there the militia's resolve was reinforced by support from professional army officers loyal to the Republic and – most importantly of all – by the regular police forces) (Assault Guards, Civil Guards and (in Barcelona) the Catalan government's own police, the Mozos de Escuadra).[63] In the cases where the rebels took control in July of cities in which the left was strong – most notably in Seville (the most revolutionary city in Andalusia and the key to control of the region), Zaragoza (Aragon) and Oviedo (Asturias) – these tended to be victories achieved because the working-class forces lacked coordination or were surprised or outmanoeuvred in some way. Nevertheless, no city in Spain was held for the Republic without the assistance of at least some part of the police.[64]

In Valencia, the ambivalent attitude of the garrison's military commander prolonged the political limbo until the last day of the month. Distrusting his intentions, the workers' organisations had declared a general strike on 19 July and surrounded the garrisoned troops. In an attempt to break the stalemate and avoid bloodshed, on 21 July Giral's government appointed a delegate body for the whole of the Valencia region which was to take power in Valencia (capital) in the government's name.[65] But the central state's writ had ceased to run in Valencia. In the streets Falangists killed workers and workers burned churches. The CNT,

---

[63] In Barcelona the (loyal) military commander of the Catalan region (General Llano de la Encomienda) did not have the military forces to defeat the rebels. The fact that he could count on the police was absolutely crucial: Barcelona had 3,000 Civil Guards, 3,200 Assault Guards and 300 Mozos de Escuadra, a total of 6,500 men against 2,000 military rebels. For the police role in Barcelona, see Escofet, *Al servei de Catalunya i la República* and V. Guarner, *L'aixecament militar i la guerra civil a Catalunya* (Barcelona, 1980) – Escofet was councillor for public order in the Catalan government and Guarner his *jefe de servicios*.

[64] According to R. Salas Larrazábal, just over half of the Civil Guard remained with the Republic, along with 60 per cent of the Carabineros (customs police) and 70 per cent of the Assault Guards. In Guadalajara there was Civil Guard support for the militia and at Jaen the corps remained loyal to the Republic. In Malaga the militia had the Assault Guards on their side. In Zaragoza, there was no such support: Casanova, *Anarquismo y revolución* and J. Cifuentes Chueca and P. Maluenda Pons, *El asalto a la República. Los orígenes del franquismo en Zaragoza (1936–1939)* (Zaragoza: Institución 'Fernando el Católico', 1995). (For an important critique of the consequences of the Republic's failure after 1931 to demilitarise the police, see M. Ballbé, *Orden público y militarismo en la España constitucional*, pp. 317–96, especially pp. 394–5.) For General Aranda's deceit in Oviedo (he proclaimed his loyalty to the Republic, sent the Asturian miners off to liberate Madrid, and then pronounced for the rising), see summary in Thomas, *Spanish Civil War*, p. 236. Oviedo was besieged by Republican forces (miners' militia predominantly) until October 1936, when rebel troops would succeed in breaking through: see the collective works *La guerra en Asturias* (Madrid, 1979) and *Historia General de Asturias* (Gijón, 1984), vol. 9; Fraser, *Blood of Spain*, pp. 250–4.

[65] Bosch Sánchez, *Ugetistas y libertarios*, p. 18. Decree of 22 July (in the *Gaceta de Madrid*) stipulated that its jurisdiction should cover the provinces of Valencia, Alicante, Castellón, Cuenca, Albacete and Murcia.

which trusted neither the military nor the Madrid government, had already taken the lead in establishing a joint union (CNT–UGT) executive committee which demanded to be armed against potential rebellion. (In its eyes the delegate body was discredited from the outset because it was headed by Martínez Barrio, who had just attempted to treat with the military conspirators.) Then on 25 July a party of Civil Guards, sent along with worker forces to help take Teruel, turned their guns on the militia en route and passed to the rebels.[66] This provoked a rebellion in the barracks, and a number of pro-Republican soldiers fled with arms. This in turn permitted an assault by the workers' militia, assisted by loyal Civil Guards, on 31 July. The assault extinguished the military threat, but it also signalled the end for the tenuous hold of Madrid's delegate body, which was now eclipsed by the unions' executive committee (Comité Ejecutivo Popular).

Elsewhere, however, the military rebellion succeeded rapidly and relatively easily within the first two days (18–19 July) – most notably in the conservative rural Spain of the north down to the centre, where it had a significant measure of civilian support extending to the popular classes. While the Basque industrial heartland of Bilbao (Vizcaya) was held for the Republic (if soon territorially isolated from it), the northern Carlist strongholds of Navarre and Alava as well as virtually the whole of Old Castile/Leon, with all its major centres (Burgos, Valladolid, Zamora, Salamanca all the way down to Cáceres in Extremadura), plus the Canary Islands were in rebel hands.[67] By 22 July Galicia in the north-west corner would also be almost entirely rebel-controlled in spite of desperate resistance in the left's urban bases, most notably in the ports of Vigo and La Coruña. Nevertheless, by the end of July 1936 the rebels had in fact failed to take control of more than a third of Spain's national territory.

In the other two thirds of Spain power was, as we have seen, almost everywhere intensely fragmented. The dominant view of this situation – whether in memoirs or subsequent historical analysis – has tended to be negative. But this assumes an exclusively 'top-down' perspective on the committee phenomenon and one, moreover, strongly influenced by a retrospective appreciation of the escalating military threat faced by the Republic. If we view the committees 'from below', however – from the contemporary perspectives of rank-and-file participants at the moment

[66] Jackson, *The Spanish Republic and Civil War*, p. 265; Bosch Sánchez, *Ugetistas y libertarios*, p. 19.
[67] Of all the Balearic Islands (Majorca, Minorca, Ibiza and Formentera) only Minorca was held for the Republic (until its surrender in 1939) – although Ibiza and Formentera were briefly retaken by Republican forces in August 1936 and held until late in the year.

they were mobilised by the left's local leadership cadres – then we have to understand that 'resistance' to the rebels was spurred predominantly by the possibility of direct action to transform the local environment, the lived unit of experience or *patria chica* – be it village, town or urban neighbourhood – by means of gaining control over decisions affecting daily life.

Everywhere the coup had been quelled – aside from the Republican Basque Country – there was a mushrooming of locally oriented solutions to the organisation of everyday life: from transport, communications and water supply to the cooperativisation of food supplies, workshops, newspapers, restaurants and barber shops. Money was frequently abolished and a system of coupons or *vales* to cover basic needs was instituted by individual village or urban committees – and, particularly in the latter case, these were often issued by many different committees simultaneously.[68] In some areas agriculture, industry and commerce were partly collectivised.

But although committee and militia were widely established forms of organisation and all owed their *initial* existence to the powerful centrifugal charge of the military coup, this does not mean that they were qualitatively similar beyond superficial aspects of nomenclature. What committee and militia 'meant' was strongly inflected by the regionally diverse historical experiences and political cultures to be found among Spain's proletarian constituencies. While the committee phenomenon was everywhere particularist,[69] few sectors of Spain's working classes (leadership cadres included) possessed the kind of ideological collateral which allowed them to think of the committees as the building blocks of a new order.[70] Within these variables, the direction/potential of committees and militia was also significantly shaped by the rapidity with which the imperatives of military defence impinged upon them.

Madrid saw union and neighbourhood committees formed as well as collectives and cooperatives overseen by worker committees both in the municipal sector and to some extent in private industry, commerce and the service sector. But this occurred on a significantly smaller scale than in Barcelona and it was driven more by practical imperatives

---

[68] R. Abella, *La vida cotidiana durante la guerra civil. La España republicana* (Barcelona: Planeta, 1975), pp. 17, 88.

[69] Cf. the refusal of collectives to pay state taxes, 'which only support good-for-nothings (*gandules*) and police harassment', Abella, *La vida cotidiana durante la guerra civil*, p. 89.

[70] Nor indeed was localism necessarily radical simply because it excluded the notion of the state: see M. Vilanova, 'L'Escala y Beuda: dos formas de propiedad y de lucha social durante la guerra civil', *Historia y fuente oral*, 3, 'Esas Guerras' (1990), 39–66.

than by popular ideological and cultural preferences.[71] The two cities were the only Spanish ones to have a population exceeding 1 million in 1930. But although Madrid was an important administrative centre, it was not yet a significant industrial one. Moreover, the difference between Madrid's 40,000 building workers and 25,000 metalworkers and Catalonia's 200,000 textile workers, 70,000 metalworkers and 70,000 building workers was not just one of scale; it also represented a step change in the range and potentialities of labour culture.[72] In Madrid the close proximity of rebel columns (initially to the north and later from the south) concentrated attention on the need to guarantee the coordinated economic/military supply and transport services essential to the emergency defence operation. Thus an estimated 30 per cent of Madrid's productive industry was brought relatively rapidly under military or government control[73] – with union cadres serving as the *instruments of this process*. The UGT, as the dominant labour union in the Madrid area, had always been far less interested than the CNT in syndical economic control. But, in practice, the Madrid CNT also came to accept government control as necessary in the circumstances. CNT members worked alongside those of the UGT in war production – even if some tensions remained between the respective leaderships over questions of organisational prerogatives.[74] In the Madrid area the CNT's militia forces were also less inclined to dispute the need for centralised organisation and discipline.[75]

In Asturias too, in the isolated (non-Basque) north, the pressures of the two-pronged rebel military advance on the city of Oviedo, besieged by Republican forces, concentrated minds on issues of military defence.[76] This would go some way towards facilitating the reconstruction of centralised political power *within the region*. But equally significant here was the special political and syndical culture of the north.[77]

While both the CNT and the UGT in the north had remained open to the use of direct action into the 1930s, they were also far less uniformly hostile to the idea of parliamentary and other political strategies for

---

[71] The expropriation of small businesses or industries was very rare. Although a notice might announce 'here one works collectively', it usually referred to a newly brokered profit-sharing scheme, not workers' control: Thomas, *Spanish Civil War*, p. 293.

[72] Fraser, *Blood of Spain*, p. 295. In Madrid industry meant small workshops, while in Barcelona these existed alongside large-scale factories.

[73] S. Payne, *The Spanish Revolution* (London: Weidenfeld & Nicolson, 1970), pp. 236–7.

[74] The Madrid FAI was less reconciled to government control, however.

[75] See chapter 3 below.

[76] Fraser, *Blood of Spain*, pp. 240–1. There is a nicely observed sense of the isolation of Asturias in Thomas, *Spanish Civil War*, p. 310; on the north see also Jellinek, *The Civil War in Spain*, pp. 407–16.

[77] See, the introduction and chapter 1 above.

achieving social reform. This underlying sympathy between the two had been the key to their successful pre-war collaboration in the Asturian Workers' Alliance. Although this had failed everywhere else in Spain as the intra-left unity initiative it was intended to be, in the north it had provided the organisational matrix for the famous armed rising of October 1934.[78] (Less spectacularly, but even more crucially, the experience of organising emergency supply and defence functions during the rising would provide a blueprint for collaboration and survival in July 1936.) The impassioned amnesty campaign to free the thousands imprisoned after the failure of October 1934 was a key process in forging closer CNT–UGT leadership collaboration in the north. It reinforced a common understanding among socialists and anarchists there of the importance of a left politics of pragmatism geared to intermediate goals. In the process, a certain ideological heterogeneity was also given its head, which then came to be reflected in the solutions given to homefront organisation during the war.[79]

There was, thus, a reasonably cooperative relationship between the CNT's war committee, based in its stronghold, the port city of Gijón, and the socialist-led Popular Front committee in Sama de Langreo, in the heart of the mining belt. CNT leaders were as concerned as their socialist counterparts to counteract the hyper-fragmentation of power symbolised by the seemingly endless replication of local neighbourhood committees.[80] The same CNT leaders were also instrumental in ensuring that Bank of Spain funds in Gijón were handed over to the Popular Front committee, thus effectively securing them for government use. Nor did the CNT's war committee oversee any systematic purge of the police force in Gijón, still less establish parallel security forces on a par with the patrol committees being formed at the same time in urban Catalonia.

Although there was conflict in Gijón over the anarchists' desire to expropriate small traders and shopkeepers, in other respects the CNT and UGT concurred.[81] The CNT accepted the Sama de Langreo Popular Front's veto on any interference with the property or individual commercial rights of rural smallholders whose farms constituted the predominant form of agriculture in the region. Thus agrarian collectivisation

---

[78] See chapter 1 above.   [79] Radcliff, *From Mobilisation to Civil War*, pp. 305–7.
[80] Fraser, *Blood of Spain*, pp. 240–1.
[81] For the long history of anarchist mobilisation around issues of popular consumption in Gijón, see Radcliff, *From Mobilisation to Civil War, passim*. But even on this issue the northern CNT leadership was remarkably conciliatory: Fraser, *Blood of Spain*, p. 244; Jellinek, *The Civil War in Spain*, pp. 407–16.

was never seriously on the agenda in Asturias[82] – even though such rural constituencies had significantly less economic and political power than did their Catalan or Levantine counterparts. (Not least because Asturias had no urban middling classes of any significance outside rebel-held Oviedo.) The regional CNT and FAI also accepted the UGT's line on pre-existing industrial property rights in Asturias. Workers' control committees existed – UGT-led in the coal mines and CNT-directed in the steel works. But their function was largely one of monitoring production – itself left largely in the hands of such politically reliable foremen and engineers as had not fled or who could be procured from elsewhere. Given the UGT's dominance in the mines, the production committees were overseen almost from the beginning by a central government representative.[83]

Economic innovation and cooperativist/committee activity in Asturias was heavily concentrated on organising the practical needs of urban life and, in particular, the supply of food and essential services (including education). As well as being eminently pragmatic, this also responded to a deeply ingrained community-based idea of politics that was further reinforced by the isolation of the Republican north in 1936–7.[84] Although private distribution systems continued, the Asturian Popular Front was collectively responsible for underwriting the consumption of poorer sectors of the population.[85] It was thus an attempt to deliver – within the ever-increasing constraints of the war[86] – what had been the Asturian Front's political agenda between the February 1936 elections and the military rising: namely the 'reclaiming of the Republic' for worker constituencies and for social reform, by means of extra-parliamentary (but legal) mass political mobilisation.

From the above analysis is thus becomes clear why CNT leaders in the north were far less resistant than their counterparts elsewhere to the dissolution of their own war committee. While defence imperatives obviously figured in the calculation, they had no serious ideological qualms. The northern CNT joined the new provincial Popular Front committee,

---

[82] A few large landowners who were pro-rebel were expropriated in November 1936, but this was the exception rather than the norm: Fraser, *Blood of Spain*, p. 243 (n. 1).

[83] Thomas, *Spanish Civil War*, p. 310.

[84] See Radcliff, *From Mobilisation to Civil War*, pp. 279, 307.   [85] Ibid., pp. 306–7.

[86] Food supply posed a challenge not least because from early September the Republican north was isolated from both France and the rest of the Republican zone except by sea. There were droll remarks about cats being afraid of Gijón's inhabitants (Thomas, *Spanish Civil War*, p. 311). The food problem, though acute, was eased by the relative lack of population pressure and then by evacuation in 1937.

which, though socialist-led, moved to Gijón in September 1936. Nor, in spite of some organisational conflicts with its other members, did the CNT oppose what was effectively the 'bottom-up' reconstruction of government power. New town councils were set up in September–October 1936 – the earliest this process occurred anywhere in Republican territory.[87]

A not dissimilar picture would also emerge in August and the following months in the Valencia region.[88] There the Popular Executive committee allowed the multiform committees which had mushroomed during the emergency defence to be replaced by a reconstructing Republican government authority. Thus by September 1936 all three provinces in the region (Valencia, Castellon and Alicante) would have re-established local Popular Front authorities through which the Republican government gradually recuperated its power.[89] For although the Valencian CNT was influential, its regional federation was the heartland territory of *treintismo*, a reformist syndicalism far less hostile to the state's political power than its radical libertarian counterparts in adjacent Catalonia.[90] This political outlook also explains the extent of the Valencian CNT's own efforts to articulate the atomised rural collectivisation carried out by local committees which had fragmented the region's economy to such an extent that it was jeopardising basic processes of distribution and supply crucial to Republican defence.[91] The CNT also faced the thorny issue of *ad hoc*/indiscriminate 'requisition', a collateral effect of the emergency defence which, as elsewhere, was threatening to alienate middling social constituencies.[92]

For in Valencia the CNT had to recognise the sociologically divided nature of the region. While it was strong in urban areas – and especially in the port of Valencia – its rural base was somewhat weaker.[93]

---

[87] As part of this process, in September the Madrid government appointed the Asturian Popular Front leader, veteran socialist Belarmino Tomás, as governor of Asturias and León; in November the Popular Front committee was renamed the Council of Asturias and in December the Consejo Interprovincial de Asturias y León.

[88] I use 'Valencia region' here to denominate the provinces of Valencia, Castellón and Alicante (known collectively as the País Valenciano or Levante).

[89] Bosch Sánchez, *Ugestistas y libertarios*, p. 41.

[90] Ibid., p. 22 citing the Valencian CNT on 'the committee plague'. For a discussion of *treintismo* see chapter 1 above.

[91] Bosch-Sánchez, *Ugestistas y libertarios*, pp. 19, 22–3, 38–9.

[92] Note the acute comment by syndicalist leader J. López from *Fragua Social* (Valencia: CNT press) on 'una masa permanentemente sublevada que pedía víveres' (a perpetual mass revolt demanding foodstuffs) in Bosch Sánchez, *Ugestistas y libertarios*, p. 19 (inc. n. 6); see also p. 22. There were also serious clashes over requisition between peasants and militia in Aragon: see chapter 4 below.

[93] Bosch Sánchez, *Ugetistas y libertarios*, pp. 45–6.

Moreover, in the Valencian countryside important rural constituencies of smallholding and tenant farmers were bastions of social and often political conservatism.[94] In the latter case this was inflected by strong regionalist sentiments. But though these distanced Valencia's middling classes from the ultra-centralist ideals underpinning the military rising,[95] these social constituencies were, nevertheless, hostile to the collectivism associated with the proletarian defenders of the July days.[96] In fact, agricultural collectivisation in Valencia, though not negligible, would still remain marginal to the economy of the region *as a whole*.[97] But fears of what might happen remained prevalent among tenants and smallholders, fuelled by the knowledge of incidents where CNT cadres on the ground had exercised coercion. Thus mutual distrust and sharp social divisions between individualists and collectivists, as well as the increasing influence of Republican state agencies, would set the stage for future confrontations in the Valencian countryside – in spite of the regional CNT's overall pragmatic commitment to the voluntary principle.

In the rural zones of neighbouring Catalonia the CNT–FAI leadership similarly acknowledged the rights and property of the populous class of rural smallholder and tenant farmers. What made Catalonia different, however, was its urban dimension – in particular Barcelona (Spain's only metropolis) and its surrounding industrial belt. There a unique configuration of industrial production and urban life had, over decades, produced a rich and complex set of popular and proletarian cultures unparalleled anywhere else in Spain. Among some sectors of Barcelona

---

94 Ibid., pp. 23, 47–8; Thomas, *Spanish Civil War*, p. 305; Jackson, *The Spanish Republic and the Civil War*, pp. 246, 264.

95 For the fate of Luis Lucia, leader of the Valencian Derecha Regional (Regional Right) (which was a constituent part of the mass Catholic Party (CEDA) prior to the war), see P. Preston, *Comrades* (London: HarperCollins, 1999), p. 326; Thomas, *Spanish Civil War*, p. 242 (and n. 1).

96 'Speaking to them about collectivisation was like speaking to them in Greek', as one local CNT leader observed, Bosch Sánchez, *Ugetistas y libertarios*, p. 48.

97 Rural expropriation and agrarian collectivisation occurred most notably in Aragon and in the Republican centre-south (New Castile downwards). (For Aragon, see discussion and note below.) There was also a considerable amount in the provinces of Toledo and Guadalajara: see Bosch Sánchez, *Ugetistas y libertarios*, p. 372 for useful comparative statistics and also J. Casanova (ed.) *El sueño igualitario. Campesinado y colectivizaciones en la España republicana 1936–1939* (Zaragoza: Institución Fernando el Católico, 1988), *passim*. On Jaén see L. Garrido González, *Colectividades agrarias en Andalucía: Jaén (1931–1939)* (Madrid: Siglo XXI, 1979). There is substantial individual memoir material on collectivisation both by Spaniards and non-Spaniards. This is of variable quality, but with the proviso that such material always offers a 'worm's-eye view' it also provides invaluable insights into the passionate commitment and hope – also a condition of history – which fuelled collectivisation as a cultural as well as a social and economic endeavour. For a brief, useful summary of the historiographical debate see J. Casanova, 'Anarchism, Revolution and Civil War in Spain: The Challenge of Social History', *International Review of Social History*, 37 (1992), 398–404.

labour it had also produced a much more explicit and focused hostility to the political, social and economic status quo. These perceptions were also mediated by libertarian ideas, thus consolidating a collective awareness of integral *dispossession* rather than just of poverty or political inequality. The failed military coup, in provoking the collapse of state institutions, thus bequeathed a real legacy of revolutionary social conflict. The emergency defence of 18–19 July offered workers the chance to go further. They created a network of popular committees, collectivised industry in significant quantities[98] and implemented a range of cooperative experiments in the organisation of social life. In neighbouring Valencia industrial workers resisted the coup with a general strike but then used their leverage far more conventionally to try to gain improved pay and conditions from their employers.[99] Set against this, the specificity of urban Catalonia becomes clear. Moreover, the experiment stretched beyond into the adjacent rural zone of eastern Aragon. Catalan anarchists carried collectivisation to its villages.[100] Thus, under the jurisdiction of libertarian Barcelona, Aragon became the agrarian hinterland of Catalonia's urban revolution.[101]

In the rural south of Spain too, land was frequently collectivised by villagers in the days after the coup attempt.[102] The UGT's agrarian federation, the FNTT, was involved along with the CNT. In contrast to the process in Aragon, collectivisation in the south had deep roots in the pre-war period, driven by ideological opposition to the social, economic and political effects of the *latifundia*. The fact that the land expropriated belonged almost entirely to (often absentee) pro-rebel elites made collectivisation a less immediately fraught political issue for the Republican authorities than was the case elsewhere, as did the involvement of the UGT, which was much more government-friendly than the CNT's

---

[98] Most industrial and commercial collectivisation occurred in urban Catalonia, with a concentration in the Barcelona area; see chapter 4 below.

[99] Bosch Sánchez, *Ugetistas y libertarios*, p. 29.

[100] Casanova, *Anarquismo y revolución*, pp. 36, 218; W. L. Bernecker, *Colectividades y revolución social. El anarquismo en la guerra civil española 1936–1939* (Barcelona: Crítica, 1982), pp. 251–2 (German original, *Anarchismus und Bürgerkrieg. Zur Geschichte der Sozialen Revolution in Spanien 1936–1939* (Hamburg, 1978).

[101] For more on Aragon, see chapters 4 and 5 below. For more on collectivisation therein, see Casanova, *Anarquismo y revolución* and 'Anarchism and revolution in the Spanish civil war: the case of Aragon', *European History Quarterly*, 17 (1987); J. Casanova, *El sueño igualitario*; G. Kelsey, *Anarchosyndicalism, Libertarian Communism and the State: The CNT in Zaragoza and Aragon* (Amsterdam, 1991); P. Broué and E. Témime, *The Revolution and the Civil War in Spain* (London: Faber & Faber, 1972); important oral testimonies in Fraser's *Blood of Spain*.

[102] Garrido González, *Colectividades agrarias en Andalucía: Jaén (1931–1939)*, pp. 27–37; Bosch Sánchez, *Ugetistas y libertarios*, p. 372.

southern federations.[103] Inevitably, however, given the chaotic aftermath of the coup, the overall effect was one of serious fragmentation. Even in the province of Jaen, where the FNTT's influence was predominant, collectivisation was occurring beyond the control of union leaderships, and village committees were often hostile (as they also were in other regions) to any interference from outside.[104] On the other hand, there were villages where the coup seemed to induce paralysis and once committees had established themselves, they did very little.[105] Given that the immediately pressing need was for the collection of the harvest which was essential to the supply of urban Republican zones,[106] both scenarios presented problems. A significant proportion of the collectives in the south-west would be felled rapidly in August and September by the rebels' military advance. But those that remained, in the Republican south-east and in Jaen, would soon be the object of concerted government efforts to impose state regulation and control.[107]

From this brief survey of developments across Republican territory it is clear that the local forms of social and economic reorganisation born out of the emergency defence were everywhere highly atomised. This reflected the tendency of most people to identify exclusively with their village or neighbourhood of origin (*patria chica*) – a normal consequence in an underdeveloped state which lacks an entirely unified, interdependent economy. Committees and emergency defence did not everywhere produce collectivisation, however. And where it did occur, urban or rural, it too was fragmented, a heterogeneous and uneven mix of forms.[108] It was, moreover, frequently beyond the control of even those regional UGT and CNT leaderships struggling to articulate it. In Aragon, as we have seen, agrarian collectivisation was impelled by urban-based cadres from neighbouring Catalonia. And virtually everywhere it was developed, apart from in the Republican south, the movement lacked a strong pre-war collectivist tradition.[109] Heterogeneous and highly 'invertebrate', most of

---

[103] The FNTT represented the interests of the landless in search of land. However, the UGT's involvement also points to another set of opinions which had historically fed into the debate around southern collectivisation: those of specialists (economists and agronomists) who saw it as a means of rationalising southern agriculture as part of a plan to stimulate and modernise the Spanish economy.

[104] Thomas, *Spanish Civil War*, pp. 305–6; Abella, *La vida cotidiana durante la guerra civil*, p. 89.

[105] Jaén examples in Thomas, *Spanish Civil War*, pp. 306–7.

[106] Garrido González, *Colectividades agrarias en Andalucía: Jaén (1931–1939)*, p. 57.

[107] For a discussion of this, see chapters 4 and 5 below.

[108] Bosch-Sánchez, *Ugetistas y libertarios*, pp. 31–9; Fraser, *Blood of Spain*, p. 232 (n. 3); Thomas, *Spanish Civil War*, pp. 306–7.

[109] For a rare exception in the Valencia region, see Bosch Sánchez, *Ugetistas y libertarios*, p. 36.

these local initiatives were only made possible by the paralysis of the state, which, for a time, also paralysed the social opposition to collectivism.

Even in the one possible exception to this picture of contingency – urban Catalonia – the fact that revolutionary forms of social and economic organisation had the opportunity to develop derived in significant measure from the region's considerable distance from the front line of military defence in 1936. Barcelona was the Republican city farthest from the military front. The fact that its collectivist initiatives were impelled by radical libertarians certainly did not help infuse them with the need for any greater economic or political articulation. But it was also more generally true that outside Madrid and the central zone there was still no sense of the need for centralisation. This was because there was still no real consciousness of 'the war'. Thus, while in some areas of rebel Spain the first waves of conscription were being organised within three weeks of the coup, in this same period in Republican territory we cannot refer in any meaningful sense to a single 'Republican' war effort, still less to a single goal. The energy, enthusiastic improvisation and heterogeneity of the emergency defence were initially its strength, but they would soon come to symbolise its underlying weakness.

What would 'bring the state back in' to the Republican equation was the encroaching experience of the war in the south. The Republicans would soon be confronting much more than a series of ill-coordinated and (until then) only very partially successful garrison revolts. Early on 19 July, as Franco himself arrived in Tetuán, a 200-strong contingent of troops from North Africa (indigenous troops (*regulares*) commanded by career officers (Africanistas)) landed at the mainland port of Cadiz in the far south-west. The workers' movement there had declared a general strike, offering fierce resistance to the African veteran and Carlist sympathiser General José Enrique Varela and his supporters *in situ*.[110] The arrival of the Moroccan troops not only assured Varela's victory at Cadiz, but also underwrote the rebel order in the whole area of Cadiz–Algeciras–La Línea. This African contingent – supplemented by a few other relatively small-scale transfers from Morocco[111] – would also participate in the repression of popular resistance in Seville.

[110] Cadiz was apparently called 'Rusia Chica' ('Little Russia') by the right because of the strength of socialist support there. On the rising in Cadiz, see A. Garrachón Cuesta, *De Africa a Cádiz y de Cádiz a la España Imperial* (Cadiz: n.p., 1938); F. Espinosa Maestre, *La justicia de Queipo. (Violencia selectiva y terror fascista en la II División en 1936) Sevilla, Huelva, Cádiz, Córdoba, Málaga y Badajoz* (Seville: Centro Andaluz del Libro, 2000), pp. 57–72.

[111] Preston, *Franco*, p. 152; M. Alpert, *La guerra civil española en el mar* (Madrid: Siglo XXI, 1987), p. 86.

More extensive troop transportations were supposed to follow since the rebels intended to use the Army of Africa (including Spain's Foreign Legion – the *tercios*) as their shock troops to extinguish popular resistance, thus guaranteeing their control. But the insurgents' plans were thwarted by the rebellion of the navy crews (on the main fleet of warships sailing south towards Algeciras) against their pro-rebel commanders.[112] The Straits were effectively blocked.[113] This meant that the rebels' southern advance was also blocked as they could not now get their crucial professional forces to the mainland. At the same time, the levels of popular resistance the rebels had met meant that their bid for power had been aborted in many areas, and Mola's northern advance, also hindered by a lack of munition, was halted at the Guadarrama sierra outside Madrid. It was clear to the insurgent leaders that as the balance of power stood, a rebel victory seemed a remote possibility.

It was at this point on 19 July that Franco, coordinating the southern campaign from Tetuán, called for assistance from Italy and, in view of Mussolini's initial refusal to supply transport planes, a few days later on 22 July Franco petitioned Hitler directly. The provision of aircraft by Hitler[114] (and simultaneously by Mussolini, who had revised his opinion by 27 July[115]) to fly the Army of Africa to the mainland effectively gave the rebels the forces with which to turn a foundering coup into a war. By the end of July there was an air ferry of troops from Morocco to Seville which in ten days saw 10,000 troops transferred. (By 5 August there would also be troop ships crossing the Straits under Italian air cover. The Republican navy could do little to stop this – causing significant Loyalist demoralisation – since its ships were debarred from refuelling

[112] D. Sueiro, *La flota es roja* (Barcelona: Argos Vergara, 1983). There had also been a similar sailors' rebellion in the south-eastern port of Cartagena. J. Martínez Leal, *República y guerra civil en Cartagena (1931–1939)* (Murcia: Universidad de Murcia, 1993), pp. 169–85.

[113] In fact a trickle of African troops continued to come across the Straits from Tetuán in small transport planes: Preston, *Franco*, p. 154. But this was neither substantial nor rapid enough to provide the insurgents with a mainland army.

[114] Ibid., pp. 156–62. Hitler sent (in what was known as 'Operation Magic Fire') thirty Junker JU-52 transport aircraft. Franco had approached Hitler directly after initial requests direct to the German Foreign Office had been rebuffed; see P. Preston, 'Mussolini's Spanish Adventure: From Limited Risk to War', in P. Preston and A. Mackenzie (eds.), *The Republic Besieged: Civil War in Spain 1936–1939* (Edinburgh: Edinburgh University Press, 1996), p. 21.

[115] For a variety of reasons – mainly to do with his understanding of Britain's pro-rebel position and an awareness that France and (initially) the Soviet Union would not aid the Republic – Mussolini reversed his initial decision. He did this in ignorance of Hitler's decision to assist Franco, even though the Duce's decision was taken at more or less the same time as Hitler's: Preston, 'Mussolini's Spanish Adventure: From Limited Risk to War', in Preston and Mackenzie, *The Republic Besieged*.

or using the port facilities at Gibraltar by the British authorities[116] there (as they were also debarred from Tangier in spite of its free port status[117] and further harassed by the presence of German warships patrolling the Moroccan coasts). The Germans also sent some Heinkel fighters and volunteer pilots and mechanics from the Luftwaffe. Within a week of petitioning, the rebels were thus receiving regular supplies of armaments and ammunition from both Nazi Germany and Fascist Italy. Between the end of July and October 1936 868 flights were to carry nearly 14,000 men plus artillery and 500 tons of equipment to mainland Spain.[118] Courtesy of their fascist suppliers, the insurgents were now escalating their offensive against the Republic. They would strike with all the force of superior firepower and technological advance that their foreign backers could provide. It was to be the agrarian south, inevitably, which first felt the full blast of the escalation.

Much of the south had been held by the Republic in the initial phase of the rebellion (see map 1). Indeed, a significant portion would never be conquered militarily by the insurgents: the south-east coast, from Alicante down through Cartagena to Almeria (rebel conspiracies were defused or resisted in all three[119]) and the interior down to and including much of Jaen province (where no rising occurred)[120] remained Republican until the surrender at the end of March 1939.

The highly conservative city of Granada, 93 kilometres south of Jaén, fell to the military rebels on 20 July, although fierce residual resistance continued for several days in the working-class district of the Albaicín, which was bombed and shelled into submission. A ferocious repression followed. The military authorities gave the Falangist death squads free rein to liquidate the left extra-judicially. The *paseos* on which the

---

[116] The British naval authorities actively invited Franco to make a formal request that Republican ships be excluded both from the port facilities and from Gibraltar's territorial waters. E. Moradiellos, 'The Gentle General: The Official Perception of General Franco during the Spanish Civil War' and P. Preston, 'Mussolini's Spanish Adventure: From Limited Risk to War', both in Preston and Mackenzie, *The Republic Besieged*, p. 4 and p. 38 respectively.

[117] The pro-Franco sympathies of Italy's Minister Plenipotentiary in Tangier, De Rossi, who was also Chairman of the Control Committee administering the port, ensured the exclusion of Republican ships from Tangier: Preston, 'Mussolini's Spanish Adventure: From Limited Risk to War', in Preston and Mackenzie, *The Republic Besieged*, p. 31.

[118] Preston, *Franco*, pp. 161–2.

[119] M. Ors Montenegro, *La represión de guerra y posguerra en Alicante (1936–1945)* (Alicante: Instituto de Cultura Juan Gil-Albert, 1995); V. Ramos, *La guerra civil (1936–1939) en la provincia de Alicante* (3 vols., Alicante: Biblioteca Alicantina, 1974), vol. 1, pp. 85–111. Martínez Leal, *República y guerra civil en Cartagena*, pp. 169–85; R. Quirosa-Cheyrouze y Muñoz, *Política y guerra civil en Almería* (Almería: Cajal, 1986), pp. 113–20; Thomas, *Spanish Civil War*, pp. 242, 251.

[120] F. Cobo Romero, *La guerra civil y la represión franquista en la provincia de Jaén (1936–1950)* (Jaén: Diputación de Jaén, 1993).

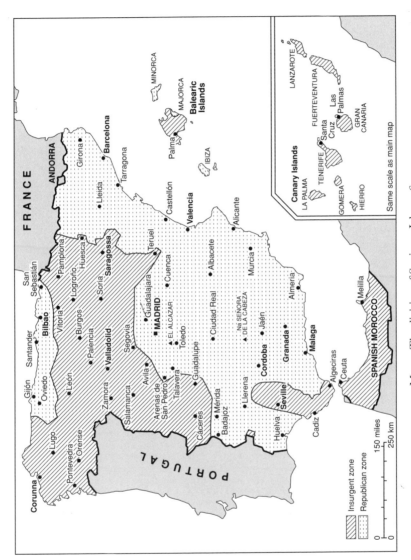

Map 1 The division of Spain 22 July 1936

FRANCE

ANDORRA

PORTUGAL

SPANISH MOROCCO

MINORCA

MAJORCA

Balearic
Islands

IBIZA

Palma

Corunna

Lugo

Pontevedra

Orense

Gijón

Oviedo

León

Santander

San
Sebastián

Bilbao

Vitoria

Pamplona

Logroño

Huesca

Girona

Barcelona

Tarragona

Lleida

Zamora

Salamanca

Valladolid

Palencia

Burgos

Soria

Saragossa

Teruel

Castellón

Valencia

Alicante

Segovia

Avila

Arenas de
San Pedro

Talavera

Guadalupe

Cáceres

Mérida

Badajoz

Llerena

Huelva

Cadiz

Algeciras

Ceuta

Melilla

Seville

Córdoba

Granada

Malaga

Almería

Murcia

Jaén

Nª SEÑORA
DE LA CABEZA

Ciudad Real

Toledo

EL ALCÁZAR

MADRID

Guadalajara

Cuenca

Albacete

Canary Islands

LA PALMA

GOMERA

HIERRO

TENERIFE

Santa
Cruz

GRAN
CANARIA

Las
Palmas

FUERTEVENTURA

LANZAROTE

Same scale as main map

Insurgent zone

Republican zone

0   150 miles

0   250 km

Falangistas took their victims – who ranged from the poet Federico García Lorca through liberal professionals to labour activists, rank-and-file workers and Popular Front supporters of any kind – ended in execution against the cemetery wall.[121] The scenes were such that they drove the caretaker insane. Thousands met their deaths in the *paseos* as the rebels directly removed their 'red' opponents while also ensuring the submission of recalcitrant sectors of the population through this non-exemplary, generalised terror.[122]

Much of the south-west had been initially held for the Republic – the major exceptions being the isolated enclaves of Seville – General Queipo de Llano's fief – and Cordoba.[123] (Though in the south, as elsewhere, the insurgent military had to liquidate many army officers – including high-ranking ones – who refused to rebel.[124]) But once the highly trained and well-armed Army of Africa had reached the mainland *en masse*, there was little pro-Republican sectors of the population could do. Although they were numerous, these civilian resisters had no military training or experience and scant arms. (In fact, to speak of the southern defenders of the Republic as 'militia' is rather misleading.) The African Army troops swept out from Seville (capital) on a campaign of wide-scale repression in the province. (The precedent here had been set in

---

[121] I. Gibson, *The Assassination of Federico García Lorca* (London: W. H. Allen, 1979); R. Gil Bracero, *Granada: jaque a la República* (Granada: Caja General de Ahorros de Granada, 1998).

[122] All the rebels' political opponents were described as 'red'. But the term was also applied indiscriminately to entire social constituencies – predominantly to the urban and rural working classes, but also to Republican-identified intellectual and liberal professional sectors, including regional nationalists in Catalonia and the Basque Country. In the post-war period 'red' came to mean whomever the rebel victors chose so to label as a means of removing either their lives or their civil rights.

[123] For the military rising and ensuing repression in Seville (capital), see A. Bahamonde y Sánchez de Castro, *Un año con Queipo: memorias de un nacionalista* (Barcelona: Ediciones Españolas, n.d. [1938]), pp. 23–7; J. de Ramón Laca, *Bajo la férula de Queipo: como fue gobernada Andalucía* (Seville: Imprenta del Diario Fe, 1939), pp. 18–20; A. Braojos Garrido, L. Alvarez Rey and F. Espinosa Maestre, *Sevilla 36: sublevación fascista y represión* (Seville: Muñoz Moya y Montraveta, 1990), esp. pp. 211–21; J. Ortiz Villalba, *Sevilla 1936: del golpe militar a la guerra civil* (Cordoba: Diputación Provincial de Sevilla, 1998); Espinosa Maestre, *La justicia de Queipo*, pp. 73–117; I. Gibson, *Queipo de Llano: Sevilla, verano de 1936* (Barcelona: Grijalbo, 1986), pp. 80–92. There is also N. Salas, *Sevilla fue la clave: república, alzamiento, guerra civil (1931–1939)* (2 vols., Seville: Castillejo, 1992), vol. 1, pp. 281–363, vol. 2, pp. 409–91 – although its hagiographical aspect in regard to Queipo de Llano leads the author to make some dubious assertions (see Espinosa Maestre, *La justicia de Queipo*, pp. 46–7, 56–7, 95, 319 for a critique of Salas' work). For Cordoba, see below.

[124] J. Vila Izquierdo, *Extremadura: la guerra civil* (Badajoz: Universitas Editorial, 1983), p. 57. 'Conspirators were, in the main, *africanistas* removed from active commands in late February 1936: they had in most cases to get rid of Azañista garrison-commanders before "pronouncing" against the government', R. H. Robinson, *The Origins of Franco's Spain* (Newton Abbott: David and Charles, 1970), p. 376, n. 3; Cordón, *Trayectoria*, p. 224; Thomas, *Spanish Civil War*, pp. 250, 266 (for a list of the six generals and an admiral shot by the rebels).

Asturias in October 1934, when, at Franco's initiative, they had been used violently to repress the workers' rebellion in the northern mining *cuenca*.[125] The Republic's agrarian reform was thus reversed and land and power handed back to the *latifundistas* (owners of the large estates), who often rode along with the army to reclaim their lands *manu militari*.[126] Rural labourers were killed where they stood, the 'joke' being they had got their 'land reform' at last – in the form of their burial plot.[127] In pueblos across the rebel-held south there was systematic brutality, torture, shaving and rape of women and mass public killings (of both militia fighters and civilians – male and female) in the aftermath of conquest.[128] Where there was a particularly strong radical or collectivist tradition or where there had been land occupations or militancy in the spring/summer 1936 or after the rural landworkers' strike of June 1934 or as a consequence (though this more rarely) of the October 1934 revolt, the apoplectic rage of a feudally minded ruling elite saw villages wiped off the map by repression.[129] (And when, at the end of the war, the repression was extended and institutionalised by the triumphant rebel forces throughout

[125] As the war minister's special adviser, Franco had effectively been in charge of the Asturian repression: Preston, *Franco*, p. 103.

[126] Salas, *Sevilla fue la clave*, vol. 2; 'El comienzo: la "liberación" de Lora del Río (1936)', in *Cuadernos de Ruedo Ibérico* (Paris, 1975), pp. 46–8. For the case of Arahal (Seville), see Fraser, *Blood of Spain*, p. 158 (n. 1); Salas, *Sevilla fue la clave*, vol. 2, pp. 623, 650–1; and Carmen Muñoz, 'Masacre fascista en Arahal (Sevilla)', *Interviu*, 91 (9–15 Feb. 1978), pp. 38–41 (of interest for its oral testimonies; the figures cannot be corroborated). *Latifundistas* rode with the army columns across the south: for Cordoba, see L. Collins and D. Lapierre, *Or I'll Dress You in Mourning* (London: Weidenfeld & Nicolson, 1968), pp. 85, 93–7. For the repression in Cordoba, see F. Moreno Gómez, *La guerra civil en Córdoba (1936–1939)* (Madrid: Alpuerto, 1985), *passim* but esp. pp. 284–325; Espinosa Maestre, *La justicia de Queipo*, pp. 119–24.

[127] Zugazagoitia, *Guerra y vicisitudes*, p. 84; F. Moreno Gómez, 'La represión en la España campesina', in J. L. García Delgado (ed.), *El primer franquismo: España durante la segunda guerra mundial* (Madrid: Siglo XX, 1989), p. 192.

[128] J. T. Whitaker, 'Prelude to World War: A Witness from Spain', *Foreign Affairs*, 21(1) (October 1942), 104–7 and (same author) *We Cannot Escape History* (New York: Macmillan, 1943), pp. 111–14; E. Taylor, 'Assignment in Hell', in F. C. Hanighen, *Nothing but Danger* (New York: NTC, 1939), pp. 68–73; Buckley, *Life and Death of the Spanish Republic*, p. 235; M. Koltsov, *Diario de la guerra española* (Madrid: Akal, 1978), pp. 96–7; Moreno Gomez, *La guerra civil en Córdoba*, p. 265 (for women's deaths see pp. 80, 86, 373); A. Braojos Garrido *et al. Sevilla 36*, p. 244. For incitement to rape, cf. Gibson, *Queipo de Llano*, pp. 160–1, 431 and G. Brenan, *Personal Record 1920–1970* (London, 1974), p. 297; Castilla del Pino, *Pretérito imperfecto*, p. 196. For more on rape/other punishment of republican women and its significance, see discussion and notes below. See also below for the repression in Extremadura.

[129] Moreno Gómez, *La guerra civil en Córdoba* (e.g., case of Palma del Río, pp. 377–82 and continuing into autumn in conquered territory – the case of Fuenteovejuna, pp. 438–43) and F. Moreno Gómez, 'La represión en la España campesina', in García Delgado, *El primer franquismo*, p. 191; F. Espinosa Maestre, *La guerra civil en Huelva* (Huelva: Diputación Provincial de Huelva, 1996). (Although isolated from the rest of Republican Spain by the rising at Seville, Huelva, with its 'red' miners, had initially been kept for the Republic only to fall to the rebels after a delayed rising by the Civil Guard. The large number of *huidos* (fugitives often operating as guerrillas)

the south in the form of highly summary legal proceedings, rural workers would be found guilty in mass 'trials' and executed – without any
apparent intended irony – for the crime of military rebellion.) The colonial mentality permeating the rebels' southern campaign is more then
amply demonstrated by Franco's letter to Mola of 11 August. In the
context of explaining that the conquest of Madrid remained the military priority, Franco stressed the need to annihilate all resistance in the
'occupied zones', especially in Andalusia.[130] As Army of Africa troops
under Varela swept south-eastwards to connect up Seville with the other
rebel enclaves of Cordoba and Granada during August and September
1936,[131] this process of removing the 'dangerous element' ('elemento
peligroso') continued.[132]

But the main thrust of the rebels' advance from the south was in
the direction of the greatest prize – the capital, Madrid. They saw it as
the hub of Republican resistance whose conquest would win them the
war. Franco, having landed in Seville on 2 August, directed the Army
of Africa's troops. The bulk of these, under the overall command of
Lieutenant-Colonel Juan de Yagüe, a veteran of the Moroccan wars and
the most influential military supporter of the Falange, had begun the
march up towards the capital. Taking village after village as they went,
the columns left a trail of carnage and terror in their wake.[133] Ultimately
there was nothing the towns' hastily organised defenders – still less an

who became the premier target of rebel repression was a result of the virtual impossibility
of escape, surrounded as Huelva was by hostile territory.) For later repression in Malaga and
(later again) in Jaén, see E. Barranquero Texeira, *Málaga entre la guerra y la posguerra* (Malaga:
Arguval, 1994), pp. 199–228 and Cobo Romero, *La guerra civil y la represión franquista en la provincia
de Jaén*; Richards, *A Time of Silence*, pp. 130–1.

[130] Preston, *Franco*, p. 165. Note also Franco's frequent requests to Italy for chemical weapons in
1936–7, which reflected his earlier experiences in North Africa, A. Viñas, *Franco, Hitler y el estallido
de la guerra civil* (Madrid: Alianza, 2001), pp. 29–112, esp. pp. 109–12.

[131] L. M. de Lojendio, *Operaciones militares de la guerra de España 1936–1939* (Barcelona, 1940), p. 108;
J. M. Martínez Bande, *La campaña de Andalucía* (Madrid, 1969), p. 73ff. There was a failed
Republican attempt to reconquer Cordoba on 20 August (under Miaja): see Thomas, *Spanish
Civil War*, pp. 380–1, 490, 493, 494. Moreno Gómez suggests that Miaja's military strategy was
deeply flawed, *La guerra civil en Córdoba*, pp. 368–9.

[132] Moreno Gómez, *La guerra civil en Córdoba*, pp. 438, 463–4 (where he cites radio broadcasts by
a Franciscan priest on the necessary cleansing of red elements ('it is imperative that we uproot
and destroy the poisonous and degenerate seed of marxism from the soil of the fatherland. Exile
is not enough: we have to obliterate it'). The result of this is described in Collins and Lapierre,
Or I'll Dress You in Mourning, pp. 93–9.

[133] Thomas, *Spanish Civil War*, pp. 373–4, who remarks (quoting the Portuguese press) on the severe
level of repression – a thousand deaths at Almendralejo (including those of 100 women) on
6 August. Both Gerald Brenan and Herbert Southworth comment on the initial openness of
reporting of these southern massacres in the Portuguese press, Brenan, *The Spanish Labyrinth*
(1943; Cambridge: Cambridge University Press, 1990), p. 322 and H. R. Southworth, *El mito de
la cruzada de Franco*, 2nd edn (Barcelona: Plaza & Janés, 1986), p. 218.

atomised rural labour force – could do to protect Republican land and labour reforms, or their cherished collectives, pitted as they were in open country against lorry-loads of seasoned troops, artillery and German and Italian air bombardments. They would fight desperately as long as they had the cover of buildings or trees. But the defenders were not trained in elementary ground movements or even in the care and reloading of their weapons. Moreover, as reports of the atrocities committed by Yagüe's troops mounted, even the rumoured threat of being outflanked was enough to send them fleeing, abandoning their weapons as they ran. A vast army of refugees fled before Yagüe's army northwards.

On 10 August the Army of Africa reached Mérida, an old Roman town near Cáceres (most of which was rebel-held from early on[134]). Mérida was an important communications centre between Seville and rebel-friendly Portugal. Its defenders went out to engage the oncoming rebel troops outside the town, fighting ferociously in the battle for the River Guadiana. This was the first serious opposition the Africanistas had encountered. But the resisters could not hold them and they broke through to the town.[135] Shortly afterwards, initial contact was made with General Mola's forces. The two halves of rebel Spain were thus joined into what would come to be called 'the National zone' ('la España nacional'). In Mérida, meanwhile, the executions began with those of the entire defence committee.[136]

Yagüe then turned west to capture the frontier town of Badajoz, the capital of Extremadura. On 14 August his forces reached the outskirts of the walled city, where the garrison commander was in charge of a small nucleus of soldiers and several thousand inexperienced civilian resisters[137] – many armed only with scythes and hunting shotguns. The inequality of the contest was increased by the fact that the defenders had to put down a Civil-Guard mutiny which undermined their material, energy and confidence just as they had to confront the besieging troops.

---

[134] For the rising and repression see J. Chaves Palacios, *La represión en la provincia de Cáceres durante la guerra civil (1936–1939)* (Cáceres: Universidad de Extremadura, 1995).

[135] On the battle for Mérida, see J. Chaves Palacios, *La guerra civil en Extremadura* (Mérida: Junta de Extremadura, 1997).

[136] This included two women, Rita Aznar and Anita López: Vila Izquierdo, *Extremadura: la guerra civil*, p. 46; López is also mentioned by Hugh Thomas (apparently also citing the Portuguese press), *Spanish Civil War*, p. 373 and by Víctor Chamorro, *Historia de Extremadura* (6 vols., Madrid: Víctor Chamorro, n.d. [1985]), vol. 5. Shirley Mangini's more recent enquiries confirm López's existence (and profession – a pharmacist) but no more. S. Mangini, *Memories of Resistance. Women's Voices from the Spanish Civil War* (New Haven/London: Yale University Press, 1995), p. 75.

[137] Estimates for the number of militiamen range from 8,000 (Thomas, *Spanish Civil War*, p. 373) to 3,000. Later estimates suggest that the original 3,000 from Badajoz grew by around another 2,000 as refugees fled the rebels, Vila Izquierdo, *Extremadura: la guerra civil*, p. 50.

Nevertheless, the resistance was solid. A built-up city was a much harder target than untrained fighters scattered around villages or in open country. It would take two assaults by artillery and bombs before Yagüe's shock-*tercios* could breach the city walls. Once they succeeded, however, a savage repression ensued. Initially, there was chaotic, indiscriminate slaughter and looting in the streets by *tercios* and *regulares* (enraged among other things because this first experience of solid resistance had caused serious casualties amongst their own ranks). Later, the more systematic repression began. Falangist patrols stopped workers in the street to check if they had fought to defend the town. They would rip back their shirts to see if their shoulders bore the give-away bruising of rifle recoil. The defenders were herded into the bullring-turned-concentration camp and machine-gunned in batches. After the first night the blood ran 'palm-deep' according to the witnesses interviewed by American journalist Jay Allen, whose famous report on the Badajoz massacre catapulted the Spanish war into newspaper headlines throughout Europe and America.[138] The shooting at Badajoz would continue for weeks (and the provincial repression for months after).[139] No less an authority than Yagüe himself would soon confirm the witnesses' accounts of repression when, interviewed by another American journalist, John T. Whitaker (who accompanied him for most of the march on Madrid), he made his – now famous – reply: 'Of course we shot them. What do you expect? Was I supposed to take four thousand reds with me as my column advanced racing against time? Was I supposed to turn them loose in my rear and let them make Badajoz red again?'[140] Bodies were left for

---

[138] 'After the first night the blood was supposed to be palm-deep on the far side of the lane. I don't doubt it. Eighteen hundred men – there were women, too – were mowed down there in some twelve hours. There is more blood than you would think in 1,800 bodies.' Jay Allen, report in the *Chicago Tribune*, 30 August 1936 – although the massacre was first reported by two French journalists and by a Portuguese reporter, Mario Neves. The latter's (censored) report appeared on 17 August 1936 in the *Diario de Lisboa*. In 1982 Neves finally returned to Badajoz, where he was interviewed for the Granada Television series *The Spanish Civil War*: Vila Izquierdo, *Extremadura: la guerra civil*, pp. 54–8. Neves' memoir is in *La matanza de Badajoz* (Badajoz: Editorial Regional de Extremadura, 1986) (Portuguese original, *A chacina de Badajoz* (Lisbon, 1985)). The volume also contains the text of his original newspaper reports. According to Jay Allen's original *Chicago Tribune* article, war booty – gold watches and jewelry from the dead citizens of Badajoz – went on sale in Portugal at bargain prices.

[139] Contemporary journalist accounts refer to approximately 2,000 people killed in the initial mass executions in the bullring. Recent area studies of the repression estimate that some 5,000 people were killed in Badajoz province. Chaves Palacio, *La guerra civil en Extremadura*; F. Espinosa Maestre, *La justicia de Queipo*, pp. 161–87; J. Casanova, in Juliá *et al.*, *Víctimas de la guerra*, pp. 77 and 194 for the repression in Badajoz during 1937–8, in the context of the ongoing war effort and shifting position of military fronts.

[140] M. Neves, *La Matanza de Badajoz* (Badajoz, 1986), pp. 13, 43–5, 50–1. See also Jay Allen, 'Blood Flows in Badajoz', in M. Acier (ed.), *From Spanish Trenches: Recent Letters from Spain* (London: The

days in the streets to terrorise the population[141] and then heaped together in the cemetery and burned without burial rites. Simultaneously, the 'liberation' of territory by the rebels would be celebrated by the reopening of churches, by masses and baptisms and other public religious ceremonial.

The fall of Badajoz sealed the Republic off from Portugal while it gave the rebels unrestricted access to the frontier with the power that had been their first international ally.[142] From the beginning, Oliveira Salazar had permitted the rebels to use Portuguese territory to link their northern and southern zones. (The Portuguese police also repeatedly returned refugees to certain death.[143]) Indeed, access to Portuguese help had been an important factor in Franco's decision to forego the more direct route from Seville to Madrid across the Sierra Morena via Cordoba. This had also wrong-footed the Republicans, who concentrated their exiguous military defensive forces in the region (under General Miaja) on the Madrid–Cordoba line. Now, with all the south-west coast from Cadiz to Huelva and the entire land border with Portugal beyond under rebel control, Yagüe's forces continued from Badajoz up the roads north-eastwards towards Madrid (see map 2).

The columns split for a time to cover roughly parallel routes. The first route took one of the three columns through Trujillo to Navalmoral de la Mata (occupied on 23 August). To the east lay the valley of the River Tagus, which offered no serious natural obstacles. The collectives formed after the March 1936 land occupations were easy targets on whose members hard deaths were inflicted. Massacre at the hands of the Army of Africa was, once again, the brutal lesson meted out to those who had dared to challenge the socio-economic status quo. On the route taken southwards through the Guadalupe mountains, however, the remaining two Moroccan columns had a more difficult time. Here they were met by Republican government troops from Madrid under General José Riquelme. In Medellín part of one column came close to destruction

Cressett Press, 1937), pp. 3–8; Whitaker, 'Prelude', pp. 104–6; J. J. Calleja, *Yagüe: un corazón al rojo* (Barcelona, 1963), pp. 99–109.

141 This was a constant feature as the rebel columns moved up through the south towards Madrid, although international press agencies usually censored this kind of detail. Various journalists' testimonies about Santa Olalla and Talavera de la Reina are cited in H. R. Southworth, *Guernica! Guernica! A Study of Journalism, Diplomacy, Propaganda and History* (Berkeley, Calif.: California University Press, 1977), pp. 53, 420–1 (n. 69). See also Espinosa Maestre, *La justicia de Queipo*, pp. 189–204.

142 Portugal's unfettered support was taken by Mussolini to indicate Britain's essentially pro-rebel sympathies, which, in turn, spurred his own intervention: Preston, 'Mussolini's Spanish Adventure: From Limited Risk to War', p. 38.

143 These included the socialist deputy for Badajoz, Nicolás de Pablo.

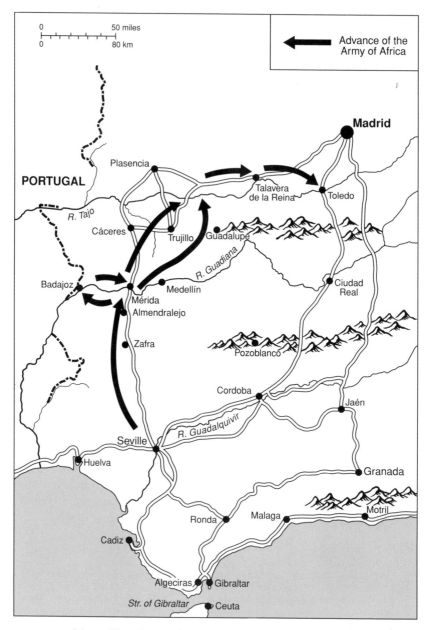

Map 2 The advance of the Army of Africa August–October 1936

at the hands of the Republican air squadron, organised by the French writer André Malraux, in its first serious engagement. While it could not challenge the faster Italian fighter planes that gave the rebels local control of the air,[144] the Republic's overriding military weakness at this stage remained its inexperienced militia.

Untrained in elementary ground movements, the militia were constantly being outmanoeuvred by the *tercios* and *regulares* and forced to retreat. In the harsh conditions of the barren Tagus valley on the approach to Talavera, the vulnerability of their fighters meant that retreat was the only option for the Republican commanders. While the volunteers themselves still seemed to believe that their (undoubted) bravery would find its own recompense, the government simply could not afford to risk all their men in a general engagement. Unpreparedness and lack of training forced constant Republican retreat all the way back to Talavera itself. There, defensive positions were established to the fore of some 10,000 volunteer fighters inside Talavera. But at dawn on 3 September the Moroccan columns surrounded the town and, having taken the aerodrome and railway station on the outskirts, assaulted the centre, overwhelming its defenders in street fighting. In a bare month the rebels had advanced almost 500 kilometres. And now the last important town between the rebels and Madrid had fallen.

The August defeats and ensuing repressions continued into September – terrible and seemingly inexorable. There was little or nothing unarmed or poorly armed and untrained workers and landless peasants could do against the highly disciplined and well-equipped insurgent forces. Their bravery was epic, but on all the evidence it was failing. Even occasions of prolonged resistance were not that plentiful, and when they occurred were usually based on natural obstacles or the advantage of urban terrain.[145] But the rebels had already launched a war which could not be won militarily unless the Republicans could meet and hold them in pitched battle. Moreover, on each occasion that resistance was broken,

---

[144] There were some Republican air raids in the early weeks of the war against rebel-held towns, including Granada, Cordoba, Segovia and Valladolid. These resembled First World War raids in terms of intensity and casualties caused. It was, of course, German and Italian firepower that enabled the rebels to achieve levels of destruction on a par with those seen in the Second World War.

[145] 'Militia units were able to put up sporadic resistance in some places by dint of the energetic effort of their leaders, but, even so, time and again this failed to prevent the flattening of the resistance and ensuing disorderly retreat – notwithstanding which there could be many instances of militia bravery during the fighting itself.' This was the opinion of Vicente Rojo, future chief of staff of the Republican Army, in V. Rojo, *Así fue la defensa de Madrid* (Madrid: Comunidad de Madrid, 1987), p. 60.

the, quite literally, *terrible* price paid had an ever more devastating (and unaffordable) impact on Republican morale.[146]

Terror had always been a key weapon in the Army of Africa's armoury. In the aftermath of the military rising it was first seen in evidence in the bloody repression of the working-class neighbourhoods of Seville (capital). In one of these, Triana, Army of Africa soldiers[147] rounded up all the men they found, knifing many of them to death in the streets.[148] Now in the 'long-haul' war in the south, mass terror was being deployed to facilitate a rapid military advance on Madrid and to 'pacify' the conquered territory, consolidating rebel control so nothing might jeopardise that advance. But the rebel commanders' deployment of mass terror was about more than short-term tactics. While Badajoz was undoubtedly a message aimed specifically at those in Madrid contemplating resistance,[149] in targeting specific social sectors *en masse* – whether or not they were active combatants – the rebels were in fact redefining 'the enemy' as an entire social class – the proletariat produced by modernisation and perceived (by the rebels and their elite civilian backers) as 'out of control'.

What occurred in the killing fields of the south was highly visible because of the presence of numerous foreign war reporters. The scale of the immediate repression also marked out the south. But it is important to remember that a similarly Dantesque repression was simultaneously being enacted *everywhere* in rebel-held territory. Moreover, it was happening in places controlled by the rebels from the outset: where there was no objective military threat, no significant political resistance and no Army of Africa – in short, where one would be hard-pressed to find a 'war-situation' at all.[150] Nor is it feasible to argue that much of the initial

---

[146] For the cumulative psychological effect of this on the militia's capacity to contribute to the defence of Madrid, see Cox, *Defence of Madrid*, p. 70.

[147] These soldiers belonged to a small advance contingent flown across in a Fokker from Morocco.

[148] Some women were also taken prisoner. There are eye-witness accounts in Braojos Garrido *et al.*, *Sevilla 36*, pp. 211–21 (La toma de los barrios populares). A laconic reference to the 'pacification' of Triana is in the account of rebel journalist M. Sánchez del Arco, *El sur de España en la reconquista de Madrid* (Seville: Editorial Sevillana, 1937), pp. 31–2.

[149] Through both the refugees and the French press, news of the massacre soon spread throughout the whole Republican zone: Cordón, *Trayectoria*, p. 256.

[150] It is regularly adduced that the southern repression was uniquely attributable to a strategy of war elaborated by the rebels in view of their own numerical exiguity in relation to the bulk of the civilian population. Zamora is a good example of repression where the rebels were in control from the outset: see P. Fidalgo, *A Young Mother in Franco's Prisons* (London: United Editorial, 1939), *passim* and R. Sender Barayón, *A Death in Zamora* (Albuquerque: University of New Mexico Press, 1989), pp. 106ff. In western (rebel-held) Aragon too there was a vicious repression out of all proportion to the resistance offered: see J. Casanova *et al.*, *El pasado oculto. Fascismo y violencia en Aragón (1936–1938)* (Madrid: Siglo XXI, 1992); Cifuentes Chueca and Maluenda Pons, *El asalto a la República. Los orígenes del franquismo en Zaragoza (1936–1939)*, pp. 44–83 and A. Cenarro,

violence stemmed, as in the Republican zone, from 'uncontrollable' groups. For nowhere in the rebel zone was there a collapse of public order. Falangists and other vigilante volunteers of the right could at any time have been disciplined by the military authorities who underwrote public order from the beginning. Not only did this not happen, but military and civilian-instigated repression existed in a complementary relationship. The military authorities were, thus, sanctioning widespread terror throughout rebel territory.[151] Indeed, the director of the coup, General Mola, had both envisaged and announced the need for just such an extensive application: 'we have to terrorise, we have to show we are in control by rapidly and ruthlessly eliminating all those who do not think as we do'.[152] In both northern and southern Spain the terror had a common political-strategic dimension: violent repression functioned as public spectacle and threat, as a means of liquidating opponents which would also enforce orthodoxy among those left alive, thus increasing the level of social control exercised by the military authorities.[153] If anything distinguished the south from the north, it was a quantitative, not a qualitative factor. In the rural south the social structure of the population meant that there were far more 'enemies' to be dealt with. The presence of a populous, professional killing machine in the Army of Africa facilitated the 'solution', although Falangists and other right-wing civilian volunteers played their part too. In the northern half of Spain the military was short of personnel, which explains why, from the outset, Carlist *requetés* and other right-wing volunteers played a more prominent role in the killing process. It may also be possible to show that the rebel forces doing the killing in northern parts of Spain had a different cultural perception of their victims from those in the south. But they still saw killing them as the solution.[154]

El fin de la esperanza: fascismo y guerra civil en la provincia de Teruel (1936–1939) (Teruel: Diputación Provincial de Teruel, 1996), pp. 67–91.

[151] Cenarro, *El fin de la esperanza*, pp. 73–5; C. García García, 'Aproximación al estudio de la represión franquista en Asturias: "paseos" y ejecuciones en Oviedo (1936–1952)', *El Basilisco*, 2 (6) (1990), 76.

[152] This principle was established in Mola's series of confidential instructions initiated on 25 April 1936: G. Cabanellas, *La guerra de los mil días* (2 vols., Buenos Aires: Grijalbo, 1973), vol. 1, pp. 304–5; F. Bertrán Güell, *Preparación y desarrollo del alzamiento* (Valladolid: Librería Santarén, 1939), pp. 119–24. See also text of Mola's 'Bando de declaración del estado de guerra, 19 July 1936, in E. Mola, *Obras completas* (Valladolid: Librería Santarén, 1940), pp. 1173–76.

[153] Such as the sudden increase in church attendance among the urban liberal middle classes: Castilla del Pino, *Pretérito imperfecto*, p. 212 and cf. C. Barral, *Años de penitencia* (1975; Barcelona: Tusquets, 1990), pp. 75–6.

[154] Whether there was a quantitatively greater rebel repression in the south *overall* (in terms of the percentage of the total population of Extremadura and Andalusia) we cannot yet know

Also significant is the *manner* in which the 'enemy' so often met his or her death at rebel hands: the mass public executions (sometimes with the victims roped together) followed by the exhibition of corpses in the streets for days, the mass burning of bodies,[155] the quasi auto-da-fé of a socialist deputy in the Plaza Mayor of Salamanca or the fact that executions in the centre/north of the rebel zone often took place on established saints' and feast days.[156] Both physical and psychological torture were also habitually inflicted on prisoners, and they were also publicly humiliated – especially the women prisoners.[157] All these forms of violence (in which I include the humiliation) were functioning as rituals through which social and political control could be re-enacted. Thus the

definitively. One would need to be able to compare each and every Spanish province from 18 July 1936 up to and including at least three years of 'post-war' (i.e. post-1939) repression. At the moment (March 2002) any conclusion is provisional, as only half of Spain's provinces have been researched (and some, to date, only studied in part): see Juliá *et al.*, *Víctimas de la guerra*, pp. 407–12 for an explanation of the state of current research and tables of findings to date. The known figures for the south – and especially Badajoz – are very high. But as yet we lack any figures for Galicia or for Castilian provinces such as Guadalajara and Cuenca, where the indications are of heavy repression.

[155] The exhibition and burning of corpses took place most infamously at Badajoz, but both occurred in other places (north and south), and everywhere mass graves were to be found. Sender Barayón, *A Death in Zamora* (bodies at the roadside, p. 137; common graves, pp. 149–50, 155, 162, 163); García García, 'Aproximación al estudio de la represión franquista en Asturias', pp. 69–82 (includes information on different kinds of *paseo*, on common graves, bodies on the streets and *razzias* (searches) of working-class areas).

[156] The Salamanca incident (involving the death of Andrés y Manso in the first days after the rising) is described in a letter from Julio Alvarez del Vayo (16 April 1937) in the Archivo de Barcelona (AB), Azaña's correspondence RE 135 (carpeta 11 (5)) and L. González Egido, *Agonizar en Salamanca. Unamuno, julio–diciembre 1936* (Madrid: Alianza, 1986), p. 82. Also the similar execution of a socialist leader in Calatayud was reported in *Heraldo de Aragón* (Zaragoza) and then *by El Socialista* (Madrid): R. Abella, *La vida cotidiana durante la guerra civil*, p. 38. There are many accounts reporting the auto-da-fé atmosphere which permeated rebel Spain: see A. Ruiz Vilaplana, *Doy fe... un año de actuación en la España nacionalista* (Paris: Editions Imprimerie Coopérative Etoile, 1938); various authors (inc. Flory), *Galice sous la botte de Franco* (Paris, 1938); A. Bahamonde, *Un año con Queipo* (for Andalusia). For the south see also Moreno Gómez, *La guerra civil en Córdoba*, p. 287. Such spectacles continued well into the war, for example the 'terror and fiesta' in the main square (called the Plaza del Torico) of Teruel (Aragon), Cenarro, *El fin de la esperanza*, p. 75 and García García, 'Aproximación al estudio de la represión franquista en Asturias', pp. 74–5. On public executions during religious festivals, see J. de Iturralde, *El catolicismo y la cruzada de Franco* (Bayonne, 1955), pp. 88–9, 93 (the festival of the Virgen del Sagrario in Pamplona); Altaffaylla Kultur Taldea, *Navarra 1936. De la esperanza al terror* (2 vols., Tafalla: author-editor, 1992) and Fraser, *Blood of Spain*, p. 165.

[157] See Fidalgo, *A Young Mother in Franco's Prisons*, *passim* and p. 24 for a variation on the *ley de fugas* – for which see also Muñoz, 'Masacre fascista en Arahal (Sevilla)', p. 38; García García, 'Aproximación al estudio de la represión franquista en Asturias', pp. 74–5, 82. For ritual public humiliation of Republican prisoners, see also Espinosa Maestre, *La justicia de Queipo*, pp. 209, 217–22; S. Ellwood, 'Spanish Newsreels 1943–1975: The Image of the Franco Régime', *Historical Journal of Film, Radio and Television*, 7 (3) (1987), 230–1; Braojos Garrido *et al.*, *Sevilla 36*, p. 244; Castilla del Pino, *Pretérito imperfecto*, p. 205. On the rape and other punishment of women, see discussion below.

violence was also a form of exorcism of the underlying fear of loss of control which was the subconscious linkage uniting the military rebels with their various groups of civilian supporters.[158]

All those against whom violence was done belonged to groups whose accelerating political mobilisation (channelled by the Republic) constituted a threat to the ultra-hierarchical, monolithic national order on which Spain's past (and future) national 'virtue' and greatness were perceived as being founded. (Local studies of the repression demonstrate quite clearly that those targeted the length and breadth of rebel Spain were precisely those on whom the Republic's reforming legislation had conferred social and political rights for the first time in their lives.[159]) No area of Spain was exempt from this threat, and thus no area could be exempt from the 'cleansing' repression.[160] The dialectic of fire and sword, the necessary suffering of the 'heretic' is reminiscent of Counter-reformation values and norms.[161] But in the interior landscape of rebel leaders and many of their followers these melded with other more 'modern' discourses of disease and *racial* impurity in which the Republicans' 'marxist barbarism' was explained as a lethal virus, the germ of 'anti-nation' which if not 'cleansed' out to the last trace, would contaminate the healthy body of 'Spain'. Disease equalled disorder and, more significantly, vice versa.[162] Likewise, the widespread complicity of

[158] Also suggestive here – if indirectly so – are the anxiously repeated references juxtaposing Africanista terror and the rebel army's restitution of 'tradition' in Sánchez del Arco, *El sur de España en la reconquista de Madrid*: see, for example, p. 164.

[159] While unskilled urban and rural labourers bore the brunt of the repression in the south, in other zones of distinct social composition there was still a notable level of repression falling on various kinds of leaseholding peasantry who had disputed the terms of their leases under the impetus of Republican leglisation: Cenarro, *El fin de la esperanza*, pp. 88–9; J. Casanova, 'Guerra civil ¿Lucha de clases? El difícil ejercicio de reconstruir el pasado', *Historia Social*, 20 (1994), 135–50.

[160] The lexicon of cleansing and 'public hygiene' is also to be found in the Republican zone, although not in the discourse of the state/political leaders of the Republic: J. Casanova, in Juliá *et al.*, *Víctimas de la guerra civil*, p. 70.

[161] The expectation that the Republican population should *suffer* is repeatedly pronounced by rebel cadres and supporters of all kinds. For example, the intelligence officer in Burgos who in 1937 in response to his Quaker interlocutors' concerns about how there was significantly greater material deprivation being endured by the Republican population commented that 'just as soon as we can get things cleaned up in the North then there'll be more suffering there too': Dan West, 'Needy Spain', Reports from the field, vol. 2 (report authored Feb. 1938), FSC/R/Sp/4. For an analysis of the political functions of 'suffering' and 'penitence', see Richards, *A Time of Silence*.

[162] See, for example, the comments of two rebel press officers: first, Captain Rosales (on the taint to Spain's bloodstream which had come through the industrial cities of the coast), cited in M. Richards, *A Time of Silence*, p. 62 and those of the Africanista Captain Gonzalo de Aguilera (Conde de Alba de Yeltes), in Whitaker, 'Prelude to World War', pp. 107–8 (Whitaker judged his social and political ideas to be typical of 'scores and hundreds of others on the Franco side'). (Whitaker also discusses Aguilera in *We Cannot Escape History*, pp. 108–9); see also Charles Foltz,

priests in the denunciation, killing and torture of those deemed opponents has to be understood as an active element within this ideological
framework rather than a response to popular anti-clerical violence in
Republican territory.[163]

In view of these discourses and where they led, it is probably too restric-
tive to categorise only the war in the south as colonial. Franco's specific
reference to Andalusia as an 'occupied zone' has tended to highlight the
south. Certainly there was a reciprocal influence between *latifundismo*'s
feudal values and the colonial experience of the Africanistas (an interchange intensified by the contiguity of Africa and Andalusia). But above
and beyond this, the entire rebel project was constructed as a colonial
enterprise in which the target was Spain as a whole.[164]

In the decades after the loss of the remnants of Spain's empire in 1898,
the military elite developed an ideological identity for themselves as the
defenders of the unity, hierarchy and (thus) the cultural and political

Jr (who also considered Aguilera's views typical of the landowning elite's), *The Masquerade in Spain*
(Boston: Houghton Mifflin, 1948), p. 116; P. Kemp, *Mine Were of Trouble* (London: Cassell, 1957),
p. 50; Neves, *La matanza de Badajoz*, p. 60. Further testimonies in Southworth, *Guernica! Guernica!*,
pp. 50–3. Also P. Preston, 'Slaves, Sewers and the Nationalist Uprising' (unpublished essay on
Aguilera). Consider also the self-revealing anecdote that some among the rebel political class
believed that the Republicans were plotting to infect them with epidemic disease: Southworth,
Guernica! Guernica!, pp. 463–4 (n. 43). Likewise, General Mola's later outburst (in April 1937,
to the Condor Legion's General Sperrle) about the need to wipe out the industrial centres if
Spain was to be healed, in A. Viñas, *Guerra, dinero, dictadura. Ayuda fascista y autarquía en la España
de Franco* (Barcelona: Crítica, 1984), pp. 102–3. There were also tests conducted in 1938–9 on
Spanish Republican and International Brigade prisoners by a military psychiatrist, Antonio
Vallejo Nágera, in search of the 'bio-psychic roots of Marxism', A. Reig Tapia, *Ideología e historia:
sobre la represión franquista y la guerra civil* (Madrid: Akal, 1986), p. 28; Richards, *A Time of Silence*,
pp. 57–8.
[163] Kemp, *Mine Were of Trouble*, pp. 76, 80; Moreno Gómez, *La guerra civil en Córdoba*, pp. 463–4;
Fraser, *Blood of Spain*, pp. 116, 166; Mario Neves, the Portuguese journalist who reported the
Badajoz massacre, recalled similar comments by a priest: see Neves' interview in *The Spanish
Civil War* (Granada Television, 1982), episode 2 ('Revolution, Counter-Revolution and Terror').
A similar picture obtained in the north: see Fidalgo, *A Young Mother in Franco's Prisons*, pp. 14–15;
Sender Barayón, *A Death in Zamora*, p. 163; A. Cenarro, *Cruzados y camisas azules. Los orígenes del
franquismo en Aragón 1936–1945* (Zaragoza: Prensas Universitarias de Zaragoza, 1997), pp. 203–4
and (same author) *El fin de la esperanza*, pp. 89–90; García García, 'Aproximación al estudio de
la represión franquista en Asturias', p. 78. For continuing violence in the post-war period, see
M. Torrent García, *¿Que me dice Usted de los presos?* (Alcalá de Henares: Talleres Penitenciarios,
1942) – Torrent's behaviour is discussed by H. Southworth in P. Preston (ed.) *Spain in Crisis*
(Hassocks: Harvester Press, 1976), p. 272; and in *El mito de la cruzada de Franco*, pp. 320–1;
F. Arrabal, *Carta al General Franco* (Paris, 1972), p. 159; Preston, *Franco*, pp. 323–4.
[164] The conquering rebel armies would enter northern cities in the same manner as those in the
south, in the spirit of *razzia* (a term of nineteenth-century North African derivation meaning a
raid or hostile incursion for the purposes of conquest and plunder), J. A. Sacaluga , *La resistencia
socialista en Asturias 1937–1962* (Madrid, 1986), pp. 5–6. See also the description by a pro-rebel
priest (Father Alejandro Martínez) of the army's entry to Gijón (Asturias) in October 1937, when
they 'sacked it as if it were a foreign city': 'it was as if a "certain species" had to be liquidated',
Fraser, *Blood of Spain*, pp. 424–5.

homogeneity of Spain.[165] In the process, they effectively internalised the empire: first, in the sense that metropolitan Spain itself became the empire (according to the monarchical constitution, the colonies had, anyway, been *provinces* of Spain), and second, in that many within the military elite interpreted their defence of 'Spain' as an *imperial* duty.[166] By the 1930s this defence was directed against both disintegrative regional nationalisms and the working class as the bearers of political change and cultural difference.

The cultural difference which sparked the most vehement, pathological loathing and, in turn, some of the most extreme cases of ritual, violent humiliation was digression from rigid gender norms. Women who took part in the armed resistance (*milicianas*) and others identified as 'red' were shot alongside men. Many were also raped before they were killed. More frequently, defeat was branded upon 'red' civilian women by means of shaving their heads and administering doses of castor oil with the inevitable consequences (although sometimes these punishments were also the prelude to murder).[167] The evident misogyny of rebel elites was rooted in the same fear of losing control: hence the consistent displays of

---

[165] For the impact of imperial decline and re/degenerationist thought on the development of the Spanish right's ideology into the civil war period, see M. Richards, 'Civil War, Violence and the Construction of Francoism', in Preston and MacKenzie, *The Republic Besieged*, pp. 197–239 and Richards, *A Time of Silence*.

[166] For the concept of internal colonialism where rival nationalisms are developed by antagonistic groups within a state, see M. Hechter in J. G. Kellas (ed.), *The Politics of Nationalism* (Basingstoke: Macmillan, 1991).

[167] There is a significant amount of women's memoir material which attests to these *consistent forms* of rebel attack on women. See picture of women of various ages with shaved heads (Montilla, Cordoba) in Moreno Gómez, *La guerra civil en Córdoba*, p. 93. Contemporary right-wing accounts also make reference to shaving, for example journalist Cecil Gerahty's *The Road to Madrid* (London: Hutchinson, 1937), p. 95. References also in Collins and Lapierre, *Or I'll Dress You in Mourning*, p. 97; García García, 'Aproximación al estudio de la represión franquista en Asturias', pp. 79–80; Fraser, *Blood of Spain*, p. 272. There are also reports of atrocities against women (who subsequently became refugees) in Quaker correspondence, FSC/R/Sp/1 file 1 (Barcelona 1936–7). Such punishments continued to be meted out by victorious Falangists in village and town in the immediate post-war period. See also Y. Ripa, 'La tonte purificatrice des républicaines pendant la guerre civile espagnole', *Identités féminines et violences politiques (1936–1946). Les cahiers de l'Institut d'Histoire du temps présent*, 31 (Oct. 1995), 39–51. Women political prisoners also continued to suffer rape during police interrogations. T. Cuevas, *Cárcel de Mujeres* (Barcelona, 1985) and translated as *Prison of Women: Testimonies of War and Resistance in Spain* (Albany, N.Y.: State University of New York Press, 1998); Giuliana di Febo, *Resistencia y movimiento de mujeres 1936–1976* (Barcelona: Icaria, 1979), pp. 18–20, 88, 107; F. Romeu Alfaro, *El silencio roto: mujeres contra el franquismo* (n.p.: n.p., 1994), p. 40; C. García, *Las cárceles de Soledad Real. Una vida* (Madrid: Ediciones Alfaguara, 1982), p. 97 mentions a gaol rape of which there are many reports; cf. Fidalgo, *A Young Mother in Franco's Prisons*, p. 22; J. Doña, *Desde la noche y la niebla. Mujeres en la cárceles franquistas* (Madrid, 1978; 2nd edn, 1993), p. 171; Richards, *A Time of Silence*, pp. 52, 55, 64. For women's undocumented disappearances, see Cenarro, *El fin de la esperanza*, pp. 80, 89–90.

pathological hatred manifested towards even the *memory* of the *milicianas* in the post-war years.[168]

'Red' women in general were obsessively reduced to their sexuality by rebel commentators who thus projected their own fears onto the Republican enemy.[169] In the same vein, note the myth of rape vouchers supposedly distributed as payment to the Republican militias. In fact, it was Africanista officers themselves who came closest to realising this when they paid Moroccan troops in war booty that included access to 'red' women. The contradictory layers of rebel pathology also led to peculiar philosophical debates between officers over whether such women were still not fundamentally 'Spanish' (i.e. 'white' in a different sense) which made handing them over to the *regulares* a questionable action.[170] Even within their own terms of reference this seems a pointless debate, since Republican women were regularly subjected to severe physical abuse (including rape) by assorted 'Spanish' sectors within the rebel camp.[171]

All kinds of women were imprisoned – from teenagers to seventy-year-old grandmothers. Many were imprisoned with their babies, sometimes newborn. Conditions were infrahuman, and not infrequently the

---

[168] Hate-filled commentaries accompanying pictures of *milicianas* were published in the post-war Francoist press, including in Sección Femenina women's magazines.

[169] For the extraordinary case of General Queipo de Llano's sexual psychopathology – as manifest in his Seville radio broadcasts – see Brenan, *Personal Record*, p. 297; I. Gibson's *Queipo de Llano* reconstructs the text of these broadcasts. On war, sexuality and loss of control, see also the thought-provoking analysis in J. Labanyi, 'Women, Asian Hordes and the Threat to the Self in Giménez Caballero's *Genio de España*', *Bulletin of Hispanic Studies*, 73 (1996), 377–87 – see esp. p. 382 (for his hysterical denunciation of Madrid as a whore and Medusa from the pulpit of Salamanca Cathedral) and p. 385 (for Labanyi's fruitful incorporation of Theweleit's concept of war as the 'ultimate permissible "controlled explosion" of the self').

[170] See Whitaker, 'Prelude to World War', pp. 106–7 and Taylor, 'Assignment in Hell', p. 61 for an example of racist theories among southern landowners and rebel officers. At the same time, both they and priests waxed lyrical about the cleansing services offered by the African troops, their underlying racism buried here beneath the image of these troops as part of the larger imperial enterprise embodied in the 'Crusade', A. Lunn, *Spanish Rehearsal* (London: Hutchinson, 1937), p. 66; Sánchez del Arco, *El sur de España en la reconquista de Madrid*, pp. 95, 165, 205, 248 ('at the hour of liberation [of the Alcazar of Toledo] women of Castile received from African hands a bread as white as Communion bread . . . [the war] was a Mudejar enterprise against the Asiatic hordes' (p. 205).

[171] War rape is a complex issue for which a growing theoretical and comparative bibliography exists. But neither the Spanish Civil War nor post-war repression have yet been subject to such analysis (although see Alberto Reig Tapia's comments in *Ideología e Historia*, p. 145 and Espinosa Maestre, *La justicia de Queipo*, pp. 249–55). My purpose here, however, is purely to locate the subject in the broad context of rebel pathologies. There was no comparable phenomenon of consistent, mass physical abuse of women in Republican territory as contemporary pro-rebel commentaries note: see, for example, Sánchez del Arco, *El sur de España en la reconquista de Madrid*, p. 55 and H. R. Knickerbocker, *The Siege of the Alcazar* (London: Hutchinson, 1937), p. 86. Subsequent research also bears this out, including in respect of nuns: S. Juliá *et al.*, *Víctimas de la guerra*, pp. 140, 152–3. (Few female religious were killed, and their sexual intimidation was rare.)

children died. Indeed, this seems to have been part of the punishment for their gender transgression: one prison offical remarked that 'red' women had forfeited their right to nourish their young.[172] Nursing mothers were shot along with the grandmothers and teenagers. For the child survivors the price of nourishment (via Falangist social welfare) involved what one witness (herself a prisoner) described as 'moral suffering: obliging orphans to sing the songs of the murderers of their father; to wear the uniform of those who have executed him; and to curse the dead and blaspheme his memory'.[173]

In the end, what the military, Falangists and other rightist volunteers did to Republican men and women responded to something other than tactical necessity in a military conflict. The startling uniformity of the degradation and objectification inflicted upon Republican prisoners – and in particular the remarkable need of their captors to break not only their bodies but also their minds before killing them (and, even where they were not killed, to leave them, as it were, psychologically 'reconfigured' by their experience of prison/repression) – was servicing the underlying rebel project: to (re)build a homogeneous/monolithic and hierarchised society.[174] The rebels' objective and the insistent desire to reach the inner life of the 'enemy' correspond very closely to what, in another national context, we would term fascist.[175] It has been powerfully argued that fascism is a kind of 'colonialism come home': in both there is a need to subjugate – if not annihilate – the threatening 'other'.[176] Yet the 'other' – or outgroup – is also crucial to the process of national reordering.[177] For the rebel (and later Francoist) project of national reordering, the Spanish working classes became what the Jews were to that other, more notoriously renowned Volksgemeinschaft. 'Biological' racism is,

---

[172] Fidalgo, *A Young Mother in Franco's Prisons*, p. 28.   [173] Ibid., p. 31.

[174] For a strikingly similar attempt to refix the identities of political prisoners by coercing them into signing declarations of 'repentance', see the case of post-civil war Greece in the essay by Polymeris Voglis in M. Mazower (ed.), *After the War was Over. Reconstructing, the Family, Nation and State in Greece 1943–1960* (Princeton, N.J.: Princeton University Press, 2000), p. 77.

[175] Cf. H. Arendt, *The Origins of Totalitarianism* (New York, 1966), p. 245.

[176] For fascism as 'colonialism come home' in relation to the ideas of both Hannah Arendt and postcolonial theorists Fanon and Césaire (whose phrase it is), see D. Stone, 'Ontology or Bureaucracy? Hannah Arendt's Early Interpretations of the Holocaust', *European Judaism*, 32 (2) (1999), 11–25. (Although Arendt is herself referring to the common *territorial* expansionism of fascism and colonialism.) On the Spanish right's internalisation of the empire, see H. Graham, 'War, Modernity and Reform: The Premiership of Juan Negrín', in Preston and Mackenzie, *The Republic Besieged*, p. 178 (n. 40) and 'Popular Culture in the Years of Hunger', in Graham and Labanyi, *Spanish Cultural Studies*, p. 238.

[177] On the instrumentality of German antisemitism and the organisational function of outgroups, see Arendt, *The Origins of Totalitarianism*, pp. 238, 226, 241 (respectively).

after all, ultimately explicable as a cultural category: thus one would always expect the specificities of a given national history and 'tradition/myth' to construct both the outgroups and the arguments which justify their exclusion/annihilation. Thus the crucial instrument of Franco's Volksgemeinschaft was the Castilian Catholic Church – both as an organisation and in terms of a particular construction of Catholicism whose political function was to subjugate and exclude.[178] The project would remain confined within Spain. But no less than the German variant, it required the brutal eradication of 'disorder' and the subjugation of difference and change. Like Nazism (and, in a substantially different socioeconomic context, Stalinism) the Spanish rebels used 'massacres . . . for the purpose of establishing a circumscribed, rational political community'.[179] On this reading, then, Mola's war directives encapsulate not a strategy but a pathology.

As Yagüe's forces conquered Talavera de la Reina on 3 September, the needs of an escalating war situation were forcing themselves acutely on socialist, communist (and to a lesser extent republican) political leaders in Madrid. They were learning a hard and crucial lesson – paid for in blood by the thousands of militiamen and women who fought and died in the south. The Republic could not now win unless it was able to meet the rebels in pitched battle. And that meant – sooner or later – having to confront the cumulative material and technological expertise of their Axis backers – including the most sophisticated military-industrial complex of the day, the Nazi state gearing itself up for war.[180]

The Republic, as the legitimately elected government of Spain, had straightaway (19 July) attempted to secure war material for itself from the western democracies. But initial promises from the French Popular Front government were withdrawn in the face of British disapproval

---

[178] Catholic organisation and discourse provided the mediating device whereby the regime integrated and nationalised the bulk of the Spanish population: see A. Botti, *Cielo y dinero. El nacionalcatolicismo en España (1881–1975)* (Madrid: Alianza Universitaria, 1992).

[179] Arendt, *The Origins of Totalitarianism*, p. 186. The repression carried out by the rebels in Spain both during and after the civil war was vastly more violent and extreme than anything which occurred in Italy under Mussolini. We have known this empirically for some time. Yet few analytical conclusions have yet been drawn. The first Spanish work to deal with the civil war repression as a whole (as opposed to empirical local studies which limit themselves to quantifying deaths), S. Juliá *et al.*, *Víctimas de la guerra civil*, still implicitly treats rebel repression and popular violence in Republican territory as if they meant the same thing. For the opposing view, see A. Reig Tapia, *Ideología e Historia* and (a brief encapsulation in) Cenarro, *El fin de la esperanza*, pp. 68–9.

[180] For the Republican (defenders' and civilians') culture shock faced by modern warfare (planes and bombs), see Cox, *Defence of Madrid*, pp. 15, 30, 32.

and opposition from the bulk of the French Radicals whom the social-ist premier Leon Blum feared would jeopardise his domestic reform programme if he insisted on official French military aid to the Spanish Republic.[181] In Britain, unease at the potentially destabilising impact of conflict in Spain crossed into overtly pro-rebel attitudes in some quar-ters of the policy-making establishment. (The Spanish Republic was perceived as less capable than the rebels of guaranteeing capital and property – not least in respect of significant British investment in Spain. The fact that it was precisely the act of military rebellion itself which had provoked the violence and disorder that so shocked British diplomats and political leaders did not, however, seem to register in these circles.) British fears and hostilities obliged Blum, also acutely aware of France's vulner-able defences, to sponsor Britain's preferred policy of 'Non-Intervention' in Spain. By 24 August the diplomatic consensus for this was achieved when Nazi Germany agreed to join (primarily to lock France into the agreement and thus tie Blum's hands). As the Axis powers were in effect already intervening with impunity, what the policy amounted to was an arms embargo imposed in practice exclusively against the Republic.[182]

As a result of this, the Republican leaderships were reduced in August and September to scrambling for arms piecemeal through *ad hoc* pur-chasing agents. For many reasons this was both a hideously expensive and highly inefficient process – not least because the plethora of Spanish buying agents, dispatched by the many Republican committees and thus acting independently of each other, ended up competing to purchase scarce material thus driving the already high prices higher still.[183] All this was, of course, a direct result of the organisational dislocation and fractured communication channels caused by the rebellion. Yet given the Republic's near total international isolation, its ability to withstand the Axis-backed insurgents – indeed, its very survival – depended absolutely on coordinating its efforts and on maximising its internal resources. Nor

---

[181] G. Howson, *Arms for Spain* (London: John Murray, 1998), pp. 21–6. The Radical Pierre Cot, who was Blum's air minister, supported the Republican cause.

[182] The Non-Intervention committee set up to administer the agreement was inaugurated in London on 9 September. Representatives were present from every European country except Spain itself, Portugal (which had formally agreed to Non-Intervention under great pressure from its ally Britain) and Switzerland, which also accepted the policy but declined to compromise its neutrality by attending the committee's discussions: M. Alpert, *A New International History of the Spanish Civil War* (Basingstoke: Macmillan, 1994), pp. 40–61.

[183] For more on the acute problems of procuring war material, see chapter 3 below.

in the period from 18 July to early September did there appear to be much prospect of foreign assistance for the Republic from any other quarters. Not only were Britain and France tied into Non-Intervention, but so too seemingly was the Soviet Union. Once it became clear that the offer of French military aid was in great danger of stalling, prime minister Giral hastily dispatched a desperate request to the Soviet Union.[184] But although Stalin was prepared to send a few military advisers, he hesitated before the Republican request for military hardware – fearful of the destabilising potential of an escalating conflict in Spain, given the vulnerability of the USSR's own frontiers.[185] Faced with these hesitations, and rebel advance, the Republic's own initiative was clearly going to be imperative. A single, overarching political structure – Republic-wide – was the *sine qua non* for planning or implementing a single, coordinated war effort. This was evident to most among the Madrid leadership – anarcho-syndicalists included. But it was probably best learned by Juan Negrín, the socialist deputy soon to become the Republic's new finance minister.

Meanwhile, the war was bearing down on Madrid from the south. It was physically manifest in the tide of refugees who poured in having fled before the rebel army. To the north at Guadarrama lay the rebels' other forces under Mola. On 23 August the military airfield at Getafe, on the city's perimeter, was bombed, and on the 25th that of Cuatro Vientos – even closer. On 27–8 August the population of Madrid suffered their first air raids – indeed, the first of their kind to occur anywhere in Europe. Their occurrence led to the formation of house committees in each residential block to implement basic civil defence measures (such as

---

[184] The Republic's emissary, the distinguished legal historian and former education minister Fernando de los Ríos, arrived in Paris on 23 July. Given the climate of embarrassment and fear he encountered there in the parliamentary Socialist Party and the waves being made by the conservative press, it cannot have taken him very long to realise how precariously placed was the whole question of Republican aid: Howson, *Arms for Spain*, pp. 24–5. Giral's request of 25 July to the Soviet government is reproduced in R. Radosh, M. R. Habek and G. Sevostianov (eds.), *Spain Betrayed. The Soviet Union in the Spanish Civil War* (New Haven/London: Yale University Press, 2001), p. 21.

[185] F. Schauff, 'Hitler and Stalin in the Spanish Civil War 1936–1939', unpublished research paper (presented at the Annual Conference of the Society for Historians of American Foreign Relations, Toronto, 24 June 2000), p. 8. According to Schauff, 'informally and during Stalin's holidays it was agreed that the Soviet Union would send instructors to Spain. At the beginning of August, two were selected and a group of about a dozen Red Army officers were sent to Spain later that month.' But at the start of September, Litvinov, the People's Commissar of Foreign Affairs, informed the Soviet ambassador to Madrid that there would be no arms sent to Spain for the moment. See also D. Smyth, 'Soviet Policy Towards Republican Spain: 1936–1939' pp. 92–3 and P. Preston, 'Mussolini's Spanish Adventure: From Limited Risk to War', pp. 39–40 both in Preston and Mackenzie, *The Republic Besieged*.

listening for sirens – the signal to go down to the cellars – or attempting t
ensure a black-out). Gradually, as the socialist and communist leadership,
in Madrid organised civil defence mobilisation, the war began to enter
popular consciousness. It was now an only too tangible reality – perceived
directly through personal experience and in the news/rumours of incessant defeats borne by the refugees. On 21 September Yagüe's troops
would take Santa Olalla, mounting a public execution of 600 militiamen in the main street of the town: 'they were unloaded and herded
together. They had the listless, exhausted, beaten look of troops who
can no longer stand out against the pounding of German bombs.'[186]
The conviction was growing among the Madrid-based leaders of the
Republic that something else was needed: the 'apocalypse' had to be organised.[187] The defeats in the south and the aerial bombardments were
a constant reminder of the need for military preparation and popular
mobilisation, in both of which the Spanish Communist Party especially
would soon show itself to excel.

The scale of the challenge facing the Republic also made changes
in government essential. By September it was clear that Giral's all-
republican cabinet could not command the political respect or support
of a broad enough spectrum of Republican Spain. Its credibility was
tainted by popular memories of earlier republican attempts to treat with
the rebels. Its authority was further undermined by the string of military defeats and by public-order disasters. The loss on 3 September of
Talavera, to the south-west of Madrid, and of Irún on the border with
France at the western end of the Pyrenees, intensified the Republic's
physical vulnerability. The inability of Irún's defenders to hold on –
munition-starved and bombed by Italian planes – meant that the rebels
acquired some thousand square miles of fertile farm land, densely populated, with many important factories. It was also a major strategic defeat,
cutting off the Republican Basque Country, Santander and Asturias from
France and the rest of the Republic.[188] Worker confidence in the republican leadership was reduced to virtually nil. But as great, if for different
reasons, were the anxieties to which middling social constituencies within

---

[186] In the words of American journalist John T. Whitaker, 'Prelude to World War', *Foreign Affairs*,
21 (1–4) (Oct. 1942–July 1943), 105–6.
[187] André Malraux's famous metaphor in his novel *L'Espoir* (Paris, 1938); see also Cox, *Defence of
Madrid*, p. 28.
[188] Previously Spanish militia had been able to pass through France from the Catalan frontier to
the Basque side. For their part, the rebels could now travel by rail all the way from Hendaye
(France) to Cadiz on the south-west coast: J. M. Martínez Bande, *La guerra en el norte* (Madrid:
San Martín, 1969), pp. 91–2.

its territory were still prey. 'Bottom-up' violence continued in the form of *paseos* and *sacas* (the removal from gaol and assassination of imprisoned rightists). On 23 August, as news of the mass killings at Badajoz began to circulate in Madrid and as the bombers closed in on the capital, there occurred a notorious loss of control in the Cárcel Modelo (Model Prison). In unclear circumstances a fire broke out inside, attracting a hostile crowd to the prison. After panicked staff had fled, and before the socialist militia, the Motorizada, could arrive on the scene, the building was assaulted by the crowd and some 70 political prisoners (out of approximately 3,000 held) – including numerous prominent conservatives and right wingers – were shot, more or less by 'popular acclamation'.[189] As a result, the government immediately moved to establish a system of popular courts (the Tribunales Populares) in an attempt to forestall any recurrence of such devastation.[190]

Republican-zone violence was thrice negative. First, it was preventing the minimal inter-class consensus necessary to create the coherent structures essential for the successful prosecution of an escalating war. Second, in that it was perpetrated by the least powerful sectors of society, it remained very uneven and incomplete – in contrast to what was occurring in rebel Spain – and thus left social and political opponents in place, later to demand counter-measures (or to contribute to erosive fifth-column activities). Third, and not least, the *paseos* and *sacas* meant that the Republic risked political defeat by alienating the liberal capitalist democracies – something which a good many CNT leaders understood just as well as did their republican, socialist and communist counterparts.

The detonation of the military coup in July had blasted open the fault lines running deep in Spanish society. It destroyed the fragile anti-oligarchical Popular Front alliance of urban and rural workers with middle-class sectors and thus precipitated a state crisis of unprecedented proportions. Almost everywhere within the atomised regions and localities (apart from the Republican Basque Country[191]) the military rebellion had unleashed conflict between antagonistic social constituencies. The coup had failed on its own terms – in that it did not achieve complete political and territorial control of Spain. However, the level of

---

[189] Zugazagoitia, *Guerra y vicisitudes*, pp. 128–30; Borkenau, *The Spanish Cockpit*, pp. 125–6; Fraser, *Blood of Spain*, pp. 175–6; Thomas, *Spanish Civil War*, p. 404. The Model Prison incident was the most notorious, but both before and after there were also other *sacas* from both the Modelo and Madrid's other prisons: Porlier, Ventas and San Antón.

[190] See chapter 3 below for discussion of Republican public-order policy.

[191] See chapter 3 below.

fragmentation thereby provoked had pushed the Republic far back from a reasonable starting point for fighting the kind of war rapidly being imposed on it. In retrospect, therefore, it is possible to see the coup as an inadvertent strategic success. This was especially the case given that the rebels – by the use of terror and with an authoritarian Catholic lowest common denominator – would have a much easier time uniting their fragments.

The challenge facing the veteran socialist union leader Francisco Largo Caballero, appointed to replace Giral as prime minister on 4 September 1936, was, first and foremost, to legitimise *Republican government* in the eyes of the proletarian forces who had led the emergency defence. This would permit the rebuilding of military and civilian state structures capable of erecting an adequate front-line military defence, while also articulating and mobilising the Republic's internal resources against the rebels and their fascist backers, and mending political fences with the western democracies in whose eyes the Republic had been diminished by its loss of public, political control in the aftermath of the July days. The support of Britain and France (or at least their genuine neutrality) was a basic condition of Republican victory. For unless the embargo underlying Non-Intervention was lifted, it would be impossible, in the medium term, for the Republic properly to undertake the enormous task of military and state reconstruction necessary to wage the full-scale war now looming. In the mean time, while embargo was a reality, it was imperative that the Republicans cement the home front in order to ensure as wide as possible a social mobilisation of the Republican population behind the war effort.

Such a mobilisation, in turn, however, required the establishing of a new *modus vivendi* between the proletariat in arms and the Republic's middling classes. Both represented fragments of social constituencies. The loss of large sections of the landless proletariat in the rebel-conquered south-west, plus radical urban centres like Seville, Zaragoza and Oviedo, meant the amputation of much of the social base which might have driven a more radical wartime political agenda; while the middling-class sectors still with the Republic were those of the historically separatist north and confederal north-east (Vizcaya and Catalonia). The challenge for the Republican government would therefore be how to instil war consciousness and, linked to that, an idea of the 'necessary state' in the differing social constituencies which made up its base.

The opposition of some working-class sectors, but also strongly regionalist middle-class constituencies, to the central state-building enterprise would lead to bitter, energy-diverting social and political conflicts in the Republican zone which impeded and undermined the war effort. But they could scarcely be avoided. A Republic that was in the process of reconstructing (post-coup) its democratic forms could not, without annihilating its own *raison d'être*, solve this dilemma in the fashion of the rebels: by the mass physical liquidation of the enemy or the blanket use of terror as a weapon of social control.

CHAPTER 3

Building the war effort, building the state for total war (September 1936–February 1937)

You who will emerge from the flood
In which we have gone under[1]

On 4 September 1936 Republican president Manuel Azaña formally confirmed the appointment of a new government to replace Giral's. The new prime minister was the veteran socialist union leader Francisco Largo Caballero, who also took charge of the war portfolio. His supporters had been arguing for some time that he was the only figure capable of bringing the whole of organised labour, including the CNT, on board the war effort. Prieto and his supporters in the PSOE also recognised the truth of this and told Azaña so – in spite of their own profound political differences with Largo. The new cabinet comprised twelve ministers. There were four republicans, including one from the Catalan Esquerra. (Basque nationalist (PNV) representation would come later in the month when Madrid agreed to a Basque autonomy statute.[2]) But the three Madrid-based republican representatives, including ex-premier Giral himself as minister without portfolio, were very much on the cabinet's margins. Its core was provided by the Socialist Party, which had six ministers. In addition, there were two from the Communist Party (PCE) in agriculture and education.

Largo's value as prime minister was chiefly a symbolic one: his leadership gave an impression of political unity under left leadership which was designed to pacify the radical mood of the Republic's proletarian defenders. Workers saw Largo as a guarantee of their interests and, in particular, of no compromise with the military conspirators.[3] A cabinet

---

[1] 'To those born later', Bertolt Brecht.
[2] Largo originally (5 Sept.) designated the PNV's leader, José Antonio Aguirre, as his minister for public works. There then followed negotiations over the 'price' of Basque participation. After the central government had agreed to promulgate the Basque statute forthwith, Manuel de Irujo joined the cabinet as minister without portfolio, *Gaceta de Madrid*, 26 Sept. 1936.
[3] Graham, *Socialism and War*, pp. 55–9.

led by him was thus the only viable way of rescuing the concept of government, which had suffered greatly as a result of the military rebellion and subsequent republican temporising with the rebels.[4] Largo's symbolic importance thus overrode the considerable reluctance of President Azaña, the republicans and the parliamentary Socialist Party to accede to left socialist leadership of the new cabinet.[5] They would all have preferred a republican-led cabinet reinforced by PSOE participation – something the Soviet leadership had also actively sought, and for the same reason – the more favourable impression such a government line-up would have on western government/policy-making opinion internationally.[6] But this sort of coalition was vetoed by Largo at the start of September, just as he had vetoed a republican-socialist government back in May. Largo's insistence had also carried the day over the inclusion of the Communist Party in the cabinet. Stalin had opposed this, but Largo made his own acceptance of the premiership conditional on it[7] – fearful that, otherwise, the PCE would gain political credit at socialist expense from the freedom of opposition.

Largo was widely perceived among working-class constituencies as a symbol and guarantee of left unity and proletarian ascendancy. But it was in fact Largo's underlying reformism which made it 'safe' for Popular Frontist socialists and republicans to accept his appointment in September 1936.[8] If nothing else, the experience of 1934–6 had made it clear to Indalecio Prieto, his close friend and colleague Juan Negrín and the rest of their, like-minded, collaborators in the parliamentary PSOE that the socialist left had no viable ideas or strategies of its own. (On hearing that Largo was to form a government, Negrín remarked that it was the victory of October 1934 and worse than if the rebels had taken Getafe (the military airfield near Madrid). But this was certainly not an expression of trepidation about any radical policy potential.[9] Negrín was alluding instead to the likely international ramifications of such a

---

[4] Koltsov, *Diario de la guerra española*, p. 62.

[5] Azaña had no real input in Largo's appointment except for formal endorsement. On parliamentary socialist rationale and preferences, see Graham, *Socialism and War*, pp. 56–7.

[6] Azaña's continuity in the presidency was a crucial source of legitimacy *vis-à-vis* international observers. For the Soviet perspective, see A. Elorza and M. Bizcarrondo, *Queridos camaradas. La Internacional Comunista y España 1919–1939* (Barcelona: Planeta, 1999), pp. 308–12.

[7] Bolloten, *SCW*, p. 121; Elorza and Bizcarrondo, *Queridos camaradas*, pp. 312–13.

[8] On the socialist left see Graham, *Socialism and War* and 'The eclipse of the socialist left 1934–1937' in Lannon and Preston, *Elites and Power in Twentieth-Century Spain* and Juliá, *La izquierda del PSOE*.

[9] Zugazagoitia, *Guerra y vicisitudes*, pp. 154–5; M. Ansó, *Yo fui ministro de Negrín*, p. 151; see also Pascua's comments in Alvarez, *Juan Negrín (Documentos)*, pp. 278, 281. The socialist left's ideological sterility and strategic bankruptcy were nowhere clearer than in the procedural techniques through which they chose to continue waging war inside the Socialist Party while the Republic itself was fighting for its life: Graham, *Socialism and War, passim*.

government line-up as well as to the party left's political mediocrity and strategic bankruptcy.) This deep and savage division inside the socialist movement, however, meant that Largo's cabinet was badly fragmented. The three members of the UGT-identified left socialist contingent (with the premiership/war, interior and foreign ministry portfolios) scarcely communicated with the three parliamentary socialist ministers (Prieto in the navy/air ministry, Negrín in the treasury and the veteran socialist Anastasio de Gracia, who was in charge of industry and commerce).

Such atomisation at the heart of the cabinet might have mattered less if the left socialists had themselves formed a strong, coherent nucleus for government. But this was far from the case. In terms of hard policies, developments during 1934–6 had revealed that the socialist left was in practice indistinguishable from the rest of the PSOE. Largo, a veteran, reformist union leader, probably saw his own arrival at the premiership as setting the seal on his camp's *organisational* victory in the internecine socialist conflict. With a few notable exceptions, the socialist left derived from and identified with the trade union rather than the socialist parliamentary party, and there was a certain tendency among the left's members – Largo included – to perceive political office in terms of the institutional advantage which could accrue to the UGT. Largo was nevertheless well-meaning, strong on patriotic duty and very concerned to acquit himself honourably as prime minister. But he had little grasp of the magnitude of the task awaiting his government as the military rebellion escalated to full-scale war in the south, and he would prove a disaster as war minister.

Indeed, the PSOE split itself revealed just how little real political expertise the party left could call upon. Largo's choice of the ex-Radical socialist Angel Galarza (only recently affiliated to the PSOE) as his interior minister underlines this weakness.[10] Galarza was widely perceived as something of a political opportunist. Nor, in the event, would he prove a successful or efficient interior minister.[11] In all, Galarza's appointment did little to reinforce left socialist coherence or credibility in the cabinet. This was, moreover, all the more significant as the left's third ministerial appointee to the foreign ministry, Julio Alvarez del Vayo, was moving away from his close personal allegiance to Largo towards the Spanish Communist Party. It is likely that Largo's political adviser, Luis

---

[10] The alternative was the landworkers' union (FNTT) leader Ricardo Zabalza: del Rosal, *Historia de la UGT*, vol. 2, pp. 526–7. Julián Zugazagoitia in *Guerra y vicisitudes*, pp. 152–3 tries to make the best of it – but the implication even here is that Largo did not have a lot of options to choose from.

[11] Graham, *Socialism and War*, pp. 63–4.

Araquistain, was the left's preferred candidate for the foreign ministry portfolio. But his appointment was vetoed by President Azaña, who regarded Araquistain as the brains behind the May 1936 cabinet fiasco (when Largo had blocked Prieto's bid for the premiership – with deadly results). After the war, Largo's political-military secretary, José María Aguirre, would claim that Araquistain had been vetoed as a result of Soviet pressure over armaments.[12] But the Soviet Union had not yet decided on intervention and, irrespective of the Soviet opinion of Araquistain, both republicans and parliamentary socialists were already vehemently opposed to him.[13]

Parliamentary socialists and republicans both sought a smaller, more homogeneous Popular Front cabinet staffed by themselves, with token Catalan and Basque representation and supported by the Communist Party from outside the government. Such a line-up would have been better able to address the urgent problems of military reorganisation and state infrastructural rebuilding which were looming large by September. Internal party political tensions would still have existed to some extent, of course, but such a government's political expertise and international perspective and connections would have allowed it to compute more rapidly the policy implications for the Republic of fascist intervention and the war in the south. But such a Popular Front government would not have had the confidence of the proletarian forces at the forefront of the July defence – and most particularly the CNT's cadres, whose support was absolutely crucial to war mobilisation. Largo's appointment was, therefore, inescapable.

[12] Aguirre in an undated (but post-1945) note to Araquistain's son (Araquistain correspondence, legajo 71, no. 22a (AHN) and again in a series of articles in *Informaciones* 8–10 Nov. 1977, published under the pseudonym A. Vélez. Aguirre claims Largo told him (i.e. on 3 Sept. 1936) that del Vayo was 'a Soviet agent'. Bolloten cites this testimony without comment, *SCW*, pp. 123–4. But the language suggests a suspicious amount of prejudice of hindsight. (Indeed, only a few pages earlier (p. 120) Bolloten himself refers to the still functioning relationship between Largo and del Vayo in September 1936 and elsewhere in his book gives a highly critical assessment of Aguirre, whom Bolloten knew personally during the war, as a 'young upstart...arrogant and inexperienced' which must also cast doubt on his testimony, *SCW*, p. 353.) Azaña's memoirs make no reference to the episode.

[13] Stalin only finally made up his mind to send the Republic war material in mid September, Elorza and Bizcarrondo, *Queridos camaradas*, pp. 314, 317, 322–4; Howson, *Arms for Spain*, pp. 124–15; F. Schauff, 'Hitler and Stalin in the Spanish Civil War', unpublished research paper (presented at the Annual Conference of the Society for Historians of American Foreign Relations, Toronto, 24 June 2000), p. 8. While Araquistain's left socialist political trajectory scarcely recommended him to a Soviet leadership concerned to assuage France and Britain, the harsh view presented by the Comintern representative to Spain, Vittorio Codovilla, must be understood in the context of an attempt to deflect Comintern secretariat criticism from himself: Elorza and Bizcarrondo, *Queridos camaradas*, pp. 315–16, 319–20.

Bringing the CNT into government was the biggest political challenge facing Largo Caballero's government. The prime minister himself was from the outset concerned to 'implicate' the CNT in governmental responsibilities in order to defuse their potential criticisms of cabinet decisions. Largo was anxious, as ever, about the UGT's 'credit'/'credibility' and fearful of the CNT stealing a march over the socialist union now that its leadership was fulfilling a governmental function. But at root, the imperative of CNT inclusion in the Republican cabinet, even more than Largo's own appointment, derived from the need to relegitimise and consolidate Republican government and state functions so badly eroded by the military rebellion. However, this internal political imperative conflicted greatly with the political requirements of the international situation. The overriding fear within the Popular Front – should anarchists be included in the government – was of confirming the hostility of the western democracies whose material support (and, first and foremost, the lifting of the Non-Intervention arms embargo) remained their primary/immediate goal. Although not blind to these image problems, the PCE was more flexible. The Comintern was clear about the need to rein in the CNT in Barcelona, but it also appreciated that CNT support would be crucial to the effective war mobilisation of Republican society.[14] (Its references to the need to separate 'good' anarcho-syndicalists from the 'lumpen' and 'low lifes' represent an initial attempt to skirt the political dilemma posed by the CNT.[15]) But neither parliamentary socialists nor republicans were comfortable with the idea of anarcho-syndicalist representation, and President Azaña was vehemently opposed.[16]

Indicative of this fear and unease was the fact that Largo initially offered the CNT's national committee just a single ministry in September. Unsurprisingly, this was rapidly rejected by a majority of its regional federations[17] as beneath the CNT's (political) dignity and due, given its size/strength and the key role it had played in the emergency defence

---

[14] The PCE reinforced with favourable comments all the signs of reformist ascendancy in the CNT: for example the public recognition within the CNT of the need for centralisation to serve the war effort, *Guerra y revolución en España*, vol. 2, pp. 52–4.
[15] Cf. André Marty's report (10 Oct. 1936), Elorza and Bizcarrondo, *Queridos camaradas*, p. 327 and cf. p. 340 and *Guerra y revolución*, vol. 2, pp. 10–11, which insists on the same manichean division within the CNT.
[16] M. Azaña, *Apuntes de memoria y cartas*, ed. de Enrique de Rivas (Valencia: Pre-Textos, 1990), p. 26; S. Juliá, 'Presidente por última vez: Azaña en la crisis de mayo de 1937', in A. Alted, A. Egido and M. F. Mancebo (eds.), *Manuel Azaña: Pensamiento y acción* (Madrid: Alianza Universidad, 1996), p. 246.
[17] Plenary session of regional federations held 3 September 1936, C. Lorenzo, *Los anarquistas españoles y el poder 1868–1939* (Paris: Ruedo Ibérico, 1972), p. 180.

of the Republic. The same national plenum which rejected the single ministerial portfolio did, however, accept the *principle* of CNT participation in government. The fact that the text of the CNT resolution made such participation conditional on the prior restructuring of government and state along syndical lines should not deflect our attention from the crucial importance of this decision, which was taken – albeit as a result of much heated debate – only three and a half months after the apparent victory of the purist anarchist currents at the Zaragoza congress in May 1936.

Throughout September 1936 the CNT – in the form of successive plenary meetings of its regional federations – continued to argue with a lone voice that the Republican government should be reconstituted in the form of a National Defence Council. The Popular Front groups would all be represented on this, but majority control would be split between five CNT and five UGT members. The CNT's proposal met with steely resistance, however, from all these other groups, including the UGT. Then, on 24 September, the CNT accepted the dissolution of the Catalan Anti-fascist Militia Committee – until then the most important source of political authority in the region – whereupon the CNT's representatives entered the Catalan regional government effectively as ministers.[18] The precedent was thus set and on 18 October the delegates at the CNT's national plenum of regional federations finally agreed to allow participation in the central Republican government *tout court*, something which the CNT's ultra-pragmatic general secretary, Horacio Prieto, had been advocating since the formation of Largo's government itself.[19]

But even for the pragmatic syndicalists in the CNT, Largo needed to offer more substantial representation in the cabinet for them to feel able to justify participation before their own membership. In the ensuing negotiation process Largo revealed himself as the most resolute champion of a conventional, bourgeois government structure. In this he was in part undoubtedly concerned to calm British and French fears over the Republic's perceived radicalism. Alongside this one can also detect the veteran UGT fighter concerned not to give any advantage to the CNT. Most significantly, however, in his championing of the Popular Front government mode, Largo revealed that the socialist left – for all its radical rhetoric between 1934 and 1936 – was as comfortably anchored as the parliamentary wing of the PSOE in the 'old liberal' world

[18] For events in Catalonia after 18 July 1936 and an analysis of the CNT's wartime political evolution, see chapters 4 and 5 below.

[19] Lorenzo, *Los anarquistas españoles y el poder*, p. 185. (Lorenzo was Horacio Prieto's son.)

of bourgeois political hierarchy and limited popular mobilisation.[20] The outbreak of war, in bringing Largo Caballero to power, fully exposed the contradictions underlying the socialist left.

The UGT leadership had all along continued to share with its parliamentary PSOE counterpart a very singular view of the socialist movement's 'manifest destiny', according to which it would inherit the state. This implicit statism meant that the union's national executive had been as profoundly traumatised by the events of July–August 1936 as its party counterparts. For the rebellion's disintegrative impact took its toll on the UGT's organisational hierarchy as much as on party political and state structures. Local union committees acted autonomously even when they claimed a UGT denomination. Neither Largo Caballero nor the rest of the union leadership had any intention of supporting such localist initiatives, which significantly undermined their own control of the UGT. It is in this context that one must understand the leadership's energetic and persistent calls from the start for the nationalisation of industry. Certainly there were cogent reasons for this in terms of articulating an integrated national war effort. But an equally crucial agenda here was ensuring the rearticulation of the UGT itself and the recovery of leadership control.[21] The entire historical experience of the UGT, and in particular the increasing identification with state power in the 1920s and 1930s, informed the decision of Largo Caballero to pursue both aspects of this agenda (i.e. the concentration/rationalisation of war production and the Spanish socialist movement's consolidation of political power) from government after September 1936 – rather than by making an alliance with the CNT.

But although Largo Caballero instinctively favoured a moderate political course, his premiership was marked by a certain sense of policy limbo. For Largo was reluctant to undertake any overt or vigorous policy for which he might be criticised by one or other popular consistency, and especially where his action could be construed as endorsing the 'old' hierarchies of power against the workers. The impact of this contradiction would weigh heavily from the start on the Republic's most imperative task – the rapid reconstruction of its defensive military capacity.

The impact of the rebel coup had left Largo's predecessor, Giral, with no option but to enact the formal dissolution of the army. The degree of organisational disruption caused by the rebellion varied from area to area – the centre (Madrid) zone being *relatively* less affected. But nowhere in Republican territory was it possible to deploy army units in the rapid

[20] See chapter 1 above.   [21] Graham, *Socialism and War*, p. 185.

and reasonably coherent way the rebels could.[22] Even in Madrid, when the Republican government was using regular troops, these constituted the remains of units dislocated by their commanders' departure which were then lumped together with militia forces and often put under the command of any available lieutenant, sub-lieutenant (*alférez*) or sergeant, even though they were often strangers to the men they were required to direct.[23] And nowhere did Republican militarised forces exceed 2,000 at the outset. Moreover, the massive distrust of the officer class *per se* which the rebellion had caused everywhere among the Republic's proletarian defenders made a symbolic break with the old army structures crucial to successful military mobilisation thereafter. Giral had appointed a committee headed by Captain Eleuterio Díaz Tendero,[24] formerly prominent in the progressive republican army organisation the UMRA (Unión Militar Republicana y Antifascista). This committee investigated the political reliability of all those officers who remained at the Republic's disposal, removing those whose loyalty was materially in doubt.[25] But the underlying conservativism of the Spanish officer corps would clearly create an enormous – and in many ways irresolvable – problem for the Republic at war in its attempts to ascertain military loyalty.

Even before Largo came to power, it had been realised by Giral and others that any successful attempt at military rearticulation had to start from the basis of the militia. Initially – on 3 August – Giral's government had decreed the creation of a volunteer army on the French revolutionary model – something both more conducive to the republicans' ideological framework and comforting to their sense of order than the perilously un-predictable, multi-form militia units.[26] But the militia – dynamised by the sheer centrifugal force unleashed by the rebellion and buoyed up by the popular anti-militarism it had magnified – simply could not be sidelined.

The protagonism of the militia thus required other measures designed to lay the basis of centralised control. This process began with the decree

---

[22] See Cordón, *Trayectoria*, p. 250 for some idea of the huge extent of the fragmentation the coup caused in the officer corps.

[23] Even in the Madrid military region it has been calculated that the forces remaining to the republicans were 70 officers and 1,313 NCOs and soldiers out of a previous base of more than 828 officers and 10,425 NCOs and men. This was just not enough to allow the conventional restructuring of an armed force. Alpert, *El ejército republicano*, p. 30; Azaña, *Obras completas*, vol. 3, p. 487.

[24] Cordón, *Trayectoria*, pp. 235–6; Alpert, *El ejército republicano*, pp. 17, 367.

[25] In the Civil Guard a high proportion of its officers – perhaps in excess of 40 per cent – were removed by the Republican authorities after 18 July 1936 – in spite of the corps's initial role in the suppression of the rebellion. Alpert, *El ejército republicano*, p. 25 (and see pp. 20–32 for an estimate of the military forces available to both sides).

[26] Cordón, *Trayectoria*, p. 249.

of 8 August creating a new Inspectorate of Militias covering the central zone, the south and the Valencian area. (The centrifugality unleashed by the coup meant that both Catalonia/Aragon and the north were still beyond the reach of Madrid's authority.) The Inspectorate's brief was to end irregular or arbitrary militia requisitioning. By the end of the month its operations had grown to such an extent that it had entirely superseded the original volunteer battalion initiative, whereupon the government formally recognised the militia as the building blocks of the new army.[27] By 16 August the Inspectorate had decreed conditions of service for those militias which agreed to be regulated by it (food and 10 pesetas a day for each *miliciano*). At one level this was welcome to militia members because it rationalised and thus (in theory at least) speeded up what was a notoriously haphazard system of payment and provisioning.[28] But standardisation was effectively the first stage in the process of militarisation because it required the presence in each militia of an army quartermaster's (Intendencia) official to ensure the proper utilisation of public funds.[29] The connection between payment and control was thus established, and by the end of the month the government was already threatening to withhold militia wages in those cases where the requisite membership lists had not been forwarded to the authorities.

This militia system, already in the course of transformation, was thus inherited by Largo with the premiership in September. In theory (and rhetorically) he entirely approved the principle of accelerating the creation of a new Republican army (Ejército Popular). The series of devastating militia defeats in the south made the military case unanswerable. Moreover, the initiative also offered a powerful means of reinstilling the centralised political order he instinctively sought in the Republican zone. In practice, however, there was often rather more ambivalence in Largo's manner of proceeding. He knew that endorsing the policies required to achieve militarisation would inevitably bring him into head-on conflict with some sectors of the organised working class, including even some socialist sectors, with unavoidably negative consequences for his personal reputation within the labour movement and the left as a whole. This is

---

[27] Decree of 28 August, *Gaceta de la República*.

[28] 'The *miliciano* can never be sure when he's going to be paid, nor does he know who is paying him – the (military) unit he's in, his union, political party or the War Ministry.' C. Contreras (Quinto Regimiento), in *Milicia Popular*, 6 Sept. 1936, cited in Alpert, *El ejército republicano*, p. 39.

[29] M. Azaña, *Apuntes de memoria y Cartas*, ed. de Enrique Rivas (Valencia: Pre-Textos, 1990), p. 68 refers to the mayhem in the early days of a huge excess of rations paid in excess of active militiamen; see also I. Diéguez's report to the Madrid Defence Council on 12 Dec. 1936, J. Aróstegui and J. A. Martínez, *La Junta de Defensa de Madrid* (Madrid: Comunidad de Madrid, 1984), pp. 341–2.

no doubt one reason why Largo undermined the fundamental rationale of militarisation established by his general staff by tacitly allowing the CNT to form some homogeneously anarchist military units.[30] And if this happened on the centre front, then clearly the chances of his taking a resolute stand in the near future on the matter of the military incorporation of Catalonia and the Aragon front under central government control were distinctly remote. Largo's reluctance to take unpopular action – although probably largely unconscious – derived no doubt in part from the same prickly sense of amour-propre that underlay his infamous dogmatism. At root, Largo did not really understand either fast enough or fully enough the imperatives of Republican militarisation. His lack of ease with the idea also stemmed from the fact that he had not grasped that what was being advocated – above all by example in the PCE's Fifth Regiment – was light years away from any attempt to resurrect an *ancien régime* army.[31] This also underlay his reluctance to put his weight behind an effective programme of military conscription. A decree mobilising all able-bodied men aged between twenty and forty-five passed on 29 October was simply not enforced.[32] Similarly, Largo was not prepared to gainsay the bureaucracies of the UGT and CNT building federations, which refused to exert influence on their members to build trenches after working hours.[33] In overall terms, Largo's resolve was inhibited by the enormous weight of the contradiction between the grass-roots radicalism whose symbolic guarantor he had become and the moderate course which his political preferences and past practice dictated.

Throughout the second half of September the PCE's leaders, and in particular Antonio Mije, one of the Republic's four deputy commissar generals, did their utmost to impress upon Largo the desperate need to accelerate militarisation and civil defence in Madrid. Mije also suggested a four- or five-member war council to overcome the problems inherent in the unwieldy and lumbering (although still politically necessary) form of the Popular Front cabinet. But the prime minister rejected all these proposals out of hand, adducing practical difficulties, even though the military case the communists made was unanswerable. Largo undoubtedly felt overwhelmed by the desperate circumstances, but it was a culpably obtuse response which he gave to Mije's observation that the way to stop militia fleeing under attack was not to shoot the offenders but to dig

[30] Bolloten, *SCW*, pp. 331–2.
[31] Azaña, 'Cuaderno de la Pobleta', *Obras completas*, vol. 4, p. 862.
[32] Bolloten, *SCW*, pp. 346–7.
[33] Jackson, *The Spanish Republic and the Civil War*, p. 312; cf. D. Ibárruri, *En la lucha. Palabras y hechos 1936–1939* (Moscow: Editorial Progreso, 1968), pp. 59–65; Azaña, *Obras completas*, vol. 4, p. 819; Preston, *Comrades*, p. 292.

proper trenches: according to Largo, Spaniards were too proud to hide in the ground.[34] After the fall of Toledo on the 28th, Mije pointed out to Largo that the same would happen in Madrid unless they speeded up fortification work. He proposed a joint war ministry for which Largo and Prieto would be responsible. For obvious reasons of a personal and (in the circumstances) petty nature – namely his enmity with Prieto – Largo rejected the suggestion instantly. By October, Mije – for all his jovial Andalusian personality – was frustrated and exhausted. It had become clear that anything emanating from the PCE leaders would instantly be rejected by Largo for reasons of personal or organisational jealousy. For this reason, in October the Soviet ambassador, Rosenberg, took the brunt of trying to persuade Largo of the need to accelerate the defence of Madrid – something which indicates just how crucial Stalin deemed the survival of the Republic to be as an advance front to defend Soviet frontiers against Nazi aggression. In time, the tensions between Largo and the PCE would be replicated between premier and ambassador. We shall return to these in due course, but it is important to emphasise at the outset that their *origin lay, not in arguments over the unification of the socialist and communist parties* but in the clash over the speed of implementation and quality of Republican defence policy and, thus, in Largo's running of the war ministry.

To Largo's suspicious narrow-mindedness, we also have to add the massively debilitating consequences of his extremely bureaucratic approach. To be sure, the Spanish left as a whole was politically inexperienced by dint of its lengthy exclusion from power. But Largo's particular inability to evaluate the bigger picture, or to discriminate between the issues on which he really needed to focus as wartime premier and those more trivial matters which could be delegated to others, seriously inhibited the Republic's recovery capacity. Some sense of being out of his depth seemed to convert itself into an exaggerated doggedness (if Largo didn't understand the point, everything stopped in its tracks until he had) which only magnified the effects of his inefficiency.[35] This already difficult situation was made worse by certain other understandable physical

---

34 Elorza and Bizcarrondo, *Queridos camaradas*, p. 325, citing André Marty's Comintern report of 10 Oct. 1936. This is echoed in other memoir literature; for examples see Thomas, *Spanish Civil War*, p. 432. Koltsov's diary entries for September/October abound with scathing references to Largo's imbecility in matters military – see the heavy irony in the entry for 30 Sept. 1936 (points 8 and 9).

35 Cordon, *Trayectoria*, pp. 258–61 (especially p. 261); Koltsov, *Diario de la guerra española*, p. 62 records Prieto's withering insights. Koltsov was beside himself over Largo's inefficiency and procrastination (p. 191). In its very precision and lack of stridency, Cordón's assessment is particularly damning; also Gabriel Jackson's comments on cabinet meetings, *The Spanish Republic and the Civil War*, p. 366.

limitations. At sixty-seven years of age, and in less than robust health, Largo apparently saw no reason why the larger crisis should cause him to modify his night-time routine and regularly retired between eight at night and eight in the morning – during which time he was rigidly *incomunicado*. While it was quite reasonable for Largo to bar individual militia leaders' direct access to his person (indeed, the Militia Inspectorate forbade this), as war minister, he needed to be more flexible with officers of the general staff.

These deficiencies of prime ministerial leadership as well as the general cabinet fragmentation made the crucial work of military and state-administrative reconstruction more difficult. It also meant that in both areas crucial reconstruction work was being carried out initially in isolated pockets, both by individuals and small groups, usually without much specific government guidance or support.[36]

As we have seen, the Militia Inspectorate provided a key base from which to begin centralising control on the Madrid front. More than any other body, it did most every day, both practically and psychologically, to articulate a vast array of disparate militia forces formed in the July days, shaping them into the Republic's first battalions. It was the Inspectorate which did much to free up the war ministry from the incessant and (inevitably) unstructured demands of individual militia leaders.[37] The Inspectorate itself was reorganised on 20 October, when it passed directly under the control of the military chief of operations on the central front, being renamed the Comandancia Militar de Milicias. Through both its control of militia payment[38] and through the dissemination of a constant stream of circulars and instructions it instilled the need for discipline, endlessly arguing/reiterating the point that the militias were now no longer autonomous forces but part of a larger defensive enterprise. An idea of the Comandancia's efficacy can be gauged from the fact that by the end of the month some of these battalions were being successfully incorporated into the Mixed Brigades (Brigadas Mixtas), the integrated, autonomous units being established on the central front as the basis of the new Republican army under construction.[39]

---

[36] Elorza and Bizcarrondo, *Queridos camaradas*, p. 326.
[37] Cordón, *Trayectoria*, pp. 241, 258, 260. Cf. J. López in Bosch Sánchez, *Ugetistas y libertarios*, p. 19.
[38] Within the Commandancia's territory such payment ceased to be transmitted via parties or unions from around 21 October 1936.
[39] Thus, a Mixed Brigade would incorporate cavalry, heavy and light artillery, a signal corps and sappers, as well as infantry troops, in order to make the brigade a flexible and independent unit. For more on the Mixed Brigades, see Alpert, *El ejército republicano*, pp. 76–80. For the reorganised Comandancia de Milicias and its achievements under its director, Servando Marenco, see Alpert,

Largo's appointment, and that of Colonel José Asensio[40] (whom Largo promoted to General) as his under-secretary at the war ministry, also marked a process of evolution towards the construction of a central general staff, the lack of which was making it impossible for the Republic even to begin to develop an overarching strategic plan. Yet prioritisation, not least of scarce resources, was essential if it was to sustain a war effort against the better-supplied and equipped rebels. The July rebellion had obviously left the pre-war general staff, as part of the state, in chaos. There was a desperate shortage of capable military staff, yet, given the circumstances, very few of the available officers were trusted. The government relied on a small group of fervently republican officers – Hernández Sarabia, Casado, Menéndez, Estrada, Fontán, Fé and Cordón – to begin the enormous task of reconstruction.[41] Antonio Cordón, supported by his colleagues José Martín Blázquez and José Cerón, directed a kind of emergency substitute known as the Secretariado Técnico (Technical Secretariat) from the war ministry which began the long task of reconstructing crucial war-related services such as communications, transport, munitions, supplies and medical services.[42] The first full new general staff was announced by Largo on 5 September. There were few names from the pre-war body, while it included those – most notably Casado, Rojo and Cordón (the latter at the head of the operational section) – who would later be key figures in the new Republican army. But in September, with the continuing removals of officers whose loyalty was considered doubtful and the ongoing battle to bar the militia's direct access to the war ministry, it would be the end of the month before any real semblance of a new order of command appeared.

pp. 38–40, 377 (on Marenco himself – who was a (not previously prominent) officer from the Cuerpo de Intervención Militar). On the battalions, see Alpert p. 42 and appendix 3, pp. 320–2; and on the building of the new Republican army in autumn 1936 'en tierras manchegas', R. Salas Larrazábal, *Historia del ejército popular de la república* (4 vols., Madrid: Editora Nacional, 1973), vol. i, p. 545.

[40] Asensio had been serving as a militia commander at the start of the war on the Guadarrama sierra front, north of Madrid, where he met and impressed Largo Caballero: Bolloten, *SCW*, p. 280.

[41] For biographical details on these officers, see Alpert, *El ejército republicano*, appendix 13, pp. 359–88; M. T. Suero Roca, *Militares republicanos de la guerra de España* (Barcelona: Península, 1981). For Cordón see also the very positive description in J. Martín Blázquez, *I Helped to Build an Army* (London: Secker and Warburg, 1939), p. 279. Cordón, a professional army officer of one-time monarchist convictions, had, like Casado, conspired against the Primo dictatorship and then retired, along with many other pro-Republican officers, from the active scale under Azaña's military reform law of 1932: Alpert, *El ejército republicano*, p. 12.

[42] Cordón, *Trayectoria*, pp. 233–4, 260; Martín Blázquez, *I Helped to Build an Army*. The latter was a professional officer who eventually left Spain in spring 1937, exasperated with what he saw as the irremediable chaos and incompetence of the Caballero government.

The daunting task of military reorganisation was made more difficult precisely because of the rising's political implications. The distrust of military power meant that civilian-political vigilance of its new forms was inevitable.[43] Indeed, the rebellion had problematised the notion of the military having *any* autonomous sphere of power – even in technical matters. Witness the many highly laboured references to the subordinate function of the military staff in the overall process of wartime decision making – for example when the government publicly announced its objective of a single Republican command (*mando único*) on 16 October.[44] The widespread civilian incumbency in posts which required specialist military knowledge, and which thus necessitated the additional allocation of a 'military adviser', has often been interpreted as the implementation of some abstract revolutionary goal. In fact it was a direct response to the military coup. Post-rebellion, a certain duplication of functions was as inevitable as it was understandable at various levels in the Republican zone. But the enduring effects were, nevertheless, negative. First, because such duplication used up time and human resources that could scarcely be spared. Second, because it reinforced the military–civilian divide which the Republic, gearing itself for war, could also ill afford.

This psychological divide placed tremendous pressure on the hundreds of professional army officers serving the Republican war effort. For them the rising had produced an enormous culture shock. They had been betrayed by the conspiratorial actions of their own comrades, which had ripped away their social and professional terms of reference.[45] On top of this came the Republic's own post-coup purge of officers, which further increased their sense of alienation. At any time, problems caused by shortage and dislocation could be turned into accusations of treason and crypto-fascism. The feeling of being continually under suspicion and required to prove oneself daily (at the same time as risking one's

---

[43] Thus in November Largo reformed the Consejo Superior de Guerra to include wider ministerial participation for all the main political groupings in the Republic.

[44] The *Gaceta de la República* for 16 October 1936 stated that 'the Chief of Staff (Estado Mayor Central) would not function as an executive body itself but rather as a consultative one assisting the executive power', cited in Alpert, *El ejército republicano*, p. 72. There are echoes here of the post-coup fears of independent military action. A further, related problem would be the refusal of Republican governments to pass from a 'state of alarm' to a 'state of war' because – as a result of the non-occurrence of pre-war public-order reform, this would still have meant ceding supreme control to the army. See chapter 1 above and chapter 6 below.

[45] Cordón, *Trayectoria*, p. 253; J. I. Martínez Paricio (ed.) *Los papeles del General Rojo*, 2nd edn (Madrid: Espasa-Calpe, 1989), pp. 76–7, 81.

life at the front) caused extremely high levels of stress and illness.[46] Even for those whose Republican political identity was clear, the world they knew had gone.[47] The new one was either hostile or offered few known points of reference in terms of organisation or values. The state was still in chaos, its sustaining political forces (republicans and socialists) either consumed or badly fragmented by the crisis. Yet there was one party – albeit still on the sidelines – with a very clear line on military and rearguard organisation which spoke directly to their sense of order and discipline. It is in this very particular and desperate context that we have to understand the appeal of the Spanish Communist Party to regular army officers on the centre front – *whether or not they actually joined the party*. What the PCE offered them was an alternative family/a refuge of structure in culturally dysphoric, structureless and traumatic post-coup times, and a source of collective protection; and, not least, the party reaffirmed their patriotism and sense of civic value, both severely damaged by the rebellion.[48] These motives predominated in the gravitation to the party of officers whose social and political values were usually quite conservative. Antonio Cordón, who would become more closely identified with the PCE than many others, also shared these reasons for joining the PCE at the start of the war.[49]

While this could be seen as a constructive trend, much less fortunate was the hostile disdain of the militia displayed by many of the officers who remained to serve the Republic at war. Indeed, this included convinced republican officers and even some of those who joined the PCE (although not Cordón). Whether because of their professional training or the trauma of post-coup disarticulation, these officers – including some of high rank – were insufficiently flexible to adapt to the irrefutable reality: that the militia represented the only available material out of which to construct the army needed to resist the rebels and their fascist

---

[46] Alpert, *El ejército republicano*, p. 87; Cordón, *Trayectoria*, p. 233; Rojo's letter to Indalecio Prieto, September 1937 in Martínez Paricio, *Los papeles del General Rojo*, documentary appendix (no page number); also cf. p. 73.

[47] Cordón, *Trayectoria*, p. 233.

[48] For the sense of 'family betrayal' which professional officers serving in the Republican zone felt towards the rebel military, their sense that the latter had caused their own plight, see *Los papeles del General Rojo*, pp. 77, 81.

[49] Cordón, *Trayectoria*, pp. 236–8; Martín Blázquez, *I Helped to Build an Army*, p. 241; I. Falcon, *Asalto a los cielos* (Madrid: Temas de Hoy, 1996), p. 166, according to all of which he joined the party in July 1936. Also corroborated by the little-known memoir by Colonel Eduardo Cuevas de la Peña, who would serve as Republican Director General of Security in 1938, cited in Bolloten, *SCW*, p. 607.

backers. It would seem that this was a failing of the otherwise talented General Asensio, Largo Caballero's anchorman in the war ministry.[50] Another case in point was the irritation which some officers displayed at the ubiquitous mediation of party and union representatives in the Republic's decision-making processes. But as Cordón replied to his exasperated friend and colleague José Martín Blázquez, this was simply the way things were since the coup, and one had to operate accordingly.[51] But this response indicates in Cordón a degree of psychological flexibility which was comparatively rare among Spanish officers of that time – and unsurprisingly so if one considers the nature of their professional education. But the prejudices and abrasive behaviour of some army officers only reinforced the hostility of the militia volunteers, which, in turn, 'confirmed' military antipathy and antagonism. This vicious circle was of itself wasteful of the energy and potential of both sides. Moreover, it made the function of the political commissariat an absolutely vital one.

Although the political commissariat was only formally constituted by Largo in mid October,[52] the very nature of the conflict meant that in fact political commissars had existed in everything but name almost from the very start. They provided the vital link between military and *miliciano* (since, as already mentioned, it was common practice for militias to have a professional military adviser attached). The commissars explained the rationale of orders, looked after the practical welfare of the men and reminded them of the *raison d'être* of the war. In the initial stages especially, the function of the commissar was particularly important as a shock absorber. Even though the commissar (or political delegate, as they were initially often called) never intervened in matters of military policy, given the militias' antagonism towards the professional military the delegate's presence was seen by the men as a kind of guarantee of their own interests.[53]

As the war went on, the commissars' other functions of practical welfare and political education would become paramount as the Republican army, forged to meet the needs of modern warfare, was forced to engage in a long, attritional conflict in conditions of persistent, morale-sapping material inferiority. In spite of the commissariat's objective importance, however, it never ceased to be vehemently denounced both by many

---

[50] For more on this see the discussion of the fall of Malaga (Feb. 1937) later in this chapter.

[51] Martín Blázquez, *I Helped to Build an Army*, pp. 207, 240–2.

[52] *Gaceta*, decrees of 16 and 17 Oct. 1936; also see Alpert, *El ejército republicano*, p. 182.

[53] The commissars provided a kind of temporary 'quarantine' service for professional officers. The expression is from Guillermo Cabanellas, *La guerra de los mil días*, p. 529.

1 Francisco Largo Caballero (seated, first on left), veteran socialist leader and prime minister of the Republican wartime government from September 1936 to May 1937 (Ministerio de Educación, Cultura y Deporte, Archivo General de la Administración)

2(a) Madrid front December 1936–January 1937. An image which conveys the abrupt encounter between military front and urban space in Madrid. A casualty is borne away by stretcher through the damaged streets of the capital. We see houses and shops scarred by gunfire and two sandbagged shelters in front of the buildings. The 'front' is just outside the frame (see plate 2(b)), barely one block beyond the set of sandbags on the top lefthand edge of the photograph. (Vera Elkan Collection (HU 71664) Photograph courtesy of the Imperial War Museum, London)

2(b) A panoramic shot of the 'front' which lies just beyond the range of plate 2(a). The sandbags on the righthand side of this photograph are the same ones which appear on the top lefthand edge of plate 2(a) (Vera Elkan Collection (HU 71662) Photograph courtesy of the Imperial War Museum, London)

3(a) 'Emulate the hero of the people' ('¡Imitad! al héroe del Pueblo')
Wall poster mobilising military and homefront effort by appealing to the memory of
the legendary anarchist leader Buenaventura Durruti, killed on the Madrid front in
November 1936 and rapidly converted into an icon of Republican resistance
(Ministerio de Educación, Cultura y Deporte, Archivo General de la Guerra Civil
Española (Kati Horna Collection))

3(b) Wall posters, the most prominent reading '¡Unión! ¡Disciplina! ¡Socialismo! ('Unity! Discipline! Socialism!) (Abraham Lincoln Brigade Archives Collection, Tamiment Library, New York University, Albert Harris Collection)

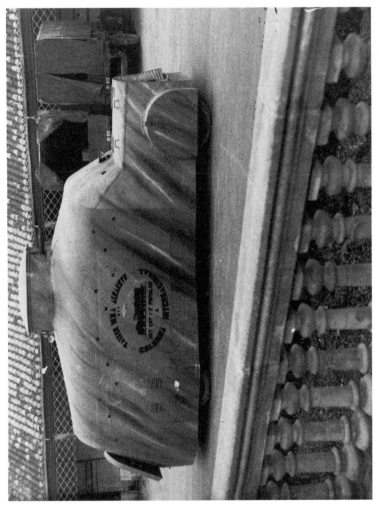

4 Home-produced armoured car c. January 1937 destined for use by the International Brigades (Vera Elkan Collection (HU 71512) Photograph courtesy of the Imperial War Museum, London)

5 Soviet journalist Mijaíl Koltsov flanked by two commanders from the German Thaelmann battalion in Madrid c. December 1936–January 1937. Koltsov was one of Stalin's key political observers inside Republican Spain (Vera Elkan Collection (HU 71579) Photograph courtesy of the Imperial War Museum, London)

6 This photograph shows Santiago Carrillo (centre), the Socialist Youth leader who at twenty-one became general secretary of the mass socialist-communist youth organisation (JSU) and Councillor for Public Order on the Madrid Defence Council (November 1936). The JSU epitomised the accelerated popular mobilisation occasioned by the war, as a result of which many young people were catapulted into positions of major political and military responsibility in Republican Spain. Not least because of this, the JSU also focused the bitter organisational rivalry between socialists and communists. In the post-war period Carrillo would become the long-serving general secretary of the exiled Spanish Communist Party (PCE). On Carrillo's left is the PSOE journalist Julián Zugazagoitia, Minister of the Interior from May 1937 until April 1938 and one of Juan Negrín's close political collaborators. In 1940 he would be handed back to Franco by Vichy France and shot. To Carrillo's right (in profile) is Fernando Claudín, then a Communist Youth leader and member of the JSU executive and later a leading member of the PCE executive and party theorist until his public dissent in 1964. (Fred Copeman Collection (HU 34724) Photograph courtesy of the Imperial War Museum, London)

7 A gathering in Barcelona in late 1936 of the Catalan Pioneers, a Popular Front youth group (Fred Copeman Collection (33003) Photograph courtesy of the Imperial War Museum, London)

8 Parade in support of the construction of the Popular Army, Barcelona, c. February
1937 (Fred Copeman Collection (HU 33009) Photograph courtesy of the Imperial War
Museum, London)

9 Postcard issued to underline the importance of women's factory labour in supporting the Republican war effort. The image reinforces the gendered division of labour that had been challenged during the period of Republican emergency defence, but which was being reconstructed in the course of 1937 (Ministerio de Educación, Cultura y Deporte, Archivo General de la Guerra Civil Española)

10 Republican government ministers visiting the Madrid front in November 1937. From the left, José Giral (foreign minister), prime minister Juan Negrín, President Manuel Azaña, accompanied by General Miaja (Ministerio de Educación, Cultura y Deporte, Archivo General de la Administración)

11 Shattered houses (with suspended bicycle) after air raids in Barcelona, January 1938 (Fred Copeman Collection (HU 33151) Photograph courtesy of the Imperial War Museum, London)

12 Residents of a Republican home for child refugees in 1938 demonstrating
co-educational principles in action. The boys were required to fulfil their share of the
domestic tasks. (Fred Copeman Collection (HU 33143) Photograph courtesy of the
Imperial War Museum, London)

13 Republican wall newspaper calling for unity and solidarity in the war effort. It contains extracts from prime minister Juan Negrín's Thirteen Points, the Republican government's declaration of war aims, published on 1 May 1938. These stressed the war effort as one to guarantee the independence of Spain (implicitly understood as from the invading forces of Germany and Italy). As well as pictures of soldiers, nurses and workers, the wall newspaper features images of the charismatic Spanish communist leader La Pasionaria (Dolores Ibárruri) (centre) and of the two Republican premiers, Juan Negrín (top, centre) and Generalitat leader Luis Companys (top, right) (Fred Copeman Collection (HU 33062) Photograph courtesy of the Imperial War Museum, London)

14 Soldiers of the Republican Army crossing the River Ebro in July 1938 by means of one of the pontoon bridges laid down after the initial boat crossing (Fred Copeman Collection (HU 33117) Photograph courtesy of the Imperial War Museum, London)

15 Wounded Republican soldier on an ambulance train during the battle of the Ebro, 1938 (Fred Copeman Collection (HU 34628) Photograph courtesy of the Imperial War Museum, London)

16 War memorial, Serra de Pàndols (Catalunya) built by International Brigaders (under the supervision of Percy Ludwick, chief engineer of the 15th Brigade) to commemorate a number of their comarades killed during the battle of the Ebro in 1938. Unlike other Brigade and Republican war memorials, it survived destruction by the victors because of its remote position in mountainous territory. The monument was restored in 2000 by a team of Spanish volunteers led by the historian Angel Archilla. (Photograph from the private collection of David Leach, director of the documentary film *Voices from a Mountain: British Volunteers in the Spanish Civil War* (2001) and reproduced here with his kind permission)

professional army officers who disliked what they saw as interference in their sphere[54] and from various civilian political quarters, mainly on account of the accusation that the commissariat was a vehicle of Communist Party aggrandisement.

This view was obviously shaped retrospectively by the clientelist political rivalries and organisational hostilities between the PCE and other groups in the Republican camp which would mount across the war period for a variety of reasons. But the function of the commissar was not invented by the PCE, for all that it was strongly advocated and first implemented in communist units.[55] Nor did the party have any particularly overriding *executive* influence in the formation of the commissariat proper in October. If one looks back at 1936, the relationship between the PCE and the political commissariat can be seen for what it mainly was – an organic one emerging from the PCE's understanding of the limitations of the militia forces and the imperatives of Republican military defence. There would be more communist commissars not because of any conspiracy but because in 1936 no other political group really grasped (and certainly Largo did not) the fundamental importance of the institution to a viable war effort. Moreover, this lack of understanding stemmed logically from the resistance among both the republican and the socialist leaderships in the pre-war period to new forms of politics involving mass mobilisation. It was, then, only the PCE that initially prioritised the appointment of high-quality and experienced personnel as commissars.[56]

Much less controversial, indeed highly welcome to army officers, republicans and PSOE leaders, was the PCE's vocal commitment from the start to the creation of a unified political-military command (*mando único*) and militarisation.[57] The PCE stressed the need to put in place new training structures for both officers and soldiers. As a working example of what it advocated, the party created a prototype of the new militarised force in the Fifth Regiment (Quinto Regimiento).[58] Its nucleus was the

---

[54] Cordón, *Trayectoria*, p. 263.

[55] The idea had a pedigree stretching back through the Russian Civil War all the way to the French or American revolutionary armies of the eighteenth century, as various authors have indicated – see Cordón, *Trayectoria*, pp. 262–3 and C. Blanco Escolá on Rojo's ideas, 'El centenario del General Rojo', *El País*, 14 Sept. 1994. For PCE advocacy through *Milicia Popular* (the newspaper of the party's military formation, the Fifth Regiment) see Alpert, *El ejército republicano*, pp. 176–8.

[56] For a sensible summary of views on the commissariat's genesis and development, see Alpert, *El ejército republicano*, pp. 180, 183.

[57] D. T. Cattell, *Communism and the Spanish Civil War* (New York: Russell & Russell, 1965), pp. 86, 230 (n. 5).

[58] On the Regiment's name and origins, see Alpert, *El ejército republicano*, pp. 48–9.

PCE's militia, the MAOC,[59] run since 1933 by Juan Modesto, who had served in Morocco as an NCO. It was the only party militia that had undertaken any real military training before 18 July 1936. To the MAOC were added forces from the fifth of the original volunteer battalions, plus some extra numbers from the united socialist-communist youth organisation, the JSU. The autonomous form of the Fifth Regiment's own fighting units (each carrying its entire military infrastructure within itself) was adopted as the blueprint for the Mixed Brigades, the basic unit of the new army. (These would be built up into the first of the Republic's operational armies, the army of the centre, whose model was then 'exported' to build the armies of the east, Levante and Extremadura in the course of 1937.[60]) At its peak in October it was estimated to be some 20,000 strong.[61] But although the Fifth Regiment contained fighting units, its key function would be as a transitional training formation which then generated other battalions.[62] Apart from its extremely realistic attitude to the needs of war, the Fifth Regiment's utility lay in its stress on discipline and in the organisational model it provided. The PCE had always been extremely clear about the need for the primacy of military authority in the army and for new forms of hierarchy and discipline.[63] The difference between the *ancien régime* army and the new Republican one lay not in the removal of these principles but in their qualitative transformation through a process of broader military reorganisation which would be catalysed by the desperate defence of Madrid in November and December.

It was the kind of work undertaken so singularly by the Fifth Regiment that underpinned Largo Caballero's two decrees of 30 September 1936 formally militarising the militia. Under its terms all politically sound

---

[59] Milicias Antifascistas Obreras y Campesinas.

[60] Alpert, *El ejército republicano*, p. 82. For an estimate of the strengths of the various components of the Republican army (Centre, Aragon, East (Valencia region/Levante), South (Andalusia and Extremadura), Basque Country, Santander and Asturias) in the winter of 1936–7, see Thomas, *Spanish Civil War*, p. 542 (based on Salas Larrazábal's figures in *Historia del ejército popular de la república*, vol. 1, pp. 528–30). Whether or not these figures were initially inflated, Michael Alpert suggests that by spring 1937 reality had caught up with them and that by July 1937 the Republic had over half a million men under arms, *El ejército popular*, p. 87.

[61] Report by Marty: Elorza and Bizcarrondo, *Queridos camaradas*, p. 328.

[62] The Regiment probably trained in the region of 25,000 men during the five months when it was active – a significant achievement given the fact that the PCE was coming from the political margins: Alpert, *El ejército republicano*, p. 54.

[63] See, for example, Pasionaria's explanation of what militarisation involved (for the home front too) in *Mundo Obrero*, 25 Sept. 1936, reprinted in D. Ibárruri, *En la Lucha*, pp. 54–6 and Carlos Contreras' articles in *Milicia Popular*, Aug. 1936, cited in Alpert, *El ejército republicano*, p. 51. (Contreras was the pseudonym of the Italian communist Vittorio Vidali.)

officers and NCOs (*suboficiales*) would pass to active service in the army,[64] while men would be distributed to companies and services as required by the general staff. The militia battalions were to form the basis of the Mixed Brigades. The decrees also established new minimum and maximum ages for military service of 20 and 35 years respectively. From 10 October on the central front, and from 20 October elsewhere, the new militia battalions were subject to military justice.[65] They were also numbered in an attempt to erase the political identity of the constituent militias, whose names were forbidden to be used in official documentation.

In practice, the militarisation process would take months to effect, given the scale of reorganisation necessary, the severe lack of middle-ranking officers/NCOs directly to command men and the ingrained hostility of many (but far from all) *milicianos* to the centralisation inherent in the process and, especially, to the loss of militia names. These problems were worse in Catalonia and Aragon, where, as we shall see, it would be over half way through 1937 before the militia began to be properly integrated.[66] Even on the central front, militia identities within the new military formations endured well into spring 1937[67] – encouraged by the ambivalent messages coming from Largo Caballero himself.

Paradoxically, this situation was also exacerbated by the inflexibility and overly bureaucratic style of the new general staff. While perfectly competent in conventional military terms,[68] it failed to make the necessary organisational and procedural allowances for the unconventional circumstances in which it was operating and for the resulting shortages of officers and trained men. Its only concession was itself distinctly bureaucratic: the general staff provided lengthy and fairly empty 'ideological' preambles when circularising (even fairly simple) orders to demonstrate that these did not offend against soldiers' rights or egalitarian principles. What would have been more useful would have been a greater degree of organisational flexibility. But the legacy of the coup itself worked against this as the professional military, under pressure as such and aware of the mutual lack of trust between themselves and the popular forces they were called upon to mould, took refuge in conventional forms and

---

[64] 'Pasarán a las escalas activas del Ejército'. [65] Alpert, *El ejército republicano*, pp. 72–4.

[66] The problem of non-integration in the Basque north was somewhat different since it had to do with the competition for authority between the central government and the Basque government rather than with a conflict over the type of structures *per se*. The Basque nationalist militia were subject to military discipline from the start, see chapters 4 and 5 below.

[67] An April circular reminded units that numbers, not names, must be used to designate themselves at all times, Alpert, *El ejército republicano*, p. 75.

[68] For further general staff reorganisations in October and late November 1936, see ibid., pp. 70–1.

procedures. Their almost fetishistic drive for rigidly centralised bureaucratic structures outstripped that of the rebels in practice[69] and, beyond a
certain point, was not necessarily the most effective means of transforming the hybrid Republican forces – a resistance movement *sui generis* –
into a functioning army that could take on a 'modern' opposition.[70]
(Indeed, it seems quite likely that some of the tensions between officers
and troops that tend to be interpreted as *ideological* in origin could in fact
have been mitigated by a more flexible and intelligent form of military
organisation.)

In order to function, this army-in-the-making not only had to be
trained, however; it also had to be equipped and armed. The fact that
the Republic was, from the start, being obliged to undertake this from
a position of clear material inferiority put an absolute premium on
the maximisation of its internal resources. (On the Madrid front the
rebels noted that they were picking up Republican munitions that had
been produced in the Toledo arms factory only days before.[71]) As Non-
Intervention had deprived the Republic of any hope of credits from the
Western democratic governments, as well as effecting an arms embargo
which was forcing it to procure arms at extortionate prices on the black
market, the first priority was to consolidate existing financial resources
and to develop a strategic plan for their use.

The first major task here, as the capital Madrid came under greater
and greater threat from rebel forces advancing from the south, was for
the Republic to secure its gold reserves in a place where they could readily be converted to meet war needs. The – inevitably secret – decree to
mobilise the gold reserves was one of the last made by Giral's republican

---

[69] M. Alpert, 'Uncivil War – the Military Struggle', *History Today*, 39 (March 1989), 14.

[70] On the vexed question of the Republic's 'failure' to wage a guerrilla war, see Ronald Fraser's
judicious summary, *Blood of Spain*, p. 330 (n. 2). The new Republican Army would include
a guerrilla unit trained by one of the Soviet Union's premier advisers, Alexander Orlov. It
carried out sabotage and other specific tasks (for example freeing prisoners) behind enemy
lines: see A. Orlov in *Forum für osteuropäische Ideen und Zeitgeschichte*, 4 (2000), 235–7; E. P. Gazur,
Secret Assignment. The FBI's KGB General (London: St Ermin's Press, 2001), pp. 57–78. But the
Republic never waged a full-scale partisan war (even though Orlov would claim a high (possibly
exaggerated) level of partisan activity). That it did not do so indicates something important
about the politics of the Popular Front alliance and (even more crucially) its perception of the
international political environment. But one should also remember the practical context here
and keep hindsight at bay. The Republican government began by throwing all its resources into
fighting a war on Franco's terms in the belief that it could win. It hoped that Non-Intervention
would not hold. It had no way of knowing either that it would or that Germany and Italy would
massively escalate their aid to the rebels in spring 1937. After that, all the Republic's resources
were locked into a different kind of war *just to stay alive*.

[71] Sánchez del Arco, *El sur de España en la reconquista de Madrid*, pp. 134–5. He also refers to Madrid
troops using taxis, which rather belies the otherwise carefully worked-up impression that the 'red
army' was awash with hardware, p. 112.

cabinet on 30 August 1936 before it gave way to Largo Caballero's. After consultation with high-ranking representatives of the Bank of Spain, Giral and his ministers, though cautious and conservative by instinct, came to realise that the escalation of the war made imperative the rapid mobilisation of the country's major convertible resources. Otherwise, the Republic would simply not have the means to continue waging war.[72] With the arrival of the new cabinet, it then fell to Juan Negrín, as treasury minister, formally to carry out this policy, overseeing the transfer of the gold from Madrid to the Republican-held naval base of Cartagena on the south-east coast. The first transportation occurred on 15 September, part of the reserves being sent to France (either directly or indirectly) as part of the Republic's ongoing strategy of gold sales to the Bank of France.[73]

As the rebels increased their military pressure on Madrid, the impact of the arms embargo began to bite. The Madrid government was, moreover, experiencing real difficulties with western banks. They were delaying the transfer of funds urgently required by its agents and diplomats to purchase war material.[74] From this the Republicans drew the only sensible conclusion possible: that were they to place their financial resources – the lifeblood of the future war effort – in the Western capitalist sector, these would risk being frozen. The partisan logic of Non-Intervention scarcely gave the Republicans cause for optimism.

From mid September it was also becoming apparent that the Soviet Union was inclining towards the option of aiding the Republic in order to avert its immediate military defeat. This saw a concerted effort by the Republican government to consolidate diplomatic communications in order to reinforce this inclination. Marcel Rosenberg, the Soviet ambassador, arrived in Madrid in the third week of August to establish the first embassy in Spain since the act of diplomatic recognition back in June 1933.[75] (It would be the end of 1936, however, before the embassy

---

[72] Angel Viñas' exhaustive, technical research on the gold's shipment is published in his study *El oro español en la guerra civil* (Madrid: Instituto de Estudios Fiscales, 1976) and summarised in *El oro de Moscú. Alfa y omega de un mito franquista* (Barcelona: Grijalbo, 1979), see pp. 74–86, 110–11; also A. Viñas, 'Gold, the Soviet Union and the Spanish Civil War', *European Studies Review*, 9 (1) (Jan. 1979), 107–9 and 'The Financing of the Spanish Civil War', in Preston, *Revolution and War in Spain*, pp. 266–83.

[73] Viñas underlines this continuity of policy, *El oro de Moscú*, pp. 27–41, 66–94. By the end of March 1937, the Bank of France had purchased at least 26.5 per cent of the gold reserves held in Madrid at the start of the war: Viñas, 'Gold, the Soviet Union and the Spanish Civil War', p. 108.

[74] Viñas, *El oro de Moscú*, pp. 91–2, 218–27; E. Moradiellos, *Neutralidad benévola* (Oviedo: Pentalfa, 1990), pp. 207–9.

[75] This act of recognition was effectively frozen throughout the period of conservative government (1933–5). Nor would the republican administration elected in February 1936 get around to

was functioning, and acute staff shortages remained a constant problem throughout the war.[76]) On 16 September, as the first consignments of gold headed for Cartagena, the Republican government approved the setting up of an embassy in the USSR. Marcelino Pascua, whose name had already been suggested for the post three years earlier, was appointed to head the mission.[77] A medical doctor like Negrín and a former colleague of the finance minister's in their days in the Residencia de Estudiantes,[78] Pascua arrived in Moscow in early October to face the daunting and difficult task of setting up a functioning embassy from scratch.[79]

Pascua's brief was to promote more substantial Soviet aid to support the Republic. But he found Stalin and his lieutenants already persuaded of this need. By the end of September it was manifest that the military situation was threatening the Republic's very survival, and for Stalin Republican collapse was an alarming prospect. It meant that France would have three fascist states on its borders and would be less likely than ever to make a wholehearted commitment to an anti-German alliance. It also meant that German firepower would be freed up for an attack against vulnerable Soviet frontiers. This context is crucial to any assessment of the motives for Stalin's decision to intervene at precisely this point. A Soviet military historian, Yuri Rybalkin, has suggested that Stalin's offer

unfreezing diplomatic relations prior to the war. Some of Rosenberg's Soviet colleagues doubted that he had the personal qualities for the job: Gazur, *Secret Assignment. The FBI's KGB General*, pp. 55–6.

[76] Elorza and Bizcarrondo, *Queridos camaradas*, p. 329; Marchenko, the chargé d'affaires, would still be complaining to Litvinov about this more than a year later. A boost to 35 had been promised – but it never materialised. For most of the civil war there were only four people working in the embassy, or five if we include Marchenko's wife: Schauff, 'Hitler and Stalin in the Spanish Civil War', p. 20. Rosenberg's second-in-command was Gaikis, who would take over from him in March 1937. Rosenberg and Gaikis did not get on and it seems clear that Gaikis reported back to Moscow on Rosenberg. But there was no obvious political reason for their disagreement. Gaikis may simply have been ambitious. But he too would be removed after several months: Schauff, 'Hitler and Stalin in the Spanish Civil War', p. 19.

[77] Pascua was one of the members of the Fabian-esque Escuela Nueva (New School), which had argued for the PSOE's alignment with the Third International at the beginning of the 1920s. Losing this argument, they formed the PCOE, but many, including Pascua, returned to the PSOE. Falcón, *Asalto a los cielos*, p. 138. On the New School see Meaker, *The Revolutionary Left in Spain 1914–1923*.

[78] Madrid University's student residence, which was also an elite powerhouse of Spanish intellectual and artistic development in the inter-war period.

[79] Viñas, *El oro de Moscú*, pp. 154, 156. Pascua was bitterly critical of republican inaction after February 1936 because the total absence of Spanish diplomatic infrastructure in Moscow made his difficult brief even harder – especially in a political culture as distinct as the Soviet Union's. Cf. Falcón, *Asalto a los cielos*, p. 138. The purges also made Pascua's work more difficult. He would complain that he could never reach the same Soviet personnel on any two consecutive occasions – which made it very hard to complete any piece of business: Schauff, 'Hitler and Stalin in the Spanish Civil War', p. 20.

of more substantial and technologically advanced aid was the result of an informal assurance at the end of September that its cost would be covered in full by the transfer to Russia of Spanish gold reserves.[80] Given the Republic's clear international isolation and war needs, it may be that such an informal assurance was given. Intervening to save the Republic would require the dispatch of precious war material from Soviet factories. So, given the Soviet Union's imperative of national defence, it may also be that the gold reserves were seen as constituting a guarantee (and important psychological reassurance) that these could be replaced rapidly should a crisis situation occur. But whether the gold was the single deciding factor is still not clear. We do know, however, that once the Soviet Union had the gold, it would subsequently manipulate the exchange rate in its favour, ensuring that the Republican government paid high prices for its aid.[81] But this was not necessarily a preconceived plan. Soviet intervention in Spain was marked by contingency – so there is no reason to suppose that it did not apply in this respect too. Moreover, nor was Soviet intervention particularly consistent in terms of narrow or pecuniary self-interest. In 1936 the Soviet government would dispatch at least 50 per cent (and probably more) of its precious total annual production of military aircraft to Republican Spain. Later in the war too the Soviet government would provide substantial credits to the Republic when it knew that it had virtually no chance of recouping them.[82]

We do not know whether it was a Soviet or a Spanish Republican representative who first uttered the words proposing the transfer of gold. But its significance is less than many commentators have supposed. In so far as the Republican government was under pressure, this derived not from its Soviet interlocutors but from the knowledge of its precarious international situation.[83] The Republic's objective was to accelerate the mobilisation of its gold reserves in such a way as to guarantee the foreign exchange necessary to fight the war. Given that Non-Intervention had already produced worrying restrictions on the Republic's economic room for manoeuvre, instant convertibility could only be assured if the gold left Spain. In the existing political climate nor was there was much

---

[80] Howson, *Arms for Spain*, pp. 127–8 cites Lt-Col. Rybalkin. (Stalin had already permitted Republican purchases in the Soviet Union of low-grade armaments which were shipped to Cartagena, the first arriving on 4 October: Howson, p. 126.)

[81] Ibid., pp. 146–52.

[82] The aircraft tally may have been higher because Soviet production targets for arms were rarely fulfilled in the second half of the 1930s as a result of the disorganising effects of the terror: Schauff, 'Hitler and Stalin in the Spanish Civil War', pp. 10, 17. On the credits see chapter 6 below.

[83] Viñas, 'Gold, the Soviet Union and the Spanish Civil War', pp. 111–12; Howson, *Arms for Spain*, p. 128.

choice of destination other than the Soviet Union or Mexico. In terms of its financial and infrastructural capacity for assisting the Republic, then the Soviet Union's resources were obviously incomparably greater than those of a small country like Mexico. Thus it was that Largo Caballero formally proposed the transfer of Republican gold reserves in a letter dated 15 October which was couriered by the Soviet trade attaché, Stashevsky.[84]

The gold transfer obviously took place in the utmost secrecy – both because it constituted the crux of the Republic's resistance strategy and also because of the hostile propaganda potential it inevitably provided. Negrín, in overseeing the transfer, was implementing Republican government policy, not formulating it himself. Much has been made of his frequent communication with Stashevsky. But both Negrín and Indalecio Prieto (as navy and air minister) were in close consultation with Soviet representatives (in Prieto's case, particularly with ambassador Rosenberg). Nor is this surprising in the circumstances, given the weighty cabinet responsibilities borne by the two Spaniards.[85] In actioning the gold transfer, Negrín was, moreover, acting with the full knowledge and support of the most senior representatives of Republican constitutional and governmental authority – which obviously included President Azaña, premier Largo Caballero and Prieto himself.[86] The mobilisation of the gold also involved senior Republican civil servants, including both of Negrín's deputies in the finance ministry, the left republican Méndez Aspe and Negrín's under-secretary, the socialist Jerónimo Bugeda. As Angel Viñas also indicates, the shipment was witnessed by representatives of the Republican executive, legislature and judiciary – among them the former republican premier José Giral, who was then minister

---

[84] Viñas, *El oro de Moscú*, pp. 166, 288. Thereafter the Republic's negotiations and purchase of war material were channelled (and foreign exchange raised) via banks connected with the associates of the Soviet National Bank (Gosbank) and then charged against the Spanish gold deposits.

[85] Cf. Bolloten, *SCW*, pp. 138–44. But there is nothing conclusive here and Bolloten's perspective is (like that of so many of the memoir sources he cites) heavily coloured by a *post hoc* Cold War reading of Negrín's premiership. Note, however, that Santiago Garcés, a Carabinero captain and colleague of Negrín's who would later head Republican military intelligence (SIM) and who witnessed meetings between Negrín and Stashevsky, was clear about the fact that it was Negrín who set the agenda and controlled the proceedings: Bolloten, *SCW*, p. 909, n. 27.

[86] Graham, *Socialism and War*, pp. 132–3; Viñas, *El oro de Moscú*, pp. 52–5, 112, 251–3, 314, who also points up (pp. 52–3) Azaña's resounding silence on this issue in what are otherwise voluminous memoirs of the civil war period; Vidarte, *Todos fuimos culpables*, pp. 536–9. The lengthy polemic over responsibility and knowledge has to be understood in the context of the post-war battle – both for political leadership of the Republicans in exile and for Allied support to dislodge Franco – in a burgeoning Cold War environment. Prieto's denials are absurd and, quite literally, incredible, as even the most Cold warrior-like of his colleagues (such as Luis Araquistain and Rodolfo Llopis) were aware (see Graham, *Socialism and War*, p. 279, n. 28).

without portfolio in the Largo Caballero cabinet.[87] Moreover, Negrín's punctilliousness in ensuring that each stage of the transfer was carefully documented stands in contrast to Largo's own irritation at these safeguards, underscoring Negrín's own highly developed sense of the great responsibility incumbent on those serving the state.[88]

Negrín had reluctantly accepted the treasury post at Prieto's behest as part of the PSOE national executive's team in the September cabinet.[89] Like the rest of his parliamentary socialist colleagues, he had a very low opinion both of Largo's leadership capacity and of the general political calibre and organisational abilities of the PSOE left which backed him.[90] Negrín thus saw himself as an embattled outpost of orderly government amid the tide of deadly, if well-intentioned, disorganisation and inefficiency in Largo's cabinet. He knew that he held a portfolio which was absolutely crucial to the survival of a Republic struggling under the crushing weight of economic embargo – an 'iceberg' of which the specific diplomacy of Non-Intervention was only the tip. In such circumstances foreign exchange was lifeblood. Negrín was shrewd enough to know that 'the war ends for the Republic the day the last gold peseta does'.[91] Accordingly he saw his function as the husbanding of resources

---

[87] Viñas, *El oro de Moscú*, pp. 250–1 and 'Gold, the Soviet Union and the Spanish Civil War', p. 112. The kinds of fantasy of 'Negrín's treason' recounted in books like *Chantaje a un pueblo* (Madrid: Toro, 1974) by veteran Valencia socialist and Caballero-supporter, Justo Martínez Amutio (see p. 42) are scarcely worth refuting since the evidence is so clearly against them. But Marcelino Pascua's withering assessment rings true – that it was an empty, scandal-mongering book in which the author attempted to substantiate his claims by the old trick of presenting himself as something he never was – part of the inner circle of Republican policy makers: Pascua to Viñas, 13 February 1977 (point 6), *caja* 8 (13), Pascua's personal archive (AHN).

[88] Zugazagoitia, *Guerra y vicisitudes*, p. 301; Gazur, *Secret Assignment. The FBI's KGB General*, p. 87.

[89] Negrín's reluctance in Zugazagoitia, *Guerra y vicisitudes*, pp. 154–5, confirmed by Negrín in his speech to the Cortes, 30 Sept. 1938 (Valencia: Ediciones Españolas, 1938), p. 4, and in the *Epistolario Prieto y Negrín. Puntos de vista sobre el desarrollo y consecuencias de la guerra civil española* (Paris: Imprimerie Nouvelle 1939), p. 40. Also Gabriel Jackson's comments on cabinet meetings, *The Spanish Republic and the Civil War*, p. 366.

[90] The negative attitude was mutual. For Largo's hostility to Negrín and Negrín's sense of party discipline ('estoy con mi partido hasta en sus errores'), see Graham, *Socialism and War*, pp. 93–4.

[91] Cf. 'A state at war, to be victorious, needs a treasury as strong as its army.' Both opinions were voiced by one of Negrín's deputies in the treasury, the socialist Jerónimo Bugeda, at the important PSOE national committee meeting held in July 1937 in Valencia. His report is the closest we come in documentary form to Negrín's own political-economic testimony. Stenographic record of Bugeda's report (pp. 46–7) in the Archivo Histórico de Moscú, Fundación Pablo Iglesias; see also Graham, *Socialism and War*, p. 108. On Bugeda's role in the treasury, see also Negrín's letter of 23 June in *Epistolario Prieto y Negrín*, pp. 41–2; Viñas, *El oro de Moscú*, esp. pp. 211–16. Also correspondence on Soviet credits between M. Pascua and Negrín, 22 June 1937–11 March 1938, AHN/MP, *caja* 2, *carpeta* 2, including the (undated) report (c. mid 1937) 'Ante la perspectiva de una larga lucha', which makes the case for the necessity of such credits because of the international economic isolation of the Republic and the likely prolonged nature of the war.

for a long struggle. In the pursuit of this goal, first in the treasury and later as prime minister, Negrín would implement policies designed to concentrate all economic and political decision-making within the central Republican government. This is the key to Negrín's immense importance during the civil war and to the controversies which surround him to this day.

Economic centralisation brought Negrín immediately into conflict with the Republic's procurement committee (*comisión de compras*) in Paris as he sought to bring all channels of arms purchasing under the direct authority of the treasury and thus under his personal control. The procurement committee was created by Luis Araquistain, Largo's political lieutenant and Republican ambassador to France (until May 1937). Araquistain's objective had been to end the chaos he had encountered in September on arriving in Paris, where scores of individual Spaniards were milling around attempting to purchase arms in the name of the myriad Republican committees which had dispatched them. Indeed, these agents often ended up driving the already high prices higher by bidding against each other – such was the general dislocation and lack of communication as a consequence of state fragmentation after the coup. Araquistain complained that Negrín simply ignored his requests for funds, with the result that potential arms purchases were lost.[92]

The lack of trust between Araquistain and Negrín was in part the product of pre-existing political and personal antagonisms. Their estrangement dated back to the May 1936 cabinet crisis and the socialist left's obstruction of Prieto's bid for the premiership. The left's role in helping block PSOE access to the cabinet was the issue which had finally broken, *de facto*, the organisational unity of the socialist movement,[93] and it was something that Negrín and his parliamentary colleagues held Araquistain primarily to have been responsible for engineering.[94] But while it is true that funds were on numerous occasions

---

[92] Araquistain's requests to Negrín, 9, 25 Feb. 1937 and his sarcastic comments to fellow left socialist Julio Alvarez del Vayo, foreign affairs minister (22 Feb. 1937) in legajo 70/81, Araquistain's correspondence (political documentation) AHN. Rivas Cherif wrote on 26 February 1937 to Azaña (his brother-in-law) that Araquistain was fuming and had proclaimed that Negrín needed shooting, Archivo de Manuel Azaña, *caja* RE 137 (16) (Archivo de Barcelona).

[93] Graham, *Socialism and War*, pp. 34–41 and 'The Eclipse of the Socialist Left 1934–1937', in Lannon and Preston, *Elites and Power in Twentieth-Century Spain*, pp. 134–9; see also chapter 1 above.

[94] Araquistain's letter to Negrín, 2 March 1937, accusing him of sabotaging his ambassadorial work and claiming that this was because he disapproved of Araquistain's having ever been appointed, *legajo* 35, 8–20, Araquistain correspondence (political documentation), AHN. For the pre-war conflict in the PSOE, see chapter 1 above.

not released to the Paris committee, it seems unlikely that Araquistain's accusation of a vendetta against himself has any truth in it, however understandable his irritation at the delays.[95] Structural difficulties and fractured communication channels played a far greater role than Araquistain supposed. But Negrín's 'parsimony' was also reinforced by his awareness of the staggering waste involved in arms procurement via the committees. While the Paris-based one may have constituted an improvement on the state of affairs Araquistain had encountered, the committee was still unwieldy since its membership, like that of Largo Caballero's cabinet, had to reflect the full configuration of the Popular Front. This meant that there was a great deal of internal politicking and dissension which significantly reduced its efficacy, while the problem of the committee duplicating material purchased through other sources remained. In December, in a joint bid by Negrín and Prieto to overcome these problems, the Paris committee would be wound up and its brief transferred to the newly created armament and munitions department (Comisaría de Armamento y Municiones) within Prieto's navy and air ministry.[96]

But we should remember that, ultimately, the inefficiency and waste involved in Republican procurement was a structural consequence of the embargo itself. Non-Intervention ruled out most of the useful government-to-government aid channels (the upcoming Soviet aid notwithstanding). In so doing it obliged the Republic to submit to the vagaries of the arms market and to the dealings of some extremely dubious private intermediaries. We should also remember that the Republic's leading cadres – most of whom were liberal professionals – were ill-equipped to deal with this jungle, having neither adequate contacts nor the requisite technical expertise. The Republican purchasers were made doubly vulnerable to a startling array of middlemen and assorted opportunists, who invariably demanded grossly inflated rates of commission, precisely because of their lack of alternative channels. The fact that Non-Intervention forced the Republic to rely on a series of ever more byzantine routes and procedures to obtain arms and war material also meant cumulative qualitative, as well as quantitative, disadvantages. When the purchased material arrived (which was not always the case), weapons were often found to have incompatible ammunition, or their instructions to be in some obscure foreign language. On other occasions, what arrived bore no relationship to the 'specification'. Moreover, the material invariably lacked any technical or logistical back-up, vastly

95 Viñas, *El oro de Moscú*, pp. 230–6.   96 Ibid., p. 231.

reducing its utility. To add insult to injury, the ratchet effect produced by Non-Intervention – which had effectively created a black market in arms – meant that these substandard goods habitually cost the Republic hugely 'over the odds'. The haemorrhaging of time and money that Non-Intervention inflicted at the start of the war, solely upon the Republic, was absolutely devastating.[97] Moreover, nor would Soviet assistance release the Republic from the obligation of paying these crippling prices *for the duration of the war.* For much of that assistance came not through the supplying of domestically produced armaments (which though good were also very expensive), but through Soviet procurement of arms for the Republic on the international market – where, thanks to Non-Intervention, black-market prices obtained just the same.

It is in this context that we have to understand Negrín's ongoing battle to maximise foreign exchange and to establish a central government monopoly on the deployment of state economic resources. This was not, however, a politically neutral agenda. Through treasury centralisation policies Negrín was seeking to re-establish an orthodox capitalist economic order in Republican Spain. He began by overhauling the structure and technical working of the treasury itself, although there was a continuity of personnel – the ministry staff being chiefly republican technocrats and senior state functionaries.[98] From the start, Negrín's aims would bring him into conflict with union and neighbourhood committees over control of resources, supply policy and the thorny question of requisitioning.[99] And the same objectives would later mean that he clashed with a variety of regional and sectoral institutions – radical/proletarian, but *also* bourgeois – whose economic and political prerogatives challenged the realisation of Negrín's goal and ideal: the reconstruction of the central liberal state.

This preference for state building had been evident in Negrín long before his arrival at the treasury in September 1936. Believing as he did in the idea of a 'rational' or 'guardian' state, Negrín had never been interested in parliament as an oratorical arena which derived from Mediterranean-clientelist practice. From the beginning, when Negrín had first been elected to the Republican Cortes in 1931, he had committed

[97] The complex history of Republican arms purchasing under the vicious conditions of Non-Intervention is unravelled in Gerald Howson's excellent study, *Arms for Spain.* See also his *Aircraft of the Spanish Civil War* (London:Putnam Aeronautical Books, 1990), which, in spite of its specialist format, has a considerable amount on the effects of Non-Intervention embedded within it.
[98] Names and details in F. Vázquez Ocaña, *Pasión y muerte de la segunda República española* (n.p.: Editorial Norte, (1940?)), p. 61; Viñas, *El oro de Moscú*, pp. 81, 210–18.
[99] Vázquez Ocaña, *Pasión y muerte*, p. 59.

himself to the technical, behind-the-scenes work in parliamentary committee. (He was a member of the treasury budgets committee.) In terms of both Negrín's personality and political objectives, even then he was more concerned with renovating, with establishing underlying structures in order to make things work.[100]

It was Negrín's experience in the very first stages of the post-coup conflict which galvanised his understanding of the need to concentrate political and military as well as economic authority. When not engaged directly, along with his parliamentary socialist colleagues, in the task of holding together the remnants of government fabric from the presidential office or navy and air ministry in Madrid, Negrín would often hitch a ride in a militia lorry in order to observe at first hand the Republican military defence on the Guadarrama sierra, north of the city, often in far from secure conditions.[101] From these trips he returned unequivocally convinced of the need to galvanise Republican defences by means of a thoroughgoing programme of militarisation.

An even stronger drive to state building in Negrín, however, came in response to the explosion of popular violence detonated by the military rising. The *paseos* had posed a serious dilemma for Negrín, even leading him to question for a time the validity of his commitment to the Republican cause.[102] What confirmed that commitment was, first, Negrín's awareness of the rebels' dependence on large-scale foreign fascist assistance both to launch and to fight the war and, second, a growing realisation that the rebels were committing genocide.[103] But the eradication of the *paseos* in Republican territory remained for him the essential precondition of constructing a legitimate state/political order.[104]

---

[100] Even later, as wartime premier, Negrín would never be very 'visible'. There are very few photographs of him – at any stage in his life – since he actively discouraged even his children from taking them: Jackson, *The Spanish Republic and the Civil War*, p. 392; Vázquez Ocaña, *Pasión y muerte*, pp. 78–80. He also refused to sit for Jo Davidson, the American artist who sculpted many leading Republican figures during the war: C. de la Mora, *In Place of Splendor*, p. 366. Even the grave in which Negrín was buried in November 1956 in Père Lachaise (Paris) bore no name. Interestingly, Negrín's future military opposite number, Vicente Rojo, displayed similar traits: Martínez Paricio, *Los papeles del general Rojo*, p. 16.

[101] Zugazagoitia, *Guerra y vicisitudes*, pp. 122–3; Ansó, *Yo fui ministro de Negrín*, pp. 140, 151; also M. Pascua, cited in S. Alvarez, *Negrín (Documentos)*, p. 280.

[102] Negrín to the French ambassador Morel, J. Marichal, *El intelectual y la política* (Madrid: CSIC, 1990), p. 100.

[103] For a discussion of rebel violence, see chapter 2 above. Negrín refers (via Bugeda) to the threat of Spain's economic colonisation by Germany and Italy in the economic report to the PSOE National Committee, July 1937. This then becomes a major plank of Negrín's public campaign to maintain popular resistance: see chapter 6 below.

[104] Cf. Negrín's reported comments in early September 1936 on the importance of constitutionality to the Republic, 'No tenemos, no podemos tener otra divisa de guerra' ('we simply cannot allow any "war currency" but this'), Ansó, *Yo fui ministro de Negrín*, p. 251.

The killings of detained rightists in Madrid's Model Prison on 23 August brought the situation to crisis point. More than any other single incident, the prison killings have come to symbolise the loss of state control in Republican territory. President Azaña was so devastated by the events, which for him vitiated the very essence of the Republican cause, that he considered resigning.[105] But even without his departure the incident did significant damage to the Republic's standing internationally – and precisely in the western democracies whose support was so desperately being courted.

In an attempt both to limit the political damage and to channel popular anger, the Republic immediately set up the Popular Courts (Tribunales Populares) to try those accused of supporting the rebellion.[106] Composed of a jury of representatives from all the Popular Front parties and presided over by a professional judge, assisted by two others, these tribunals were designed to put an end to the period of *paseos* and summary 'justice'. Gradually over a period of months these would indeed subside.[107] But it was an uphill struggle. The coup had capsized the judiciary as it had every other instrument of state action, and there was a resulting shortage of career judges and magistrates. Nevertheless, the popular court system constituted the first step in returning to the state its defining function and basis of power – a monopoly on 'legitimate violence'. While the juries found for or against the defendant, the judges were responsible for sentencing. But even though harsh sentences were passed, including capital sentences, most of those brought before the Popular Courts escaped with their lives.[108] Punishment most frequently took the form of social disciplining via the prison system (which included work camps where prisoners were deployed in fortification and other war-related work[109]). Nor was it government policy that drove the capital sentences passed in the Popular Courts. This would change

---

[105] Among the dead was his old colleague, the founder of the Reformist Party, Melquíades Alvarez. Fraser, *Blood of Spain*, p. 176.

[106] A. Reig Tapia, *Violencia y terror. Estudios sobre la guerra civil española* (Madrid: Akal 1990), p. 121; 'Justicia republicana', in *Justicia en guerra (Jornadas sobre la administración de justicia durante la guerra civil española: instituciones y fuentes documentales)* (Salamanca, 26–8 November 1987) (Madrid: Ministerio de Cultura, 1990), pp. 19–245; G. Sánchez Recio, *Justicia y guerra en España. Los Tribunales Populares (1936–1939)* (Alicante: Instituto de Cultura 'Juan Gil-Albert', 1991); Fraser, *Blood of Spain*, pp. 177–8. For the equivalent within the system of military justice, see Alpert, *El ejército republicano*, pp. 213–14.

[107] Between 50 and 70 per cent of the civilians who died violently in the Republican zone did so during the summer of 1936: Juliá *et al.*, *Víctimas de la guerra civil*.

[108] Julián Casanova gives an overview of the operation of the courts in various areas, ibid., pp. 161–8.

[109] Sánchez Recio, *Justicia y guerra en España*, pp. 176–9; (same author) 'Justicia republicana', pp. 30–6; Aróstegui and Martínez, *La Junta de Defensa*, p. 241.

later in the war in other sorts of Republican courts[110] as deteriorating internal conditions and external circumstances led to an increase in fifth column activity and other sorts of individual behaviour harmful to the war effort. But in the Popular Courts, in addition to jury-led motives of popular retribution, it also seems probable that harsh sentences were sometimes the result of the personal agendas of individual judges – either because they feared for their own lives or, in some cases, in order deliberately to accelerate the discrediting of the Republic on a public-order ticket.[111] Although we still lack a comparative analysis of rebel and Republican penal policy, it is clear that there was no equivalent in Republican Spain of the mass regime-sanctioned killing that occurred throughout the rebel zone. Nevertheless, the Republic did pass (and implement) death sentences from the time of the Popular Courts onwards, which reversed the regime's pre-war abolition of the death penalty in the civil code.[112]

Although this was a retrograde step in humanitarian terms, not all liberals in the Republican camp were equally disturbed by the restitution of the death penalty. For Negrín, 'legitimate violence' had always included the state's recourse to capital punishment for exceptional crimes which threatened its stability. For example, in 1932 Negrín had argued strongly that the Republic was too weak to do other than execute the military ringleaders of the failed August coup attempt.[113] (These included the man who became the original titular head of the July 1936 rising, General José Sanjurjo, then leader of the Civil Guard.) For Negrín, as a liberal, legitimacy in this context resided in the fact that violence as a facet of state power was not arbitrary but limited by constitutional law subject to revision by collective consent.

By this criterion, the 'popular justice' of the irregular patrols was considered to be entirely beyond the pale because it was bound by no due process. As a result, from mid September 1936 the Republican government promulgated a series of measures intended ultimately to disarm and disband all non-state police forces operating on the civilian front. As a first step, the Milicias de Vigilancia were set up[114] to replace the myriad and multi-form 'patrols' which had emerged during the July days.

---

[110] See chapter 6 below for summary forms of justice in the workings of the Tribunales de Guardia and the Tribunales de Espionaje y Alta Traición.

[111] Fraser, *Blood of Spain*, p. 178.

[112] The Republic had abolished the death penalty in the civil code in 1932.

[113] Vidarte, *Todos fuimos culpables*, vol. 1, p. 213.

[114] *Gaceta de la República*, 17 Sept. 1936. In theory these militias (Milicias de Vigilancia de Retaguardia (MIVR)) were also constituted to reflect the membership of the Popular Front alliance.

These patrols, like some of the militia columns discussed earlier, had a reputation for violence and looting which terrified the urban and rural smallholding middle classes of Republican Spain – even those who had no *direct* experience of the patrols. Indeed, the insidious threat of the patrols[115] was probably more corrosive over time than more dramatic incidents such as prison massacres and *sacas* – even though these had more international impact. The lack of any external control on the patrols facilitated their infiltration by numerous undesirables including crypto-rebels bent on mayhem to discredit the Republic, as well as a variety of lumpen elements, some of whom had been released when the prisons emptied in the wake of the rising.[116] While the Milicias de Vigilancia represented a certain concentration of coercive force in a quasi-governmental direction, the forms of repression for which they were responsible (including executions) were highly contingent, constitutionally dubious and no doubt sometimes driven by particularist political agendas.[117] This situation made it easier for the Republican government to avoid any debate about radical, innovatory forms of justice, allowing it to present full judicial and police normalisation as a purely humanitarian campaign against the arbitrary abuse of power which would be equally beneficial to all citizens.

The fact that one of the other consequences of the rebellion had been an intensification of inter-union violence between sectors of the CNT and UGT bases also reinforced the government's case here.[118] Even though the meanings of this intra-union violence were somewhat different from that practised by patrols on shopkeepers and smallholders, its very occurrence allowed the state to claim that the order it sought to reconstruct was 'class-blind'. In October the government began its attempt to remove weapons from the hands of private citizenry, which, in theory, included both the committees and workers' patrols.[119] In reality, little happened. Many of the municipal authorities that were supposed to

---

[115] Fraser, *Blood of Spain*, p. 177.

[116] Vidarte, *Todos fuimos culpables*, vol. 2, p. 531. See chapter 2 above for similar problems affecting some militia columns.

[117] For the important case of Madrid, see I. Gibson, *Paracuellos cómo fue* (Barcelona: Argos Vergara, 1983), pp. 42, 224–5.

[118] For a discussion of this intra-union violence in terms both of antagonistic social constituencies of workers and specific organisational rivalries, see chapters 1 and 2 above. For the way in which UGT–CNT clashes – above all in Barcelona – were about conflicts between middling- and working-class sectors (or white- and blue-collar workers), see chapters 4 and 5 below.

[119] Decree of 27 October 1936 required the handing over to the municipal authorities of all 'long arms' (i.e. rifles and machine guns): Morrow, *Revolution and Counter-Revolution in Spain*, p. 58.

drive the process scarcely existed. Moreover, the memory of the military rising (frequently seconded by sectors of the police forces) meant that there was significant worker resistance to police normalisation. It was to be a very slow process, above all in Barcelona, where social resistance was greatest.[120] Nevertheless, the October decree established an important precedent for subsequent state action.

For many in positions of Republican authority, however, not only were the patrols and popular justice questionable, but so were the myriad party and union committees criss-crossing Republican territory. Largo Caballero himself came, like many veteran union leaders in the UGT and the CNT, to adopt the pragmatic view that unless the fragmentation of military, economic and political power was corrected, the Republic would never be in a position to hold its own against the rebels and their backers. It is in these terms that we can explain both his public support for militarisation (the September and October decrees providing for the formation of regular regiments), his implementation during October of decrees limiting the scope of industrial and agrarian collectivisation[121] and, in the same month, the formal (if often not yet *de facto*) re-establishment of municipal authorities. But other ministers – and most notably Negrín – were opposed to the popular committees *on principle* because they were the antithesis of liberal constitutional order. Whether the committees had proved themselves good, bad or indifferent at coping in the period of the Republic's emergency defence was ultimately beside the point, since their very existence was an affront to governmental legitimacy and authority.

Although the months of September and October were a time of continuing political contradiction and confusion, in retrospect we have to understand them as a necessary and unavoidable stage in the slow recuperation of a liberal Republican order. While we should not discount humanitarian motives, Republican government measures obeyed a particular political logic. They were aimed above all at reassuring middling social constituencies whose confidence was crucial to the restitution of a functional level of cohesiveness on the Republican home front. Without this there could be neither an adequate level of domestic political support for the Republic nor the practical mobilisation of human resources imperative for the war effort. But for all their clear intent, government initiatives were as yet extremely 'weak' in practice. For all Negrín's iron

---

[120] See chapters 4 and 5 below.
[121] For more on industrial and agrarian collectivisation, see chapters 4 and 5 below.

resolve, there was still a fundamental lack of working structures and personnel to enact them. The government's authority continued to suffer the serious damage and dislocation deriving from the rebellion. Moreover, the military crisis rapidly supervening on the Madrid front was about to deal it a further substantial blow.

By the end of October 1936 the rebels were on the outskirts of Madrid. This was somewhat later than it might have been owing to Franco's earlier detour to Toledo to relieve the rebels holding out in the Alcázar (a triumph which greatly consolidated his own leadership position[122]). This delay gave the Republicans vital time to begin organising the city's defences. Soviet aircraft and tanks made their first, crucial appearance on the central front (24 October), to wild popular enthusiasm. But the mobilisation for civil defence was slow and knowledge of its real requirements lacking. The Republic's military situation remained critical. In line with cabinet guidelines, the press had previously been largely triumphalist, but this was changing in Madrid and, anyway, the unpalatable reality was increasingly common knowledge.[123] In this context, on 4 November Largo Caballero announced the entry into his government of four members of the CNT.[124] The result was an unwieldy cabinet of eighteen,[125] no less internally fragmented than before. But in other important ways the inclusion of the CNT was a positive sign. The military crisis had forced the realisation that – notwithstanding British and French government opinion or President Azaña's personal opposition[126] – a viable Republican war effort depended upon full-scale worker mobilisation and this, in turn, required bringing the CNT fully on board. Although the CNT had four titular cabinet portfolios, these really amounted to two politically significant posts: the moderate syndicalist Juan Peiró and his colleague Juan López took over industry and trade between them,[127] while the strong man of the Catalan FAI, Juan García Oliver, was given the justice

[122] Preston, *Franco*, pp. 169–80. The rebels conquered Toledo on 28 September.

[123] Aróstegui and Martínez, *La Junta de Defensa*, p. 40: on press triumphalism, see Zugazagoitia, *Guerra y vicisitudes*, pp. 173–5 and G. Woolsey, *Malaga Burning* (Paris, Reston: Pythia Press, 1998), p. 51 (first edition entitled *Death's Other Kingdom* (London: Longmans, Green & Co., 1939)).

[124] For the best account of the prior negotiations both inside the CNT and between it and the government, see Lorenzo, *Los anarquistas españoles y el poder*, pp. 177–90. Also, Casanova, *De la calle al frente*, pp. 181–6. For a full discussion of the implications for the CNT of entry to government, see chapter 4 below.

[125] For a full list see Bolloten, *SCW*, p. 203.   [126] Azaña, *Obras completas*, vol. 4, p. 592.

[127] For the pre-war syndicalist–radical anarchist division, see chapter 1 above. For its impact during the war, see chapters 4 and 5 below. Peiró was one of those handed back to Franco by Vichy France. He was executed in 1942. See his collected writings, *Escrits 1917–1939*, ed. P. Gabriel (Barcelona: Edicions 62, 1975) and a smaller pre-war selection in *Trayectoria de la CNT (Sindicalismo y anarquismo)* (Madrid: Ediciones Júcar, 1979).

portfolio.[128] His fellow FAI member, Federica Montseny, daughter of the anarchist intellectuals Federico Urales and Soledad Gustavo, became health minister and thus the first woman in Europe since Alexandra Kollontai to occupy a ministerial post of cabinet rank. It seems likely that the appointment of a CNT minister to the justice portfolio was made with the intention of reining in the patrols, thus bolstering government authority while tying the CNT's credibility to this most sensitive of tasks. Above all, however, the CNT's presence in government was intended to reduce – or at least equally apportion – the political fall-out as the government abandoned Madrid.[129]

Although the capital was not crucial to the military prosecution of the war, its loss would mean a major and unaffordable blow to the Republic's already precarious legitimacy both in the eyes of its own population but even more importantly with the very political establishments in Britain and France whose support the regime was so desperately seeking. (Thus Largo's own view of Madrid as little more than a 'stomach' was rather too reductive.[130]) Indeed, the rebels' eagerness to conquer Madrid sprang precisely from an understanding of its political significance. Nevertheless, on 6 November the Republican government took the decision to leave because virtually no one believed the capital could be held. The under-secretary of war, General Asensio, had come to be highly pessimistic, which doubtless explains why the prime minister chose this moment to offer the combined defence portfolio to his rival Indalecio Prieto. Unsurprisingly, Prieto refused, seeing it as an attempt to saddle him with the defeat.[131] In the circumstances, a strategic case could be made for government departure from the capital,[132] but the secret and rushed manner in which this occurred on 6 November created an overwhelming impression of panicked flight. The political damage done to Republican government credibility – and the PSOE's in particular – would prove considerable. Others too paid the political price. It cost the CNT's *éminence grise* and chief architect of its ministerial participation,

---

[128] The choice of ministerial incumbents in all cases was the CNT's own – and concretely Horacio Prieto's as general secretary.

[129] This is conveyed very well in J. García Oliver, *El eco de los pasos* (Paris: Ruedo Ibérico, 1978), pp. 303–4.

[130] Aróstegui and Martínez, *La Junta de Defensa*, p. 66.

[131] Zugazagoitia, *Guerra y vicisitudes*, p. 178.

[132] For example, that it would be militarily more efficient to let Madrid go, thereby gaining more time to build up the new Republican army under construction on the centre front ('en tierras manchegas'). See Koltsov, *Diario de la guerra española*, p. 191, who makes it clear that this view originates with Asensio; Salas Larrazábal, *Historia del ejército popular de la República*, vol. 1, p. 545.

Horacio Prieto, his post as general secretary. Whether or not he directly advised the CNT ministers to accept the government's departure remains unclear. But the CNT ministers must themselves have felt under great pressure to accept government discipline given what was at stake. Horacio Prieto nevertheless stepped down to appease those in the CNT who believed that it should have abandoned the government rather than acquiesce.[133]

In the event, the government relocated to Valencia rather than to Barcelona, where President Azaña had taken up residence towards the end of October.[134] The choice of Valencia seems largely to have been decided personally by Largo Caballero subsequent to the cabinet meeting of 6 November, which approved – somewhat stormily – the Madrid departure. No official explanation was ever given for the choice, and contemporary commentators offer us little clear information.[135] The key could very well lie in the notorious treatment to which several government ministers (though not Largo himself) were subjected just outside Madrid by militiamen belonging to the del Rosal column. Its checkpoint at Tarancón refused to let them pass, threatening them with execution as cowards for abandoning Madrid.[136] The ministers in question (including Julio Alvarez del Vayo, the PCE's Jesus Hernández and the CNT's Peiró and López) were forced to retreat, finding their way out to Valencia by the back roads instead. Not only was this deeply humiliating for the individuals concerned, but it also served as a brutal reminder of the fragility of Republican government authority beyond the limits of the capital. Nor would it be the last occasion on which PCE leaders were obstructed by anarchist checkpoints as they went about government business.[137]

---

[133] F. Montseny, *Mis primeros cuarenta años* (Barcelona: Plaza y Janés, 1987), pp. 105–6; Peirats, *La CNT en la revolución española*, vol. 1, pp. 219–21; Lorenzo, *Los anarquistas españoles y el poder*, pp. 177–206. Lorenzo claims (p. 206) that the CNT ministers accepted the government's departure without consulting Prieto. García Oliver says that Prieto was consulted. This discrepancy is discussed by Aróstegui and Martínez (*La Junta de Defensa*, pp. 59–60), but they draw no conclusion. In spite of Prieto's resignation, he continued to be a key figure in the political evolution of the anarchosyndicalist organisation during the war: see chapters 4 and 5 below. (The new secretary was Mariano R. Vázquez: Casanova, *De la calle al frente*, pp. 186–7.)

[134] For Azaña's departure from Madrid, see his *Apuntes de Memoria*, pp. 79–83.

[135] A summary in Aróstegui and Martínez, *La Junta de Defensa*, pp. 57–61, which also indicates how the manipulation of the issue in subsequent political disputes makes it even harder to clarify the original decision.

[136] Zugazagoitia, *Guerra y vicisitudes*, pp. 180–1; Vidarte, *Todos fuimos culpables*, vol. 2, p. 531; Bolloten, *SCW*, p. 206; Carrillo, *Memorias*, p. 190. A full résumé of memoir sources is in Aróstegui and Martínez, *La Junta de Defensa*, pp. 60–1.

[137] See Aróstegiu and Martínez, *La Junta de Defensa*, pp. 236–8 for the cases of Mije and Pablo Yagüe; Gibson, *Paracuellos*, pp. 207–8. Later on also Pasionaria and others were prevented by an anarchist frontier committee from crossing the Catalan border into France (in spite of carrying passports), where they were due to embark on a propaganda and aid-seeking tour.

In these terms, then, Barcelona represented a veritable lion's cage – the heartland of radical anarcho-syndicalism and hostile territory *par excellence* where the battle against governmental authority was being waged more fiercely than anywhere else. The Madrid government would, moreover, be doubly a target: not only was it a government, but it was the *central* government and as such symbolised Castile's historical controlling pretensions. The very fact that the Catalan government (Generalitat) was at this stage prepared to accept its presence offers some indication of the parlous state of its own political authority in Catalonia in the early months of the war. Valencia, on the other hand, also offered the government a base deep in the home front,[138] but one where the CNT moderates (*treintistas*) were strong and thus the anarcho-syndicalists – at least at leadership level – would be significantly less unfriendly.

Meanwhile, in Madrid, rumours of the government's departure spread like wild fire, eliciting responses of popular anger and consternation, but also of some cynicism and fatalism. These latter feelings were intensified by the evident paralysis of government functions in the city: once the cabinet had gone, ministerial buildings emptied rapidly as terrified civil servants packed their bags. Even those not set upon immediate departure seemed locked into a panic-induced torpor.[139] The mood amongst those charged with Madrid's defence was one of quiet desperation. Largo Caballero had left the task in the hands of General José Miaja, appointed for the purpose as commander of the Madrid military area. He had instructions to liaise with General Sebastian Pozas, the new commander-in-chief of the centre army, and to establish a defence council. In the precipitousness of the government's departure the sealed written orders to Miaja and Pozas became mixed up and each initially received the other's envelope.[140] This chaos reinforced the general feeling that Miaja was being sacrificed to a hopeless task – as did the otherwise inexplicable instruction (ignored by Miaja) not to open his envelope until 6 o'clock on the following morning of 7 November. Indeed, these orders from the government specified guidelines for troop withdrawals on the fall of the city but made no mention of defence provisions.[141] The government

---

[138] Valencia was an oasis, with plentiful food in the early months of war – a marvel to the hungry eyes of refugees from Madrid: Abella, *La vida cotidiana*, pp. 134, 160–2.

[139] Zugazagoitia, *Guerra y vicisitudes*, pp. 182–3.

[140] The accusation that this was a deliberate act of sabotage by Asensio has no real basis, although it is repeated in the memoirs of those hostile to Asensio such as Santiago Carrillo and Politburo member and ex-minister Jesús Hernández. Aróstegui and Martínez, *La Junta de Defensa*, p. 64.

[141] A. López Fernández, *Defensa de Madrid* (Mexico: Editorial A. P. Márquez, 1945), pp. 147–50; Aróstegui and Martínez, *La Junta de Defensa*, p. 72. A copy of Miaja's orders is in Rojo, *Así fue la defensa de Madrid*, pp. 255–6.

even gave orders that the anti-aircraft guns be removed to Valencia.[142] Miaja himself certainly believed that Largo Caballero – and thus really General Asensio – had chosen him to implement the surrender of Madrid precisely because they saw him as expendable.[143] Since Miaja's failure to recapture Cordoba in August – a failure which reinforced the intense popular distrust of the professional military in general[144] – his reputation had been under something of a cloud. In September he returned to command troops in the Valencia region, where he came up against the reality of state collapse. Military structures were in disarray, and soldiers and police were being directed by a plethora of party and union committees – nominally under the authority of the Popular Executive Committee. Miaja had to contend not only with his personal aversion to this situation but also with the hostility which greeted him. The general had already been outspoken about his lack of faith in the Republic's ability to resist when he declined to continue as defence minister in Giral's August cabinet, at the same time opposing the arming of the popular militia.[145] Moreover, it seems very probable that, before the war, he was a member of the conservative officers' association, the UME (Unión Militar Española), and his wife and children were still in the rebel zone.[146] Incidents of sabotage by officers on the Madrid front during October[147] further increased popular suspicions, making them an ever-present and sapping occupational hazard for all those professional officers serving the Republic.

It was thus in this context of personal and professional alienation, abandoned, so it seemed, by almost the entirety of the Republican political class, and with no concrete defence plan in place, that Miaja and his exiguous military personnel faced an organisational challenge of staggering dimensions: to build both the military and civil defence of Madrid while also administering the city, feeding its refugee-swelled population and tackling the running sore of intimidatory violence and killing by self-appointed patrols and other uncontrollable elements, including

---

[142] Aróstegui and Martínez, *La Junta de Defensa*, p. 60; Santiago Carrillo interviewed in Gibson, *Paracuellos*, p. 202.

[143] For a resumé of the available memoir sources and an extremely sharp assessment of Miaja's situation, see Aróstegui and Martínez, *La Junta de Defensa*, pp. 70–2; General Pozas also recalled Miaja's rage over this in an interview with B. Bolloten (Mexico, 1939), *SCW*, p. 285.

[144] Zugazagoitia, *Guerra y vicisitudes*, p. 110.

[145] López Fernández, *Defensa de Madrid*, pp. 63, 65. (Pozas, on the other hand, accepted its necessity.)

[146] The evidence for UME membership is summarised in Aróstegui and Martínez, *La Junta de Defensa*, pp. 68–9 and Bolloten, *SCW*, p. 291. After five months in a rebel gaol Miaja's family was freed in a prisoner exchange.

[147] Cox, *Defence of Madrid*, p. 29.

crypto-rebels. Miaja was, moreover, facing these demands with fragmented and debilitated state agencies and a shortage of civilian personnel.[148] In such circumstances, it is, then, unsurprising that he accepted with alacrity the organisational support and man and woman power which the Spanish Communist Party offered.

The PCE had resisted the government's evacuation longest, giving in only when it became clear that further opposition risked breaking up the cabinet.[149] Individual PCE leaders may have had private doubts about the feasibility of defending Madrid, but Comintern discipline determined that the party as a collective entity would concentrate its organisational efforts and best leadership cadres in the capital. The key importance of PCE support for Miaja was prefigured in the pressing demands facing him on the night of 6 November: the military defence, maintaining calm amongst the civilian population and containing the fifth column. Miaja immediately consulted Major Vicente Rojo, who was to act as his chief of staff. Rojo was a practising Catholic, but he had a pre-war reputation in the army as a liberal and educated moderniser. Throughout November Rojo would be, from behind the scenes, the real architect of Madrid's military defence: an achievement which would take him on to be probably the single most important military figure inside the Republic and from May 1937 chief of its general staff.[150] On the Madrid front military authority lay with Rojo and his officers who were directly responsible to Miaja. The general also contacted and briefed all the political forces that had militia active on the Madrid front. Among these briefings the most crucial was with Mije, Santiago Carrillo and José Cazorla, the latter two leaders of the youth organisation, JSU.[151] From the very start

---

[148] While Aróstegui and Martínez's very thorough analysis suggests that there were still basic governmental structures in place, these still needed reactivating and staffing: *La Junta de Defensa*, pp. 62–3.

[149] The official PCE history of the war simply refers to cabinet unanimity in the decision to leave Madrid, *Guerra y revolución en España*, vol. 2, pp. 140–1. There is little specific on the PCE ministers' interventions in memoir accounts by their cabinet colleagues, but Largo quite correctly saw the PCE suggestion that the government's departure be publicised *beforehand* as an implicit blocking tactic: 'Notas históricas de la guerra en España 1917–1940' (Ms, Fundación Pablo Iglesias, Madrid), p. 482. The PCE also leaked news of the government's departure in an attempt to galvanise the formation of immediate defence measures.

[150] Rojo's function in Madrid was very much an anonymous one until an article by the *Pravda* correspondent Koltsov in the PSOE newspaper *El Socialista* (21 Dec. 1936) drew attention to his key role: Aróstegui and Martínez, *La Junta de Defensa*, p. 77; Martínez Paricio, *Los papeles del general Rojo*, pp. 86–7; see also Koltsov's diary entry for 10 Nov. 1936, *Diario de la guerra española*, p. 236; also C. Blanco Escolá, *Franco y Rojo. Dos generales para dos Españas* (Barcelona: Editorial Labor, 1993). For more on Rojo see chapter 6 below.

[151] This preceded a further meeting on 7 November with both Mije and the socialist deputy and commissar general, Crescenciano Bilbao. See Aróstegui and Martínez, *La Junta de Defensa*,

the communists had argued strongly and consistently for militarisation and had constructed the Fifth Regiment as an exemplar. The party had an important war commissar in Mije and experienced military commanders such as Juan Modesto, and had long demonstrated its general support for professional army officers in the difficult circumstances of the times. It is clear that the party endorsed the principle of separating military and civil functions in the defence of Madrid. The PCE's uncompromising line on public order was also crucial to Miaja. As elsewhere, this appealed to those socially conservative middling sectors whom otherwise the Republic ran the risk of permanently disaffecting. But even more importantly, given Madrid's position on the front line with the enemy at the gates, a tough public-order policy was a crucial weapon in the battle to neutralise an acutely effective and dangerous fifth column that had been finding it easy to pass military and political intelligence to the enemy on the perimeter.[152] Thus the core responsibilities given to the communists on the still-to-be-configured Defence Council reflected Miaja's belief that they would deliver what he needed.

The Defence Council was formally constituted on the evening of 7 November. At this meeting the component organisations of the Popular Front nominated their own representatives for the portfolios allocated to them by Miaja as a result of his consultations during the previous twenty-four hours. Under the presidency of Miaja, the PCE had war, public order (Carrillo) and – through the UGT incumbent – supply. Mije's function in war was essentially that of coordinating Council resources in order to meet Miaja's orders and requirements for the military defence. The supply portfolio went to the communist Pablo Yagüe of the Madrid UGT's bakers' and confectioners' union (Artes Blancas). Here the party's known preference for centralisation and the reconstruction of government control in the economic sphere must certainly have recommended itself to Miaja after his own experience of fragmented committee power in Valencia. The Madrid CNT (including Libertarian Youth) was allocated war industries and information, while the republican groups Republican Union and Republican Left covered finance and communications respectively. Ex-CNT moderate Angel Pestaña's tiny Syndicalist Party was responsible for evacuation, and the PSOE for the Council's administrative post (Secretariado).[153] Thus constituted, the Council would run

---

pp. 66–8 and pp. 75–9 for the complex set of meetings and consultations over the period 6–7 November before the Council was formally constituted.

[152] See Council minutes, ibid., p. 447.

[153] For a full breakdown of Council membership, see ibid., pp. 76–7.

the capital and organise its civil defence throughout November – thereby overseeing not only the first but also the most intense process of civil mobilisation seen in the Republican zone during the war. References abound to the extraordinary atmosphere of exhaustion and elation in Madrid during November 1936 – with the seventh as the day of 'iron in the soul'. It was an experience which went deep, many participants remembering those days as the most intense experience of their lives.[154] The days of urgency in Madrid generated a high political profile for the Council which would bring it rapidly into mounting conflict with the Valencia government, whose own reconstructing authority had been set back by its departure. Matters were made worse by the fact that the government, convinced that the Council would not survive, had neglected to specify its own understanding of the Council's political role. The ensuing conflict was multifaceted, as we shall see. It stemmed from the power fragmentation that still plagued the Republic. But unlike Barcelona or even Bilbao, 'Madrid' did not in any real sense represent a separate or antagonistic political project to that of the Republican government in Valencia.

General Miaja's function at the head of the Council was essentially a symbolic one. He was not a gifted military strategist or technician. (Indeed, his expendability was part of the reason why he had been chosen.) Nor was Miaja possessed of particular administrative talent. But he turned out to be a reasonably good manager of people and he had the good fortune to have allocated, and to choose for himself, some gifted and efficient collaborators. On the military side, he could rely on the vision and abilities of Vicente Rojo. Miaja's political collaborators were, for reasons already explained, often communists. But this was not invariably so: his *aide-de-camp* was a *cenetista*. Nor was Miaja blind to the party political/clientelist implications of his strong reliance on PCE cadres.[155] The fact that Miaja took the party card proffered by the PCE tells us little more than that political membership was vital in a traumatised Republican polity otherwise lacking adequate or credible organic structures.[156] As Miaja himself commented, faux-naively, in November to the Italian socialist leader, Pietro Nenni, 'I'm further to the left than you. You're in

---

[154] This is remarkable in most memoirs, but see the best example in Margarita Nelken's preface to López Fernández, *Defensa de Madrid*.

[155] R. Gullón, 'Justice et guerre civil: souvenir d'un procureur', in C. Serrano (ed.), *Madrid 1936– 1939. Un peuple en résistance ou l'épopée ambiguë* (Paris: Editions Autrement, 1991), p. 235.

[156] Miaja collected party and unions cards in the spirit of the true stamp collector, according to R. Malinovski, *Bajo la bandera de la República* (Moscow, 1975), cited in C. Zaragoza, *Ejército popular y militares de la República 1936–1939* (Barcelona: Planeta, 1983), p. 278. (The (rare) Malinovski volume is a collection of testimonies by the most important of the Soviet advisers who served in Republican Spain.)

the Second International, but, me, I'm a member of the Third – even though I'm a political illiterate!'[157] In fact, Miaja was an old-style military conservative who came to keep a faith of sorts with the wartime Republic – even though he had once sworn to Azaña (when the latter was war minister in 1933) that there was nothing for it but to shoot the socialists.[158] But Miaja never acquired much grasp of the liberal democratic principles underlying the Republican war effort: witness his half-joking – but nevertheless illuminating – retrospective comments that a Republican victory could potentially have made a political career for him akin to Franco's. Santiago Carrillo would also later claim that in 1937 Miaja even suggested it would be no bad thing for front-line morale if the PCE 'took things in hand' and put an end to the internal political 'wrangling' in the Republican government – an opinion which rings true because it reflects the underlying cultural comfort which many army officers derived from democratic centralist discipline.[159]

Although many have passed judgement on Miaja's (very real) military and political limitations – his 'provincialness' – he was shrewd enough to understand that as head of the Council his key function was to navigate and adjudicate as best he could its internal organisational political conflicts in order to deliver the wherewithal of military and civil defence. Miaja's vanity was certainly titillated by the popular acclamation accorded him as the 'hero of Madrid' by thousands of ordinary *madrileños* – especially women. (Miaja's commitment to the Republic was, like Rojo's – who may also have had pre-war ties with the UME[160] – in a sense 'made' by his experience of popular resistance in Madrid.[161])

[157] P. Nenni, *La guerra de España* (Italy, 1958; 4th Spanish edn, Mexico: Ediciones Era, 1975), p. 124.

[158] Azaña, *Obras completas*, vol. 4, p. 589.

[159] The (unsourced) post-war comments are cited in Cortada, *Dictionary of the Spanish Civil War* and Carrillo's anecdote in his *Memorias*, p. 246; Azaña also transmits this current of opinion in *Obras completas*, vol. 4, p. 603. Miaja's personality and abilities have always excited strong opinions for and against, and all have to be understood in the context of their political provenance and chronology. For a resumé of sources with a sharp analysis of the interpretative difficulties, see Aróstegui and Martínez, *La Junta de Defensa*, pp. 68–75. But, on a close reading, these differences of opinion rarely amount to outright contradictions about Miaja – something I have tried to indicate in my own analysis here.

[160] Rojo always denied it. See resumé of evidence in Aróstegui and Martínez, *La Junta de Defensa*, p. 69. Barring the outright forgery of documents by the rebels (given that they were produced in the context of the *Causa General*), this would seem to suggest that there was a connection – unless Rojo's 'ficha' (record card) resulted from his being 'signed up' by military colleagues – not beyond the bounds of possibility, particularly in the case of the 'list' of members apparently seen by Largo Caballero.

[161] For a sense of this, see the text of the dedication (to the anonymous Spanish women of the home front) in Rojo's book, *Así fue la defensa de Madrid*, written in exile (although the experience had a stronger impact on Rojo, who was altogether more serious and deeper thinking).

But Miaja understood the underlying importance of his function as the 'necessary hero' in whom the population could trust, projecting a confident but empathetic authority and an absolute faith in victory. This is not the same, however, as saying that he believed in his own myth, for all that he perceived – and was prepared to use – the opportunity it afforded for personal advancement. Indeed, he displayed a robust and ironic sense of humour in regard to his 'myth', awarding his 'hero's' medals to a field hospital.[162] Miaja's bluff bonhomie rang hollow to informed military and political observers, including Prieto and, later, Negrín.[163] But it was an important part of Miaja's appeal to Madrid's civilian population and to its soldiery – as Azaña recognised. Troop morale was a material condition of Republican survival, and for many of them Miaja remained a 'un gran jefe' (a leader they believed in and felt loyalty to). The importance of this myth lay in its ability to galvanise and channel the collective endeavour of defending the capital. By the same token, the myth or image was not – as is often suggested – uniquely created by the PCE.[164] But the communists' particular understanding of the requirements of mass mobilisation led them to disseminate it very energetically.

The especial importance of the PCE to Miaja came from its unique profile: the fact that its uncompromising position on militarisation, political and economic centralisation and public-order policy was married to an especial organisational dynamism. Although one must be careful not simply to take the party's own propaganda at face value, there is no doubt that there was an aura of vitality and positive thinking (a sense of 'can do') about the PCE which made a great impression in a situation where such qualities were at a premium. Miaja himself summarised it excellently when he commented – again to Nenni – 'the communists are more capable and determined. The socialists have to talk about it, weigh up the pros and cons, before they act. They have an enormous capacity for sacrifice but little sense of initiative. With the communists it's actions rather than words – or at least if they discuss it's *after* they've taken action. In military terms that is a distinct advantage.'[165] The PCE's profile derived to a great extent from party discipline. But communist dynamism was also about numbers. For even before the Madrid defence

---

[162] Gullón, 'Justice et guerre civil', p. 236.

[163] For the views of both Prieto and Negrín (the latter thought that Miaja was a dolt), see Azaña, *Obras completas*, vol. 4, pp. 639, 678, 767.

[164] Aróstegui and Martínez, *La Junta de Defensa*, p. 75.

[165] Nenni, *La guerra de España*, p. 124; other witnesses also reinforce this view, for example the *News Chronicle* journalist Geoffrey Cox, letter to the author, 3 Dec. 1999.

accelerated the process, the wartime PCE was expanding. A wide variety of new members – especially the young – were joining party organisations, especially the joint communist and socialist youth organisation, the JSU, whose leadership was fast moving into the PCE orbit.

The PCE's connection to the Soviet Union gave it a tremendous boost in October. For Soviet aid offered the besieged population of Madrid crucial psychological support at a devastating moment of complete international isolation. It is this that explains the sudden craze among the city's population for Soviet objects and images – hats, badges, mobilisation posters and the like – and the warm reception given to Soviet films.[166] Films about the Bolshevik revolution and the civil war would be used to boost troop and civilian morale throughout the battle for the capital.[167] But most effective of all here were the Soviet tanks and planes, in action on the Madrid front by late October. Also important were the military advisers sent under Soviet auspices. There would never be that many of them – between six and eight hundred at any one time across the whole Republican zone and a maximum of 3,000 personnel during the war.[168] But they played a vital role. Contrary to the impression often given, however, this was predominantly a subordinate, technical role: the 3,000 included many engineers, interpreters and technicians of various kinds and not least the pilots and tank drivers.[169] For the Republican general staff, led by Rojo, was in desperate need of those with a practical knowledge of how to wage war in modern, mechanised conditions.

This need, and the gratitude and appreciation it initially stimulated, did not of course preclude the emergence of tensions between Spanish commanders and Soviet military advisers. In the course of time there would be real conflicts over organisational prerogatives and protocol. But

---

[166] Cox, *Defence of Madrid*, pp. 51, 72, 153; López Fernández, *Defensa de Madrid*, p. 162; Carrillo, *Memorias*, pp. 185, 200; Zugazagoitia, *Guerra y vicisitudes*, p. 128, who memorably conveys what Soviet support meant in his image of a pure oxygen shot. Cf. M. Azaña, *Causas de la guerra de España* (Barcelona: Crítica, 1986), p. 50 (text written in 1939).

[167] R. Cruz, '¡Luzbel vuelve al mundo! Las imágenes de la Rusia Soviética y la acción colectiva en España', in R. Cruz and M. Pérez Ledesma (eds.), *Cultura y movilización en la España contemporánea* (Madrid: Alianza Universidad, 1997), p. 302. Alpert, *El ejército republicano*, p. 53 refers to the frenetic pace of such showings on various fronts and how – on one day alone (27 December 1936) – there were six showings in the vicinity of Madrid.

[168] These figures derive from an estimate of Soviet human war losses 1935–41 published by the Russian Ministry of Defence in 1998. I am grateful to Frank Schauff for providing me with this material and for making the important point that the Soviet leadership's main concern was that its technicians gain valuable *military* experience from their engagement with the Axis in Spain. See also Schauff, 'Hitler and Stalin in the Spanish Civil War', p. 9. Cf. Azaña's figure (provided by Largo) of 781 Russians in Republican Spain in spring 1937, *Causas de la guerra de España*, p. 50.

[169] Cox, *Defence of Madrid*, p. 168; Zugazagoitia, *Guerra y vicisitudes*, p. 128; cf. P. and A. Abramson, *Mosaico roto* (Madrid: Compañía Literaria, 1994), especially pp. 67–87.

it is misleading to explain these in terms of a fundamental disagreement over military strategy, still less in terms of Stalin's desire to control the Republican war effort. This would have run counter to his whole strategy in Spain and, in any case, would have been physically impossible. First, because Soviet personnel in Spain were too sparse (particularly political 'advisers' proper – as opposed to specialist technical personnel). Second, because there was also a tremendous *discontinuity* of personnel. Staff were constantly being recalled and replaced as a consequence of the vast purges then gripping the Soviet Union.[170] The disagreements between Soviet military advisers and Spanish officers were often a complex mix of the cultural, personal-psychological and military-procedural. Many of the Spaniards were ambivalent about the presence of foreigner advisers *per se* – especially ones whose ideas and strategies might reveal their own shortcomings. Some of the advisers lacked tact, failing to grasp this human dimension, while others were high-handed, but others too were reasonably discreet in handling prickly Spanish male, military amour-propre.[171]

The Soviet Union did not, of course, send fighting troops to Spain in the way that Germany and above all Italy would, increasingly, for the rebels. But the Comintern's organisation of a volunteer force, the International Brigades, which began to arrive in Spain in October 1936, provided the Republic with a core of experienced fighters who could be thrown into the breach to gain time.[172] The International Brigades symbolised the Popular Front in arms. Their bulk was constituted by so-cialists, communists, trade unionists – politically conscious workers from across the world, but in the main from the continental European core of

---

[170] Schauff, 'Hitler and Stalin in the Spanish Civil War', pp. 10–11, 19–20. For a useful attempt to explain the sociology of the purges, see F. Schauff, 'Company Choir of Terror: The Military Council of the 1930s – The Red Army between the XVII and XVIII Party Congresses', *Journal of Slavic Military Studies*, 12(2) (June 1999), 123–63.

[171] Cf. Col. Sverchevsky ('Walter') to Voroshilov, retrospective report on military advisers, doc. 77 (undated but c. August 1938) in R. Radosh, M. R. Habek and G. Sevostianov (eds.), *Spain Betrayed. The Soviet Union in the Spanish Civil War* (New Haven/London: Yale University Press, 2001), pp. 491–4; Bolloten, *SCW*, p. 278 cites Rojo's endorsement of Republican military supremacy against other testimonies which he seems to think argue the opposite. As cited, however, they fit entirely with the analysis I propose here. It is also interesting to compare the 1945 and 1975 versions of *Defensa de Madrid*, the memoir by A. López Fernández, Miaja's personal secretary. The earlier version talks about various tensions between Spanish commanders and Soviet advisers (for example p. 298), while the 1975 edition converts everything into a single patriotic reaction against Stalin's bid for hegemony in Spain. Observations on the cultural differences between Spanish officers and Soviet advisers are in Gullón, 'Justice et guerre civil', in Serrano, *Madrid 1936–1939*, pp. 238–9. See also the illuminating anecdote in L. Crome, 'Walter (1897–1947): A Soldier in Spain', *History Workshop Journal* 9 (spring 1980), 121.

[172] Elorza and Bizcarrondo, *Queridos camaradas*, p. 324.

France, Italy and Germany. Initially, the Republic's military command hoped to use the Brigades in flank attacks on rebel lines while the militia defended the capital itself. But such was militia demoralisation after the tide of previous defeats that this plan had to be abandoned and the Brigades used in the defence of Madrid itself.[173] But crucial though they were, neither this emergency use of the Brigades nor Soviet military technology/advice could in itself have saved Madrid. To hold the six-mile front along which the rebels were attacking required an enormous effort of domestic militarisation as well as mass mobilisation on the civil-defence front.[174] And as Miaja's comments intimate, it was here that the PCE's superior discipline and organisational dynamism would really tell.

One of the most important sources for the sustained mobilisation which the PCE began via the Fifth Regiment was to be found in the united youth organisation (JSU). Expanding rapidly after 18 July, it would provide vital forces not only for the Fifth Regiment but also then for other battalions. Eventually some 70 per cent of the JSU's total force[175] would be sustaining the Republican war effort at the front. JSU members contributed significantly to the political commissariat too. These developments need to be set in the context of a wider process of political and social modernisation already in train and further accelerated by the rebellion of 18 July. As Comandancia de Milicias records show, recruitment to the militia, far from deriving from the 'people in arms' as a whole or from the *organised* proletariat, came overwhelmingly from the young (in this case male), unskilled and *previously unmobilised* sectors.[176] A similar phenomenon of rapid youth mobilisation (of both sexes) underpinned the vertiginous growth of the JSU across late 1936 and into 1937, upon which an important part of the PCE's strategy of permanent political mobilisation was built.

The PCE used Soviet images to stimulate both military and civilian mobilisation in Madrid. Propagandistic parallels were drawn between the achievements of the Bolsheviks' revolutionary army and the potential of the new Spanish Republican army under construction. But there was no lack of awareness among the party's leaders of the great differences

---

[173] Cox, *Defence of Madrid*, pp. 69–70.

[174] There were about 57 militiamen for every one brigader on the Madrid front initially. With brigader reinforcements this became 32 to one. But the ratio would have increased again with the arrival of militia from Catalonia and other areas: ibid., p. 106.

[175] Carrillo, *La juventud, factor de la victoria* (speech to PCE Central Committee 6–8 March 1937) (Valencia, 1937).

[176] Alpert, *El ejército republicano*, pp. 41 (n. 25), 62. The political as well as military mobilisation of youth was a cross-organisational phenomenon: Fraser, *Blood of Spain*, p. 371.

between the two historical situations that scarcely favoured the Spanish Republicans. Most critical was the disparity of military training. In the case of the Russian Civil War the mass base of the revolutionary army had already received basic training for (First World) war service, which also meant that arms were available. Spain had been neutral in the 1914–18 war. And in 1936, apart from the lack of arms, there were very few soldiers integrated in the militia. Most *milicianos* had never handled a weapon before or received any training – hence their vulnerability, as we have seen, as they faced rebel tanks, aviation and the Army of Africa's cavalry and troops in open terrain. The defence of Madrid too meant *regular* warfare – although in streets, this time, not in open spaces – which at least reduced the militia's disadvantage. But military training remained the vital ingredient – hence the importance of the Fifth Regiment, and also of the International Brigades, from whose example the Spanish troops learned tactics as well as discipline. Trained and, above all, highly mobile, the Brigades took the lead in November in holding up the Army of Africa's troops in the open scrubland of the Casa de Campo outside Madrid. Then, by mid month, they were confronting them in bloody hand-to-hand fighting in the buildings of the University City on the western perimeter of the capital. Among the rapidly learning Spanish troops, the political commissars played a vital role at this stage in preventing retreat under fire. Meanwhile, as well as training, the local fighting forces on the Madrid front were also receiving reinforcements from other areas of the Republican zone. They came via Valencia. As one contemporary commentator pointed out, Franco committed a major strategic error in not making the closure of the Madrid–Valencia road his target from the outset. Disdainful of his opponents, he spoke of letting the 'red rats flee'. But 'the tide which flowed on it was not a rabble moving to Valencia, but an army to Madrid'.[177]

Among the reinforcements came several thousand Catalans, including anarchists of the Durruti column.[178] The battle for Madrid was the forcing house of anarcho-syndicalist pragmatism. Durruti himself came rapidly to understand that the Republic's survival depended upon its ability to put an army in the field and that all such armies required discipline and a command structure.[179] Among the CNT militia active on the

[177] The quotations are from the *News Chronicle* and *Daily Express* correspondent, Geoffrey Cox, *Defence of Madrid*, p. 111.

[178] R. Sanz, *Los que fuimos a Madrid* (Toulouse: n.p., 1969).

[179] See also the revealing Defence Council minutes for 14 November 1936 (in Aróstegui and Martínez, *La Junta de Defensa*, pp. 301–2). The Comintern representative, André Marty, opined

Madrid front there was relatively little opposition to this, as they learned the reality of these needs through their own hard fighting experience. The Madrid CNT as an organisation also proved adept at producing mobilising propaganda as excellent as the PCE's. The issue which confronted anarchists and communists in Madrid was never in fact militarisation *per se*: it was political power, including that which flowed from control of the militarisation process, as well as from the parallel one of reconstructing civilian police forces behind the lines.[180] It is simply wrong to see the CNT – anywhere in Spain – as an anti-militarist monolith.[181] Nor indeed was libertarian anti-militarism itself a single, homogeneous phenomenon. There were, of course, many instances of militiamen leaving their columns rather than submit to a militarisation with which they profoundly disagreed.[182] But in a rural society like Spain, resistance to it was also often driven by practical needs (militarisation would prevent peasant-soldiers dividing their time between their land and the front).

The death of Buenaventura Durruti on 20 November saw the birth of an anarchist icon but also the death of a living symbol which the Republic at war could ill afford to lose. He died in the environs of the University City while returning from a tour of duty, probably as the result of the accidental discharge of a weapon – either his own or that of one of his guards.[183] The tragically arbitrary circumstances of Durruti's demise were suppressed, however, because all sections of the Republican leadership were fearful – not only of feeding internecine political feuds, but also, quite simply, of demoralising the troops battling to hold Madrid. For the CNT his death would prove a watershed.[184] But the liberal Republic also needed heroes like Durruti. The protection of the legendary anarchist's reputation was also a means of protecting what

favourably in October 1936 on the pragmatism of both Durruti and García Oliver: Elorza and Bizcarrondo, *Queridos camaradas*, p. 327, as did CNT newspaper editor Jacinto Toryho, *No eramos tan malos* (Madrid: Toro, 1975), p. 136. This acceptance of discipline also holds true for other anarchist leaders on the Madrid front, such as Cipriano Mera: Bolloten, *SCW*, pp. 326–9.

[180] The same was true for the POUM, which consistently argued for a centralised army with a single command – as copious articles in its own and the CNT press indicate. The real debate was over who should control the army, how it should be organised, and, above all, what kind of social, economic and political order it should be defending: Morrow, *Revolution and Counter-Revolution in Spain*, p. 71.

[181] Ibid., p. 7; Casanova, *Anarquismo y revolución*, pp. 111–13 (who also indicates the multiple meanings of 'anti-militarism').

[182] B. Bolloten gives several examples, including that of the Iron Column: *SCW*, p. 420.

[183] For a forensic résumé, see chapter 5 below.

[184] For a discussion of Durruti's death in the context of the internal crisis of the CNT, see chapter 5 below.

the Republican authorities chose to present as Durruti's endorsement of state, as well as military, reconstruction – encoded in the famously resonant (but apocryphal) slogan 'we will renounce everything except victory'.[185]

Victory – or indeed survival – at Madrid also demanded a major effort of organisation on the civilian front. The waves of refugees arriving in the capital had begun the process whereby the war entered popular consciousness. This was reinforced by civilian involvement in fortification work that accelerated in November. But it was the devastating impact of the civilian-targeted waves of air raids between 14 and 23 November, led by the German Condor Legion, which brought home the reality of modern war to the population of Madrid.[186] But far from undermining civilian morale, as Franco had hoped, the bombing reinforced it. Many saw it as proof of what the refugees told of rebel atrocities to the south and thus acquired a furious determination never to submit to the barbarism of their compatriots. There would be no gas attacks, however, on either military or civilian targets. It was too indiscriminate a weapon. The front lines were too close, winding their way in irregular, snake-like fashion, while the political topography of the city meant that – even without a strong wind – Franco would necessarily have risked gassing his own supporters.[187] Madrid's trade unions acted as agents of government, implementing war measures according to their specialist competences – in communications, transport, supply, fortifications, war-material production and other civil-defence tasks. Both socialists and communists took the lead in establishing house or block committees on a neighbourhood basis to organise civil defence. These committees also had responsibilities for investigating government housing decrees to deal with refugee housing needs and other war-related contingencies, and they also played

[185] Although Durruti himself never spoke these words, the slogan was invented by the CNT: see C. Ealham, editor's introduction to J. Peirats, *The CNT in the Spanish Revolution*, vol. 1 (Hastings: The Meltzer Press, 2001), pp. xii–xiii. Cf. Geoffrey Cox's view of Durruti as a 'binding force' for Republican/Popular Front unity, *Defence of Madrid*, pp. 139–41. A classic defence of Durruti as a radical anarchist and intransigent opponent of militarisation is to be found in A. Paz, *Durruti. The People Armed* (New York: Free Life Editions, 1977) and *Durruti en la revolución española* (Madrid: Fundación Anselmo Lorenzo, 1996). But this interpretation is contested: see Casanova, *Anarquismo y revolución*, p. 144 and *De la calle al frente*, pp. 186–7, 251.

[186] Cox, *Defence of Madrid*, pp. 114–31; G. Hills, *The Battle for Madrid* (London: Vantage Books, 1976), pp. 105–8; Fraser, *Blood of Spain*, p. 175 (n. 1).

[187] For more on gas, see Cox, *Defence of Madrid*, p. 199. Franco did, nevertheless, request poison gas bombs from Italy in August 1936: P. Preston, 'Mussolini's Spanish Adventure: From Limited Risk to War', in Preston and Mackenzie, *The Republic Besieged*, p. 49. For more on Franco and his contemplated use of gas, see A. Viñas, *Franco, Hitler y el estallido de la guerra civil* (Madrid: Alianza, 2001), pp. 29–112.

a role in checking the activities of fifth columnists.[188] In an important way too they represented the beginning of the reconstruction of the relationship between government and populace shattered by the rebellion.

But again it was the PCE in Madrid which led the way, quantitatively and qualitatively, with organisational initiatives to link the home front to the military front. The party would attempt to develop such initiatives in other parts of the Republican zone, but these were arguably never as successful as the 'prototype'.[189] Catalysed by the Madrid campaign, at the heart of the PCE's strategy was the Fifth Regiment. Integral to its functioning were welfare and support services. The Regiment had medical and auxiliary training facilities (a school for nurses) and forged links with women's organisations, most notably the Popular Frontist Association of Anti-fascist Women (AMA) to provide support for soldiers' families (which included provision of a nursery). The Regiment also developed links with specific war production factories through an 'adoption' scheme. It initiated literacy and general educational courses, organised talks, film showings and exhibitions, and through its press and poster campaigns promoted both its ideas on the new army and enhanced communication between military and civilian fronts. The Regiment also originated the idea of using loudspeakers to transmit Republican propaganda to the rebel trenches. In keeping with the philosophy underpinning its work, by the end of 1936 part of the Regiment's barracks was also converted to create the Casa del Combatiente – recreational and educational facilities for soldiers' use which anticipated the Republican Army's own Hogar del Soldado.[190] But by then the Regiment would be winding down, as some 70 per cent of its base had been incorporated in the Mixed Brigades and its separate support functions reverted, where appropriate, to the Republic's central general staff. (Its purpose served, the Fifth Regiment would be formally dissolved on 27 January 1937.) Through the Fifth Regiment, the PCE demonstrated not only its considerable practical organisational skills but also that it understood, as no other Republican group did, that the looming challenge of total war

---

[188] For a vivid depiction of Madrid's population waking up to the war, see Cox, *Defence of Madrid*, pp. 31–7.

[189] See Mary Low's comments on the 'gaps' in cultural mobilisation in Barcelona, where there was a rapid resurgence of commercial popular entertainment: M. Low and J. Breá, *Red Spanish Notebook* (London, 1937; San Francisco: City Lights Books, 1979), pp. 224–7.

[190] Alpert, *El ejército republicano*, p. 54. On the PCE's cultural and educational work, see C. Cobb, *Los milicianos de la cultura* (Bilbao: Universidad del País Vasco, 1994) and 'The Educational and Cultural Policy of the Popular Front Government in Spain 1936–9', in Alexander and Graham, *The French and Spanish Popular Fronts*, pp. 246–53.

required new *forms* of organisation. These had, by addressing welfare and morale, to ensure the permanent physical and psychological mobilisation of both military and civilian fronts so that each understood its relation of mutual interdependence and the overarching reasons for the fight. It was this understanding and the PCE's ability to act efficiently upon it which gave it the edge over both the CNT and the socialists.

The appeal of the communists, in Madrid first and foremost, was to young people across a range of social classes. As the then JSU leader and later (dissident) Communist Party theorist Fernando Claudín acutely remarked: 'they were attracted by the party's military virtues and by a simplified ideology in which the idea of revolution was identified with anti-fascism mingled with patriotism'.[191] To this should also be added the attraction of the modern and novel. For the 'Soviet Union', whatever else it may have represented in 1930s Spain, conjured up a powerful image of political and cultural modernity which was especially appealing to young (but also to some not so young) Spaniards seeking a model, or at least examples, of change which might offer pointers for their own situation and aspirations. Or, as a cultural theorist might put it, the PCE was appealing to (and influencing) the Republican popular imaginary. This also needs to be understood in the broader context of the cultural and social reception of images of the Soviet Union across the 1920s and 1930s in Spain – an important topic that still awaits its researcher.[192]

Nor was the phenomenon of youth protagonism confined to the communist base. The JSU's leaders were also by and large in their late teens and early twenties. This reflected a post-1918 generational shift. But the Republic at war saw this generational shift become a veritable revolution as these 'young' youth leaders were given major national political responsibilities. Contemporary observers remarked on the youth of many of the Madrid Defence Council members: for example, JSU general secretary Santiago Carrillo was only twenty-one years old when he was appointed

[191] F. Claudín, *The Communist Movement. From Comintern to Cominform* (Harmondsworth: Penguin, 1975), pp. 230–1. This was generally important – not just to young people – as PCF leader Maurice Thorez remarked at the start (September 1936). The PCE offered 'very simple formulas, popular formulas' which, above all, 'appealed to a sense of national pride': Elorza and Bicarrondo, *Queridos camaradas*, p. 318.

[192] 'Russia together with other expressions of modernity such as "aviation, the radio, the telephone gave life great interest"', E. Montero, 'Reform Idealised: The Intellectual and Ideological Origins of the Second Republic', in Graham and Labanyi, *Spanish Cultural Studies*, pp. 131–2. A suggestive preliminary study is Cruz, '¡Luzbel vuelve al mundo! Las imágenes de la Rusia Soviética y la acción colectiva en España'; also E. Ucelay da Cal, 'Socialistas y comunistas en Cataluña durante la guerra civil: un ensayo de interpretación', in S. Juliá (ed.), *Socialismo y guerra civil, Anales de Historia*, vol. 2 (Madrid: Fundación Pablo Iglesias, 1987) p. 306.

its Councillor for Public Order.[193] The war also saw an important gender shift as large numbers of young women joined the JSU and took up active war-related roles on the civilian front. (This provoked another 'civil war within the civil war' waged in many Spanish families in the Republican zone as young women defied social convention to stay out late at night on account of their JSU responsibilities.)

The most striking feature of communist membership in the war period, however, was its *hybridity*. This is true whether one looks at younger or older constituencies – the party proper or the youth movement, or the various other Popular Front organisations, for example and most importantly that for women (the AMA), which the party originated. This hybridity is true for the Republican zone more or less as a whole – although the configuration of motives leading people to join the party, or at least to participate in Popular Front organisations, varied from area to area. In Madrid and on the centre front the impact of the war was naturally paramount. We have already discussed the particular case of professional army officers. But given the general, 'neo-clientelist' context[194] which encouraged political membership of some kind or other as a form of political and social protection in uncertain and chaotic times, many men at the front opted for the Communist Party because it was the best-organised, most disciplined and most efficient formation. This was also true for many already subscribed as republicans or socialists as well as those (a majority) who had not previously belonged to any political organisation.[195]

In Catalonia, where the military conflict remained a more distant prospect for longer, the appeal of the Communist Party was still very considerable (although here it was a separate party, the PSUC, which retained a strongly Catalan nationalist steer[196]). Communist appeal was notable too in the eastern coastal region of Valencia, which always remained 'behind the lines'. In both places, and especially Catalonia, the appeal was predominantly because the communist parties offered the most robust defence of private property and 'law and order' in areas which had been more affected than had Madrid by challenges to the social and economic status quo: thus peasant smallholders and the owners of industrial workshops and commercial premises joined the PCE or

---

[193] Cox, *Defence of Madrid*, p. 110; López Fernández, *Defensa de Madrid*, p. 207; Aróstegui and Martínez, *La Junta de Defensa*, p. 80.

[194] Cf. Azaña's shrewd if cynical assessment, *Causas de la guerra de España*, p. 51.

[195] Martín Blázquez, *I Helped to Build an Army*, p. 205. For the organisational chaos in the PSOE caused by enthusiastic rank-and-file 'fusionism', see Graham, *Socialism and War*, pp. 75–6.

[196] See chapter 4 below.

the PSUC in droves.[197] By the same token, the total lack of any such threat in the Republican Basque Country, as well as the overwhelming nationalist political loyalties of the lower-middle classes (encadred in the PNV),[198] meant that the PCE remained a marginal party. The same was true in the other area of the Republican north, Asturias. There, the only significant middling class of property holders to whom the PCE might have appealed was located in the regional capital of Oviedo, which was held by the rebels.

But for all its new appeal to middling social constituencies in various areas of Republican Spain, the PCE retained its pre-war working-class membership. Indeed, it expanded this. The inter-class nature of the wartime Spanish Communist Party – evident too in the JSU and the women's organisation, AMA, is the crux of the party's importance during the war. For what the PCE was able to achieve, at least for a time, was the recreation of the inter-class Popular Front alliance exploded by the military rebellion – within itself as a mass organisation. The hypothesis proposed here about the importance of the PCE as a producer of integrating, patriotic images and symbols for a fractured Republican society/polity (in which, otherwise, there were *far too many* conflicting symbols) needs more theoretical exploration than can be afforded it here. Indeed, it also needs more empirical research.[199] But what is clear is that the PCE's ability to address and incorporate a range of different social and political constituencies, and to vary political discourses accordingly, meant that the PCE was the first party on the left to go a significant way to realising the fundamental challenge of Spanish politics since 1931: that of achieving mass political mobilisation *across class boundaries*. This pursuit of a politically and socially modernising (but not a socialist) national project had been prefigured in the pre-war speeches of the PSOE leader Prieto, who was challenging his own party to take the lead here.[200] But

---

[197] The fact that, unprecedentedly, the Comintern allowed two (organisationally separate) communist parties – the PCE and the PSUC – to hold official representation for one country, Spain, is indicative of the crucial importance of Catalonia to the Popular Front alliance/industrial war effort as the basis of a viable Republican defence strategy.

[198] See chapter 4 below.

[199] There is some – as yet unpublished – theoretical work on the PCE's cultural-political functions during the war by M. T. Gómez, 'El largo viaje/The Long Journey: The Cultural Politics of the Communist Party of Spain 1920–1939', Ph.D. thesis, McGill University, Montreal, 1999, and much that is open to this interpretation in C. Cobb's *Los milicianos de la cultura*. But we need to ground this in an empirical social history of the wartime Spanish Communist Party – something we as yet lack.

[200] Graham, *Socialism and War*, p. 16. Prieto's speeches in *Discursos fundamentales*; see, for example, p. 185 (Cine Pardiñas (Madrid), Feb. 1934), p. 279 (Ejea de los Caballeros (Aragon), May 1936) and pp. 255–73 for his visionary speech, 'La conquista interior de España' (Cuenca, 1 May 1936).

it was to be the wartime PCE that finally acted upon Prieto's strategy of 'thinking as republicans'. As a result, there was increasingly little that we would commonly identify as 'communist' in the *content* of either the wartime PCE's political discourse[201] or its cultural policy, which was liberal democratic through and through.[202] What was radical (i.e. new or even 'communist') about the PCE in the war was not the content of its policies but its organisational techniques. By marrying the two, the wartime PCE would thus become the best republican party Spain had ever known.

The inevitable question that arises is why the Spanish Socialist Party was not fulfilling this key role. Until the military coup of 18 July it had had a much higher profile than the PCE. Indeed, the socialists (party and union) constituted Spain's only mass parliamentary political movement of the left in the pre-war period. Madrid especially had been a socialist fief in the political sphere.[203] The image of the government's abandonment of Madrid in November 1936 damaged the PSOE most of all the political forces in Republican Spain, since it formed the nucleus of the 'fleeing' government. Moreover, the PSOE national executive committee also decamped to Valencia, thus giving the impression of systematic leadership withdrawal. The socialists further erred in sending relatively unknown rank-and-file members (Máximo de Dios and Fernando Frade) to represent the party on the Defence Council – because it was perceived as an ephemeral body.[204] The PCE, in contrast, appointed national and provincial leaders: Mije, and Isidoro Diéguez of the PCE's Madrid executive, as well as members of the JSU executive. (The fact that the CNT's national leadership had also 'departed' Madrid was crucially compensated for by its ministers in the Valencia cabinet, Montseny and García Oliver, constantly moving between the two cities.) Many individual socialists – known and unknown – did stay behind in Madrid to fulfil important public responsibilities related to the city's defence and

---

[201] See Pasionaria's speech of 23 May 1938 to the PCE's central committee in which she reiterates the policy with unprecedented force in the light of the acute military crisis of those days. See also the comments of Vincent Sheean, an American journalist who heard the speech, that she 'was asking these people to stop being Communists altogether, at least until the war was won'. Sheean is cited in Preston, *Comrades*, p. 302.

[202] This is the conclusion drawn in Gómez's thesis. In my opinion, it is also the conclusion to be drawn from Christopher Cobb's work. The PCE's sectarianism was organisational, not ideological – a point which some of Cobb's reviewers have failed to understand (see, for example, J. M. Fernández Urbina in *Historia Contemporánea*, 13–14 (1996)).

[203] Although, as we have seen in chapter 1, the UGT in Madrid was being challenged by the CNT in certain sectors in the 1930s: Juliá, *Madrid, 1931–1934*.

[204] Aróstegui and Martínez, *La Junta de Defensa*, p. 77. Frade leaves Madrid so Máximo de Dios becomes the acting councillor: S. Carrillo interviewed in Gibson, *Paracuellos*, p. 203.

administration: for example Carlos Rubiera, who served as civil governor and then in a variety of war-related committee functions such as evacuation and supply[205] and Julián Zugazagoitia, the editor of the most influential socialist newspaper.[206] But this presence did little to counter the prevailing impression of PSOE paralysis.

An obvious major contributory factor to the erosion of PSOE prestige was the lack of support for the Republic from the organisations of the Second (Socialist) International. By contrast, the optimism generated by Soviet military aid procurement and Comintern support – in the shape both of the International Brigades and of a high-profile European solidarity movement gathering humanitarian aid and lobbying for the lifting of Non-Intervention – rubbed off heavily onto the PCE. But the passivity of the Second International is far from the whole explanation for PSOE eclipse. For the socialists were already in massive internal crisis *before* the war.

The adult party was seriously divided, and the resulting paralysis had encouraged the departure of the Socialist Youth (FJS), which, as we have seen, decided, without the approval of the PSOE, to merge with its Young Communist counterpart in spring 1936.[207] This was a step that marked the beginning of the end for the party's control of its youth movement. But although the PSOE would blame much of its wartime plight on this loss, the departure of the FJS was itself a symptom rather than the underlying cause of socialist crisis. The reasons for this were bound up with the very identity of the PSOE/UGT as a political entity. In sum, as we have seen in the introduction and chapter 1 above, the very values that had shaped the Spanish socialist movement historically meant that neither the PSOE nor the UGT was able to respond effectively to the pressing political challenge of mass political mobilisation. Historically, the socialists had sought to guarantee what they saw as the organisational health of the movement by demanding a high level of political awareness of their militants. The mass political mobilisation on the agenda in the 1930s meant that the UGT was obliged to accept new recruits with a lower level of both general and political education. But there was

---

[205] Rubiera was appointed civil governor on 8 October 1936. He was a stalwart of the skeletal Madrid socialist organisation during the war who fulfilled various war-related functions and was later part of the PCE–PSOE liaison committee in the capital. On Rubiera, see Graham, *Socialism and War*, pp. 123, 201, 239, 242.

[206] On Madrid, as on the war in general, Julián Zugazagoitia's memoirs are among the three or four most important we possess. (Both Rubiera and Zugazagoitia were executed by the Franco regime in 1939 and 1940 respectively.) On the PSOE in Madrid, Santiago Carrillo is right about the impression but wrong on the details – interview in Gibson, *Paracuellos*, p. 217.

[207] See chapter 1 above.

no real understanding of how to integrate these constituencies into the socialist movement and, moreover, there was an unwillingness to do so (although this was largely unconscious) for fear of the organisational consequences. At root, Spain's socialist leaders – whether from party or union – saw politics as still the province of an elite inside parliament rather than of a rapidly mobilising population pressuring for social change from the streets. This underlying tension in the socialist movement was already sapping its energies by the spring of 1936, and that, in turn, had encouraged the departure of the Socialist Youth.

What was pressing before, however, became imperative after 18 July. Mass mobilisation was now the *sine qua non* of Republican survival. Yet the socialists became even more fearful of party expansion at such an 'abnormal' time. Hence the endlessly repeated advice from veteran leaders not to 'pescar en río revuelto' ('fish in troubled waters').[208] As a result, the wartime PSOE lost militants to the PCE – including some very high-profile ones like the socialist deputy for Badajoz, Margarita Nelken, the soul of Madrid's defence.[209] Indeed, that her allegiance to the PCE was made through the transformative experience of the siege makes her case emblematic. In the end, the war would see the final crystallisation of the PSOE's internal political crisis in the emergence of two opposing rationales among socialists. There were those, like Largo Caballero and many of his old union retainers (both reformists *and* radicals), for whom even the war effort had to come second to the protection of socialist organisational 'heritage' (although no doubt they never consciously mooted it in such terms).[210] What this meant was keeping out threats new and old: fifth columnists/crypto-rebels, communists and the 'ill-fitted' of all kinds. Alternatively, there were PSOE/UGT members – including leaders such as Prieto, Ramón Lamoneda (the wartime PSOE general secretary) and Juan Negrín himself – for whom the party was an *instrument* for achieving national political reform. For this group the war was being fought as a last-ditch attempt to salvage the very possibility of such change, and thus, if need be, it would be worth sacrificing the Socialist Party to the battle. Unfortunately for the PSOE, many of the socialists who believed this also came to the conclusion that they could best ensure the maximisation of their own wartime efforts from the ranks of the Spanish Communist

[208] Graham, *Socialism and War*, pp. 118–19.

[209] She was famous for her rousing radio speeches: Zugazagoitia, *Guerra y vicisitudes*, pp. 186–8; Aróstegui and Martínez, *La Junta de Defensa*, p. 63 and P. Preston, 'Margarita Nelken', in *Doves of War. Four Women of Spain* (London: Harper Collins, 2002), pp. 297–407.

[210] For more on this see the discussion of the May 1937 cabinet crisis in chapter 5 below. New members did join the wartime PSOE, but its growth was much slower than the PCE's.

Party. This was a decision based primarily, if not exclusively, on organisational criteria rather than ideological differences. Indeed, one could see the wartime PCE here as picking up the socialists' 'historic' objective of renovating the state.[211] And nowhere was the PCE's contribution to the renovation of government authority earlier evident than in the besieged city of Madrid in winter 1936.

One of the Defence Council's major objectives during this period was the evacuation of the civilian population from the capital. Evacuation in some form had been occurring since October, given the need to disperse the accumulated waves of refugees from further south who had fled there ahead of the advancing rebel forces. But from 7 November the situation became acute. Madrid's population of 1 million now stood at some 1,300,000, swelled by troops and refugees. The additional pressure on food and increasingly exiguous housing increased further with the siege-induced displacement of Madrid's own residents from the south and parts of the west of the capital. The shock of the initial rebel assault did persuade some to depart the city. But the bulk of *madrileños* were extremely reluctant to leave or indeed to let their children go to unknown conditions and anonymous carers – even though this meant the greater safety of the Valencia and Catalan regions behind the lines. (Although as time went on and the food supply[212] and living conditions deteriorated this reluctance would decrease, especially when the children were known to be heading for the children's residences (*colonias infantiles*) set up by various Spanish and foreign refugee agencies.) The only really willing adult evacuees were those who followed family members taking up government-related employment in Valencia.[213] People had a strong attachment to their *patria chica*.[214] This intensified what were also very real fears about the fate of their houses and remaining belongings if they left. The Madrid authorities were technically responsible for ensuring that these came to no harm. But, in an emergency war situation with so much else for the hard-pressed authorities to oversee, ordinary people were, quite understandably, dubious. Moreover, everyone remembered

---

[211] It is for these reasons that Burnett Bolloten's presentation of wartime Spanish socialists turned communists as 'submarines' is fundamentally wrongheaded. He ignores the context and texture of the 1930s – that is, historical chronology – interpreting the actions of the political actors through a *post hoc* (and therefore anachronistic) Cold War interpretative schema. *SCW*, *passim*.

[212] As Quaker sources indicate, it rapidly became difficult to procure the *range* of foods needed to meet the nutritional needs of growing children; also Cox, *Defence of Madrid*, p. 155.

[213] López Fernandez, *Defensa de Madrid*, pp. 227–8.

[214] There was some ironic humour too about the Junta trying to get the inhabitants to 'do a bunk' like the government: ibid., pp. 225ff.

the mayhem of the early weeks when 'patrols' and, indeed, individuals had been free to appropriate virtually whatever they liked. This was no longer the case, but the memory was still a vivid one.[215] Then there were mothers, sisters and wives who were reluctant to abandon male family members on the Madrid front or whose vital source of employment was in Madrid. (Adult males required express permission to be evacuated.[216]) The Junta and its dependent bodies waged a continuous propaganda campaign in favour of civilian evacuation, covered the cost of the journey and guaranteed accommodation at the other end. But popular reluctance was hard to diminish. Moreover, there were also serious material restrictions on the rate of evacuation: vehicles and petrol were in extremely short supply and there existed intractable organisational impediments deriving from the fragmentation of state power.[217] In the course of November (when the rate of evacuation was at its highest) some 250,000 people left. By 9 December the Junta reported that the figure stood at over 300,000.[218] The evacuation was ongoing into 1937, but at a decreasing rate. Transport still presented problems, but the decrease was mainly about people's reluctance to leave – in spite of numerous deaths in the air raids. In view of the increasing pressure on resources (including human ones), the difficulty of guaranteeing civilian safety and the growing fear of contagious disease, Council measures were passed at the end of 1936 to require the evacuation of non-essential groups. But these were only ever seriously enforced for transit refugees.[219] Towards the end of March 1937 the Council would claim a total of 700,000 evacuations. But this was undoubtedly an exaggeration, being based on the statistics for valid ration cards issued in the city.[220]

From the Council's perspective, a greater level of civilian evacuation would have been useful. Apart from important humanitarian objectives,

---

[215] A. Jacob to J. Reich, 10 April 1937, FSC/R/Sp/Box 1, file 2.

[216] Originally interpreted as males between sixteen and fifty-five, this was amended to between twenty and forty-five at the beginning of 1937: Aróstegui and Martínez, *La Junta de Defensa*, p. 183.

[217] Ibid., pp. 176–7. The railway system was used, but road was the predominant means.

[218] My calculation is based on Aróstegui and Martínez's Council-based figures, ibid., pp. 178, 180.

[219] Ibid., pp. 180–1, 183–4.

[220] Ibid., p. 188. The number 700,000 is an overestimation even taking into account those who organised their own departure without accessing Council facilities (and thus did not figure in the statistics). It may be that transit refugees have inflated the figure. The analysis is based primarily on Aróstegui and Martínez's work and on material from the Friends Relief Council (Quaker) archive. (The 1930 census registered a population of 952,832 for Madrid capital and 1,383,951 for the whole province.)

it would also have made it easier to identify and contain the serious danger posed in a besieged city by the clandestine activities of spies and saboteurs. It was the presence of such a fifth column, with the enemy at the gates of the city, which made public-order policy so serious and fraught an issue. In particular, there were fears that, should the rebels break through to the capital, their military capabilities would receive a significant boost from the incorporation of the expertise of officers currently imprisoned in Madrid's gaols and, above all, those in the Model (Modelo) Prison, which was right on top of the rebel lines west of the city. As a result, Largo Caballero had instructed his interior minister, Galarza, to implement the transfer of such high-risk prisoners (and especially army officers) out of Madrid to gaols further inside the Republican home front. But, with the typical lentitude afflicting all process in the Largo government, no transfer had yet been effected when the government itself left Madrid on 6 November.

It was thus the Madrid Defence Council which inherited responsibility for the transfer. But, by definition, this meant that it did so at precisely the moment when the Madrid military situation went critical. The city was under siege, with an enemy at the gate that had already shown it possessed remarkably accurate military and political intelligence on the Republic.[221] A number of foreign enemies and legations were sheltering armed pro-rebel refugees.[222] Even without the fifth column's contribution the Republican defence was highly precarious. *Madrileños* had already experienced air raids and were fearful of more. If the rebels broke through, would there be atrocities in Madrid like those in the south reported by the refugees? The mood in the city was tense. Nor were such apprehensions limited to the ordinary population. The nerves of those political cadres who had remained to staff the Council were also taut: the government had gone, they were alone with so much to organise and with so few means. Maybe tomorrow they would wake up to the rebels in the city and their own executions? The sense of living on the edge, of there only being two choices in the fight – survival or obliteration – enveloped the November days, hugely increasing the fear of – and animosity towards – the enemy within.

[221] Cox, *Defence of Madrid*, p. 175; Aróstegui and Martínez, *La Junta de Defensa*, p. 447.
[222] Defence Council minutes 14 and 24 November, reproduced in Aróstegui and Martínez, *La Junta de Defensa*, pp. 303, 326–7; see also memoir material: J. de Galíndez, *Los vascos en el Madrid sitiado* (Buenos Aires: Ekin, 1945); A. Núñez Morgado, *Los sucesos de España vistos por un diplomático* (Buenos Aires, 1941); F. Schlayer, *Diplomat in roten Madrid* (Berlin, 1938); Claude Bowers, *My Mission to Spain* (New York: Victor Gollancz, 1954).

The initial transfer or prisoners, as arranged by the government before its departure, took place over 7–8 November, during which period there were evacuations from Madrid's four gaols, including the Modelo.[223] A number of convoys set out for gaols beyond Madrid – in Alcalá de Henares, Chinchilla and Valencia's San Miguel de Los Reyes. But most never reached their destination, and none at all made it from the largest single evacuation – that of 970 prisoners from the Modelo. Some 1,200 prisoners were shot in the villages of Paracuellos del Jarama and Torrejón de Ardoz, situated on the Aragon road on the outskirts of Madrid.[224] Throughout the rest of the month and into early December – effectively until the end of the siege – there was a series of further smaller prison evacuations that each time ended in the killing in this same area of a percentage of the prisoners under transfer.[225] There had been *sacas* before in Madrid and in other Republican towns, and these continued into December 1936. They were invariably the result of popular violence when angry crowds assaulted prisons following some provocation, such as news of atrocities in the rebel zone or – most frequently – after air raids.[226] But Paracuellos was different. Those implicated here in extrajudicial murder were the security forces charged with the prisoner transfers – that is, the very representatives of Republican political authority whose re-emergence was supposed to halt such abuses.

Precisely because of this, Paracuellos would become a major plank in the Crusade martyrology confected to legitimise the Franco regime after the war. The events were presented as proof of an orchestrated killing machine sanctioned at the highest level by those exercising power in the Republic. Given the anti-communist tenor of the Crusade, the accusation was levelled particularly at Santiago Carrillo, leader of the PCE from 1960, who, on 6–7 November 1936, as JSU secretary, had become the Madrid Defence Council's Councillor for Public

---

[223] The others were San Antón, Porlier and Ventas; for gaol locations see map in Gibson, *Paracuellos*, p. 128.

[224] Because the rebels held the first part of the Valencia road on the exit from Madrid, Republicans had to make a detour along the Aragon road and then descend to join the Valencia road further along – see map, ibid., p. 128.

[225] The material used in this section comes mainly from Gibson, *Paracuellos* and, to a lesser extent, from Carlos Fernández, *Paracuellos del Jarama: ¿Carrillo culpable?* (Barcelona: Argos Vergara, 1983).

[226] The gaol in Guadalajara was assaulted in December with fatalities, and a similar attack was narrowly averted in Alcalá de Henares: Gibson, *Paracuellos*, p. 178. For a discussion of this phenomenon and other examples, see chapter 2 above. Rebel air raids even succeeded in breaking the social peace prevailing in the Republican Basque Country: there was a *saca* in Bilbao at the end of September 1936 and again on 4 January 1937, when some 200 prisoners were killed. For the war in the Republican Basque Country see chapters 4 and 5 below.

Order.[227] Also targeted was Carrillo's then deputy, the twenty-four-year-old Segundo Serrano Poncela, like Carrillo a former Socialist Youth leader and JSU executive member. This targeting occurred in spite of the fact that until 22 November the orders for prison transfers were signed by interior minister Galarza's deputy director of security (DGS), the policeman Vicente Girauta Linares.[228] In spite of the sound and fury of Francoist denunciatory propaganda, however, there is no hard evidence that Carrillo, Serrano Poncela or anyone else with ministerial or political responsibility[229] issued orders for the prisoners to be killed. Certainly there is no solid basis for the conjecture (originating in Crusade literature) that in signing evacuation orders Republican officials were in fact giving coded orders to kill.[230] Moreover, if the prisoner deaths at Paracuellos were the result of a 'well-oiled' killing machine, how was it that, on each occasion (excepting 7–8 November) a proportion of the evacuated prisoners reached their end destination of prison?[231]

On the existing evidence it seems no less possible or likely that what occurred was the result of the anger and outrage felt by the mix of Milicias de Vigilancia and regular police forces (the, then militarised, Assault Guards) who undertook the various transportations.[232] These

---

[227] Such was the perceived potency of Paracuellos that the episode would be reactivated in 1977 by those hostile to the process of democratic transition then under way – see list of Paracuellos dead republished, with a highly inflammatory commentary, by the extreme rightwing newspaper *El Alcázar*, 3 January 1977. The ensuing polemic led to the production of a number of examinations, including J. Bardavío, *Sábado Santo Rojo* (Madrid: Ediciones Uve, 1980) and those by Gibson and Fernández.

[228] Girauta Linares, who left for Valencia on 22 November, was a member of the Cuerpo de Vigilancia: Gibson, *Paracuellos*, p. 261.

[229] See the accusations against Girauta Linares' superior, the army officer and freemason Muñoz Martínez, who was Director General of police in Galarza's ministry: R. Casas de la Vega, *El terror: Madrid 1936* (Madrid: Fénix, 1994), pp. 193–5 (also pp. 78–9, 105–12). For Girauta and Koltsov, see pp. 198–206.

[230] Gibson forgets his own caution over the limitations of testimonies from the Causa General (the Franco regime's (inchoate) state lawsuit against the defeated) as source material (see *Paracuellos*, pp. 20–2) when he then adduces such a testimony as the *sole* proof of Serrano Poncela's involvement, *Paracuellos*, p. 97. On the lack of evidence against Carrillo in the Causa General see also Bardavío, *Sábado Santo Rojo*.

[231] The expression is Gibson's in *Paracuellos*, p. 233, but the idea comes from the Causa General.

[232] Gibson never really addresses this crucial issue. But it is clear from his account and others that as well as militia forces, regular police were also involved in some capacity – certainly in the later *sacas* and quite probably in the ones of 7–8 November too. Schlayer, the German diplomat who investigated the prisoner disappearances, refers to 'state police' recruiting militia for the task – as Gibson notes on p. 114. Gibson's suggestion that it was Assault Guards is corroborated by other testimonies such as Gullón, 'Justice et guerre civil', in Serrano, *Madrid 1936–1939*, p. 235. The fact that the Assault Guards were militarised is also probably reflected in Carrillo's reference to the evacuee prisoners being in military custody: interview with Gibson, *Paracuellos*, p. 197.

were the days of the major battles in the Casa de Campo. On 15 November rebel forces crossed the River Manzanares into the University City, where there was fierce hand-to-hand fighting. From the fourteenth, heavy air raids were again being targeted directly against civilians. There were also gruesome episodes such as the one in which the body of a Republican fighter pilot, dismembered by the rebels, was dropped back over Madrid.[233] Fears of the enemy within (and we should remember that General Mola had named them as such) increased as the threatening presence of the enemy 'without' loomed large. To understand why Paracuellos happened we have to return the events to the historical circumstances of November 1936 and the unique and acute vulnerability of Madrid under siege. At one point the rebel front was only some 200 metres from the Modelo Prison.

In so far as any influence was exercised by Comintern and Soviet political representatives over what happened to the prisoners, it was also an indirect one. The well-documented concern of the journalist and high-ranking political observer Mijail Koltsov about Madrid's hostile prison population derived from the Russian experience of revolution and war under siege conditions.[234] But his concern registered only because it resonated with the anxiety already felt by the Republic's defenders. Francoist sources repeatedly claimed there was intervention by the Soviet secret police (NKVD). But this remains highly speculative.[235]

---

[233] Koltsov, *Diario de la guerra española*, p. 250; Gibson, *Paracuellos* records Carrillo and other witnesses on this, also citing the contemporary press reports, p. 219.

[234] Koltsov, *Diario de la guerra española*, pp. 191, 206–7.

[235] Such an intervention by the NKVD in 1936 risked damaging the careful strategy of Popular Front and attempted rapprochement to Britain and France of which Stalin still had real hopes. But given the acute *military* crisis in Madrid in November 1936 we cannot rule it out. As Burnett Bolloten relates, there was a Comintern presence in the Modelo Prison. Members of the First International Brigade had been sent in at the height of the danger of rebel army breakthrough to Madrid on 7 November in order to replace the ordinary prison warders in the guarding of military inmates: see Schlayer, *Diplomat in roten Madrid*, pp. 118–19. The Spanish police doubtless listened to the opinions of Soviet intelligence advisers. But, as with Koltsov, these would have been *additional* influences, not 'directives' which determined the course of events. Alexander Orlov, who was NKVD chief in wartime Republican Spain, shed no light on his role to his US debriefers of the 1950s. Nor does the NKVD material available to date refer to the Madrid events: see J. Costello and O. Tsarev, *Deadly Illusions* (London: Century, 1993), *passim*. The authors assume that Republican Spain was a blank screen to be 'written' on by the Soviet operatives. But the archival evidence they present often undermines this assumption. Indeed, they cite Orlov himself complaining precisely about the *lack* of efficient internal police security in Republican Spain (see pp. 255–6, 264–6). It is also worthy of note that although 'Soviet influence' is the background mantra in Francoist material, the real focus is always on the Spanish protagonists. A more recent study of Orlov offers (with some lapses) a slightly more nuanced view of Soviet intervention and Orlov's role: Gazur, *Secret Assignment. The FBI's KGB General*, pp. 29, 49–51, 332–4.

By dint of their office, Carrillo and Serrano Poncela obviously bore a general political responsibility for what happened. But this responsibility was one of default. Instead of intervening to prevent – or at least to revisit the supervision of – further transfers as soon as it became apparent that something was amiss (that is, within a day or so of the first transfers of prisoners failing to arrive at their destination),[236] Carrillo and Serrano Poncela turned a blind eye.[237] Carrillo's subsequent insistence that he only even heard the name 'Paracuellos' after the war is clearly not credible.[238] Nevertheless, in one important respect, Carrillo consistently relates a central emotional truth about how it felt inside Madrid in November 1936: given the magnitude of what people were undergoing in the defence of the city – the gargantuan effort of organisation, the miltary struggle, the deaths in battle and in air raids behind the lines – when the rumours came of prisoner killings on the outskirts they seemed somehow remote and, in the immediate scheme of things, of secondary importance.[239]

The fact that Defence Council measures on public order brought a rapid general improvement in the security of the population at large was no doubt a contributory factor here. For it had been the widespread and unpredictable rough justice of the night-time 'patrols' inside the city which most fed public anxieties. Although it would take until the early months of 1937 properly to eradicate such phenomena, the Council at least reduced their occurrence inside Madrid to isolated, sporadic

---

[236] R. Gullón, 'Justice et guerre civile: souvenir d'un procureur', p. 234.

[237] I have chosen not to discuss Carrillo's subsequent denunciation of Serrano Poncela here. First, because it does not bear on the main thrust of my argument. Second, because it remains difficult to substantiate and highly controversial in view of Serrano Poncela's increasing political alienation from the JSU during the civil war. (By 1938 he was helping the Socialist Party executive in its attempt to re-establish a separate Socialist Youth: see Graham, *Socialism and War*, pp. 30–1, 226–31 – Serrano Poncela was the author of an important report on the JSU passed to the PSOE executive in 1938 (Graham, p. 297, n. 31).)

[238] Interview with Ian Gibson in 1982, *Paracuellos*, p. 230 and in Carrillo, *Memorias*, pp. 208–11. On 11 November Carrillo reported on the prison transfer question at a special meeting of the Defence Council chaired by Mije in Miaja's absence. But the minutes are extremely brief and oblique. Even from these, however, there is a sense that Carrillo and the others present have some sense of the looming problems of prisoner security: see text of minutes in Aróstegui and Martínez, *La Junta de Defensa*, pp. 295–6 (see also pp. 230–3).

[239] Interview with Gibson, *Paracuellos*, pp. 219–21. Note also the format of the Defence Council minutes for 16–30 November (reproduced in Aróstegui and Martínez, *La Junta de Defensa*). Before and after these dates, Council meetings are identified by day, month and year. But the entries for these dates – the most intense of the siege/fighting – are almost always indicated just by the day. This was moment zero: there was no sense of an 'after time'. None of this meant, however, that the Republican government considered the Paracuellos killings to be unimportant. Even so, there was no attempt either at cover-up or justification by recourse to *raison de guerre*: Cox, *Defence of Madrid*, p. 183.

instances.[240] This cumulative, collective improvement in public order also saw the ending of the prison *sacas*. The CNT's new prison delegate, Melchor Rodríguez, who took up his duties on 4 December, increased security measures around prison transfers and forbade nocturnal ones.[241] But crucially too, the ending of the siege itself reduced the tension in the city enormously. In all, fifth column activity was largely brought under control by the actions of the Council and would only reappear as a notable problem when the material conditions on the home front began seriously to deteriorate in late 1937, thus providing a new series of opportunities.

But it is also vital to understand that the Council's public-order measures, including those specifically directed at the control of fifth columnists, represented something more than themselves. They were also part of the dense battle for political power being waged inside the Republican polity. In Madrid, the Council's drive against the uncontrollables and the fragmentation of political power saw it close the private prisons and interrogation centres previously operated by various political organisations and, in particular, the communists and anarchists. But this consolidation of public-order machinery, in accordance with central government directives, did not end the organisational struggle; it simply reconfigured it. It is in these terms, therefore, that one needs to understand much of the conflict between the PCE and the CNT on the Council right up to its dissolution by the Valencia government towards the end of April 1937.

The JSU's José Cazorla, who had replaced Carrillo as Public-Order Councillor in December 1936, consolidated control of the police and implemented rigorous investigative and punitive measures against those suspected of pro-rebel subversion and fifth column activities – either sabotage or, at the worst end of the scale, conspiracies in the army or violence aimed at discrediting the Republic internally and externally. In the latter cases, he instituted a system of preventive detention of suspect individuals pending the outcome of further police investigations leading either to punishment (often in work brigades) or evacuation from Madrid.[242]

[240] Aróstegui and Martínez, *La Junta de Defensa*, pp. 228, 230, 444; Cox, *Defence of Madrid*, p. 179; López Fernández, *Defensa de Madrid*, pp. 245–9; Gibson, *Paracuellos*, pp. 194–6; Fraser, *Blood of Spain*, p. 177.

[241] Aróstegui and Martínez, *La Junta de Defensa*, p. 261 (n. 102). He remains a controversial figure, however. See the startling instance recalled by Cazorla in the Defence Council minutes of 15 April 1937, cited in Aróstegui and Martínez, p. 446.

[242] Ibid., pp. 234, 241, 447.

These measures were rapidly denounced by the CNT on the Council as a covert means of persecuting its members. It accused Cazorla of illegal detentions and, later (in April), of trumping up espionage charges against *cenetistas*. This would explode into a damaging slanging match in the press – in spite of censorship regulations, which were heeded by none of those involved. The CNT complaints were not always without substance.[243] But Cazorla was strongly driven by the need to eradicate a real and present danger to Republican security: the case he made powerfully to the Council in session (on 15 April) was, indeed, unanswerable in its essentials – hence the significant personal embarrassment of the CNT's representative (Marín) in having to insist on the contrary.[244] In particular there was the delicate matter of pro-rebel embassies in Madrid serving as a base for fifth column conspiracy. The Popular Courts often simply acquitted people on whom they had no case notes without conducting any independent investigations (since they did not have the resources). A proportion of these individuals, it was well known, subsequently holed up in the embassies in question. Cazorla, prepared to take swingeing action and deal with the constitutional issue later, had many of them rearrested at the doors of the Courts.[245]

But although Cazorla could justify his public-order policy, the police personnel (new or old) who implemented it may sometimes have had rather more mixed motives when *cenetistas* were involved. Some no doubt had directly party-political motives. But many of the Madrid policemen involved would have been 'new', not 'old' communists – i.e. they would have acquired a PCE membership card after 18 July 1936. They were, thus, exactly the same policemen who had dealt with the CNT before the war, with exactly the same attitudes. Cazorla was open about the occurrence of some grave irregularities – including killings, kidnappings and other forms of coercion. But he was on record as acting against every case brought to his knowledge. Cazorla put his finger on the root cause of the problem when he remarked that 'today it is easier to get away with being a thief than it ever was before – because the state is in

---

[243] For a detailed and suggestive analysis of internal conflict on the Defence Council see ibid., pp. 136–42, pp. 226–42.

[244] Ibid., pp. 440–54, especially pp. 445–9 for Cazorla's major intervention and p. 449 for Marín's discomfiture: 'I'm in an awkward position, I have to represent the collective position of the Organisation [Madrid CNT]; I can't go and say to them that Cazorla's explanation has convinced me.'

[245] See ibid. for Cazorla to the Council, minutes of 19 Feb., p. 411 and 27 Feb., pp. 421–2, where he gives convincing reasons for some of these detentions. The embassy problem is present throughout the minuted discussions: see also p. 446 (15 April 1937).

disarray'.[246] Unfortunately that disarray also facilitated dubious behaviours inside the reconstructing agencies of the state. But nor did the
CNT occupy the moral high ground here. There were cases in Madrid
and elsewhere of illegal detention and the extortion of funds by individuals who claimed libertarian affiliation.[247]

The PCE representatives on the Council also retaliated, predictably,
but also with some truth, by recalling how, whenever there was insubordination to government instructions (of whatever kind), there would
always be *cenetistas* involved somewhere. Indeed, the Madrid CNT rather
disarmingly confessed that it could not change overnight the deeply ingrained anti-authoritarian attitudes of many of its supporters – war or no
war.[248] As a result, in this instance the CNT was unable to avail itself of
the support of republican and socialist members who, otherwise, sought
to maintain the PCE and CNT in equilibrium on the Council.

Although there was an ideological backdrop to the confrontation between the CNT and PCE in Madrid, there was no equivalent of the
confrontation looming by early 1937 between anarchists and communists in Catalonia over government directives to disarm the home front
and centralise food supply policy. The Madrid CNT held the key Council portfolio of war industries. This required it to oversee the industrial
mobilisation upon which the supplying of the crucial central front depended. This direct and immediate responsibility for maintaining the
front – in particular guaranteeing the rapid and reliable movement of
supplies and personnel – made the centralisation of such functions a
much less polemical issue in Madrid than it was in Catalonia (at least
as far as local CNT *leaders* were concerned).[249] In Madrid the root of
PCE–CNT conflict was an organisational struggle for power in the capital, as the socialist Councillor Máximo de Díos would openly identify in

---

[246] 'No tenemos un Estado organizado', ibid., p. 446. Although the Council gave Cazorla a public
vote of confidence in April (with the CNT abstaining), the very occurrence of such incidents
in his sphere of responsibility led to some private criticism from the other political groups
(Aróstegui and Martínez, p. 255, n. 112). The ensuing enquiry into the Cazorla affair exposed
some dubious activity by individuals in his employ: Broué and Témime, *The Revolution and the
Civil War in Spain*, pp. 273–4. Nothing was proven against Cazorla personally. Cazorla, who
stayed behind as part of the PCE's first cadres in clandestinity, was imprisoned and executed by
the Franco regime: see the recent memoir by his widow, Aurora Arnaiz, *Retrato hablado de Luisa
Julián. Memorias de una guerra* (Madrid: Compañía Literaria, 1996). Cazorla emerges as scrupulous
(see, for example, p. 34) though prepared to be tough and to take unpopular decisions if his
political responsibilities required it.
[247] Aróstegui and Martínez, *La Junta de Defensa*, p. 448.
[248] Ibid., p. 238 and p. 416 for similar intervention by Marín (CNT), minutes of 19 Feb. 1937.
[249] For the situation in Catalonia, see chapter 4 below.

February 1937.[250] Indeed, the very fact that political parties and trade unions were required to fulfil crucial public and social service functions because of the deficiencies of the state was another factor exacerbating the organisational competition between them.[251]

The comments of another witness on the 'rough' or unpolished quality of the political discussion at Madrid Council meetings also offer a key here:[252] it is important to remember that, in addition to the pressing circumstances of the war, democratic politics in Spain were very recent. The impact of the war massively accelerated popular participation in government process and fora. A good proportion of those involved in the Council had had little or no previous jobbing political experience. It is important to factor in this 'immaturity', as well as the accompanying hangover from clientelist political modes, in order to understand the organisational confrontations in council chamber, police station and street in wartime Madrid.[253] The production of mobilisation propaganda was also part of this organisational contest. Along with the PCE, the CNT also participated energetically in the task. Here the PCE used Soviet images and symbols in order to compete with the CNT for popular support. But this was a *domestic* war of symbols in which the Soviet Union had no role other than as a depository of images.

Although the PCE was a major player in the internal conflicts in the Madrid Council, this was not as some mythic instrument of Soviet pressure. The disputes had little to do with Stalin or the Comintern. Indeed, pushed to an extreme, this fierce organisational contest prejudiced Stalin's overarching objective of keeping the Republican coalition afloat and the CNT on board the war effort. Moreover, once the Soviet Union had begun to offer support to the Republic, the main medium of Soviet–Spanish relations shifted to diplomatic channels broadly construed.[254] By 1937 various kinds of liaison related to military support/advisers, Soviet intelligence activity, and even some matters concerning the International Brigades were occurring via channels other than

---

[250] 'Lo que aquí existe es una lucha de organizaciones', Aróstegui and Martínez, *La Junta de Defensa*, p. 238.

[251] For example, the unions oversaw various kinds of benefit – unemployment, sickness and accident – while both parties and unions provided canteens and nurseries, organised civil defence, and ran searches for refugees/displaced persons on behalf of families.

[252] According to Miaja's secretary, the General had a bell which he would ring furiously to bring meetings to order: López Fernández, *Defensa de Madrid*, p. 259.

[253] The stenographic record of the Council's deliberations – reproduced ibid. – offers invaluable insights into this (and its deleterious effects in wartime): see, for example, minutes of 19 February (especially Cazorla, p. 410) and 15 April 1937, pp. 440–54.

[254] Cf. Bolloten, *SCW*, p. 589; Schauff, 'Hitler and Stalin in the Spanish Civil War', p. 18.

the Comintern's. This was in part a consequence of the heavy purge going on inside the Comintern itself. As a result, its role in Republican Spain was in a sense shrinking as it shifted back to more specifically PCE-related matters, although again with the emphasis strongly on how best to achieve practical wartime mobilisation.[255] This shift was also heralded in the one instance where the Soviet Union did make a political preference strongly known in regard to the Madrid Defence Council. Although the PCE was clearly in agreement,[256] it was primarily through diplomatic channels (including ambassador Rosenberg) that representations were made in early November 1936 to debar the POUM, as a dissident communist (and for the Comintern a 'trotskyist') party. As a result, the POUM's exclusion was accepted without even being discussed by the Council in session.[257]

But one must keep the Soviet veto in perspective. While it indicated Spanish Republicans' preparedness to take on board Soviet political sensitivities because of their own military and defence requirements (that is, to ensure Soviet support), it is important to remember that excluding the POUM was not in itself a source of particular conflict or difficulty for any of the groups. The POUM was a very marginal political force in Madrid.[258] Certainly no other group on the Madrid Council had any political empathy with it. Socialists and republicans were hostile and the CNT largely indifferent. The Madrid POUM's exiguousness ruled out any real political hostility such as existed in Catalonia, where CNT–POUM organisational rivalry was an important feature of the Republican landscape. But even so, the Madrid CNT clearly felt no need to object on political principle to the POUM's exclusion. Indeed, the only criticism of this, or indeed any, kind was made (implicitly) by the newspaper of Angel Pestaña's Syndicalist Party when it carried a

---

[255] Elorza and Bizcarrondo, *Queridos camaradas*, pp. 14, 329. This interpretation is also sustained by recent research on Soviet–Republican Spanish relations during the war: Frank Schauff, doctoral thesis, 'Sowjetunion, Kommunistische Internationale und Spanischer Bürgerkrieg 1936–1939', University of Cologne, 2000. Cf. also the clear division of labour between Soviet representatives charged with military, diplomatic and Comintern functions: Gazur, *Secret Assignment. The FBI's KGB General*, p. 334.

[256] Aróstegui and Martínez, *La Junta de Defensa*, p. 130 (and n. 76).

[257] Ibid., pp. 79, 80–1.

[258] Statistical information about POUM membership outside Catalonia (i.e. in Madrid and Valencia) is sparse, but there is no doubt that the party was tiny in Madrid. Some statistics, including a figure of 70 for Madrid (area) membership in 1936, are in Durgan, *B.O.C. 1930–1936*, pp. 556, 559. The Madrid POUM was to the left of the Catalan party – being mainly constituted from Andreu Nin's tiny Left Communist component (Izquierda Comunista): Morrow, *Revolution and Counter-Revolution in Spain*, p. 85. For the POUM in Catalonia see chapters 4 and 5 below.

note from the POUM executive criticising the Council for weakening the fight for a revolutionary victory over fascism by excluding it.[259] (The Syndicalist Party was itself represented on the Council, in spite of being even smaller than the POUM and having no militia presence.) Across November and December, as the POUM also came under attack in Catalonia, its public criticisms of the Soviet leadership, the Republican government and the Madrid Council became increasingly vehement. In response, it was made harder and harder for the POUM to function politically in Madrid, and this culminated in the Council's closure (in January 1937) of POUM press and radio in the city.[260] But given the full-time demands of the war effort and the significant energy required even to keep relations between the Coucil's constituent groups on an even keel, no one had the time or inclination to worry overmuch about the fate of a group as marginal as the POUM.

The inherent source of conflict in the Madrid Council was not Soviet interference but the fraught nature of relations with the central Republican government in Valencia – a conflict which would eventually lead to the Council's dissolution in April 1937. This difficulty was partly structural in origin and partly personal. Both aspects were encapsulated in the deep mutually antagonistic relationship between Largo Caballero and General Miaja. The Council's inevitably high political profile during the November days seemed to threaten reconstructing government authority, already dealt a further blow by the cabinet's departure. In Miaja Largo saw both an insubordinate general and a popular hero whose fame detracted from his own prestige. Both men had a wide streak of vanity which increased the antagonism between them. In their excessive concern to protect their own reputations and bask in popular acclaim they were very alike. The subjects of many of their running disputes seem scandalously petty given what was at stake in November. (And in this respect the prime minister's capacities outdid the general's.[261]) But at root the fundamental question was one of hierarchies of power. Once the immediate danger to Madrid had passed by the end of November 1936,

[259] Aróstegui and Martínez, *La Junta de Defensa*, pp. 130–1.
[260] Broué and Témime, *The Revolution and the Civil War in Spain*, p. 254; Aróstegui and Martínez, *La Junta de Defensa*, p. 376 (minutes of meeting of 29 Jan. 1937); Bolloten, *SCW*, p. 298 and n. 83, p. 835. Bolloten looks for a hidden, conspiratorial explanation of the measures against the POUM and entirely ignores the force of the reasons given – the destabilising impact of its vehement anti-government criticisms in wartime.
[261] López Fernández, *Defensa de Madrid* (1945), pp. 169–70, 190ff., 281, 285ff. The first of these references describes Largo's outraged sense of protocol when Miaja authorised the purchase of a consignment of zips for pilot uniforms – which, in theory, required the war minister's approval.

Largo insisted that the Council be restructured. The ensuing change of nomenclature was highly significant: henceforward the Council was to be called the Under-Council (Junta Delegada) and its members were no longer 'councillors' (*consejeros*) but 'delegates' (*delegados*).[262]

But the conflict of competences with Valencia would be ongoing and evident across the range of the Council's responsibilities. In the vital function of supply, for example, the government was determined to reimpose its control in the Madrid area over and above the Council's. Supply centralisation was opposed by many of the local neighbourhood committees in Madrid. But, unlike the contemporaneous conflict over the same issue in Catalonia, Madrid's again lacked an overtly ideological dimension. Although there were some tensions deriving from people's commitment to *patria chica*, there was no head-on clash over supply policy between the CNT and the PCE on the Madrid Council.

Nevertheless, all the internal conflicts and those between Council and government involved an expenditure of energy and time that could be ill afforded in the circumstances. Against such a background of government dissatisfaction, it would be the conflict over public order that eventually brought matters to a head. Cazorla's confrontation with the CNT exploded into the press, thus giving the rebels a useful opportunity to make damaging propaganda about Republican disorder with an international audience in mind. This probably accounts for the precise timing of Valencia's move against the Council. Nevertheless, the decision to replace it with a reconstituted municipal authority was entirely in line with zone-wide Republican government directives first issued in December 1936 as part of the ongoing process of state reconstruction.[263] Neither the PCE nor the CNT would express surprise. Indeed, the PCE was already publicly calling for the Council to be dismantled in the cause of the *mando único* (single military and political command) it so strongly advocated.[264]

For all that premier Largo Caballero accused the Council of having pretensions to autonomy, in fact it signified a crucial intermediate stage in the process of Republican state reconstruction (from the bottom up as well as from the top down) which would then be 'exported' with greater difficulty to other parts of Republican territory in the course of 1937. For although in Madrid they knew that there was a full-scale war on

---

[262] The basic distribution of functions remained the same, however: for a list of Council members as of 15 January 1937 (and until its dissolution), see Bolloten, *SCW*, p. 296.

[263] The decree dissolving the Madrid Defence Council came on 21 April 1937. Largo gave no particular explanation.

[264] Aróstegui and Martínez, *La Junta de Defensa*, p. 142.

by the end of 1936, few elsewhere in the fragmented Republican zone perceived this imperative. In Barcelona, the experience of emergency defence – street fighting and the storming of rebel garrisons – had not, of itself, produced any sense of the need to build a war machine. And given the strength of nationalist feeling in Catalonia, still less was it accepted that this had necessarily to see the centralisation of political and military power in order to organise total mobilisation of domestic (human and material) resources. In the Republican Basque Country a rigid nationalist political agenda would also conflict with the needs of the war effort, as we shall see in the next chapter.

The battles to defend Madrid continued through the first quarter of 1937. There was bitter fighting and enormous casualties resulted, especially among the International Brigades in their role as shock troops. The battle of Jarama (5–24 February), fought to keep the Madrid–Valencia road open, would see the decimation of its British contingent and savage losses among the American brigaders. The price was great, but so was the prize: Madrid was to be a major defeat for the rebels. As their forces dug in around the capital's perimeter, the war turned into one of attrition. But for all the psychological boost which the successful defence of Madrid provided, in the harsh light of day the Republic was badly isolated by the economic blockade which underlay the diplomacy of Non-Intervention. It was facing the onslaught of 'violent modernity' in the form of full-scale warfare, courtesy of the rebels' fascist backers. Moreover, Soviet aid was insufficient to do more than keep the Republic afloat. In Valencia, some minds were concentrating ever more on the growing imperatives of state centralisation in order to accelerate the maximum mobilisation and co-ordination of the Republic's internal resources. Only by so doing could it engage in and survive the looming war of attrition.

In order to provide an infrastructural basis for such a programme of political and economic centralisation, the Popular Front was formally reconstituted in Valencia in January 1937 on the basis of an alliance between the parliamentary PSOE and the PCE. It was agreed that it should work towards establishing a network of inter-party liaison committees (*comités de enlace*). The idea was that these would function in all areas of home front war organisation at local, provincial and national level, providing personnel and coordination to compensate for the weaknesses and gaps in Republican governmental machinery.[265] But immediately Largo Caballero and his supporters accused the PSOE executive of

---

[265] For the origins and political dimension of the *comités de enlace*, see Graham, *Socialism and War*, pp. 74–8. The circular was published in *El Socialista*, 7 Jan. 1937.

factional manoeuvring against themselves. Although Prieto, the executive's *éminence grise*, may have had some idea of this, far more important in his calculations was the role of the inter-party liaison committees in supporting the war effort. Indeed, the Caballeristas' reaction here prefigured what would rapidly become their obsessive trait: they would interpret every policy or strategy of the PSOE executive solely in terms of its tactical impact on the internal socialist war which they were determined to play out, come what may. They quite forgot that, beyond the relative tranquillity of their bolt hole in behind-the-lines Valencia, there was a real and very brutal war being fought for stakes which made those of the internal organisational 'war' appear trivial indeed.[266]

The understanding between the national leaderships of the socialist and communist parties was, then, based on a set of shared political preferences and the common objective of centralisation to serve the war effort. The PSOE was as keen as the PCE to accelerate militarisation at the front and liberal normalisation on the home front. The need for these things was brought home forcibly to Prieto by his experience in the navy and air ministry. He was constantly having to manage crises without any real organisational back-up or even decently articulated communication channels. In terms of the home front, the target in the spring of 1937 remained the regularisation of the state police forces. These were crucial in the battle to centralise economic power being waged by Negrín in the treasury.

Negrín spent the last months of 1936 and the beginning of 1937 building up the Carabineros. Recruiting heavily from PSOE affiliates, he made the force directly responsible to himself as minister.[267] It was deployed to curb the activities of the (mainly CNT-related) internal checkpoints and frontier controls on the French–Catalan border in order to recoup state control over foreign exchange. These, usually self-appointed, controls also interfered with the free movement of ministers and personnel on government business.[268] In the medium term, the Carabineros would

---

[266] This story is told in Graham, *Socialism and War*. For the 'peacetime' atmosphere in the Valencia region see various memoirs including López Fernández, *Defensa de Madrid*, p. 145 ('ciudad de las flores' – 'city of flowers'); Cox, *Defence of Madrid*, p. 212.

[267] Zugazagoitia, *Guerra y vicisitudes*, p. 179; Morrow, *Revolution and Counter-Revolution in Spain*, p. 68. The Carabineros were first brought under treasury control as a result of General Sanjurjo's attempted coup against the Republic in August 1932: see Payne, *Spain's First Democracy*, p. 100. On Negrín's use of them, see Vázquez Ocaña, *Pasión y muerte*, p. 59; Alpert, *El ejército republicano*, p. 306. The PSOE 'ring fence' around the Carabineros would only be breached after the division of Republican territory in April 1938: see chapter 6 below.

[268] This particularly enraged Negrín, for whom state prerogatives were an overriding value. See F. Vázquez Ocaña, *Pasión y muerte*, p. 59, also his article in Alvarez, *Negrín (Documentos)*, pp. 252–3;

also be deployed to reinforce Assault Guards and National Republican (ex-Civil) Guards in Negrín's bid to impose state control over socialised industries. The thrust of Negrín's economic strategy was thus consonant with the liberal statist political values which he, probably most of all the PSOE leaders, endorsed.[269] But he also understood that accelerating the centralisation of domestic industrial resources was crucial to compensate for the increasing scarcity of external supply which Non-Interventionist embargo would invariably mean.

It was in the logic of the PCE's commitment to an inter-class policy of Popular Front that the party would grow closer to the PSOE's parliamentary wing and away from its former (pre-war) socialist left allies grouped around Largo Caballero. While Prieto was delighted by the transformation in the PCE's policies, the socialist left, acutely aware of the PCE's rapid wartime growth, and smarting from its loss of control over the socialist youth, was becoming increasingly hostile. The powerful discourse of unity suffusing the Popular Front period in Spain had intensified after 18 July, and by 1937 the PCE was calling for the PSOE to merge with it in a single party of the left (Partido Unico). Caballero's supporters reiterated their historic complaint that the communists were intent upon absorbing the socialist movement. But the case of the JSU notwithstanding, the Caballeristas' anti-communist broadside, like their criticism of the PSOE, ignored the wartime imperatives fuelling the unity drive which also made it an initially appealing prospect to many rank-and-file party and union members.

The Caballeristas, immensely shrewd and self-protective in matters of organisational prerogative, were nevertheless right to discern a streak of competitiveness in the PCE. This was epitomised in Vittorio Codovilla, the Argentinian communist who had been Comintern representative in Spain since 1932. By the end of 1936 Codovilla had come to be Largo Caballero's *bête noire*, so insistent was he that the premier should give a strong steer to socialist-communist unification.[270] But Codovilla's obsessive ambition for the PCE derived far less from his Comintern function than it did from a trait of personality. Codovilla had effectively 'gone

---

Largo Caballero, 'Notas históricas de la guerra en España 1917–1940', p. 986. Negrín's strong opinions on the obligations of individuals to the state (for example in the payment of taxes) come through clearly in the economic report to the PSOE National Committee, July 1937.

[269] Negrín's treasury work represented in microcosmic form his larger goal of putting the state 'back on track' – cf. his hatred of the 'arbitrary spirit' of the July days, Vázquez Ocaña, *Pasión y muerte*, pp. 59–60; Negín to Prieto, letter of 23 June 1939, *Epistolario Prieto y Negrín*, p. 42.

[270] Elorza and Bizcarrondo, *Queridos camaradas*, pp. 329–30; Largo Caballero, 'Notas históricas', p. 265 and *Mis recuerdos*, pp. 210–12.

native' in Spain and looked upon the PCE as his personal creature.[271] This became a particular problem after the Comintern's adoption of the Popular Front strategy. For while democratic centralism remained unbreachable, there was, nevertheless, an attempt to foster the organisational capacities and talents of indigenous Communist Party leaderships.

The effects of the war itself would to some extent counteract Codovilla's influence. The huge scale of practical demands meant that the PCE's own leadership cadres had to take the strain. And, in a fast-moving war, that meant they were also taking political initiatives and gaining experience, becoming, in some ways, a real leadership.[272] Communication between the PCE and the Comintern was, moreover, slow and frequently out of synch. The Spanish Politburo often found itself 'on its own' in situations which demanded rapid political responses. Codovilla's influence was great but, in the maelstrom of war, with all its myriad demands, not even he could be the 'one-man executive' often claimed. Nevertheless, Codovilla's overbearing behaviour and ambitions were a problem, and from the beginning of the war he was increasingly the target of Comintern criticism for a variety of reasons – although he would not be removed from Spain until September 1937.[273]

Largo Caballero interpreted Codovilla's insistent demand for party unification as an expression of Soviet leadership intent. But in this he was mistaken. Throughout the winter of 1936 and spring of 1937 Stalin's primary concern was not to upset Largo Caballero and his wing of the socialist movement since they held crucial cabinet posts and this would have risked destabilising the Republican alliance and thus the war effort. Stalin knew that Largo was the best guarantee of keeping the CNT on board the war effort. Internationally too, Largo was saying the kind of things about the parliamentary democratic nature of the Republic and its war aims which Stalin believed should bring Britain and France to reconsider their position on Non-Intervention.[274] Codovilla's insistent

---

[271] Elorza and Bizcarrondo, *Queridos camaradas*, p. 337; Falcón, *Asalto a los cielos*, pp. 144–6; Carrillo, *Memorias*, pp. 262–3.

[272] T. Rees, 'The Highpoint of Comintern Influence? The Communist Party and the Civil War in Spain', in T. Rees and A. Thorpe (eds.), *International Communism and the Communist International 1919–43* (Manchester: Manchester University Press, 1998), pp. 143–67.

[273] See chapter 6 below. A. Elorza and M. Bizcarrondo suggest that the delay was because the Comintern was very short of suitable representatives, *Queridos camaradas*, pp. 319–20. But Frank Schauff has suggested that it was simply evidence of the arbitrariness and irrationality that afflicted Soviet procedures: 'Failure in Emergency: The Spanish Civil War and the Dissolution of the Comintern' (unpublished research paper, presented at the University of Bristol, 1 Mar. 2001), p. 25.

[274] Graham, *Socialism and War*, p. 89; Elorza and Bizcarrondo, *Queridos camaradas*, p. 329.

pursuit of party unification from November 1936 was, then, going directly against Stalin's policy. But the reciprocally slow and cumbersome process of communication between the Comintern and Republican Spain obscured this fact for a time.[275] Eventually, however, on 8 January, the Comintern telegraphed Stalin's urgent instructions that the PCE should backpeddle on party unity and instead promote unity of action, via the mooted liaison committees and other avenues.[276] Particularly to be discouraged were high-profile cases such as that of Margarita Nelken, the PSOE leader and parliamentary deputy who had joined the PCE in November 1936 during the siege of Madrid.[277] Stalin's instructions would also seem to shed some light on why Nelken never rose to prominence in the wartime PCE in spite of her undoubted talent, intelligence and passionate commitment to the Republican cause.[278]

But if Stalin saw the fortunes of the PCE in contingent terms, this was precisely because he was enormously exercised by the need to ensure a viable Republican war effort. And the primacy of this objective meant that he instructed his diplomatic representatives, and in particular the Soviet ambassador in Valencia, Marcel Rosenberg, to visit Largo daily to discuss practical matters of war policy. But this was a thankless task, as the PCE leader Mije had already discovered. Rosenberg and Largo were soon as much at loggerheads as Largo and Mije had been earlier.[279] The prime minister would accept no advice on war ministry matters even though such advice was seriously necessary. When it came from a *foreigner*, it was even easier for Largo to deflect it by a display of outraged patriotism. No doubt the emotion was genuine. But that did not resolve the underlying problems in the war ministry.

Then came the devastating news of the collapse of the southern city of Malaga, taken by Franco's Italian allies on 7 February. The repression that ensued in the city – in spite of the lack of military resistance – saw some 4,000 people shot in the week after conquest (and executions on

---

[275] Cf. Carr, *The Twilight of the Comintern*, pp. 3–32.

[276] Elorza and Bizcarrondo, *Queridos camaradas*, pp. 338–9 (n. 80 cites the Comintern archive reference for the telegram); Schauff, 'Hitler and Stalin in the Spanish Civil War', pp. 10–11.

[277] Zugazagoitia, *Guerra y vicisitudes*, p. 187; also the less famous case of Francisco Montiel (PSOE deputy for Murcia) and author of the February 1937 agitprop pamphlet 'Por qué he ingresado en el Partido Comunista' (Barcelona, 1937).

[278] Preston, *Palomas de guerra* (Barcelona: Plaza & Janés, 2001), pp. 315–18 (and in English in *Doves of War*, pp. 360–6).

[279] Elorza and Bizcarrondo, *Queridos camaradas*, p. 338 have critical details from Codovilla's December 1936 report (Largo didn't understand the concept of a Popular Army or *mando único*; he didn't have the required sense of urgency about creating war industries; he communed only with his ministry bureaucrats).

a massive scale would continue for months).[280] Refugees fleeing the repression eastwards along the coastal road to Almería were bombed and machine gunned from the air, shelled from the sea and pursued by a motorised column.[281] All the reasons why Malaga had fallen endorsed the criticisms of Largo's leadership. Above all, it brought home the vulnerability of the Republic's military defence for as long as the civilian front was not brought fully under centralised government control.

Malaga's geographical isolation had exacerbated the problem of arms shortage, which, in turn, intensified various forms of internecine political conflict among the Republicans holding out there.[282] In particular, anarchists and communists clashed over the forms of defence strategy to be adopted. Both the arms shortages and the internal political conflicts damaged morale, as, no doubt, did the awareness that the hard-pressed government was concentrating its organisational energies mainly on the central Madrid front. During the second half of January, as rebel troops advanced towards the city, Malaga suffered severe bombing raids. There were no anti-aircraft guns (rare anyway in Republican cities), yet it was the end of the month before the government sent planes and (some) artillery. Although shortage rather than political malice was the underlying reason for the delay, it is also true that the government felt that matériel sent to Malaga would be poorly deployed.

Indeed, much more could have been achieved by way of military organisation had it not been for the fragmentation of political authority in Malaga. The political committee and civil governor were neither active in practical, war-related matters nor in contact with each other. This was exacerbated by the total disconnection of political bodies in the town from the military authorities based just outside it.[283] These various sorts of internal disarticulation led to fatal inefficiencies: crucial infrastructural repair work was not undertaken (for example of a bridge), which

---

[280] Franco told the Italian ambassador, Roberto Cantalupo, that Malaga was a particularly 'red city': Jackson, *The Spanish Republic and the Civil War*, p. 345. On the repression and Malaga's place in the rebels' pathological firmament, see Richards, *A Time of Silence*, pp. 41, 62; Juliá *et al.*, *Víctimas de la guerra civil*, p. 201.

[281] '100,000 fugitivos – suicidios – madres que matan a sus hijos', Azaña, *Apuntes de Memoria*, p. 73; for an oral history account see R. Fraser, *In Hiding. The Life of Manuel Cortes* (London: Allen Lane, 1972), pp. 149–52; other eye-witness accounts in T. C. Worsley, *Behind the Battle* (London: Robert Hale, 1939), pp. 179–208; A. Bahamonde, *Un año con Queipo*, pp. 126–36.

[282] As elsewhere, of course, these labour conflicts had pre-war histories. At the end of 1936 the UGT in Malaga had written to the national executive begging for arms – which meant prestige – and informing the committee that they had agreed to fuse with the local CNT since they had arms. Actas de la UGT, 9 December 1936. (The UGT executive forbade the merger, of course.) Vidarte, *Todos fuimos culpables*, vol. 2, pp. 649–50.

[283] Borkenau, *The Spanish Cockpit*, p. 219.

hindered the delivery of arms even when these were eventually made available. Nor were there enough fortifications – a situation worsened by the desertion to the rebels of the two commanders in charge. The lack of anti-tank trenches of adequate quality explains the very rapid progress of the Italian forces. The isolation of the civilian and military fronts from each other, which the visiting Austrian writer Franz Borkenau remarked, was in part a result of the fragmentation of political authority. But it was also a result of prevalent military attitudes.

Malaga, like other peripheral fronts, had seen less progress towards militarisation. The defence forces were no longer the 'militia' of summer 1936, but in terms of training and mentality they were still a body of men in transition.[284] Yet military professionals, like Colonel Villalba, who was in charge, were far too inflexible in their understanding of what constituted 'troops' and 'strategy' to be able to respond effectively. The tragedy of Malaga was that the resources the military commanders wanted were simply not available, while those they had on hand they proved unable or unwilling to use. Villalba did not understand his 'troops' and they did not trust him.

After Malaga's collapse, questions were immediately asked about the responsibility borne by the Republic's military strategists and the southern commanders on the ground. In particular, there was a redoubling of the criticism of General Asensio, Largo's under-secretary of war and the main impeller of military strategy in the ministry. The PCE had long been critical of him, but now so too were socialists and republicans, including President Azaña.[285] These assessments all carried a heavy political charge since they implicitly cast doubt on Largo Caballero's judgement in choosing his ministerial collaborators.[286] On 14 February a public demonstration in support of Largo arranged by the Valencian UGT was transformed by the organisational efforts of the PCE into a show of support for *mando único*, a clean-out of the military command structure, boosting the war industries programme and, perhaps above all, for the genuine implementation of military conscription.[287] The voluntary recruitment favoured by Largo was falling off and Malaga served to clarify the urgency here. The PCE's use of street mobilisation was

---

[284] Ibid., p. 220 and cf. pp. 215–16.

[285] Bolloten accepts that '[Asensio] was defeated by a broad opposition spanning the political spectrum from the Anarchosyndicalist to the left Republican ministers', *SCW*, p. 355.

[286] PCE criticism of the pernicious influence of Largo's personal entourage was constant through to the May crisis of 1937: see Manuel Azaña's diary entry for 20 May 1937, *Obras completas*, vol. 4, p. 592.

[287] R. Llopis, *Spartacus*, 1 October 1937, pp. 6–7; *El Socialista* 14 Feb. 1937; Bolloten, *SCW*, pp. 360, 345.

deprecated as cheap populism by republican and, especially, socialist leaders – even those hostile to Largo. But the fact remained that the PCE had not invented popular lack of confidence in the professional military – with distrust inevitably surging on occasions of defeat – and it was less the need for military resignations that the PSOE disputed than the PCE campaign itself.[288]

In response to mounting pressure inside and outside the cabinet, to which the CNT also contributed,[289] Largo finally agreed to remove Asensio on 21 February along with Generals Martínez Monje (head of the southern army) and Martínez Cabrera, the chief of the Republican general staff.[290] Asensio was a far from incapable officer, if conservative and conventional in matters of military organisation. He was also very ambitious. This would explain his brutal contempt for fleeing militiamen.[291] Asensio took no account of their lack of training and on one occasion, in the crisis conditions of autumn 1936 on the Madrid front, had had thirty of them shot for leaving their positions.[292] This brought him into conflict with the PCE. The party wanted to impose as strict a military discipline as Asensio, but understood that first it was necessary to train and prepare men who had started out as militia *volunteers*. Asensio's abrasiveness had certainly been an important contributory factor in Largo's decision to move him from his field position to the war under-secretaryship in October 1936 when the Madrid front was in grave disarray and militia morale low because of past defeats.[293]

In the case of Malaga, Asensio probably believed that it could not be held with only the militia to defend it. He even seems to have considered,

---

[288] As the PSOE press makes clear – see *El Socialista* between 12 and 20 February 1937.

[289] Bolloten, *SCW*, pp. 355–9.

[290] Martínez Cabrera's critics saw him as the epitome of a fossilised Republican General Staff: Alvarez del Vayo to Araquistain 11 Feb. 1937, Araquistain correspondence, Leg. 23 no. 112b.

[291] Cordón, *Trayectoria*, pp. 261–2. Cordón was a professional army officer under the pre-war Republic, and he had also served in Africa. In spite of his PCE affiliation, his assessment of Asensio is astute. There is a party-driven zeal to the criticism and also a puritanism that may or may not be related. But the basic assessment fits with other (often at least partially positive) assessments of Asensio: Zugazagoitia, *Guerra y vicisitudes*, pp. 166–9 (also pp. 117–18, 160). Biographical sketches of Asensio are in M. Teresa Suero Roca, *Militares republicanos de la guerra de España*, pp. 27–52; Zaragoza, *Ejército popular y militares de la República*, pp. 221–3.

[292] H. E. Knoblaugh, *Correspondent in Spain* (London/New York: Sheed & Ward, 1937), pp. 45, 210. It was to this reputation that Indalecio Prieto referred in February 1937 when he remarked that Asensio's 'antecedentes' (record) made him disinclined to support him against his critics.

[293] The more emollient General Pozas replaced Asensio on 22 October 1936. Rojo, *Así fue la defensa de Madrid*, pp. 27–8, 40–1; Cox, *Defence of Madrid*, pp 69–70. Bolloten claims that Asensio was moved exclusively because of PCE pressure on Largo, *SCW*, pp. 280–1. But this does not tally with Largo's general recalcitrance in the autumn of 1936 in all matters of war policy and especially where the PCE was concerned.

somewhat controversially, that the consequent shortening of the Republican front would be an advantage.[294] Certainly his appointment of the expendable Villalba, with his chequered professional history and ordinary military record, lends credence to this interpretation (and indeed one is reminded of Asensio's earlier thinking in respect of Miaja on the Madrid front).[295] Although Asensio thus laid himself open to charges of negligence in respect of the Malaga front, there is nothing which necessarily indicates that he was a saboteur. On the other hand, Colonel Villalba's precipitate departure from Malaga more than twelve hours before the rebels arrived left a seriously negative impression.[296] His role in the defeat – along with that of Asensio, Martínez Cabrera and Martínez Monje – would be the subject of judicial investigation. The case against them was eventually quashed and all would be rehabilitated to a greater or lesser extent. But given the especial fragility of civil–military relations in Republican Spain, none would serve again in pivotal, active military commands.[297]

But the removal in February 1937 of those held to be militarily responsible for the loss of Malaga did little to resolve the underlying tensions between the Republican alliance and Largo Caballero over his running of the war ministry and the need to accelerate military, political and economic centralisation. The attack was spearheaded by the PCE. But, contrary to what is frequently suggested, its criticism of Largo's performance as war minister was not simply a 'cover' for communist organisational ambitions. In any case, there was a rather more complex picture of organisational rivalries being played out between socialists, anarchists and communists. When Asensio was sacked after Malaga there were also several other sackings of PCE members and sympathisers in

---

[294] Cordón, *Trayectoria*, pp. 291–2.

[295] Villalba had been pro-rebel in July 1936. But, at the head of the Barbastro barracks (Huesca), he decided at the last moment not to join the rising, Cordón, ibid., pp. 292–5; Thomas, *Spanish Civil War*, p. 239; Bolloten, *SCW*, p. 846, n. 6.

[296] Villalba was apparently allowed back into the Francoist army reserve after the war: Alpert *El ejército republicano*, pp. 387–8. Given his behaviour in July 1936 (see preceding note) it can only be assumed that he made an excellent retrospective case for himself as a fifth columnist.

[297] Asensio wrote a memoir, *El General Asensio. Su lealtad a la República* (Barcelona, 1938) while in prison awaiting trial over the Malaga affair. He had powerful supporters, including Rojo, by then Chief of the Republican General Staff, whose letters are cited in Asensio's book, pp. 110–11. Negrín also supported him: see Zugazagoitia, *Guerra y vicisitudes*, pp. 453–4. After his rehabilitation Asensio was appointed military attaché to Washington in January 1939 and would later be identified with Negrín and the SERE in the immediate post-war period: Graham, *Socialism and War*, p. 272, n. 21; Alpert, *El ejército republicano*, p. 361. Martínez Cabrera was later appointed military governor of Madrid. He would support the Casado rebellion at the end of the war and was shot by Franco: Alpert, *El ejército republicano*, pp. 377–8.

the war ministry, most notably of Cordón, who was sent to the Cordoba front.[298] Moreover, it is also clear from the Comintern archival sources now available that war policy, rather than socialist–communist unification, was the nub of the dispute between PCE and premier and, above all, *between Largo and the Soviet Union's diplomatic representatives* throughout the first four months of 1937.[299] In Catalonia, the fall of Malaga also galvanised the PSUC. It organised a big demonstration in Barcelona on 28 February, with the participation of soldiers, to mobilise political and popular support for the immediate militarisation of the militia on the Aragon front and the call up of the 1934–5 military roll. To the same end it also created the Committee for the Popular Army.[300]

It was only later that the issues of war policy and party unification came to be seen as two sides of the same coin in Largo's confrontation with the PCE. This interpretation has persisted largely as a result of historians (including me) too readily accepting the conflation of these two questions in both Largo's own memoirs and those of his supporters.[301] Instructions from Stalin had been received by the PCE Politburo on 8 January that Largo was to be conciliated. It is then highly unlikely that Codovilla would have been belligerent over party unification after this date. He could have continued to be belligerent over war policy, but Largo refers

---

[298] Bolloten presents intra-political conflict as if it were uniquely the result of PCE (and/or Comintern) ambitions (i.e. a kind of 'one-way traffic'), but his own evidence contradicts this: *SCW*, pp. 355–8; also Cordón, *Trayectoria*, pp. 296–8.

[299] Elorza and Bizcarrondo, *Queridos camaradas*, p. 337. The same point is made in the memoirs of Pasionaria, Carrillo and Irene Falcón. See also Koltsov, *Diario de la guerra española*, pp. 352–3: 'Everyone speaks ill of Largo Caballero: his enemies shout from the rooftops while his supporters whisper criticism . . . The old man is inflexible too, he shouts, won't let anyone gainsay him, he "decides" military matters as minister of war and all the rest as premier. If only that were true! The problem is his decisions don't resolve anything. Crucial documents on military operations just pile up without being looked at, still less dealt with.' I would like to make the immensely novel suggestion that we take Koltsov literally here. The subtext of PSOE–PCE rivalry should never be taken as the only message.

[300] Bolloten, *SCW*, p. 419; see Abella, *La vida cotidiana*, pp. 228–9 and Low and Breá, *Red Spanish Notebook*, p. 217 for the previously voluntary form of much defence work in Barcelona.

[301] Bolloten, *SCW*, p. 352; Graham, *Socialism and War*, p. 90. Innumerable memoirs and secondary sources do the same. In the end, however, we have all relied on Largo's interpretation. Largo Caballero, *Mis recuerdos*, pp. 210–12 and *Notas históricas*, pp. 264–5, 698. The former is Largo's published memoir. It was written up after his release from a German concentration camp in 1945 when he had no access to his papers. Largo Caballero died in 1946, but the memoir was only published in 1954 (first edition). Its brief, elliptical and highly impressionistic form makes it a problematic source for historians. Largo had, however, written a much fuller set of memoirs between 1937 and 1940 while he had access to his papers. These ('Notas históricas') c. 1,500 pages of manuscript can now be consulted in the Fundación Pablo Iglesias in Madrid (to date only the pre-war section has been published). At times the case made by Largo and his supporters is so exaggerated that it appears as if the war itself is just an excuse for the PCE's campaign against themselves.

only to one wartime meeting with Codovilla – and that in relation to the party question. This must have taken place before 8 January and probably at the end of 1936. Largo gives no date in his memoirs,[302] and precisely because he does not the incident blends into his increasingly heated interchanges with Soviet ambassador Rosenberg, which led to their famous confrontation at the end of January 1937.[303] The subject here was, once again, war policy (and, most particularly, Asensio). Largo in fact says as much later in his memoirs.[304]

What makes Largo's conflation of the issues seem something more than forgetfulness – or even telescoping – is that it occurs not only in his published recollections, which were constructed from memory after 1945 without the benefit of access to his papers, but also in the documentary-based manuscript version written between 1937 and 1940. In this Largo also presents his February 1937 meeting with the Republican ambassador to Moscow, Marcelino Pascua,[305] as yet a further attempt to force unification between the PSOE and the PCE.[306] But this seems highly improbable. Between the Rosenberg incident and Pascua's visit to Valencia, Malaga had fallen. The viability of Republican defence policy – broadly understood – was, from the point of view of the Soviet leadership, now the issue eclipsing all others and surely the main reason behind Pascua's exceptional trip. Ostensibly he had come to hand-deliver a letter from Stalin. But this was merely an introductory note[307] to a verbal presentation for which we have no record other than the reference to proposed party unification in Largo's memoirs.[308] Pascua may have raised

---

[302] Largo Caballero, 'Notas históricas', p. 265 and *Mis recuerdos*, pp. 210–12.

[303] Dated by Bolloten, *SCW*, p. 350; Thomas, *Spanish Civil War*, p. 533 also gives the meeting as the end of January (but offers no source).

[304] The infamous meeting between Largo and Rosenberg (Alvarez del Vayo in attendance) which ended with the ejection of the ambassador from the premier's office is described by Largo himself as a marathon session about Asensio, *Mis recuerdos* (1976), pp. 180–1.

[305] *El Socialista*, 12 Feb. 1937.

[306] Largo Caballero, 'Notas históricas', vol. 2, pp. 264, 698.

[307] Dated 4 February, it is reproduced in L. Araquistaín, *Sobre la guerra civil y en la emigración* (Madrid: Espasa-Calpe, 1983), p. 240.

[308] Pascua's own archive contains some private notes written following the May 1937 crisis. He comments that Largo was a notoriously incapable prime minister in a war where the element of international great power intervention was decisive and that he wasted crucial and irreplaceable time in both the military and internal political spheres. Pascua also says of Largo that 'no correspondía la suma de sus calidades a lo que reclamaba/requería el mito...limitado por la formación intelectual que había recibido' ('the real Largo's talents did not match up to what the myth demanded...he was limited by his background and education') – all of this in Pascua's private notes on 'Largo Caballero's socialism' and 'the fall of May 1937', Pascua correspondence, *caja* 5 (6) (AHN). There is an interesting echo too in the comments on Largo made by a *News Chronicle* journalist in March 1937: 'I had shaken hands with that shabby myth, Largo Caballero,

the matter of Asensio, or more generally the loyalty and competence of Republican military personnel. But it also seems likely that he would have been bearing a message that reiterated Stalin's concern that the Popular Front alliance should adhere to parliamentary politics and market economics both to reassure Britain and France and also to keep middling social sectors in the Republican zone on board the war effort. On 21 December Stalin had sent a letter to Largo outlining the importance of these matters. But in his reply of 12 January Largo expressed himself rather lukewarmly about the 'parliamentary institution' in Spain (no doubt thinking back to the conservatives' philibuster of social reform legislation in the pre-war period).[309] After the military defeat at Malaga it became crucial to clarify Largo's mind for him. Surely the real point of Pascua's visit was that he, as a Spaniard, might be able to convince where Rosenberg had failed. But given Largo's previous berating of his own foreign office minister Alvarez del Vayo for supporting Rosenberg,[310] this tactic was scarcely likely to work. Indeed, it is clear from Largo's memoirs that he was immensely irritated by any reminder – from whatever quarter – that the wartime Popular Front alliance had to be politically and economically liberal or else it would not survive. Largo also refers indirectly to his tiredness at being told 'the lessons of the Russian Civil War'.[311] No doubt there was an element of prickly patriotic pride and 'culture clash' here. But it is worth bearing in mind that what this 'lesson' also amounted to was being told that his great rival Prieto's pre-war strategy of republican-socialist alliance was indeed the only valid one.[312]

War policy would become the absolutely critical issue from the middle of March – ironically, as a result of the Republic's success at Guadalajara. In retrospect, the victory was one of imposing a stalemate rather than

---

whose vanity did so much to dissipate the early strength of Republican Spain', Philip Jordan, *There Is No Return* (London: Cresset Press, 1938), p. 18.

[309] Text of both letters reproduced in *Guerra y revolución en España*, vol. 2, pp. 101–3.

[310] Largo Caballero, *Mis recuerdos*, pp. 180–1; Bolloten, *SCW*, pp. 348–9 cites the published post-war recollections of the Caballerista deputy, Ginés Ganga.

[311] Largo Caballero, 'Notas históricas', vol. 2, pp. 691, 694.

[312] See chapter 1 above. In his public pronouncements during the war Largo had already accepted this. Cf. his speech to the Cortes on 1 Feb. 1937 calling for social and economic normalisation on the basis of the market ('ya se ha ensayado bastante') and the UGT executive's manifesto following the fall of Malaga: 'Ha llegado el momento de dejar en suspenso el logro de nuestros más preciados ideales . . . Igualmente hay que suspender, por ahora, toda inovación en los métodos económicos y sociales con vistas al futuro' ('The moment has come for us to postpone our most cherished political goals . . . Likewise, all innovation in social and economic affairs – that will have to wait'), reproduced in *El Socialista*, 12 Feb. 1937. But the private political 'reckoning' in someone like Largo, who did not relinquish grudges easily, was quite another matter. The evidence of his rancour fills the pages of the 'Notas históricas' for the war period and may well be one reason why their publication seems to be indefinitely delayed.

making a positive advance. But it meant that the Madrid front was now stable, with no possibility of a rebel breakthrough to the capital in the foreseeable future. On realising this, Franco's fascist backers drew the fateful conclusion that only by massively escalating their aid would the rebels be assured of victory. This escalation meant that from late March 1937, Germany and (especially) Italy were effectively at war with the Republic.[313] The stakes in the Republic having a centralised and rationalised strategic plan for military, economic and civilian resistance had just risen a hundredfold. And no single minister understood this better than did Negrín from the treasury. Rosenberg was replaced as ambassador by his more emollient chargé d'affaires, Leon Gaikis.[314] But time was ever more at a premium, and it was becoming clear that Largo Caballero's control of the defence ministry was an anachronism the Republic could increasingly ill afford.

With the battle for Madrid indicating that the Republic could successfully resist, even the notoriously pessimistic President Azaña began to think in terms of an outcome other than defeat. His deduction would lead him in the direction of exploring the possibilities of a mediated peace. In fact, Franco's rebels would never be interested in mediation. But Azaña's reactions in the wake of Guadalajara constitute the remote origins of the polemic over a putative mediated peace that, in time, would become the explosive centre of political strife inside the Republic.

The PCE's rise to become a political force of the first magnitude in the first year of the wartime Republic has to be understood within the context of the internationalisation of the Spanish conflict and the growing importance of Soviet aid to the Republic. But, as we have seen, there were also important structural political reasons for PCE ascendancy. The PCE assumed the mantle of progressive republicanism. Above all, it served to bring the previously unmobilised – both middle and working class – to the state. 'Hybridity' – or class heterogeneity – is the most oustanding characteristic of the wartime Spanish Communist Party as it constructed

---

[313] While Hitler remained relatively cautious about committing German resources to rebel Spain – sending important equipment and the crack, technologically advanced, but small Condor Legion – Mussolini ploughed in money and material: 'financial and physical resources [were] deployed on a scale which severely diminished Italian military effectiveness in the Second World War', P. Preston, 'Mussolini's Spanish Adventure: From Limited Risk to War', in Preston and Mackenzie, *The Republic Besieged*, pp. 22, 48–51; I. Saz Campos, *Mussolini contra la II República: hostilidad, conspiraciones, intervención (1931–1936)* (Valencia: Edicions Alfons el Magnànim, 1986).

[314] Bolloten, *SCW*, p. 383. On Stalin's general instructions that Soviet political/diplomatic personnel in Spain should be conciliatory, see Schauff, 'Hitler and Stalin in the Spanish Civil War', pp. 10–11. On Rosenberg's lack of the appropriate social skills, see Gazur, *Secret Assignment. The FBI's KGB General*, p. 56.

itself during 1936–7. This can be seen as part of a broader modernisation process speeded up by the war itself. Of particular importance here was the communist mobilisation of youth in the united youth organisation (JSU) and its associate bodies. As a result, the PCE was creating within its own organisational structure a model for the inter-class alliance sought by republicans and socialists since 1931 in order to provide the social base of a reforming regime. It is in this frame that we have ultimately to understand the growing organisational antagonism between the PCE and Largo Caballero's sector of the socialists. But the issue of war policy remained the *primary* source of conflict between these two groups during 1936–7: a fact that has been somewhat obscured by the overwhelming emphasis placed by the Caballeristas on the Comintern's putative agenda of absorption. An organisational rivalry certainly existed, and it would become more acute as time went on. But this would have less to do with the Comintern than it did with the struggle for power between competing groups *inside* the Republican polity.

In spite of this emergent conflict, however, the early months of 1937 saw the Popular Front, as the 'least weak option', being reconstructed as the basis of the Republican war effort. With the eclipse of republicanism, its new axis was provided by the PSOE–PCE alliance. The attitude of the socialist who led the cabinet was deeply antagonistic to this alliance. In the medium term, this was a problem that would require resolution. In the immediate term, however, the viability of the Popular Front project depended on the full incorporation to the war effort both of the Republican Basque Country (Vizcaya) and of Catalonia. In the latter, however, the battle was still being waged to establish government authority. It is thus to the situation of revolution and war in Catalonia that we now turn.

CHAPTER 4

Challenges to the centralising Republic: revolutionary and liberal particularisms in Catalonia, Aragon and the Basque Country

To articulate the past historically [...] means to
seize hold of a memory as it flashes up in a moment of danger.[1]

In Catalonia as elsewhere the collapse of the state, combined with the protagonism of organised labour in resisting the military rebels, saw the emergence of worker committees to rearticulate crucial supply, transport, defence and public-order functions. But unlike anywhere else in Republican Spain, the Catalan anarcho-syndicalists channelled the power which their pivotal defence role – and the armed strength underpinning it – gave them to spearhead in Barcelona and in other urban centres[2] a wide-ranging programme of industrial and commercial collectivisation in a bid to reinvent not only the economy but also social and cultural life on anti-capitalist lines.[3]

The unparalleled range of what was attempted in Barcelona in the months after the July days cannot be explained purely in terms of Barcelona's greater distance from the active front of the war[4] compared to Spain's other capital, Madrid. Certainly an emergency war footing would have required a different prioritising of radical energies in Barcelona. But no amount of distance from the war could have made 1936 Madrid a revolutionary city. What occurred in Barcelona was rooted in the unique scale and richness of its popular and proletarian cultures. Formed in the crosscurrents of resistance to a multi-layered

---

[1] Walter Benjamin, 'Theses on the Philosophy of History', VI.
[2] In some of these other industrial towns – for example in Lleida, Tarragona and Girona – the dominant political force was the dissident communist POUM rather than the CNT. Relations between the two organisations are discussed later in this chapter.
[3] ' "The revolution of July 19" was incomplete, but that it was a revolution is attested to by its having created a regime of dual power', Morrow, *Revolution and Counter-Revolution in Spain*, p. 23.
[4] Barcelona militias went to attempt the taking of Zaragoza (in rebel hands) and then some (including Buenaventura Durruti) to fight on the Madrid front.

liberal commercial and artisan-industrial[5] development evolving over decades and unparalleled anywhere else in Spain, these worker cultures were shaped by the radical heterogeneity of a cosmopolitan port city, but also by the federal political traditions and civic dynamism of the bourgeois metropolitan culture against which they defined themselves.[6]

But for all that Barcelona was uniquely advanced within Spain, it was still a place where 'modern' and 'pre-modern' worlds of popular and labour cultures merged or, indeed, were actively linked through the direct-action practices of the CNT, which constituted the dominant form of labour organisation in the city. The Catalan CNT's praxis had been forged in the brutal labour wars waged by industrialists and the Restoration state police on an unskilled and overwhelmingly immigrant workforce in the years after the First World War. But the flexibility of the CNT's organisational structures and direct-action tactics meant that its mobilising capacity extended beyond strictly libertarian-identified workers through street sellers, the itinerant and the unemployed via a grey area of semi-illegality to the underworld of petty crime: from the politically conscious and organised to the 'lumpen', the CNT's influence reached out across the myriad overlapping worlds of the urban poor of 'outcast Barcelona'.[7]

Heterogeneous and amorphous though some of these CNT constituencies were, in their political and economic dispossession all shared a common resistance – whether visceral/intuitive or consciously ideologised – to liberal economic order and the machinery of the liberal state. What the Spanish state meant to the poor and marginalised was basically still the police and the army. It was thus associated with punitive functions: with conscription and indirect taxation, when not with direct persecution, especially of the unionised. The general brutality of daily life – for example a highly exploitative private housing market or the ever-present problem of food procurement – also generated neighbourhood support networks (often centred around women's activities) into which the CNT could plug and which it, reciprocally, politicised: the

---

[5] Although there were some very large concerns, industry in Barcelona – textile in the main – was still mostly organised on a small scale in the 1930s as family-run businesses and workshops: Shubert, *A Social History of Modern Spain*, pp. 15–16, 119–21.

[6] For details of the city's industrial development, demographic growth, urbanisation, and more complex sociological stratification compared to elsewhere in Spain, see Ealham, 'Policing the Recession', pp. 27–30; also E. Ucelay da Cal, 'Catalan Nationalism: Cultural Plurality and Political Ambiguity', in Graham and Labanyi, *Spanish Cultural Studies*, pp. 145–7. See also chapter 1 above.

[7] The term is used by Christopher Ealham in his thesis 'Policing the Recession', and borrows from Gareth Stedman Jones' study of the world of nineteenth-century London's poor and dispossessed, whose image so terrified the affluent classes.

libertarians and the inhabitants of 'outcast Barcelona' were, for a time at least, one in their social war against the liberal state.

In its essentials, that relationship had remained intact, as we have seen, during the Republican years between 1931 and 1936. The conditions of daily existence for many reinforced the arguments of radical anarchists in the FAI[8] that the Republic was but a new façade for the old order. By 1936 many in the CNT doubted whether liberal governance (that is, constitutional politics and a market economy) could effect structural social and economic change.[9] But even after the coup-induced implosion of the liberal state, it was only Barcelona that possessed sufficient 'collateral' to confront liberal social and economic order with anything approaching an alternative project.

But although Barcelona was a unique proletarian centre in 1930s Spain, and the CNT's articulating political power singular therein, the imperatives of the post-18 July 1936 situation would deepen ideological divisions and reveal organisational flaws in the anarcho-syndicalist movement which together seriously undermined it. These, in turn, opened up opportunities to the political opposition. For even in the days of emergency defence against the military rebels, Catalonia – and even Barcelona capital – never ceased to be contested political space.

When Barcelona's workers faced down the military rebellion in the streets, they did so in a context where the rural and urban middle classes were far more uniformly hostile than any other sector of Spain's bourgeoisie to the ultra centralism of the military insurgents. The Catalan bourgeoisie was also resistant to the relatively more subtle, but equally real, centralist values of the Spanish liberal republicanism in power in Madrid since 1931. But neither of these hostilities meant that there was any less of a contradiction between the anarchist and liberal federalist visions of Catalonia's politico-social order after the rebel military had been defeated. While the worker militia had support from both municipal and state police in Barcelona and while Catalanist values sometimes influenced friendly officers to hand over weapons, we must remember that Luis Companys, president of the Generalitat (the Catalan regional

---

[8] The Anarchist Federation of Iberia (Federación Anarquista Ibérica): see introduction and chapter 1 above. There was an overlap between male youth gangs engaged in petty crime and the FAI's 'grupos de afinidad' (cells of young libertarians dedicated to direct action – such as robbery and, sometimes, assassination – as acts 'against the state'), Ealham, 'Policing the Recession', pp. 17, 327–8, 346–70 and 'Pimps, Politics and Protest' (unpublished article), pp. 4–5.

[9] Although most still voted for the Popular Front coalition in the February 1936 elections, this was overwhelmingly motivated by the desire to secure the release from gaol of thousands of political prisoners to whom the Front's electoral programme promised immediate amnesty.

government), and leader of the (until then) hegemonic liberal-left Catalanist party, the Esquerra (ERC), never formally sanctioned the arming
of Barcelona's militia forces.

Once the anarchist movement-in-arms had, nevertheless, subdued the
military rebellion in Barcelona, the expropriationary new order emerging implied immediate jeopardy for the social and economic interests
of Catalonia's urban and rural middle classes, large sections of which
constitued the Esquerra's own base.[10] The coup-induced collapse of the
region's liberal political structures and state institutions, in particular
related to law and order, meant that there was no physical means of
repression available to protect private property/capital. (Once the city
was secure against the rebels, both Civil and Assault Guards would be
dispatched to the front – such was the distrust of the corps among worker
constituencies.) This is the context that explains the purposeful humil-
ity of Companys' comments to the CNT-FAI leaders who met with the
Generalitat on 20 July:

> Today you are the masters of the city and of Catalonia ... You have conquered
> and everything is in your power. If you do not need me or want me as President of
> Catalonia ... I shall become just another soldier in the struggle against fascism.
> If, on the other hand, you believe in this post ... I and the men of my party ... can
> be useful in this struggle.[11]

Companys was performing a strategic retreat in order to achieve by
lateral means two key objectives on behalf of the political class and social
groups he represented: first to keep the concept of government legality formally in play and second to persuade the anarcho-syndicalists
that their revolution needed a central governing body. In both, Companys was successful. The CNT agreed to the formation of a Central
Anti-fascist Militia Committee (21 July 1936)[12] whose legitimacy was thus
implicitly determined by Generalitat sanction. In the circumstances, this
was a staggering concession on the CNT's part. Through it the Catalan
government was able repeatedly to assert its legal existence. Nor should
we consider this a question of mere form or rhetoric: it constituted the

---

[10] The Esquerra contained both urban professionals and white-collar sectors as well as the Unió
de Rabassaires or rural tenants' and sharecroppers' union. The Rabassaires were the especial
base of Companys himself. See chapter 1 above.

[11] The report of Companys' address is to be found in a number of texts and memoirs. These are
listed in Bolloten, *SCW*, p. 389 (n. 17), from whom I also take these translated extracts.

[12] The Committee had 15 members: CNT/FAI (5), UGT (3), POUM (1), Rabassaires (1), PSUC
(1), liberal republicans (4): full details are in *Solidaridad Obrera*, 21 July 1936. See also Morrow,
Revolution and Counter-Revolution in Spain, p. 21; Broué and Témime, *The Revolution and the Civil War
in Spain*, pp. 131–2.

first material stage in the battle to re-establish the Generalitat as the instrument through which liberal order could be reimposed.[13] The CNT's ascendancy was reflected in its control of the central committee's key departments of defence, transport and public order. But the last of these would rapidly become the supreme focus of tension in the battle for political control waged over the next twelve months between the CNT and its liberal Catalan opponents. For the latter understood, quite correctly, that if they could reconstruct their coercive force, then all other forms of liberal reconstruction would be possible – as indeed they proved to be. All of which leads one to ask the fundamental question of why the CNT-FAI agreed in the first place to share power on the Central Anti-fascist Militia Committee.

The answer to that question lies in the ideological and organisational specificities of the CNT-FAI. Its historical trajectory had scarcely equipped it with either a political blueprint for the seizure and exercise of power or the organisational structures through which to realise this. At the time and since *cenetistas* have represented their behaviour as a conscious/willed rejection of 'bolshevik methods'.[14] But, in reality, it was the limitations in the CNT's 'invertebrate' organisational forms that clinched matters here. The CNT still had very few vertically structured industrial unions in 1936, and the CNT's own structure was a highly decentralised one. As neither the national committee nor the regional confederal committee in Catalonia had executive power over its constituent union sections, nor did they have particularly good communication channels. So the dissemination from top to bottom of information – even leaving aside the vexed question of instructions – remained a difficult if not impossible task.[15]

---

[13] For a suggestive comment on the cultural dimension of this consolidation – via the amalgamation of worker demonstrations and the civic symbols of Catalan nationalism (music, flags, police wearing nationalist insignia) – see H. D. Freund, in 'The Spanish Civil War. The View From the Left', *Revolutionary History*, 4(1–2) (winter 1991–2) 321.

[14] As late as May 1936 radical libertarian sectors of the CNT were still stressing 'revolutionary spontaneity' as the means and autonomous rural communes as the goal. Cf. the editorial line of the influential anarchist theoretical review *La Revista Blanca*, and the lack of any detailed strategy (linking ideas and practice) evident at the CNT's Zaragoza congress (May 1936). On this see W. Bernecker, '"Acción directa" y violencia en el anarquismo español', in J. Aróstegui (ed.), 'Violencia y política en España', *Ayer* (Madrid), 13 (1994), 181 ff.

[15] Cf. 'Only a party with an iron discipline could have taken power – a party organised as if it were a military unit, with its revolutionary general staff, its centralised and hierarchised structures . . . In the CNT . . . to get something accepted, a militant had to argue at length and *do the rounds* convincing people [in the various regional organisations]. How on earth – in such conditions – could the CNT have taken power, *even if its 'leaders' had wanted to? The anarchists had no effective organisational machinery with which to fight*: the risings of 1932 and 1933 had already demonstrated that' (my italics). Lorenzo, *Los anarquistas españoles y el poder*, pp. 192–3. See also chapter 1 above.

The lack of industrial unions and of centralised CNT executive power also made lateral communication between unions difficult. None of these things had ever been absolutely crucial before.[16] The libertarians' strength – particularly in Barcelona – lay in their 'bottom-up' mobilising ability. But after 18 July 1936, the libertarian order needed 'top-down' political articulation and a political 'head' in order to defend itself. Ironically, the lack of such facilities was itself an indication of how successful purist anarchists had been in blocking the initiatives of pragmatist-syndicalist currents in the CNT right up to 1936.

In July 1936, the radical anarchist leaders in Catalonia, for want of any alternative political blueprint and also because, by confusing armed strength with the totality of power, they believed that they were more powerful than they were, opted to utilise the political experience, personnel and central apparatus of the Catalan government. In all of this, the CNT were ceaselessly encouraged by Companys, an immensely shrewd politician who rapidly assimilated the rhetoric of 'the revolution', using it with consummate skill throughout the long summer, autumn and winter of 1936,[17] even as he denounced libertarian 'excess' and campaigned for regional government control of industry and the municipalisation of services.

Companys could take heart from the rich base of social constituencies supportive of liberal order to be found in Catalonia: ranging from tenant farmers and sharecroppers – the majority of the rural Catalan population – through urban white-collar workers, state functionaries, liberal professionals and the owners of small businesses and industrial workshops to the security forces (police and Republican army officers). Although the existing political institutions of Catalonia had been battered by the coup, they still had this strong social base beneath them. These constituencies had not often been on the front line against the rebels, to be sure, but nor had they evacuated the zone or passed to tacit support of the rebels. The situation in Barcelona thus resembled that of 'dual power' in Petrograd in 1917. But Catalan liberalism (represented by the Generalitat inside the Central Militia Committee) was stronger than its Russian counterpart since it rested on a sounder social base.

[16] Although they had hindered effective strike action in the 1930s – see chapter 1 above.
[17] 'Intoxicated with their control of the factories and the militias, the anarchists assumed that capitalism had *already* disappeared in Catalonia. They talked of the "new social economy" and Companys was only too willing to talk as they did, for it blinded them and not him', Morrow, *Revolution and Counter-Revolution*, pp. 42–3. Companys' credibility derived from his special relationship with the CNT – forged in the political battles against the central state in the pre-war decades when he had acted as a labour lawyer for arraigned *cenetistas*.

But Companys also had to recognise that his own party, the Esquerra, was an insufficient instrument to deliver the goal of liberal political and economic reconstruction. The coup attempt had dealt an immense shock to both its organisational dynamic and the confidence of the leadership. Paradoxically, the impact had been so great precisely because the Esquerra's hegemonic status in Catalonia between 1931 and the 1936 coup meant that no clear distinction had ever been made between the functions/apparatus of the party and those of the Catalan government.[18] In addition, Catalan liberals, although relatively more 'modern' than the rest of progressive republicanism in Spain, still lacked adequate experience and understanding of what the arduous task of grass-roots political organisation required. What was needed, then, on the wild new frontier of political life in post-revolutionary Catalonia was a new kind of party, able to mobilise its base 'bottom-up' (taking a leaf out of the CNT's book) and also unafraid to enter the fray because it had no pre-existing organisational stakes or power base to protect – only everything to gain.

The political force which emerged to fill this political space was the PSUC (United Socialist Party of Catalonia), formed on 23 July 1936 from the merger of four smaller parties: (in ascending order of size), the minuscule Catalan Proletarian Party, the Communist Party of Catalonia, the Catalan section of the PSOE and the Socialist Union of Catalonia (USC), a Catalanist social democratic party.[19] The most important force in the new party, both quantitatively and qualitatively, was the USC, led by the ambitious Joan Comorera. At the time of the merger the party was still on the margins of political life, unable to compete with the Esquerra's umbrella appeal to rural as well as urban constituencies. In urban centres outside Barcelona the USC had also been contending with serious competition from the Workers and Peasants Bloc (BOC), which

---

[18] Esquerra dominated from the 1931 elections that brought the Second Republic to power. The Catalan autonomy statute was passed in September 1932. For Catalan politics 1931–6, see chapter 1 above.

[19] The Catalan Communist Party was the Catalan section of the official, Comintern-affiliated Spanish Communist Party (PCE). Estimates of the precise membership levels of the four groups vary, with PCE sources tending to give a slighly higher figure for the communists over the PSOE's Catalan section. But all figures indicate the minuscule size of the Proletarian Party (PCP) and the USC's numerical dominance. The likely approximate figures for July 1936 are: PCP (c. 80); Catalan communists (max. 400); Catalan PSOE (c. 600); USC (c. 2000). Bolloten, *SCW*, p. 397 has a selection of figures and sources. The unified PSUC still only had somewhere between three and five thousand members at its creation (and almost certainly nearer three), as compared to a POUM membership of between six and eight thousand. For PSUC, see Joan Comorera (USC/PSUC leader), 'Catalonia, an Example for Unity', *Communist International*, April 1938, p. 376. On the PCP, see Ucelay da Cal, 'Socialistas y comunistas en Cataluña durante la guerra civil: un ensayo de interpretación', p. 309.

in September 1935 had amalgamated to form the POUM – a process that made it the largest socialist party in Catalonia.[20] Comorera saw the merger as a major opportunity for the USC to overtake the POUM (or, more exactly, its major component, the BOC) as well as offering a chance to compete with the Esquerra.

But it was the exceptional agenda precipitated by the July days and the common fear of CNT armed dominance which served both to clarify Comorera's own mind about the PSUC merger and to overcome Catalan PSOE resistance. The prospect of leadership of the new party doubtless also influenced Comorera. While the Comintern's delegate to Catalonia, Ernö Gerö (Pedro), had exercised his good offices in the discussions *en route*, it is not credible to suggest that Gerö's intervention was the determining factor in Comorera's course of action. Far more influential was the overwhelming instrumental sense among the entire political class of the liberal left in Catalonia that a common defence of social 'normality' was imperative in the aftermath of the July days.[21] An alliance reinforced by the organisational expertise and resources of a Comintern espousing Popular Frontist moderation seemed a very small price to pay to facilitate this process.[22] But only by taking on board the thrust of Comorera's policies since 1931 can we appreciate the crucial explanatory context for the formation of the PSUC. The emergence of the PSUC responded to an underlying logic which went back deep into the interstices of Catalan Republican politics of the pre-war period – although this seldom seems to be recognised in the dominant explanations of the party's origins.[23] What this means, moreover, is that the tendency of most of the Anglo-American historiography to present the PSUC as the Communist Party of Catalonia *tout court* is highly problematic. Nevertheless, the fact that the PSUC had come into being largely around the USC's Catalanist agenda, but that the Comintern had admitted the PSUC simply as 'the United Socialist Party of Catalonia' hints at the serious tensions which would subsequently arise.[24]

---

[20] See chapter 1 above.

[21] Although – as we saw in chapter 1 – the USC congress had ratified entry to the PSUC in May 1936, the other component parts' ratification conferences were still ongoing when the war erupted. The final PSUC 'unity congress' scheduled for the end of August would never take place.

[22] It is odd that Burnett Bolloten's own empirical analysis broadly supports the argument I elaborate here, yet his conclusions – a prime example of the mythologisation of Gerö's influence – then largely contradict his own analysis: *SCW*, pp. 386–404.

[23] See chapter 1 above for a discussion of the politics of the Catalan left 1931–6.

[24] Cf. Togliatti, *Escritos sobre la guerra de España*, p. 247. This was the first time the Comintern had ever recognised more than one party in a single country.

For Comorera, with his Catalan-focused agenda, the PSUC's dynamism made it an ideal vehicle to attract sectors of the Esquerra base as well as previously unmobilised sectors of Catalonia's middling classes. Comorera's aim was to overtake the POUM and permanently eclipse the Esquerra by demonstrating that the PSUC was better able to defend middling economic interests. This task was facilitated by the fall-out from the coup. As the PSUC issued robust press attacks on CNT 'disorder', recruits flocked to the party (and concomitantly to the Catalan UGT[25]). Nor was there an urban predominance here, for the PSUC also recruited well among small and medium owner-farmers, tenant farmers and sharecroppers, many of whom had previously held Esquerra membership.[26] All these sectors – which together constituted the majority rural population of Catalonia – had in common a sense of unease provoked by the apparent libertarian ascendancy in the region. This also intensified the importance of being able to 'prove' one's political loyalty, which, as elsewhere in Republican Spain, saw a generalised rush after 18 July to acquire a party or union membership card as a means of reinforcing one's personal security.

Requisitioning by the CNT's supply committees was the main focus of peasant hostility in Catalonia, as we shall discuss later. But collectivisation also provoked anxiety. This was the case even though many had no direct experience of it. For in Catalonia, where large estates were the exception, the CNT-FAI had tacitly accepted the strength of the rural majority of smallholders, tenants and sharecroppers and had largely respected their property and individualist forms of farming.[27] In neighbouring (eastern) Aragon, meanwhile, some three-quarters of the land was collectivised.[28] Catalan collectivisation, like Valencia's,[29] tended thus to focus on industry – starting with those of Francoist supporters[30] – as well as artisan, commercial and service-sector activity in and around

---

[25] See more detailed discussion later in this chapter.
[26] For a breakdown of PSUC social constituencies and membership figures, see Bolloten, *SCW*, p. 399.
[27] 'Oases in the middle of small estates, [the collectives] were the exception rather than the rule', Broué and Témime, *The Revolution and the Civil War in Spain*, p. 158; Bolloten, *SCW*, p. 395.
[28] Broué and Témime, *The Revolution and the Civil War in Spain*, pp. 158–9; Fraser, *Blood of Spain*, pp. 348–50; Casanova, *Anarquismo y revolución*, pp. 119–29.
[29] Bosch Sánchez, *Ugetistas y libertarios*, pp. 23–31, 383–6 – this also stresses the heterogeneity of such 'intervened' forms.
[30] Some sectors of the Catalan big industrial bourgeoisie did support the rebels. But compared to what happened in the Basque Country (discussed later in this chapter) Catalonia's very particular and gradual process of industrial and commercial development had produced a much stronger liberal autonomist bourgeoisie (in both cultural and political terms) which, consequently, supported the Republic.

urban nuclei (hence the PSUC's appeal to groups like the shop and office workers' union, CADCI). As the conflict over requisition indicates,
where agriculture was concerned, the CNT intervened in distribution
systems rather than in those of production.[31] This is not to say that
confrontations over rural collectivisation did not sometimes occur – the
CNT could not entirely control the actions of pro-collectivist enthusiasts
in its cadres.[32] Nor did it mean that the very existence of alternative
economic forms in Catalonia did not itself worry and demoralise the
rural middle classes. But what close scrutiny of rural Catalonia reveals is
the extent to which the CNT's own power base was far from secure.

The situation of hung power in Catalonia was precisely what made
the adjacent territory of Aragon so important to the CNT. Not only was
it Catalonia's war front; it was also the agrarian hinterland of its urban
revolution. But 'revolutionary Aragon' was not quite the bulwark it first
appeared. The CNT's pre-war strongholds had been in the urban centres of western Aragon – Teruel, Huesca and the anarcho-syndicalists'
second 'capital', Zaragoza – which had all fallen to the rebels in July.[33]
The UGT had also had its real strength in the western zone. Paradoxically, it was eastern Aragon, with no large centres and, consequently, a
much lower level of political mobilisation in the pre-war period, which
remained to the Republic. Wartime collectivisation in eastern Aragon
occurred largely through the initiative of Catalan (and some Valencian)
anarchist militiamen who carried the new order to its villages.[34] Although
the CNT had little by way of previous roots in the area, nor did they
encounter any organised political opposition, for the obvious reason that
Republican political institutions/the state had collapsed.[35] The republicans, who had been a significant presence in pre-war municipal politics,
had no means of opposing anarcho-syndicalist initiatives in the villages.

---

[31] This pattern also holds true for the Valencia region: Bolloten, *SCW*, pp. 57–9.
[32] There were clashes in the Valencia region, Catalonia and Castile. One bad example occurred in
      January 1937 in La Fatarella (Tarragona, close by the Ebro River/Aragon border), where thirty
      peasants resisting collectivisation were killed: Broué and Témime, *The Revolution and the Civil War
      in Spain*, p. 228. For Cullera (Valencia), see Bosch Sánchez, *Ugetistas y libertarios*, p. 122.
[33] See map, Casanova, *Anarquismo y revolución*, p. 99.
[34] Ibid., pp. 127–88, 218 and 32–9; M. Cruells, *Mayo sangriento. Barcelona 1937* (Barcelona: Edito-
      rial Juventud, 1970), p. 12. Some CNT leaders who managed to escape from western Aragon
      also participated. See the nuanced and richly informative oral testimony-based account of the
      Aragonese collectives in Fraser, *Blood of Spain*, pp. 348–71.
[35] In spite of the version in the PCE's official history of the war, it was not so much the CNT *as the
      effects of the military coup* that disarticulated Popular Front committees and closed party premises
      in Aragon: *Guerra y revolución en España*, vol. 1 pp. 29–30. Hence also the inoperativeness of the
      Republican agriculture minister's measures of 10 August 1936 putting abandoned land under
      municipal control: Casanova, *Anarquismo y revolución*, p. 129.

For in Aragon, as elsewhere, the republicans lacked a mass base. None of this necessarily meant that collectivisation was imposed on a uniformly unwilling rural population. There were rural labourers who took little persuasion. Moreover, collectivisation emerged, as it did elsewhere, as a response to the desperate need to re-establish shattered communities and essential economic functions.

But in Aragon (east and west) there was also a very high percentage of small farmers who already possessed land – albeit that many had quantities too small to be economically self-sustaining.[36] They would have preferred 'the revolution' to have improved their economic situation by consolidating their private landholdings. But, equally, they felt unable to remain outside the collectives – even though this was in theory possible for Aragonese small farmers – because of a deep sense of insecurity in the political environment in which they were living.[37] After all, during August and September 1936 the CNT was the *only* organising political presence in eastern Aragon. Moreover, it had also prohibited salaried labour there.[38] This meant not only that some more prosperous individuals could not recruit labour (formally or informally), but also that other small farmers were deprived of working as such – a means by which they had previously supplemented (whether in cash or kind) their meagre incomes from their own land. Given the levels of hardship endured by many of the peasant farmers in Aragon, they were not all necessarily, *a priori*, opposed to collectivisation – although they were certainly ignorant about it. But once the militias began to engage in arbitrary requisition – as they did almost immediately in Aragon – then disaffection among the peasantry occurred rapidly.[39] And with disaffection came the seeds of opposition which would then give other political groups their opportunity to recruit.[40]

Eastern Aragon was, moreover, a weakness the Catalan *cenetistas* could ill afford, in view of their isolation in their own region. Not only were they up against liberal Catalonia, bolstered by Comorera's PSUC, but they were also increasingly estranged from the POUM. Overlaying the

---

[36] Casanova, *Anarquismo y revolución*, pp. 40–50.

[37] Ibid., p. 126; Fraser, *Blood of Spain*, pp. 348–9, 352–3. In villages for which we have testimonies (and probably in many more for which we do not) the very real, *practical* difficulties of making the collectives viable meant that moral pressure was exerted to ensure everyone joined.

[38] Broué and E. Témime, *The Revolution and the Civil War in Spain*, p. 159; Casanova, *Anarquismo y revolución*, p. 125; Fraser, *Blood of Spain*, p. 355.

[39] Lorenzo, *Los anarquistas españoles y el poder*, p. 120; Casanova, *Anarquismo y revolución*, p. 111.

[40] As Casanova's research (in *Anarquismo y revolución*) makes quite clear, pro- and anti-collectivist positions were part of a broader struggle for political *power* in Republican Aragon. For more on this see chapter 5 below.

ideological rift, there were strategic political disagreements and organisational rivalries between the CNT and the POUM (and its forerunner BOC) that stretched back years. The BOC/POUM were highly critical of the libertarians' dogged anti-politicism, which, they argued, left Barcelona's industrial proletariat defenceless. Nor had the CNT been able to ignore the BOC since, as we have seen, its mix of Catalanism and radical politics had given it a solid base among skilled workers and other urban and rural lower-middle class sectors. But the BOC also set its sights beyond them. With the Catalan CNT's membership crisis after 1931[41] and the internal dissension over *treintismo* and the FAI's violent direct action, the BOC rather over-optimistically thought that it had spied an opportunity to break the CNT's hegemonic relationship with the immigrant, unskilled industrial workforce of Barcelona capital. In 1932 the BOC had called upon the CNT dissenters to unite with them in a new *political* union leadership in Catalonia, whereupon the regional CNT responded by expelling the BOC-led trade unions in Lleida, Tarragona and Girona.[42] These inter-organisational antagonisms were doubtless also fuelled by the fact that many of the key socialist leaders in Catalonia (and not a few beyond) had served their political apprenticeship in anarcho-syndicalist ranks before moving on or, as the *cenetistas* understandably interpreted it, becoming renegades.[43]

During the July days of 1936 the CNT and POUM militia fought in unison. (While the CNT's control was uncontested in Barcelona capital, the POUM had strongholds in other urban centres of the region, most notably in Lleida.[44]) But there was clearly a connection between the pre-war tensions and the fact that the CNT, by agreeing to such a high level of representation on the Central Anti-fascist Militia Committee for the Catalan liberal republican parties, the UGT and the PSUC (some eight posts in all), allowed the POUM to be relegated to more of a minority voice than its strength and role in the July days elsewhere in the region warranted. In acting thus, the CNT may have believed that it was ridding itself of a troublesome competitor. But the CNT was also

[41] Tavera and Vega, 'L'afiliació sindical a la CRT de Catalunya: entre l'eufòria revolucionària i l'ensulsiada confederal 1919–1936'. See also chapter 1 above on the CNT crisis.

[42] Durgan, *BOC 1930–1936*, pp. 163–6. Barcelona capital remained the CNT's fief: Durgan, 'Trotsky, the POUM and the Spanish Revolution', p. 59. The union expulsions led to the formation of a separate POUM union federation (FOUS) which in May 1936 merged – disastrously – with the Catalan UGT (see chapter 1 above).

[43] For more on the phenomenon of the *tránsfuga* (political renegade), see the discussion on the May days in chapter 5 below.

[44] This was basically the BOC's old base. Lleida was dubbed 'Mauríngrad' after the BOC leader, Joaquín Maurín.

blocking out the POUM's valuable critique of the shortcomings in its own revolutionary structures and strategy. It is important to keep in mind this troubled relationship between the CNT and POUM because it was to have material effects on the development of the Catalan political scene between July and December 1936.

Within ten days of the creation of the Central Anti-fascist Militia Committee, the CNT-FAI had also consented to Companys' formal reconstitution of an all-liberal republican Generalitat (on 31 July).[45] Companys' attempt to strengthen his hand by including three PSUC members in the economy, supply and agriculture portfolios had to be abandoned because of CNT-FAI opposition. But the more important point here is that the anarcho-syndicalists did not object to the formation of the cabinet *per se*, or to the fact that, thereafter, the Central Militia Committee was formally responsible to it *as a subcommittee of the Generalitat*.[46] It was as if the old Catalan anarchist mentality of the 'division of labour' between bourgeois 'politics' and the syndicalist ambit of the workers was still operating to blind the CNT to the dangers of permitting the further consolidation of its antagonists in a situation of dual power – especially when the sudden, unexpected bonus of freedom from Madrid's control made the reconquest of political power an even more seductive prospect for the Catalan bourgeoisie. At best the CNT's armed strength in the July days had given it a temporary advantage in Catalonia at a moment when power – in the fullest sense of the term – hung in the balance. But dual power is a situation that always begs resolution. By allowing its opponents back into the political game, which the CNT did when it had initially agreed to Esquerra, Rabassaire, PSUC and UGT representation on the Anti-fascist Militia Committee, the anarcho-syndicalists were undermining their own position.[47]

At the end of September 1936 this conflict entered a new phase when the CNT agreed to the dissolution of the Central Anti-fascist Militia Committee and joined the Generalitat. Two months of war – even if

---

[45] Headed by Companys' party colleague Joan Casanovas, the cabinet contained six Esquerra members (including one from the Rabassaires), one representative of Acció Catalana and one 'independent' – an army officer, José Sandino – in the defence portfolio. (Sandino would continue in this function in the Generalitat cabinet formed on 28 September with CNT membership.) For full details of the 31 July cabinet, see *Guerra y Revolución en España*, vol. 2, pp. 18–19.

[46] Freund, 'Dual Power in the Spanish Revolution', p. 324.

[47] Nor can these concessions be attributed to some disembodied/abstract sense of political magnanimity on the part of the libertarian movement (cf. García Oliver's analysis in Abad de Santillán's *Por qué perdimos la guerra* (Buenos Aires: Editorial Imán, 1940), p. 255). This is not to suggest that such sentiments were absent from his mind or from those of the other CNT-FAI leaders in Barcelona on 21 July 1936, but rather that the underlying reasons for the outcome lie elsewhere, as will be discussed below in chapter 5.

that war was not on Catalonia's threshold – had taken their toll on the
CNT's leaders.[48] The militia defeats in the south and on the approach
to Madrid as well as the bleak international horizon weighed heavily
on libertarian hopes everywhere.[49] As we have seen too, prime minister
Largo Caballero was determined to bring the CNT into government. As
a result, in late September the CNT in plenary session sanctioned the
principle of an anarcho-syndicalist governmental presence by reference
to the overwhelming necessity of the situation.[50] But the simultaneous
attempt to justify the decision on the grounds that the emergency situation had transformed the very nature of government and the state is
indicative of how the intense crisis of Republican defence had exposed
the CNT's underlying lack of political acumen:

[t]he government has ceased to be a force of oppression against the working
class, just as the state is no longer the entity that divides society into classes. Both
will stop oppressing the people all the more with the inclusion of the CNT.[51]

The fact that these were the words of Diego Abad de Santillán, one
of the leaders of the Catalan FAI, also nullifies the argument that the
controversy over entry to government neatly split purists from pragmatists (or *treintistas*) along the lines of the pre-war conflict.[52] In fact,

---

[48] The organisation publicly admitted that they had been moved by 'the difficult situation on certain [military] fronts': quoted by Jellinek, *The Civil War in Spain*, p. 497.

[49] Cf. 'Those who talk of implanting a perfect economic and social system are friends who forget that the capitalist system has . . . international ramifications and that our triumph in the war depends greatly on the warmth, sympathy and support that reaches us from outside', Juan Peiró, in talk on Radio CNT-FAI, 23 Oct. 1936, quoted in Broué and Témime, *The Revolution and the Civil War in Spain*, p. 207 (Peiró, a moderate syndicalist and close colleague of Angel Pestaña, had become industry minister in the central government formed by Largo Caballero on 4 November 1936). Peiró criticised radical anarchists' practice in the war for having alienated the small peasantry: Abella, *La vida cotidiana durante la guerra civil*, pp. 89–90. For the pre-history of this intra-CNT dispute, see chapter 1 above.

[50] 'The CNT considers as essential its participation in a national body (organismo nacional) equipped to take on the task of war leadership and political and economic consolidation.' Extract from plenary resolution in Peirats, *La CNT en la revolución española*, vol. 1, p. 200. Cf. 'The respon-sibility both before History and their own consciences of those who, being in a position to facilitate the creation of an instrument of national defence (órgano nacional de Defensa) fail to do so, is enormous.' Extract from post-plenary statement, Peirats, p. 202. The fact that the word 'government' is studiously avoided indicates the CNT's awareness of its acute political dilemma. See also V. Richards, *Lessons of the Spanish Revolution*, 2nd edn (London: Freedom Press, 1972), p. 68. A slightly different, but not incompatible assessment of the September plenum is in Lorenzo, *Los anarquistas españoles y el poder*, pp. 184–5.

[51] The commentary appeared on 4 November 1936 in the CNT press (*Solidaridad Obrera*) and is cited in Peirats, *La CNT en la revolución española*, vol. 1, p. 220. Translated extracts appear in Broué and Témime, *The Revolution and the Civil War in Spain*, pp. 207–8.

[52] This remains true, in spite of the fact that Abad de Santillán was the first to criticise this 'short-sightedness' after the war in *Por qué perdimos la guerra*, p. 116 (a translated extract is in Broué and Témime, *The Revolution and the Civil War in Spain*, p. 208).

all sections of the movement were understandably overwhelmed by the Republic's increasingly desperate military (and international) situation.[53] Although a Catalan regional plenum at the beginning of September had agreed CNT entry to the Generalitat, the Catalans would continue to oppose CNT entry to the Largo Caballero government until mid October 1936.[54] The logic here derived from the belief that whereas the Catalan anarchists were collaborating with the Generalitat from a position of strength, the CNT's inclusion in the central government would lead only to endless compromises and the defeat of its revolutionary political goals. But it was precisely to this that the CNT's presence in the Generalitat too would lead.

In the composition of the 28 September cabinet we can see embedded the strategy of the CNT's opponents. The anarcho-syndicalists' economic control was now formally 'contained' by the Esquerra. (Josep Taradellas, appointed premier by Companys, also held the finance portfolio, while agriculture was in the hands of the Rabassaires.[55]) The dissolution of the Central Anti-fascist Militia Committee meant that the CNT committees had effectively been decapitated. Moroever, in the press and public fora, liberal commentators/politicians from the Esquerra and the PSUC (as well as other, smaller parties) had started to attribute all economic dislocation and inefficiency to the *forms* of CNT control *per se*, even though many of the problems they identified were intractable ones, deriving from the macro-economic and territorial dislocations of the war – industrial regions cut off from their suppliers of raw materials, productive regions from their markets and so on. It was the overarching crisis of the war which allowed the liberal political agenda underpinning this campaign to be submerged beneath high-minded denunciations of committee and collectivist inefficiency and abuses (which certainly existed) and impassioned exhortations to a – very necessary – unification of economic production. But what had opened the door to this liberal counter-attack was precisely the CNT's inability to articulate the committees politically. The fact that the only centralised forms of organisation available belonged to their political enemies was now forcing

[53] Cf. the comments of the Catalan FAI's premier leader, Juan García Oliver, also quoted in Broué and Témime, *The Revolution and the Civil War in Spain*, p. 208. Ironically (if unsurprisingly), the most voluble critics of the CNT's change of stance came from those national sections in the AIT (Anarchist International) with minuscule organisations: Casanova, *Anarquismo y revolución*, p. 147. Ideological differences aside, there is an interesting parallel, I think, in the criticisms of the POUM's governmental collaboration made by the exiguous Bolshevik Leninists of Trotsky's Fourth International.

[54] Lorenzo, *Los anarquistas españoles y el poder*, pp. 188–9.

[55] Full cabinet list in Bolloten, *SCW*, pp. 402–3. The PSUC had two portfolios – public services and labour/public works.

anarcho-syndicalists into one of two positions, neither of which was feasible: a political 'compromise' with liberal order or an all-out defence of
the collectives. But the latter implied a defence of economic decentralisation that was difficult to sustain in the conditions in which the civil
war was being fought. Moreover, it laid pro-decentralisation currents of
anarcho-syndicalism wide open to the attacks of their political enemies.

Agrarian collectivisation was slowly but surely being circumscribed.
The famous Republican decree of 7 October 1936 only legalised collectives when they occupied land belonging to those who had supported the
military rising – this, according to Republican law, was the *only* legally
expropriable land.[56] All Republican agricultural decrees, including that
of October, functioned to appease and protect (mainly small and middling) landholding sectors that had not actively demonstrated themselves
to be pro-rebel. Tenant farmers of six years' standing acquired the right
to buy their land outright or by means of redemption payments.[57] By
February 1937 the Generalitat would also make all Catalan tenant farmers owner-occupiers. In that these transactions reinforced the concept
of private property, they fell full square within the logic of the inter-
class Popular Front alliance and, as such, found their most energetic
upholders in the PSUC and the PCE. The latter was also responsible
for the Republican agriculture ministry and its agrarian reform institute,
the IRA. While the IRA would provide finance and technical support
for legally constituted collectives in the whole of the Republican zone
throughout the war, the price was state supervision, and many CNT
collectives held out against registration.[58] Again, the fact that political control belonged not to the anarcho-syndicalists but to their opponents would prove fatal. Without access to state funds (banks, gold etc.),
credit or external trade, the viability of the collectives reduced over time.
Lack of financial control meant that there was no means of capitalis-
ing them – so new machinery, fertiliser and specialist agronomist advice
were hard to come by. Lacking access to resources and in the face of the
inevitable increasing dislocation of wartime, even the ideologically committed minority would become weary and disillusioned by what all too
often ended in such circumstances as the collectivisation of shortage and

---

[56] Republican government thinking on all other collectivisation (in industry, the public services and
transport) was codified in its 24 October 1936 decree.

[57] Central (Giral) government decree of August 1936 in Broué and Témime, *The Revolution and the
Civil War in Spain*, pp. 164–5; Fraser, *Blood of Spain*, p. 372. For the Generalitat's January decrees
indemnifying individuals (other than pro-rebel sectors) for property lost to collectivisation since
18 July 1936, see Payne, *The Spanish Revolution*, pp. 290–1.

[58] Fraser, *Blood of Spain*, p. 373 (n. 1).

poverty.[59] The dissolution of the Central Anti-fascist Militia Committee also loosened the ties between Barcelona and Aragon. The Anti-fascist Militia Committee had had titular responsibility for overseeing the region's political and military affairs.[60] But a plenum called on 6 October by Aragonese anarcho-syndicalists to discuss the CNT's recent entry to the Generalitat decided – in the face of opposition from the Catalan representatives – to establish their own (all-anarchist) regional council – the Council of Aragon.[61] This was a response to Aragon's very real isolation from the Republican government in the aftermath of the coup. There was too a clear element of regionalist sentiment reacting against the perceived 'colonisation' by 'Catalonia' and, most concretely, by Catalan and Valencian anarchist columns.[62] The Council's primary purpose was to coordinate Aragon's highly fragmented collectivised economy. And in spite of its provenance, the Council would play a crucial interventionist (that is, quasi-governmental) role – fixing prices and salaries and organising the exchange of commodities within the region. But by far the most urgent task facing the Council at the time of its birth was to combat the plague of irregular militia requisition – amounting often to sheer armed despoliation – which was fast alienating the Aragonese peasantry even as it undercut the fragile viability of the new collectives. (In spite of the Council's efforts, however, such 'requisition' would continue even after the militarisation of the Aragon front in spring–summer 1937.[63])

Inevitably, there were also practical and political problems within the collectives.[64] In a region where average educational standards were low, there was, from the start, a lack of personnel with the requisite administrative or technical expertise. This created an opening for PCE criticisms that the CNT was accepting those of dubious political loyalties provided

---

[59] Cf. 'As an economic system it was producing a conglomeration of self-contained barter markets grinding slowly towards stagnation as the general economy ran down', R. Carr, *Spain 1808–1975* (Oxford: Oxford University Press, 1982), p. 660. It may be also that the departure of more engagé sectors to the activated front from August 1937 also contributed to this stagnation in Aragon as those (older men) left behind had neither the will nor the enthusiasm to confront the increasing material problems: Fraser, *Blood of Spain*, p. 371 (n. 1).

[60] Although in practice there was virtually total military decentralisation on the Aragon front: Casanova, *Anarquismo y revolución*, p. 109.

[61] Pleno de Bujaraloz: Casanova, *Anarquismo y revolución*, pp. 133–40. Nominal military responsibility for the Aragon front remained with the Generalitat (p. 134).

[62] Fraser, *Blood of Spain*, p. 350.

[63] Casanova, *Anarquismo y revolución*, p. 111. (In practice, each military unit continued to have its own autonomous supply section.)

[64] About which CNT internal documentation – as opposed to its press and political propaganda – was quite frank: Casanova, *Anarquismo y revolución*, pp. 3–4; see also Fraser, *Blood of Spain*, pp. 354–71 and Broué and Témime, *The Revolution and the Civil War in Spain*, pp. 164–5 for an astute and perceptive summary of the complex issues surrounding collectivisation.

they had the requisite skills.[65] At the same time, for socially conservative sectors of the Aragonese peasantry, revolutionary goals of social equality were harder to deal with than the practical rigours of wartime requisition. But equality – even for those who sought it – proved difficult to achieve in practice, and under the dislocations of war the adequate distribution and exchange of products was a fraught process. All of these things opened up space within the Council for socialists, communists and republicans to compete for the political support of the rural constituencies of eastern Aragon. Although there were ideological differences between these organisations, much of the mutual recrimination that everyone else was harbouring political undesirables merely indicates the problematic heterogeneity of the social base that the Republic was required to integrate.

Before the Largo Caballero government would recognise or communicate with the Aragon Council, it insisted that it be reconstituted to reflect the political configuration of the Popular Front alliance. (Neither the central Republican government nor the Generalitat had been remotely happy with the Council as an entirely anarchist body. But while the Generalitat saw its very existence as an infringement of its own powers, the anarchist ministers in the central government managed to persuade Largo Caballero to take the path of conciliation rather than confrontation with the Council.) Agreement was reached by the end of 1936 and henceforward the Council was composed of an equal number of CNT and Popular Front representatives, though presided over by the *cenetista* Joaquín Ascaso, cousin of the famous anarchist leader Francisco Ascaso, who had been killed in action during the July days.[66] But the erosion of the CNT's 'hegemony' on the Aragon Council occurred so rapidly thereafter as to suggest that, in fact, it had never had more than an appearance of control. The collapse of the state had not entirely dislodged the principle of its legitimacy – as we have seen in the Catalan case. And this was something upon which the CNT's political opponents in Aragon could build from the beginning of 1937. Moreover, in addition to the ongoing *internal* political struggle for influence and members, there was also the overriding issue of war needs that pointed to centralised political and economic control. The Council's *raison d'être* was as an instrument of political and (above all) economic articulation. But this still only responded to regional needs. The Council controlled resources that it converted into foreign exchange, spending it in ways that, while not improper, did not necessarily respond to larger war priorities. For example, its purchase

[65] Fraser, *Blood of Spain*, pp. 347, 362, 363–6.
[66] For a full list of members and posts, see Casanova, *Anarquismo y revolución*, p. 141 (and on Joaquín Ascaso, pp. 134–5).

of tractors and other agricultural machinery may have increased production in those collectives that received them, and certainly there was an improved quality of life for the collectivists.[67] But it was a decision taken without reference to overall Republican need/deployment of resources. In the end, then, the Council was a localism 'writ large'. Above all, there was the as yet unresolved problem of properly articulating and supplying Aragon's military front. Once it became necessary to activate the front, then the Council's days would be numbered – as would be the Generalitat's titular military responsibility for it.[68]

Meanwhile, the CNT's political control went on unravelling inside Barcelona capital. On 9 October 1936 the Generalitat decreed the re-constitution of all local committees as municipal bodies with the same composition as itself in a bid to liquidate anarcho-syndicalist power on the ground.[69] The Esquerra was amazed to find the CNT's ministerial representatives acquiescing. But by this stage it was too late for them to oppose what were, in effect, the consequences of power sharing in July.

From late September to December, Comorera and the PSUC spear-headed an increasingly bitter propaganda campaign against the embattled CNT supply committees. Keen to re-establish the free market in staple goods sought by their supporters (smallholders, traders and shopkeepers), the PSUC publicly blamed the supply committees (and, implicitly, all forms of collectivisation) for the increasingly acute food shortages facing the population.

The Catalan liberals' primary objective, however, remained full control of public order in Catalonia, since a monopoly of coercive force was the *sine qua non* of all other change. From the Generalitat's Home Office, Artemi Aiguader, the Esquerra's risk-taking political operator, set his sights on the CNT's *de facto* control of the defence/security portfolio.[70] At the same time, a number of decrees were issued with the aim of disarming the worker committees. On 27 October the central Republican government decreed that all 'long arms' (i.e. rifles and machine guns) held by 'private citizens' were to be handed over to the 'municipal authorities'.[71] But this would inevitably be a slow process – especially in Catalonia. It would take months for the municipalities to start

[67] Fraser, *Blood of Spain*, p. 356. [68] See chapter 5 below.

[69] An indication of the difficulty of implementation is in M. Vilanova, 'L'Escala y Beuda', *Historia y Fuente Oral*, 3 (1990), 53.

[70] Bolloten, *SCW*, p. 858, n. 42. On Aiguader, see Cruells, *Mayo sangriento*, p. 49.

[71] Morrow, *Revolution and Counter-Revolution in Spain*, p. 58. For the continuing 'unofficial' use of petrol as part of this conflict (illegal detentions occurred by car), see E. Ucelay da Cal, 'Cataluña durante la guerra' in (various authors) *La guerra de España* (Madrid: Taurus, 1996; 1st edn 1986), p. 327.

functioning, and neither these, nor the end of the Anti-fascist Militia Committee, nor CNT representation in the new Generalitat had, of themselves, liquidated dual power. A network of defence committees as well as factory and neighbourhood committees still functioned through-out Barcelona, even if they had been decapitated. These committees generally chose to interpret the arms decree as still permitting the re-tention of such weapons for their own collective use. In the long run, however, the October decree would set the precedent for a withdrawal of worker patrol and committee arms from the home front. Liberal gov-ernments in Madrid and Catalonia were seeking to return a monopoly of firepower to the police as the agents of the state – although this process was explained and justified purely in terms of garnering all resources for the military front.

To this end, the police were being consolidated. After having been formally dissolved in the aftermath of the coup, both the Assault Guards and National Republican (i.e. ex-Civil) Guards were by the end of 1936 subject to central government reforms – the same reforms which saw the building up of the Carabineros.[72] By the end of 1936 they were involved in skirmishes – which inside three months would escalate into bloody confrontations – with the CNT's control committees on the Franco-Spanish/Catalan border (at places such as Figueras and Puigcerdá) as treasury minister Negrín sought to exert economic control over crucial foreign exchange for the central Republican government.[73] Although this encroachment by 'Madrid' was far from welcome to the Catalan nationalists in Esquerra and PSUC, such was their desire to see social and economic normalisation that it ensured their interim support for Negrín's initiative. However, it was to be the looming political crisis over the POUM's ministerial presence in the Generalitat in November 1936 that provided the first golden opportunity significantly to consolidate liberal governmental authority in Catalonia in terms of both public order and economic policy.

This opportunity was provided by the eruption inside Republican Spain of another dispute – the increasingly bitter one raging in the

---

[72] C. Semprún-Maura, *Revolución y contrarrevolución en Cataluña (1936–1937)* (Barcelona: Tusquets, 1978), p. 237. On the Republic's – essentially failed – pre-war reform of the police/public order (they were not demilitarised), see Ballbé, *Orden público y militarismo en la España constitucional*, pp. 317–96 (partic. pp. 391, 393) and chapter 1 above. For the Carabineros, see chapter 3 above.

[73] Factory delegates in socialised industries would go abroad to arrange imports and exports direct: Morrow, *Revolution and Counter-Revolution in Spain*, p. 20. Another major focus of the battle between government and unions over control of foreign exchange was waged in the Valencian region over the collection and export of oranges/citrus fruit by a UGT-CNT consortium, CLUEA: Bosch Sánchez, *Ugetistas y libertarios*, pp. 380–3.

international communist movement. In late August, the POUM publicly denounced the execution by Stalin of Zinoviev, Kamenev and other old-guard Bolsheviks.[74] It did so in spite of a strong current of opinion in the party that urged caution so as to avoid any further deterioration of their own relations with the Comintern-aligned PCE and PSUC.[75] By November, the POUM's press criticism had escalated, in significant part goaded by the party's exclusion from the Madrid Defence Council.[76] The Catalan POUM now openly accused the Comintern of pursuing the containment of the Spanish Revolution because it was out of step with the Soviet government's defence needs – especially as the revolution offered no sectarian advantage since the Comintern did not control it politically.[77] These public criticisms are enough to explain the hostility to the POUM exhibited by Moscow and the Comintern. Moreover, while the party was not Trotskyist, the fact that Trotsky's former (albeit now politically estranged) secretary, Andreu Nin, and his small Communist Left Party also formed a minor component of the POUM clinched the Comintern's determination to remove it from the political scene in Spain.

This might have been rather more difficult to achieve, however, had the POUM's political position not already been weakened by its ambiguities.[78] The party publicly espoused a radical anti-capitalist ideology for furthering both the July revolution and the war effort. Yet since the February 1936 elections, the POUM had supported the liberal-left Popular Front alliance. Moreover, its own party base in Catalonia also depended significantly on sectors of the urban and rural lower-middle classes who, while they were Catalanist and politically to the left of the Esquerra, were far from revolutionary or socialist in their outlook.[79] It

---

[74] V. Alba, *El marxismo en España 1919–1939. Historia del B.O.C. y del P.O.U.M.* (2 vols., Mexico: Costa-Amic, 1973), vol. 1, p. 316 quoting *La Batalla* (27 August 1936).

[75] V. Alba, *Historia de la segunda república española* (Mexico: Libro Mex, 1960), p. 255 and *El marxismo*, vol. 1, p. 317.

[76] See chapter 3 above.

[77] *La Batalla*, 14 and 18 November 1936 (respectively for two criticisms) – cited in Bolloten, *SCW*, pp. 408 (n. 25), 410.

[78] The Madrid POUM was to the left of the Catalan party – being mainly constituted from Andreu Nin's tiny Communist Left component plus a few Bolshevik-Leninists: Durgan, *B.O.C. 1930–1936*, pp. 556, 559; Morrow, *Revolution and Counter-Revolution*, p. 85. The POUM's Valencia branch constituted the 'right' of the party in that it entirely supported the Republican government alliance: Morrow, *Revolution and Counter-Revolution*, p. 66; Bolloten, *SCW*, p. 860 (n. 12).

[79] The POUM justified its support of the Popular Front for tactical reasons, but it caused a definitive break between Trotsky and Nin. For the tensions inside the POUM and between the POUM and (Spanish and non-Spanish) Trotskyists, see Durgan, 'Trotsky, the POUM and the Spanish Revolution'. For the importance of the POUM's Catalanist discourse, see the way in which the party press (*La Batalla*) frames its criticism of measures to bring both the Generalitat and Catalan militia under the authority of the central government's war ministry in late March 1937, article

was the concerns of these middling sectors that lay behind the POUM's post-July days professions that it would 'uphold [the middle classes'] economic claims... within the framework of the revolution'. At the same time the POUM sought to distinguish itself from the PSUC, which it denounced as guilty of capitulating to its middle-class constituency, becoming its mere instrument.[80] But it is difficult to see how the POUM could have squared this particular circle. The party's dilemma after 18 July 1936 arose from the conflict between the radical ideological project it enunciated in its wartime publications and the nature of its social base.[81] This conflict was probably much more acute because of the absence of the POUM's undisputed leader, Joaquín Maurín, who was in prison in the rebel zone.[82] The former leader of the BOC, Maurín was an experienced politician who understood his Catalan base. Those who replaced him were activists and theorists, but none had Maurín's strategic talent. The POUM's new helmsman, Andreu Nin, was not able to invest the party's radicalised discourse with a matching practice. Indeed, some have gone as far as to argue that Nin's dogmatism wasted six years of the BOC's rich populist political practice and thus facilitated the PSUC's stealing of POUM's political discourse, strategies and base.[83] Nor did the POUM have real political allies. Indeed, the POUM's very ambiguities meant that groups which were otherwise politically antagonistic to each other (i.e. the CNT, the PSUC and the Esquerra) could come together temporarily over their common hostility to the POUM.

For all his perceived radicalism, it was Nin who took the POUM into government in spite of the reservations of the party left.[84] (Like the CNT,

---

cited in Bolloten, *SCW*, p. 420. (The editorial was written by the POUM (and ex-BOC) leader, Enric Adroher (Gironella).)

[80] 'It is one thing to attract the middle classes to the revolution and another to form a coalition giving them a decisive role as a governing force... but we uphold their economic claims... within the framework of the revolution', *La Batalla*, 23 Feb. 1937.

[81] There is little to suggest the POUM's crucial political ambiguities in George Orwell's diary account, *Homage to Catalonia* (first pub. 1938) – an omission which problematises his explanation of later political developments upon which so many accounts still ultimately rely.

[82] J. Maurín, *Cómo se salvó Joaquín Maurín. Recuerdos y testimonios* (Madrid: Júcar, 1980); Bolloten, *SCW*, p. 405.

[83] Ucelay da Cal, 'Socialistas y comunistas en Cataluña durante la guerra civil', p. 312; see also J. Miravitlles, *Episodis de la guerra civil espanyola* (Barcelona: Editorial Pòrtic, 1972), p. 178. Interestingly, another Catalan historian, Borja de Riquer, has recently commented upon the resemblance between the POUM and the PSUC during the war in the matter of nationalism. Both had party bases that were substantially Catalanist, yet had leaders (or at least some leaders) who did not want to recognise it. Borja de Riquer during the Escorial summer school, Madrid, July 2001 ('Entre la ética y el extremismo: los personajes de la guerra civil').

[84] Fraser, *Blood of Spain*, p. 341; Bolloten, *SCW*, p. 861 (n. 15). For a bolshevik-leninist critique, see Morrow, *Revolution and Counter-Revolution*, pp. 54–7.

he too was up against the enormous political responsibility of the war.) Once there, Nin took a conciliatory line over the question of unions versus soviets as the appropriate instrument of revolution. But the CNT still remained hostile. Nin's policy in the Generalitat justice portfolio was also a source of friction with CNT radicals.[85] Moreover, the POUM's numerous criticisms of CNT excess in the implementation of wartime collectivisation introduced yet further tensions to the relationship.[86] As we have already seen, the CNT viewed the POUM as a potential rival. At the same time, both the Esquerra and (more realistically) the PSUC were interested in attracting sectors of the POUM's urban base. The old USC Catalanist agenda, as much as the new Comintern one, was now driving the PSUC to compete with the POUM for the political loyalty of lower-middle-class sectors in the region. The hybridity of the Popular Frontist model no doubt also sharpened Comorera's expectations of a parallel success among industrial workers in Catalonia. The PSUC could now seek to recruit simultaneously from both Esquerra and POUM bases just as, elsewhere, the PCE was acquiring a cross-class membership through the adoption of the same model.

After the POUM's public criticism of the Soviet Union, the PSUC demanded its exclusion from the Generalitat on 24 November. A great deal of emphasis has been laid here on the intervention of the Soviet Consul-General in Barcelona, Vladimir Antonov-Ovseenko, in persuading Companys and the Esquerra to accept this.[87] That such intervention occurred is clear. But given that this intervention and influence were suggesting a political direction which all Catalan liberals were in any case keen to take, it is something of a nonsense to argue that the outcome was purely the product of Soviet 'duress'. What Antonov-Ovseenko offered Companys was a largely superfluous reminder of the liberal Republic's precarious international position. Nor did Companys need to be reminded that the POUM's presence in the Generalitat was an additional obstacle to liberal normalisation.

The PSUC's demands for POUM exclusion opened the way for a vehement Esquerra denunciation of 'committee chaos'. Companys made

---

[85] V. Alba, 'De los Tribunales Populares al Tribunal Especial', in *Justicia en guerra*, pp. 226–7, 229–30. For the underlying ideological hostility of the CNT to the POUM – which was rooted in the memory of Trotsky's role in the repression of anarchists during the Bolshevik Revolution – see Bolloten's comments on the POUM's impracticable plan to bring the exiled Trotsky to Barcelona, *SCW*, p. 859 (n. 3).

[86] The POUM press between July and December 1936 attests to this: see examples/summary in Bolloten, *SCW*, p. 863 (n. 48).

[87] For example, ibid., p. 411; Cruells, *Mayo sangriento*, p. 29.

no specific reference to the POUM, but demanded 'a strong government with plenary powers, capable of imposing its authority on everyone'.[88] The CNT instantly rejected this, well understanding that it rather than the POUM was Companys' real target. Indeed, the PSUC made this absolutely explicit. After echoing Companys' declarations on the need to concentrate all power in the government, Comorera went on to demand that dual power in Catalan defence and public order now be ended *de facto* as well as *de jure* by the dissolution of both the CNT's defence and security committees.

Faced by this Esquerra–PSUC line-up, the libertarians cannot have failed to perceive the political dangers for themselves. But this did little to reduce their ambivalence towards the POUM. Moreover, in terms of the hard currency of political power in Catalonia in 1936, both the POUM's increasing marginalisation (as the PSUC expanded) and its internal political tensions meant that the CNT did not interpret the POUM's presence or absence as making any strategic difference to its own position. So, when the PSUC offered a deal, the CNT accepted: it would drop its opposition to POUM exclusion from the cabinet and the PSUC would drop its call for the dissolution of the defence and security committees.

On 16 December, after four days of cabinet crisis, the new line-up was announced. Out of a total of eleven portfolios, the Esquerra had four (including the Rabassaire-held post of agriculture), the PSUC three and the CNT four. There was still a stand-off in public order: the Esquerra's Aiguader retained the Home Office portfolio, but the CNT committees continued to function. A crucial shift had nevertheless occurred in the economic posts. Why the CNT allowed this constitutes far more of a conundrum than does its position on the POUM.[89] Not only was the CNT's economy brief overseen, as before, by Taradellas' control of finance, but now Comorera also had control of the crucial supply portfolio.[90] The battle to 'free the market' was about to begin.

This was a battle in which the Esquerra wanted the same outcome as the PSUC – the restitution of liberal economic order. But it was less prepared than the PSUC to take the strain in the bruising confrontation that loomed.[91] In part this was because the Esquerra was still recovering

---

[88] *Solidaridad Obrera*, 9 Dec. 1936.
[89] The ostensible reason was the CNT's prioritising of the war portfolio in the Generalitat. So in the December crisis they relinquished supply in exchange for this: see Fraser, *Blood of Spain*, p. 375 (and n. 1) for the recollections of Juan José Doménech, the CNT's outgoing councillor for supply.
[90] Comorera and Doménech had in fact swapped posts from the previous (September) cabinet, with Doménech now in public services.
[91] During 1936 the Esquerra press was far less explicit in its anti-CNT stance than was the PSUC's, Bolloten, *SCW*, pp. 410, 862 (n. 39).

from the erosive impact of the July coup. But it seems highly likely that it was also a conscious tactic of Companys to allow the PSUC to do its 'dirty work' in the expectation that this would, in turn, erode the fast-growing PSUC[92] and allow the Esquerra to reclaim its hegemonic position in the Catalan arena. Increasing tensions in the 'hybrid' PSUC between centralist and Catalanist currents would give Companys and the Esquerra both the will and the opportunity seriously to recontest the political arena.

The fall of Malaga in early February 1937 and the hard fighting continuing around Madrid intensified Republican government demands that all political, economic and military decision-making power be invested in itself. The Spanish Communist Party was also spearheading demands for the proper implementation of conscription – again to be controlled by the central government. Companys had already experienced this pressure first hand in December 1936 when Antonov-Ovseenko reinforced the Republican government's agenda by linking Soviet military aid to Catalonia not only to the POUM's political exclusion,[93] but also to the Generalitat's acceptance of a single Republican political and military command – something far more politically unpalatable.[94] The Esquerra's highly developed sense of its nationalist prerogatives was seriously offended. In turn this would lead the party into a complicated political balancing act: supporting the CNT at strategic moments, albeit at the risk of alienating some of their own middle-class supporters – to the benefit of the PSUC. The Esquerra was of course keen to see the PSUC drive for economic normalisation, but it also needed a means of resisting that party's centralising tendencies. The PSUC too trod a fine line here, however. Its dynamic defence of liberal order had brought it the political

---

[92] Although I know of no figures for the first six months of the war alone, the PSUC grew from little over 3,000 to c. 50,000 members by March 1937. This compares with c. 30,000 claimed by the POUM in December 1936. See Bolloten, *SCW*, pp. 399, 405 for PSUC and POUM figures respectively.

[93] There may well also have been a psychological link between the worsening climate of denunciation inside the Comintern, the simultaneous fall of Malaga and the intensification of Comintern concerns about 'the enemy within' in Republican Spain (interpreted as both the POUM and potentially traitorous army officers): Elorza and Bizcarrondo, *Queridos camaradas*, p. 340.

[94] The evidence for this is hearsay (i.e. there are no corroborative testimonies from participants – Companys, Taradellas, Antonov-Ovseenko – see Cruells, *Mayo sangriento*, p. 29) and comes, moreover, from hostile sources, for example Rudolf Rocker (the German anarchist and AIT representative in Republican Spain), in *Extranjeros en España* (Buenos Aires, 1938), p. 91. Nor are the textual extracts from Bolloten's interview with Companys' lieutenant, Serra Pàmies, in Mexico in 1944 necessarily as unambiguous as Bolloten's deductions imply: Bolloten, *SCW*, pp. 411, 863 (n. 49). However, that a Soviet diplomatic representative should have made strong representation in favour of a single command is consonant with Stalin's preoccupation with the viability of the Republican military defence.

support of the Catalan middle classes. But whereas in the rest of the Republican zone the PCE's appeal was to a great extent built upon its identification with *mando único*, for the PSUC the pursuit of such policies – necessary though they may have been to the war effort – risked alienating their recently acquired party base. Partly these differences in perspective were about the nearness or distance of the war/military front. But at root it was the old liberal rivalry of unevenly developed Spain where economic and industrial power in Catalonia confronts political authority in Madrid (or, in this case, Valencia).

The pressure applied by less Catalanist-minded sectors within the PSUC (i.e. those deriving from the former Catalan sectors of the PSOE and the PCE and maybe some new membership constituencies too) was itself part of the longstanding battle between centralist liberals and Catalan nationalists, even if its most efficient *conduits* during the civil war were the peninsular communist parties and the Comintern.[95] But the Republic's worsening military situation was an objective pressure affecting *all* Republican political sectors alike. Comorera's increased criticism of the POUM's public anti-Sovietism in February 1937 also has to be understood as a response to this. Nor were these conflicts and pressures inside communist ranks materially different from those that increasingly divided the CNT's national leadership from sectors of the anarcho-syndicalist movement in Catalonia. For wartime imperatives were also turning the CNT's ministers and its national committee into a conduit for central government policies which sought to keep the Catalan anarchists compromising inside the Generalitat.[96] Thus far the Catalan liberals could agree. But what they failed to recognise was that while it was feasible to 'contain' the CNT's regional leadership, anarcho-syndicalist social constituencies were quite another matter. It was in the daily lived experiences of these groups and the meanings they ascribed to such experiences that we find the crucial motive force for the build-up of social and political tension in urban Catalonia across the winter and spring of 1937.

Meanwhile, the prosecution of the war under the highly unfavourable conditions of Non-Interventionist embargo was also increasing the pressure on the central government to bring the Basque Country more closely

---

[95] The three PSUC leaders in the December 1936 Generalitat were appointed simultaneously to the PCE's central committee: Pedro Checa, *A un gran partido una gran organización* (PCE agitprop pamphlet, Valencia, 1937), p. 23, which lists Central Committee members.

[96] For this 'assimilation' of CNT leaders and its political and organisational consequences, see chapter 5 below.

under its control – in accordance with *mando único*. Indeed, until the government properly controlled Basque military forces and, crucially, its iron- and steel-producing industrial plant, then 'the Republican war effort' would remain, in a crucial sense, unrealised. But against this aim was ranged a powerful regional particularism – no less recalcitrant for being entirely liberal, in contrast to Catalonia's liberal and revolutionary varieties.

The military rebellion of 18 July 1936 had opened up the internal cleavages in the Basque Country. Those areas least affected by modernisation – those which were agricultural, least urbanised and the strongholds of political traditionalism – split off from the industrialised, urbanised and more socially heterogeneous parts. Instantly removed from the Republic's orbit was Navarre, as the centre of Carlism, a bastion of the ultra anti-Republican right.[97] Most of Alava was also in rebel hands, as well as the majority of Guipúzcoa by September. The Republic retained the Basque industrial heartland – Vizcaya – and some adjacent territory, also of a mainly industrial character.[98]

But this internal separation did not much facilitate an easier fit between the Republican Basque Country and the rest of the Republic. The military defence of Vizcaya was undertaken by a combination of social groups: Basque and immigrant workers encadred in the trade unions STV and UGT respectively, and the strongly nationalist lower-middle classes represented by the Basque Nationalist Party (PNV). But it was the PNV that dominated the politics of Vizcaya. It did so, moreover, in the name of a provincial social base significantly more conservative than the profile projected by the 'capital' city, Bilbao, whose secular and workerist components chimed more easily with the rest of Popular Frontist Spain.[99]

In Bilbao itself there had been no military rising. Both army and state security forces remained loyal to the Republic. Nevertheless, in the Basque Country as elsewhere, political power fragmented under the impact of the rebellion. Defence Juntas emerged in a number of places, including Bilbao and San Sebastián (the capital of Guipúzcoa), each of which initially acted independently. The PNV had relatively more

---

97 There was, nevertheless, a significant *repression* in Navarre which suggests that the appeal of the rising was far from universal: see Altaffaylla Kultur Taldea, *Navarra 1936. De la esperanza al terror* (Tafalla: Altaffaylla Kultur Taldea, 1986) and E. Majuelo, *Lucha de clases en Navarra (1931–1936)* (n.p.: Gobierno de Navarra, 1989).

98 For example Eibar, which was Guipúzcoa's main industrial centre.

99 The PNV was electorally dominant in Vizcaya by dint of its *provincial* control. It did not have a majority in the industrial capital of Bilbao.

influence in Bilbao's. And with Republican attrition in Guipúzcoa and the fall of San Sebastián in the first weeks of September, the Defence Junta of Vizcaya emerged as the main body, overseeing both military defence and organisation of the civilian front.

Unlike elsewhere, however, political fragmentation in Vizcaya never produced a viable challenge to liberal economic order or any revolutionary experimentation with social life. Private property was guaranteed by the continued political dominance of the Basque Nationalists, backed up by the moderate social democratic Basque component of the PSOE. Unlike what happened elsewhere in Spain to the political representatives of the middling classes, the PNV's influence survived the formal break in institutional political continuity provoked by the military rebellion. But the PNV in Vizcaya was doubly cut off from Madrid and the Giral government – by dint of both its territorial separation and the state crisis triggered by the coup. In the absence of government directives and structures, the immediate needs of Basque defence saw the formation of militias on the basis of political parties and unions. But here too the PNV was soon in control. At the beginning of August, the party, along with its sister formation the ANV and the Basque labour union, STV, formed nationalist volunteer battalions (obeying military-style discipline from the outset), in order to wage a war on two fronts: first against the rebels and second against the radical left minority inside the Basque Country, which the PNV's Manuel de Irujo described as 'extremist elements brought into the house'.[100] There were some (mainly anarchist) workerist manifestations in San Sebastián in the immediate post-coup days, but they were quickly contained.[101] By August, liberal order reigned to such an extent that it appeared almost as if Basque society had experienced no break with the pre-coup world. The most striking indicator of this was the degree of religious normality in Vizcaya. Two churches were burned down in San Sebastián in July. But this was an exceptional occurrence. The PNV ensured that the churches remained open and that religious observance was still a public matter.[102] Indeed, it was common for each Basque nationalist battalion to have its own chaplain.

[100] F. de Meer, *El Partido Nacionalista Vasco ante la guerra de España (1936–1937)* (Barañáin-Pamplona: Eunsa, 1992), pp. 128–9; for Irujo, see A. Lizarra, *Los vascos y la República española* (Buenos Aires: Ekin, 1944), p. 95.
[101] Broué and Témime, *The Revolution and Civil War in Spain*, pp. 138–9. San Sebastián fell to the rebels on 13 September.
[102] J. P. Fusi, 'The Basque question 1931–7', in Preston, *Revolution and War in Spain*, pp. 183–4. (Leading Basque prelates were caught between their desire to defend Basque nationalist rights and their hostility to Republican anti-clericalism. The Castilian hierarchy protected them from rebel ire but also pushed them to line up with the rest of the Spanish Church.)

This social normality in the Basque Country was very welcome to the Madrid government. But other tensions between it and the PNV would soon surface in relation to the imperatives of the war effort, making for an uneasy relationship right through to the fall of Bilbao in June 1937. In the first instance, Madrid was not even sure that the PNV would bring Vizcaya into the Republican alliance. The PSOE – and in particular Prieto with his extensive Basque contacts – was aware of the fragility of the PNV's allegiance, especially given the breakdown of liberal order and eruption of anti-clerical violence in much of the rest of the Republican zone. After all, the commercial middling classes constituting the heart of Basque nationalism were largely defined by their Catholicism. It cemented a set of social values which, while not those of the rebels, were still clearly conservative. As such, the collectivisation of industry in Catalonia had also delivered a considerable shock in Vizcaya.

Largo Caballero had originally designated the PNV's leader, José Antonio Aguirre, as his minister for public works on 5 September 1936. Aguirre rejected the offer, whereupon there followed labyrinthine negotiations over the price of Basque participation.[103] The military pressure on the Basque defence was temporarily eased in mid September, when Mola's troops came up against the mountain chain separating Vizcaya from Guipúzcoa and Alava. But Madrid still had grounds to fear that the PNV might strike out alone and convert Junta power into an independent Basque Republic.[104] Indeed, the PNV made a pact with Largo Caballero only because his government was prepared to offer the PNV's key goal: the autonomy statute – something the rebel alliance would never have ceded, as Aguirre well knew. This awareness was reinforced, moreover, by the fact that the repression in Alava and Navarre included nationalist priests among its victims. For the Basque nationalists the statute was interpreted as a device that would permit the Basque Country after the war to 'secede' culturally and to some extent politically from the Republican centre.[105] But in addition to passing the stalled Basque autonomy statute,[106] the PNV also demanded

---

[103] De Meer, *El Partido Nacionalista Vasco*, pp. 137–56.

[104] See Irujo's comments, Lizarra, *Los vascos y la República española*, p. 81.

[105] There were, however, a minority in the PNV (the most doctrinaire followers of party founder Sabino de Arana) who refused to take sides in the civil war because they considered it a 'war between Spaniards' and thus none of their concern. If there had to be a Basque representative in the Madrid government they insisted that it should *not* be a PNV representative: de Meer, *El Partido Nacionalista Vasco*, p. 138.

[106] Indeed, this had been Prieto's strategy since April 1936 in order to tie the PNV to the Republic: ibid., pp. 67–72. Prieto as minister of air/navy negotiated the last stages of the statute. For the process which had led to the stalling of the statute, see chapter 1 above.

that Madrid permit the formation of a Basque government. This was a harder condition for the centre to meet in view of the desperate fragmentation of political power against which it was already struggling. Nor did PNV personnel have any obvious leaders with experience of the crucial areas of government: defence, economic policy and international relations. But in spite of the reluctance of Madrid (and on this issue Largo Caballero and Prieto entirely agreed) in the circumstances, the central government had to show willing in order to maintain Basque morale. Moreover, there were also pressing practical considerations. The fall of Irún on 5 September – only six weeks into the conflict – meant that the Republican Basque Country was isolated not only from the rest of Republican territory but also from France. Whatever Madrid's ambivalence concerning regional nationalist pretensions, it made sense to have an organisational structure that could articulate the fragmented power of the Juntas. Irujo joined the central cabinet as minister without portfolio in late September.[107] The ensuing hardening of rebel attitudes and the bombing of Bilbao also contributed to the sense of the PNV having crossed the Rubicon into the Republican alliance. The Basque Statute was approved by the Republican Cortes on 1 October and a Basque government formed on 7 October under Aguirre. It was configured to reflect the Republican alliance, though excluding the CNT, which remained a marginal force in the Basque Country. A majority of the posts went to the PNV, the real political power behind the new government.[108] At the same time, the Republic dispatched part of the Republican navy to Bilbao with arms and munitions to seal its pact with the Basque Nationalists.[109]

Given the fact that the Republican government was also instrumentalising the statute to commit the PNV fully to the war effort, the political transaction was in fact a reciprocal one. But even though the PNV would strongly associate itself with the principles of constitutionalism underpinning the Republican alliance, its other members still regarded Basque

---

[107] *Gaceta de Madrid*, 26 Sept. 1936.

[108] For constitution of the Basque government, see de Meer, *El Partido Nacionalista Vasco*, p. 181. On the evidence here (pp. 141–2) the author seems to exaggerate the significance of Basque socialist and communist support for a regional government. But the presence of local loyalties was, nevertheless, a generic political factor across the north and thus, as elsewhere, an obstacle to the centralisation of the Republican war effort.

[109] M. González Portilla and J. M. Garmendía, *La guerra civil en el País Vasco* (Madrid: Siglo XXI, 1988), p. 69; de Meer, *El Partido Nacionalista Vasco*, p. 176. Such aid would prove scanty, however: Salas Larrazábal, *Historia del ejército popular de la república*, vol. 1, pp. 369–72. In general, Republican ships were handicapped by the lack of naval bases in Republican hands on the Cantabrian coast. M. Chiapuso, *El gobierno vasco y los anarquistas* (San Sebastián: Ed. Txertoa, 1978), p. 79.

loyalty as fraught and conditional.[110] For one thing, it was clear that the Basques envisaged a *defensive* war of position to protect the territory of Euskadi. The question of contributing manpower or economic resources to other Republican fronts would be much more fraught.[111] Moreover, it was known that part of the PNV leadership favoured negotiating separately with the rebels.[112] Their reasons were in part pragmatic – they did not believe that the Republic could win against Franco's professional army backed by Italy and Germany. But ideological reservations about the Republic were also present, and indeed increased when the CNT joined the Madrid government in November 1936. The knowledge that this pactist group inside the PNV had taken soundings with the rebels through intermediaries in Alava, and that it was attempting to involve the Vatican in a mediatory role, reinforced Republican suspicions.[113] Nor did it help that the brunt of the fighting in the north up to the fall of San Sebastián was borne by socialist, anarchist and communist militias rather than the Basque Nationalist forces.[114] San Sebastián was evacuated on 11 September by retreating anarchists who operated a scorched earth policy before crossing into France. The fact that the Basque Nationalist militia were not prepared to do the same increased suspicions of their disloyalty among the workers' militia. In addition, tensions arising over questions of military, political and economic jurisdiction would lead to increasing antagonism between Aguirre at the head of the Basque administration and the reconstructing power of the central Republican government under Largo Caballero.

---

[110] Cf. Aguirre's claim that the PNV had civilised the war, in J. A. Aguirre, *Veinte años de gestión del Gobierno Vasco (1936–1956)* (Paris, 1956). Jackson, *The Spanish Republic and the Civil War*, p. 387 summarises the substantive political differences between the Basque Nationalists and rebels/traditionalist right (Carlists). However, constitutionalism as a war banner was stronger in Aguirre and (above all) Irujo than in other PNV leaders. See de Meer, *El Partido Nacionalista Vasco*, pp. 153–4 and p. 254 for the view that their promotion of humanitarian policies, such as prisoner exchanges, had greatly increased the Republic's international standing as a whole.

[111] This has been a controversial point, but de Meer offers a convincing circumstantial testimony, *El Partido Nacionalista Vasco*, pp. 151–2. Aguirre would offer to send Basque troops to the Catalan front in July 1937, but that offer was part of a different and complex political context when the defence of Vizcaya itself was no longer a possibility: Chiapuso, *El gobierno vasco y los anarquistas*, pp. 225–8.

[112] De Meer, *El Partido Nacionalista Vasco*, pp. 236–7.

[113] Ibid., pp. 137–56 is illuminating on the differences of political perspective within the PNV leadership; see also Thomas, *Spanish Civil War*, p. 431. Nor did these attempts at procuring mediation ever properly stop (de Meer, p. 240). The attempts are usefully summarised in M. Tuñón de Lara, 'Algunos problemas historiográficos de la guerra civil en Euskadi', in M. Tuñón de Lara (ed.), *Gernika: 50 años después (1937–1987)* (San Sebastián: Universidad del País Vasco, 1987), pp. 136, 144–5.

[114] De Meer, *El Partido Nacionalista Vasco*, pp. 113, 129–30.

Largo dispatched the efficient though abrasive Captain Francisco Ciutat as the central government's Commander-in-Chief to coordinate the 'Army of the North'. But Ciutat had to accept the reality of separate militia forces in Vizcaya, Santander and Asturias, which he consequently advised separately. Relations between Ciutat and Aguirre were poor. The fact that the captain, like so many professional officers, had joined the PCE guaranteed Aguirre's enmity.[115] Ciutat's relatively lowly rank also made it easier for Aguirre to resist. But although the PNV did not like the idea of an integrated Northern Army, the underlying point at this stage was that it saw no reason to cede military control in Euskadi's defensive war of position to a central government whose own authority was so weak. The PNV's uncertainty as to what the Largo government represented politically also reinforced the Basque Nationalists' idea of a defensive war, as did the low priority given by Madrid to the Basque front. Aguirre was determined that the PNV should control all areas of military authority even when this meant removing those who had acquired some real practical experience in the early months.[116] By late October, all the Republican militia within the Basque Country were militarised into battalions dependent on the Basque defence ministry – also held by Aguirre. By the same token, the Basque concept of defensive war also militated against its economic and military cooperation within the rest of the Republican north. This was particularly the case as the PNV disliked what it saw as the workerist tenor of the other Republican authorities in the north.[117]

But while the PNV's quite specific political agenda did not help matters, intense localist allegiances existed across the whole of the Republican north.[118] There would be some instances of troop exchanges – for example of Basque forces to Asturias in February 1937 and of brigades from Asturias and Santander to the Basque front the following April.[119]

---

[115] J. Ambou, *Los comunistas en la resistencia nacional republicana. La guerra en Asturias, el País Vasco y Santander* (Madrid: Editorial Hispamerca, 1978), p. 145. Some in the CNT militia also distrusted Ciutat, but whether this was about more than the abiding military–civilian tensions of the post-coup period it is difficult to gauge: Chiapuso, *El gobierno vasco y los anarquistas*, p. 59.

[116] Chiapuso, *El gobierno vasco y los anarquistas*, p. 63 (and p. 192 for Aguirre's sense of himself as a 'providential leader'). The Basque socialist and later government minister, Paulino Gómez, was removed from the war post that he had held under the Junta de Vizcaya.

[117] Ibid., p. 195.

[118] 'Localism (el espíritu de la patria chica) prevailed to the point of aberration', Ibid., p. 60. In this respect, the Basque CNT agreed with the constant refrain of its northern communist counterparts: Ambou, *Los comunistas en la resistencia nacional republicana*, pp. 58, 59, 75–6, 135, 143, 248.

[119] Tuñón de Lara, 'Algunos problemas historiográficos de la guerra civil en Euskadi', p. 138.

But the reciprocal effect of these enduring localisms, combined with an insufficiently strong central government, cumulatively impeded vital economic cooperation between Asturias, Santander and the Basque Country in the key period of Largo's premiership (which was precisely when the Republicans had preparatory time), just as they impeded the coordination of military planning and strategy.[120] The Communist Party in Asturias argued for just such a coordination. But it was far less influential within the Asturian Popular Front alliance than were its counterparts in Catalonia or Madrid.[121] Moreover, its calls for *mando único* were neutralised by the increasing hostility towards it of sectors of the Asturian socialist movement with whom it was competing for members. Nor, crucially, was there any force in the Basque government at this time to argue against the PNV's concept of a purely defensive war. The Basque socialists – the second most influential political force in Vizcaya – accepted the PNV's war policy, at least in part to consolidate the PNV's Republican allegiance. But so too did the Basque Communist Party, until, under the pressure of the spring 1937 rebel offensive, it was obliged to reform its policy line in the direction of greater support for *mando único* and the incorporation of Basque resources to the greater war effort.[122] But by then it would be too late.

In early November 1936 Ciutat was replaced as commander in the north by General Llano de la Encomienda, as preparations were put in train for military action designed to take the pressure off Madrid. Its specific objectives included the retaking of Vitoria (the capital of Alava) and of Irún – in order to reconnect the Republican Basque Country with France. When the action began in late November 1936 Llano de la Encomienda was in command. But control of the Basque forces was

---

[120] Chiapuso, *El gobierno vasco y los anarquistas*, pp. 63, 125, 195, which suggests Basque political reserve towards 'socialist' Asturias and indicates the free market nature of the economic exchange within the north. For Basque factories supplying the Asturian front, see Ambou, *Los comunistas en la resistencia nacional republicana*, p. 129.

[121] From December 1936 Asturias was administered by an inter-provincial council, the Consejo Interprovincial de Asturias y León: Ambou, *Los comunistas en la resistencia nacional republicana*, p. 75.

[122] Ibid., pp. 60–1; Thomas, *Spanish Civil War*, p. 541. Pressure came from the rest of the PCE in the north. The Basque communist general secretary, Juan Astigarrabía, who had also represented the party in Aguirre's government, was obliged to perform an 'autocriticism' in July 1937 and was expelled from the party: Elorza and Bizcarrondo, *Queridos camaradas*, p. 334. Text of Astigarrabía's 'self-criticism' in PCE civil war archive, microfilm XVII. He was, in a sense, taking the blame for having pursued an ultra Popular Frontist line but one which ended by conflicting with overall Republican war needs. Thereafter the PCE in the Northern Council of Asturias and León would clash increasingly with the rest of the Asturian Popular Front (republicans and anarchists, but predominantly the PSOE/UGT) over their tolerance of localism and insufficiently energetic pursuit of centralising war measures: Fraser, *Blood of Spain*, p. 245.

mediated by Aguirre. He was fixed upon the idea of a military victory to bolster the PNV's authority. Yet once again the defensive mentality infusing the Basque nationalist forces militated against this. Nor had militarisation modified the homogeneous political identity of the various Basque battalions. The notion of Basque political separateness and the war on two fronts meant that Aguirre insisted on maintaining the political purity of his nationalist soldiers (the *gudaris*).[123] For the same reasons, until early May 1937 Aguirre managed largely to resist the appointment of political commissars – who elsewhere were an important generator of discipline and fighting cohesion.[124] Nor was the morale of the equally homogeneous Basque CNT battalions improved by the PNV's insistent exclusion of the organisation from government and wartime decision-making processes.[125] Political tensions between the PNV and the CNT would have an even more deleterious effect in spring 1937, as we shall see. Aguirre was clearly determined to maintain PNV control of the Basque government. This being the case, for reasons of morale and military efficiency, he should have accepted the need to break up the political homogeneity of all the Basque units – even at the (inevitable) cost of breaking up that of the *gudaris*. That he would not meant that Aguirre's political agenda undermined the overall fighting efficiency of the forces in Euskadi. The military objectives of the Basque campaign of winter 1936 remained unachieved in what was the only real action prior to the Francoist offensive against Vizcaya launched in late March 1937. By that time, however, it would be too late to transform the Basque battalions into an offensive force, even though a central Republican government would soon emerge in which Aguirre had greater political confidence and which, in turn, better understood the strategic importance of the Basque/northern front.

But there was also an underlying clash of economic priorities be-tween successive central Republican governments and the PNV. This clash ultimately derived from the cleavage the military rebellion had exposed within the Basque bourgeoisie. As we have seen, it was the less economically powerful sectors – the commercial middle classes,

[123] Tuñón de Lara, 'Algunos problemas historiográficos de la guerra civil en Euskadi', pp. 133, 137; de Meer, *El Partido Nacionalista Vasco*, p. 233. Left party members were also excluded from the Basque motorised police.

[124] Chiapuso, *El gobierno vasco y los anarquistas*, p. 197; Ambou, *Los comunistas en la resistencia nacional republicana*, pp. 60–1; Tuñón de Lara, 'Algunos problemas historiográficos de la guerra civil en Euskadi', p. 139.

[125] Chiapuso, *El gobierno vasco y los anarquistas*, pp. 64, 117, 122.

professional/service sectors and small-scale producers – who were prepared to bargain support for the Republic in return for the autonomy statute. Aguirre himself is a good example of the kind of people the PNV represented. His father owned a chocolate factory in Getxo. In contrast, the Basque industrial grande bourgeoisie, which had always been politically and culturally centralist (*españolista*) because of its long economic integration with Madrid through the banking system, was entirely pro-rebel.[126] It had thus retired (as had its Catalan counterpart[127]) to southern France or rebel-held territory in the north – predominantly Biarritz and, after 13 September, San Sebastián. There they planned the economic reconstruction of industrial Vizcaya while awaiting its 'liberation' by Franco's forces. But, in economic terms, the PNV demonstrated by its actions (or, rather, the lack of them) that it remained more committed to preserving the overall 'normality' of the Basque economy – that is, including the property rights and profits of pro-rebel big industrial capital – than it was to contributing Basque economic resource to the broader Spanish Republican war effort.

For a start, the Aguirre government sought to maintain a peacetime economy in the Republican Basque Country. Its predecessor, the Junta de Vizcaya, on which the PNV had not been quite as influential, had been relatively more assertive with regard to wartime imperatives.[128] It had 'intervened' arms factories in Eibar, Durango, Guernica and Bilbao. But Aguirre was not prepared to militarise heavy industry. By spring 1937 the PNV's public discourse would finally be moving in the direction of such intervention. But it was only in June, when Bilbao was already in grave peril, that the PNV finally agreed measures to intervene Basque industries.[129]

From October 1936 the PNV tried desperately to find alternative export markets for Basque industrial goods to replace those lost abroad or through the region's isolation from the rest of Spain. But the party's efforts were often covertly sabotaged by the very industrial concerns it was

---

[126] See introduction and chapter 1 above.

[127] The Lliga's Francesc Cambó and other leading figures were also resident in (or visited) San Sebastián, planning for a Catalan industrial 'liberation'. On this group, see Richards, *A Time of Silence*, pp. 74–5, 123, 124–5. See also Borja de Riquer, *El último Cambó 1936–1947* (Barcelona: Grijalbo, 1997).

[128] Constitution of the Junta in Chiapuso, *El gobierno vasco y los anarquistas*, p. 43. Chiapuso (p. 69) accuses Basque socialists and communists of paying too little attention to economic organisation at the start – thus the PNV was unopposed in government.

[129] González Portilla and Garmendía, *La guerra civil en el País Vasco*, pp. 89–91; Chiapuso, *El gobierno vasco y los anarquistas*, p. 199.

attempting to assist. The PNV's inexperienced *laissez-faire* combined with this industrial sabotage (effectively amounting to a fifth columnist activity) has been assessed as being more responsible for Vizcaya's plummeting industrial production during winter 1936 and spring 1937 than was the evident shortage of raw materials stemming from its isolated and blockaded position.[130] If the PNV had been entertaining hopes of winning over some of the big industrial interests by demonstrating their probity as caretakers of capital and property, then they were to be disappointed.[131]

The Catalan and central governments had to buy Basque steel 'cash up front' during the war – as if they were ordinary commercial customers.[132] Nor were pesetas acceptable. The Basque government demanded gold or foreign exchange of Valencia and Catalonia in exchange for industrial goods and materials. In part this was an attempt by the PNV to secure the wherewithal for its own purchases abroad – whether of food supplies or war-related materials – which also had to be made in hard currency. The central Republican government paid credits to the PNV to support its contribution to the war effort, but it refused to allow Aguirre directly to deploy a portion of central gold or foreign reserves.[133] In part this was because they were at a premium and needed to supply the Madrid front. But it was also because allowing the Basque government to deploy such resources directly was perceived as further fuelling PNV pretensions to sovereignty for Euskadi. It is clear that such pretensions existed. Moreover, the wartime situation had allowed an extension of the Basque government's statutory political and military responsibility.[134] But the complexities of assuring transactions and their delivery were

[130] González Portilla and Garmendía, *La guerra civil en el País Vasco*, pp. 84–91. Rebel control of the air and occupation of Oviedo with its rail heads also put Asturian coal largely out of reach: Jackson, *The Spanish Republic and the Civil War*, p. 378 – although Chiapuso suggests that Republican vessels could have been deployed here but were not for lack of planning and foresight, *El gobierno vasco y los anarquistas*, pp. 79–80. (For Basque industry after rebel take-over, see Richards, *A Time of Silence*, pp. 110–13.)

[131] See revealing anecdote about Aguirre's propping up the publication of *El Noticiero Bilbaíno*, Chiapuso, *El gobierno vasco y los anarquistas*, p. 78.

[132] This is of course *implicit* in the peacetime economy status outlined by González Portilla and Garmendía in *La guerra civil en el País Vasco*. Chiapuso, *El gobierno vasco y los anarquistas*, pp. 102, 111, 122 and Broué and Témime, *The Revolution and the Civil War in Spain*, p. 167 refer as well to Asturian coal also having to be bought – which reminds us of the general drag of particularisms on the war effort.

[133] González Portilla and Garmendía, *La guerra civil en el País Vasco*, pp. 73–4; Chiapuso, *El gobierno vasco y los anarquistas*, pp. 114–17.

[134] De Meer, *El Partido Nacionalista Vasco*, pp. 253–4; Chiapuso refers to the printing of Republican Basque paper money which was used to pay their soldiers (as also occurred in Catalonia): *El gobierno vasco y los anarquistas*, p. 208.

indeed greater in the case of the isolated and blockaded north.[135] Thus a practical case could have been made for the Basque government's direct deployment of state capital resources. A solution might have been for the central government to bargain this against the PNV's militarisation of its war industries. Both the Basque and greater Republican war efforts needed the Basque economy to be fully militarised in order to control and stimulate production. But this question went straight to the heart of the contradiction between the economic and political imperatives of the Republican war effort. For reasons of both internal and international politics, it demanded an integrated, inter-class alliance. But this, in turn, precluded breaking the economic deadlock in the Basque Country. The fall of Malaga in February 1937 impressed upon the Basque authorities the need to consolidate their defences. But the resistance to a Republican single command remained. And while the PNV's political discourse began recognising the need for interventionist measures in the economy, in practice, nothing would happen until too late, when Vizcaya was on the threshold of military defeat.[136]

In other economic areas too the PNV's ability to adapt to the needs of the war was curtailed by its political outlook. It was insufficiently prepared to intervene in the growing war-related problems of the home front – and, in particular, the hoarding of paper money and coins by affluent sectors, which was never adequately tackled.[137] The lack of money in circulation did for a time help to contain inflation on basic goods and limited to some extent the scope of the black market – as did Vizcaya's physical isolation and the consequent (and increasing) difficulties of importation. The PNV's supply policy was to some extent interventionist – perhaps initially in response to the early refugee influx of at least 100,000 people, mainly from Guipúzcoa.[138] But it balked at price and rent controls that would have particularly assisted the most vulnerable sectors of the urban population – especially as time went on and the problems of food speculation and price inflation inevitably made themselves felt. But the sectors worst affected here did not belong to the

---

[135] Tuñón de Lara, 'Algunos problemas historiográficos de la guerra civil en Euskadi', pp. 135, 139, 141.

[136] For example the Basque government decreed the seizure of safety deposit box valuables in Basque banks in May 1937 – by which time the contents of many of these had probably already been removed by their owners: González Portilla and Garmendia, *La guerra civil en el País Vasco*, p. 74.

[137] Ibid., pp. 70–4.

[138] Ibid., pp. 94–5, 75 (n. 13). Ration cards were distributed as a preventive measure on 18 September: Chiapuso, *El gobierno vasco y los anarquistas*, p. 58.

PNV's constituency. They belonged to those of the UGT and CNT. The CNT was by far the most vocal critic of the PNV's conservative economic policy, which would lead to the imposition of increasingly severe censorship on its press and the banning of its meetings.[139] But the CNT's overall marginality in Vizcaya meant that it could do little about this state of affairs. The fact that both the Basque socialists and communists more or less supported the PNV's economic policy had the effect of neutralising the CNT's criticism. More pressure on the PNV might at least have forced it to employ innovative measures to solve wartime problems: for example the deployment of refugees as industrial labour or, at the very least, as agricultural labour to allow marginal land to be brought under cultivation in order to ease food shortages – ever present and increasing under conditions of Non-Intervention. But such a use of refugee labour would have involved large-scale trade union mobilisation in civilian front war organisation, as was happening elsewhere in the Republican zone. This would, in turn, have required a redistribution of wartime (as well as, potentially, of post-war) social and political authority in the Basque Country which the PNV was not prepared to contemplate.

The PNV's conservative notions of political and cultural order also meant that it looked askance at the influx into Vizcaya of Guipuzcoan refugees.[140] The rising xenophobia in bourgeois Bilbao directed against the perceived migrant and worker tenor of this influx echoed some of the fears then also being expressed in more conservative nationalist circles in Catalonia with regard to the CNT's urban constituencies of 'immigrant' labour – although, in the latter case, xenophobia as such was less overt.

The authorities in Vizcaya were fortunate, however, in that the structure and pattern of Basque industrial development meant that they did not face any problem of mass urban provisioning comparable to the one challenging the Catalan authorities in Barcelona. (The ribbon development of industry and the greater prevalence of the 'mixed worker' in Vizcaya meant that a proportionally greater part of its urban population retained ties to the countryside, and thus easier access to alternative

---

[139] Chiapuso, *El gobierno vasco y los anarquistas*, pp. 68–70,117–19, 123. As one moderate anarcho-syndicalist leader put it (p. 117): 'These *gudaris* are more reactionary than the Carlist militia.' ('Estos gudaris son más carcas que los requetés.') See also chapter 5 below for the PNV's attempts to obstruct production of the CNT's main press, *CNT del Norte*. And while Basque nationalists did suffer repression at rebel hands, one should note that there were those who went on to fight for Franco and even to staff the prison brigades in which Basque leftists served (Chiapuso, p. 242).

[140] Ibid., p. 79. Also pp. 136–7 for the insularity of the bulk of the rural nationalist base which reinforced these xenophobic sentiments.

sources of food – something which immigrant industrial worker populations in urban Barcelona did not have.) Nevertheless, the onset of the
rebel offensive against Vizcaya at the end of March 1937 saw a significant build-up of refugees in Bilbao, whose population had by this point
more than quadrupled as a result – from 120,000 to 500,000. Under this
pressure the Basque government initiated refugee evacuation in early
May 1937, thus contributing to the growing subsistence crisis in urban
Catalonia.[141]

[141] Ibid., p. 206 refers to the initial evacuation of women, children up to 15 and persons over 65.
It is also clear from the profile we have of the Basque child refugees sent to England that agency-
and government-assisted refugees represented predominantly less affluent social sectors: see
J. Fyrth, *The Signal was Spain. The Aid Spain Movement in Britain 1936–39* (London: Lawrence and
Wishart, 1986), pp. 220–42. Other sectors had long since made private arrangements which
usually took them to France.

CHAPTER 5

The Barcelona May days and their consequences
(February–August 1937)

I am not fighting this war so a stupid, provincial separatism can
sprout up again in Barcelona . . . I'm fighting for the sake of Spain.
For her past greatness and future possibilities. Those who imagine
otherwise are mistaken. There is only one nation: Spain.[1]

Whether or not Negrín realised what he was saying when he spoke
of having delivered better public order than any government of the
previous fifty years . . . is irrelevant: neither do pigs know they stink.[2]

By early 1937 living conditions in Barcelona and the other urban centres
of Catalonia were coming under strain from the economic dislocations
occasioned by the war.[3] The region's high pre-war population density
(already double the rest of Spain's) was exacerbated by the major and
relatively continuous refugee influx from Madrid, from Malaga in the
south (from February 1937) and by late spring from the north.[4] By the
end of 1936 there were already somewhere between 300,000 and 350,000
refugees in Catalonia.[5] In addition, there were many evacuees who had

---

[1] Juan Negrín in conversation with Julián Zugazagoitia in July 1938, cited in Zugazagoitia, *Guerra
y vicisitudes*, p. 454.

[2] G. Munis, *Jalones de derrota, promesa de victoria. Crítica y teoría de la revolución española (1930–1939)*
(Mexico, 1948; Madrid: Zero, 1977), p. 502.

[3] J. M. Bricall, *Política econòmica de la Generalitat (1936–1939)*, 2nd edn (Barcelona: Edicions 62, 1978),
pp. 33–40 – although the situation was not necessarily worse in Barcelona capital than in the
other urban centres of Catalonia. Moreover, in absolute terms, the food situation at the start of
1937 was worse in Madrid (Friends Service Council (hereafter FSC)/R/Sp/4).

[4] The first refugees (women and children) left Asturias for Catalonia in February 1937, but the big
influx began in the spring with Basque refugees and continued via the Gijón convoys of October
when Asturias was on the verge of defeat.

[5] Bricall, *Política econòmica*, p. 93 gives the lower figure (based on Generalitat estimates). The higher
estimate is drawn from Quaker sources which cite National Refugee Council (i.e. central Republican government) sources. The Republican government defined a refugee as: 'anyone, with the
exception of combatants or men in good health aged between 20 and 45 years, who has been
obliged to change residence on account of the present war and is not hostile to the regime but
lacks the means to support themselves and is not sheltered by family or friends'. Figures and
definition in FSC/R/Sp/2, file 4. The refugee influx from Malaga also supposed cultural (and
class) tensions as well as a quantitative problem, FSC/R/Sp/1 (files 1–2, reports/corresp. from

moved to live with relatives, but who were not dependent on any refugee agencies – domestic or foreign – and thus did not figure in the formal statistics. But even excluding this group, the refugee population represented some 10 per cent of the region's total population by the beginning of 1937. This precipitated an urban resource crisis which was initially manifest in the form of infrastructural overload. (Catalonia had the most developed municipal services in Spain, but this could not prepare it for the scale of social welfare demand the war would produce.) By December 1936 there were shortages of basic foodstuffs and other staples which fuelled inflation, in spite of official price controls.[6]

The onset of war had disrupted industrial production in urban centres. This led to sectoral unemployment[7] and to the disruption of normal rural–urban commercial exchange.[8] Both left the poorer sectors of urban Catalan society exposed, and the immigrant working class most of all.[9] Without family contacts in rural Catalonia and with the least monetary resources, they lacked the wherewithal to engage in the barter economy that was already appearing.[10] This situation was mitigated in the early months after the coup by the emergency provision of communal kitchens and, more crucially, by collective means of food-procurement – neighbourhood and workplace food cooperatives – organised in the period of CNT ascendancy.[11] Such grass-roots initiatives often connected up

Barcelona 1936–7). Also FSC/R/Sp/4, reports 1936–8, report of 19 May 1937 describes Malaga refugees (this time in Murcia) as 'wild' and 'half Moors' and very frightened of 'lists' for fear of what their exposure to state or public authorities might mean.

6 Both the Generalitat and the central Republican authorities had decreed price controls after 18 July, but these had little effect: Bricall, *Política econòmica*, p. 106 (n. 14), p. 111; Abella, *La vida cotidiana durante la guerra civil*, pp. 192–3.

7 Bricall, *Política econòmica*, pp. 85ff.

8 Ibid., pp. 137–40; E. Ucelay da Cal, *La Catalunya populista. Imatge, cultura i política en l'etapa republicana (1931–1939)* (Barcelona: La Magrana, 1982), pp. 309–10.

9 The analysis in this section should not be taken as implying that conditions for the poor and most economically vulnerable were, *in absolute terms*, worse in urban Catalonia than elsewhere in the Republican zone. This is a difficult matter to assess, and the situation changes across the war period. But by December 1936 things were extremely hard for the urban poor – a constituency more numerous in the Catalan capital than anywhere else and one constantly growing through the refugee influx. The point of the analysis here is rather to indicate how the acute deterioration of material conditions (*crisis de subsistencias*) was subjectively experienced, interpreted and reacted to by those constituencies at the receiving end.

10 Widespread barter – properly speaking – emerged during the second half of 1937: Bricall, *Política econòmica*, pp. 141–2. But by the end of 1936 those with enough resources were certainly using them to obtain agricultural produce direct – either with money or in exchange for other goods – often luxury/specialist or imported (such as coffee or tobacco). As Quaker reports indicate, city shops still had plenty of goods to sell in late 1936 and early 1937, only these were often tinned reserve stocks or luxury products which scarcely addressed the gathering staple food crisis: see Ucelay da Cal, *La Catalunya populista*, pp. 315–16.

11 Bricall, *Política econòmica*, pp. 148–9; Ucelay da Cal, *La Catalunya populista*, p. 313.

with the CNT supply committees, which played a major role in feeding working-class neighbourhoods. In the absence of rationing,[12] these mechanisms were the key to the survival of the urban poor as shortages had increased over the autumn and winter of 1936.

By December 1936, however, the bread shortage was acute.[13] The material hardships indicated by food queues and accelerating inflation fuelled popular support for CNT- and POUM-led campaigns for the implementation of rationing. But the initial response of PSUC leader Comorera, now in control of the supply portfolio after the December cabinet reshuffle, was publicly to accuse his CNT predecessor, Juan José Doménech, of incompetence and to abolish the supply committees.[14] These had become the focus of smallholders' hostility because they regarded the prices at which they were required to sell as unfair and perceived the transaction to be based on implicit (when not explicit) coercion.

For both the PSUC and the Esquerra, getting rid of the supply committees had more to do with eroding the political power of the CNT than it did with economic deregulation *per se*. Nevertheless, Comorera and his colleagues do seem to have believed that the urban food shortage in Catalonia was mainly the result of peasant hoarding rather than dearth. Allowing prices to increase was thus seen as a way of resolving the problem by giving Catalan smallholders the necessary incentive to sell.[15] The PSUC referred to its economic deregulation as 'Catalan NEP'.[16] But the party's optimism was badly misplaced. Catalonia's macro-economic situation was quite unlike that of post-civil war Russia.

Catalonia was a net importer of staple foodstuffs. At least half of the region's wheat consumption was normally dependent on imports from other parts of Spain or abroad. But the wartime division of Spain had

---

[12] Although rationing was formally introduced for Barcelona by Generalitat decree on 13 October 1936, the system had not yet been implemented: Bricall, *Política econòmica*, p. 150.

[13] Quaker sources remark on the population's reluctance to change its eating habits – even though substitutes for bread were available at this stage – because of the cultural importance of bread at a meal. FSC/R/Sp/1, correspondence/reports from Barcelona 1936–7, letter to London office, December 1936. Where poorer constituencies were concerned at least, bread had a value beyond the material – what has been called 'the sacralisation of bread' inherent in societies existing on the edge of hunger: Simeón Riera, *Entre la rebelió y la tradició*, p. 244.

[14] By decree of 7 Jan. 1937.

[15] By autumn 1936 Generalitat publicity posters were issuing pleas against hoarding and speculation; see, for example, Fontseré's November 1936 poster reproduced in Bricall, *Política econòmica*, p. 96 (no. 9). Although the committees were the primary target of smallholders' hostility, by spring 1937 the (restored) municipal authorities were also being criticised for paying low prices for crops in order to generate extra income for local government services (Bricall, p. 148).

[16] Payne, *The Spanish Revolution*, p. 289.

separated food-producing areas from their natural markets.[17] Nor was the problem susceptible to solution under wartime conditions. Although grain was imported from abroad on occasions, both the Generalitat and the central Republican government were increasingly limited in their ability to purchase foreign wheat as the value of the Republican peseta fell and the Non-Intervention arms embargo obliged them to concentrate virtually all foreign exchange on the covert purchase of war material ('cash up front') on the international arms market.[18] The lack of wheat and other basic foodstuffs in Catalonia was, then, the result of an absolute shortfall, massively exacerbated by the continually increasing refugee population. Moreover, given the circumstances just described, the shortages could only get worse as time went on.

For this very reason the Republican authorities needed strict central control over domestic economic resources in order to be able to prioritise their use. In Russia, the Bolsheviks had relaxed their centralised control to implement the New Economic Policy (NEP) only *after* the defeat of the White armies. For the Spanish Republic, its version of that battle still lay ahead. Moreover, it was up against an enemy far more efficiently aided and supplied by its European backers than Russia's White armies had ever been. The mass, modern war – driven by German technological aid – made the urban population of Catalonia and, especially the industrial workforce at the heart of armaments production, vital to the Republican war effort. Guaranteeing an equitable rationed minimum of essential foodstuffs for this sector would probably have been beyond the organisational capacities of the Republican state in 1936–7. But even the political will to achieve this was absent because it ran counter to the liberal economic orthodoxies which still underpinned the Republican political alliance.

After the abolition of the committees, bread shortages increased and prices rose further. In theory, overall staple-food prices were now under Generalitat control. But the technical complexities of setting up price-control mechanisms plus an ambivalence to such controls in the PSUC[19] made for quite a different daily reality at the stores and stalls of urban Catalonia. The CNT and the PSUC engaged in mutual recriminations over the cause. The anarcho-syndicalists denounced it as retail

---

[17] Bricall, *Política econòmica*, pp. 137–40; Ucelay da Cal, *La Catalunya populista*, pp. 309–10.

[18] Howson, *Arms for Spain, passim.*

[19] The PSUC had even objected to the Esquerra's mild streamlining measure back in August 1936 which required the peasantry to sell its produce through a single body in order to control prices, *Guerra y revolución en España*, vol. 2, p. 31.

speculation by the middle-men of the UGT-affiliated Federation of Small Traders and Manufacturers (Gremis i Entitats de Petits Comerciants i Industrials (GEPCI)) founded by the PSUC at the start of the war,[20] while the PSUC blamed the legacy of CNT inefficiency and poor harvests, made worse by the collectives. In fact, both the CNT and the PSUC faced a complex array of economic problems in the supply portfolio, with only limited organisational resources and controls at their disposal.[21] The CNT had been responsible for supply functions during the period of greatest fragmentation. The harvest had not long been gathered in, but although that meant there were stocks to cushion the situation, the peasantry was attempting to thwart the purchasing committees. As a result, by early December the CNT had already begun to campaign against speculation.[22] When the PSUC took over, government authority was being reconstructed, but it still had to contend both with real shortages and with administrative disorganisation in Generalitat structures. Speculation also went on growing, as did food distribution difficulties arising from a serious lack of transport (and petrol) in the Republican zone.

Food shortages, inflation, speculation and the emerging black market were all symptoms of a war-induced economic crisis. Tackling that crisis, however, involved a political choice. The shift from CNT supply committees (for all their very real shortcomings) to government price controls signified that the industrial workforce and the urban poor were to be required to bear the brunt of Catalonia's growing wartime subsistence crisis on behalf of the rest.

With both prices and the scale of refugee need continuing to increase, the Generalitat was obliged to implement rationing in Barcelona in February.[23] But the system was extremely inadequate. In practice, staple goods were frequently unavailable through the rationing system.[24] Moreover, rationed goods were supplied to neighbourhoods in an extremely haphazard way that took little account of different population densities. Inevitably it was the urban poor in the cramped housing conditions of

---

[20] A. Balcells, *Trabajo industrial y organización obrera en la Cataluña contemporánea 1900–1936*, pp. 157–8; Bolloten, *SCW*, p. 397.

[21] CNT control of supply (July–December 1936) saw a 47 per cent price increase, while the next six-month period under PSUC supervision saw a further 49 per cent increase, according to figures produced by the Servei Central d' Estadística de la Generalitat de Catalunya cited in Bricall, *Política econòmica*, pp. 137–8.

[22] Abella, *La vida cotidiana durante la guerra civil*, p. 193.

[23] It was extended thereafter to other municipalities of the province and region: Bricall, *Política econòmica*, p. 150.

[24] Originally bread, potatoes, sugar and eggs were rationed (dairy produce was generally in short supply), and soon olive oil was added. The list increased as the war went on: ibid., p. 150.

inner-city Barcelona and the densely populated working-class neighbour-hoods beyond the Eixample[25] who suffered most through the system's shortcomings. The already scarce resources in such areas were subject to added pressure too, with the influx of war-displaced persons to stay with family members or friends.[26] The food depots frequently ran out of food before everyone in the long queues had been served.[27]

Nor was it the urban working class alone who suffered from this situ-ation. There were also large numbers of middle-class families of modest means – the natural supporters of Esquerra and PSUC – who could not afford high market prices either and who were equally outraged by the evidence of speculation and the emerging black market. The manifest lack of a guaranteed minimum in the life of so many urban dwellers provoked street demonstrations against the food shortages from early 1937 onwards and, most notably, on 14 April, the sixth anniversary of the Republic's birth, following a sudden and sharp price hike.[28] Many of the street protests against bread shortages and high prices, running through from February to May, were led by women – apparently replicat-ing the role they had taken in subsistence crises in many Spanish towns across many decades.[29] But these wartime protests were different in that many were directly politically mediated. The CNT, FAI and POUM all instrumentalised such demonstrations as a plebiscite against Generalitat economic policy, and they also boycotted the Republican commemora-tion on 14 April. But a greater number of protests were mobilised by women's associations affiliated to the Popular Front. In Catalonia this allowed the food protests to be channelled by the PSUC in order to bolster the case for 'strong government'.[30] At the same time as Popular Frontist mobilisation was accelerating in Barcelona, however, the CNT remained plugged in, in a rather less 'modern' or 'organised' way, to

[25] This district, built during the nineteenth-century expansion of the city, was where the most affluent sectors of Barcelona's bourgeoisie traditionally resided.
[26] No figures available – but thousands of such people existed, as Quaker relief reports indicate (FSC). Thus, in spite of relief agencies' utilisation of the empty houses of the bourgeoisie, there was still a lot of extra population pressure in poor neighbourhoods.
[27] Long bread queues and the subsequent problems of malnutrition are well documented in the reports and correspondence of Quaker relief workers in Barcelona (Sants and San Andrés were estimated to be the neediest neighbourhoods); also Morrow, *Revolution and Counter-Revolution in Spain*, pp. 64–5.
[28] Prices rose another 13 per cent on top of a nearly two-thirds rise since July 1936: Fraser, *Blood of Spain*, pp. 375–6; Morrow, *Revolution and Counter-Revolution*, pp. 64–5; Bricall, *Política econòmica*, p. 137.
[29] M. Seidman, *Workers Against Work. Labor in Paris and Barcelona during the Popular Fronts* (Berkeley: University of California Press, 1991), p. 138.
[30] Ucelay da Cal, *La Catalunya populista*, pp. 315, 316; Cruells, *Mayo sangriento*, p. 31.

other social strata where the daily impact of *laissez-faire* – more silent, but no less profound – was priming a time bomb of social protest of a different kind.

Extreme material hardship was scarcely a stranger to the urban working class, or to other poor and marginal sectors of 'outcast' Barcelona. There had also been shortages when the CNT committees were in place. Moreover, in so far as these were the result of speculation, it would have been very hard for the CNT – especially in a Popular Front mode which precluded or restricted coercion – to have controlled that process even if it had retained charge of the Generalitat supply portfolio after December 1936. Nevertheless, the continuing deterioration in the city's supply situation and increasing inflationary pressure after January 1937 were interpreted by at least some of the social constituencies who looked to the CNT as other than merely war-induced incremental hardship. In the daily battle for survival, shortages, inflation, middle men and the black market[31] were read by sectors of the poor as the outcome of the economic normalisation occurring in parallel with the process of reconstructing state political authority inside the Generalitat. To understand how and why this link was made, we need to remember the context of repressive continuities experienced by poor and marginal social constituencies in their ongoing war with the liberal state.

In the flux following the defeat of the military coup in July 1936 the possibility of social and economic change had been glimpsed. But with the reconstitution of the Generalitat the full weight of institutional disapproval fell on collective grass-roots food procurement initiatives. The abolition of the supply committees was the culmination of a larger process of eroding such initiatives daily.[32] This also witnessed scenes – familiar from the pre-war period[33] – of the police clearing street sellers[34] and breaking up food protests, as well as now protecting commercial quarters from 'popular requisition'. Clearing itinerant vendors could of course be publicly justified as a move against the abuses of the black market, but it was a government measure which also erupted in unforeseen ways into the fragile economies of the urban poor.

Popular protest grew across the early months of 1937. The poor of Barcelona had no rights to assistance from the refugee agencies in their

---

[31] Morrow, *Revolution and Counter-Revolution in Spain*, p. 78; Semprún-Maura, *Revolución y contrarre-volución en Cataluña*, pp. 240ff.; Abella, *La vida cotidiana durante la guerra civil*, p. 196.

[32] Ucelay da Cal, *La Catalunya populista*, p. 313.

[33] Ealham, 'Policing the Recession', pp. 192–3. See also chapter 1 above.

[34] For example after the municipal ordinance of 10 November 1936, cited in Ucelay da Cal, *La Catalunya populista*, p. 320. See also Abella, *La vida cotidiana durante la guerra civil*, p. 188.

daily struggle for survival. Even in those industries converted to war production, workers' wages failed to keep up with inflation. But many families had lost their male breadwinner, while some had never had one. This produced intolerable strains on working women since wartime food procurement was itself a full-time job, especially for the poorest.[35]

While the poor fought local battles for material survival much as they had done before the war, at regional level, the Generalitat was preparing its own final push on public order. The early months of 1937 saw the imposition of tighter police discipline as Assault Guards and National Republican Guards were merged into a single Catalan police corps and prohibited from membership of any political party or trade union.[36] While such a measure was still difficult to enforce, it did achieve the major goal of putting the workers' patrols beyond the law while also debarring their members from the unified police (and, therefore, from any legitimate policing functions).[37] In reality, however, the patrols went on existing – *now in open conflict with the state*. The tension mounted further on 12 March when the central Republican government ordered all worker organisations, committees, patrols and individual workers to hand over their arms – long and small – within forty-eight hours.[38] This confrontation over public order led to the dissolution of the Catalan cabinet on 27 March when the CNT's representatives withdrew. But the ensuing three-week crisis concluded in a very similar cabinet configuration on 16 April. Still entrenched in the Generalitat's Home Office, the Esquerra's Artemi Aiguader stepped up his war against the patrols. Along the French/Catalan border, there were fatalities in the escalating clashes now occurring between Carabineros and CNT patrol committees over control of customs posts which the committees had held since July 1936.[39]

One of these incidents in particular suggests how these confrontations were many-stranded. They connected up with ancient border disputes pitting local smugglers against those upholding the fiscal prerogatives of

[35] The Quaker wartime reports contain much devastating evidence of this. As a result, children also had to spend long hours in food queues.

[36] Bolloten, *SCW*, pp. 417, 865 (n. 25) cites *Diari Oficial* of 4 March 1937. The ban on political membership was originally a central government decree (of 28 Feb. 1937) applying only to the Carabineros (Customs Police), but then extended to the Catalan police force at the beginning of March 1937.

[37] As part of this normalisation of public order, 3 March 1937 saw the Generalitat dissolve the CNT-controlled defence committee, creating another one, under cabinet control and with the power to dissolve all local police and militia committees.

[38] Morrow, *Revolution and Counter-Revolution*, p. 73.

[39] Broué and Témime, *The Revolution and the Civil War in Spain*, pp. 281–2.

the political centre – whether Spanish or French–[40] as well as with more recent conflicts over state control, or stemming from acute social conflicts between the Catalan labour unions. On a day in late April at Puigcerdá, Catalan police engaged in fire, shooting dead a number of anarchists, including the influential Antonio Martín, old-guard radical anarchist and ex-smuggler turned CNT customs chief.[41] When this incident occurred, the police detachment had been returning from Molins de Llobregat having arrested its CNT leadership for supposed involvement in the earlier assassination of UGT leader and PSUC member Roldán Cortada on the 25th. As he was an ex-*treintista* (and the secretary of Rafael Vidiella, another leading PSUC politician who had once been in the anarchist movement[42]), suspicion fell on the CNT even though it had publicly condemned the murder and called for a full enquiry. From the time of these incidents political tension was mounting in the whole of the Baix Llobregat area of Barcelona province.[43]

There were longstanding tensions between the CNT and the UGT stretching back into the pre-war period, as we have already seen. But these escalated after 18 July 1936 and led to the assassinations of both anarchist and socialist leaders and militants in various areas of Republican Spain, but notably in Barcelona.[44]

After the military coup of 18 July 1936 the Catalan UGT began to expand hugely, for much the same reasons as the PSUC, as lower-middle-class commercial and white-collar sectors – often previously

---

[40] Cf. P. Sahlins, *Boundaries: The Making of France and Spain in the Pyrenees* (Berkeley: University of California Press, 1989), pp. 103–33.

[41] An exhaustive account is in J. Pons i Porta and J. M. Solé i Sabaté, *Anarquía y República a la Cerdanya (1936–1939). El 'Cojo de Málaga' i els fets de Bellver* (Barcelona: l'Abadia de Montserrat, 1991) and for Martín especially, pp. 21–46, 133–73. Martín had apparently belonged to the Los Solidarios direct-action group, along with Ascaso, Durruti and García Oliver. See also M. Benavides, *Guerra y revolución en Cataluña* (Mexico: Ediciones Roca, 1978), pp. 344, 351–62; Jellinek, *The Civil War in Spain*, pp. 544–5; Broué and Témime, *The Revolution and the Civil War in Spain*, pp. 282, 293–4 (n. 36); Thomas, *Spanish Civil War*, pp. 311 (n. 2), 653 (n. 1); Ucelay da Cal, *La Catalunya populista*, p. 304 (n. 23).

[42] Thomas, *Spanish Civil War*, p. 300 (n. 2). Close to Largo Caballero before the war, Vidiella had resigned from the PSOE national committee in May 1936 and gravitated – with some reservations – towards a working relationship with the Catalan communists in the PSUC: Graham, *Socialism and War*, p. 111; Bolloten, *SCW*, p. 398. He replaced Nin as Generalitat Justice councillor in December 1936, moving to the labour/public works portfolio in April 1937. He was also a freemason: Ucelay da Cal, 'Socialistas y comunistas en Cataluña durante la guerra civil', p. 306, n. 12.

[43] Peirats, *La CNT en la revolución española*, vol. 2, pp. 137–8; Ucelay da Cal, *La Catalunya populista*, p. 303; Broué and Témime, *The Revolution and the Civil War in Spain*, p. 282.

[44] Graham, *Socialism and War*, p. 64. The UGT union leader, Desiderio Trillas (shot dead on 29 July 1936), was an ex-*cenetista*: Balcells, 'El socialismo en Cataluña hasta la guerra civil', p. 33; Jellinek, *The Civil War in Spain*, p. 343. For the pre-war history of this conflict, see chapter 1 above.

unorganised (or only organised as isolated trade/technical associations) – joined party and union[45] in search of protection in a hostile, apparently anarchist-dominated political environment. Indeed, it was the joint Esquerra/PSUC rearguard action against the CNT that underlay the compulsory sindicalisation decree issued in Catalonia in December 1936. After this, the Catalan UGT expanded rapidly, membership extending to the self-employed and small businesses, in the shape of the Small Traders and Manufacturers Federation (GEPCI). The identification in popular perception of GEPCI with increased economic speculation was a further source of social friction between the Catalan UGT and the CNT.

But everywhere, not just in the GEPCI, the newly politically mobilised urban lower-middle classes perceived party and union membership as a form of professional advancement or career opportunity. For the PSUC in Catalonia (as the PCE elsewhere) was the major articulator of the Popular Front war effort and provider of government/service cadres.[46] As white-collar staff joined the Catalan UGT, so it also became the organisational bulwark of internal resistance to socialised factory systems.[47] (White-collar employees, and even skilled workers sometimes – because they had more bargaining power, or for other more subjective reasons – usually felt little sense of solidarity with more precariously placed sectors of labour.) It was consistently the office and professional staff who saw CNT industrial controls as the 'problem'[48] and supported increased governmental intervention at the factory assemblies that the Generalitat required in each workplace to ratify its socialised status.[49]

Although the CNT's radical middle-level cadres were dug in on the factory committees, this was more a case of siege conditions once the anarcho-syndicalists had lost political control in the Generalitat. (In particular, the erosion of CNT economic control went back to their acceptance of Companys' suggestion of a Council of Economy with an explicitly centralising brief, although, as it had been government that

[45] For example, the shop and office workers' union (CADCI) joined the Catalan UGT in August 1936: Balcells, *Trabajo industrial y organización obrera en la Cataluña contemporánea 1900–1936*, pp. 156, 157–8; Bolloten, *SCW*, p. 416.

[46] For a similar modernising role played by another European Communist Party, see Mark Mazower on the transition between clientelist structures/networks and mass mobilisation in occupied Greece, *Inside Hitler's Greece. The Experience of Occupation 1941–44* (London/New Haven: Yale University Press, 1993).

[47] Cf. Balcells, *Trabajo industrial y organización obrera en la Cataluña contemporánea 1900–1936*, p.158.

[48] Abella, *La vida cotidiana durante la guerra civil*, p. 229.

[49] C. Vega, A. Monjo and M. Vilanova, 'Socialización y hechos de mayo', in *Historia y Fuente Oral*, 3 (1990), 95.

had held the gold and controlled the banks from the start, credit starvation was always going to be a major problem for all the collectives –
industrial and agricultural.[50] Moreover, the 'syndical capitalist' attitudes
which inevitably resulted made the collectives easy targets for their political enemies, who could, quite truthfully, point to the damage being
done to the war effort by individual collectives seeking to protect their
resources from 'outsiders'.[51]) The CNT was unable to prevent the Generalitat from gradually circumscribing socialised industry in Catalonia –
which was the intention behind successive decrees from December 1936
onwards.[52] It was the scale and entrenchment of socialised industry
in Catalonia (and especially urban Barcelona) which created an unprecedented political problem for the liberal Republican alliance – even
though worker-intervened industrial forms existed in many places: in
Madrid, Valencia, Alicante and Almeria and in Malaga (prior to February 1937).[53] By April 1937 the Generalitat was refusing to certify factory
councils' ownership of exported goods tied up in foreign ports pending
the resolution of legal suits lodged by former owners.

In its impatience, the Generalitat shifted in April from indirect political
manoeuvring within individual factories. (Government officers would
exploit internal differences in the assemblies between blue-collar and
administrative staff, or they would manoeuvre with UGT officials or,
very occasionally, with syndicalist sectors of the CNT.) Instead they sent
in the police, which, on at least one occasion, saw the surrounding of a
factory at the time of the vote.[54] For politically active sectors of the labour
rank and file, such a blatant use of the police clearly reinforced what they
already knew: at the heart of the battle to control Barcelona's factories

[50] Industrial collectives in financial straits also began to look to state intervention to solve their
problems: Fraser, *Blood of Spain*, pp. 211, 230, 231–2, 578.
[51] Broué and Témime, *The Revolution and the Civil War in Spain*, pp. 163, 169.
[52] Morrow, *Revolution and Counter-Revolution*, pp. 51, 60–2. Generalitat measures included: classifying
firms into industrial groups (26 Dec. 1936); a statute increasing the powers of the government
representative within the factory (30 Jan. 1937); the introduction of a 'certificado de trabajo'
(21 Feb. 1937) and reintroduction of the dismissal procedure as per contract laws of November
1931 (24 Feb. 1937); the stipulation that the statutes of firms had to be presented to the Juntas
de Control Económico Sindicales for approval (30 March 1937): see Vega *et al.*, 'Socialización y
hechos de mayo', p. 100, n. 4. Creeping governmentalisation was facilitated by the fact that the
CNT had never really developed its ideas on industrial (as opposed to agrarian) collectivisation:
Fraser, *Blood of Spain*, p. 212. None of the measures fostered by the CNT industry minister, Peiró,
facilitated 'worker control' in any real sense.
[53] Beyond Catalonia the central government had been more successful in installing appointee
directors and confining factory committees to routine matters.
[54] A summary of tactics is in C. Vega *et al.*, 'Socialización y hechos de mayo', pp. 97–8 (dissuasion
at Hispano-Suiza; CNT/UGT manoeuvrings at Casa Girona and coercion at the Trefilería
wirework factory, pp. 94–6 of same article).

there was a political agenda. Consubstantial with this, moreover, was the restitution of power to the very police forces that, prior to the military coup, had been the instrument of capital and state – whether monarchist or Republican.

But the perception of police ubiquity also influenced broader social sectors of 'outcast Barcelona'. For them too the revanche of the 'state' – or, at any rate, a hostile form of order – was embodied in the repressive power of its security forces. The police were remembered for their eviction of rent strikers in the pre-war period, and for their front-line role in the implementation of Republican policies of social control which rigorously invigilated public spaces and criminalised the unemployed. That many of the Catalan policemen enforcing the 'new' liberal order had gravitated to the PSUC after 18 July 1936 meant no more than that they had swapped the moribund conservatism of right-wing republicanism for a more dynamic brand – just as in 1931 they had turned to republican conservatism upon the eclipse of the dynastic variety. In so far as the role of political parties had a higher profile, this reflected the relative underdevelopment, historically, of the liberal state in Spain. The strength of lower-middle-class and white-collar sectors in Catalonia, plus the particular circumstances in which the war was being fought, conditioned the means by which private property and liberal order was defended. Nevertheless, what was primarily significant about the PSUC here was not that it was 'communist', but that it came to be so closely identified with liberal state building and the economic establishment – not least by the police operatives who joined it. They were now in the civilian 'front line', enforcing liberal order in the factories and on the streets of Barcelona.

By April 1937 worker patrols had already been excluded from all police functions in the other major Republican cities of Madrid and Valencia. State enforcement in Catalonia, and Barcelona especially, was bound to be more complex given the strength of popular resistance. (The after-effects of political scandal probably also impacted here. The chief of police, Andreu Reverter (of the radical nationalist Estat Català), detained in November 1936 for bribery and corruption, was also accused of plotting to assassinate CNT leaders and of involvement in a plan to call upon the French to intercede to procure a separate Catalan peace with Franco.[55] Although the latter never progressed beyond the

---

[55] Morrow, *Revolution and Counter-Revolution*, p. 68, reported from *Solidaridad Obrera* (Nov. 1936); M. Low and J. Breá, *Red Spanish Notebook* (1937; San Francisco, 1979), pp. 214–15; Ucelay da Cal, *La Catalunya populista*, p. 295; C. Rojas, *La guerra en Catalunya* (Barcelona: Plaza & Janes,

political fantasies of assorted Catalan nationalists, even the rumours of such a thing would have been enough to slow up the campaign against forms of worker popular power and especially the worker patrols.) But after the April 1937 cabinet crisis, Aiguader gave orders that the arms decrees were to be rigorously enforced. During the second half of the month, workers in Barcelona were disarmed on sight by the police – except, that is, where the police could be outnumbered and themselves disarmed.

The political temperature rose further as Roldán Cortada's funeral turned into a demonstration of state power in the form of a long march past of armed police and troops. While this also reflected middle-class fears that the recent violence might herald a return of the feared *paseos*, the blatant rehearsing of the state's repressive capacity and moral panic-inducing editorials in Barcelona's liberal republican press (including *Treball*, the PSUC newspaper)[56] were fatal components in the accumulation of social and political tensions (*crispación*). According to one source, three hundred workers were disarmed in the last seven days of April.[57] It was this escalating confrontation over arms which catalysed the dense web of conflicts, bringing the city to the brink of street fighting.[58]

In an attempt at containment, the traditional First of May (May Day) labour demonstrations were suspended throughout Catalonia. But then, on the afternoon of Monday 3 May, a detachment of police attempted to seize control of Barcelona's central telephone exchange (Telefónica) in order to remove the anarchist militia forces inside. (Their presence dated back to the July days of 1936 when the militia had taken the Telefónica, along with other key buildings in central Barcelona, from the occupying military.) But what this amounted to was the ejection of the CNT from the union control committee – also comprising UGT representatives and a government delegate – thereby depriving the anarcho-syndicalists

---

1979), pp. 120–1; Thomas, *Spanish Civil War*, pp. 524–5. Joan Casanovas (while he was Catalan premier in the autumn of 1936) proposed that Catalonia should try to negotiate a separate peace with Franco, with international guarantees. But this was a maverick line. It did not reflect Companys' thinking or that of the Esquerra in general: J. Benet, *La mort del President Companys* (Barcelona: Edicions 62, 1998), p. 119.

[56] Cf. M. Cruells in the *Diari de Barcelona*, 1 May 1937, 'En la diada d'avui comencem la neteja del baix fons de la Revolució. Cada organització tindrà la seva feina.' ('Today we must begin the cleansing operation to remove the dregs of the Revolution. Each organisation will have a share in this task.') Cited in M. Cruells, *Els Fets de Maig*, p. 40. It is also interesting to compare the subtext of such editorials with the degenerationist and social darwinist discourses – languages of anxiety all – which emerged in Catalanist discourse after the First World War, C. Ealham 'Policing the Recession', pp. 17–19, 34–40 (see also note below on the Barri xinès).

[57] Morrow, *Revolution and Counter-Revolution*, p. 73.   [58] Cruells, *Mayo sangriento*, pp. 27–43.

of access to information which was now vital to sh⌐
political position. Moreover, the building itself was⌐
painful memories since the CNT's bitter strike def⌐
   News of the attempted seizure spread rapidl⌐
neighbourhoods of the old town centre and p⌐
city was on a war footing, although no organisatⱢ⌐
government – had issued any such command. By 4 May ⌐
up in the city centre, there was a generalised work stoppage and ⌐
street fighting erupted. In its origins, this conflict set the Catalan goverℶ⌐
ment, state agencies and their political defenders against all those who,
for whatever reasons, opposed the expansion of state jurisdiction. The
events would be complicated by a further conflict – between competing
centralising and regionalist liberal agendas inside the Republican polity.
But it is important to make the distinction here between the underlying
causes of the May days, and the 'high political' opportunities and consequences which *then* emerged from the evolution of the conflict in both
street and cabinet office.

   The key to anti-state popular mobilisation lay in the close relationship
between mid-level cadres (shop stewards and branch activists) of the
CNT's *comités de base* (both neighbourhood[59] and factory committees) and
militant, mobilised sectors of the industrial working class, many of whom
had been the shock troops of earlier labour wars in the city.[60] Although
the CNT's committee structure had been decapitated by the process
of state political reconstruction spearheaded from the Generalitat, the
grass-roots committees still existed and could thus provide, together with
the worker patrols, the organisational sinews of collective resistance in
May.[61]

   The assault on the Telefónica focused the resisters' energies on the city
centre where all the political and economic machinery of government
was concentrated – in close proximity to the most volatile of popular neighbourhoods, the Barri xinès (literally, 'Chinese Quarter'), which
had long constituted the front line between 'respectable' and 'outcast'

---

[59] These were also known as *comités de defensa confederal* (CNT-FAI), Peirats, *La CNT en la revolución española*, vol. 2, p. 192.

[60] Obviously this sector had been reduced by its protagonism in the militias. But the infrastructural needs of the home front, especially industrial war production, meant that many CNT shop stewards and workers had been 'mobilised' in their jobs.

[61] Freund, 'Dual Power in the Spanish Revolution', pp. 326–7; Low and Breá, *Red Spanish Notebook*, pp. 221–2; Peirats, *La CNT en la revolución española*, vol. 2, p. 192; Broué and Témime, *The Revolution and the Civil War in Spain*, p. 287; Fraser, *Blood of Spain*, pp. 381, 382; cf. also C. Ealham's comments on the low public profile of pivotal branch activists, 'Policing the Recession', p. 148.

celona.[62] Indeed, the force of the initial May explosion is explicable only if one bears in mind the longstanding connection between the 'outcast' city and the CNT. While the appearance of the barricades constituted an act of conscious 'political' contestation, the CNT's direct action was also mediating more amorphous, 'pre-political'[63] forms of popular resistance. The CNT was, once again, functioning as a lightning conductor in inner-city Barcelona, transforming both a shared history of persecution and the perception among the city's marginalised of the connection between state action (public order, food supply and so on) and the brutality of daily life into generalised support for street action as active protest 'against the state'.[64] This was what confronted liberal Catalonia and its police force in central Barcelona on 4 May.[65]

As late as the evening of 3 May, with an equilibrium of forces inside the Telefónica and an armed stand-off around it, the Generalitat could have averted the explosion in the streets. But it would have required a climbdown over the police seizure and the removal of police chief Rodríguez Salas, who had led the assault (as he had also led the earlier one into Molins de Llobregat when Antonio Martín had been killed). It would probably also have required the resignation of the ERC's abrasive Artemi Aiguader, who, as Generalitat Home Office minister, had formally authorised the Telefónica raid.[66] But far from backing down,

---

[62] The Barri xinès, as the hub of 'lawlessness' and moral iniquity inspired anxiety because of its close proximity to the financial and political centres of bourgeois Barcelona (even 'Imperial Barcelona' in the language of early Catalan nationalism – according to which planned urban development provided a vital key to social control): Ealham, 'Policing the Recession', p. 18.

[63] Ucelay da Cal, *La Catalunya populista*, pp. 321–3. However, anarchist beliefs were no less a response to 'everyday experience' than other forms of political behaviour.

[64] These connections also make somewhat questionable the implicit assessments in some work on the history of industrial socialisation in Barcelona. (There is an example in Vega *et al.*, 'Socialización y hechos de mayo', which is largely based on oral testimony fifty years on.) In referring to the 'passive role' of the bulk of the affected Barcelona work force, this seems to be taken as meaning such people had no views on state or government actions. I would argue this ignores the broader context of daily life, above all around the issue of food supply, which must inevitably have shaped opinions.

[65] J. M. Bricall's *Política econòmica* perhaps underplays the fairly steep learning curve of Catalan politicians regarding the need to be interventionist in matters of wartime staple food pricing and supply (or, at least, this is a consequence of the thematic rather than chronological structure of his book – see, e.g., p. 105). The social protest of May would be a major political object lesson for the PSUC and ERC that, in wartime, some level of economic interventionism was required to protect liberal social order. The PSUC's supply policy too, presented in full at the third congress of the Catalan UGT in November 1937, surely owes something to the experience of May 1937: Bricall, p. 155. Bricall's own data implicitly endorses this interpretation: see pp. 107–8.

[66] Cruells, *Mayo sangriento*, pp. 48–9; Bolloten, *SCW*, p. 431, pp. 869–70. Bolloten makes much of Rodríguez Salas' PSUC membership and Aiguader's contacts with the PSUC. Doubtless the PSUC's general political abrasiveness appealed more to Aiguader – for reasons of his own style and personality – than it did to his other Catalanist cabinet colleagues. But Bolloten's

Companys issued a press communiqué to the effect that it would be necessary to 'clear the streets',[67] a sentiment which echoed the Esquerra's
stock-in-trade denunciations of the dangerous classes threatening the
good order and livelihoods of bourgeois Barcelona. Clearly both the
ERC and PSUC, as the driving forces in the cabinet which had been
in session throughout the evening, wanted to force the issue over the
telephone control committee as part of their onward consolidation of
government power. However, it also seems likely that they did not yet
realise what this would involve. Lulled into a false sense of security by
the CNT leadership's quiescence, Companys expected at most to have to
engage in political arbitration with CNT representatives *after the event* –
in spite of the fact that the police action breached the agreement enshrined in the February collectivisation decree. No one in the Catalan
cabinet had reckoned with the force of the ensuing popular explosion
on 4 May. This saw the Generalitat and other government buildings
armoured and barricaded against attack, while whole neighbourhoods
of the city rapidly became no-go areas for the police.

The capital's industrial satellites were solidly behind the CNT,[68] as
were the worker districts of the industrial periphery and neighbourhoods such as Sants, San Martí and Gràcia, situated just around the
perimeter of the Esquerra's fief, the predominantly middle-class Eixample. Although violent incidents occurred in some of the peripheral
areas, there was no serious challenge here to the worker patrols.[69] Police

own research findings indicate how all the Catalan cabinet, minus the CNT, was supportive of
Aiguader's objectives. (The criticisms made by Companys' cautious political lieutenant, Josep
Tarradellas, were purely about *tactical* matters: Azaña, *Obras completas*, vol. 4, pp. 577–8 (Cuaderno
de la Pobleta, entry for 20 May (1937).) In the end, however, the speculation over who in the
cabinet knew *in advance* about the Telefónica initiative is not particularly meaningful. Aiguader
may have leaked information to the PSUC some days before the police assault: Fraser, *Blood of
Spain*, p. 377.

[67] 'There are armed groups on the streets...we have no option but to clear them': Cruells, *Mayo
sangriento*, p. 58.

[68] Such as Granollers, Mataró, Terrassa and Sabadell. Also Badalona – a small city to the north of
Barcelona – and Hospitalet de Llobregat, a major immigrant quarter to south of capital. POUM
strength was in the urban centres of Barcelona *province* – but not in or around the capital itself.

[69] Fraser, *Blood of Spain*, p. 378. In spite of government decrees, the worker patrols went on functioning throughout the May events. It was only after they were over, with responsibility for public
order in Catalonia transferred to the central Republican government, that the worker patrols
were wound down in June: Cruells, *Mayo sangriento*, p. 77; Solé i Sabaté and Villaroya i Font, *La
repressió a la reraguarda de Catalunya*, p. 205. There were also cases of local loyalties overriding the
dominant political divisions – for example patrol members belonging to state-identified republican parties, in particular the ERC, withdrawing at the start of May to avoid any potential
confrontation with *cenetistas* who were also neighbours and sometimes even friends. I am grateful
to Chris Ealham for this information. Fraser, *Blood of Spain*, p. 294 (n. 1) gives an example of how
some working relationships continued post May days even across the POUM–PSUC divide.

action was focused on the city centre as the hub of political power. But the peripheral neighbourhoods were also perhaps left alone for fear of the resulting violence spilling over into the Eixample, which was surrounded by hostile territory.[70] It is certainly the case that throughout the May street protests the areas of uncontested CNT strength virtually encircled the city.[71]

On 4 May there were violent confrontations across the city. There were lengthy cabinet deliberations with the CNT's national and regional leaderships. Also present were García Oliver, CNT justice minister in the central government, and Pascual Tomás and Carlos Hernández Zancajo, representing the UGT's national executive committee. Both were close to Largo Caballero and keen to find a resolution to the Catalan crisis that did not unduly undercut the CNT leaders' political position. For Largo and his supporters were now looking to the CNT for backing in their own deepening conflict with the Spanish Communist Party over organisational control of the UGT throughout the Republican zone.[72] Nevertheless, the UGT leaders also represented the wishes of the Valencia government, whose overrriding objective remained, necessarily, a ceasefire. By the evening of 4 May, Companys was amenable to discussing the political compromise he had refused twenty-four hours earlier. In changing his stance, Companys was effectively recognising the unforeseen gravity of the situation on the streets. For this was now posing a direct threat to Catalan autonomy.

In his dealings with the central Republican government, Companys had since July 1936 assiduously cultivated the picture of Esquerra populism as a vital device for controlling the CNT. This was intended to keep at bay any attempt by 'Madrid' to recoup the *de facto* expansion of Catalan statute powers – especially in regard to the army and finance – which had occurred in the wake of the military rising. Inside the Generalitat too, although the Esquerra had mainly sided with the PSUC, Companys had nevertheless wanted to keep the CNT in the game as a

---

[70] Although a proportion of the Eixample's mansions lay empty after 18 July 1936 – their occupants never having returned from their summer residences (in the Pyrenean zone or southern France) where the rebellion had surprised them – the neighbourhood was still home to a substantial number of lower-middle-class households.

[71] See plan of Barcelona, map 3; Josep Costa of the Badalona CNT commented that the CNT had Barcelona surrounded: Fraser, *Blood of Spain*, p. 380; Bolloten, *SCW*, p. 432 (though he mistakenly includes Sarriá).

[72] Carlos Hernández Zancajo led the UGT's urban transport federation, whose Catalan contingent had virtually ceded from the national federation because it supported the PCE. For the wartime intra-union dispute, see Graham, *Socialism and War*, pp. 167–218.

counter-weight,[73] in spite of the difficulties this posed,[74] in order to en-sure Esquerra hegemony. In particular, Companys was concerned not to let the centralising sectors inside the PSUC gain the upper hand for fear that they would permit Catalan economic resources to pass under the control of the Valencian government – as the logic of *mando único* dictated.

But now, faced with the May days, the central government repeat-edly refused Companys' requests for police reinforcements, unless he also surrendered the Generalitat's control over public order and military affairs in the region. The PSOE, republicans and communists in the Valencia government were all unsympathetic to Catalan particularism and wanted a public-order crack-down. But Largo himself was increas-ingly aware of the strategic importance of the CNT given his growing isolation in the cabinet. As a veteran populist union leader with a rad-ical reputation, moreover, Largo also wanted to avoid an outcome that involved his dispatching police to fire on workers.

But by the end of 4 May it was too late for Companys to avert the acceleration of violent confrontation. The CNT leadership – national and regional – desperately sought to broker a ceasefire on the basis of the cabinet compromise. But they were, for a time at least, swept aside by the sheer force of what was happening down on the streets. When García Oliver, once the strongman of Barcelona's July days, broadcast his appeal for a ceasefire from the Generalitat on the night of the 4th, many *cenetistas* hearing him from the other side of the barricades were convinced that he had been taken hostage. Soon incredulity gave way to a dominant mood of embitterment at what was interpreted as the leadership's betrayal of core anarchist values. In particular, García Oliver's attempt to claim as his brothers all those who had died, on whichever side of the barricades, was instantly scorned with a savage and sardonic amazement that has reverberated in the memoirs of the revolutionary left ever since:

García Oliver . . . in a speech which was teeth-grating to the *poumistas* and *cenetisas* who heard it . . . told, in a voice charged with pathos, how he had arrived at his beloved city to find a dead *cenetista* lying in the street, whereupon he knelt and laid a kiss upon his forehead, after which he did the same for a dead *poumista*, and then, 'crossing over the road he espied another body in police uniform, so kneeling again, overcome with emotion, he kissed this one too . . .' And, so he

---

73 For example, as late as April Tarradellas defended the CNT's record in administering the war industries: Morrow, *Revolution and Counter-Revolution*, p. 77 (this was not, of course, an endorsement of socialisation itself).

74 It was a difficult balancing act for Companys since the Esquerra's membership was, as a whole, more conservative than he was.

claimed, he went on, planting kisses willy-nilly on whatever corpses he came across . . . In fact he did no such thing, as all the dead were in the mortuary, and, anyway, García Oliver took very good care not to stop on his *car* journey to the Generalitat – and he was also very careful to avoid the city centre.[75]

In the black humour of the barricades, García Oliver's speech was christened 'The Legend of the Kiss' after a famous light opera.

But, in spite of mounting anger and incomprehension among their Catalan cadres, the CNT-FAI national and regional leaderships repeatedly refused to sanction armed action of any kind in Barcelona. The fact that this included the FAI as much as the CNT, with its *treintista* heritage, indicates the enormous impact of the war on the political consciousness of anarcho-syndicalist leaders. Nor can this be satisfactorily explained as the corrupting effect of political power, as the consolatory but also highly reductionist post-war anarchist history tells it. More than anything, people like García Oliver held back in May because they saw the bigger picture, not only – or even necessarily primarily – in terms of the overriding imperatives of the war against Franco, but also in terms of the overall balance of firepower *within Republican Spain*. Beyond Catalonia and Aragon, the CNT had always been a politically subordinate force.[76] This was even more evident in the war period since the military rebels, in rapidly conquering western Andalusia (including Seville) and the urban centres of western Aragon, had deprived the anarcho-syndicalists of key strongholds.

The CNT could certainly have 'taken out' the state in urban Catalonia. But holding Catalonia as a whole would have required calling upon their troops from the Aragon front. Moreover, either courses of action would have brought them up against the central Republican government. Its more powerful propaganda machine and greater media access could

---

[75] 'García Oliver . . . [en] una alocución que hizo rechinar los dientes a los del POUM y a los cenetistas . . . en tono patético, dijo que al llegar a su querida ciudad y encontrar en la calle un muerto de la CNT, se arrodilló y le besó en la frente, después hizo lo mismo con otro muerto poumista, y cuando "cruzado en la acera vio un muerto con el uniforme de guardia, se arrodilló, emocionado, y lo besó . . ." Y así, según él, fue besando a diestro y siniestro, a tantos muertos como iba encontrando . . . Claro es que no besó a muerto alguno, porque todos estaban en el depósito de cadáveres, y además, en su marcha hacia la Generalitat, "su coche" no paró ni un minuto y se guardó muy de pasar por el centro de la ciudad.' A. Bueso, *Recuerdos de un cenetista* (2 vols., Barcelona: Ariel, 1976, 1978), vol. 2, p. 243. (Adolfo Bueso was a member of the BOC in the early 1930s and in the CNT printers' union. Because of the importance he attributed to political action he sided with the *treintistas* when the split occurred.) Fraser, *Blood of Spain*, p. 379.

[76] Even within Catalonia the CNT was now 'in conflict with *all* organisations comprising the other social layers', as Helmut Ruediger, vice-secretary of the AIT (Anarchist International) and present in Barcelona during the events, indicated: Souchy *et al.*, *The May Days. Barcelona 1937* (London: Freedom Press, 1987), pp. 71–2.

easily have portrayed the CNT as the betrayers of the Spanish proletariat who had turned their backs on the war. There was inevitably a
lack of knowledge and understanding elsewhere of what was occurring
in Barcelona – even the POUM's small sections in Madrid and Valencia
were uneasy[77] – and the fact that Barcelona was the Republican city
farthest from the battle front was a gift to hostile propaganda. Moreover, the Republican government was already poised to intervene: had it
been faced with an all-out CNT challenge, it would surely have drafted
in far greater numbers of troops and police to take on 'revolutionary
Barcelona'. Otherwise it could not have guaranteed the Aragon front or
retained liberal state control over Catalonia's war industries – even more
essential now as Basque industry came under massive rebel attack in the
north. The Republic itself might well not have survived such a massive
escalation of armed internecine conflict, but, either way, the CNT would
certainly have gone down in the blood bath.

Thus the CNT-controlled anti-aircraft guns on Montjuïc hill, trained
on the government buildings below, remained silent. The armoured-car
attacks on government buildings occurred only as sporadic and uncoordinated attempts by individual groups of CNT resisters and were easily
repelled. The CNT's most seasoned and best-equipped fighters, the five
hundred or so men left from the Durruti column (now commanded by
Ricardo Sanz), which had fought on the Madrid front, were instructed by
García Oliver to obey the orders dispatching them to Aragon.[78] Those
CNT militia members on the Aragon front who had shown a willingness
to come to the defence of their comrades in Barcelona were ordered to
remain at the front. The POUM leadership in Barcelona also sent the
same instructions to its divisions.

What transpired on the Aragon front itself is, however, less clear. The
evidence that exists is fragmentary and at times contradictory.[79] Bitterly

---

[77] Fraser, *Blood of Spain*, p. 384 (n. 1). The Valencian POUM was unambiguously Popular Frontist
and therefore tended to be criticised by Nin's sector in the party.
[78] Ibid., p. 380. Sanz was one of Fraser's interviewees. Sanz's own memoirs, however, make no
specific reference either to his own role in May 1937 or to the situation on the Aragon front: *Los
que fuimos a Madrid*, pp. 137–46.
[79] J. Coll and J. Pané, *Josep Rovira. Una vida al servei de Catalunya i del socialisme* (Barcelona: Ariel,
1978), pp. 163–75, esp. 171–3; for Rovira's own trial testimony and proceedings (he was the head
of the POUM's 29th Division on the Aragon front) see Alba and Ardevol, *El proceso del P.O.U.M*,
pp. 493–529; Broué and Témime, *The Revolution and the Civil War in Spain*, p. 284; Bueso, *Recuerdos
de un cenetista*, vol. 2, p. 246; Bolloten, *SCW*, pp. 452, 875 provides a summary of the available
sources. To my reading, official republican, Communist Party and POUM-friendly reports do not
absolutely contradict each other. But sources favourable to the government side – and therefore
keen to justify the ensuing repression – suggest that far greater numbers of men abandoned the
front, with the express intention of going all the way to Barcelona.

disappointed and confused though many *cenetistas* and *poumistas* were, overall, military discipline remained intact – in spite of the inactive state of the front probably adding to the temptation. A group of CNT/POUM troops did get part of the way to Lleida. But they returned to the front once they were assured that government forces would desist from besieging the CNT and POUM headquarters there – a pattern of attack being replicated by pro-government forces in a number of other urban centres in Catalonia.

In Barcelona, however, all CNT action remained defensive. This situation was the despair of the POUM's Catalan leadership – and specifically of Andreu Nin, who during 3–4 May argued to no avail with the CNT's regional leaders that they must support the cause of their workers on the barricades. When it was clear that they would not, however, Nin too pulled POUM militants back from the brink, refusing to sanction joint armed action with CNT cadres, even though in some places joint defence and neighbourhood committees already existed.[80] Neither the POUM nor, still less, the Spanish Bolshevik Leninist groupuscule[81] orbiting the party nor the handful of radical anarchist activists who made up the Friends of Durruti (Amigos de Durruti)[82] had the organisational purchase to intervene in a politically decisive way in the May events. Indeed, it could be argued that the POUM's published proclamations of ideological support for those at the barricades and its public articulation of what the May days meant functioned in some ways as a compensation for the party's relative political marginality.

The POUM's intention in calling upon the CNT to back their workers at the barricades was to strengthen the resisters' hand in subsequent negotiations with the Generalitat.[83] Nin and his executive colleagues were as aware as García Oliver that the overall balance of forces within Republican Spain was against those at the barricades. For this reason, the POUM leadership, like the CNT's, rejected outright the Friends of Durruti's published manifesto of 5 May, which attempted to rally

---

[80] The POUM youth wing, JCI, was the most prominent sector in favour of joint action with the CNT cadres: see JCI leader Wilebaldo Solano's testimony in Fraser, *Blood of Spain*, pp. 380–1.

[81] Estimated at between 10 and 30 individuals: Bolloten, *SCW*, p. 860 (n. 11).

[82] This was a splinter group formed by those from the Durruti militia column who refused to be incorporated in the Republican Army. For a summary, see Fraser, *Blood of Spain*, p. 381 (n. 1). Also Bolloten, *SCW*, pp. 420, 866 (n. 49); Casanova, *Anarquismo y revolución*, pp. 245–7; Semprún-Maura, *Revolución y contrarrevolución en Cataluña*, pp. 249–50, 273; Durgan, 'Trotsky, the POUM and the Spanish Revolution', p. 59.

[83] Defensive resistance was the intent behind all the POUM's May manifestos: see the material cited by Semprún-Maura, *Revolución y contrarrevolución en Cataluña*, pp. 275–6.

resistance behind a Revolutionary Junta.[84] But Nin still sought to convince the CNT of the need for unified resistance in Barcelona as a bargaining counter in order to prevent the unleashing of a blanket repression afterwards.[85]

The CNT leadership was, however, reluctant to sanction even this form of tactical resistance. The fact that it did not could certainly be counted a serious strategic error, for it exposed not only the POUM but also the CNT's cadres to the full blast of state political repression from 7 May onwards. But it is vital to remember the intensity of the pressures deriving from the war situation.

Since 18 July 1936 these had also reinforced the (pre-war) 'politicising' currents inside the anarcho-syndicalist movement led by the *de facto* general secretary Horacio Prieto.[86] (Prieto saw the CNT's incorporation into government as a logical *progression* of its role in the emergency structures of committee power.[87] And he and others viewed the Council of Aragon as performing classic governmental functions.[88]) The year 1937 also saw a series of internal organisational changes in the CNT designed to erode the old confederal autonomy – for many synonymous with the CNT – and to centralise power in the hands of the national committee.[89] This cracked down on the FAI's direct-action groups, excluding them as such from the organisation. A much tighter editorial control of the confederal

---

[84] Cruells, *Mayo sangriento*, p. 70; Broué and Témime, *The Revolution and the Civil War in Spain*, p. 284; Semprún Maura, *Revolución y contrarrevolución en Cataluña*, pp. 281–2 – who wrongly dates the manifesto as 6 May. According to Juan Andrade, Nin's executive colleague, Spanish Trotskyists (i.e. the diminutive group of Bolshevik-Leninists who belonged to the Fourth International) who were present in Barcelona in May also agreed with the POUM's assessment of the situation – in spite of the triumphalism of their public manifestos: Fraser, *Blood of Spain*, p. 388 and Morrow, *Revolution and Counter-Revolution in Spain*, pp. 143–4. For a generally more orthodox Trotskyist assessment of the genealogy of revolutionary failure/the May events, see analyses by H. D. Freund and J. Rous in 'The Spanish Civil War. The View From the Left', pp. 317–28, 345–402.

[85] Testimonies of Solano and Andrade in Fraser, *Blood of Spain*, pp. 381–2; Bolloten, *SCW*, p. 435.

[86] Prieto had resigned as general secretary in November 1936 after the CNT ministers had accepted the government's departure from Madrid (see chapter 3 above), but he continued to advise the acting general secretary, Mariano R. Vázquez.

[87] Lorenzo, *Los anarquistas y el poder*, pp. 178–9; Prieto, *El anarquismo español en la lucha política*, p. 11.

[88] J. Gómez Casas, *Los anarquistas en el Gobierno 1936–39* (Barcelona: Bruguera 1977), pp. 128, 148–9; although the national committee were fundamentally unfavourable to the uncompromising political direction taken by the Council and ultimately refused to defend it against government intervention in summer 1937: Casanova, *De la calle al frente*, p. 232.

[89] Semprun-Maura, *Revolución y contrarrevolución en Cataluña*, pp. 242–52. For a sharp analysis of internal renovation in the CNT, see J. Casanova, *Anarquismo y revolución*, pp. 144–50 and *De la calle al frente*, p. 227. Casanova indicates a decrease in the two-way flow of initiatives inside the CNT after 18 July 1936 even though the leadership cadres remained largely unchanged. This is unsurprising as this internal battle over organisational forms in the CNT-FAI predates the war: see chapter 1 above.

press was implemented – over and above the norms of wartime censorship.[90] Bureaucratic controls were imposed. None of this occurred simply because the CNT was collaborating with the Popular Front alliance, but that collaboration accelerated the process of CNT centralisation, which was, in some ways, a form of political modernisation.[91]

In none of its armed uprisings across the Republican years since 1931 had the FAI ever won out against the forces of the state. In some ways it seemed as if the Barcelona events were finally illuminating that pattern of defeat. Certainly García Oliver's plea to his comrades on the barricades 'not to cultivate the mystique of the dead hero' seems haunted by such an awareness.[92] The escalation from military coup to full-scale civil war had widened the fault line in the CNT until by May 1937 the organisation was itself divided by the barricades. The Barcelona May days in effect constituted the CNT's own 'crisis of modernity'.[93]

A transformation certainly occurred in the representation of the CNT's dead across the first ten months of the war. Gone by May 1937 was the cult glorifying the fallen warrior and martyr, such as that which grew up around the figure of the veteran anarchist leader Francisco Ascaso, killed in the assault on Barcelona's Atarazanas barracks in the July days or that which suffused the collective narrative of the Iron Column.[94] Or, supremely, the mythologising, quasi-religious aura and the exhortation to

---

[90] S. Tavera and E. Ucelay da Cal, 'Grupos de afinidad, disciplina bélica y periodismo libertario 1936–1938', *Historia Contemporánea*, 9 (1993), 167–90, esp. 177, 185.

[91] These changes culminated in the decisions of the FAI plenum of July 1937. Partly this was about legalising the FAI so it could participate in Republican political institutions. But the process of change went deeper: Lorenzo, *Los anarquistas españoles*, pp. 228–9; Peirats, *La CNT en la revolución española*, vol. 2, pp. 241–54; Jellinek, *The Civil War in Spain*, p. 571–2.

[92] 'No cultivéis en este momento el culto a los muertos.' The speech, broadcast on the night of 4 May, is cited by many authors, including Cruells, *Mayo sangriento*, p. 63 and Semprún-Maura, *Revolución y contrarrevolución en Cataluña*, p. 267.

[93] As we have seen earlier, syndical reformers in the CNT had been driven, even before the 1930s, by a desire to find some way out of the increasingly unequal (and therefore erosive) confrontations between radical workers/anarcho-syndicalist cadres and the state. (For even in Spain the relative increase in the technological/operational sophistication of the security forces had opened up a distance between them and their anarcho-syndicalist opponents in the social war.) The CNT leadership's public insistence that the May events had resulted from 'foreign' influence (see, for example, Cattell, *Communism and the Spanish Civil War*, p. 145) also needs to be understood in this context – as a means of deflecting attention and responsibility from these racking internal conflicts (both within the CNT and between it and other Spanish organisations).

[94] 'Iron Column. Impassioned fighters for the Idea. Hearts of fire in the service of liberty. Visionaries, whose hopes are set on a shining, humane tomorrow. Their flesh has suffered the prisons of Reaction. They are the sons of those ones murdered by the Civil Guard with their "Ley de Fugas" (shot in the back "while attempting to escape"). Martyrs, martyrs, martyrs...Ascetics with no divine master. Anarchists: victory is yours!', from the Iron Column's newspaper, *Línea de Fuego*, 24 Oct. 1936, cited in Casanova, *Anarquismo y revolución*, p. 113.

emulatory mourning[95] evident at the funeral of Buenaventura Durruti, who had died on the Madrid front in November 1936:

They embalmed the body, and put it on show, and even now one can look through an opening into the tombs and see their leader sleeping under glass... They had brought him back from the Madrid front so that the Anarchists could look at his wounded body and decide by what treachery he had been killed. It was too difficult for them to admit that he had been shot like any ordinary man.[96]

Durruti had been the comrade-in-arms of both García Oliver and Ascaso in the brutal Barcelona labour wars of the 1920s. The 'three musketeers' of popular legend, Durruti, Ascaso and García Oliver had created the most famous of all the anarchist direct-action groups, Los Solidarios, to confront the hired gunmen of the monarchist state. But in spite of the stories of fascist or communist snipers and internal betrayal, in Madrid in 1936 there was neither conspiracy nor martyrdom: if Durruti's end symbolised anything, then it was the brutal happenstance of death in war.[97]

The CNT's reportage on leaders, such as Domingo Ascaso (the brother of Francisco), who died in the course of the May events in Barcelona, was, in contrast, deliberately low key.[98] No longer were they martyrs to the cause. The CNT's supporters were now being exhorted to respect other types of leader: the politician and office-holder rather than the street fighter or radical egalitarian. But, in fact, even though Durruti was perceived by many as the latter two, the call to emulate him was already, by November 1936, an ambiguous one. The transformation of his image represented the anarcho-syndicalist movement's coming to terms with the war. García Oliver as minister also underwent a notable

---

95 'imitad al heroe del pueblo' ('emulate the hero of the people'), Abella, *La vida cotidiana durante la guerra civil*, pp. 163–8.

96 Low and Breá, *Red Spanish Notebook*, pp. 215, 216.

97 For a resumé of earlier theories on Durruti's death, see Casanova, *Anarquismo y revolución*, p. 251 and (more extensively but very unclearly) in Paz, *Durruti en la revolución española*, pp. 689–714. On Durruti's death through the accidental discharge of a weapon at close quarters, the forensic opinion of Dr Santamaría, Jefe de Sanidad of the Durruti Column (who carried out the post-mortem), appears compelling. This is cited in J. Arnal, *Yo fui secretario de Durruti. Memorias de un cura aragonés en las filas anarquistas* (Zaragoza: Mira Editores, 1995), p. 119. Even though the CNT leader Federica Montseny was still referring to the unexplained nature of Durruti's demise in her (extremely bland) memoirs of 1987, Arnal (p. 201) claims that she had verbally confirmed the truth to a Spanish journalist well before their publication. See also testimony of Clemente Cuyàs, in 'Así murió Durruti', *El País*, 11 July 1993. Paz's ostensibly extensive analysis, *Durruti en la revolución española*, pp. 715–24 sheds little light.

98 Cf. Casanova, *Anarquismo y revolución*, p. 252.

reconstruction. He, unlike Francisco Ascaso and Durruti, had outlived the time when 'heroes' could credibly take on the state single-handed.[99] Anarchist iconography serves thus as a cultural 'barometer' registering the expansion of state political authority.[100]

Yet we cannot simply point to the CNT's leaders as the conscious 'authors' of these changes. Certainly for some the war had reinforced pre-existing views in favour of modifying anarcho-syndicalist practice to allow the incorporation of the CNT within parliamentary politics. But for many more – although they did not consciously moot it, still less articulate it in public – the war's overwhelming practical imperatives had greatly problematised ideological resistance to centralised forms of organisation. Yet most of these resources remained in liberal hands. This, plus the limited capacity of CNT organisational forms to integrate and centralise, saw the force of attraction exerted by the liberal state over anarcho-syndicalist leaders increase as the war itself escalated. The very real needs of the war effort saw both CNT and FAI leaders increasingly incorporated into the governing machinery of the liberal state, leaving isolated and uncomprehending sectors of their own cadres and social base whose daily experience led them to continue to resist its encroachment.

The Barcelona radicals had no organisational means of coordinating the fight back from the CNT's grass-roots committees – decapitated by political developments inside the Generalitat. Above all, the historic radical anarchist hostility to the formation of industrial unions in the CNT would now come back to haunt them. In the spring of 1937 the CNT was still in the early stages of transforming its unions into industrial ones.[101] If such structures had existed, then the battle for industrial production in the city which had raged across the months since the military coup might have been harder for the government to win. Their lack points up the flaw in explanations of anarchist failure that posit a binary choice: 'the revolution *or* the war'. But radical anarchists could not 'make the revolution' for the same reasons that they could not take the lead in waging the war: they lacked the requisite structures in which to coordinate it.

---

[99] Consider also the fact that the CNT national committee would end by expelling the Council of Aragon's leader, the veteran radical Joaquín Ascaso (cousin of Francisco and Domingo), from the organisation in September 1938: Casanova, *De la calle al frente*, p. 233.

[100] We should also note that in April 1938 the Republic would posthumously confer on Durruti the rank of Lieutenant Colonel: Paz, *Durruti en la revolución española*, p. 726.

[101] It was February 1937 before industrial union structures even existed in the CNT in some crucial war industries – such as metalurgía, Vega *et al.*, 'Socialización y hechos de mayo', p. 100 (n. 6); Fraser, *Blood of Spain*, p. 544 (n. 3).

The CNT-FAI's identification with localist popular resistance needs, thus, to be problematised rather more than it has been. Such an identification undoubtedly indicates the anarcho-syndicalists' superior understanding of the dynamics of popular mobilisation – of its basis in local imperatives and community goals (whether in terms of a factory, urban neighbourhood or village) and of its value as a liberating, socially and culturally transformative process – as compared to the Popular Frontist concentration on end result (mobilisation for the war effort). But CNT radicals' identification with community rather than state and their heroisation of the popular defence obscure serious ideological and strategic contradictions: the internal division in the anarcho-syndicalist movement threatening since 1931 had by May 1937 opened into an abyss.

By 5 May the tide had begun to turn against the resisters. The Telefónica workers surrendered to the besieging police, and those behind the barricades, bereft of orders from their leaders – other than one urging them to 'return to work'[102] – remained confined to the defensive as their positions crumbled. Beyond Barcelona too, police and pro-government forces, emboldened by the anarcho-syndicalist stalemate in the capital, made concerted assaults on CNT and POUM premises and CNT-held telephone exchange buildings in a number of towns across Catalonia, including, most notably, Tarragona and Tortosa.[103] The striking similarity of this police action – in both timing and pattern of attack – suggests a common set of orders emanating from government authorities in Barcelona.[104]

Midday on 5 May saw the formation of an emergency four-man cabinet of Esquerra/Rabassaire, CNT and UGT representatives which excluded all those who had previously occupied ministerial posts.[105] The absence of any representative with a named PSUC affiliation might be interpreted as an attempt at cosmetic conciliation. But the new cabinet's line on public order was as uncompromising as that expressed by Companys on the eve of the conflict on 3 May. The central government in Valencia confirmed its assumption of Catalan public order shortly after the proclamation of the new Generalitat. The urgency was increased by

---

[102] Broadcast by radio and 'signed' by the local union federations of both the CNT and UGT: Semprún-Maura, *Revolución y contrarrevolución en Cataluña*, p. 277.

[103] Cruells, *Mayo sangriento*, pp. 86–90; B. Bolloten summarises a number of contemporary press and other sources, *SCW*, pp. 452, 875 (n. 19); Semprún-Maura, *Revolución y contrarrevolución en Cataluña*, pp. 284, 287–9; Souchy, *The May Days*, pp. 95–100.

[104] Semprún-Maura, *Revolución y contrarrevolución*, p. 287; Cruells, *Mayo sangriento*, p. 90.

[105] Bolloten, *SCW*, p. 441. This comprised Esquerra (Martí Feced), CNT (Mas), UGT (Sesé) and Rabassaires (Pou): Cruells, *Mayo sangriento*, p. 67.

the fact that President Azaña, traumatised by his experience of being trapped by the street fighting in the Catalan parliament building in central Barcelona, was threatening to resign.[106] This had to be avoided at all costs since it would have obliterated the Republic's democratic credibility at the very moment when it was intensifying diplomatic efforts in an attempt to procure the lifting of Non-Intervention. Azaña was desperate – as indicated by his suggestion to his close friend Prieto, the navy and air minister, that he should order the Republican airforce to bomb clear the short route from his residence to the port. This would have been like dousing the May fires with petrol. But it took Prieto and other leading republican figures to spell out the implications of the president's imprisonment to Largo Caballero, whose personal dislike of Azaña had been fed by the preceding months of prickly interchange between the two. Indeed, quite staggeringly, Largo did not see fit to communicate personally with the President of the Republic throughout the whole of the May crisis.[107] It was Prieto who arranged, on his own ministerial responsibility, the sending of two Republican warships to Barcelona. These docked on 5 May, with orders to assist the Generalitat, but, first and foremost, to evacuate the president.[108] The central government also announced the dispatch of militarised police units to Barcelona. But even as late as 5 May, Companys was hoping that a rapid, determined push on the part of what were, for a short while at least, still Generalitat-controlled police forces inside Barcelona might bring the situation sufficiently under control for Valencia to reconsider its decision. Unfortunately, the violence on the streets exploded again, this time entirely shattering Companys' coping strategy.

On the afternoon of 5 May, Antoni Sesé, front-rank leader of the Catalan UGT and new Generalitat minister, was shot dead outside a CNT union building as he was being driven to assume his governmental responsibilities. It is not possible to say for certain who killed Sesé or why.

[106] Zugazagoitia, *Guerra y vicisitudes*, p. 268. The Catalan parliament building was situated in the old Ciutadella arsenal: M. Vázquez Montalbán, *Barcelonas* (London: Verso, 1992), p. 127; Azaña's diary account of the May events is in the 'Cuaderno de la Pobleta' (20 May 1937), *Obras completas*, vol. 4, pp. 575–88. The telegraphic recordings of Azaña's communications with Valencia between 4 and 6 May are in the Servicio Histórico Militar (Madrid) legajo 461.

[107] S. Juliá, 'Presidente por última vez: Azaña en la crisis de mayo de 1937', in A. Alted, A. Egido and M. F. Mancebo (eds.), *Manuel Azaña: pensamiento y acción* (Madrid: Alianza Universidad, 1996), pp. 249–50. (Although the telephone lines were down, the telegraph system functioned throughout.)

[108] Bolloten, *SCW*, pp. 448–9; Cruells, *Mayo sangriento*, p. 71. Prieto was disparaging about Azaña's preference for days of dread to a few moments' resolution (i.e. making the short trip from the palace to the port along the Paseo de Francia): Zugazagoitia, *Guerra y vicisitudes*, pp. 268–9. Azaña finally left for Valencia by air on 7 May: Vidarte, *Todos fuimos culpables*, vol. 2, p. 666.

Of all the hypotheses which have circulated, the least likely would still seem to be that he was killed, in a kind of doomsday scenario, by someone connected to the ultra-centralist current in the PSUC in order to force a central government crack-down on Catalan autonomy. Even if one accepts the rather too conspiratorial notion that Sesé's dissident communist past (he had been a member of the BOC in the pre-war period) made him 'expendable' in the eyes of centralist PSUC sectors, such a strategy still entailed enormous risks which could have sent the situation in Barcelona spinning completely out of control. But whatever the source of the bullet which killed Sesé – and it could, conceivably, have been a stray, like the one which killed Domingo Ascaso[109] – the circumstances of Sesé's death were sufficiently ambiguous, and the atmosphere of reciprocal mistrust generated by days of inter-organisational bloodletting so absolute, for the accusation that he was shot by an anarchist sniper to be believed.[110]

Probably more than any other single incident, it was Sesé's death which precipitated the political intervention of the central government. In a context where the continuation of violent street confrontation signalled the continuing jeopardy of state authority, the symbolic significance of a minister's demise was not lost on either the Catalan cabinet or Valencia. The Generalitat was now wide open to the charge that it had failed to contain a rising tide of disorder which was threatening the Republic's very capacity to resist militarily. Valencia's appointee to the public order portfolio, Colonel Antonio Escobar,[111] was seriously wounded when shot at on his arrival in Barcelona. And production in Barcelona's war

---

[109] Cruells, *Mayo sangriento*, p. 69.

[110] Ibid., pp. 67–9 (in particular, what Cruells terms 'the atmosphere of personal extermination' which affected all the participants, p. 67); Peirats, *La CNT en la revolución española*, vol. 2, p. 151; Semprún Maura, *Revolución y contrarrevolución en Cataluña*, p. 276; Bolloten, *SCW*, p. 453, who quotes PSUC leader Serra Pàmies' 1944 testimony (p. 875, n. 29) on Sesé's political past. (Sesé had stood as a BOC candidate for the Cortes in 1931 – polling some 500 votes.) See also Ucelay da Cal, 'Socialistas y comunistas en Cataluña durante la guerra civil', pp. 305–6, 308, and p. 311 (on Sesé himself) – and see also chapter 1 above. Anarchist commentator Agustín Souchy also refers to the possibility of a PSUC assassination in his contemporary (1937) account, published in Buenos Aires. But mainstream nationalism still held sway in the PSUC (as Bolloten attests, *SCW*, p. 448). The involvement of a PSUC 'fringe' seems unlikely – although it cannot be ruled out entirely. Virtually all parties and organisations had their 'uncontrollables' – see the discussion later in this chapter.

[111] A cavalry colonel, Escobar had been head of the Civil Guard in pre-war Barcelona and thus pivotal in the defeat of the military rising. A conservative of profound Catholic faith (appearing as Colonel Ximénez in Malraux's *L'Espoir*), he would end the war as Commander-in-Chief of the Army of Extremadura. He supported the coup which displaced the Negrín government (see chapter 7 below) and was shot in February 1940 by the Franco regime: J. L. Olaizola, *La guerra del General Escobar* (Barcelona: Planeta, 1983).

industries had been disrupted by the generalised work stoppage since 4 May. Valencia's take-over of the public order and defence briefs in Catalonia meant that the Generalitat lost precisely those functions – deriving from the 1932 statute – which were most highly charged in terms of nationalist identity. Companys personally authorised the hand-over, but in the circumstances he had little real choice.[112] It meant the loss of Catalan control over police and army in the region, but this still left the Generalitat's political-administrative and, most importantly, its *economic* control intact. Behind Valencia's partial political intervention there lay the tacit threat of the complete suspension of the Catalan Statute – something Companys obviously wanted to avoid at all costs.

Bitter battles would lie in store as the Generalitat sought to defend its 'statutory' sphere of economic influence against a central government increasingly desperate to centralise economic power as the impact of Non-Intervention provoked mounting material crisis by late 1937.[113] But bitter though this later jurisdictional conflict was between 'Madrid' and 'Barcelona', it should not obscure the fact that in May 1937 Companys' primary objective remained the restoration of liberal political and eco-nomic control in Catalonia. The 5,000 central government troops and police who arrived in Barcelona late on Friday 7 May – soon to be rein-forced by several thousand more[114] – enacted a repression which would guarantee the very liberal order that the ERC, PSUC and Catalan mid-dle classes had sought to reconstruct and defend since July 1936.[115] It was only once this had been secured that Companys began to criticise central government infringement of Generalitat powers.

With the arrival of police detachments from Valencia, the May days were effectively over. State repression was, however, only just beginning. All of the CNT leaders' painstaking efforts during 6 and 7 May to secure a

---

[112] Cruells, *Mayo sangriento*, p. 74; Bolloten, *SCW*, pp. 437, 451 (also see nn. 15 and 16, p. 874); Broué and Témime, *The Revolution and the Civil War in Spain*, p. 285.

[113] See chapter 6 below.

[114] *Solidaridad Obrera*, 9 May 1937; Bolloten, citing this and other contemporary press reports, calcu-lates that twelve thousand arrived in total over a few days: *SCW*, p. 460 (inc. n. 63).

[115] The fact that the new arrivals' conquering cry was the leitmotiv of the left – ¡U.H.P.! (¡Uníos Hermanos Proletarios! (Workers Unite!)) – was an example of the classic process whereby the legitimising discourse of 'the revolution' is assimilated all the better to consolidate a conserva-tive order. Much the same purpose was served by the fact that Valencia's incoming nominee as Barcelona police chief was Lieutenant Colonel Emilio Torres Iglesias, the former chief of the anarchist militia column, Tierra y Libertad (Land and Freedom): Cruells, *Mayo sangriento*, pp. 80–1; Semprún-Maura, *Revolución y contrarrevolución en Cataluña*, p. 285; Broué and Témime, *The Revolution and the Civil War in Spain*, p. 285. Comparative examples of this process might include the Liberal discourse of post-unification Italy or the French Radical Party's use of the symbols of 1789.

peace 'with guarantees' came to nought. Indeed, even as they negotiated in Barcelona, government troops *en route* to the city were participating in acts of violent reprisal which dismembered the anarcho-syndicalist movement. Symbolic acts – such the burning of the confederal flag – were rapidly followed by the burning of CNT premises, and soon a veritable wave of *paseos* was unleashed in which many *cenetistas* would be killed.[116]

Companys' promise that there would be neither victors nor vanquished rang hollow as Republican prisons began to fill up with those held in 'preventive detention' (*prisioneros gubernativos*) and thus with little hope of a trial.[117] On the streets, Valencian troops and Catalan police behaved like occupiers, routinely demanding identity papers, tearing up any CNT union cards they found and humiliating their owners.[118] But it was scant revenge, given the dominant tenor of regret among the police and pro-government forces in general that the barricades had come down before they had finished the job.[119] It is difficult not to hear echoing in these sentiments the old attitudes of official Barcelona to the 'rabble'.[120] But the Republican state had to tread a fine line between punishment and the needs of wartime mobilisation.

Barcelona's proletariat may have been the beating heart of the barricades, but it was also the crucial centre of the Republic's war industry. Factory production was gradually starting up again after 7 May, and assuring it against further disruption was vital, not only in view of the external arms embargo but also with the mounting rebel threat to war production in the north. Thus, while punishment for the May days was

---

[116] Cruells, *Mayo sangriento*, pp. 86–90; Peirats, *La CNT en la revolución española*, vol. 2, pp. 157–61; Semprún-Maura, *Revolución y contrarrevolución en Cataluña*, pp. 284, 287–9; Souchy, *The May Days*, p. 98; Solé i Sabaté and J. Villarroya i Font, *La repressió a la reraguarda de Catalunya*, vol. 1, pp. 212–16, esp. pp. 213–14; Bolloten, *SCW*, p. 452, p. 875 (n. 19).

[117] By July 1937 the CNT estimated that 800 of its members were in gaol in Barcelona alone: Morrow, *Revolution and Counter-Revolution in Spain*, p. 144; E. Goldman, 'Political Persecution in Republican Spain', *Spain and the World*, 10 Dec. 1937, also cited in Souchy, *The May Days*, pp. 104–7; Peirats, *La CNT en la revolución española*, vol. 2, pp. 263–4; Solé i Sabaté and Villarroya i Font, *La repressió a la reraguarda de Catalunya*, vol. 1, pp. 217–24, 260 and pp. 279–86 on Republican work camps.

[118] Cruells, *Mayo sangriento*, p. 83; Bolloten, *SCW*, p. 456. This form of disciplining was fairly indiscriminate, however, since the Generalitat had decreed compulsory unionisation at the end of 1936.

[119] Cruells, *Mayo sangriento*, p. 79.

[120] Cf. Comorera's pre-war comments (as USC leader) on anarchism as the ideology of 'sub-human' and 'degenerate' individuals and 'underworld parasites', Ealham, 'Policing the Recession', p. 354. See also the comments of exiled conservative Catalan nationalists that the Francoist 'clean-up' of the radical left in Catalonia in 1939 had saved them a task: R. Abella, *Finales de enero, 1939. Barcelona cambia de piel* (Barcelona:Planeta, 1992), p. 50.

essential in order to guarantee future labour discipline, this had to be an exemplary punishment which did not directly victimise the CNT since its cadres still had the potential to disrupt production.

While the Generalitat took the opportunity discreetly to annul its previous decree measures recognising socialised control in industry,[121] the results of Republican government *realpolitik* were twofold. First, there was conciliation with the CNT leadership, whose political subordination increased as divisions in anarcho-syndicalist ranks grew more acute in the wake of the May débâcle. The CNT would never have more than an emblematic government presence after May 1937 and in fact never took up their seats in the Generalitat – at root because they could not come to terms with their new political marginality therein.[122] Second, there was a political scapegoating of the POUM. (Indeed, the CNT leadership's muted response to this is an important indication of its acceptance of Popular Frontism in the service of the war effort.[123]) The POUM's public (and much published[124]) identification with those resisting on the barricades, combined with its relative political marginality, made it the ideal target for the symbolic function required by the Republican state *pour encourager les autres*. On 16 June, in the wake of the fall of Bilbao, the industrial powerhouse of the Republican north, the POUM executive committee was arrested.

The fact that the POUM was also the target in internecine wars in the communist movement facilitated the Republican government's objectives by increasing the party's isolation. But it is important to stress that these two processes of targeting the POUM had separate agendas and, moreover, ones which rapidly came into conflict with each other. The Republican authorities needed to make an example of the POUM by bringing the full weight of liberal law and order to bear on its leaders.[125] But the very basis of liberal legitimacy – the constitutionality of the state – was daily being violated in the latter weeks of June as the Spanish Communist Party, Comintern representatives and some Soviet police personnel set up private interrogation centres (*checas*) on Republican state territory – but beyond the control of its constitutional

---

[121] Morrow, *Revolution and Counter-Revolution in Spain*, p. 62. For the consequences of this on the ground see M. Vilanova, 'L'Escala y Beuda', *Historia y fuente oral*, 3 (1990), 53. As regards any assessment of output levels in collectivised industry, there are no meaningful terms of comparison, first, because Catalonia had not previously produced war *matériel* and second, because it was being produced during the war in extraordinarily difficult economic and logistical circumstances.

[122] Bolloten, *SCW*, pp. 494–7.   [123] Casanova, *Anarquismo y revolución*, pp. 251–2.

[124] The POUM press, *La Batalla*, was suspended at the beginning of June.

[125] Members of the POUM executive would stand trial in October 1938: see chapter 6 below.

authorities – wherein they assaulted and assassinated anti-stalinist dissidents with virtual impunity.

The intention here is not to suggest that Republican order was somehow less implacable (although it was less lethal, at least in the short term[126]). Rather it is to indicate that Comintern activity was directly challenging the 'monopoly of legitimate violence' on which state authority depended. This is very well illustrated in the story told by POUM executive member Juan Andrade of his transfer from Madrid to the state gaol in Valencia. The justice minister, Manuel Irujo of the PNV, sent a detachment of Assault Guards whose main purpose was the surveillance not of the POUM prisoners but of the accompanying communist policemen in order to ensure that Andrade and his colleagues reached their destination safely.[127]

Andrade's account raises a crucial further question, however. What were the respective roles of the Comintern and the Spanish Communist Party in the repression of the POUM?[128] While the ideological attack on anti-stalinist dissent was prepared in Moscow, there were simply not enough Comintern functionaries in Republican Spain to have carried out – or even supervised – a systematic political repression of the POUM.[129] The priorities and attention of the Soviet leadership were until 1939 largely absorbed by domestic policy – a focus which was massively reinforced by their own purges.[130] Undoubtedly Comintern

---

[126] Later, imprisoned members of the POUM were caught between communist revenge and Francoist punishment as Francoist troops bore down on Barcelona in 1939: J. Gorkin, *Caníbales políticos. Hitler y Stalin en España* (Mexico, 1941); G. Regler, *The Owl of Minerva* (London: Rupert Hart-Davis, 1959), pp. 324–5; Fraser, *Blood of Spain*, p. 389 (n. 1); Thomas, *The Spanish Civil War*, p. 876. On POUM and other left prisoners, see Goldman, 'Political Persecution in Republican Spain', pp. 105–7; Broué and Témime, *The Revolution and the Civil War in Spain*, p. 315.

[127] Fraser, *Blood of Spain*, p. 389; on the detentions see also A. Súarez, *El proceso contra el POUM* (n.p.: Ruedo Ibérico, 1974), pp. 83–7.

[128] The POUM's own criticisms were in 1937 focused on the sectarianism of the PCE, for example in their letter to Republican president Azaña in December 1937: copy in Azaña's personal archive, AB (*apartado* 7, *caja* 137, *carpeta* 9).

[129] As we already know from E. H. Carr's study, *The Twilight of the Comintern*, it was a creaky, ramshackle affair. The war in Spain severely tested its really quite meagre organisational and personnel resources. As far as Soviet personnel in general were concerned, although we do not have exact figures, current research estimates only a few dozen, and an absolute maximum of thirty, high-ranking functionaries for the entire war period (i.e. certainly far fewer at any one time) in Republican Spain. And while there was a relatively greater presence of Red Army personnel (c. 3,000 and between 600 and 800 at any one time), they were overwhelmingly absorbed by military functions (which includes those performed by civil engineers and interpreters). I am grateful to Frank Schauff for this information.

[130] G. Roberts, 'Soviet Foreign Policy and the Spanish Civil War 1936–1939', in C. Leitz and D. J. Dunthorn (eds.), *Spain in an International Context 1936–1959* (Oxford/New York: Berghahn Books, 1999), p. 91; Schauff, 'Hitler and Stalin in the Spanish Civil War', pp. 19–20.

perceptions of the events in Barcelona were coloured by the rarefied atmosphere in the Soviet Union. (This was borne to Spain by Stepanov, who had arrived in the wake of the military débâcle at Malaga (in early February 1937) seeking explanations for it in terms of 'spies and traitors'.[131]) But, once again, it is important to remember that, whether in respect of Malaga or the Barcelona events, Stepanov's accusations found a reply, in so far as they did at all, only because they chimed with the desperate domestic circumstances of the Republic and, given these, the very real and reasonable fear in a civil war of 'the enemy within'. Moreover, his continuing tirades in 1937 against 'trotskyism and its helpers' can themselves also be read as an indication of the Comintern's frustration that the multiple and fissiparous political life of the Republic was not in fact reducible to the 'redemptive' two-dimensional prescriptions to which its reports and advice tended.

In the aftermath of the May days, moreover, Comintern personnel in Spain seem notably to have targeted their aggression on *foreign* dissidents (often themselves exiles).[132] Why this was so lies beyond the scope of this book. However, as all epoques have guiding mind-sets, and inter-war Europe's derived heavily from forms of social darwinism, it does not seem too speculative to suggest that the imperative within stalinism to 'cleanse' the heterodox from the Comintern was akin in many respects to other contemporaneous pathological hatreds of ambiguity and otherness, in which we could also include – albeit in a minor category – the moral panics of official Barcelona faced with the urban 'rabble'.[133]

It is also vital to ask whether the initially semi-autonomous police action against the POUM obeyed rationales other than the Comintern's. The order to arrest the POUM originated inside the police force, not in the cabinet.[134] The violence and unconstitutional methods used by

---

[131] Elorza and Bizcarrondo, *Queridos camaradas*, pp. 340–1, 387, 395.

[132] Cf. Jellinek, *The Civil War in Spain*, p. 337.

[133] Cf. P. and A. Abramson, *Mosaíco roto*, p. 206. For this very reason it also becomes problematic to write the history of the May days and their political ramifications exclusively from the perspective of Comintern sources. A recent example of the resulting distortion is in chapters 7 and 9 of Antonio Elorza and Marta Bizcarrondo, *Queridos camaradas*. What the 'enemy within' represented in rebel Spain was a contaminant in a moral/social Darwinian sense: see chapter 2 above. There are echoes of this at times in locally produced Republican propaganda (against 'rightists' and 'hidden enemies'). And although this did not perform the same macro-political function in Republican Spain, it would be useful to explore some of the parallels.

[134] POUM youth leader Wilebaldo Solano referred explicitly to 'the police coup of 16 June 1937': Bolloten, *SCW*, p. 891 (n. 84); Zugazagoitia (then interior minister), *Guerra y vicisitudes*, pp. 291–4; M. Irujo comments on an 'arbitrary police order', cited in Peirats, *La CNT en la revolución española*, vol. 3, p. 234; Suárez, *El proceso contra el POUM*, pp. 83, 101–4; Alba, 'De los tribunales populares al Tribunal Especial', *Justicia en guerra*, p. 232. Cf. Azaña, diary entry 18 Oct. 1937, *Obras completas*, vol. 4, p. 828. Note in particular Azaña's comment that what was happening in the police was worse than Nin's disappearance itself.

the police after the May events are still routinely attributed to their Communist Party membership. However, many of those involved were 'new' communists, but 'old' policemen (and, sometimes, long-serving professional army officers, as in the case of the then Director General of Security, Colonel Antonio Ortega, with whom the order for the arrests orginated.[135]) So the violence raises far wider questions about the abiding failure of the Republic since 1931 to reform (i.e. demilitarise) police culture and practice. The democratic Republic was barely five years old when the war exploded. But the Spanish security forces, whether army or police, had a much longer tradition of taking matters into their own hands and acting unconstitutionally.[136] Moreover, the onslaught against the POUM came after the exposure of a network of Falangist activity and fifth column sabotage. To expect the 'old' police or military mentality to have drawn a distinction between different sorts of anti-governmental rebellion in wartime is unrealistic – especially when the left was, anyway, a target with which many policemen were more comfortable. If we look again at what was happening, a much older and more deeply ingrained political culture than stalinism begins to be apparent behind police zeal. Additionally, as in other aspects of the post-May repression, there was also a strong clash of regional cultures – for these were Madrid's security forces repressing the Catalan left.[137]

The notorious case of the kidnapping and murder of POUM general secretary Andreu Nin remains a conundrum. Nin was separated off from

[135] Ortega was a long-serving professional army officer of moderate republican sympathies who had joined the PCE in the war: Zugazagoitia, *Guerra y vicisitudes*, p. 292. Ricardo Burrillo, the Barcelona police chief who signed the order for Nin's detention, was also an army officer and Assault Guard commander (Suárez, *El proceso contra el POUM*, p. 83) and another wartime recruit to the PCE. He was reputed to have been involved in the pre-war assassination of Calvo Sotelo in July 1936; his career bespoke a certain ruthlessness and he was clearly not averse to the use of political violence. But none of these attributes were suddenly acquired simply because Burillo had joined the Communist Party: V. Alba and M. Ardevol (eds.), *El proceso del P.O.U.M.* (Barcelona: Lerna, 1989), p. 73. Burillo's military career went into decline in 1938 and he ended the war, like a number of other professional officers who had been wartime communists, opposed to the PCE. See biographical sketch in C. Zaragoza, *Ejército popular y militares de la República* (Barcelona: Planeta, 1983), pp. 232–5 and entries for both Burillo and Ortega in Alpert, *El ejército republicano*, pp. 364, 381.

[136] Even the Soviet intelligence chief, Alexander Orlov, would himself comment on this, cited in Costello and Tsarev, *Deadly Illusions*, p. 300 and P. and A. Abramson, *Mosaíco roto*, p. 190. This is also borne out by some of the testimonies gathered in Alba and Ardevol, *El proceso del P.O.U.M.*, for example the circumstances of POUM leader Jordi Arquer's temporary release and the exchange between him and Jaume Aiguader (then Esquerra minister in the Negrín cabinet), pp. 539–40; also Gorkin, *El proceso de Moscú en Barcelona*, p. 236. For more on the unconstitutional behaviour of the police, see the discussion about the militarisation of Republican society at war in chapter 6 below.

[137] For a suggestive reference to their hostility to the speaking of Catalan, see Súarez, *El proceso contra el POUM*, p. 103.

the rest of the POUM executive. His personal history may provide the explanation here.[138] Nin had lived in the Soviet Union throughout the 1920s. He had been an executive member of the Red International of Labour Unions. Then in 1926 he had joined the Left Opposition, acting for a time as Trotsky's secretary. All of this bound him inextricably into the inner circle of the Bolshevik old guard in a way that the rest of the POUM leadership was not. But the implication here is that Soviet operatives were responsible for his murder. A massive amount has been claimed and conjectured about this. But the fact remains that we still do not know exactly what happened to Nin or who was involved. To date nothing in the Comintern archives has shed any further light on the affair. The NKVD material that has so far surfaced is less than conclusive, while the NKVD archives themselves are not on open access.

A Catalan Television documentary on Nin's assassination (*Operació Nikolai*) made in the early 1990s claimed to offer definitive proof that it was orchestrated by Alexander Orlov, the NKVD chief in Spain.[139] But in spite of its claims, the documentary raised more questions than it answered – in particular about what clearly emerges as the key role of the Spanish police service in Nin's detention, torture and killing, although this is never directly commented on in the programme.[140] On 24 July 1937 Orlov sent a coded report to Moscow which has been interpreted as referring to his involvement in the Nin assassination – although the details remain obscure.[141] Certainly we know that evidence was forged in a vain attempt to link Nin, via the Falange, to Franco and Nazi Germany. Orlov may have been involved, and he would certainly have known about the forgery. He was also involved in – or at least knew about – the liquidation of foreign dissidents, such as the Austrian socialist Kurt Landau.[142] But Orlov, having fled to the USA in August 1938 to avoid being purged, always denied all personal knowledge of Nin's assassination. In the 1950s he claimed that it had been carried out by a

[138] For a brief political biography, see Durgan, 'Trotsky, the POUM and the Spanish Revolution', p. 69 (n. 5).

[139] M. Dolors Genovès, 'Operació Nikolai', Televisió de Catalunya, 1992.

[140] The video also has a transcript – see pp. 15–18 for information on police involvement. The Republican interior minister at the time, the socialist Julián Zugazagoitia, also referred to police responsibility – although he emphasised the problem of post-18 July recruitment to the security forces, Alba and Ardevol, *El proceso del P.O.U.M.*, p. 549. For more on the police's role in the Nin case and the repression of the POUM, see chapter 6 below.

[141] The report is cited in Costello and Tsarev, *Deadly Illusions*, p. 291. But see the comments on this book's particular bias in Gazur, *Secret Assignment. The FBI's KGB General*, p. xvii.

[142] Orlov's report to Moscow of 25 August 1937, cited in Costello and Tsarev, *Deadly Illusions*, p. 286; Gorkín, *El proceso de Moscú en Barcelona*, pp. 220–1; Thomas, *The Spanish Civil War*, p. 706.

special Soviet flying terror squad unconnected to the NKVD in Spain. This served the dual purpose of delivering the line his US hosts wanted to hear at the height of the Cold War and avoiding incriminating himself. (Orlov was then seeking the right to permanent US residence and fearful of anything that might prejudice the decision, especially in view of some hostile questioning over his role in Spain from immigration service officials.[143]) But then in 1968, in response to a questionnaire put to him by the historian Stanley Payne, Orlov retracted his earlier explanation claiming that what had happened to Nin was all the work of Spanish communists.[144] There was no obvious political motive for the change of line. So why did Orlov revise his account? He died in 1973 without making any further clarification. None of these unknowns rule out the involvement of Orlov and/or other Soviet personnel in Nin's death.[145] Indeed, there can be little doubt that Orlov, as intelligence chief, would have been privy to the details.[146] But it is quite conceivable that Orlov was assisting the Spanish communists in an enterprise that also served his general purposes in, as he saw it, cleaning up security risks on the Republican home front. After all, Orlov was empowered to take specific initiatives of his own without consulting Moscow.[147] With so many unanswered questions about the role of the other Spanish communist parties – PCE and PSUC – in the POUM repression, and the separate, though overlapping, issue of 'new communists' and 'old' police culture, as historians we should take care not to accept too readily the idea of sole Soviet authorship.[148] Indeed, given the sheer density and multiplicity of the political conflicts in the wartime Republic, its very simplicity should give us some pause for thought.

From the pattern of communist intervention in the arrest and re-arrest of Andrade and his POUM executive colleagues, it could be construed that the object was to ensure that the party executive was subject to formal criminal proceedings. They were originally arrested in Barcelona

---

[143] Costello and Tsarev, *Deadly Illusions*, pp. 352, 356. Marcelino Pascua also pointed to the evident unreliability of Orlov's testimony given the context in which it was produced: M. Pascua to A. Viñas, 13 Feb. 1977, AHN/MP, *caja* 8 (13).

[144] Bolloten, *SCW*, p. 509. The Orlov questionnaire has now been published in English in *Forum für osteuropäische Ideen und Zeitgeschichte*, 4 (2000), 238–43; see also Gazur, *Secret Assignment. The FBI's KGB General*, pp. 337–8, 340, 341–5.

[145] Orlov's own musings on the role of PCE leader Jesus Hernández also raise the knotty question of whether any putative Comintern involvement in the Nin affair need have been synonymous with a Soviet government directive: Gazur, *Secret Assignment. The FBI's KGB General*, pp. 344–5.

[146] Cf. G. Brook-Shepherd's preface, ibid., p. xiii.

[147] Costello and Tsarev, *Deadly Illusions*, p. 272.

[148] See chapter 6 below for the rise of police and intelligence service influence in 1938 – as the Republican home front became increasingly militarised.

by communist police from Madrid and taken to police cells in Valencia (thereafter being transferred to the state gaol).[149] Had the objective been liquidation, it seems unlikely that Valencia would have been their destination – as the case of Nin, arrested separately, would seem to bear out (although the killing of Nin may ultimately have resulted from the failure of his gaolers to extract a 'confession' to POUM espionage). When international pressure procured the release of Andrade and his colleagues, they were instantly re-arrested by communist police and this time taken to a *checa* in Madrid. As police action was now clearly occurring without any constitutional check, their lives were indeed at risk. But as a result of government pressure they were transferred several weeks later (at the end of July) to state custody in Valencia prison.[150]

Especially after the disappearance of Nin it was vital to the Republic's international credibility as a democracy that due process was followed in the detention of the POUM executive and that its members' safety was guaranteed. Negrín was no less concerned here than Prieto, Irujo and Zugazagoitia (in the interior ministry). (Indeed, provided the POUM leaders could be shielded from irregular police action, they were rather safer inside state prison than they would have been on the streets – given how high political tempers were running in some quarters.) Negrín differed from his cabinet colleagues, however, over how far they should take the investigation of Nin's disappearance.[151] Given it was a *fait accompli*, Negrín was determined to limit the damage that revelations of PCE and Soviet involvement would do to the political coalition underpinning the Republican war effort. But this did not mean that Negrín was simply sanctioning what the PCE wanted. After all, the prime minister had effectively sacked Ortega.[152] Equally, Comintern reports of this time expressed unhappiness at the government's obstruction of the 'war' against the POUM.[153] No doubt Negrín's own political antipathy to the POUM after May 1937 – which owed nothing to the PCE – made it easier for

[149] Súarez, *El proceso contra el POUM*, p. 84.

[150] The Suárez account also makes it clear, however, that, prior to their (second) departure for Valencia, the POUM executive members had already been transferred from *checa* to state gaol in Madrid – presumably also because of government pressure: *El proceso contra el POUM*, p. 85. Andrade's account is in Fraser, *Blood of Spain*, pp. 387–9. Republican state prisons also held foreign dissidents as well as Spaniards: Morrow, *Revolution and Counter-Revolution in Spain*, p. 145; E. Goldman, 'Political Persecution in Republican Spain', *Spain and the World*, 10 December 1937, also cited in Souchy, *The May Days*, pp. 104–7.

[151] Prieto, *Convulsiones de España*, vol. 2, p. 117.

[152] Zugazagoitia, *Guerra y vicisitudes de los españoles*, pp. 292–3.

[153] Elorza and Bizcarrondo, *Queridos camaradas*, pp. 378–9.

him to deal with the ethical implications of his decision over Nin. Negrín had few hesitations about bringing the POUM to trial because, in the middle of a war, its leadership had publicly (in its press) approved rebellion against the Republican state. His rationale around the POUM was essentially no different from the one that he had followed in 1932 when he demanded that the full force of the law be brought against the leaders of the anti-Republican military rebellion. But precisely because this was Negrín's reasoning, precisely because of the supreme importance which he had always accorded Republican state authority, it was imperative that the judicial enquiry and trial of the POUM affirm that same authority and the constitutional legal principles on which it rested.

What was happening to the POUM clearly served the party political interests of both the PCE and the PSUC. However, the party leaderships were less interested in the repression of individual POUM dissidents *per se* – indeed, there is some indication that the PCE, like the Republican government, was wary of a backlash.[154] Rather, the thrust of the two Spanish communist parties' post-May days attacks on the POUM was a strategic offensive designed to procure the party's total exclusion from the political life of the Republic at war. We still do not know enough about the dynamic of this wartime conflict inside the communist movement in Spain.[155] Two things, however, are clear. First, the PSUC was not a bystander in the process.[156] Its leaders would subsequently stress the role of the Spanish Communist Party in POUM repression, arguing that in the small world of Catalan communism, where organisational loyalties had been extremely fluid until 1935 and where all the leaders knew each other personally, it would have been impossible for anyone in the PSUC to believe that the POUM leaders were fascist agents (as was the Comintern's justificatory line).[157] This is no doubt true – and certainly the communist policemen sent to arrest the POUM leaders came from Madrid.[158] However, there were plenty of other tensions and

[154] Ibid., p. 378; Fraser, *Blood of Spain*, p. 388.
[155] Casanova, *Anarquismo y revolución*, p. 247. It is clear that the PCE mounted a well-organised anti-POUM propaganda campaign which involved high-pressure tactics and intimidation: Gorkín, *El proceso de Moscú en Barcelona*, p. 250; Alba and Ardevol, *El proceso del P.O.U.M.*, p. 541.
[156] Cf. Súarez, *El proceso contra el POUM*, p. 88.
[157] See PSUC leader Pere Ardiaca's testimony in Fraser, *Blood of Spain*, p. 390. POUM leader Andrade's comments distancing *both* PSUC *and* PCE from responsibility for the repression should be seen in the context of the post-war tendency of POUM survivors to construct the Comintern as the monolithic author of their political downfall: Fraser, *Blood of Spain*, p. 388.
[158] Súarez, *El proceso contra el POUM*, p. 101.

disagreements which could have provoked PSUC violence against the POUM during the May Days.[159]

In the pre-war Republic many acute intra-organisational conflicts on the left had been played out violently. The coming of the war did not wipe out these memories or the patterns of dispute which had originated the conflicts. Indeed, as these frequently arose over issues of political influence, clientele and membership rivalries, the circumstances produced by rebellion and war, if anything, intensified such clashes in the Republican zone – hence the emblematic importance of the *tránsfuga* (political renegade).[160] These clashes occurred, as we have seen, between *cenetistas* and *ugetistas*, between socialists and communists and between the rival branches of Catalan communism. Part political, part organisational, part personal, these disputes also led to physical violence against individual *poumistas*. But while this constituted in part 'communist' violence, it cannot accurately be subsumed under the term 'stalinist', in the sense that it was not a response to a Comintern game plan. Once the street fighting had erupted in Barcelona, it precipitated a quantity of bloodletting on all sides. The CNT, UGT, PSUC and POUM, as well as other lesser players, were all involved as the 'ghosts' of decades of labour wars and political infighting stalked the streets and meeting rooms of Barcelona.[161]

---

[159] Not the least of which were intense intellectual jealousies in what was a very small world. The most bitter personal animosities were those between the BOC members who had joined the POUM in 1935 and those who had joined the PCC (soon the PSUC). Indeed, the personal hatreds between POUM and ex-PCC people were in general the most intense. We need to think back to the process by which both the POUM and the PSUC were formed (see chapter 1 above). As Enric Ucelay da Cal has pointed out, the disputes between the two parties would be made more complex because – in spite of how they are frequently portrayed – *both* the POUM and the PSUC contained social democratic and 'neo-bolshevik' components, 'Socialistas y comunistas en Cataluña durante la guerra civil', p. 311. The traces of these disputes even appear embedded in the narrative of POUM leader Julián Gorkín's own memoir, *El proceso de Moscú en Barcelona*: see, for example, pp. 227, 246 – although, of course, the author himself interprets these details as proof of something else entirely.

[160] In Catalonia people usually passed from the CNT to the sphere of left parliamentary politics (UGT and communist parties). This sort of *tránsfuga* was a fairly common phenomenon on the inter-war Spanish left: examples include Roldán Cortada, Rodríguez Salas (see Bolloten, *SCW*, p. 417) and Rafael Vidiella (Sesé's replacement). Andreu Nin's own political trajectory went from left Catalanism through the PSOE and the CNT onto Bolshevik-Leninist ranks. Anarchist commentators have always been at pains to point out that the CNT had no *institutional* history of taking reprisals against *tránsfugas* (see J. Peirats, in Souchy *et al.*, *The May Days*, p. 20). But it must have exacerbated other intra-left organisational tensions. As chapter 1 above also indicates, there was, additionally, a great deal of 'traffic' up to 1935 between the various socialist and communist organisations in Catalonia. Reflecting the pattern elsewhere in Spain, some leading members of the Esquerra also passed to the PSUC in summer and autumn 1936: Ucelay da Cal, 'Socialistas y comunistas en Cataluña durante la guerra civil', p. 311.

[161] Cruells, *Mayo sangriento*, pp. 62, 69; Ucelay da Cal, 'Socialistas y comunistas en Cataluña durante la guerra civil', p. 313.

Even the ritualistic reciprocal tearing up of union and party cards in the days after the May streetfighting could also be seen as a point where 'top-down' state repression met this clientelist intra-party conflict.[162] The recruitment of 'opportunists' was another constant and widespread accusation levelled by each of the Republic's political groups against the rest since the start of the conflict. Socialists blamed republicans and communists;[163] republicans blamed the communists, and everyone blamed the CNT, who, in turn, blamed the communists and republicans.[164] The most numerous – namely the anarcho-syndicalists and the communists – were both accused by leading socialists on various occasions of violent outrages against their membership which the denouncers publicly identified as forming part of a brutal battle for party-political/organisational advantage within the Republican home front.[165] The CNT's (militia) recruitment from among prison populations freed at the start of the war was not easily forgotten.[166] But by early 1937, as the socialists were suffering a degree of organisational eclipse from which the PCE was benefiting, there were also various denunciations of a similar type levelled against communist office-holders – for example a scandal involving the detention of PSOE militants in Murcia led to the dismissal of the civil governor.[167]

It would have been extremely difficult, given the war, for those joining Republican political organisations to have been screened – even if the

---

[162] *Spain and the World* press report, 22 Sept. 1937, in Souchy *et al.*, *The May Days*, p. 100; Cruells, *Mayo sangriento*, p. 82. See also Azaña's acute remarks about inter-party competition for members, Azaña, *Obras completas*, vol. 4, p. 593.

[163] Graham, *Socialism and War*, *passim*.

[164] Cf. CNT's jaundiced view of the political 'promiscuity' of Left Republicans in Aragon: 'son del último que viene (they follow whoever's in political fashion): with the Republic in 1931; with the right and Gil Robles during the black biennium (1933–5); after the military rising with the CNT and now, once again, with the government' (Teruel province), letter from CNT union, November 1937, cited in Casanova, *Anarquismo y revolución*, p. 223.

[165] In so far as the PSOE (though not the UGT) remained mostly outside this argument, it was because the war had supposed a 'membership crisis' of sorts for a variety of reasons. See chapter 3 above for a discussion of these. (Our knowledge of this crisis does not come from membership figures – which for the war are hard to come by (especially for the PSOE) – and, in any case, difficult to interpret in such an exceptional period. Rather, we know of this crisis from the consistent, across the board discussion of it by a variety of socialist party and union leaders: see Graham, *Socialism and War*, *passim*.)

[166] Ibid., p. 63; Vidarte, *Todos fuimos culpables*, vol. 2, p. 656; G. Morón, *Política de ayer y política de mañana* (Mexico: n.p., 1942), pp. 77–8; Broué and Témime, *The Revolution and the Civil War in Spain*, p. 273.

[167] Graham, *Socialism and War*, p. 63; Morrow, *Revolution and Counter-Revolution in Spain*, pp. 73–5. Although Morrow alludes to it, I purposely do not cite here the famous polemic involving Cazorla and the Madrid Defence Council which erupted in April 1937. As I explain in chapter 3 above, this was a significantly more complex conflict which developed from the perilous and fraught front-line position of the capital city.

will had existed. But infighting was inevitable anyway in a context of accelerated mass political mobilisation. The war had massively inflated the reciprocal currency value of political membership in a society in which deep-rooted traditions of political nepotism and 'fixing' (*enchufismo*) combined with low levels of political education.[168] A 'penumbra' certainly existed at the edges of the most successful and competitive organisations where political clientele met criminal fraternity. Precisely what relationship these elements had to the political activities of the communist and anarcho-syndicalist organisations, however, is rather harder to assess. The input of these and other 'uncontrollables' is, by definition, an imponderable. But once meltdown had occurred in Barcelona on 4 May, the ensuing confusion in the region offered opportunities for the 'resolution' of all manner of scores – at least some of which would not have been directly related to the big political issues at stake. State control was significantly greater than in July 1936, but it seems reasonable to assume that there would still have been elements of lumpen activity under the blanket of May. As we have already seen, *paseos* were notorious for providing a useful cover for acts of personal as well as political revenge and for outright criminal activity.[169]

There was some evidence that 'uncontrollables' on the fringes of the CNT may have been responsible for the killings of the leading Italian anarchist Camillo Berneri and his secretary Francesco Barbieri, whose bodies were found on the streets of central Barcelona, near the Generalitat building, during the night of 5–6 May.[170] Their deaths have frequently been attributed to Comintern activity, but largely speculatively, on the basis of the political context in which they occurred.[171] A search was made of Berneri's flat on 4 May by two men 'wearing red armbands' who carried away documents. The CNT press report of 11 May which broke the news of the double assassination was censored to prevent its identifying the searchers as PSUC policemen. But we do not really know

---

[168] The very ambiguity of 'communist police action' as discussed here is itself indicative of the still relatively weak nature of state-derived professional identities as against those of political parties whose force of attraction still depended at least in part on clientelist practices (i.e. parties were still viewed as offering access to direct material benefits, career advancement etc.).

[169] See chapter 2 above for these problems in relation to the July days of 1936; also chapter 3 on the Madrid Defence Council, public order and the occurrence of kidnapping and extortion 'scams' involving its employees.

[170] Cruells, *Mayo sangriento*, p. 69; Semprún-Maura, *Revolución y contrarrevolución en Cataluña*, pp. 279–81.

[171] The report in the CNT press, *Solidaridad Obrera*, on 11 May 1937 (see Peirats, *La CNT en la revolución española*, vol. 2, pp. 148–50) linked the killings to the disappearance of the Russian dissident communist Marc Rhein: Broué and Témime, *The Revolution and the Civil War in Spain*, p. 305 (also pp. 285–6); Souchy *et al.*, *The May Days*, pp. 40–2, 105.

whether the larger group who came to arrest Berneri and Barbieri on 5 May were also PSUC affiliates, or, indeed, even police at all.

While some CNT sources held to the theory of PSUC police involvement,[172] the CNT's official report on the events, published in June 1937, accused pro-Fascist elements of the radical Catalan nationalist party, Estat Català, of colluding in the killings with agents of the Italian secret police (OVRA). There is a great deal of circumstantial evidence to recommend this explanation.[173] However, other intelligence which came to leading members of the PSOE in government also suggested that Berneri and Barbieri may have been killed on the orders of Angel Galarza, interior minister in Largo Caballero's central government, in order to prevent Berneri going public on Galarza's involvement in the embezzlement of public funds.[174] Galarza, apart from being a fairly incompetent minister, was a late-comer to the PSOE who had a very dubious reputation among his colleagues as something of an opportunist and sharp operator reminiscent of the 'old world' of monarchist politics.[175] According to this intelligence report, Galarza's 'fixer' was an Italian anarchist called Gigi-Bibi who had already employed other Italian anarchist contacts in Barcelona to secure some of the incriminating documents in Berneri's possession. Although none of this is conclusive, Galarza could easily have ordered a police search and then taken other measures accordingly. Indeed, his 'anarchist' contact could conceivably have been an OVRA agent himself. Although the OVRA's activity in Barcelona was relatively marginal, we do know that its agents kept Berneri under close surveillance and it is quite possible that, to this

---

[172] Cf. A. Souchy, *Los sucesos de Barcelona* (Valencia: Ebro, 1937, transl. as *The Tragic Week in May*, a publication of the CNT-FAI's external information service which Souchy directed) and Souchy's own essay in *The May Days* (1987), p. 42.

[173] See Bolloten, *SCW*, pp. 453, 875–7 for a resumé of the available literature and current state of the enquiry on Berneri's death. Souchy also implies the possible removal by those searching Berneri's flat on 5 May of Berneri's manuscript dealing with Mussolini's expansionist Mediterranean policy: *The May Days*, p. 42.

[174] Copy of (anonymous) report, dated 24 Nov. 1937, found in the correspondence of Luis Araquistain, political lieutenant of Largo Caballero and his ambassador in Paris until the cabinet changes of May 1937. See Howson, *Arms for Spain*, pp. 225–7.

[175] Certainly there were complaints in the PSOE about the dubious characters sometimes to be glimpsed 'in the wings' of Galarza's ministerial suite: Graham, *Socialism and War*, pp. 63–4, 99; Vidarte, *Todos fuimos culpables*, vol. 2, pp. 673, 655, 862; Jellinek, *The Civil War in Spain*, p. 558. The 'old politics' represented by Galarza would also be integrated to the *new* Francoist order. For, in the rebel zone, although there was never any crisis of political order, networks of corruption also existed. The point about the Republican zone is that although these old behaviours were still present, they were also beginning to come up against other political values – such as those of the 'public-service' state – which carried the transformative potential for new professional identities and a different political culture.

end, they may have infiltrated foreign anarchist groups operating in the city.[176]

Certainly there were particular aspects of CNT practice which might be said to have facilitated infiltration – whether by Italian or Spanish fascists[177] or by those involved in straightforwardly criminal pursuits. However, the fact that the wartime 'penumbra' spread wider than the CNT-FAI suggests that this picture is best explained in relation to the generally destabilising impact of coup and war. These had produced a 'wild new frontier' environment which saw gangsterism and local feuds, political or otherwise, waged in the space still unfilled by reconstructing state power.[178] It was this that probably explains the intensity of the post-May days violence in the smaller towns of the Barcelona area.[179] For onto state repression – in the form of the police-led attacks on Telefónicas and CNT/POUM premises – were grafted other sorts of score-settling in more opaque, but still often very violent, local conflicts. This was the picture not only in Catalonia but also in neighbouring Aragon.[180]

Although many imponderables remain over the May days, it is at least clear that the events cannot be reduced to a Cold War parable of an alien stalinism which 'injected' conflict into Spanish Republican politics. The Comintern's 'clean-up' of dissident communists in Barcelona in May and June 1937, ethically unattractive though it was, constituted but one element in a bigger picture. Nor can it even explain everything that happened to the POUM.

In the wake of the May events, the POUM would be made a political example in a way no other Republican group was. But how, why and (crucially) *when* that happened all make for a far more complex story than the one habitually laid down in the existing martyrologies of POUM demise – as we shall see.[181] Moreover, if we always compose the party's history backwards from the May days – and in particular from the atrocious murder of Nin – then we shall never understand the political and

---

[176] See the work of C. Rama (ed.), *Camillo Berneri: Guerra de clases en España 1936–1937* (Barcelona: Tusquets, 1977) and *Fascismo y anarquismo en la España contemporánea* (Barcelona: Bruguera, 1979). See also S. G. Pugliese, *Carlo Rosselli: Socialist Heretic and Antifascist Exile* (Cambridge, Mass.: Harvard University Press, 1999).

[177] In contrast to Madrid, however, the *indigenous* fifth column in Barcelona was, as yet, marginal. It would only become a force of any significance in the grim days of 1938 when the Republic faced an utterly bleak international horizon and was on the edge of material collapse. See chapters 6 and 7 below.

[178] Cazorla himself points this out: see minutes of the Madrid Defence Council reproduced in Aróstegui and Martínez, *La Junta de Defensa de Madrid*, p. 446.

[179] Cf. Cruells, *Mayo sangriento*, p. 90.   [180] Casanova, *Anarquismo y revolución*, pp. 253–63.

[181] For an analysis of the proscription of the POUM in the context of the Republic's deteriorating wartime situation in 1938, see chapter 6 below.

cultural complexity that made the POUM what it was – with everything that 'complexity' signifies in terms of *internal* tensions. In this respect, we should remember too that the POUM had had its own experience of violent internecine conflict earlier in the war.[182] This stemmed from a particular genealogy across the 1930s which had brought the POUM to encapsulate within itself the major political division between radical politics and liberal political reform now rending the wartime left as a whole.[183]

Finally, we can conclude that the May days were an urban rebellion, directed against state power and reflecting the particular configuration of CNT strength – and weakness – in Catalonia. This is confirmed by the fact that the last act of the May days took place, not in Catalonia, but in neighbouring Aragon – the agrarian counterpart of 'red' Barcelona. The city's physical barricades had been dismantled, but Aragon's institutional barricades against central state power still remained, in the form of the governing Council of Aragon, backed by the armed strength of CNT and POUM cadres on the eastern (Aragon) front. The central government's appointment on 5 May of General Pozas as commander of the Eastern Army, as well as military head of the Catalan region, set the stage for the subsequent military offensive in Aragon which would take place in August.

What would open the way for Aragon to be brought fully into the orbit of the central Republican government, however, was the crucial change in the constellation of that government – a change also detonated by the May day events in Barcelona. The PCE's discontent with Largo's running of the war ministry had already reached critical mass before May. In all respects, the party's criticism reflected the collectively held view of Largo in the cabinet: he was inept, devoid of his own ideas, and made policy with a cabal of military and civilian supporters of questionable abilities and (in some cases) perhaps dubious loyalty too; he neither consulted the cabinet nor convoked the High War Council (Consejo Superior de Guerra).[184] It had taken Largo until the beginning of March to get the Generalitat to agree to submit the Catalan militia to the control of the Valencia war ministry.[185] By mid April the PCE had been given the go-ahead by the Comintern to find a way of separating Largo from the war brief.[186] But this did not mean removing him as prime minister. Stalin

---

[182] See the suggestive testimony of Paul Thalmann to B. Bolloten, *SCW*, p. 860 (n. 12).
[183] Cf. Ucelay da Cal, 'Socialistas y comunistas en Cataluña durante la guerra civil', p. 311.
[184] Azaña, *Obras completas*, vol. 4, pp. 591–2, 594–5; Elorza and Bizcarrondo, *Queridos camaradas*, pp. 340–1, citing Stepanov's Comintern report of 17 March 1937.
[185] Salas Larrazábal, *Historia del ejército popular*, vol. 4, pp. 1042–5; Bolloten, *SCW*, p. 419.
[186] Elorza and Bizcarrondo, *Queridos camaradas*, p. 341.

saw Largo as performing a vital political role – and one in which he could not easily be replaced. It was the symbolism of Largo that guaranteed for the Republican alliance sectors of the labour movement and political left – especially in the CNT – who might not otherwise support the war effort but who were crucial to it.[187] Largo's premiership was, however, already extremely problematic, given that he was now estranged from virtually the entire cabinet. What most concerned republicans and parliamentary socialists – and perhaps above all President Azaña – was the war's crucial international-diplomatic dimension. None were unaware of Largo Caballero's domestic usages. Nevertheless, both republicans and socialists were desperate for a prime minister with a greater intellectual grasp of the vital importance of international diplomacy to the Republic's fate.[188] They wanted someone 'fluent' in such milieux who could plead the Republic's case, indeed who, in his own person, encapsulated the liberal democratic principles being defended in arms. For the socialists too, there was also the ongoing friction with Largo and his supporters over the liaison committee policy with the PCE. For those socialists who identified with the PSOE leadership, the Caballeristas were not only ignoring party discipline in voicing their opposition, but were also undermining a policy whose primary rationale was the practical support of the war effort and the government.

Once the May day protests had exploded in Barcelona, the issue of public order rapidly focused minds in the Valencia cabinet. The assassination of Generalitat minister Sesé on 5 May increased the republicans' resolve to find a firmer hand for the helm: someone who was prepared to crack down even if it meant unpopularity with some sectors of organised labour and the left.[189] The PCE leadership was also clear about this

---

[187] The same conclusions on Stalin's position here have also been reached independently by Frank Schauff, in 'Sowjetunion, Kommunistische Internationale und Spanischer Bürgerkrieg 1936–1939', doctoral thesis, University of Cologne, 2000 and in his unpublished research paper 'Failure in Emergency: The Spanish Civil War and the Dissolution of the Comintern', p. 27. It would be Largo's own refusal to separate the two ministerial portfolios which made inevitable his departure from the cabinet in May.

[188] Cf. 'One of the main reasons [Largo] had to be replaced was because of his evident and notorious incapacity as prime minister, at least during such a war which was complex and exhausting not only because of its internal dimension but also because of the powerful influence of certain great powers whether they intervened militarily or held back from the conflict – *there was a complex diplomatic configuration in which precious, and irrecuperable, time was lost both in the military and political spheres*' (my italics). Undated comments in the personal archive of PSOE member and Republican ambassador M. Pascua, *legajo* 5, *carpeta* 6 (doc. 8 in series although unnumbered).

[189] Irujo, in the name of the PNV's parliamentary group, called for a new prime minister who could 'impose constitutional order and the rule of law on the home front and put an end once and for all to the uncontrollables, to committees and to other kinds of violence': M. Irujo, cited in H. Raguer, *La pólvora y el incienso. La iglesia y la guerra civil española (1936–39)* (Barcelona: Ediciones Península, 2001), p. 325.

and, by 7 May, the basis of an anti-Largo cabinet alliance had formed between republicans and communists.[190] The PSOE national executive was no less a part of this alliance. But it kept a lower profile – something which reflected Prieto's preference for behind-the-scenes manoeuvring, but also the party leadership's not inconsiderable collective fears that too obvious an attack on Largo would exacerbate the internal divisions in the socialist organisation – something they were keen to avoid at all costs since it would further advantage PCE recruitment. The republicans also remained cautious about a full frontal attack on Largo. The May events were themselves a reminder that excluding him from the cabinet itself might provoke further destabilising popular protests in the streets and workplaces of other Republican cities. The conundrum preoccupying republicans, communists and the PSOE was just how powerful Largo Caballero really was.

On Thursday 13 May, during an extremely acrimonious evening cabinet meeting, the crisis finally broke. The PCE had tabled a severe criticism of Largo's war and public-order policy. When the premier refused to accept any of it, the two communist ministers walked out of the meeting. Largo was all for continuing the meeting, but Indalecio Prieto reminded him that the PCE's withdrawal constituted a government crisis and that the president needed to be informed immediately. At this point, Largo seems to have been looking to Azaña to back his formation of a new cabinet entirely excluding the PCE. Largo was also much exercised by the communists' demand – raised as part of their broader public-order concerns – that the POUM be declared an illegal party after its involvement in the May day events. Although the prime minister felt no sympathy for the POUM's political stance, he was reluctant to bear the personal responsibility for state action against any organisation of the left. Partly this was an ethical concern, but partly it reflected his anxiety over the damage which would inevitably be done to his reputation as leader of the UGT if he were to become publicly associated with the repression of the POUM. Largo's concern that the courts should opine on the POUM before the government acted was constitutionally impeccable. But the Republic was at war, fighting for its life, and the events in Barcelona could easily have capsized Republican resistance. Moreover, that Largo could have believed that it was feasible to exclude the PCE from the cabinet is the clearest possible indication of his limited political understanding. Neither the international nor domestic situation nor his own political isolation in the cabinet permitted it.

[190] M. Azaña, *Obras completas*, vol. 4, pp. 591–2; Graham, *Socialism and War*, p. 91.

Largo was also up against President Azaña's own intense – if still dissembled – dislike of him. Azaña had been opposed to his appointment as premier back in September 1936 and had not changed his opinion since – finding Largo obtuse and obdurate. The president had wisely kept his own council on this matter (Largo certainly had little idea how much he was disliked), but now Azaña glimpsed the opportunity to acquire a prime minister on his own wave length. His desire so to do had, of course, been galvanised by the fact that Largo had ignored him entirely during his anguished days of virtual imprisonment in Barcelona. At the same time, however, Azaña was determined that Largo's removal should not be seen as a presidential caprice. He knew that this would only bolster the outgoing premier's credibility. Largo's removal had to come as a consequence of his rejection by the Republican political alliance – *including* the parties that represented working-class constituencies.

The verbal sound and fury on 14 May from Largo's unconditional backers in the UGT executive as well as CNT threats of mass protest action momentarily fazed the PSOE – as it did some republicans, including the Republic's vice-president, Martínez Barrio.[191] By the end of that same day, however, it had become clear that Largo was not going to negotiate with the PCE. Instead he was hoping simply to put off the crisis by disappearing to conduct military operations in Extremadura. Their success, so Largo hoped, would be enough to silence the PCE and end the crisis in his favour. Given the general lack of confidence in Largo as war minister, Azaña viewed this scenario with not much less scepticism than he did the Caballeristas' totally impracticable scheme to foment an anti-Francoist rebellion among the Rif tribes of Spanish Morocco.[192] The Extremaduran offensive – never in fact implemented – was intended to take the pressure off the north, while also cutting Franco's troop supply lines in the south. Whether it could ever have achieved the

---

[191] Azaña, *Obras completas*, vol. 4, pp. 596–7.

[192] See ibid., pp. 589, 594 for his cogent views on the Moroccan plan (and a shrewd assessment of Largo's naive belief in popular uprising as a mystical event). As has been demonstrated, there were structural political reasons why the proto-nationalists with whom the Caballeristas (particularly Carlos de Baraibar) were in contact (and to whom they were paying substantial sums of money) *could not deliver* what they promised: R. M. de Madariaga, 'The Intervention of Moroccan Troops in the Spanish Civil War: A Reconsideration', *European History Quarterly*, 22 (Jan. 1992). Prieto debunked the Moroccan plans along similar lines: see *Guerra y Revolución*, vol. 3, p. 80 (n. 3). There is information on de Baraibar's role as go-between in Araquistain's papers, *legajo* 25, B30. Pascua also points out that Largo and de Baraibar were financing the Moroccan plan without telling Negrín in the treasury. Pascua (who would take charge of the Republic's Paris embassy in June 1938) also cites reports critical of Largo's Moroccan scheme from the Spanish consul general in Rabat (French zone), 12, 28 May and 23 June 1937, AHN/MP, *caja* 2 (14.4).

latter objective is questionable – not least because of the Republic's lack of an offensive capability. In the event, the Republic would opt instead to activate the eastern (Aragon) front to relieve pressure on the north. It is certainly true that the PCE dragged its feet over Extremadura. But so did Prieto. General Miaja, who had had his own severe conflicts with the prime minister, also procrastinated over the dispatch of troops from Madrid to participate in the operation. There was a fear of uncovering the Madrid front – where Franco's best troops were concentrated – and a shared conviction that Largo was militarily incompetent. Both sentiments existed in their own right rather than merely as foils for other personal or political agendas. The strategic value of the Extremaduran offensive was also somewhat dubious given that the rebels had access to Portuguese roads, air bases and telephone facilities.[193] Moreover, the fact that no evidence of any detailed military dispositions for the operation was ever found in the war ministry suggests that the reservations of those opposing Largo were well founded.[194]

But if the outcome of the May cabinet crisis can be said to have had an architect, it was the PSOE's Indalecio Prieto.[195] The sheer unconstitutionality of Largo's *ad hoc* postponement of the cabinet crisis provoked him into action – doubtless strongly encouraged by Azaña, who was particularly exercised by such things given what little remained of constitutional etiquette during wartime with parliament closed. Azaña, unlike many of his republican colleagues, was unworried by the noise from Largo's backers because he believed that they overestimated their leader's strength in the UGT.[196] (Largo's base there had, anyway, been undermined by the split in the national executive – several members of which now backed Prieto and the PCE.[197]) Thus, on the evening of 14 May it was the PSOE which forced wide open the political crisis by withdrawing its appointees from the cabinet. Prieto himself remained, as

---

[193] Araquistain would make great claims for the Extremaduran offensive in his pamphlet *El comunismo y la guerra de España*, first published in France in 1939 (and reproduced in L. Araquistain, *Sobre la guerra y en la emigración* (Madrid: Espasa-Calpe, 1983), p. 218). Some of these claims were subsequently endorsed by Francoist military historians – see R. Salas Larrazábal, *La historia del ejército popular*, vol. 1, pp. 1076–83. The plan of operations also appears in Colonel José Manuel Martínez Bande's *La ofensiva sobre Segovia y la batalla de Brunete* (Madrid: San Martín, 1972), pp. 237–40. But such historians also had a clear political agenda. With this in mind, Salas' sudden belief in the offensive capacity of the Republican army is, to say the least, remarkable.

[194] Prieto and an (unnamed) officer of the Republican general staff, both interviewed by G. Jackson, *The Spanish Republic and the Civil War*, p. 372, n. 13.

[195] The key link between Azaña and Prieto throughout the May crisis is the republican former premier, José Giral. A close friend of Azaña's, Giral had also relied heavily on Prieto's advice during his premiership at the start of the war – see chapter 2 above.

[196] Azaña, *Obras completas*, vol. 4, p. 596.   [197] Graham, *Socialism and War*, pp. 168–70.

ever, in the wings, sending his fellow PSOE ministers, Juan Negrín and the veteran socialist Anastasio de Gracia (labour minister), to inform Largo of the party's decision.[198]

Largo's manner of confronting the situation amply demonstrates his political limitations. First, a fit of pique, then an attempt to ignore all his opponents entirely – but this without offering any further incentive to the CNT to close ranks with his supporters in the UGT. The cabinet which Largo proposed to Azaña on 17 May was an instrument designed to punish the PSOE executive and, above all, Prieto. The plans to do so predated the crisis by some months, however. Already in early March Araquistain had tabled proposals to Largo which were similar in their overall design (of marginalising the Caballeristas' socialist rivals in the cabinet) to those of 17 May.[199] In the latter the PSOE would have been reduced to 2 ministries out of 14. Negrín remained in the treasury. But Prieto was relegated to a combined ministry of trade, industry and agriculture.[200] (The PCE, however, retained two posts – although swapping agriculture for labour.) But there was even worse to come. In spite of the PCE's key demand that Largo relinquish the war portfolio – tacitly seconded by the PSOE and the republicans – Largo had augmented his responsibilities here to oversee a new ministry absorbing Prieto's former navy and airforce brief. To cap it all, the CNT was thrown mere scraps – the now politically marginal post of justice, as well as that of health. As the CNT lost no time in pointing out, this showed a fine lack of gratitude (among other things) on the premier's part, since it put them on an equal footing with the PCE – the party that had initiated the crisis.[201] Immediately the CNT made it known that it would not participate in any cabinet in which it did not retain control of the trade and industry portfolios. Finally, the unwieldiness of the cabinet – against which Azaña had expressly warned – indicated Largo's stubborn adherence to an antiquated political formula whereby peripheral portfolios (and non-portfolio posts) were allocated proportionally to *all* groups in the Popular Front coalition – a practice which generated a monster entity entirely

---

[198] Largo Caballero, *Mis recuerdos*, p. 205; Graham, *Socialism and War*, p. 97.

[199] Graham, *Socialism and War*, pp. 92–3. Prieto was allocated public works. The other PSOE minister was, as before, Anastasio de Gracia in the labour post.

[200] Azaña, *Obras completas*, vol. 4, p. 601. A full list of Largo's proposed cabinet is in *Guerra y revolución en España*, vol. 3, p. 81. The Left Republicans had two ministries (public works and propaganda), as did the PSOE and PCE. Republican Union had one (communications/merchant navy) and the Basque and Catalan nationalists (PNV and Esquerra) had a minister without portfolio apiece.

[201] There was extensive coverage of the CNT's reactions in the press. A collection of related cuttings is also to be found in the Archivo Histórico Nacional (SGC), Salamanca, serie Bilbao, *carpeta* 39.

inappropriate to the tight communication and cooperation required in wartime.

But the most striking feature of Largo's proposed 'solution' to the cabinet crisis was his absolute refusal to relinquish personal control of the war ministry. He maintained this position even though he knew that it was the one non-negotiable issue with the PCE and that neither the PSOE nor the republicans would accept a cabinet without communist participation. Moreover, Largo was holding out in almost complete political isolation. Behind him he had only his old retainers on the, now divided, UGT executive. Largo had boxed himself into a political corner. As a result, the inevitable came to pass: Largo resigned on 17 May. The question which immediately arises, however, is why, if Largo set such store by the war ministry, did he not fight for it by making a political deal with the CNT – his only potential allies for such a ministerial combination? One answer would be that Largo and his supporters were poor strategists. But that is stretching credibility when the CNT option was so glaringly obvious.

In fact, Largo's inability to take the only route out of the cul-de-sac in which he found himself obeyed a much older political rationale: that of the entrenched organisational values of the Caballerista union bureaucracy.[202] By the time the May crisis broke, Largo and his union old guard were engaged in a battle with the PCE for control of the UGT whose origins lay in the pre-war period. By spring 1937 it was also clear that the united youth organisation (JSU) had exited the socialist orbit entirely. This organisational conflict entirely shaped Largo's understanding of what was at stake during the May crisis. Araquistain had warned him on the eve of the cabinet crisis that socialist-communist rapprochement – and maybe even a merger – was inevitable given the international configuration, and that setting his face against it absolutely would guarantee his own eclipse as Prieto's star rose.[203] But the political values underpinning Largo's worldview made it impossible for him to accept that the war effort constituted an overriding imperative, requiring certain political alliances – such as the one the PSOE executive was actively pursuing with the PCE. Largo saw himself as a lone champion of socialist (and above all UGT) organisational integrity. Prieto was consorting with the 'enemy'. In Largo's eyes, this alone was enough to debar him from the war ministry – possession of which was pivotal to *political* ascendancy in

---

[202] For more on these, see chapters 1 and 3 above.

[203] Araquistain to Largo Caballero, 2 May 1937 in AH-26-36 (Madrid); Nenni, *La guerra de España*, pp. 48–9.

the wartime Republic. It was this same 'logic' which prevented Largo from making concessions to the CNT – an even older enemy in his long war of organisational position on behalf of the UGT.[204] Hence his total lack of response to the CNT, which, already by the early weeks of March, was calling for a pre-emptive union alliance to head off the hostile party forces in the cabinet. That Largo behaved thus in May 1937 tells us something else too about his unspoken political assumptions – although it is something deeply counter-intuitive, and thus difficult to grasp for any observer operating with historical hindsight. For socialist organisational integrity to have been more important to Largo than winning the war (for this is the logical conclusion of his stance), then, at some level, he has to have assumed that, even if the Republic lost, there would still be some point to that 'integrity'. In other words, Largo was scripting Francoism as if it were going to be a rerun of the Primo de Rivera dictatorship of the 1920s. According to this scenario, even if no democratic regime existed in post-civil-war Spain, there would still surely be a space for a 'responsible' trade union – namely the UGT. Nor was Largo the only socialist leader with union ties who would think in this way.[205] Moreover, such tacit assumptions would become more prevalent through 1938, feeding misguided 'pro-negotiation' currents as the Republic's military position grew more fragile.[206]

In the last analysis, the May cabinet crisis had exposed both Caballeristas and the CNT to the consequences of their political contradictions and their inability to lay the basis of a strategic alliance over the period 1934–6.[207] By 1937 Largo Caballero, as titular head of the 'socialist left', found himself without any solid political base.[208] But even then, he was unwilling to offer political concessions to the CNT. On its own, the anarcho-syndicalist movement lacked, as we have seen, the organisational capacity to articulate a political alternative to the Popular Front. In fact the UGT had some similar defects.[209] But, in any case, the

---

[204] Juliá, 'Presidente por última vez: Azaña en la crisis de mayo de 1937', p. 251; although it seems to me that Juliá's analysis exaggerates the magnitude and coherence of the 'union threat' to the Republican alliance of political parties (see p. 249). On this see Graham, *Socialism and War*, pp. 92–3.

[205] Cf. the views of Julián Besteiro in 1939, *Obras*, vol. 3, pp. 435–7, cited in Preston, *Comrades*, pp.187–8. See also chapter 7 below.

[206] See chapters 6 and 7 below.   [207] See chapter 1 above.

[208] H. Graham, 'The Erosion of the Socialist Left 1934–1937', in Lannon and Preston (eds.), *Elites and Power in Twentieth Century Spain*, pp. 127–51.

[209] It was not designed to allow easy or regular communication 'horizontally' between the intermediate levels of the various industrial federations – as opposed to communication at the apex, between the national executives of each federation.

radical minority in the UGT to whom the CNT might have appealed for support[210] had never occupied the primary leadership positions in the union hierarchy. This remained in the hands of cautious bureaucrats whose spirit was epitomised by Largo himself. Isolated and faced by the united opposition of his parliamentary socialist, communist and republican cabinet colleagues, Largo was obliged to resign the premiership. He had been ousted not by a stalinist plot, as he and his supporters would later insist, but by the entire Republican alliance. As the PSOE's general secretary Ramón Lamoneda would later pointedly comment: 'Caballero always claimed to have been "kicked out by the Communists", which was in part true, since everyone kicked him out, from Azaña to Martínez Barrio.'[211] And the CNT stood by while this happened – alienated by Largo's political parsimony – a bitter reminder of the old prewar antagonisms. The fact that the Caballerista power base was so badly eroded by 1937 facilitated Largo's ejection from the cabinet. But the common purpose of republicans, socialists and communists was crucial to its realisation.

President Azaña had achieved his wish. But if Largo's removal came through the collective decision of the Republican alliance, the president was singularly more personally proactive in the selection of PSOE finance minister Juan Negrín as the new premier. That said, the range of individuals fulfilling the minimum criteria from which the president had to choose was not very great. Neither a republican nor a communist was feasible: the former because he would have lacked credibility inside Spain, the latter because not only would it have been deeply divisive inside the Republic, but it would also have destroyed its international campaign to secure the lifting of Non-Intervention. The new prime minister had perforce to be a socialist. But he could not be a Caballerista since none of them would never have accepted the subordination of the trade unions which had long been the objective of republicans, communists and parliamentary socialists alike – redoubled after the May events in Barcelona. Nor, in any case, would it have been easy to find someone of the requisite calibre in Caballerista ranks. (Indeed, only Araquistain appeared prime *ministrable*. But Azaña would never have appointed the

---

[210] The aspirations of a radicalised rural base after the February 1936 Popular Front elections saw some collaboration between the CNT and sectors of the UGT landworkers' federation, the FNTT, in the south: Payne, *Spain's First Democracy*, pp. 301–3. This political constellation would reappear in late 1937 as part of the Caballeristas' ongoing war for control of the UGT: Graham, *Socialism and War*, pp. 198–218.

[211] R. Lamoneda, 'El secreto del anticomunismo', unpublished post-war writings, ARLF-166-40, p. 6 (Fundación Pablo Iglesias, Madrid).

man he saw as the architect of the May 1936 crisis which had kept Prieto out of the premiership at such a critical juncture.[212]) By a process of elimination, therefore, the new premier had to be a parliamentary socialist. The expected choice was Prieto himself – for his grasp of political realities both domestic and international, his strategic intelligence, ministerial experience and sheer drive, as well as his pivotal role inside the Spanish socialist movement and close friendship with the president. But, as Azaña himself indicated, Prieto was needed for that most crucial of cabinet responsibilities: the war ministry.[213] Indeed, the consolidation of land army, airforce and navy in a single ministry, thus rectifying the anomaly pending since 4 September 1936, had not been the least of the goals of the cabinet front against Largo in May. With all his faults, Prieto was truly irreplaceable in the war ministry. The premiership, on the other hand, required someone of a less emotionally volatile nature than Prieto. It also needed someone who had good – or at least neutral – relations with all sectors of the Republican alliance. But Prieto was at loggerheads with an important sector of his own movement. Nor were his relations with the CNT good. Hence Azaña's preference for 'the calm energy' of Negrín.[214] His republican convictions would not recommend him to the CNT, but at least he was (as yet) a neutral figure in their eyes, unlike Prieto. Likewise, Negrín, although clearly identified with the PSOE executive and Prieto, had not been prominent in the internecine socialist conflict. Moreover, Azaña and Prieto were in perfect agreement that the multi-lingual and cosmopolitan Negrín, with a good network of contacts in Europe, was the Republic's international politician *par excellence.*[215]

But in spite of Azaña's very clear statement that he himself chose Negrín, as well as the evident rationale behind the appointment, a great deal of mythology has grown up suggesting that Negrín was the Communist Party's candidate or, even more fantastically, that he was imposed by the Soviet Union. Much of this mythology derives from particular and contentious interpretations of Negrín's policies as prime minister in the later stages of the war and not least from the voluminous and

---

[212] See chapter 1 above.

[213] Negrín would himself be both premier and war minister later in the war. But that was the result of the political crisis in the PSOE which saw Prieto, as the only other feasible incumbent, depart the cabinet (and, in effect, active political life). See chapter 6 below.

[214] Azaña, *Obras completas*, vol. 4, p. 602.

[215] For a biographical sketch of Negrín, see H. Graham, 'War, Modernity and Reform: The Premiership of Juan Negrín', in Preston and Mackenzie (eds.), *The Republic Besieged*, pp. 163–6.

vehemently anti-communist post-war writings of Indalecio Prieto.[216] But the fact remains that in May 1937 Negrín was as much Prieto's choice as he was Azaña's and for precisely the same reasons: his ability to articulate the Republican alliance internally, his republican convictions, singular political intelligence and international fluency. And while it is true that Negrín's profile was conducive to Stalin's political objectives in supporting the Republic, it makes no sense to claim this as the driving force behind his premiership: first, because of the role played by Azaña and Prieto, second, because, as we now know, Stalin had been far from adverse to Largo's remaining as premier and third, because, in any case, neither the Soviet Union nor the PCE was in a position to 'impose' a premier on the Spanish Republic in May 1937. Negrín had a good working relationship with Stashevsky, the Soviet commercial attaché, with whom he was necessarily in frequent contact in his capacity as treasury minister. But Negrín's relations with Soviet personnel were no different from or indeed closer than Prieto's. In fact, socialists as diverse as Araquistain and PSOE executive member Manuel Albar repeatedly commented on the excellence of Prieto's relations with both Soviet diplomatic personnel and the PCE.[217] Negrín was aware and concerned far earlier than Prieto about the negative impact of inter-party competition within Republican state bodies, as a result of which he debarred members of the PCE from the reorganised Carabineros. It was also Prieto who suggested in spring 1937 that the PSOE accept the PCE's proposal of merger for the sake of the war effort.[218] Negrín was opposed (as, in the event, was the PSOE national executive – with the exception of Jerónimo Bugeda). Had relations not been good between Prieto and the PCE, the party would scarcely have joined the rest of the cabinet in strongly backing him for the war portfolio, which it considered a far more pivotal post than the premiership – as the clash with Largo indicates.

[216] From *Cómo y por qué salí del ministerio de defensa nacional. Intrigas de los rusos en España* (Paris, 1939) to the anthology *Convulsiones de España* (3 vols., Mexico City, 1967–9) passing through a torrent of similarly directed spoken and printed words in the intervening years (until Prieto's death in 1962). Some were republished inside Francoist Spain in 'explanatory' editions courtesy of the regime's policemen-ideologues: see *Yo y Moscú* (Madrid, 1955) (prologue, commentary and notes by Mauricio Carlavilla).

[217] Graham, *Socialism and War*, pp. 132–3 (see also n. 29 for Lamoneda's comments to the same effect).

[218] Ibid., p. 132; Vidarte, *Todos fuimos culpables*, vol. 2, pp. 620–1; Nenni, *La guerra de España*, pp. 48–9 (n. 16), in which he also cites a characteristically pithy encapsulation by Lamoneda of Largo Caballero's apparent *volte-face* on socialist-communist unification.

The new Negrín government emerged in mid May 1937 just as the rebel offensive against Vizcaya was reaching its height. The then six-week-old assault on the Republican Basque Country demonstrated the profound change in how the rebels were fighting the war. Franco, although still obsessed with taking Madrid, had been persuaded by his German advisers in the wake of the Guadalajara débâcle of the need to expand his armed forces through mass conscription. An expanded army, however, required equipping. Hence the campaign against the Republic in the industrial north acquired added urgency. The large army put together by Mola was backed by air support from the small but well-equipped Condor Legion and by Italian air units – both under German command but ultimately at Franco's orders. The air attacks began with Durango on 31 March and reached their crescendo on 26 April when the small town of Guernica, the symbolic seat of Basque nationalism, was annihilated by three hours of saturation bombing. (It had no anti-aircraft defences.) Franco's key strategic target in the attack was not a military one, however, but rather morale: Guernica was intended to kill the Basque appetite for resistance. And in an important sense it achieved this, along with the vast toll of human destruction.[219] Two days later, Mola publicly linked the fate of Guernica with that of Bilbao, declaring 'we shall raze Bilbao to the ground'.[220] Franco himself was more concerned to acquire its industrial capacity than to see it destroyed as a source of moral pollution, as Mola sought. Nevertheless, in other respects Franco was no less committed to the 'redemption' of the Basque region, as of everywhere else in the Republican zone, through violence and the mass physical elimination of his opponents.[221] Throughout April the rebels inflicted increasing artillery and aerial bombardment against which the defenders – virtually devoid of aircraft – could do little. The terror this produced increased political divisions within the ranks of Vizcaya's defenders, ensuring the gradual collapse of resistance.

In March, as the Catalan cabinet crisis had raged over the public-order question and the disarming of the worker patrols, the Basque president, Aguirre, had had his own smaller-scale show-down with the CNT in Bilbao. The ostensible issue was the ongoing dispute over production

[219] From a market-day population of some ten thousand people, the Basque government estimated the death toll at 1,645 with a further 889 injured.

[220] Bilbao was first bombed on 31 August 1936 and repeatedly in September, including with leaflets threatening a brutal bombing campaign and other reprisals if the Basques resisted: Tuñón de Lara, 'Algunos problemas historiográficos de la guerra civil en Euskadi', p. 134.

[221] Preston, *Franco*, pp. 240–2, 245.

of the CNT's press.[222] On 24 March, the CNT's print workshop was expropriated by the Basque government and the CNT's regional committee arrested temporarily as a security measure. Basque nationalist troops were also sent to surround garrisoned CNT troops, whom they had been told were about to rise against the government.[223] The build-up of tension in Catalonia had brought calls from some sectors of the PNV for the disarming of the CNT's battalions or their decanting into disciplinary brigades. The Basque Communist Party – to which the government had ceded the CNT's printing premises – seconded these calls. But Bilbao was not Barcelona and Aguirre was almost certainly more concerned to discipline a marginal and (as he saw it) troublesome political force in the knowledge of the coming rebel offensive. But CNT morale was damaged. It opted to produce its paper in Santander, where a more liberal censorship operated.[224] And for all it was a lesser political force in the north, CNT support was a necessary component of Basque military resistance.

Faced by a seriously worsening military situation in the wake of the bombing of Guernica, the Basque government formally declared the creation of an Army of Euskadi.[225] Then, as the Italians crossed the ría de Guernica and tensions escalated in Barcelona, Aguirre assumed its supreme command on 1 May. This was communicated to Largo Caballero on 5 May when the street war in Catalonia was already a fact. The horror with which some sectors of the PNV contemplated the unfolding of events in Catalonia – which they saw as confirming all their doubts about the Republic – further impelled the party's ongoing attempts to seek a separate mediated peace with the rebels. But these attempts proved fruitless – as would all subsequent ones.[226]

The emergence of the Negrín government on 17 May went some way towards stabilising the fears of Aguirre and the PNV. The new premier, for all he represented *mando único*, also symbolised the victory of Republican normality over the 'dangerous classes' of Barcelona. On the positive side too was the appointment of Prieto to a new unified defence ministry. This, as well as the appointment of Colonel Rojo, the architect of Madrid's defence, as the new chief of the general staff, overcame at least some of Aguirre's reservations about accepting military instructions

[222] Chiapuso, *El gobierno vasco y los anarquistas*, pp. 117, 130ff.
[223] Ibid., pp. 141–8.   [224] Ibid., p. 194.
[225] By decree published in the *Diario Oficial del País Vasco*, 26 April 1937.
[226] De Meer, *El Partido Nacional Vasco*, pp. 410–550.

from the centre. Prieto appointed General Mariano Gámir Ulibarri to command the newly formed 'Army Corps of the Basque region' (Cuerpo del Ejército del País Vascongado).[227] Although the avoidance of the word 'Euskadi' is to be noted, this measure nevertheless recognised that there was no such thing as an overarching 'Army of the North'. Henceforward Llano de la Encomienda would command the forces in Santander and Asturias, while Gámir – to whom Aguirre handed over command – oversaw those of Vizcaya. Relations were improving now that Vizcaya was the object of serious strategic attention from the Republican chief of staff. Gámir arrived to take up his command at the end of May. The conversion of the Basque battalions into Mixed Brigades got underway and Aguirre's former reluctance to accept political commissars was overcome. In spite of the Basque units' retention of their specific political identities, their performance improved.[228] But it was probably already too late. Moreover, there was an ongoing and increasingly anguished conflict over the lack of aircraft to defend Bilbao.

Although this dearth of air support provoked from the isolated, besieged Basques angry accusations of treason and would subsequently give rise to a bitter polemic over responsibility for the fall of Vizcaya between Largo, Prieto and Aguirre,[229] the fact was that the Republic did not have the requisite planes to defend the north against the rebels' plentiful German and Italian air support. (Indeed, the German aircraft in the north were the best ones deployed throughout the entire war.) The situation was compounded by a variety of other factors: inadequately functioning communication channels, some practical incompetence and competing needs (as well as rivalries) on the centre front. But the main problem remained the lack of both planes and pilots. While Largo had passed the responsibility on to his military command, Prieto made desperate personal attempts to find more air cover. But often the planes procured never made it to their destination. Non-Intervention meant that some were impounded in France while others crashed, turned back or went off course because of bad weather or technical insufficiencies. Modifications were made to increase flight capacity in order to allow

---

[227] On Gámir, see appendix on army officers in Alpert, *El ejército republicano*, p. 371.

[228] This may have been attributable in significant part to the withdrawal of Aguirre from military command responsibilities: Thomas, *Spanish Civil War*, p. 687. Certainly the other components of the Vizcaya and northern Popular Fronts were unimpressed by Aguirre's abilities in this area.

[229] J. A. Aguirre, *Informe del Presidente Aguirre al gobierno de la República sobre los hechos que determinaron el derrumbamiento del frente del Norte* (Bilbao, 1978), especially, pp. 353–62 (for exchange of telegrams between Largo, Prieto and Irujo). The loss of the north was also grist to the mill of the internal battle in the PSOE: Graham, *Socialism and War*, pp. 134, 279 (n. 35).

direct flights from the central front to Vizcaya, thus avoiding the perils of the stop-over in French territory. But even so, it is unlikely that many arrived in the north.[230]

Under such conditions, Bilbao's defenders stood little chance. They had no means of inhibiting the technique of ground attack from the air being developed by Franco's Condor Legion strategists. During the second half of May, the rebels closed the siege ring around Bilbao. During the first days of June, Condor Legion planes and artillery bombarded the 'Iron Ring' – the double ring of trenches cut into the hills outside the city. Even apart from the fact that the structural plans had earlier been betrayed to the rebels, these fortifications were in any case inadequate. Uncamouflaged and lacking in depth, they had been built by engineers and architects with purely civilian experience. Moreover, the defenders were up against the most powerful guns ever deployed by the Germans in Spain. Anti-aircraft guns – superfluous in view of the Republic's lack of planes – were also deployed as light field artillery. The trenches were pulverised by tracer shells and the defence ring breached on 12 June.

With the memory of Durango and Guernica still fresh, the Basque government made a strategic decision, in consultation with the military command, to evacuate Bilbao and continue the fight from other fronts.[231] But this was also a key political decision driven by the PNV's desire to protect Basque capital and property. This was further demonstrated by Aguirre's absolute refusal to allow the implementation of a scorched-earth policy. Prieto's orders to destroy heavy industrial plant were ignored and *gudaris* posted to protect such installations (armaments and explosives factories, steel-making plants, shipyards and heavy engineering works) in case other groups, most notably the Basque CNT, tried to implement Prieto's instructions.[232] For a week Asturian, Santander

---

[230] The question of aircraft numbers in the defence of Vizcaya is a fraught one with complex and fragmentary sources that do not agree: Tuñón de Lara, 'Algunos problemas historiográficos de la guerra civil en Euskadi', pp. 141–3. While Howson does not provide a specific breakdown for the Basque campaign, his overall assessment/figures confirm the dearth: Howson, *Arms for Spain*, pp. 141–2, 209–10, 212–13, 234–5, 255–7, 302–3. (Cf. Tuñón de Lara's (unreferenced) estimate of a rebel air strength tenfold the Republic's and of one hundred planes sent from the central (Madrid) front of which only one-third arrived.) It must be borne in mind also that the Republic could not afford to uncover the central front.

[231] The rebels had feared a repeat of the siege of Madrid in Bilbao: Preston, *Franco*, p. 280.

[232] Zugazagoitia, *Guerra y vicisitudes de los españoles*, p. 312; Chiapuso, *El gobierno vasco y los anarquistas*, pp. 215–17; Ambou, *Los comunistas en la resistencia nacional republicana*, p. 147. (Plant was later destroyed in Santander, but Ambou remarks that much was not in Asturias – if for different reasons, Ambou, p. 236); Tuñón de Lara, 'Algunos problemas historiográficos de la guerra civil en Euskadi', p. 143 (the Basque police (*ertzainas*) also guarded churches, other religious buildings and prisons).

and Basque units retreated westward – and thence by boat to France, or directly to Santander and Gijón to carry on the fight. On 19 June the rebels entered Bilbao without opposition.

The loss of Vizcaya redoubled Negrín's determination to impose a uniform Republican order on the rest of the zone. First in the firing line was Aragon. Whereas Largo Caballero had implictly legitimised the Council of Aragon by engaging in a discussion of its sphere of influence and competences, the highly centralist Negrín simply ignored it, refusing to answer any requests for 'clarification of status'. Although the Council had agreed in June to abolish its public-order section (in order to demonstrate an acceptance of government authority here), it was accused by the Popular Front parties of not fulfilling this promise. The Negrín government's first real 'communication' with the Council was to send in troops in August to reinstate the machinery of municipal government.

The central government's target here was not rural collectivisation *per se*, but the dissolution of the Council's political authority and the destruction of the organisational sinews of CNT power in the region: 'the moral and material needs of the war imperiously demand the concentration of authority in the hands of the state'.[233] *Raison de guerre* was here reinforcing the government's underlying beliefs – that neither political power nor the deployment of significant economic resource should be in union hands and that privatised agriculture should be afforded a greater degree of material protection.[234] Hundreds of *cenetistas* were imprisoned.[235] In allowing the departure of reluctant collectivists, the dissolution did, however, constitute an important factor in the growing crisis of the collectives. But it is important to realise that, just as the Council's political crisis (sparked by the June public-order question) was partly internal,[236] so too was the anti-collectivist polemic. When the central government sent in the army, this activated and potentialised the Council's political and social opponents inside Aragon.

[233] Text of dissolution decree, cited in Fraser, *Blood of Spain*, p. 390. Fraser himself has made the point eloquently that much Aragonese collectivisation continued to function after the enforced dissolution of the Council: P. Broué, R. Fraser and P. Vilar, *Metodología histórica de la guerra y la revolución españolas* (Barcelona: Fontamara, 1982), p. 125.

[234] Cf. the CLUEA dispute in Valencia. The Negrín government clashed with the unions over a political principle as much as over their ability to deliver a centralised operation and the foreign exchange derived therefrom: Bosch Sánchez, *Ugetistas y libertarios*, pp. 382–3.

[235] Many of the Council's political office holders as well as those accused of crimes against private property were still in prison when Franco began his final offensive against Aragon in March 1938: Casanova, *De la calle al frente*, p. 233.

[236] Casanova, *Anarquismo y revolución*, pp. 258, 264–71.

Once government troops had been sent into Aragon, the destabilisa-
tion of CNT authority created local political opportunities for others.[237]
After the harvest had safely been gathered in, the Left Republicans endorsed the Council's dissolution – in accordance with Azaña's great
wish – when the Aragonese Popular Front met in Barbastro. Having
lost out to the PCE where Aragonese peasant smallholders were concerned,[238] Left Republicans now competed to acquire the CNT's clientele in the contest for political influence within the region's new municipal
structures. For its part, the PCE was able to maintain a political influence
via both the army and the post-Council influx of Ministry of Agriculture
personnel to register the collectives and assess the status and needs of
production in the region.[239] In the latter respect, this process mirrored
what had occurred earlier and on a bigger scale in the Valencia region
as small farmers and more affluent constituencies had from autumn
1936 looked to reconstructing state agencies like the Institute of Agrarian Reform (as well as to the PCE's Provincial Peasant Federation (FPC))
as a means of mobilising against what they perceived as the threat of
collectivised economic forms.[240] But whatever the specific colour of the
politics, in Republican eastern Aragon, unlike more developed Valencia,
it was the war itself that had produced the beginnings of mass politics
proper.

The real nature of the Council's social base remains difficult to ascertain since arms were used to build it and also to dismantle it – and in
both cases those arms came from outside Aragon. The net effect of the
Council's economic intervention had been redistributive. But both its
quasi-governmental functions and the element of implicit if not explicit
duress involved in some of the collectivisation process made the Council controversial both within the CNT and beyond. In the last analysis,
it was born in, and of, an emergency, and operated in such difficult

---

[237] On post-Council politics, see ibid., pp. 264–97; Fraser, *Blood of Spain*, pp. 390–4.

[238] Casanova, *Anarquismo y revolución*, p. 221.

[239] The Agriculture Ministry's Institute of Agrarian Reform (IRA) required registration as a condition of legalisation. But this process would be obstructed by the activation of the military front
in late 1937 and ended by the rebels' final offensive in Aragon in March 1938.

[240] In Valencia it was the consolidation of government power which activated the regional conflict over collectivisation: Bosch Sánchez, *Ugetistas y libertarios*, pp. 39–49. The promulgation of
normalising legislation from August 1936 onwards – and especially the decree of 7 October so
favourable to smallholders and tenant farmers – provided anti-collectivist social constituencies
with ammunition. Many of the peasants recruited by the PCE's Provincial Peasant Federation
(FPC) had before the war been attached to Catholic unions linked to the Valencian Regional
Right (DRV) – a component of the mass Catholic party CEDA. By the end of 1936 there were
explosive social and political conflicts between 'individualists' and 'collectivists' in villages across
the Valencia region: Bosch Sanchez, *Ugetistas y libertarios*, p. 122.

conditions and was so short-lived that it is virtually impossible properly to measure it against the revolutionary schemas it enshrined.[241] What is clear, however, is that the Republican government used the evidence of local conflicts in Aragon – both of a class nature and otherwise – to justify its own intervention.[242] Thus, in the name of the war effort, republicans, parliamentary socialists and communists together brought the last independent stronghold of regional particularism in Republican Spain under the control of the central state.

But there was also another crucial factor which explains the precise timing of the Aragonese action: the need to activate the eastern front in an attempt to relieve the pressure of all-out rebel offensive against beleaguered Asturias – now all that remained of the Republican north. Since the start of the war, the rebels had kept only a bare minimum of troops on the Aragon front. As a result, the Republicans concentrated on simply maintaining their own lines. (This, aside from any political agenda, was the key to the poverty of arms among the militia. The Republic simply could not afford to divert scarce weaponry to a super-fluous front – and for the first year of the war, that status was defined by the content of *rebel* war policy.) But if the Republic now took the offensive and attacked in the east, then Franco would be forced to divert resources from the north. This, however, required the prior full military integration of CNT and POUM militia forces. But these forces had only begun to accept the authority of the Valencia war ministry in March 1937 and had a distinctly over-optimistic sense of their military capacity precisely because it had never been tested. The move into Aragon in August 1937 was thus a means of belting and bracing the militarisation of the front.[243]

A scarcely less important objective was to increase agricultural production in Aragon. With central political control in place, it was hoped that this could also be used to mitigate the acute problem of feeding the populous Republican cities – and, above all, Barcelona with its huge refugee population, now being further increased by the influx from Asturias. Implicit here was the assumption that collectivisation had diminished productivity by its inefficiency and demoralisation of smallholding constituencies. In fact, the balance sheet for collectivised wartime production

---

[241] Casanova, *Anarquismo y revolución*, pp. 319–20.   [242] Ibid., pp. 258–60.

[243] Alpert, *El ejército republicano*, pp. 82–3. The militarisation of all Catalan-originated militia in eastern Aragon was completed by the end of April 1937 – except for the POUM's 29th division, which was reorganised as a result of the political action against the POUM in summer 1937: Casanova, *Anarquismo y revolución*, p. 114.

in Aragon was far from obviously negative in 1936–7.[244] But eastern Aragon had never contained territory of sufficient yield for it to serve as an adequate emergency granary for urban Republican Spain – irrespective of the mode of production therein employed.[245] Moreover, as the war came to the eastern front, so the conditions of production deteriorated along with the supply of manpower and availability of transport. In the end, it was the war – causing economic dislocation and the shrinkage of markets – rather than political opponents or state action which was the greatest single eroder of collectivised agriculture as it was of the privatised variety. In Aragon, as elsewhere, war under conditions of Non-Interventionist embargo would erode the material fabric and the psychological resilience of collectives and collectivists as it would all other facets of the Republican home front.

[244] See Ministry of Agriculture figures for comparative regional productions in 1936 and 1937, reproduced in Thomas, *Spanish Civil War*, p. 559; Bosch Sánchez, *Ugetistas y libertarios*, pp. 378–9. Production in 1936–7 went down in both Catalonia and Valencia – where private peasant agriculture was more widespread.

[245] In the pre-war period, the three provinces of Aragon had in any case only provided 7.6 per cent of Spain's total cereal crop. Over half of that 7.6 per cent had come from Zaragoza province – of which the most productive sector was in rebel hands: Fraser, *Blood of Spain*, p. 348.

CHAPTER 6

Negrín's war on three fronts

A long time, even for heroes... [1]

When Negrín took over as prime minister in May 1937 his primary objective was to procure the lifting of Non-Intervention as the greatest obstacle to the Republic's active prosecution of the war. Within a month, the loss of industrial Vizcaya had increased his urgency. Negrín was the ideal candidate to carry the Republican war effort onto this crucial third 'front' in Europe's diplomatic arena – while also simultaneously maintaining the military front and the home-front mobilisation that underwrote it. But the start of his premiership coincided with the end of Blum's in France and Baldwin's in Britain. Neither development favoured the Republic. But, as always, it was Britain's position on Non-Intervention that held the key to its predicament.

The majority opinion in the British cabinet was certainly one of passive pro-Francoism.[2] But the crux of the problem for the Republic was the strategic role played by Non-Intervention within Britain's *overall* foreign policy. From the end of May 1937, under new prime minister Neville Chamberlain, the cabinet was steering hard for rapprochement with Italy. Britain's pivotal foreign policy goal remained the defence of its extensive imperial interests, and a *modus vivendi* with Italy in the Mediterranean was judged the best means of securing it. To this end,

---

[1] Milton Wolff, *Another Hill* (Urbana/Chicago: University of Illinois Press, 1994), p. 119.

[2] E. Moradiellos, 'The Gentle General: The Official British Perception of General Franco during the Spanish Civil War', in Preston and Mackenzie, *The Republic Besieged*, pp. 1–19. When Madrid had been besieged in autumn 1936 there had been a favourable swell of opinion in the British cabinet for granting the rebels belligerent rights. The foreign secretary, Anthony Eden, had overcome this only with difficulty. By the time of the blockade of Bilbao in late March and early April 1937, however, Eden had less difficulty in containing the staunchly pro-rebel First Lord of the Admiralty, Samuel Hoare, when he called for foodstuffs en route to the Basques to be formally classified as war material (although, in fact, the rebels were treating food as such anyway and blockading the port as if they had been granted belligerent rights.) Eden himself wanted the Royal Navy to escort British merchant ships through to Bilbao: Alpert, *A New International History of the Spanish Civil War*, p. 122.

Non-Intervention offered a useful diplomatic framework in which to stabilise relations with Italy while attempting the sought-after alliance. The
massive increase in Axis aid to Franco after March 1937 would cause
some anxiety. But British policy makers remained confident that the
power of sterling and, failing that, of the Royal Navy to blockade would
ensure a 'friendly' rebel Spain even in the worst-case scenario. Given this
reasoning, then, for the majority of the British cabinet the machinery of
Non-Intervention was a valuable resource – irrespective of Italy's persistent flouting of it. When Italian action was seen as directly damaging
British interests, such as in the sinking of merchant shipping by Italian
submarines in 1937, steps would be taken to resolve matters *beyond* the
framework of Non-Intervention.[3] Britain's persistent diplomatic utilitar-
ianism where Non-Intervention was concerned would, thus, prevent the
consolidation of the Republic's defence possibilities in 1937.

From early on in the war both the Italians and Germans had continually attacked shipping bound for Republican ports, even though they had
no authority so to do.[4] As most aid came by sea, by 1937 these attacks
were, from the start, a major threat to the Republic's ability to sustain
a military defence. Once the *Komsomol* was lost on 14 December 1936,
the Soviet Union – whose merchant marine was small and whose vessels
were dispersed across far-flung seas (the Caspian, Aral, Arctic/White,
Baltic and Black Seas and the Pacific Ocean) – required the Republic to find other sources of transport for war *matériel* it procured on the
Spaniards' behalf.[5] The Republic had begun the war with around three-
quarters of the Spanish merchant fleet.[6] But it suffered heavy losses,
which meant that it could not compensate for the lack of Soviet or other

[3] The Nyon Conference of September 1937 was convened to discuss the problem of 'unknown'
submarines interfering with British and other shipping. Italy was invited to join even though it
was an open secret that the submarines in question were Italian: Alpert, *A New International History
of the Spanish Civil War*, pp. 142–3. After Nyon, the attacks on British shipping more or less stopped.
[4] Only belligerent rights permitted the intercepting of merchant shipping on the high seas.
[5] Howson, *Arms for Spain*, pp. 130–4 (the *Komsomol* was unlikely itself to have been carrying arms);
D. T. Cattell, *Communism and the Spanish Civil War*, p. 77. Howson gives comparative details on
size and fleet tonnage, pp. 133–4. Recourse to an atlas also reminds one of how the immensity of
Russia made inordinately complex the task of fleet coordination across all the separate seas.
[6] The Republic nationalised those merchant ships in its ports at the start of the war. But vessels
at sea were often permanently lost to it, as were those docked in Germany, Italy and the USA,
where the rebels and their supporters mounted legal challenges over ownership. There is a lack
of clarity still over the size of the Spanish merchant marine. See F. and S. Moreno de Alborán
y de Reyna, *La guerra silenciosa y silenciada. Historia de la campaña naval durante la guerra de 1936–39*
(4 vols., Madrid: Gráficas Lormo, 1998) and R. González Echegaray, *La marina mercante y el tráfico
marítimo en la guerra civil* (Madrid: San Martín, 1977). It was in the region of 880 vessels, of which
the Republic had 660 and the rebels 220. I am grateful to Gerald Howson for his help with the
technical and quantitative material relating to naval strength.

vessels. Enemy action and – to a lesser extent – difficulties relating to inexperienced crew and the lack of a proper command structure eroded Republican shipping. By contrast, the rebels managed to preserve most of their smaller share of merchant vessels. But, more importantly, the German government sent ships for their use which sailed under flags of convenience (in particular the Panamanian) and were thus beyond the reach of the (in any case very short-lived) Non-Intervention naval patrols of Spanish coasts between April and June 1937. The Republic had neither the resources nor the contacts to do likewise – at least not on anything like the same scale. In addition, vessels bringing war *matériel* to the rebels from Italy were openly escorted by naval warships.

By the late summer of 1937 rebel and Axis naval aggression had virtually sealed off the Mediterranean as a supply route for the Republic. Access via the French frontier thus became vital to its survival. The Radical-led government in France that had replaced Blum's in June was continuing to operate a policy of 'relaxed Non-Intervention' ('Non-Intervention relâchée').[7] Nevertheless, this border policy was erratic. And even when the aid did pass, it constituted 'the discreet smuggling . . . of small quantities of war material and of civil aircraft in ones and twos' – which was very far from offering a basis to turn the war around.[8] For as long as Non-Intervention existed, the Republic was, in reality, condemned to a hand-to-mouth existence.

But in spite of the enormous, gathering question mark over the feasibility of maintaining – still less augmenting – war *matériel*, Negrín realised from the start that the political-diplomatic climate made it imperative for the Republic to move onto the offensive. It needed a clear military victory to demonstrate that it could hold its own (if not more) and that Franco was not heading inexorably for victory. Unlike President Azaña, who from spring 1937 was convinced that the most that could be achieved was a negotiated end to the war via international mediation, Negrín would throughout 1937 act upon his belief that the Republican war effort was a going concern.[9] If Non-Intervention could be ended and foreign volunteers withdrawn, then it might even be possible for the

---

[7] Blum remained as vice-premier (until January 1938), as did Cot in the air ministry.

[8] Howson, *Arms for Spain*, p. 233.

[9] For the differences of emphasis between Azaña and Negrín in 1937, see R. Miralles, 'Paz humanitaria y mediación internacional: Azaña en la guerra', in A. Alted *et al.* (eds.), *Manuel Azaña: pensamiento y acción* (Madrid: Alianza, 1996), pp. 263–8 and R. Miralles 'Juan Negrín: al frente de la política exterior de la República (1937–1939)', *Historia Contemporánea*, 15 (1996). These differences would begin to have serious political consequences from the military crisis of spring 1938 when the Republican zone was split into two – see below in this chapter.

Republic to win. But Negrín understood too that any negotiated settlement would also demand a resilient Republican war machine: because only from a position of strength could he force the rebels and their backers to accept something other than unconditional surrender. Partly with this in mind the Republic mounted the Brunete offensive in July on the western Madrid front. Probably the bloodiest single battle of the war,[10] fought in the extreme heat (with temperatures of over 100 degrees in the shade), this bid to raise the siege of the capital was doomed to failure by the Republic's lack of offensive capacity – to which hold-ups of material at the French frontier at a crucial moment contributed.

Even when aid did arrive in Republican Spain, the fundamental point to grasp is that its very intermittence as well as its variable quantity and quality (often unascertainable in advance, frequently different from the specifications and always so motley as to be the despair of the command[11]) made it virtually impossible for the Republic to plan very far ahead ahead or to sustain such actions as it undertook. The year 1937 did see some improvement in terms of the stabilisation of military fronts and the building up of an indigenous arms industry in Catalonia. But domestic arms production came nowhere near to meeting the needs of the army.[12] For as long as Non-Interventionist embargo existed, there could therefore be no *overall* Republican stabilisation.[13] Indeed, not even the lifting of Non-Intervention would have put the Republic on an equal footing with the rebels. Neither Britain nor France nor the Soviet Union – re-armers all – would have offered the kind of integrated state-backed military aid such as the rebels continued to be assured of from the Axis, and especially Italy. But ending Non-Intervention would, nevertheless, have given the Republic access to sufficient sources of arms properly to fight an offensive war.[14]

During the summer and autumn of 1937 the full weight of the Republic's diplomatic offensive to reverse Non-Intervention was focused

[10] In terms of the *proportion* of casualties to overall participants, on both sides.

[11] Howson, *Arms for Spain*, pp. 250–1, note **.

[12] Once the improvised Catalan war industry was up and running (by autumn 1936), it produced 6 million cartridges per month until the end of the war in Catalonia. But Mussolini could authorise dispatch of 10 million in a single month and, overall, provided 319 million for the rebels: P. Preston, 'Italy and Spain in Civil War and World War', in S. Balfour and P. Preston (eds.), *Spain and the Great Powers* (London: Routledge, 1999), p. 173. Catalan industry (which by spring 1937 was effectively *the only* Republican war industry) could muster little over half of this number. Borja de Riquer, unpublished paper on the Catalan war effort, Escuela de Verano, San Lorenzo del Escorial (Madrid), August 2000. See also J. M. Bricall, *Política econòmica*, pp. 56–72.

[13] Cf. Cattell, *Communism and the Spanish Civil War*, pp. 76–7.

[14] A. Viñas, 'Las relaciones hispano-francesas, el gobierno Daladier y la crisis de Munich', in *Españoles y franceses en la primera mitad del siglo XX* (Madrid: CEH-CSIC, 1986), p. 179.

on France.[15] Anxieties in the French government and diplomatic corps over defence vulnerability were increasing in direct proportion to escalating Axis aid to the rebels and Italian influence in the Mediterranean. At the same time, Britain's unilateral policy of rapprochement to Mussolini made France feel doubly isolated. As a protest, in July the French cabinet suspended the service of international observers on its land frontier with Spain and exerted diplomatic pressure on Britain to end Non-Intervention. A diplomatic window of opportunity for the Spanish Republic seemed to be opening. French pressure on Britain led to a proposal to Italy for the withdrawal of all foreign volunteers from both rebel and Republican zones in return for recognition of limited belligerent rights.[16]

The Soviet Union was also inclined to consider such an exchange. The outbreak of the Sino-Japanese War in early July, and its rapid escalation, was the first of several developments which, by 1938, would displace Spain from its privileged position in Soviet foreign policy.[17] Already by mid 1937 Stalin may well have been coming to believe that impossible odds were being stacked against a Republican victory.[18] But its continued *resistance* remained, nevertheless, a significant component in his strategy. Axis energies were, for the time being, tied down in Spain, and Nazi Germany thus deterred from any attack in the east. Moreover, even Non-Intervention itself – which the Soviet Union had consistently opposed once it became clear that it was not an efficient means of curbing aid to

[15] This initiative was carried forward by Negrín himself, his foreign minister Giral and also by the Republican ambassador to Britain, Pablo de Azcárate, who transferred his attention from London to Paris: E. Moradiellos, 'Una misión casi imposible: la embajada de Pablo de Azcárate en Londres durante la Guerra Civil (1936–1939)', *Historia Contemporánea*, 15 (1996), 135ff.

[16] E. Moradiellos, *La perfidia de Albión. El gobierno británico y la guerra civil española* (Madrid: Siglo XXI, 1996), p. 184.

[17] Although this had always been a *relative* privileging – given the primacy of domestic policy for the Soviet leadership up to 1939: Roberts, 'Soviet Foreign Policy and the Spanish Civil War', in Leitz and Dunthorn (eds.), *Spain in an International Context (1936–1959)* p. 91. Soviet foreign policy seems to have been made informally rather than in cabinet or politburo meetings. The Soviet bodies involved in Spain (defence, foreign affairs and Comintern) did not liaise with each other but were all individually subject to general political guidance by 'a group of functionaries around Stalin who came together in Moscow from time to time to discuss foreign policy issues'. This policy-making group included Molotov, Ezhov, Voroshilov, Litvinov and Dimitrov: Schauff, 'Hitler and Stalin in the Spanish Civil War', p. 18.

[18] Although this was not a clear position, cf. the questions being asked in an internal Comintern policy document dated 9 September 1937: '[h]ow can we achieve the break-up of the bloc currently standing against Republican Spain, and how can we achieve a change in the policies of the democratic countries? Which kind of concessions can we make to England and France . . . concessions compatible with the existence of the Spanish Republic, in order to change their behaviour? We do not have any clear thought in this matter', Schauff, 'Hitler and Stalin in the Spanish Civil War', pp. 13, 14.

the rebels – had its diplomatic uses. By maintaining a tension in British relations with the Axis (nothwithstanding Chamberlain's bid for Italian rapprochement) it impeded any putative four-power concert against the USSR – the possibility of which Stalin continued to fear.[19] But irrespective of Spanish Republican resistance, the Soviet Union could rule out neither four-power concert nor German aggression definitively. Provision for such an eventuality had to be made. So while Negrín continued to gear his diplomacy to protecting the Soviet lifeline, what Stalin probably had in his sights was ensuring the Republic's sufficient resistance capacity while at the same time reducing the call it made upon war material that was *domestically produced* in Soviet factories. Production levels in heavy industry for the period 1937–9 would be badly affected by the purges and by industrial reorganisation (a proportion, but not all, of which resulted from the purges). In some cases heavy industrial production in the Soviet Union did not reach 50 percent of the projected targets.[20] In an attempt to reduce Republican demand, by October 1937 Stalin was prepared to accept the British proposal of conceding limited belligerent rights to the contenders in Spain in return for an agreement on the withdrawal of foreign troops (even though Soviet diplomats thought it madness that Britain was prepared to concede such rights to Franco, given the potential

---

[19] Hence the Soviet Union's hostile reaction at the end of May 1937 to Prieto's wild-card suggestion that, in response to the German shelling of Almería (a virtually undefended port) the Republic should declare war on the aggressor in order either to force German withdrawal or to provoke a European war: Alpert, *A New International History of the Spanish Civil War*, p. 141; Bolloten, *SCW*, pp. 574–5.

[20] Ex-NKVD chief Orlov apparently claimed that a reconfiguration of Soviet policy was in any case made explicit to relevant Soviet personnel as early as summer 1937: Payne, *The Spanish Revolution*, p. 274; D. T. Cattell, *Soviet Diplomacy and the Spanish Civil War* (Berkeley, Calif.: University of California Press, 1957), p.115. (We still have no direct documentary evidence from NKVD sources.) E. H. Carr suggests a rather less abrupt or explicit shift, *The Comintern and the Spanish Civil War* (London: Macmillan, 1984), p. 51 (n. 22). Certainly the information we have on Soviet arms indicates the latter (Howson, *Arms for Spain*, appendix 3, pp. 278–303). Frank Schauff suggests that, in terms of overall domestic production, the proportion of Soviet war material directed to Spain between 1937 and 1939 was high – especially for planes (in the light of Howson's figures). Soviet propaganda itself obviously played a major role in shaping the Republicans' belief that the Soviet Union was stronger than it was, but holding back. As the logic of this analysis indicates, there is absolutely no sense in Burnett Bolloten's wild suppositions that the Soviet Union was exporting industrial goods and plant machinery from Republican Spain (see Bolloten, *SCW*, p. 581, n. 32 and endnote text p. 905). In extrapolating backwards from an eastern European scenario post 1945, Bolloten is leaving out of account Soviet policy priorities up to 1939. But even if these had not existed and Republican Spain had been producing something sufficiently industrially advanced to be of interest (which it was not), there were neither ships to carry it nor a viable route to take. The Soviet Union's imports from Spain were not great and, in the main, consisted of citrus fruit. But, again, once the Mediterranean became impassable (in August 1937) even this was highly problematic. 'Even in the sphere of foodstuffs the Soviet Union had to supply the Spanish Republic', Schauff, 'Hitler and Stalin in the Spanish Civil War', pp. 14, 16.

impact on its merchant shipping). The granting of belligerent rights would not have resolved the Republic's arms procurement problem, as the British plans proposed the maintenance of Non-Intervention controls. But it would, crucially, have allowed the Republic properly to defend its war *matériel* en route to Spain. Less wastage through sinkings and impoundings would clearly have been in Stalin's interests, and there were sufficient Republican warships to serve as escorts in Mediterranean waters.[21]

But the volunteer withdrawal proposals were stalled endlessly. Neither Mussolini nor Hitler was prepared to decrease assistance to the rebels. Indeed, quite the opposite: what had underlain their withdrawal from the Naval Patrol in June 1937 was the realisation that there could be no certainty of a rebel victory unless they injected *more* aid. The withdrawal of foreign combatants from Spain would have seriously damaged Franco's fighting capacity, but the Republic's hardly at all by mid 1937. As it was, however, Britain accepted the Italian insistence that the proposals for troop withdrawal should be discussed in the Non-Intervention committee rather than by the League of Nations. This was the equivalent of guaranteeing a massive delay. The Soviet Union had thus to maintain a certain level of aid. France, on the other hand, confounded by Britain's acquiescence, continued to resist pressure to close its border.

It is unlikely, however, that the League of Nations route would have yielded more. (Indeed, Azaña's apparent faith in the League's ability to oversee a viable troop withdrawal scheme sits oddly with his scepticism over Negrín's attempts to draw France away from British influence.) Negrín's resolution of 18 September 1937 to the League that foreign troops should be withdrawn from Spain, or else Non-Intervention lifted, was duly approved. But the weight of absentions, including from the key European players, ensured that it remained just a resolution. Negrín continued to work on the French as the weak link in Non-Intervention. But little was achieved. Border restrictions remained, and the noises over a French military expedition against Italian-held Majorca subsided along with French resolve.[22] Inevitably, Franco continued to procrastinate over the British plans for troop withdrawal. With the help of Germany and Italy, seemingly endless objections were raised. The debate would

---

[21] Franco's navy had more cruisers and submarines, the Republic's more destroyers: Gerö to Dimitrov, 19 Nov. 1938, Radosh, Habek and Sevostianov, *Spain, Betrayed. The Soviet Union in the Spanish Civil War*, p. 505 (doc. 80).

[22] Negrín's request for French officers to reinforce the Republican army remained as a French blind eye to the recruitment of reserve officers: Miralles, 'Juan Negrín al frente de la política exterior de la República', p. 151; Azaña, 'Cuaderno de la Pobleta' (27 September 1937), *Obras completas*, vol. 4, p. 806.

effectively be frozen until the spring of 1938. The measure of the Republic's diplomatic failure was that it could achieve neither movement on troop withdrawal nor the lifting of Non-Intervention.

Meanwhile, the fall of the remainder of the Republican north threatened. The Brunete offensive of July 1937 had been intended to take pressure off the north. But though it retarded the fall of Santander (as Franco had to divert troops[23]), it could not prevent collapse. Santander was taken by the rebels on 26 August, whereupon they opened their final northern offensive against Asturias. The Republic tried a further military diversion by activating the eastern (Aragon) front. But the underlying pattern of Brunete was repeated: a temporary success when the Republican forces took the towns of Quinto, and then Belchite on 6 September,[24] then a failure to maintain the momentum. The capture of the two towns entirely exhausted their resources. As usual the Republican forces were gravely handicapped by their lack of hardware, or at least appropriate hardware. It is also the case that the *knowledge of lack* of *matériel* had a psychologically inhibiting effect on the Republican command.[25] But there were also other sorts of troop and logistical insufficiencies in Aragon: on a front that had been inactive for months, intelligence as obvious as the location of enemy fortifications was still unavailable.[26] By 19 October Gijón had fallen, and with it what remained of Asturias was rapidly lost.

There were other factors too complicating the Republic's prosecution of the war. Not the least of these was the abiding tension between the civil and military authorities that stemmed back to the breach of trust caused by the military coup itself. The enduring suspicion of the professional military acted as an insidious and massively destructive pressure, coming as it did on top of the eternal battle against inadequate resources and undertrained personnel. This was one of the crucial ways in which the military rebellion would go on working, indelibly, against Republic long after its immediate organisational effects had been contained.[27] It

---

[23] Both rebel and Republican lines were always thinly manned outside the immediate battle areas – quite simply because the human resources available did not afford more.

[24] The towns were taken street by street and house by house and involved bitter hand-to-hand fighting which is described in Milton Wolff's autobiographical novel, *Another Hill*, pp. 69–86. The journalist Herbert Matthews described parapets of corpses and characterised Belchite after its capture as 'a fetid mass of wreckage', *Two Wars and More to Come* (New York: Carrick & Evans, 1938), pp. 301–10; see also de la Mora, *In Place of Splendor*, pp. 336–7.

[25] Rojo to Prieto, 28 September 1937, letter reproduced in J. I. Martínez Paricio (ed.), *Los papeles del general Rojo* (Madrid: Espasa Calpe, 1989) (documentary section is not paginated).

[26] Jackson, *The Spanish Republic and the Civil War*, p. 398.

[27] The trial of Asensio, Villalba and other officers for their responsibilities in the loss of Malaga (see chapter 3 above) also needs to be understood in this context. The case had been under

underpinned Negrín's opposition to declaring a full state of war in Republican territory. Prieto in the war ministry was coming to favour this by late 1937, and the chief of staff, General Rojo, deemed it essential.[28] But the prime minister stood firm. In spite of the organisational – and disciplinary – advantages that would have accrued in other respects, he would repeatedly refuse to declare a state of war until the very end, when the collapse of Catalonia was imminent.[29]

In the face of military reverses and increasing diplomatic isolation, it was vital to bolster mass political and economic mobilisation on the Republican home front in order to sustain the defensive effort at the core of Negrín's strategy. For this reason the PCE remained as crucial in 1937 to Negrín's domestic policy on the civilian front as it was to the organisation of the Republic's military defence. Not only did the party entirely endorse Negrín's drive for war centralisation, but it also offered a dynamic instrument through which to achieve the necessary psychological mobilisation of the population, as well as its engagement in war work. (This had also been the *raison d'être* of the liaison committees established with the PSOE in the spring.) The particular talent of the PCE lay in its practical application of multiple discourses of mobilisation. The effects of acutely uneven development meant that Republican society remained, inevitably, deeply fragmented during the war. The PCE's technique of adapting the register of the message to the cultural/educational level and expectations of its differing audiences[30] was thus far more effective on the ground than the PSOE's somewhat austere and demanding appeal to a civic socialism, and certainly more appropriate than Negrín's 'universal' language of constitutional liberalism, transferred, without much modification, from his interventions in European diplomatic fora.[31] The PCE was thus at the core of multiple forms of Popular Frontist political and cultural mobilisation during 1937 which criss-crossed urban and rural

---

investigation since February 1937. They were brought to trial in October, as the north was falling, and given prison sentences: Nadal, *Guerra civil en Málaga*, pp. 417–18. But the case was subsequently reconsidered and dismissed in July 1938. For the role of Negrín (who supported Asensio) see Zugazagoitia, *Guerra y vicisitudes*, pp. 453–4.

[28] Azaña, *Obras completas*, vol. 4, p. 785; *Los papeles del General Rojo*, pp. 91–2, 97–8.

[29] A state of war was declared on 23 January 1939. Negrín's earlier reluctance also stemmed from his evaluation of the military personnel available. To declare a state of war safely would have required a more plentiful supply of senior officers of Rojo's calibre. But he knew that they were relatively few. In September 1937 Negrín had lamented Miaja's lack of talent – alarmed at the prospect of his wielding such control in the Madrid area: Azaña, *Obras completas*, vol. 4, p. 767.

[30] Graham, *Socialism and War*, p. 119; Largo Caballero, *Mis recuerdos*, p. 227.

[31] The text of Negrín's wartime speeches is scattered in press and archive. A number feature in the accompanying documents volume of Alvarez, *Negrín, Personalidad histórica*, vol. 2. But it would be very useful to have an edited volume of Negrín's speeches.

worlds and different constituencies of Spaniard in terms of class, region, gender and age. In this sense, the PCE could, then, lay some claim to have constituted itself during the war as the most successful Republican party of all. For a time at least, it delivered, both within itself and the organisations of the wartime Popular Front, the counter-hegemonic, inter-class alliance that republicans and socialists had sought, but mainly not achieved, since the birth of the Republic in 1931. And for all that socialists and republicans criticised the PCE for its 'populism', this was a utilitarian populism vital to the Republic's survival in wartime.[32] The PCE could not, of course, solve the significant ideological and policy contradictions inherent in Popular Frontism in Spain. But it was precisely the PCE's discipline, deriving from its democratic centralist structure, which made it strong enough to bear them – without sustaining the organisational fragmentation that so debilitated the PSOE. This we could term the functionality of democratic centralism.

But democratic centralism did not obviate significant internal stresses in the PCE. The party's rapid growth and the influx of a lot of people without political experience took its toll on efficiency and coherence, as was noted by Comintern adviser Palmiro Togliatti, who arrived in Spain in July 1937.[33] Moreover, the fact that the PCE was incorporating disparate constituencies within itself meant that competing political and economic agendas tended to resurface inside both the party and Popular Front organisations – especially as the Republic's material conditions eroded during 1937 and into 1938. One example of this, which we shall consider later, was the increasing tension in the PSUC between Catalanists and centralisers. Another important area of wear and tear on the PCE related to Popular Frontist agrarian policy.

As we have seen, in areas like Catalonia, Aragon and Valencia, where considerable social resistance to collectivisation existed among smallholders and tenant farmers, the PCE (and the PSUC) had sought to channel that opinion.[34] From the agriculture ministry too the PCE's Vicente Uribe had promoted measures – from the decree of 7 October

---

[32] Casanova, *Anarquismo y revolución*, p. 221 cites Aragonese republicans complaining how the PCE's political line can't be sincere 'unless apostasy is the order of the day (consigna)'; for PSOE criticisms, see Graham, *Socialism and War*, p. 119.

[33] Carr, *The Comintern and the Spanish Civil War*, pp. 52–3; P. Togliatti, *Escritos sobre la guerra de España* (Barcelona: Crítica, 1980), p. 9 – introduction by P. Spriano. On Togliatti in Spain, see also his *Opere 1935–1944*, vol. 4 (Rome: Editori Riuniti, 1979) and A. Agosti, *Togliatti* (Turin: UTET, 1996), pp. 225–43.

[34] This also happened in a more low-key way in the Republican south – for example via the PCE's championing of co-operative forms over collectives: see L. Garrido González, *Colectividades agrarias en Andalucía: Jaén (1931–1939)* (Madrid: Siglo XXI, 1979), pp. 57ff.

1936 onwards – designed to protect such sectors in order to ensure their productivity for the war effort. This accorded with the respect for liberal individualism and property rights at the heart of the Popular Front. But for the PCE the essential goal by 1937 was maximising production – and no doubt, in Comintern minds, the Soviet Union's experience of civil war was influential here. In Republican Spain, however, that meant that collectivists as well as smallholders had to be kept on board the war effort.[35] (As we have seen, reining in Aragon had been more about defusing the power of the Council and activating the military front than it had been about hostility to collectivisation.) As a result, the agricultural ministry, via its Institute of Agrarian Reform (IRA), oversaw the codification of the collectives during 1937 – many of which were in the Republican south.[36] This was a means of extending state control, to be sure. But neither was it hostile to agrarian collectivisation *per se*.[37] That would not have been politic – especially given the context of pre-war collectivist culture and traditions in Castilla La Mancha and the rural south-east – where communists too were sometimes involved in these initiatives.[38] When the issue of private-property rights resurfaced in the course of the IRA's work, however, the Republic chose to postpone discussion of this as a principle. The collectivists were deemed to have usufruct. But the instances of former owners' suits being favourably adjudicated by the IRA in 1937 and 1938 created a sense of instability.[39]

It is well known that the tensions between collectivists and small farmers led to a number of violent clashes in Republican territory. But it is difficult to see how any policy option could have avoided this, given the degree of political and social fragmentation obtaining in the Republic. The PCE made certain choices both for party-political reasons and because of its understanding of war needs. But the conflicts it had to mediate as a result were already inherent in the post-coup political situation and social breakdown of forces.

As the war went on, however, the focus of conflict in the agrarian sphere would cease to be so specifically collectivism versus individualism.

---

[35] Ronald Fraser explains this dilemma well in *Blood of Spain*, p. 370.

[36] The figures suggesting a 25 per cent increase in the number of collectives between mid 1937 and late 1938 (even after the loss of Aragon) point to a furious process of registration: ibid., p. 393 (n. 1) and p. 373 (n. 1).

[37] R. Fraser summarises IRA aid to registered collectives: ibid., p. 373 (n. 1). See also Instituto de Reforma Agraria, *La Política del Frente Popular en agricultura* (Madrid/Valencia, 1937) and V. Uribe, *La política agraria del Partido Comunista*, speech given in Valencia 4 July 1937 (Barcelona, 1937).

[38] Garrido González, *Colectividades agrarias en Andalucía: Jaén (1931–1939)*; N. Rodrigo González, *Las colectividades agrarias en Castilla la Mancha* (Toledo, 1985).

[39] *Adelante*, 29 May 1937; Bolloten, *SCW*, p. 238.

By the second half of 1937, the extension of price controls brought rural producers of all sorts into conflict with government bodies. Then, as the conditions of production deteriorated further and the effects of the war began to bite in Catalonia (with an acute subsistence crisis in urban areas), tensions would erupt around the issue of military requisition from rural producers. Given that the PCE's overriding priority was the war, then, as it grew more difficult to provision the home front as well as the army, it was obliged to back state regulation not only for the collectives (in terms of wages and conditions) but also for individual farmers. By the end of 1937 the effects of prioritising war needs were beginning to be the major cause of peasant alienation and urban–rural tension.[40] And the collectives too – whether in Aragon or the Republican south – were in the end eroded as much by the deteriorating conditions of war as by any specifically anti-collectivist action on the part of PCE or government.

The very fact of the PCE's rapid political ascendancy had also instantly exacerbated the historic rivalry and longstanding organisational tensions with the PSOE/UGT. The evolution of this conflict would be further complicated by the internal division in the socialist movement, the ramifications of the PCE's links with the Comintern and the cumulatively erosive impact of the war. But it is crucial to appreciate that the breakdown in relations between the two movements sustaining the Republican polity at war came as a result of the *interaction* of these factors rather than as the consequence of a purportedly monolithic Stalinist-inspired sectarianism emanating from the PCE.

The alliance between the PCE and the parliamentary PSOE forged early in 1937 had been based on a common perception of the importance of the Popular Front and of the need for joint party action behind the war effort. As we have seen, the parliamentary socialists also intended it to facilitate the marginalisation of Largo Caballero and his supporters, whom they judged to be responsible for the damaging divisions in the movement since 1934 (and now, with the war, unaffordable). But the PCE was also increasingly embroiled in an organisational battle with Caballerista socialists over influence in the UGT.[41] This was a continuation of the pre-war 'battle' in which Largo and his veteran *ugetista* leadership were as determined to absorb the upstart young communist organisation (as they viewed it) as the PCE was to steal a march over Largo.[42] But the outbreak of the war had given the PCE certain advantages. This, in turn, intensified the party's ambitions – and in particular those of the Comintern

---

[40] For more on this see below in this chapter.   [41] Graham, *Socialism and War, passim.*
[42] See chapter 1 above.

delegate, Codovilla, who, in what became branded very much as his *own* initiative, pushed for the creation of a single proletarian party (the *partido único*). But, as we have also seen, this brought Codovilla up against Comintern instructions from Stalin not to force the issue and to be mindful of the plurality of the Popular Front in Spain. For the PCE to have behaved otherwise would have undermined Stalin's prime objective: to sustain Republican resistance. But after the military reverses of early 1937, and with immense pressure still on Madrid, Stalin had accepted the opinion emanating from the socialists and republicans in the cabinet that Largo was an obstacle to the implementation of appropriate war policy.

Once Largo Caballero had exited from government in May 1937, however, he began to construct the reasons for his departure entirely according to the old rationale he knew best: that of socialist–communist organisational rivalry. He had been ejected from government as the result of a communist conspiracy. The Caballeristas saw themselves confirmed in their suspicions by the increasing rapprochement of Prieto's socialists to the PCE and by Prieto's own 'wild card' suggestion, in the summer of 1937, that the primacy of war probably required the fusion of the PSOE and the PCE. Even though this was instantly vetoed by the PSOE executive, it fed the flames of the Caballeristas' own escalating propaganda war against the PCE. The tension was further increased on the ground by what the socialists saw as the arrogant proselytism and sectarianism of an expanding Communist Party. What was happening here was also the result of more than one factor, however.

Certainly the sectarianism inherent in the PCE's self-perception as the revolutionary vanguard party had been stimulated by its wartime successes. But it is rather too simple to explain the PCE's aggressive proselytising practice across 1937 exclusively in terms of ideology. Certainly there were those in the PCE (and the Comintern) who believed that the May days had pointed up the dangers of Popular Frontist pluralism and that it was time to revert to an earlier policy of a worker bloc led by a 'single party' of socialists and communists, inevitably under the political tutelage of the latter.[43] But these tensions were, as yet, submerged beneath disciplined adherence to the official line. At the same time, however, what wartime success had also meant to the PCE was a mass influx of new members, usually with low levels of political education. As we have seen, the circumstances of the civil war had made it important for people to join political parties and organisations for all sorts of practical

[43] Elorza and Bizcarrondo, *Queridos camaradas*, p. 451.

reasons – protection, advancement, sometimes even to ensure access to food. These new communists also contributed to shaping the wartime party by infusing communist sectarianism with old-fashioned clientelism and the politics of patronage.[44] By this I mean the politics that typified pre-Republican Spain. Clienteles served political parties in return for protection and favours. The coming of the Republic had initiated a process of change, with the PSOE symbolising a new ethos of public service. But the change was still in its infancy when the war erupted. Political culture and people's mentalities at local/village level were still, for the most part, framed by an older understanding of politics. The pervasive culture of clientelism influenced the left as much as the right. Many of the new recruits to the PCE saw the party in these terms and were deeply hostile to members of the PSOE as potential rivals for job preferments or other favours. But all political groups operating in the Republic were affected to some extent by clientelist assumptions. They fed internecine conflict and the left's continuing obsession with *tránsfugas*. Indeed, Largo Caballero's own input in the conflict with the PCE was in part constructed via his immense anger at finding that the old-guard UGT leadership had, for the first time ever, a serious rival for its members' allegiance within the socialist camp itself. Largo would rewrite the script of the May cabinet crisis in the light of what was, by late 1937, an increasingly bitter and rarefied battle with the PCE inside the UGT. He began to see himself as the great anti-communist warrior, defending the organisational integrity (and, not coincidentally, his own control) of the UGT.

Fortunately for the broader needs of the war, Prieto and the PSOE executive held firm to its policy of inter-party liaison with the PCE. But there were ominous signs as some local and provincial party sections, hostile to the new communists' thrusting ambition, challenged the authority of the PSOE executive and began to withdraw from the liaison committees.[45] As their own relations with local PCE organisations deteriorated, so Largo's increasingly public anti-communism began to chime with their own experience. His political demise, in retrospect, was acquiring a whole new, and powerful, meaning. Once again, Largo Caballero's influence would be based on a symbolism that hid a far more complex and contradictory reality. But this time, unlike in September 1936, his symbolic power would hinder, not help, the beleaguered Republic.

---

[44] Until we have a thoroughgoing social history of the PCE in the 1930s, this must remain a working hypothesis. But the circumstantial evidence, even thus far, is compelling. This facet of the PCE is an important, albeit implicit, theme in Graham, *Socialism and War*.

[45] Ibid., p. 80.

The containment of this potentially very damaging situation between the PSOE and the PCE was assisted by the fact that Stalin reined in Codovilla. In September 1937 he was recalled to Moscow and Togliatti took over his role as Comintern delegate, with Stepanov remaining as deputy and Gerö continuing in Barcelona.[46] Togliatti was keen to ensure good relations with the PSOE in order to strengthen the Popular Front and thus Republican resistance. He thus sought to stabilise the liaison committee initiative and contain the PCE's more zealous advocates of communist vanguardism and the 'single party' (such as Dolores Ibárruri).[47] For these tactical reasons, but also perhaps because of his own political understanding of Popular Frontism, Togliatti was critical too of the Comintern's idea that the PCE should press for new elections to be held in the Republican zone.[48] In fact, the proposal drew no real support and thus died on the drawing board in the autumn of 1937. Negrín replicated his response to the calls for a single party: he procrastinated amiably. The PSOE executive did likewise – although some criticism was expressed of the shortsightedness of the proposal in terms of the negative international diplomatic reaction it would provoke – crucially in Britain. Socialists and republicans also believed that the coup had made the renovation of the parliamentary assembly desirable. But they also knew that it would have to wait until the war was over. This was for practical reasons, but also because the legitimacy of the electoral results would depend on the balloting of the entire Spanish population. Even the PCE's own leaders saw that their identification with the electoral initiative would be counter-productive as it would isolate and thus weaken the party.[49]

But nor is it as clear as has been suggested that Stalin had taken up the idea of elections with the intention of promoting the political

---

[46] These changes followed Togliatti's September report, which was very critical of Codovilla's highly dictatorial style. On this see also Falcón, *Asalto a los cielos*, pp. 144, 150–1, 160. Togliatti's report is in *Escritos sobre la guerra de España*, pp. 143–50 and Carr, *The Comintern and the Spanish Civil War*, pp. 94–8.

[47] Togliatti wrote to Moscow in November about what he saw as the worrying extent of Codovilla's sectarian influence on Ibárruri: Togliatti, *Opere 1935–1944*, pp. 288, 291 (also in Togliatti, *Escritos sobre la guerra de España*, pp. 149, 164); Elorza and Bizcarrondo, *Queridos camaradas*, p. 417 and for a summary of Togliatti's goals and influence, Rees, 'The Highpoint of Comintern Influence? The Communist Party and the Civil War in Spain', in Rees and Thorpe (eds.), *International Communism and the Communist International 1919–43*, pp. 157–8. There are conflicting views of Togliatti's own leadership style. But he was certainly significantly less interventionist than Codovilla: Schauff, 'Failure in Emergency: The Spanish Civil War and the Dissolution of the Comintern', p. 28; Carrillo, *Memorias*, p. 263.

[48] Togliatti's report of 30 August 1937 cited in Elorza and Bizcarrondo, *Queridos camaradas*, p. 401. In full in Togliatti, *Escritos sobre la guerra de España*, pp. 126–42.

[49] Elorza and Bizcarrondo, *Queridos camaradas*, pp. 404–5.

career of the PCE – still less a fully fledged 'popular democracy' in Republican Spain.[50] There seems to be a strong element of post-1945 hindsight operating in such assessments and a concomitant tendency to downplay the contingencies of the time in shaping Soviet policy.[51] War needs remained the determining factor in Stalin's view of the Republic. The autumn and winter of 1937 saw the final loss of the north and hard fighting in Aragon which exposed the continuing weak points in the Republican army. And all the time the enemy was getting stronger. The Axis had made clear its determination to arm and supply the rebels unto total victory. The fact that it was at *this* point that Stalin thought of looking towards the consolidation of the PCE's organisational protagonism in the Republican polity – and, above all, towards maintaining its high profile in the army – strongly suggests that the goal was to throw the PCE into the breach to ensure that the Republic would be able to go on resisting.

Although party-political interests played a part, this imperative of re-sistance also underlay the PCE's confrontation with Prieto in the defence ministry over his desire to downsize the Political Commissariat in the au-tumn of 1937.[52] Prieto's October reforms were intent upon reducing both the numbers of commissars and their authority – especially at the lower levels of the army. In effect, Prieto was seeking to depoliticise the army and, as he saw it, to reinforce the hierarchy of command[53] (although in fact it was envisaged that commissars would go on existing at the higher levels – in brigades, divisions and armies). Prieto's measures were intended to have the same 'normalising' functions as those which, for ex-ample, prevented soldiers from participating in political demonstrations

[50] See, for example, ibid., pp. 384–405 (esp. p. 402).

[51] The very structure of Elorza and Bizcarrondo's *Queridos camaradas* encourages this since it sepa-rates the discussion of Comintern ideological influence/political objectives in Republican Spain from its discussion of the impact of the war (i.e. Republican resistance capacity) on Soviet/PCE policy – as if the former were somehow fixed and independent of the latter. But the balance of current research indicates precisely the 'complex, contradictory and uncertain' nature of Soviet policy in Spain. It was 'driven as much by circumstances as anything else', Roberts, 'Soviet Foreign Policy and the Spanish Civil War', p. 83. Note also that the Kremlin never sought to integrate the various Soviet bodies involved in Spain (defence, foreign affairs, Comintern) – which also suggests contingency over a monolithic agenda: Rees, 'The Highpoint of Communist Influence? The Communist Party and the Civil War in Spain', p. 160; Gazur, *Secret Assignment. The FBI's KGB General*, p. 334.

[52] A. Elorza and M. Bicarrondo (*Queridos camaradas*, p. 408) emphasise Prieto's anti-communism over his 'defeatism' as the main motive for Comintern opposition to him as minister in late 1937. But this would seem to introduce a false distinction. As the Comintern interpreted the situation by late 1937, the PCE's pro-active military presence was the only reliable guarantee of the Republic's continued resistance.

[53] Broué and Témime, *The Revolution and the Civil War in Spain*, p. 314; Alpert, *El ejército republicano*, pp. 184–9.

and increased army pay differentials (5 October 1937). It is also worth reinforcing the point that political affiliation of *any sort* was considered undesirable, not just communist affiliation. There is no doubt that many professional officers were keen to see such a normalisation. But in their enthusiasm to return to what they knew they tended to forget that the Republic was not fighting a war in 'normal' conditions. And it was precisely this fact that made the role of the commissar as crucial in 1937–8 as it had been, in a different way, in 1936.

In waging their own 'war' to look after the physical and psychological welfare of their men, the commissars were the Republic's best guarantee of morale and discipline in the face of the permanent, cumulative and highly erosive material inferiority and the structural handicaps under which it was forced to fight.[54] In fact the kind of political education commissars pursued was frequently low grade and very general – for example explaining the Republic's war of national independence to what were, by the second half of 1937, units of recruits rather than volunteers. From the start of the war it had been the PCE that had recognised the importance of the Commissariat, contributing its best men. But Prieto continued to be exclusively exercised by the party-political, including clientelist, aspects of the PCE's strong influence in the Commissariat. By 'uprooting' it and repeatedly challenging new PCE nominations, however, he can only have undermined the institution's efficiency. He clearly thought that a price worth paying in order to achieve a better party-political balance inside the Commissariat. And indeed this helped to damp down the tensions between PSOE, CNT and PCE *on the home front*. But whether it was a price worth paying in terms of the *army*'s cohesion and efficiency is more uncertain.

Nor can Prieto's campaign be seen purely in terms of his desire to professionalise Republican institutions. Negrín yielded to no one in prizing the independence of state authority.[55] But without a victory in the war he knew that there would be no Republican state. And, as Negrín himself recognised, PCE commissars, like PCE army commanders, were almost invariably good, and frequently the best the Republic possessed. Prieto was normally no less given to intelligent pragmatism than Negrín. Except, that is, in matters where he sensed his own political reputation

---

[54] De la Mora, *In Place of Spendor*, pp. 352–3.

[55] I omit entirely from the discussion here the vexed question of how Soviet military advisers related to the command structures in the Republican army. We simply do not as yet have the means of corroborating or disproving the claims about Soviet autonomy made in some of the memoir literature.

to be endangered. Prieto's 'war against the communists' in 1937–8 had a clear political meaning. However, it was not the meaning that he subsequently came to invest it with in his voluminous post-war writings. The seamless narrative of Prieto as the great anti-communist warrior opposing the Soviet Union's bid to satellitise the Republic through the PCE was a *post hoc* construction, increasingly determined by the exigencies of Republican exile politics in an environment of intensifying Cold War antagonisms.[56] (In the latter half of the 1940s the objective of exile Republican politics was to persuade the Allied powers to intervene against Franco. Prieto consciously played the anti-communist card as a means of constructing a viable political platform from which to attract western support for a Republican option to replace Franco. The role came naturally to Prieto because he could tap his quite genuine and intensely visceral dislike of the PCE and he doubtless ended by believing that there was an absolute continuity between his wartime sentiments and post-war discourse.) By contrast, Prieto's civil wartime anti-communism in some ways recalls that of his great rival and antagonist, Largo Caballero, in the UGT. Both were fuelled in part by bruised ego and personal political rancour, and both were politically myopic in that they undermined the Republic's ability to resist.[57]

In spite of the conflict over political commissars, the Popular Front was held together by the joint efforts of Togliatti on the one side and the PSOE executive on the other. In particular it fell to the PSOE's general secretary, Ramón Lamoneda, repeatedly to mitigate the damage done by the party's high-profile, 'historic' leaders.[58] Togliatti's task was facilitated by the abiding difficulties of communication between Moscow and Spain. The habitual delays had meant that, effectively from the start of the war, the communists in Spain were making their own decisions – even if these subsequently had to be defended in terms of the broad Comintern line.[59] This situation created a certain latitude for Togliatti to continue stressing the Popular Front as a pluralistic alliance to protect

---

[56] As Lamoneda shrewdly observed, Prieto's anti-communism was a strategy for exile: Lamoneda, 'El secreto del anticomunismo', unpublished notes (FPI) cited in Graham, *Socialism and War*, p. 144.

[57] It is interesting to contrast the tenor and content of Prieto's notorious 'anti-communist' speech of August 1938 to the PSOE National Committee (as well as the extremely negative reactions it evinced) with his later, far more grandiloquent anti-communist expositions which, in an entirely different political context, met with general approval in PSOE and republican circles. On this see Graham, *Socialism and War*, pp. 142–4.

[58] For Lamoneda, see ibid., pp. 157–8.

[59] Rees, 'The Highpoint of Communist Influence? The Communist Party and the Civil War in Spain', pp. 145, 148–9, 150–2.

and foment a new democratic politics in Spain.[60] His conception chimed in important ways with republican and socialist ideas about how the war would necessitate the reshaping of the Republican polity. For all components of the Republican alliance, this had to be reinvented as something apart from the discredited oligarchic order that had backed the military rebellion. The historically very weak central state was being restored as the central instrument of economic modernisation. But for this to work (and in the immediate term for the war to be fought), it had to be underpinned by an anti-hegemonic alliance reaching across social classes (such as republicans and socialists had been seeking since 1931). It was this vital Spanish inflection of the Popular Front strategy that gave it a specific utility and resonance in the civil war.

If the Republic's military situation had stabilised rather than deteriorated after late 1937, then the Popular Front might have evolved and been strengthened. Although this is a counterfactual hypothesis, it seems reasonable, and indeed important, to make the point – not least because seldom is it made clear the degree to which the military reverses and defeats of 1938 were themselves a major cause of the Spanish Popular Front's progressive erosion and eventual disintegration. Indeed, what was often perceived – and certainly reported in hindsight – as the increased political stridency of the PCE leadership in 1938 was at least in part generated by its desire to hold the line on resistance after the military situation began steeply to decline into the spring of 1938 and the rebel armies began their drive against Aragon. In many ways too this strategy had grown apart from the Comintern's to become grafted as a *domestic* PCE agenda driven by the party's own ambitions and interests. This would be evident in the party leadership's reluctance to accept Comintern instructions in February–March 1938 that the PCE ministers should leave the cabinet in the hope of improving the Republic's standing with the British and French establishments, thus facilitating Stalin's long-sought-after diplomatic front against Hitler.[61]

It fell to the PCE, as the party most single-mindedly engaged with maintaining the war effort, to back Negrín unconditionally in his

---

[60] Togliatti was a leading member of the Comintern rather than merely its functionary. His experience in Spain would shape his strategic and conceptual thinking around the key questions of anti-fascist resistance, revolution and 'democracy of a new type' which, in turn, would later inform the policies of other European communist parties and especially his own PCI.

[61] Elorza and Bizcarrondo analyse the interchanges between Comintern and PCE in *Queridos camaradas*, pp. 410–16. Stalin's strategy here reinforces the contingency of Soviet policy in Spain. It was always adapting to changing circumstances. There was no rigid ideological blueprint – in spite of what Elorza and Bizcarrondo finally seem to suggest on p. 420.

increasingly hard line on political centralisation to ensure the concentration of scarce economic resources in central government hands. The battle with the Council of Aragon had partly been over control of foreign exchange. In Valencia too, the Republican treasury's ongoing battle to centralise control of citrus exports led to increasing (and ultimately armed police) confrontations across 1937 with the unions' collection and export agency, CLUEA – a conflict which was closely bound up with that between pro- and anti-collectivist currents in the region.[62] In Catalonia, the drive for economic centralisation also crystallised tensions between the PCE and the PSUC as well as driving a wedge between centralisers and Catalanists inside the PSUC. Both conflicts would intensify in the course of the damaging confrontation looming between Negrín and the Generalitat.

The crisis of May 1937 in Barcelona had seen the Generalitat obliged to cede control of public order to the central government. From then on, relations between the two deteriorated apace. In many ways it was a 'dialogue of the deaf'. Each side imputed the worst kind of political manipulation to the other, thus blocking any real discussion of the perspectives and needs of each. The loss of public order, the touchstone of political autonomy, had understandably traumatised Companys and the Esquerra.[63] Catalan nationalists were also aggrieved at what they saw (justifiably) as a lack of recognition from Valencia of the achievements of the improvised Catalan war industries.[64] The central government, desperate for arms and munitions (in particular because of the loss of material through Italy's torpedoing of ships) was, understandably, always demanding more. Rather less justifiably, however, the centralist prejudices of the governing majority led it to conceive the 'solution' in terms that were practically simplistic and politically highly damaging. Apparently all that was required to achieve higher production was greater

---

[62] For the CLUEA dispute, see Bosch Sánchez, *Ugetistas y libertarios*, pp. 117–23, 336–40; W. Bernecker, *Colectividades y revolución social: el anarquismo en la guerra civil española 1936–1939* (Barcelona: Crítica, 1982), pp. 123–6; Abella, *La vida cotidiana durante la guerra civil*, p. 82.

[63] Companys criticised the order dissolving the Council of Aragon as a veiled attack on Catalan autonomy; Prieto expressed extremely harsh judgements of Companys ('Companys is mad as in "should be confined to an asylum" '), Tarradellas and Comorera: Azaña, *Obras completas*, vol. 4, p. 760 and p. 802 (La Pobleta entries for 31 Aug. and 20 Sept. 1937 respectively).

[64] An improvisation memorably evoked by the historian Enric Ucelay da Cal as 'una titánica chapuza'. The most famous example of this 'dialogue of the deaf' in regard to military production is in the famous exchange of letters between Prieto and Companys in December 1937. Prieto complains about what he still needs and hasn't received, while Companys paints a picture of the staggering amount that the Catalans have achieved in such inauspicious circumstances: *De Companys a Indalecio Prieto. Documentación sobre las industrias de guerra en Cataluña* (Buenos Aires, 1939). See also Azaña, *Apuntes de memoria*, p. 82.

political will – hence the necessity of sweeping out half-hearted Catalan managers from the factories and installing government agents (i.e. engineers and civil servants) in their stead. Negrín's case for nationalisation to increase war efficiency was strongly inflected by his Spanish nationalism.[65] But if the prime minister gave a determined lead here, he found firm backing as much from the PSOE as from the PCE. For the socialists were as centralist as President Azaña's Madrid-based republicans. While the Republican President too gave indirect expression to his bitterness towards Companys and the Generalitat,[66] it was Prieto who expressed himself violently in full cabinet meetings on the subject of Catalan 'selfishness'. A month after the central government's October 1937 move to Barcelona, with the express intention of exerting greater economic control over the region, the process of factory intervention began with piecemeal take-overs.[67] After some resistance from the Catalans, it would conclude nearly a year later in August 1938 when the government assumed direct control of the region's war industries in their entirety – thus provoking the cabinet crisis that would see the departure of both Catalan and Basque nationalist ministers.[68]

The huge influx of central government personnel and civil servants to Barcelona in the autumn of 1937 stretched the already meagre supply of food and space in the refugee-packed city to breaking point. It also led to spiralling political tensions. The Spanish-speaking incomers requisitioned buildings for work accommodation. At the same time, with an international public in mind, Negrín was projecting an image of the Republican war effort as a 'Second War of Independence'. (This was

---

[65] Azaña, _Obras completas_, vol. 4, p. 701 (La Pobleta, entry for 29 July 1937); p. 745 (entry for 23 Aug. 1937), p. 823 (entry for 14 October 1937); E. Líster, _Nuestra guerra_ (Paris: Colección Ebro, 1966), pp. 244–5. See also Besteiro's comments that the vision of (a unified) Spanish history in Negrín's speech of 18 June 1938 was so reactionary that it could have been given by a fascist or a Carlist. Besteiro to Pascua, 10 July 1938 AHN/MP _caja_ 2 (16).

[66] This is apparent in Azaña's fictionalised dialogue about the war, _La velada en Benicarló_. See also various diary entries, for example _Obras completas_, vol. 4, p. 699 (28 July 1937); pp. 707–8 (29 July 1937).

[67] These factories were placed under the control of the Catalan branch of the Ministry of Defence's subsecretariat of armaments (first created in June 1937), A. Monjo and C. Vega, 'La clase obrera durante la guerra civil: una historia silenciada', _Historia y fuente oral_, 3 (1990), 88, n 13. For the intervention and ensuing tensions, see also Bricall, _Política econòmica de la Generalitat_, pp. 291–3. In its public explanation of the move to Barcelona, the central government emphasised the need for a good dialogue in order to make autonomy work. But, between the lines, the message was clear in the reference to everyone putting the war effort first. Text of broadcast speech by interior minister J. Zugazagoitia, 28 Oct. 1937, in AHN/MP, _caja_ 6 (18).

[68] For a time the Generalitat refused to allow government representatives into the factories: Fraser, _Blood of Spain_, p. 227 (n. 1). By 1938 it would even seem that the government was transferring Catalan police and even firefighters out of the region: Fraser, _Blood of Spain_, p. 383 (n. 1).

after the 'First' of 1808–14, when sectors of the Spanish population (most mythically, the popular classes of Madrid) had offered armed resistance to the new Napoleonic order.) But precisely because 1808 had subsequently been constructed as the *españolista* myth of patriotic resistance *par excellence*, this made it difficult for Catalanists to assimilate.[69] The same sort of problem supervened in the PCE's propaganda production. For all its abstract Popular Frontist discourse on national rights, the party demonstrated its complete lack of understanding of the need to make a cultural 'translation' in Catalonia of the material it produced for the rest of Republican territory. This was – strategically speaking – rather shortsighted. After all, Catalonia was the one region of Spain where the inter-class alliance – at which Popular Front aimed – had already assumed a real form by the spring of 1936. But PCE myopia should scarcely surprise – given that the official Spanish Communist Party had never had any real presence in Catalonia prior to the civil war.[70] For the same reason, it was hard for the PCE's leaders to understand the complex skein of allegiances and rivalries on the Catalan left. It was another world entirely – which they sought in vain to fathom by deploying a Manichean schema in part derived from the two-dimensional ideological categories in vogue with the Comintern, thus further straining relations with the PSUC.[71] Inside the PSUC too there was a widening divide between Catalanist social democrats and communists as the former backed Companys' growing criticism of the Negrín government while the communist sector supported its centralisation measures.[72]

Companys' criticisms of the Negrín government in the Catalan parliament found a more strident echo in the Catalanist press. There was a call for an end to the publication of newspapers in Castilian as the 'language of the coloniser'. The editor was subject to judicial action.[73]

---

[69] None of these observations is intended to imply any particular assessment of how the Catalan experience of 1808–14 (i.e. in terms of collaboration and resistance) compares with other areas of Spain. Everywhere pro- and anti-French positions were complex and contradictory. In Catalonia, as elsewhere, there were various popular rebellions against the French, and the pressures of occupation rapidly eroded *afrancesado* (pro-French) support. The different reactions in 1937–8 had more to do with *post hoc* nationalist constructions of 1808–14 (both Spanish (*españolista*) and Catalanist). Nationalist historians in Catalonia also chose – logically – to concentrate on instances of specifically Catalan rebellion against the Spanish crown.

[70] See chapter 1 above.

[71] Ucelay da Cal, 'Socialistas y comunistas en Cataluña durante la guerra civil', p. 314.

[72] Togliatti, *Escritos sobre la guerra de España*, pp. 180–1, 247–8; E. Gerö to Dimitrov, 19 Nov. 1938, cited in Radosh, Habek and Sevostianov, *Spain Betrayed. The Soviet Union in the Spanish Civil War*, p. 511; Elorza and Bizcarrondo, *Queridos camaradas*, p. 427.

[73] Azaña, *Obras completas*, vol. 4, p. 701 – which also indicates harsh PSOE press criticism of wartime Catalanism.

But in some senses the central government had itself driven up the temperature by its own political heavy-handedness. In essence, a majority in the cabinet, starting with Negrín, felt that there was far less need to placate the Esquerra now that the CNT had been domesticated.[74] And this sense no doubt also underwrote Azaña's own support for new elections in Catalonia. But this hostility towards all Catalanist claims and objections was unwise. For quite apart from the CNT's status, the long-drawn-out jurisdictional dispute with the Generalitat sapped both government and regional resources and seriously eroded Catalan morale in the process. The Republic could afford none of these things.

Precisely because of these gathering problems, the middle of August had seen a prohibition on all political street demonstrations in Barcelona aimed at damping down the myriad political discontents and suppressing overt manifestations of war weariness and other forms of defeatism. But this inevitably meant increasing press censorship too. Catalan liberals, as well as libertarians,[75] criticised this as evidence of the erosion of 'political liberty' in the Republican zone under the Negrín government. Political sensibilities were understandably bruised by Negrín's high-handed centralism. Nevertheless, in many crucial respects Negrín was as genuinely a liberal by conviction as any of his critics in the Esquerra.

The prime minister was actively pursuing domestic policies designed to consolidate a liberal market-based economy and a parliamentary polity in Republican Spain.[76] In this 'normalising' vein I place initiatives such as that of the Caja de Reparaciones, set up by Negrín under treasury auspices.[77] This body was responsible for supervising the economic restitution of expropriated property.[78] Liaison between it and the Tribunal de Responsabilidades Civiles set up (in the Ministry of Justice) to investigate complicity with the military rebellion was, in theory, intended to increase the authority of the state by making it the arbiter of restitution. But in fact, the Tribunal, unlike the Caja, was never very active. Negrín was also concerned to limit dismissals of staff from state

---

[74] Jellinek, *The Civil War in Spain*, p. 571.

[75] Tavera and Ucelay da Cal, 'Grupos de afinidad, disciplina bélica y periodismo libertario', pp. 186–7.

[76] 'We are fighting for all Spaniards... The Republican government has no enemies except those who will not accept the rule of law', Negrín's broadcast speech, 22 Oct. 1937, reproduced in *Servicio Español de Información* (Valencia), 24 Oct. 1937, copy in AHN/MP *caja* 1 (15).

[77] Although Negrín's close collaborator, the left republican Francisco Méndez Aspe, would formally take over the treasury portfolio in April 1938, in fact Negrín himself continued to be the main architect of the Republic's economic policy until the end of the war.

[78] Del Rosal, *Justicia en guerra*, pp. 239–45. See also G. Sánchez Recio, *La República contra los rebeldes y los desafectos. La represión económica durante la guerra civil* (Alicante: Universidad de Alicante, 1991).

employment to those against whom actual instances of military rebellion, treason, espionage or flight of capital could be proved.[79] Late 1937 and early 1938 would also see the public return to the Loyalist zone of some eminent politicians from the centre-right of the Republic's pre-war spectrum – including the ex-ministers Miguel Maura and Manuel Portela Valladares.[80]

Negrín's appointment as prime minister had also seen an acceleration of the process of normalising the judicial process as the Popular Courts were incorporated into the established framework of 'ordinary' justice (the Audencias Provinciales).[81] While other modifications of the judicial process under Negrín would prove controversial, as we shall see, this measure nevertheless very probably helped diminish one set of problems connected with undue political influence of a clientelistic variety as well as outright corruption in some cases.[82] In terms of guaranteeing constitutional rights, Negrín supported his interior and justice ministers, respectively the PSOE's Julián Zugazagoitia and the Basque Nationalist Manuel de Irujo, in their attempts to consolidate the normalisation of the Republican police, judicial process, courts and prison system. In the latter, length of professional service rather than political affiliation became the criteria for the promotion of staff – especially senior ones. There also occurred an unpublicised release of priests who were in prison solely because they were priests.

By the summer of 1937 private Catholic worship was effectively permitted by the Republican authorities, although churches remained closed. This *de facto* tolerance preceded Negrín's appointment as prime minister. But until Negrín there was no active and sustained cabinet support for Basque Nationalist minister Irujo's bid to initiate a gradual process of religious normalisation.[83] From May 1937 until the fall of Catalonia in January–February 1939 Negrín never ceased to support and

---

[79] Cf. decree of 25 December 1938 (published in the *Gaceta de la República*). Part of this decree is cited in Ortiz Heras, *Violencia Política en la II República*, p. 73 (n. 13).

[80] Portela attended the Cortes meeting held at the end of September/beginning of October 1937: see Azaña's La Pobleta diary entry for 30 September 1937, *Obras completas*, vol. 4, pp. 811, 807.

[81] Sánchez Recio, *Justicia y guerra en España*, p. 96.

[82] R. Gullón, 'Justice et guerre civile: souvenir d'un procureur', in Serrano, *Madrid 1936–1939*; P. Nenni, *La guerra de España* (1958; Mexico: Ediciones Era, 1975), p. 53 (although Nenni erroneously implies that the Popular Courts were entirely replaced by the Special Tribunals against espionage, treason and defeatism (created 22 June). These were in fact additional. See below in this chapter for more on the range of new courts in 1937–8.

[83] For Irujo's January 1937 proposals, rejected by the cabinet as impracticable, see M. de Irujo, *Un vasco en el ministerio de Justicia, memorias* (3 vols., Buenos Aires: Editorial Vasca Ekin, 1976–9), vol. 1, pp. 125–7. For Irujo's statement of policy intent as part of the new Negrín cabinet in May 1937, see de Lizarra, *Los vascos y la República española*, pp. 173–87.

promote initiatives to this end. It made eminent sense in public-order terms since public worship could be monitored, unlike religious ceremonies in private homes, which could be used as a cover for subversive activities – or, at the very least, to hold collections for Socorro Blanco (White Aid) in support of rebel sympathisers. But, at heart, Negrín was motivated by conviction here rather than political expediency. The absence of religious liberty was a fundamental ethical and political flaw in a Republic whose legitimacy rested, so he believed, upon its constitutionality.[84] Liberal republican ideas were shaping the Republican economy and polity, but they had to be extended out into Republican society. Progress was slow – but not because Negrín lacked the political will. Rather extreme caution and discretion in how, when and where religious ceremonial should be reintroduced were the inevitable consequence of the maelstrom unleashed by the military coup and, as part of that, of the Spanish Catholic Church hierarchy's overwhelming support for, indeed legitimation of, the rebels. This had created a dense and fraught atmosphere in Republican territory which no amount of political will from the top could conjure overnight. If the reintroduction of religious freedoms was to be successful, then it had to be taken one step at a time. On this point at least the Catalans saw eye to eye with Negrín. Ironically, the Christian democrats of Unió Democràtica found it much easier to agree with the prime minister on matters of religious policy than with their fellow Catholics in the PNV.[85]

By mid 1938 things would begin to move. The Negrín government approved a series of communications between Cardinal Vidal i Barraquer (Bishop of Tarragona, resident in Rome), his emissary, Santiago Rial (Vicar General of Tarragona) and the Vatican in the hope of normalising the (never broken) diplomatic relations between the Republic and the Holy See[86] and, most importantly, of obtaining its support for the discreet re-establishment of public worship in Catalonia.[87] Although cautious, the Vatican was not unwilling. The opposition came rather from inside the Spanish – and Catalan – hierarchy. But the government

---

[84] Negrín had never been remotely anti-clerical. For his family background and political beliefs see H. Graham, 'War, Modernity and Reform: The Premiership of Juan Negrín 1937–9', in Preston and Mackenzie, *The Republic Besieged*, pp. 163–96 and H. Raguer, 'La política religiosa de Negrín (1937–1939)', unpublished article, pp. 7–8 and (same author) *La pólvora y el incienso*, pp. 325–30, 347, 354–8. See also chapter 3 above.
[85] H. Raguer, 'La política religiosa de Negrín', pp. 6, 7 and in letter to the author, 9 Aug. 1999.
[86] A useful summary is in Lannon, *Privilege, Persecution and Prophecy*, pp. 207–8.
[87] Raguer, 'La política religiosa de Negrín', pp. 2–5; *La pólvora y el incienso*, pp. 331–58.

pressed on. In October 1938 the burial of a Basque war hero took place in Barcelona with full public religious ceremonial and several Republican government ministers in formal attendance. This statement of the Republic's commitment to a pluralism which included public Catholicism was still not an easy one to make. But it was followed up almost immediately by the creation of a specific body charged with overseeing the implementation of public worship (the Comisariado de Cultos). It was headed by an old colleague of Negrín's, Jesus María Bellido i Golferichs, like the premier a professor of physiology. With the collaboration of Unió Democràtica, and the tacit support of the Vatican, this had very nearly achieved its aim in Tarragona province when the military collapse of Catalonia supervened.[88]

Negrín's domestic policies also played a notably important role in his conception of the third, diplomatic front. Projecting a decisive image of the Republic's liberal credentials was, he knew, an important weapon in the battle to convince Britain to modify its position on Non-Intervention. But, again, it would be wrong to interpret the prime minister's strategy here as 'opportunistic' as so many commentators have done. The policies Negrín attempted to pursue inside Republican Spain during 1937 and into 1938 – religious and otherwise – were of a piece with the political, economic and cultural options he had vehemently defended since 18 July 1936 and, in their fundamentals, those he had defended since he had first entered politics in the Republican Cortes of 1931. What would steadily consume his attempts to develop the liberal political practice of the Republic – above all in its judicial practice – was the exceptional pressure of the war, mounting inexorably throughout 1938.[89] Moreover, in assessing what happened one must also remember the newness of the democratic system in Spain. The formal superstructure itself only dated back to 1931. But any kind of broader democratic culture was very much work in very early progress given the enduring consequences of underdevelopment – high levels of illiteracy and the concomitant lack of basic education. Indeed, with the possible exception of Catalonia, most

[88] Raguer, 'La política religiosa de Negrín', pp. 7–8. As Hilari Raguer's article makes clear, the Vatican was anxious that Catholic practice should be reinstated in Republican territory by means *other* than the military offensive of the victorious Francoist armies.

[89] Negrín, in his speech of 30 September 1938 to the Cortes, effectively recognised how the 'virtual state of war' (i.e. quasi-martial law) had inevitably eroded some aspects of the constitutional order built up after the July days in 1936. But he urged his critics to compare the current constitutional order with past times or with other polities at war – in effect not to judge the Republican state while it was in a 'state of emergency'. Negrín's speech is reproduced in Alvarez, *Negrín, personalidad histórica*, vol. 2 – see particularly pp. 74–5, 71–2.

middling sectors – even if reasonably educated – still operated with a highly clientelist understanding of politics.[90]

Moreover, in that the Spanish war was a *civil* war, there was the additional serious problem of a fifth column or 'enemy within'. The fifth column in Republican Spain covered a range of people and activities that expanded as the war went on. Most crucially, it involved passing intelligence to the rebels and engagement in a range of activities which either handicapped the Republican war effort (for example production of counterfeit ration books, work certificates and dispensations from military service) or demoralised the civilian population (spreading rumours of shortages, negative military reports etc.). Apart from the 'autonomous' pro-rebel groups and individuals thus engaged, there were also by 1937 articulated networks, including a Falangist one. They received financial support from wealthy rebel supporters in exile or the opposing zone. Most dangerous of all were those in direct contact with international espionage and in particular the Gestapo and OVRA (Italian secret police), both of which were active inside Republican Spain. In Madrid – where the fifth column was most active – it was often linked to sympathetic diplomatic corps via which it acquired safe houses, facilities and assured means of radio communication with the rebels.[91]

Such 'invisible' internal enemy activity posed a unique problem for the Republic.[92] In the beginning it was because state collapse had allowed such individuals and groups to act with impunity. Thereafter it was because, the Republic's critics notwithstanding, a democratic polity would always be *relatively* constrained in the methods it could employ against the fifth column. This was true even though, as the war went on, fifth column activities posed an ever greater threat to an economically besieged and internationally isolated Republic which, short of everything, had to face up to incessant offensive military action from the enemy. The rebels never had to operate under these kinds of pressures, which

---

[90] In such a context, the hugely erosive impact of the war and the pressing needs of post-war reconstruction would, by the very end of 1938, lead Negrín to posit some necessary curbing of the highly fragmented party politics of 1931–6: see Marchenko to Voroshilov (reporting conversation with Negrín of 10 Dec. 1938) in Radosh, Habek and Sevostianov, *Spain Betrayed. The Soviet Union in the Spanish Civil War* (doc. 79), p. 499. But precisely what Negrín thought and meant by this cannot be read 'transparently' from a Comintern report.

[91] On the fifth column, see J. Cervera, *Madrid en guerra. La ciudad clandestina 1936–1939* (Madrid: Alianza, 1998) and M. Uribarri, *La quinta columna española*, vol. 1 (Havana: n.p., 1943). See also discussion in chapter 3 above.

[92] 'Invisible' in the sense that these enemy spies could not be easily identified by cultural markers such as language, accent, manners or customs.

inevitably magnified internal political and social tensions. These were precisely the factors which 'armed' the fifth column so powerfully in Republican Spain. The opportunities for home-front sabotage would increase as time went on. And with an external enemy that was always winning, always advancing, fears about the enemy within (doubly dangerous because hidden) produced an ever heightening state of anxiety and tension – especially after the material and psychological crises induced by the splitting of Republican territory in April 1938 – which itself contributed significantly to justifying more repressive (and eventually quasi-militarised) judicial practices.[93]

If one takes into account these extreme circumstances, then, it is remarkable that the general historical opinion of the Republic's internal political and judicial evolution from mid 1937 should be quite so hostile. Even historical commentators who see themselves as broadly sympathetic to the Republic implicitly apply to it standards that no extant democracy has yet attained in wartime. In modern times, war has always eroded constitutional practices. In the Second World War even 'mature' democracies such as the USA and Britain modified judicial procedures and curtailed the constitutional rights of their citizens (some of whom were interned) in the name of the war.[94] But in Republican Spain democracy was only five years old when polity and society were plunged into a gruelling war and a *civil* war at that – something which is always more brutal. Inevitably the norms of such a young democratic culture could not have permeated all sectors of the state or society. Yet if one compares Republican police or judicial practices with the constitutional realities of European democracies like Britain and France during the *First World War* – a more appropriate historical comparison in this respect than the 1939–45 conflict – then the untenability and sheer anachronism of many of the criticisms of the Republic's constitutional flaws become

---

[93] Cf. Hidalgo de Cisneros' outburst of frustration at the potential cost of guaranteeing civil liberties for the enemy: de la Mora, *In Place of Splendor*, p. 344. The effects of the divison of Republican territory are discussed later in this chapter. But it is worth noting here that the existing literature ignores the scale of the resulting chaos and dislocation. There is a vivid oral account by one American International Brigader, Irving Goff, who, as a member of the Republican guerrilla corps, was sent with a colleague, Bill Aalto, to try (in vain) to stem the retreat of Republican soldiers occasioned by the breakthrough of Franco's armies to the Mediterranean. Taped interview with Jim Carriger, courtesy of Peter Carroll. The tapes are also lodged in the Bancroft Library, University of California (Berkeley).

[94] Cf. Emergency Powers Bill in Britain (May 1940), Calder, *The Myth of the Blitz*, 123. See also A. W. B. Simpson, *In the Highest Degree Odious: Detention without Trial in Wartime Britain* (Oxford: Oxford University Press, 1994).

apparent.[95] For they assess it not in the real context of its time, place and culture, but against some *idea* of Republican perfection.[96]

It was the need to respond to the very real problem of espionage and sabotage in Republican Spain that led Prieto to consolidate and strengthen the state's intelligence services. On 9 August 1937 he announced the creation of the SIM (Servicio de Investigación Militar).[97] Responsible directly to him as defence minister, the SIM functioned primarily as a military police force. But given its counter-espionage brief, it was also responsible for gathering political intelligence on – and therefore policing – the home front. The vital importance of such functions in wartime had been brought home by the May days and reinforced by the events surrounding the detention of the POUM leadership in mid June 1937. A vulnerable Republic needed its own intelligence instrument with incisive powers to separate rumour and hearsay from hard evidence of treasonous activities. In view of the scandal surrounding the disappearance of POUM leader Andreu Nin,[98] Prieto's concern about extraneous 'friendly' political agendas (namely the Soviet Union's) was scarcely surprising.[99] But as we shall see later, it is important to separate the specific political anxieties Prieto and other ministers may have had as a result of the Nin affair in 1937 from the dynamic of SIM expansion during 1938, which was overwhelmingly a response to the needs of the war.

Nevertheless, the circumstances of Nin's disappearance in June 1937 had provoked an international outcry. Negrín was swamped by telegrams and letters of protest from abroad. As well as being a foreign-policy and

[95] See, for example, B. F. Martin, *The Hypocrisy of Justice in the Belle Epoque* (Baton Rouge: Louisiana State University Press, 1984) – a useful study of the quite acute limits on *de facto* (as opposed to *de jure*) political rights under the Third Republic (an example on p. 234); Simpson, *In the Highest Degree Odious*. See also later in this chapter for the discussion of death sentences passed by the Republic's special courts.

[96] To which the enduring myth of the European and American left – 'the last great cause' – has doubtless inadvertently contributed.

[97] Decree published in the Diario Oficial del Ministerio de Defensa Nacional, Bolloten, *SCW*, p. 547. The draft text stipulating the SIM's remit was personally composed by Prieto, *Cómo y por qué salí del ministerio de defensa nacional*, p. 77. Clearly this did *not* mean that the Republic lacked intelligence-gathering instruments before this, or indeed that the SIM had a monopoly on intelligence work after its creation: D. Pastor Petit, *Espionaje. España 1936–1939* (Barcelona: Bruguera, 1977), p. 112; Payne, *The Spanish Revolution*, pp. 346–7. In the aftermath of the coup of 18 July 1936, the intelligence services had presented the Republican government with the same problem as the rest of the state apparatus: how to tell who was loyal among a personnel largely inherited from the monarchy.

[98] For the Nin kidnap and assassination, see chapter 5 above.

[99] See Orlov's comments on this as part of his questionnaire response to the historian Stanley Payne in 1968, in *Forum für osteuropäische Ideen und Zeitgeschichte*, 4 (2000), 229–50 (Orlov's comments, pp. 245–6). These are also cited in Bolloten, *SCW*, pp. 546–7.

public-relations disaster, it also undermined the fundaments of the liberal state to which the prime minister was committed. Police action was, as we have already discussed, occurring beyond ministerial control.[100] The challenge facing Negrín was to reimpose civilian political authority and to deal with the underlying problem of security – in no small part related to the increasing fears concerning espionage and fifth column activity generated by Republican political and military vulnerability. It was for both these reasons that Negrín introduced in late June a special court for espionage and treason (the Tribunal Especial de Espionaje y Alta Traición[101]), whose first task was to regain control of the process of investigating the charges against the POUM.

There seems little doubt that Soviet representatives – whether from the intelligence services or the Comintern remains unclear – helped forge a link (quite literally) to try to implicate the POUM in other ongoing discoveries of espionage activity against the Republic.[102] It is crucial to bear in mind this context of real espionage, in which the rumours against the POUM became embedded, to appreciate why the accusations were, up to a point, 'successful'.[103] The imperative of war is a violent one, not least because it renders most sorts of ambiguity 'unsafe'. Real and present danger invested the anti-POUM rumours with a power inside Republican Spain that they would not otherwise have had.[104] But the forged evidence against the party leadership was very poor.[105] It was not taken seriously by anyone in the Republican judiciary or polity who saw it. Notably disparaging were Irujo and the Esquerra's Jaume Miravitlles, Generalitat propaganda minister.[106] In the small circle of the Catalan

---

[100] See chapter 5 above.

[101] *Gaceta de la República*, 23 June 1937. Text cited in Alba and Ardevol, *El proceso del P.O.U.M.*, pp. 529–35. These courts were presided over by five judges – three civil and two military. All were ministerial appointees – respectively from justice (two civil), interior (one civil), defence (made nominations to the justice ministry for the two military positions).

[102] See chapter 5 above.

[103] Solé i Sabaté and Villaroya i Font, *La repressió a la reraguarda de Catalunya (1936–1939)*, vol. 1, pp. 243–58; Cervera, *Madrid en guerra. La ciudad clandestina*, pp. 283–337. Cervera deals with a number of fifth column networks, including the one used by Orlov to forge evidence against the POUM (p. 303). Some of the author's further deductions regarding Nin's death are, however, rather dogmatic – given the current state of our knowledge.

[104] Azaña, *Obras completas*, vol. 4, p. 692 (La Pobleta); cf. the efficacy of Franco's rumour mongering here too: Cattell, *Communism and the Spanish Civil War*, pp. 146–7.

[105] J. Gorkín, *El proceso de Moscú en Barcelona* (Barcelona: Aymá, 1974), p. 163; see Bolloten, *SCW*, pp. 513–14 for a résumé.

[106] Bolloten, *SCW*, p. 509, p. 890 (n. 58). Miravitlles' disbelief in I. Suárez, *El proceso contra el POUM* (n.p.: Ruedo Ibérico, 1974), p. 172; J. Miravitlles, *Episodis de la guerra civil espanyola*, p. 189; Peirats, *La CNT en la revolución española*, vol. 3, p. 238. Miravitlles had once been a POUM member himself: Low and Breá, *Red Spanish Notebook*, p. 202.

political left, tightly knit notwithstanding its organisational divisions, it is inconceivable that anyone believed the accusations. It is improbable too that a politician of Negrín's sophistication did not also appreciate the denseness of the political web being spun around Nin's disappearance, although the prime minister had no *specific* information: indeed, the very lack of it was precisely the measure of the crisis this supposed for Republican state authority. Negrín's comment to both President Azaña and Zugazagoitia that 'anything was possible' is reasonably astute and, taken in its full context, need not have related only to his voiced thoughts on putative Gestapo involvement.[107]

But in spite of Nin's fate and the detention by the Republican authorities of other POUM executive members, the party continued to have an organisational existence of sorts right through until the spring of 1938. The small sections of the POUM in Valencia and Castellón continued to participate in municipal politics, retaining their city councillors until December 1937.[108] In its Catalan heartland, the POUM's party-political life was more precarious. Nevertheless, a new executive was appointed to replace the imprisoned one.[109] This picture alerts us to the error of seeing the POUM's post-May 1937 experience as part of a seamless whole of imported and monolithic stalinist persecution. The specificity of the Catalan situation should also return our attention to the internal dynamic of longstanding rivalry and animosity on the Catalan left and thus to the many unanswered questions about the PSUC's part in POUM repression. Instead, the Anglo-American historiography – following somewhat uncritically the Catalan POUM's memoir material[110] – has

---

[107] Azaña, *Obras completas*, vol. 4, p. 692; Zugazagoitia, *Guerra y vicisitudes*, pp. 292–3. PSOE executive member Juan-Simeón Vidarte wrote that after the war Negín told him that he believed 'the communists' had killed Nin: *Todos fuimos culpables*, vol. 2, p. 729; also Azaña, *Obras completas*, vol. 4, p. 638.

[108] See V. Alba and S. Schwartz, *Spanish Marxism vs. Soviet Communism* (New Brunswick, N.J.: Transaction Books, 1988) for the POUM's municipal activities after May 1937. Supporting contemporary press sources are also cited by Bolloten, *SCW*, p. 890 (n. 79). An order to dissolve the POUM was issued by the examining magistrate in December 1937: Alba and Ardevol, *El proceso del P.O.U.M.*, p. 471. This would take effect in the wake of the guilty verdict at the October 1938 trial: Elorza and Bizcarrondo, *Queridos camaradas*, p. 380.

[109] Bolloten, *SCW*, p. 513, p. 891 (n. 84).

[110] In particular those by Julián Gorkín and Victor Alba, which tend repeatedly to reduce complex national political conflicts to the 'hidden hand of Moscow'. It is interesting to contrast this with the party's own criticisms in a letter to Azaña in December 1937 when the focus is entirely on the PCE's own sectarianism: POUM to Azaña, Archivo particular de Manuel Azaña (AB), *apartado* 7, *caja* 137, *carpeta* 9. Gorkín and Alba's own *bête noire*, Orlov, in his reply to Payne's 1968 questionnaire, shrewdly remarked on the evident political interest, in a post-war era of Cold War ascendancy, of reducing the POUM repression to an 'affair of the Soviets' (Orlov in *Forum für osteuropäische Ideen und Zeitgeschichte*, 4 (2000), 239). Moreover, the Valencian POUM,

tended instead to conflate the June 1937 detention and the October 1938 trial. But it was only in 1938 that the party was obliged to operate semi-clandestinely.[111] The new POUM executive was imprisoned in April 1938, when the splitting of the Republican zone sparked a major military and political crisis. The party's fate would therefore ultimately be tied up with the much larger process of militarisation happening under the impact of the war, as the rebels stepped up their offensive and as the Republic's diplomatic isolation became total and its home-front conditions desperate.[112]

As the sense of siege increased towards the end of 1937 – with the final loss of the north and the diplomatic impasse over Non-Intervention and troop withdrawal – Negrín sought the institution of special courts to tighten up prosecution of 'espionage, treason and defeatism'.[113] These emergency courts (Tribunales Especiales de Guardia), like the already functioning ones for espionage and high treason, would apply a highly summary procedure reminiscent of military courts which thus meant the suspension of normal constitutional guarantees for the defence of the accused.[114] By way of safeguard, death penalties imposed by the emergency courts had to be ratified by the cabinet. This infringement of the independence of the judiciary was criticised at the time, as it has been subsequently by historians, as unconstitutional – precisely because

while itself critical of the PCE's behaviour, was also hostile to the Catalan POUM's political position. Years later, in 1973, Joaquín Maurín himself – whose own very different experience of the war meant that he was never again able to tune in to the POUM leadership's post-Nin wavelength – would write to Víctor Alba in terms critical of the party's wartime stance: Elorza, 'La estrategia del POUM en la guerra civil', in *La II República. Una esperanza frustrada* (Actas del congreso Valencia Capital de la República) (Valencia: Edicions Alfons el Magnànim, 1987), pp. 133–6.

[111] Bolloten, *SCW*, p. 513; Alba and Ardevol, *El proceso del P.O.U.M.*, pp. 135, 145; Elorza, 'La estrategia del POUM en la guerra civil', p. 135. Orlov's own intelligence reports for spring 1938 refer to ongoing surveillance: Costello and Tsarev, *Deadly Illusions*, p. 364.

[112] Cf. Alba, 'De los tribunales populares al Tribunal Especial', *Justicia en guerra*, p. 232. The author not only ignores all of these factors, but also, unaccountably, appears to think it reasonable to compare Republican democracy in the 1930s with late-twentieth-century western models. By the same token of course, Alba's assessment thereby implicitly disregards the democratic deficits in liberal parliamentary systems today. Conversely, aspects of Julián Gorkín's own account of his experience of the Republican judicial system sit oddly with some of his political conclusions: see Gorkín, *El proceso de Moscú en Barcelona*, pp. 210–13.

[113] *Gaceta de la República*, 1 Dec. 1937.

[114] In the espionage and treason courts two out of the five judges had to be military ones: see text of foundational decree, cited in Alba and Ardevol, *El proceso del P.O.U.M.*, pp. 530–1; A. González Quintana, 'La justicia militar en la España republicana', *Justicia en guerra*, p. 186. The Emergency Courts were presided over by a professional judge but composed of military and police officials, and conviction was always based on the confession of the accused who had no counsel: Solé i Sabaté and Villaroya i Font, *La repressió a la reraguarda de Catalunya (1936–1939)*, vol. 1, pp. 268–76, particularly p. 269.

the Republic had not declared a state of war (*estado de guerra*).[115] But this assessment ignores the extraordinary fraughtness of such a step for the Republican government.

The civil war had begun with a military rebellion against the constituted civilian power. The rebels had themselves declared a state of war precisely because, according to existing public-order legislation, this conferred upon the military supreme political authority *for the duration*.[116] It is, then, entirely unsurprising that Negrín should have been reluctant to risk any of his military commanders 'confusing' the limits of military authority once again. Julián Casanova provides the key to what was happening in 1938 when he refers to summary justice being implemented in a 'virtual state of war'.[117] Negrín was beginning to operate as if a state of war had been declared – but without declaring one *de jure* – for fear that even graver unconstitutional acts might supervene. Under Negrín's system, there was summary justice, but at least it was controlled by the civilian political authority, represented by the cabinet.[118]

However, the implementation of the emergency courts provoked the resignation in December 1937 of the Basque Nationalist Minister of Justice, Irujo.[119] He could not accept them – even given the exceptional context of the war.[120] (We should also note that it was Irujo, along with Prieto, who had consistently voted against the implementation of the death penalties imposed by Republican courts – the rest of the cabinet usually voting affirmatively.) Irujo's under-secretary, Mariano Ansó, took

---

[115] The Republic was still governed under the preliminary 'state of alarm' (*estado de alarma*) that had continued, virtually unbroken, since February 1936: González Quintana, 'La justicia militar en la España republicana', *Justicia en guerra*, p. 187.

[116] The 1933 Public Order Act passed by the Azaña government had not changed the legal provisions which allowed a state of war (or siege) to be declared by the military (without consultation) – *even though this infringed the Republican constitution*. Nor did the Republic demilitarise the police. In July 1936 the rebels had simply issued a 'Bando declaratorio – del estado de guerra'. Franco would rescind these provisions by decree in 1948. On this see M. Ballbé, *Orden público y militarismo en la España constitucional*, pp. 13, 361–2. Ballbé also indicates that the provisions under the 1933 Public Order Act were even more favourable to the military than under that of 1870. The 1933 Act envisaged a war council exclusively of military representatives while the 1870 law had specified military and civilians.

[117] J. Casanova, 'Rebelión y revolución', in Juliá *et al.*, *Victimas de la guerra civil*, pp. 161–2.

[118] Negrín's justification in his speech to the Cortes (30 September 1938), reproduced in Alvarez, *Negrín, personalidad histórica*, vol. 2, pp. 71–2. See also his public reply to the Generalitat's criticisms in *La Vanguardia*, 28 April 1938 ('Justicia dura, pero justicia'), a section of which is cited in Solé i Sabaté and Villaroya i Font, *La repressió a la reraguarda de Catalunya*, vol. 1, pp. 270–1.

[119] Ansó, *Yo fui ministro de Negrín*, pp. 208–9.

[120] M. Irujo, *Un vasco en el ministerio de justicia, memorias* (3 vols., Buenos Aires: Vasca Ekin, 1976–9), vol. 1, pp. 83, 87; A. de Lizarra, *Los vascos y la República española* (Buenos Aires: Vasca Ekin, 1944), pp. 188–90; Bolloten, *SCW*, p. 514. Bolloten's insistence that the police courts were communist-driven is nowhere corroborated – not even by his own account/the material he cites.

over in the justice ministry until the cabinet reshuffle of April 1938. But Negrín personally assumed responsibility for seeing the emergency court proposals through the cabinet. To his mind, the defence of Republican democracy required exceptional measures – in wartime even more than back in 1932 when he had argued for the execution of General Sanjurjo, the leader of the abortive military coup of September. Irujo was never reconciled to this view, but he did, nevertheless, return as a minister without portfolio, persuaded by the Basque premier, José Antonio Aguirre, that the PNV's cause would be better served by maintaining a presence in the cabinet.

Criticism of the emergency courts' unconstitutionality also came from Catalan quarters. While these too had a clear ethical base, there was also a political ambiguity. When the Generalitat complained about the erosion of 'political liberty' it primarily meant the erosion of regional autonomy and of the political rights of nationalists. The Esquerra had not been averse to the central state dealing harshly with rebellious sectors of the libertarian movement or the POUM in Barcelona in May 1937. (Nin's disappearance was, of course, of a different order – although here again it could conveniently be categorised under 'the depredations wrought by Madrid'.[121]) The constitutionality of police action was an issue – but in particular because of the implications it might have for *centralising* political control. The Generalitat's main complaint against the SIM was that it amounted to a Spanish imposition, which breached the spirit of the autonomy statute.[122] SIM personnel were mainly non-Catalans drafted into the region. Their lack of 'local knowledge' may have made their actions more swingeing on occasion – although, as a military police force, nowhere was the SIM noted for its lightness of touch. Nevertheless, there was an additional cultural dimension to the SIM's unpopularity in Catalonia[123] – a point we have already noted in relation to earlier (Madrid) police action in the detention of the POUM's Catalan leadership. By the time the POUM trial came about in October 1938, the Catalan nationalists' worst fears about political centralisation would have been realised. Even so, the eventual sanction of the Republican courts

---

[121] See Azaña's bitter comments here: 'It comes as no surprise that [Companys and his supporters in the Generalitat] have exploited the Nin case. That Companys affects moral indignation and assumes the role of constitutional champion after everything that has happened in Catalonia under his presidency is intolerably cynical', La Pobleta diary entry for 28 July 1937, *Obras completas*, vol. 4, p. 699; see also Azaña, *Apuntes de memoria*, p.78.

[122] The SIM in Catalonia nevertheless had its own separate command structure: D. Pastor Petit, *Espionaje. España 1936–1939* (Barcelona: Bruguera, 1977), p. 110; Payne, *The Spanish Revolution*, p. 346 (citing Manuel Uribarri (not Ulibarri), who headed the SIM for a period during 1938).

[123] Solé i Sabaté and Villaroya i Font, *La repressió a la reraguarda de Catalunya*, vol. 1, p. 260.

against the POUM – for rebellion against the constitutional order[124] – was entirely consistent with the model of social and political order to which the Generalitat subscribed and which it had been keen to see re-established in May 1937. And, as the outcome of May had demonstrated, the Republican state was engaged upon reconstructing economic, social and cultural hierarchies appropriate to such an order.[125]

Accordingly, as we have seen, the Negrín government encouraged the return of some leading political conservatives and restored to them control of their property. Indeed, more generally too, the burden of economic decisions by Republican bodies was in favour of restoring property rights to former owners provided that no active complicity in the military rebellion could be proved. Nor were those of more conservative political persuasion targeted by the post-Popular Tribunal Republican authorities for the *mere fact* of their political opinions, previous allegiances, cultural values or economic class. Republican practice was an attempt to be consistent with the liberal principles enshrined in President Manuel Azaña's speeches and which also informed Negrín's policies: the rights of individuals over those of social groups were to be guaranteed by due constitutional process. The Republic had overcome the arbitrary power of the committees and patrols: illegal detentions and *paseos* were now rare.[126]

At the same time, there was an increase over 1937–9 in the numbers of people detained in prison and in work camps (where those detained performed war work on fortifications and the like).[127] The CNT denounced the economic and political conservatism of the 'new Republic', claiming that the increase was made up of social and political constituencies identified with itself. In other words, the Republican legal system was being used to discipline the left and ensure that it accepted the regime's political and economic authority. (In this, of course, the agenda was not essentially different from 1931–3.) But it had been the CNT's own García Oliver who had created the work camps in December 1936 in

---

[124] Alba and Ardevol, *El proceso del P.O.U.M.*, pp. 479–90, esp. pp. 485–7. The court specifically found there to be no case to answer in terms of treason or espionage.

[125] See Raguer, *La pólvora y el incienso*, pp. 328–9. For the Republic's imposition of hierarchies – apart from the obvious examples of the nationalisation of war industries and the construction of the New Republican Army, consider also the spring 1937 decree excluding militiawomen from the fronts and the fact that May 1937 saw an end to the publication of anonymous soldiers' poems (the famous *romanceros*) in favour of rather more elite focused literary production. This change is apparent, for example, from *Mono Azul*, the literary weekly published under the auspices of the Alliance of Anti-fascist Intellectuals – a body epitomising the Popular Front ethos.

[126] See Irujo cited in Raguer, *La pólvora y el incienso*, p. 329.

[127] Solé i Sabaté and Villaroya i Font, *La repressió a la reraguarda de Catalunya*, vol. 1, p. 283; pp. 281–6 includes some extracts from testimonies; Juliá *et al.*, *Víctimas de la guerra*, pp. 256–7.

his capacity as justice minister. The increase in the scale of their operations has to be understood most immediately in the context of the war and the deterioration in the Republic's position. It seems probable also that the restitution of a liberal Republican order in law, economy and society would have had a qualitative impact on the sociological profile of the Republican prison population over the war. But the very fact of war, especially a civil war, complicates the prison picture and makes this difficult to assess.[128]

As far as the overall erosion of popular morale on the Republican home front is concerned, however, we should be careful of exaggerating the impact of judicial questions in a society whose experience of constitutional rights freely exercised was still quite limited. Far more important sources of the erosion of morale among large sectors of the population were hunger, shortage and the increasingly frequent severe air raids on big urban centres against which the Republic, short of fighter planes, could offer people little protection. These problems became most acute in Catalonia. December 1937 saw the mass bombing of Barcelona. In March 1938 came a second saturation Italian bombing wave, more intense than anything inflicted on Madrid. In its effects – and probably in the intent too – the damage was overwhelmingly civilian. Delayed-fuse and lateral-force bombs were used – both designed to cause maximum civilian casualties. Diplomatic protests proved futile.[129] Wealthy districts were also bombed – including the Ritz and Hotel Majestic, where foreign correspondents were hit. But the bombing hit hardest in refugee-crammed areas. As the rebel armies advanced, so an unending flood of refugees poured into Catalonia. By late 1937 the food situation was dire. Among the urban poor, hunger bordered on starvation – as indicated in Quaker reports of wartime relief work, which include a wrenching account of conditions in one anarchist 'ragged school' in the centre of Barcelona.[130] For this besieged and bombed urban population,

---

[128] For example, the impact of black-market activities or low-grade 'fifth column' offences. P. Pagès i Blanch, *La guerra civil espanyola a Catalunya (1936–1939)*, 2nd edn (Barcelona, 1997) makes a start and bears out the libertarian/left testimonial literature. See also P. Pagès i Blanch, *La presó Model de Barcelona. Història d'un centre penitenciari en temps de guerra (1936–1939)* (Barcelona: L'Abadia de Montserrat, 1996), pp. 303–404 and C. Cañellas *et al.*, *Història de la presó Model de Barcelona* (Lleida: Pagès, 2000).

[129] After the Nyon conference in September 1937, Italy modified its tactics. The rebels were given Italian submarines and Italian aircraft on Majorca flew with Spanish markings. From then on, bombing of all Republican ports and cargo ships thus bound could be carried out with virtual impunity for the rest of the war: Alpert, *A New International History of the Spanish Civil War*, p. 145.

[130] Report dated 1 November 1937, FSC/R/Sp box 1 (file 3) and 14 December 1937, FSC/R/Sp box 5.

increasingly ground down by hunger and shortage, the situation was psychologically even harder to bear in the absence of any sign of relief or improvement on the international horizon.

Integral war weariness was, then, also part of the cumulative, collateral effect of Non-Intervention. Not only had this made it impossible for the Republic to sustain an offensive war, but it had also undercut its ability to provide adequate staple supplies to sustain the home front and compensate for the severe dislocation of the national economy. Maintaining resistance under conditions of Non-Intervention obliged the straitened Republic to spend virtually all its resources on war *matériel* and, thereafter, to concentrate its scarce staple supplies on the army. Prieto had always said that the winning side would be the one with the healthier home front. Ultimately, increasing hardship and hunger were what undermined the Republic's legitimacy on that home front.

This was also true away from the towns and cities. Hunger was not by any means a monopoly of urban dwellers. Rural populations, as producers (whether collectivist or individual) more often had direct access to food. But harvest difficulties or being on the wrong side of village power relations could cancel out any advantage here,[131] as did the abiding problem of all wars, namely that the army began to live off the land. Across the entire Republican zone, rural populations wearied of the army's 'parasitism', which compounded the other effects of economic dislocation. Complaints once made against the militia were now levelled against army units. In Aragon, where many of these retained autonomous supply functions,[132] there were criticisms of soldiers helping themselves to poultry and other produce. 'Informal' requisition often seemed little more than pillage. The CNT press warned against 'banditry' – while the PCE, which owed its political entrée to Aragonese politics to the problem of *militia* depredations, sought to impose tougher military discipline. How successful it was in ameliorating this particular problem remains unclear. Certainly there was a deterioration in the situation during the Republican military retreat through Aragon to Catalonia in the spring of 1938 when numerous violent conflicts between civilians and soldiers were

---

[131] Ucelay da Cal, 'Cataluña durante la guerra', pp. 348–9. The author makes a number of important points about the complex question of which groups went hungriest in Republican Spain during the war. However, he is rather optimistic about the fate of urban workers. Many sectors of the urban poor would not have had access to the union facilities he describes. In any case, the Generalitat's economic liberalisation had seen the abolition of the food committees responsible for provisioning poor neighbourhoods in 1936, and it had reduced the efficacy of initiatives like consumer co-operatives too (see chapter 4 above). Nor were these or the communal kitchens provided by unions immune to the growing food crisis of 1938.

[132] Casanova, *Anarquismo y revolución*, p. 111.

reported.[133] Moreover, in Aragon as elsewhere, the PCE's stringent disciplinary line in all matters would frequently be interpreted by the CNT as anti-libertarianism. The CNT regularly defended young deserters, or peasants discontented with the government's requisition of their crops – which meant, in consequence, heightened intra-organisational political tensions.[134] These were increasing more generally too by 1938 as civilians became alienated by other manifestations of militarisation such as the increased billeting of troops in houses and school buildings.[135] One can see this weariness too in the rising tide of general complaints directed against military personnel – for example the careless driving of military vehicles, which in some places had led to accidents and even fatalities.[136]

The general attrition attendant on wartime economic dislocations came to affect smallholders, tenant farmers and those in collectivised agriculture alike. They were already subject to unpopular war taxes. A shortage of labour and material (seed and fertilisers) as well as worsening conditions of production eroded both yield and producer morale.[137] Collectivists and smallholders alike would also come to criticise government measures such as the *brigadas de cultivo* (agricultural brigades) under the control of the UGT and the CNT landworkers' federations. These were workers drafted in from urban centres to replace the agricultural labour force lost to conscription or other forms of war work. In a sense, one can appreciate the complaint levelled by Ricardo Zabalza, leader of the UGT land federation (FNTT), that it would have been more effective to create general brigades for fortification work, leaving the rural population to work their own land. By the same token, such an exchange between rural and urban environments might, in different circumstances, have had the potential to forge a greater sense of national political cohesion for the Republic. But the seriously deteriorating conditions ruled out any potential for such a 'Republicanisation' or 'nationalisation' of differing political and social constituencies. Instead, the rural world turned in upon itself. Collectives as well as smallholders were quite ready to hoard food.[138] While this provoked urban complaints, a

[133] For example, soldiers taking bread from a Catalan village shot dead a CNT municipal officer attempting to stop them: Juliá *et al.*, *Víctimas de la guerra civil*, pp. 253ff.

[134] See Elorza and Bizcarrondo, *Queridos camaradas*, p. 407 for an example of how intra-organisational tensions were now bound up with economic tensions and war weariness – especially around issues of compulsory government purchase of crops.

[135] This was already a problem in Aragon by late 1937: Azaña, *Obras completas*, vol. 4, p. 812.

[136] Simeón Riera, *Entre la rebelió y la tradició*, pp. 233–4.

[137] For the exhausting conditions of production (including under fire) and its attrition of the southern collectives, see Garrido González, *Colectividades agrarias en Andalucía*, pp. 95–100.

[138] See Fraser, *Blood of Spain*, p. 371 (n. 1).

greater factor in urban shortage was the chronic lack of transport to deliver foodstuffs to consumers.[139] By 1938 the Popular Front would be undermined by these intractable practical problems as much as, if not more than, it was by specific political sectarianisms. But the language of the latter would often be used to give voice to this burden of war weariness and practical despair – a shift to which one needs to be increasingly atuned as 1938 progresses. The harsher discipline in evidence on both the military and home fronts would further contribute to this alienation – although its very intensification was also a desperate response to an increasingly impossible material situation.

Increasing frustration at the impasse the Republic faced internationally, as well as the attritional tension of maintaining a war effort under such conditions, inevitably began to deepen the political divisions in Republican ranks. The CNT's general secretary, Mariano R. Vázquez, continued to support the government while remaining deeply suspicious of the PCE. Many in the movement were much more disaffected, however, and as the military situation further deteriorated their voices would become louder. Most worryingly of all for Negrín at this stage was the accelerating strife in the PSOE/UGT. If he had to contend with CNT discontent and the low-intensity war with the Generalitat, the very least Negrín needed was to be able to rely on his own party.[140] But the Caballeristas' increasingly *public* dissidence had reached red alert by the autumn of 1937. Their battle with the PCE for organisational influence in the UGT was regularly presented as a high moral crusade against ruthless political opportunists. This inevitably found a response among all those – in the socialist movement and beyond – who had lost out in the bruising organisational struggle unleashed by the war. Largo was also able to tap into a current of incipient anti-Soviet sentiment that was beginning to appear.[141] This too had its source in war weariness and mounting frustration at Republican impasse. In such circumstances, anti-Sovietism was the inevitable counterpoint of the popular mythologisation of the Soviet Union in late 1936. The hopes then had been unrealistic, and the resulting

---

[139] This is a constant reprise in Quaker relief reports.

[140] As the veteran socialist Gabriel Morón expressed it, 'with his own party, [Negrín] felt as if he were communing with the Void', *Política de ayer y política de mañana* (Mexico: n. p., 1942), p. 109; see also Buckley, *Life and Death of the Spanish Republic*, p. 401.

[141] The government, alarmed by the likely destabilising effects should this escalate, put up discreet posters in Valencia and Barcelona to request that care be exercised in public pronouncements: Jackson, *The Spanish Republic and the Civil War*, p. 405. In Moscow, Pascua also tried to limit the diplomatic damage caused by the Caballeristas' increasingly incendiary press editorials: see AHN/MP, *caja* 2 (2) for Pascua's complaints to Negrín (letter of 28 Nov. 1937) and examples of his diplomatic notelets to Stalin.

disappointment – as Non-Intervention strangled arms deliveries and Stalin began to reassess his position – was commensurately intense. The fact that the PCE had wrapped itself in the mantle of Soviet strength – so effectively projected by its own propaganda – meant that it too would feel the full force of disappointed expectations.

But if Largo was the chief beneficiary here, he overstepped the mark when he insisted on his right to air his political grievances with the PCE publicly. The Communist Party was a crucial element in the Popular Front alliance sustaining the war effort. The Caballeristas' public and vociferous anti-communism constituted wrecking tactics of the worst sort. It was this that galvanised the PSOE executive – effectively under Prieto's direction – to remove Largo and his supporters from all positions of authority in the party. By 1 October 1937 they had also successfully evicted Largo from the UGT leadership.[142] With a war on, neither Negrín nor indeed the PSOE leadership could afford to give Largo his head – however much respect he still commanded as a 'historic' leader of the movement. The incendiary quality of the high-profile personal animosities involved in this internal socialist dispute should not obscure the fact that what was at issue in the Caballeristas' irresponsible politicking behind the lines was the very stability of the Republican home front in this most difficult of wars.

At the front itself, morale was relatively better for rather longer during 1937.[143] The political commissars had played an important role in curbing desertions and generally serving as a positive force for discipline – this not only via elementary political education but also by dispensing practical health care and general education. Looking after the welfare and interests of their men meant keeping up fighting morale – something that was doubly crucial in circumstances of such material deprivation. Prieto's attempts in late 1937 to normalise the army had, as we have seen, weakened the commissariat – especially at the lower levels of the army. Indeed, one could argue that it was precisely this erosion that intensified the need for the brutal discipline imposed by the Republican military

---

[142] For events in the party and union see Graham, *Socialism and War*, pp. 112–31, 167–89 and a brief summary in Jackson, *The Spanish Republic and the Civil War*, p. 406. Jackson tends, however, to overemphasise Negrín's direct intervention in the proceedings. Prieto was the architect. (It was Prieto's (then) political lieutenant, Ramón González Peña, the Asturian miners' leader and (significantly) a hero of the October 1934 rising, who led the ousting of Largo from the UGT executive: see Graham, *Socialism and War*, p. 178.)

[143] Although there were incidents – for example the rebellion in a unit being transferred from the Madrid front to Aragon in August 1937: Azaña (La Pobleta, 31 Aug.), *Obras completas*, vol. 4, p. 760.

police (SIM) once the Republic's military situation became critical in 1938 – a topic to which we shall return later.[144]

On 15 December 1937 the Republic launched a major offensive on the Aragon front in a further bid to seize both the military and diplomatic initiative. After the fall of the north, Franco was concentrating his forces to storm Madrid – planned for the eighteenth. Teruel was thus another attempt at a diversion. But the fact that the Aragonese city was already some two-thirds surrounded by existing Republican lines, plus the element of surprise, meant a much better chance to follow through an offensive campaign. Republican morale was good, in spite of winter weather as bitter as the fighting – which replicated the building-to-building, hand-to-hand combat of Madrid and Belchite. With rebel reinforcements rushed from the Madrid zone, it was touch and go. But the Republicans took Teruel on 7 January. They held it until late February, with International Brigade troops drafted in late January to stiffen the resistance. But the cost in casualties was huge as they were battered by heavy air and artillery attacks. Nor did the Republicans have the reserves to counter-attack outside the city. In the end the sheer weight of enemy back-up forced the Republicans to evacuate Teruel before they were encircled. They had held on so long for reasons of prestige and morale. But the cost of doing this exhausted the meagre resources of the Republican army, while, in reality, its courageous performance caused not a ripple on the international diplomatic scene.[145] Teruel was not a defeat because of logistical insufficiency or lack of training or discipline, it was a rout occasioned by material lack – of arms, artillery and, most ominously, of aircraft.

The Republic's chances of forcing international diplomatic movement, or France to break ranks with Britain over Non-Intervention, were fading. In spite of the January breakthrough in Teruel, Chautemps formally closed the French frontier, making the passage of war material even more uncertain. In reality, very little aid at all reached the Republic during the entire, *crucial* year from June 1937 to June 1938 – for the most part because of the extraordinary difficulty of getting it there. The key to the Republic's military starvation lay in its enemies' successful quarantining of its Mediterranean ports. This left only the lengthier

---

[144] This is not intended to imply that the commissariat ceased to be important. It was still instrumental in maintaining discipline during the horrendous conditions of the Ebro battle: see Alpert, *El ejército republicano*, p. 203. On both the SIM and the Ebro see later in this chapter.

[145] The desperate retreat from Teruel involved the Republic's forces fighting their way back through enemy lines. In the process they abandoned a quantity of military hardware the Republic could ill afford to lose.

routes via the Baltic Sea and the Atlantic – used by the Soviet Union from December 1937 until summer 1938.[146] But rebel control of the Straits of Gibraltar still meant that there was no direct access by sea to the Mediterranean. The odyssey of Republican war material thus concluded in an always problematic land transportation across France from the Atlantic to the Mediterranean coast where, from January 1938, it hit Chautemps's reclosed border. French policy-making circles had been in at least several minds over what to do about Spain. But by early 1938 the defence imperative was pulling the Chautemps government towards seeking its own accord with Fascist Italy. While Negrín perceived this danger, he chose to continue trying to exert a countervailing influence in the belief that the mounting tension in Europe would demonstrate the relatively small worth of such an accord and thus force France to break ranks with Britain.

Unfortunately for Negrín, however, developments in Britain would further weaken his diplomatic gambit. Italy had continued to work on deepening the rift between Chamberlain and his foreign secretary, Eden, who was increasingly concerned by the implications of massive Axis aid to the rebels. Chamberlain had himself once hoped that negotiations with Italy might yield a *quid pro quo* that would reduce its troop and armament commitment to Franco. But the nazification of Austria in February 1938 had made him doubly anxious to secure an Anglo-Italian agreement. Mainstream cabinet opinion was backing him to do this irrespective of whether concessions could be exacted from Mussolini over Spain. Eden continued to hold out against any accord with Italy or recognition of its Abyssinian empire until Mussolini had agreed to cease attacks against merchant shipping and civilian targets in Spain as well as to end CTV troop dispatch there. But Eden's views isolated him in the cabinet, thus prompting his resignation on 19 February.[147] By mid April an Anglo-Italian settlement would be a reality even though Ciano had made it clear that Italian forces would not leave Spain short of a rebel victory. Non-Intervention inspectors had been in Spain counting foreign troops since February 1938. But Franco would continue to obstruct the planned withdrawal through to June and beyond – even though he was only ever prepared to sanction it at a minimal level of a few thousand Italians. The Republic could thus bring an end neither to Non-Intervention nor to the underwriting of the rebel war effort by Axis might – evident in the massed ranks of planes, tanks, trucks and CTV troops that had confronted the

---

[146] Howson, *Arms for Spain*, pp. 235–6.   [147] Alpert, *A New International History*, pp. 143, 152–4.

Republican army at Teruel. By 9 March 1938 Franco's offensive to take control of Aragon was underway. Both Quinto and Belchite fell within the first twenty-four hours of the rebels' rapid advance.

The aftershock of Anschluss (Hitler's occupation of Austria) brought about the temporary reopening of the French frontier by Chautemps, whose government then gave way in mid March 1938 to a new one under Blum.[148] But by this stage the rebel army was heading for the Valencian coast. When it reached it, the Republic zone would be split in two. Negrín urgently petitioned the Blum cabinet for military aid on 12–14 March 1938, since such a division of territory posed an enormous challenge to Republican military viability and responding to it would require the urgent and large-scale reorganisation of the Republic's armies. But the French government showed little resolve – faced with British opposition and also its own Chief-of-Staff's warnings of a possible Axis reaction. No doubt residual political ambivalence towards the Spanish Republic in military and diplomatic circles further inhibited French action, which, in the end, was limited to a defensive measure: the stationing of more troops on the Franco-Catalan frontier.

Although some stockpiled material did start to pass across the now open border, it is unlikely that it did so on the grand scale often implied.[149] In any case, there seems to have been a fall-off in Soviet-procured aid after December 1937.[150] Certainly this was the impression in France by May 1938 – which only added to the government's reluctance to aid the Republic.[151] The Soviet Union did intervene in spring 1938 to facilitate the passage of one small arms consignment from Czechoslovakia. But it was a drop in the ocean. In other circumstances, Czechoslovakia, as the world's largest exporter of armaments, would have been an obvious source for the Republic from the start. The Soviet Union could have acted as the ostensible purchaser to procure the necessary exportation documentation – for Czechoslovakia was also a signatory to Non-Intervention. But the coolness of the Czech government towards the Soviet Union, in spite of their mutual assistance pact of 1935, had ruled this out. (As a result, the Republican ambassador in Prague, Luis Jiménez de Asúa, was obliged to do business with the usual array of dubious and corrupt 'contacts' who embroiled him in the sadly familiar round of daylight

---

[148] Although the decision to open it was taken by the outgoing Chautemps cabinet.

[149] Alpert, *A New International History*, p. 155; Moradiellos, *La perfidia de Albión*, p. 332.

[150] Howson, *Arms for Spain*, pp. 239–41 and pp. 302–3.

[151] Republican ambassador Pascua also derived the same impression from his Soviet opposite number in Paris in May 1938: Viñas, 'Las relaciones hispano-francesas, el gobierno Daladier y la crisis de Munich', pp. 176, 183.

robbery.[152]) But, in any case, by 1938 Spain was fading as the focal point of Soviet foreign policy. Escalating Japanese aggression (in the form of further expansion in China), Anschluss and, by late March, the looming, increasingly all-consuming Czech crisis itself would all stand in Negrín's way.[153] This was so especially because, in spite of cumulative German aggression, Britain was still absolutely opposed to Stalin's proposal of a grand alliance against Hitler, made at the League (of Nations) on 18 March.

Meanwhile, as rebel troops rapidly overcame Republican resistance in Aragon[154] and Barcelona was subject to savage bombing, the pressure on Negrín was mounting. President Azaña was looking for a way of opening up the question of mediation. A current of pro-mediation republican opinion was circulating around him, swelled by the adherence of Catalan and Basque nationalists as well as some *cenetistas* and members of the PSOE. War minister Prieto, in profoundly pessimistic mood, freely expressed his belief that the army was demoralised by the enemy's overwhelming military superiority, that the Republic had therefore lost and that it should sue unequivocally for peace. Britain's immovability clinched matters for Prieto. However, he had no illusions about the rebels, who were unlikely to negotiate over what they believed they could take by military action. So it is difficult to conclude other than that Prieto was at least prepared to risk that the conflict would end entirely on Franco's terms.[155] Picking up on this, the French government made an offer of mediation via its ambassador, Labonne.[156] The offer was discussed by the cabinet. But it was rejected in the face of vehement opposition from Negrín, who argued that the Axis would not allow it to prosper and that even attempting it would damage the Republican cause at home and abroad at a critical moment when it

---

[152] Howson, *Arms for Spain*, pp. 153–63,144.

[153] Roberts, 'Soviet Foreign Policy and the Spanish Civil War 1936–1939', pp. 90–1. It is as well to remember that *almost all the way through* the major crises affecting the Soviet Union's western defences (Anschluss in March 1938, Munich in September and Hitler's Prague coup of March 1939), the Soviet Union was also fighting a relatively large-scale war with Japan in the east (along the frontier of Mongolia and Manchuria): H. Ragsdale, 'Soviet Military Preparations and Policy in the Munich Crisis: New Evidence', *Jahrbücher für Geschichte Osteuropas*, 47 (1999), 216 (n. 31).

[154] For a brief summary of the rebel's drive through Aragon, see Thomas, *Spanish Civil War*, pp. 798–802. Once again, as at Teruel, the rebels' air superiority was crucial to their success.

[155] Note, for example, Prieto's scepticism when, in response to the March military crisis, the army and airforce chiefs of staff, Rojo and Hidalgo de Cisneros, proposed offering themselves to Franco in a bid to facilitate peace and mitigate its conditions for the rest of the army: Zugazagoitia, *Guerra y vicisitudes*, pp. 383–4.

[156] Zugazagoitia, *Guerra y vicisitudes*, pp. 384–5; Miralles, 'Paz humanitaria y mediación internacional: Azaña en la guerra', pp. 268–70.

could not afford to appear weak. It was this that broke open the political crisis inside the Republican cabinet. At issue were the purpose and ethics of resistance as well as the principle of prime ministerial authority.

On 16 March the PCE and CNT leaderships orchestrated a street demonstration against 'the treasonous ministers' near the Pedralbes Palace (Azaña's residence in the Barcelona suburbs) to coincide with the cabinet meeting taking place there. One week later, in a blatant breach of ministerial solidarity, not to mention press censorship, the communist education minister, Jesús Hernández, writing under a pseudonym, also attacked Prieto in the press.[157] Given Negrín's view of the press's crucial function in maintaining morale, he can scarcely have approved, if indeed he had advance knowledge. The premier, however, did know in advance about the demonstration of the sixteenth and justified it to the cabinet.[158] Indeed, he may even actively have suggested it to the PCE as a way of consolidating his own political position against the threat of Azaña's resignation and 'unconditional surrender' apparently taking shape against him in the cabinet.[159]

But in fact, the cabinet danger was – and would remain – inchoate. Negrín's policy of maximum resistance was approved in spite of republican reservations. For these did not (nor would they ever) amount to an alternative *policy*. The republicans wanted mediation, but had no concrete strategy for how it might be achieved. Having weathered the cabinet storm, then, on 27 March, an astounded Negrín heard the French ambassador, Labonne, enquire of him whether he, like Prieto, also considered the war to be lost. Until that point Negrín had been clear about keeping Prieto in the war ministry in spite of the Teruel defeat and the mounting pressure from the PCE to remove him. But the military situation was critical. Having seen the French frontier reopened in the wake of Anschluss, Negrín could now brook nothing that undermined his efforts to get the French to send arms. The thought of the impact of Prieto's tragic queen performance in front of Labonne – reprised in front of the

---

[157] Article(s) by Juan Ventura in *La Vanguardia* and *Frente Rojo*, 23 March 1938. *La Vanguardia* was more or less the Negrín government's official press medium by this stage. (Its editor was the socialist deputy, Fernando Vázquez Ocaña: see his memoir, *Pasión y muerte de la segunda República española*, p. 78.) This was not the first press attack on Prieto, however. See, for example, Dolores Ibárruri's savage speech of 27 February 1938 to the PSUC, Ibárruri, *En la lucha*, p. 249.

[158] Elorza and Bizcarrondo, *Queridos camaradas*, p. 413.

[159] Vidarte, *Todos fuimos culpables*, vol. 2, pp. 823–35, 820–1; Zugazagoitia, *Guerra y vicisitudes*, pp. 389–91; Ansó, *Yo fui ministro de Negrín*, p. 214; Togliatti, *Escritos sobre la guerra de España*, p. 193. The demonstration was an attempt to evoke the spontaneous popular disapprobation of 18 July 1936 in Madrid when Martínez Barrio sought to treat with General Mola.

entire cabinet on 29 March – was finally just too much.[160] The prime minister went back on his arrangement with the PSOE executive. He still wanted Prieto in the cabinet, but not as defence minister.[161] But Prieto, partly from conviction, partly because he felt his own political reputation to be on the line, insisted on the war portfolio as the price of his cabinet participation. His fatal obstinacy, not devoid of egoism, was reminiscent of his great rival and antagonist, Largo Caballero, almost a year previously.[162]

Prieto's intransigence meant that, in the end, Negrín had no choice but to leave him out of the cabinet that was reconstituted on 5 April. For Negrín, resistance – as the Republic's only viable option – dictated seamless public optimism from all Republican ministers. In the end, the real difference between Negrín and Prieto was not their intellectual grasp of the situation, but their subjective response to it. Negrín drew strength from adversity while Prieto seemed to cave in before the bleakness. Negrín honed down his energies to a single fierce point directed at the main strategic objective: sustaining resistance. To this end, he employed a useful psychological device: he avoided considering the whole. Instead he concerned himself with what was practically necessary to keep resistance on track in the immediate term – namely maintaining an army in the field, supplied and fed.[163] He did this not because he believed the

---

[160] Zugazagoitia, *Guerra y vicisitudes*, pp. 395–6; Negrín's own account is in *Epistolario Prieto y Negrín*, pp. 23–4 and in speech of 1 Aug. 1945, Palacio de Bellas Artes, Mexico, reported in *Novedades*, 6 Aug. 1945 – a copy of which is lodged in AHN/MP, *caja* 14 (12). In this speech Negrín says that removing Prieto was one of the hardest decisions of his life. But he had to do it because the military situation was verging on utter disaster, with the front broken and Franco's armies only an hour's march from Barcelona. Burnett Bolloten also cites Negrín's public denial that Prieto's removal was the result of Comintern or PCE pressure: 'on the graves of our war dead . . . there is not a word of truth in it', *SCW*, p. 581 quoting from *Documentos políticos para la historia de la república española*, vol. 1 (Mexico City: Colección Málaga, 1945), p. 21. Given Negrín's personal value system, that was a very powerful – and far from formulaic – oath.

[161] Negrín, *Epistolario Prieto y Negrín*, p. 55 (n. 7); see Zugazagoitia, *Guerra y vicisitudes*, pp. 402–4 for his own and the PSOE executive's attempts (in the persons of Lamoneda and Albar) to mediate between Prieto and Negrín.

[162] In particular Prieto's behaviour regarding the ambassadorship in Mexico: Zugazagoitia, *Guerra y vicisitudes*, pp. 409–10. Prieto was prepared to go in order to undertake negotiations with the Mexican government about the receipt of Republican refugees – *but only if this was an offical cabinet mandate*. As Negrín pointed out, he could not agree to this because the cabinet was a sound box. In a matter of days the credibility of the Republic's resistance policy would be in tatters. See also Negrín in *Epistolario Prieto y Negrín*, pp. 53–4 and Graham, *Socialism and War*, pp. 142–3.

[163] *Epistolario Prieto y Negrín*, pp. 26–8; Irujo, *Un vasco en el ministerio de justicia*, vol. 1, pp. 82–3; Morón, *Política de ayer*, pp. 83, 86; Zugazagoitia, *Guerra y vicisitudes*, pp. 421–2. Even hostile witnesses record this conscious attempt by Negrín to bolster morale: for example see comments ('entusiasmo ficticio', 'balones de oxígeno') by Colonel Cuevas, appointed Director General of Security in the interior ministry in April 1938, *Recuerdos de la Guerra de España* (Montauban: n.p., 1940), p. 58. For an astute summary of the essence of Negrín's wartime strategy, see Ansó, *Yo fui ministro de Negrín*, p. 215.

Republic could win militarily. Franco's destruction of a large quantity of the Republic's best troops at Teruel had put paid to whatever remained of those hopes. But Negrín did believe that the international situation had to break and that if the Republic could only hold on militarily, then that seismic political shift would save it. Franco could be forced to negotiate, but he would never do so if the Republic's will to resist were seen, even momentarily, to waver. Negrín was well aware of just how grim material conditions were for many people on the home front. But as this was part of the 'whole' that he could not significantly mitigate, he chose just to let it lie. This was also true for the closely related problem of the increasingly harsh disciplinary codes operating on both 'fronts' – military and civilian. In the circumstances it was impossible to investigate individual cases of injustice without unravelling the very fabric of 'iron resistance' ('resistencia a ultranza' – 'con pan o sin pan').[164] But both politically and socially this would become Negrín's Achilles's heel. The departure of Prieto intensified the internal tensions in the socialist movement to a point just short of open crisis.[165] As an inevitable part of this it also further incapacitated the functioning of the liaison committees between the PSOE and the PCE, also rapidly being ground down by their members' sheer physical and mental exhaustion in a war where all the exits were blocked. In addition, Negrín was now facing the estrangement of the sector inside the CNT, identified with the general secretary, Mariano Vázquez, that had until then backed his resistance policy.

The new cabinet line-up was ultimately determined by Negrín's need to have unconditional commitment to the war from his ministers. Thus the republican Giral was replaced in the foreign ministry by Alvarez del Vayo, reoccupying the post he had lost back in May 1937.[166] The removal of Giral, a very close friend of Azaña's, was also intended to obstruct the president's tendency to conduct informal diplomacy on his own account. This had always been anathema to Negrín's constitutional sensibilities, but now the backdoor diplomacy was also absolutely incompatible with his own policy strategy.[167]

---

[164] Cf. Zugazagoitia, *Guerra y vicisitudes*, pp. 420, 421–2, 429–30.

[165] Graham, *Socialism and War*, pp. 136–63.

[166] Although Negrín took personal charge of high-level European diplomacy. Nevertheless, he was clear about del Vayo's advantages over Giral: for all that foreign diplomats might wonder about del Vayo's grip on reality, he would at least never provide them with defeatist words for their governments to use against the Republic: Zugazagoitia, *Guerra y vicisitudes*, pp. 405–6, 428–9, 430.

[167] In late October 1936 Azaña had, on his own authority, sent Bosch Gimpera to London to sound out the British over mediation. The veteran socialist leader Julián Besteiro had fulfilled

The need to support the war effort had also been the crucial factor deciding the PCE's continuation in the cabinet – in the form of a sole minister – Vicente Uribe in agriculture. In mid February Stalin had sent notice that the party should withdraw because of the negative effect its presence was having internationally.[168] This indicates that Stalin had not yet entirely given up hope of shifting Britain's position on collective security – even if this had to come at the expense of the Republic – whose resistance Stalin must by now have considered to be strictly time-limited. Nevertheless, the Soviet leader had absolutely no reason to want to hasten this process and particularly not after Anschluss in March. So the PCE's leaders, who, understandably, wanted to remain in the cabinet, were able to argue both truthfully and effectively that, without them, the policy of resistance itself would be significantly weakened[169] because Negrín would find it harder to neutralise the pactist caucus gathering around the Republican president, Manuel Azaña.[170]

Jesús Hernández's departure was, nevertheless, more or less inevitable after the clash with Prieto. Hernández would become Commissar General of the Army. The CNT's Segundo Blanco replaced him in education, although his presence in the cabinet did little to counteract the CNT's growing alienation from the government. Both the home office and justice ministry had appointees who were less experienced than their predecessors but unconditionally loyal: respectively, the socialists Paulino Gómez[171] (who replaced Julián Zugazagoitia) and Ramón González Peña, the 'historic' leader of the Asturian miners' union (who replaced Irujo). Formerly closely identified with Prieto, González Peña had been engaged across 1937 in the organisational struggle to remove control of the UGT executive from Largo Caballero. Negrín himself assumed responsibility for the war ministry. Irujo remained in the cabinet as minister without portfolio, while Giral rejoined it in the same capacity. The crisis had thus been managed, allowing Negrín, along with his

a similar function when he represented the Republic at the coronation of George VI in May 1937: Miralles, 'Paz humanitaria y mediación internacional', pp. 257–8 and S. Juliá, 'Presidente por última vez', in Alted *et al.*, *Manuel Azaña: pensamiento y acción*, pp. 255–6. For Azaña's own prediction of the coming clash over the question of mediation, see his 'La Pobleta' diary entry for 7 August 1937, *Obras completas*, vol. 4, p. 716.

[168] Elorza and Bizcarrondo, *Queridos camaradas*, p. 410.

[169] See ibid., pp. 413–16 for a reconstruction of these interchanges.

[170] *Guerra y revolución en España*, vol. 4, pp. 75–6; Bolloten, *SCW*, p. 582. Nor was the PCE entirely confident about Negrín's commitment to resistance: Togliatti, *Escritos sobre la guerra de España*, pp. 200, 231; Graham, *Socialism and War*, p. 138.

[171] Gómez had done a good job in Catalonia, where he had been put in charge of public order – a responsibility incumbent on the central government since the May days: Zugazagoitia, *Guerra y vicisitudes*, p. 293.

chiefs of staff (where there was also continuity in Rojo and Hidalgo de Cisneros) to concentrate on maximising the possibilities for military resistance. The PSOE journalist, Zugazagoitia, relieved of the home office portfolio at his own request, remained close to Negrín, offering important support in his secretarial role at the war ministry.[172] Indeed, even Prieto would remain at Negrín's disposition for a time.[173] But republican and nationalist disaffection and the widening rift in the PSOE were inevitably making serious inroads into Negrín's political support base.

In the first days of April 1938 the northern wing of the rebels' advance into Aragon took the city of Lleida and then the important power station at Tremp, temporarily blacking out Barcelona and decreasing its industrial output thereafter. Meanwhile, the rebels' central units drove down the Ebro valley to the Castellón-Valencian coast.[174] On 15 April General Alonso Vega reached it at Vinaroz and split Catalonia from the centre-south zone. On the same day Britain signed the Anglo-Italian naval agreement and continued to pressure France to close the frontier – even though Britain's own merchant ships were still being sunk by Franco. As always, the assumption held – as it would most damagingly of all in the escalating Czech crisis – that there was no Axis (and more particularly no German) bluff to be called. Britain's persistent overestimation of Germany's rearmament levels eroded any belief in the strategic purpose of *diplomatic* resistance to its expansionist aims.

---

[172] On Julián Zugazagoitia's important working relationship and friendship with Negrín – which endured until virtually the end of the war – see Zugazagoitia's own memoirs, *Guerra y vicisitudes*, pp. 403–4, 407–8, 410, 411, 427–8, 434. Zugazagoitia's memoirs, first published as *Historia de la guerra en España* in Buenos Aires, 1940, are probably the best high political memoirs ever written on the civil war. As a friend of both Negrín and Prieto, Zugazagoitia tried immensely hard to prevent the clash between the two in 1938. As a veteran socialist, he was discreetly critical of what he saw as Negrín's excessive tolerance of PCE sectarianism: Graham, *Socialism and War*, p. 139, p. 280 (n. 54) and letter to M. Pascua (Paris), 25 April 1938, AHN/MP, *caja* 2 (bis) 16 (Embajada de Paris). But what finally strained the personal relations between the two was Negrín's increasingly erratic manner of working (a personality trait exacerbated as the wartime pressure on him mounted), which exasperated the punctilious and methodical Zugazagoitia. He repeatedly complains (but frequently more in sorrow than in anger) that Negrín is impossible to help. This crucial tension is already evident from the published memoirs, but it becomes much clearer when one consults his (sharp and witty) letters to Pascua, for example 11 and 26 April 1938, 5 May, 17 and 20 June and 6 Oct. 1938, AHN/MP, *caja* 2 (bis) 16 (Embajada de Paris). Nevertheless, Zugazagoitia felt compelled to withdraw from Prieto's orbit because of his 'war' against Negrín. Julián Zugazagoitia was detained by the Gestapo in France in 1940. He was handed back to Franco and executed. Memorial articles in *El Socialista* (Mexico D.F.), 1 Feb. 1942.

[173] For the *post hoc* ideological construction of the April cabinet crisis, see Graham, *Socialism and War*, pp. 136–7.

[174] For a useful map of the rebel advance, see Thomas, *Spanish Civil War*, p. 799; also Jackson, *The Spanish Republic and the Civil War*, p. 410.

Meanwhile, as Franco had more and more Italian aid and troops as well as US trucks and oil, the ruptured Republic faced a massive crisis on both its military and home fronts. Indeed, militarily, the war might even have been over at this point. In the period immediately after the splitting of the zones, the Republic's defence situation was the worst it would ever be at any point in the entire war. There was no continuous front between Vinaroz and Barcelona. If the rebels had gone straight on for Barcelona at that point, then they could not have been stopped.[175] But, to the astonishment of the Republic's political leaders and its military high command, Franco turned away from Catalonia, instead diverting his troops south for a major attack on Valencia.[176]

Communication between the two Republican zones was extremely difficult. Radio contact was uncertain and intermittent. Axis submarines bombed sea traffic, effectively putting Valencia out of reach of Barcelona, except by aircraft. But these had a limited capacity and, though relatively more reliable, they were still subject to enemy attack. Food for Catalonia had therefore to come from France. But the increasingly fraught politics of the border made it a precarious source. Catalonia, with its massive number of refugees, suffered acute food shortages. After the definitive closure of the French frontier in June 1938 a subsistence crisis of major proportions loomed.[177] But all over Republican territory, subsistence crisis and deteriorating material conditions fed an acute sense of vulnerabilty, isolation and danger.[178]

The survival of the Republic beyond April 1938 depended on the rapid reorganisation of its armies and the equally rapid political galvanisation of its home front. These were the imperatives that made the PCE indispensable to Negrín if he was to be able maintain his resistance strategy with a view to forcing Franco to the negotiating table.[179] The prime minister and the party promoted in parallel similar ideas about the war's nature and objectives. Under the banner of Unión Nacional

---

[175] J. Negrín, speech, Palacio de Bellas Artes, 1 Aug. 1945, Mexico, AHN/MP, *caja* 14 (12); Azaña, *Obras completas*, vol. 4, p. 537.

[176] Azaña, *Obras completas*, vol. 3, p. 537; V. Rojo, *¡Alerta los pueblos!* (Buenos Aires, 1939; Barcelona: Ariel, 1974), pp. 40, 46–50, 54–5.

[177] This is very clear from Quaker relief work sources. Miscellaneous field reports for 1938 in FSC/R/Sp/box 1 (file 4); /box 2 (files 3 and 4); /box 4 (field reports, vol. 2: (D. Ricart) report on Catalonia in 1938).

[178] Zugazagoitia commented to Pascua on this too, observing that Negrín's speeches of exalted resistance were failing to connect with this public mood, letter of 20 June 1938, AHN/MP *caja* 2 (2) 16.

[179] To manage the territorial division, the PCE created a double party leadership – the main one in Barcelona included Díaz, Ibárruri, Uribe, Delicado and Antón, while in Madrid, Checa, Hernández, Giorla, Mije and Diéguez functioned as a deputy leadership.

(national unity) they reinforced the civil war as primarily one *against* foreign colonisation and *for* the right to build a national polity in which Spaniards of different classes and ideas could participate.[180] The same liberal constitutionalist nationalism underpinned Negrín's war aims – the famous 'Thirteen Points' – published on 1 May.[181] This most moderate of political programmes was intended for international consumption and as a blueprint for mediation – while, inside Spain, 'Unión Nacional' was designed to attract conservative and Catholic elements in both zones who were uneasy at the increasing influence of Germany and Italy. In line with this policy, the leadership of the united socialist-communist youth organisation (JSU) proposed extending membership to Catholic youth. The move was denounced by many former young socialists who, already worried by the implications of Popular Frontism for the left, saw it as a further attempt to 'decaffeinate' the youth movement ideologically.[182]

But if 'Unión Nacional' accelerated the break-up of the JSU, nor was its espousal an easy step for the PCE. It went beyond the widely understood definition of the Popular Front and was tantamount to 'stop[ping] being Communists altogether, at least until the war was won'.[183] The PCE leaders toed the line. But that was far from meaning that all were convinced by the subordination of a specifically class-based discourse and worker interests to 'national unity'.[184] Nor were the PCE's leaders blind to the dangers involved for the party in submerging its identity in the war effort, given the political climate of mid 1938 with popular war weariness increasing apace. It meant mortgaging the party's credibility

---

[180] For example, text of Negrín's Madrid speech of 18 June 1938, '¡España para los españoles!' (published in pamphlet form, FPI); see also J. Díaz, 'Unión Nacional de todos los españoles', *Frente Rojo*, 30 March 1938, reproduced in *Tres años de lucha*, vol. 3, pp. 128–32.

[181] These were published in many places and languages. The points are listed by Zugazagoitia, who assisted in their production, *Guerra y vicisitudes*, pp. 430–2 and also in *Guerra y revolución en España*, vol. 4, pp. 88–9. The exact origin of the idea for the Thirteen Points remains unclear. But Stepanov's claim that the PCE produced the entire document, word-perfect, does not ring true: Elorza and Bizcarrondo, *Queridos camaradas*, p. 418. For an English resumé of the Thirteen Points, see Thomas, *Spanish Civil War*, p. 820 and analysis in Jackson, *The Spanish Republic and the Civil War*, p. 452. The Thirteen Points also implicitly indicated the withdrawal of the International Brigades.

[182] For the dispute in the JSU, see Graham, *Socialism and War*, pp. 69–74, 112–16, 226, 229 and 'The socialist youth in the JSU: the experience of organizational unity 1936–8', in Blinkhorn, *Spain in Conflict 1931–1939*, pp. 83–102.

[183] These shrewd words are those of the journalist Vincent Sheean, who heard Ibárruri's speech to the PCE central committee on 23 May 1938, five weeks after the territorial split: V. Sheean, *Not Peace but a Sword* (New York: Doubleday, Doran & Co., 1939), pp. 185–8.

[184] Togliatti had already censured a February 1938 speech of Dolores Ibárruri's precisely because it implicitly called for a return to a class-based politics for the wartime PCE: Elorza and Bizcarrondo, *Queridos camaradas*, p. 417. José Díaz's address 'Unión Nacional de todos los españoles', in *Tres años de lucha*, also alludes to this tension inside the party.

and reputation to a victory whose possibility seemed remote even to the most disciplined amongst them.[185] Indeed, even the Comintern saw this danger.[186] But given that maintaining Republican resistance was also in Soviet defence interests, the PCE was being impelled inexorably towards serving as Negrín's indispensable support – as 'el partido de la guerra' (the war party). Rather than the PCE using Negrín, then, it was the prime minister who found in the PCE the only instrument capable of sustaining his resistance policy and holding things together politically and militarily.[187] It would prove capable of doing so through the second half of 1938 precisely because of its iron discipline. All other Republican political organisations were now, under the immense material strains imposed by the war and through sheer human exhaustion, either hostile to Negrín's policy of holding out or else (more commonly) badly divided by the question. But the PCE would, in the end, pay a huge price for its discipline. The very fact that it was identified with holding the line meant that it would become increasingly isolated. It was the *bête noire* of many, with a variety of longstanding political grievances (much intensified precisely because of everyone's increasing sense of helplessness). But the PCE would also become the target of a rising tide of other, far more amorphous, much less overtly 'political' (but no less real) discontent which, in the end, signified, quite simply, the cumulative desperation and desolation of a war-weary population at the end of its tether.

In spite of Blum's resignation on 8 April, the new French premier, Daladier, kept the border open in spite of British pressure to close it.[188] However, this did not bode as well as first appeared for the Republic. The open border was merely a bargaining device to try to negotiate with Franco the resumption of pyrites exports to French factories. The most important figure in the new French cabinet was the foreign minister, Georges Bonnet, from the most conservative sector of the Radical Party. Insular and pragmatic, he was no less wedded to an Italian

---

[185] In October 1937 Dolores Ibárruri had agreed with Azaña that the division of Catalonia from the rest of the Republic would mean defeat: Azaña's diary entry for 13 October 1937, *Obras completas*, vol. 4, p. 820.

[186] Stepanov, cited in Elorza and Bizcarrondo, *Queridos camaradas*, p. 421 and see also pp. 417–18.

[187] Prieto was in a sense also suggesting this when he remarked, off the cuff, just after the Pedralbes demonstration 'against capitulation' that he was convinced that Negrín had asked the PCE to organise it: Zugazagoitia, *Guerra y vicisitudes*, p. 391. See also Luis Araquistain, cited in Cattell, *Communism and the Spanish Civil War*, p. 233 (n. 11); Buckley, *Life and Death of the Spanish Republic*, p. 402 and Negrín's own comments in the course of the cabinet crisis of spring 1938, 'for me today there is only one significant distinction between political parties – whether they want to continue fighting or whether they want to surrender', Ansó, *Yo fui ministro de Negrín*, p. 215.

[188] For the politics of the French border, see Moradiellos, *La perfidia de Albión*, pp. 272–85.

rapprochement than was Chamberlain, and even more to the instrumental use of appeasement. For Bonnet, whether it was Spain or eastern Europe, political guarantees for 'small' nations against Germany were an ethical-political luxury too far.

On 11 May the League of Nations also rejected the Spanish demand for an end to Non-Intervention presented by Republican foreign minister Alvarez del Vayo. Only Spain and the Soviet Union voted in favour. Negrín's intention here had been to procure an injection of military aid to bolster the military reorganisation underway after the territorial division of the Republic.[189] But now Republican military resistance and the pursuit of a diplomatic breakthrough were both tacitly aimed at forcing a mediated settlement with guarantees. Negrín was actively pursuing this.[190] As its *sine qua non* was effective Republican resistance, however, the prime minister could not make this dual policy explicit. With his eyes on both the enemy high command and his international political and diplomatic audience, the only viable public watchword Negrín could give to the Republican population was 'iron resistance'.

On 13 June the French border was finally reclosed. Franco had insisted upon this before he would settle the matter of pyrites imports that so exercised the Daladier government. Non-Intervention relâchée was over. But it was even worse for the Spanish Republic. Franco was also insisting on the return of gold reserves that it had lodged in France. As a result these funds, deposited in the Mont de Marsan, would effectively be frozen from July 1938 – even though nothing definitive had yet been agreed about the bilateral withdrawal of volunteers.[191]

By this stage too the Republic's gold deposits were perilously close to being exhausted. A year previously Negrín had warned that the war would end for the Republic the day the last gold peseta was spent. He

---

[189] See also Negrín's representations to the British government in this regard, ibid., p. 269.

[190] Zugazagoitia, *Guerra y vicisitudes*, pp. 429–30, 433; Azaña, *Apuntes de memoria*, p. 82. There is also a cryptic confidential PCE report for March 1938 referring to Negrín's travels incognito to Paris, PCE archive, film XVIII (frame 224). Apart from oblique references such as these, we still do not know very much about Negrín's secret diplomacy. He never spoke of it even to his closest collaborators. For example, around the time of Negrín's secret talks with the Francoist emissary, the Duque de Alba, in September 1938, his secretary and colleague Julián Zugazagoitia remarked that the prime minister seemed preoccupied, but all he ever spoke of was 'frivolous things like women and cabaret', Zugazagoitia to M. Pascua, 6 Oct. 1938, AHN/MP, *caja* 2 (bis) 16 (Embajada de Paris). There is little in the Quai d'Orsay or the PRO to enlighten us further. Another potential source for Negrín's secret diplomacy would be the archives of the French interior ministry – which I have not investigated to date. I am also grateful for the advice of Professor Santos Juliá and Dr Enrique Moradiellos concerning their researches in, respectively, the Quai d'Orsay and PRO.

[191] A. Viñas, 'Gold, the Soviet Union and the Spanish Civil War', *European Studies Review*, 9 (1) (Jan. 1979), 120–1.

knew that Republican resistance would be over unless he could secure credits from the Soviet Union – since nowhere else would furnish them. In July Negrín sent his former ambassador to the Soviet Union, Marcelino Pascua (from spring 1938 ambassador in Paris), back to Moscow with the request.[192] Stalin agreed to make a $60 million loan available to the Republic. This was in addition to the $70 million agreed the previous February.[193] But this second loan was made when there was virtually no gold to back it.[194] Without the July credit the Republican war effort could not have survived through the second half of 1938.[195] The fact that these credits were conceded tells us something crucial about Soviet policy towards the Republic by mid 1938. With the division of its territory, the closure of the French frontier and the escalating Czech crisis, it seems clear that the Soviet cupola no longer believed that the Republic could win.[196] But Stalin was still prepared to invest in prolonging its resistance.[197]

June would also see the crystallisation of the internal political divisions in the Republic over the feasibility of pursuing a mediated peace. Opinion hostile to Negrín's resistance policy had become more evident among republicans after the Labonne soundings in March. But Azaña, galvanised by the Republican defeat at Teruel and increasingly alienated from Negrín, was beginning to look beyond his own republican circle to disaffected socialist leaders in search of an alternative government constellation.

When Negrín was appointed prime minister, Azaña had been optimistic that here was the man who would work for the mediated peace to which he was increasingly committed.[198] But the two would come to be increasingly at odds. Azaña was certainly no less capable than Negrín

---

[192] Ostensibly Pascua's return to Moscow was for the official farewell ceremony to him as ambassador: Negrín to Pascua, AHN/MP, *caja* 14 (17), July 1938.

[193] A. Viñas, 'The Financing of the Spanish Civil War', in Preston (ed.), *Revolution and War in Spain*, pp. 271–2 and 'Gold, the Soviet Union and the Spanish Civil War', pp. 118–19. Correspondence on Soviet credits between Pascua and Negrín 22 June 1937 to 11 March 1938, AHN/MP, *caja* 2, *carpeta* 2.

[194] Viñas, *El oro de Moscú*, p. 413. M. Pascua to A. Viñas, 13 Feb. 1977, AHN/MP, *caja* 8 (13). Angel Viñas' work, *El oro de Moscú* (and the more technical volume from which it was derived, *El oro español en la guerra civil*), is our main source of information on Republican wartime financing. But, as Viñas indicates, we still know nothing about how the July 1938 credit was implemented.

[195] Viñas, 'Gold, the Soviet Union and the Spanish Civil War', pp. 120–2.

[196] Viñas, *El oro de Moscú*, pp. 406–8.

[197] Reports by Soviet diplomatic personnel in early 1938 certainly suggest a serious intention still to make Republican defence viable: see report of 25 Feb. from Soviet plenipotentiary in Britain to Voroshilov, cited in Radosh, Habek and Sevostianov, *Spain Betrayed. The Soviet Union in the Spanish Civil War*, pp. 427–8.

[198] Juliá, ' Presidente por última vez: Azaña en la crisis de mayo de 1937', pp. 255–6.

of imagining the enormous distance between the cultural and political worldviews of Republican and rebel leaderships.[199] But since mid 1937 Azaña had been consumed by one overriding objective: the desire to stop the descent into internal warfare in the Republic – which was in considerable measure a product of the impossible pressure under which it was being placed.[200]

For his part, Negrín could keep his finger on the pulse of international affairs and, most crucially, gain some sense of what was happening inside the Nazi cupola, through the confidential reports he received (until the Munich crisis of September 1938) from Jiménez de Asúa, the Republican ambassador in Prague.[201] Negrín knew that Franco would not negotiate if he thought he could win outright. Negrín also understood that others would not necessarily share his conviction and that, although what drove him was a powerful sense of patriotism, he could not expect to be popular.[202] Believing that only the projection of iron resistance could bring Franco to the negotiating table, he remained fearlessly focused on removing anyone who threatened this. Hence Negrín's dismissal of Azaña's brother-in-law, Cipriano Rivas Cherif, from his post as Republic consul general in Geneva in May 1938.[203] Partly at Azaña's instigation, Rivas Cherif had been involved in some extremely indiscreet (indeed public and entirely non-viable) soundings over mediation involving a number of South American countries.

The Rivas Cherif saga was the catalyst in the collapse of relations between president and prime minister. After May, the estrangement became personal as well as political.[204] Negrín saw Azaña as behaving unconstitutionally and wrong-headedly and damaging the Republic at

---

[199] Cf. Negrín's remarks in 1938 to the French military attaché, Colonel Morel, concerning the complete mind-set ('otro modo de pensar') separating the two sides, cited in J. Marichal, *El intelectual y la política* (Madrid: CSIC, 1990), p. 100. Azaña recounts many incidents which gave him similar pause for thought, for example his diary entry for 19 July 1937 on rebel killings in Teruel, *Obras completas*, vol. 4, pp. 685–6.

[200] See Azaña's diary entry for 29 June 1937, *Obras completas*, vol. 4, p. 638, where Prieto provides a resonant echo of these fears: '[w]e have no choice but to hang on until it all falls apart. Or until we start attacking one another, which is how I have always believed that this will end'. For Azaña's (war-long) attempts at mediation, see Miralles, 'Paz humanitaria y mediación internacional: Azaña en la guerra', pp. 257–76; Azaña, *Obras completas*, vol. 4, pp. 588, 655–6, 833; *Guerra y revolución en España*, vol. 3, pp. 179–84; Bolloten, *SCW*, p. 904 (n. 54).

[201] These dispatches can be consulted in the Archivo de Barcelona (Archivo Reservado and Archivo de la SIDE (Sección de Información diplomática especial)), in the archive of the foreign affairs ministry in Madrid.

[202] This can be glimpsed in his comment about Talleyrand to Zugazagoitia, *Guerra y vicisitudes*, p. 429.

[203] Ibid., pp. 398–400, 427; Bolloten, *SCW*, p. 926 (n. 48).

[204] Zugazagoitia, *Guerra y vicisitudes*, pp. 426–7.

a time when (in the military crisis following the territorial split of April 1938) it could not afford to appear weak.[205] Azaña saw Negrín as increasingly distant and, wrongly, assumed this to be political arrogance. Negrín's 'distance' was more the result of his reducing support base and the increasing burden that he bore personally.[206] (We must also remember that, given that Negrín rather than Alvarez del Vayo was the Republic's effective foreign minister and diplomatic negotiator-in-chief, then no one knew better than he how unpromising the environment for negotiation was – something which itself added to the pressure.) Negrín's distance was not arrogance, self-importance or disdain but rather a reaction born of an increasingly acute sense of his own responsibilities. This was coupled with an ever more uncompromising sense of the real political and ethical priorities of the situation. As he memorably remarked to one socialist colleague: 'I'm no more important than any other Spanish citizen – except when I represent those who are giving their lives for the Republic.'[207]

This context explains much about Negrín's immense anger when he learned of the political intrigues of the mediation camp in Barcelona in June. Azaña had entertained vain hopes of Prieto taking over the government in May.[208] Now he was making overtures to the veteran PSOE leader, Julián Besteiro, to bring him out of his self-imposed internal exile of municipal service in Madrid. Besteiro was openly hostile to Negrín and by this point amenable to fifth column Falangist voices intent upon persuading him that he should take over as prime minister in order to facilitate 'peace negotiations'.[209] At the time, Negrín was away from Barcelona on a tour of the military fronts in the centre zone where Franco's troops were battling in the Levante, their sights set on Castellón. Cutting short his tour, Negrín returned to Barcelona to issue his famous public denunciation of the 'charca política' (political mudhole). 'If the

---

[205] But see also Azaña for his views of Negrín's constitutionalism, *Obras completas*, vol. 4 (Pedralbes, 3 May 1938), p. 878.

[206] Negrín did have a set of socialist ministerial secretaries in the cabinet, but this was insufficient in the circumstances: Graham, *Socialism and War*, p. 158; Zugazagoitia, *Guerra y vicisitudes*, pp. 388, 417, 433–4; Azaña, *Obras completas*, vol. 4 (Pedralbes, 3 May 1938), p. 879. It is little wonder that he sometimes needed to escape to the cinema, about which Azaña would complain.

[207] 'Yo soy cualquiera – menos cuando represento a los que mueren por la República', F. Vázquez Ocaña, cited in Alvarez, *Negrín. Personalidad histórica*, vol. 2, p. 252. Fernando Vázquez Ocaña had been a PSOE deputy for Cordoba. During the war he was the editor of *La Vanguardia* and head of Negrín's press office.

[208] Azaña, *Obras completas*, vol. 4, p. 884; Zugazagoitia, *Guerra y vicisitudes*, p. 427; Graham, *Socialism and War*, p.144.

[209] Preston, *Comrades*, pp. 180–1.

people and the troops only knew the sort of things that were going on, they would sweep all of us politicians away.'[210]

In fact, Azaña's plans would never prosper. The disapprobation of Negrín's policy in republican and socialist circles never amounted to more than currents of opinion. But Prieto and, perhaps even more, Besteiro were incensed by the prime minister's words, which they interpreted as a personal attack. The episode reveals how the resolution of the spring cabinet crisis had left Negrín more vulnerable to his political enemies as he became increasingly isolated. By June, stresses inside the new UGT leadership were also being felt. Its general secretary, the veteran miners' leader and justice minister, Ramón González Peña, who had been a major player in defeating the Caballeristas in late 1937, thus returning the UGT to full support of the government, was now backing a new PSOE executive under Besteiro to explore mediation.[211]

Moreover, the CNT was now internally split over the issue of continued resistance. Already in March its former secretary general, Horacio Prieto, had publicly declared that the war was lost and it was time to sue for peace.[212] The CNT justified this stance in terms of its political hostility to the PCE, and doubtless their fierce rivalry was a salient factor here. But underlying the political invective was the shattering experience of defeat at Teruel and the subsequent rebel conquest of Aragon. Ending the war was promoted as a means of reducing hardship and suffering. It was even seen, quite startlingly, as an opportunity for rebuilding the CNT – something which suggests a syndicalist myopia akin to Largo Caballero's unspoken assumptions that once the PCE was dealt with, Francoism might not prove too bad for the union movement. Apart from the practical feasibility of resistance, however, some libertarian sectors, grouped around the FAI's peninsular committee, were also now beginning openly to question its political purpose. The commitment to liberal economics enshrined in Negrín's Thirteen Points crystallised their opposition to the CNT national committee's continuing support for the prime minister.[213]

---

[210] *The Times*, 21 June 1938; Zugazagoitia, *Guerra y vicisitudes*, pp. 443–4. On Negrín's alienation from his own cabinet as a result, see Gerö to Dimitrov, 19 Nov. 1938 (doc. 80) in Radosh, Habek and Sevostianov, *Spain Betrayed. The Soviet Union in the Spanish Civil War*, p. 506.

[211] Togliatti to Dimitrov, 19 June 1938, cited in Elorza and Bizcarrondo, *Queridos camaradas*, p. 420; cf. Graham, *Socialism and War*, pp. 213–18.

[212] CNT national plenum, Barcelona, March 1938, Lorenzo, *Los anarquistas españoles y el poder*, p. 255.

[213] Peirats, *La CNT en la revolución española*, vol. 3, p. 99 (see pp. 83–99 for the course of the libertarians' internal crisis in spring 1938). There was also internal disagreement over the attitude to take towards the government's creation of a religious body, the Comisariado de Cultos, with

In June 1938, the Italian CTV participated in attacks on Valencia which were successfully blocked by Republican fortifications. Soon, however, the Republic would go on the offensive against the CTV when, on 25 July, the Popular Army launched its surprise attack across the River Ebro. In immediate tactical terms this was designed to force Franco's troops back, thus relieving the pressure on Valencia. But, even more importantly, Negrín was gambling on the fact that by throwing everything into the offensive he could convince his audience of Great Powers – and Britain in particular – that the Republic would not easily or quickly be beaten and that they should exert pressure to bring Franco to the negotiating table to end the war.

With the element of surprise in its favour, the Republican offensive had considerable initial success – particularly because, as we have already noted, the fronts in Spain were always sparsely manned. But Franco, unlike the Republic, could readily call up trained reserves. The Republican troops dug in and endured. Battle was waged for over one hundred days. Acute blockages at the French border told on the Republic, robbing its actions of staying power.[214] Franco, calling urgently on his backers, threw everything into repelling the offensive. Most crucially, he would by the end have overwhelming air superiority.[215] (The Ebro witnessed massive air battles. Nothing like this had ever been seen before, nor would it be again until the Battle of Britain.) Republican communications were bombed to oblivion and, as so many international brigader memoirs testify, the troops were blasted off the bare and rocky hillsides by the sheer force of the incendiary material launched.

For all the Republican troops conditions worsened dramatically as the rebels' vastly superior bombing capacity began to tell. The inevitable response to terror from the skies was terror on the ground. Harsh military discipline has to be understood in the context of the scale of the military challenge and its importance to the Republic's continued resistance.[216] Moreover, while there were battle-hardened troops at the Ebro, including international brigaders, there were also many new conscripts – barely

---

responsibility for ensuring that religious liberty was *de facto* as well as *de jure*. In the end the CNT approved it. Lorenzo, *Los anarquistas españoles y el poder*, pp. 259–60.

[214] Howson, *Arms for Spain*, p. 241.

[215] The Francoist army had 225 bombers to the Republicans' 50 (although they were more evenly matched on fighter aircraft – 150 Republican to 175 on Franco's side): E. Castell, L. Falcó, X. Hernàndez, O. Junqueras, J. C. Luque and J. Santacana, *La batalla de l'Ebre. Història, paisatge, patrimoni* (Barcelona: Pòrtic, 1999), p.177. Cf. Modesto's comments to Constancia de la Mora, *In Place of Splendor*, p. 369.

[216] It is interesting to see this point made unequivocally in D. T. Cattell's 1965 study, *Communism and the Spanish Civil War*, p. 209.

trained peasant boys of seventeen and eighteen, or men in their forties, whose notion of military cohesion was slight and who were poorly able to cope with the terrible conditions of massive enemy onslaught. Had the Republic been able to institute general conscription earlier, then the worst effects of this situation might have been mitigated. But, as it was, serious disciplinary problems and, notably, a high level of desertion in the midst of a military emergency made brutal penalties unavoidable as a means of enforcing obedience. Indeed, such discipline could be life-saving and was, at any rate, indispensable to the overall maintenance of frontline resistance – as in any regular war.[217] The fact that many of the officers administering these tough disciplinary measures were communists certainly further excited sectarian political conflicts – especially with the CNT. And there is no doubt that military 'justice' could be very unjust in individual cases – again, as happens in any regular war. Sometimes too sectarian motives impelled communist commanders. But it would be a distortion to portray what was going on here uniquely in terms of the political sectarianism of 1936. By the second half of 1938 – and probably earlier – the CNT's denunciations of 'communist' violence against its militants usually referred to punishments meted out to indi-vidual soldiers who had gone absent without leave from the front.[218] While this was entirely understandable behaviour at a human level, in the military circumstances obtaining by 1938 it could not be sanctioned without risking the viability of Republican defence.

Partly there was a clash of cultures here that then translated into a clash of politics. New conscripts with very rudimentary training did not understand the iron discipline of the front. For this very reason they often gravitated to the CNT's orbit, where the political culture was more conducive to them. The rural backgrounds of the recruits were very often similar to those of the volunteers of 1936–7, whose 'anti-militarism' had reflected their desire to be able to shift between the military front and their agricultural tasks. This culture clash would also echo during the POUM trial in October 1938. The communist political commissar, Ignacio Mantecón, appearing as a witness, would denounce the fact that troops on the Aragon front had fraternised with the enemy in no man's land.[219] Mantecón's account acquired an overt political gloss. He

---

[217] Wolff, *Another Hill*, pp. 120–1.
[218] See, for example, Peirats, *La CNT en la revolución española*, vol. 3, pp. 199 (although the author himself constructs what was happening at the front entirely and utterly as evidence of the PCE's sectarianism).
[219] Alba and Ardevol, *El proceso del P.O.U.M.*, pp. 222–3; Wolff, *Another Hill*, pp. 67–9.

accused the POUM of fomenting treasonous behaviour, while also, by implication, discrediting the CNT. But it is important to understand that he was referring back to a period in early 1937 before the Aragon front had been activated and to young men who had had little or no experience of warfare or military discipline. The absence of death too had, until then, made possible those transient understandings between local boys.

But the territorially divided Republic of 1938 was a world away from Aragon in spring 1937. Behind the lines too there were increasing signs of disaffection and distress. Angry mothers demonstrated against the mobilisation of their teenage sons in the infamous 'quinta del biberón' (baby call-up).[220] The sense of siege and isolation deriving from the territorial split and war under impossible odds created a reciprocally destructive dynamic. The fear of the 'enemy within' – for the fifth column was indeed more active and more dangerous now precisely because the Republic was weaker – and the crack-down on deserters and draft dodgers (*emboscados*), to whom the whiff of treason now also attached led to the increasing militarisation of the home front. It fell to the SIM, as the military police, to track down deserters and those evading military service. In so doing it was imposing military discipline on unwilling people. This explains the increasing opprobrium attaching to the service and its increasing clashes with many sectors of the civilian population, including libertarians.

The predominance of Spanish communists in the SIM reflected the already established preference for the PCE of Spanish military and police personnel (obviously the most useful to the SIM). This is also often taken as synonymous – without the case ever being explicitly argued – with the supposed heavy influence of Soviet security advisers in the SIM.[221] But the main thrust of Russian advice was technical – on new counter-espionage techniques – rather than political. Indeed, the terror inside the Soviet Union itself between 1936 and 1938 wrought such acute destruction on Soviet and Comintern operational structures outside that efficient control of anything was probably out of the question.[222] Moreover, where the Spanish security forces were concerned, there were

---

[220] From February 1938 the Republic was calling up reservists, a process culminating in the incorporation of those due only for military service in 1940 and 1941 – hence 'biberón', which literally means a baby's feeding bottle.

[221] Most obviously in Radosh, Habek and Sevostianov, *Spain Betrayed. The Soviet Union in the Spanish Civil War*, p. 476. See also Bolloten, *SCW*, pp. 601–6. But the evidence Bolloten presents is, once again, ambiguous. See also Orlov in *Forum für osteuropäische Ideen und Zeitgeschichte*, pp. 246–8.

[222] Schauff, 'Hitler and Stalin in the Spanish Civil War', p. 19. Radosh, Habek and Sevostianov, *Spain Betrayed. The Soviet Union in the Spanish Civil War*, p. 496 (doc. 78) cite a brief note (10 Nov. 1938) from Marchenko (chargé d'affaires in Republican Spain) to Litvinov. He relays Negrín's

several other far more erosive sources of political intrigue and conflict in evidence. First, there was the underlying 'old class war' between the 'old' police (if 'new' communists) and the left – especially libertarians. Then there was the ongoing organisational competition between the PCE and the PSOE that affected the SIM as it did most other Republican entities.[223] Many saw it as being to their personal and career advantage to have the party patronage of the PCE. This slotted into a clientelist understanding of politics held by many of the 'new communists' whom the war had brought to accelerated prominence. The underlying organisational competition in the SIM had also been further exacerbated by Prieto's repeatedly unfortunate choices of individuals to head the service.[224] When Paulino Gómez took over as minister of the interior in April 1938 he had sought, with Negrín's backing, to curb PCE clientelism in the SIM.[225] But here, as in other areas of the administration, this was a delicate process – given how much the underdeveloped Republican state depended on party and union personnel to sustain crucial wartime functions. Finally, there is another dimension of this organisational competitiveness that should not be overlooked. Given that the war had brought youth to the political forefront in Republican Spain, it also seems highly probable that there was a gendered dimension to the clashes between young communist commanders and their libertarian counterparts. This was male youth proving its macho credentials as much as its political metal.[226]

---

remarks that the remaining NKVD personnel ought to keep a low profile and maintain their distance from the SIM. This desire for discretion relates to Negrín's diplomatic strategy after the withdrawal of the International Brigades, which was geared to achieving British and French support to ensure a mediated end to the war. Negrín was also concerned not to inflame anti-Soviet and anti-communist feeling, growing as a part of the general weariness and desperation within Republican Spain. Radosh and his co-editors claim, unaccountably, that the Marchenko report proves that the NKVD controlled the SIM. Even within the terms of their own argument, it seems odd to be claiming this for November 1938, when Soviet infrastructural support for the Republic was rapidly being wound down.

[223] Graham, *Socialism and War*, pp. 198–244.

[224] Negrín, *Epistolario Prieto y Negrín*, p. 33. Ex-SIM director Manuel Uribarri's own books (*La quinta columna española* and *El SIM de la República* (both Havana: n.p., 1943)) were intended as a personal defence. But their disingenuousness tends to confirm that he was not the right man for the job. For a résumé of Prieto's appointments, see Bolloten, *SCW*, p. 601. See also here Orlov's comments, decades later, that he believed the Republic had genuinely lost out because Prieto was determined to install his favourites in the SIM: Gazur, *Secret Assignment. The FBI's KGB General*, pp. 133–5. Orlov told Payne that it was as a result of this that he withdrew from SIM affairs in October 1937 to concentrate on intelligence work related to the Francoist zone, *Forum für osteuropäische Ideen und Zeitgeschichte*, p. 248.

[225] Negrín, *Epistolario Prieto y Negrín*, p. 33.

[226] There is an oblique allusion in Peirats, *La CNT en la revolución española*, vol. 3, p. 218. Santiago Garcés was twenty-two years old when he was appointed to acting head of the SIM in 1938: Bolloten, *SCW*, pp. 601–2.

The SIM had taken over the Republican work camps that now also housed deserters and draft dodgers. Conditions in these varied.[227] But violence and arbitrary treatment grew less controllable everywhere as the Republic's military position deteriorated in the chaotic conditions following the rebel advance in Aragon and the rupture of the front in April 1938.[228] An increasingly harsh military discipline was exerted upon deserters and draft dodgers thereafter. Prisoners taken at the front were also sent to the work camps. Conditions worsened for all prisoners – military and civilian. There were some deaths in the work camps – mostly from neglect. However, there was at least one instance in 1938 when the Republican authorities were forced to intervene against a work-camp regime in which prisoners who were, for example, too sick to work were being shot outright.[229] In mid August, as the Ebro battle raged, the Republican government issued an amnesty designed to get trained fighting men back from the camps and prisons to the front, where they were desperately needed.[230]

The SIM also now controlled all forms of the previously private party-political prisons – which was to be expected, given its nature and function as an instrument of the Republican state. The prisons it ran were not *checas* as conjured in both Francoist and anti-stalinist left literature – that is, they were not clandestine places of illegal detention. But the SIM did carry out unconstitutional detentions on behalf of the Republican state, and it also sometimes used torture to extract the confessions on which convictions in the emergency courts were based. It was, nevertheless, also effective in dismantling spy and saboteur networks when the Republic was at its most vulnerable.[231]

There were also cases of SIM agents being implicated in the extra-judicial killings of individuals accused of fifth column activities. Sometimes there was substance to these accusations and sometimes not. But it is significant that killings like this – many of which were carried out by ordinary civilians, not by policemen – coincided with moments of

[227] See Fraser, *Blood of Spain*, p. 179 for an early testimony.

[228] This military context of panicked chaos of defeat and retreat saw all manner of brutality – both by soldiers and against them. The International Brigades were also caught up in this: see a summary in Thomas, *Spanish Civil War*, p. 801. This may have some bearing on the recent appearance of dubiously 'retrospective' hypotheses about the brigaders having been subject to a reign of terror from the day they set foot in Spain.

[229] F. Vega Díaz, 'El último día de Negrín en España', *Claves de Razón Práctica*, 22 (May 1992), 61.

[230] *Gaceta de la República*, 18 August 1938.

[231] On SIM efficiency, see Solé i Sabaté and Villaroya, *La repressió a la reraguarda de Catalunya (1936–1939)*, vol. 1, pp. 261–2. The midwife of the SIM was the war: 'técnica y terror al servicio judicial', the authors' own résumé in Juliá *et al.*, *Víctimas de la guerra civil*, p. 244.

high military tension, when the Francoist forces were achieving major breakthroughs. This suggests that those killed, often irrespective of any particular actions, were killed for what they were seen to represent and, above all, *in lieu of that advancing enemy.* Many forms of violence would be unleashed in the maelstrom of military defeat and retreat in 1938, much of it beyond anyone's control.

This erosion of the Republic's constitutional fabric was at odds with Negrín's political principles. But he had to accept it – as a part of the 'whole' he blotted out. This was the price of maintaining resistance.[232] Negrín, however, continued to see a clear distinction between violence that was imposed by a constitutional state and arbitrary violence. While he sought to end SIM torture, he would continue to defend, against constant Catalan criticisms, the rigours of the special courts and their recourse to the death penalty.[233] The death sentences provoked protests from President Azaña and bitter debate in the cabinet.[234] But Negrín's view would prevail from April through the summer. As the two armies clashed at the Ebro, the cabinet considered a batch of capital sentences imposed by the special courts. Negrín's view was that, given the sacrifices being made at the front – including now by soldiers who were virtually children – then the home front had to be subject to a discipline worthy of that sacrifice – in short, 'this is war and it has to be for all of us'. Again he faced bitter opposition, and although 58 of the 62 death penalties were eventually approved, it was by a majority vote, not cabinet unanimity.[235]

To date we know that the Republic's special wartime courts approved (and the government endorsed) at least 173 executions.[236] Many more

---

[232] See Negrín's distressed but world-weary response 'one more horror' ('una atrocidad más') on hearing of the killing of prisoners in a work camp: Vega Díaz, 'El último día de Negrín en España', p. 61.

[233] Azaña, *Obras completas*, vol. 4 (diary entry, Pedralbes, 3 May 1938), p. 878; although, in the tinder-box atmosphere of summer 1938, it seems improbable that Negrín would have thought that simply by issuing an order to Garcés (the head of the SIM) he could eradicate all instances of torture in the cells. His denial to the journalist Henry Buckley in 1939 needs to be seen in the context of the publicity 'war' for British and French support: Thomas, *Spanish Civil War*, p. 669 (n. 5).

[234] Solé i Sabaté and Villaroya, *La repressió a la reraguarda de Catalunya (1936–1939)*, vol. 1, pp. 259–68; Juliá *et al.*, *Víctimas de la guerra civil*, pp. 248–9; Azaña (diary entry for 22 April 1938), *Obras completas*, vol. 4, p. 875 ('Little more than a week after I spoke publicly of forgiveness, they throw 58 executions at me').

[235] Solé i Sabaté and Villaroya, *La repressió a la reraguarda de Catalunya*, vol. 1, pp. 274–5; de Irujo, *Un vasco en el ministerio de justicia*, vol. 1, (1) p. 83.

[236] Solé i Sabaté and Villaroya, *La repressió a la reraguarda de Catalunya*, vol. 1, pp. 268–76; Sánchez Recio, *Justicia y Guerra en España. Los Tribunales Populares (1936–1939)*, pp. 168–75, also pp. 68–9, 70. To date, we have no figures for death sentences carried out (as opposed to those passed) by special courts outside Catalonia. But as Sánchez Recio's analysis indicates, sentence review

death sentences were commuted, while the majority of people brought before the special courts were either acquitted or received other kinds of penalties (prison sentences and fines of varying severity). In view of the civil war context, and the fact that both soldiers and civilians came before these special courts, the picture we have does not sustain an apocalyptic reading of Republican state violence. As Negrín himself observed in his public reply to his critics: 'The law is harsh, but we have to act thus against those on the home front whose actions either directly endanger soldiers' lives or undermine their heroic sacrifices. The law is harsh, but its terms are public: those who choose to break the law know, before they do so, what the penalties are and what they are risking. It's a harsh law, but no more harsh (and, in practice, less so) than those which have operated in other countries that have found themselves in circumstances similar to ours.'[237] Not everyone, however, agreed with Negrín's equation of home and military front discipline, even in the context of an increasingly bitter *civil* war and the desperate military straits of April 1938 and after. The Generalitat commissioned a legal investigation that in July 1938 reported in harshly critical terms on the constitutional irregularities inherent in the practice of militarised justice in Catalonia.

By now the 'persistent Catalanism' that Negrín saw underlying the Generalitat's criticisms was also a real bone of contention. As we have already seen, the prime minister was clear about his priority in the war: he was fighting 'for Spain'. As he had commented to Zugazagoitia in the summer of 1938, he would prefer to hand over to Franco than see Spain dismembered. All he asked first was that Franco cut his ties with the Axis.[238] But Catalan disaffection over the militarisation (and thus centralisation) of justice remained acute. It was to be one of the major causes of the cabinet crisis of mid August 1938 which saw the final departure

---

(by the special court for espionage and treason and, ultimately, by the cabinet) attenuated the practice of the special courts as a whole. Moreover, the special courts in some Republican areas (Cartagena and Castellón, for example) were notably more lenient in their general sentencing policy.

[237] *La Vanguardia*, 28 April 1938. Part of Negrín's text is cited by Solé i Sabaté and Villaroya, *La repressió a la reraguarda de Catalunya*, vol. I, pp. 270–1. The fact that the Republic's special tribunals tried both soldiers and civilians complicates the comparison with wartime justice in other cases – such as, for example, Britain or France during the 1914–18 war. But such comparisons would be unsatisfactory anyway. The appropriate comparators are necessarily other European *civil* wars. Such comparative work is in its infancy, but see J. Casanova, 'Civil Wars, Revolutions and Counterrevolutions in Finland, Spain and Greece (1918–1949): A Comparative Analysis', *International Journal of Politics, Culture and Society*, 13 (3) (2000), 515–37 and S. N. Kalyvas, *The Logic of Violence in Civil War* (Madrid: Fundación Juan March, 2000).

[238] J. Zugazagoitia, *Guerra y vicisitudes*, p. 454 and see epigraph to chapter 5.

of both the Catalan and Basque nationalists from the government.[239] The cabinet crisis also brought a conclusion of sorts to the abiding internal tensions in the PSUC. Once Companys had effectively become the leader of the opposition to Negrín's government – with Prieto's departure from the cabinet in April – the PSUC's ability to compete with the Esquerra on its own political ground was increasingly blocked. The PSUC could break out of this impasse, but only by destroying the internal equilibrium between Catalanists and communists, that is, by ceasing to 'emulate' the Esquerra, as it had been doing since July 1936, and opting instead unambiguously to back Negrín's policy of centralisation. This was effectively what happened in August when the Esquerra minister was replaced by one from the PSUC.[240]

But if the PSUC could offer some support to Negrín at cabinet level, developments inside the much more crucial PSOE were making the party ever less available as a prime ministerial instrument with which to resist capitulationary currents. In the wake of Prieto's exit from the government, the PSOE executive showed its disapprobation by refusing either to convoke the national PSOE–PCE liaison committee or to issue a joint declaration of support for the government. The Socialist Party's inner turmoil also explains why it was in April that Negrín abandoned his principle of a PSOE monopoly in the Carabineros by appointing a PSUC chief.[241] In terms of government personnel, the PSOE was still providing Negrín's major support. But war weariness at the grass roots was making the party in the centre-south zone ever less prepared to endure the friction of organisational rivalry with the PCE. Many of the inter-party liaison committees were by the second half of 1938 on the verge of collapse. Indeed, some had already been suspended.[242]

Press censorship was another source of conflict. Even though this was in PSOE hands, some leading party members (including Zugazagoitia's successor in the interior ministry, Paulino Gomez) complained that Negrín was letting the PCE get away with more than the PSOE.[243] Certainly there were notorious occasions where the PCE flouted censorship: for example the broadside against Prieto at the time of the March 1938 cabinet crisis or, later, as we shall see, the circulation of leaflets

[239] In the persons of Irujo and Jaume Aiguader.
[240] Ucelay da Cal, 'Socialistas y comunistas en Cataluña durante la guerra civil', p. 315; although in fact the conflicts inside the PSUC continued: P. Togliatti, report of 21 May 1939, *Escritos sobre la guerra de España*, pp. 248–9.
[241] Bolloten, *SCW*, pp. 609–10.   [242] Graham, *Socialism and War*, pp. 145–7, 160, 224.
[243] Ibid., pp. 158–9; Togliatti, report of 31 May 1939, *Escritos sobre la guerra de España*, pp. 232–3.

defaming the POUM in the run-up to the trial of its executive committee in October. But this evasion of censorship points not to Negrín's own partisanship but to the fissures in a state that was obliged to rely heavily on clientelist party formations.[244] After all, the Caballeristas were also freely engaging in similar sorts of partisan propaganda activity, albeit directed at other targets. Negrín was a strong believer in the pre-eminent importance of good morale on the home front. The fact that the PSOE was his *own* party too probably made him especially impatient with the continual factional sniping from the Caballeristas' remaining provincial party presses – where the steady stream of pamphlet production by the dissidents belied the fact that there was a war on.

The PSOE general secretary, Lamoneda, was keen to contain these tensions between Negrín and the party since, like Negrín, he too understood that the war effort demanded collaboration with the PCE and that, thus far, there was no alternative to Republican resistance. Moreover, Lamoneda and his fellow executive members also realised that any explosion would damage the PSOE first and foremost. In a desperate attempt to pull the party together Lamoneda tried to reincorporate in the PSOE its estranged 'historic' leaders – Prieto, Largo Caballero and Besteiro – at the August national committee, taking place on the eve of the movement's fiftieth anniversary in 1938.[245] Lamoneda's efforts were probably doomed from the start. But it was Prieto's extraordinarily politically inopportune speech to the floor that administered the *coup de grâce*. The veteran leader made no substantive political points. Indeed, he left before the agenda was debated. But the damage was done. Along with Prieto, a number of other leading PSOE members withdrew from the life of the party. These included Jiménez de Asúa, the Republican ambassador in Prague, and Fernando de los Ríos, who was ambassador in Washington.[246] Nevertheless, Prieto's speech was immediately criticised – even by friends – as the massive piece of spleen venting it was.[247] It seemed as if Prieto had decided, like Largo before him, that the war was no longer worth the political candle. If the Republic could not win, then it was time to stop sacrificing the PSOE.

The national committee meeting was taking place during difficult days on the Ebro. Rebel reinforcements were in the process of containing the Republican assault south of the river. In the wake of this, Negrín sought

---

[244] See Azaña, diary entry for 23 Aug. 1937, *Obras completas*, vol. 4, p. 745.
[245] Preston, *Comrades*, pp. 181–2.   [246] Graham, *Socialism and War*, p. 153.
[247] The episode is analysed in detail ibid., pp. 142–5; see also pp. 147–9.

The Spanish Republic at war

to clamp down on socialist dissidence in the interests of the war. But this triggered the beginning of political meltdown – particularly in the JSU.[248] To the increasingly vociferous Caballerista wing were now added the voices of many more from the pre-war Socialist Youth who were hostile to the extremes of 'unión nacional', which they saw as negating the meaning of the civil war and stripping the youth organisation of its socialist identity. The political violence exploding within several provincial youth federations – most notably Albacete and Alicante – was couched in the language of the Caballerista crusade against the PCE. But across the gruelling months of the Ebro battle, from July to November, the unravelling in the JSU was driven by a more profound disillusion: the growing awareness that no amount of political discipline or self-sacrifice on the young socialists' part could improve the Republic's military situation or make up for its lack of everything needed to wage an effective war.

The battle of the Ebro epitomised the war of attrition against the Republic, whose superhuman, long-drawn-out resistance was bought at terrible cost to the best troops of its army. Even in its vastly improved form, this army could not withstand the might of Axis supply. Both sides suffered heavy losses of troops and equipment.[249] But while for the Republic these were irreplaceable, the rebels could always bring up armed and supplied reinforcements. To do this, however, Franco was reliant as never before on the massive deployment of Axis material – and especially on German artillery and aircraft. In November, in order to secure the wherewithal to drive the Republicans back across the river, Franco finally submitted to Nazi Germany's demands for mining concessions in Spain. For Negrín this was conclusive evidence that he was fighting the war to preserve national sovereignty and prevent Spain being turned into an economic satellite of the Reich.

[248] Ibid., pp. 223–31.
[249] On the Ebro see Castell et al., *La batalla de l'Ebre. Història, paisatge, patrimoni*. Jesús Castillo Doménech has argued cogently that the strictly military outcome of the Ebro battle was more ambiguous than often claimed and that it is only subsequent political events that fix our view of Republican defeat. His key points are: (1) the Republican army of the Ebro successfully blocked Franco's attack on Valencia; (2) Franco was forced (by Republican strategy) to engage in a war of position that limited the use he could make of his superior strength (in terms of war *matériel*); (3) Republican losses (of men and material) were no greater than Francoist losses; (4) the Ebro offensive allowed the Republic to maintain its resistance beyond 1938 (the core of Negrín's strategy). In a different *international political* environment, that might have been enough to save it. Archives of the Abraham Lincoln Brigade (ALBA) website, 30 June 2000. Conventional military histories in Servicio Histórico Militar (Col. J. M. Martínez Bande), *La batalla del Ebro* (Madrid: Editorial San Martín, 1988); R. Ballester, *La batalla del Ebro* (Barcelona: Bruguera, 1974).

But it was not events in Spain that turned Republican retreat into certain defeat – it was what happened in far away Czechoslovakia. As the Ebro battle raged, the crisis broke over Nazi Germany's claims to the Sudetenland. When Britain and France capitulated to Hitler at Munich at the end of September, they signed away not only Czech independence but Spanish Republican democracy too. Had Britain stood firm over Czech guarantees, then the horizon would not have closed down so dramatically for the Republic.[250] Crucially, right up to the British and French capitulation, Stalin was, in spite of all the difficulties, prepared to mobilise Russian forces and, to this end, was in September sending Soviet planes to Czechoslovakia.[251] An agreement with Romania to allow the passage of Soviet troops was also in the offing.[252] But after the Munich meeting – to which the Soviet Union was not invited – Stalin drew his conclusions about the remoteness of any grand alliance against Nazi Germany.

Soviet foreign policy remained fluid, however. At the end of August, Stalin accepted Negrín's proposal to withdraw what remained of the International Brigades.[253] It would not affect the Republic's defensive capacity and could help counteract British hostility. Military advisers had also mainly been withdrawn by this point. But Comintern personnel remained. Credits too had been supplied to the Republic. Nor were future consignments of Soviet-procured military aid ruled out. There was no sudden cutting of ties with the Republic – even after Munich – because its resistance was still valuable. But given the Republic's diplomatic isolation and the enormous difficulty now of delivering war material to it, it seems clear that Stalin had ceased to see Republican resistance as an instrument for achieving any putative anti-Nazi alliance with the democracies. If this were now to be realised, it would be sealed over the grave of Spanish democracy.

The Munich débâcle, coming in the midst of the Ebro battle, had a devastating political effect inside Republican Spain. This was particularly true in the centre-south zone, bounded by hostile territory and the sea.

[250] M. Alpert, *A New International History*, p. 167.

[251] H. Ragsdale, 'Soviet Military Preparations', pp. 210–26, esp. 220–1.

[252] Ibid., pp. 221–3; although the poor state of Romanian road and rail links would have seriously hindered land transportation (Ragsdale, pp. 219–20).

[253] Voroshilov to Dimitrov and Manuilsky, 29 Aug. 1938, cited in Radosh, Habek and Sevostianov, *Spain Betrayed. The Soviet Union in the Spanish Civil War*, p. 469; Elorza and Bizcarrondo, *Queridos camaradas*, pp. 421–2; *International Solidarity with the Spanish Republic 1936–1939* (Moscow: Progress Publishers, 1975), p. 328; J. L. Alcofar Nassaes, *Los asesores soviéticos en la guerra civil española* (Barcelona: Dopesa, 1971), p. 150.

There, since the spring of 1938, isolation had been feeding a sense of abandonment and desolation, increased by what were now very wretched material conditions and mounting hunger for most people. Acutely aware of this situation, Negrín had secret talks in Zurich in the second week of September with Franco's emissary, the Duque de Alba. But these had only confirmed Franco's uncompromising desire for unconditional surrender. Negrín saw no choice but to continue Republican resistance to force Franco to change his mind – or, rather, to oblige others to change it for him. The withdrawal of the International Brigades[254] – which began in October – had likewise been agreed to raise the diplomatic stakes, thereby increasing the pressure on Franco.[255]

It was only now too, in October, against the calvary of the Ebro, with the Republic's political options totally closed and with Negrín increasingly fearful of internal collapse that the trial of the POUM's leaders went ahead in Barcelona. (After Munich there was clearly no longer any point in worrying about adverse British reactions to the trial.) For Negrín the POUM trial constituted iron in the soul: a symbolic punishment designed to cauterise the real fifth column. (Members of the fifth column network in which there had been a vain attempt to implicate the POUM had already been convicted.) Many have supposed that the PCE's influence was crucial here in persuading Negrín to hold the trial. The party was certainly baying for POUM blood. But just as important here were Negrín's consistently held political views and his *own* perception of the needs of the fronts. He interpreted the perspective of the ordinary combatants through the prism – indeed the prejudices – of his own vehement centralism and statism.

There had been lengthy legal wrangles between prosecution and defence council over whether the POUM case should be tried by a military or civil court. Even so, the preparation of the prosecution's case seems basically to have been concluded by June 1938 – in the run-up to the Ebro.[256] (So it had taken approximately the same amount of

---

[254] The withdrawal was announced by Negrín at the League of Nations on 21 September: Moradiellos, *La perfidia de Albión*, pp. 315–16. General Rojo had already made it clear to the prime minister that this would not damage the Republic's fighting capacity. Rojo to Negrín, 9 September 1938, reproduced in Martínez Paricio, *Los papeles del general Rojo* (in (unpaginated) documents section).

[255] Moradiellos, *La perfidia de Albión*, p. 330. The Brigades' farewell parade took place in Barcelona at the end of October. On the rebel side, there was only a token withdrawal of 10,000 Italians (CTV) in order to activate the Anglo-Italian agreement of 16 November. The bulk of the CTV – some 35,000 troops – remained until the end of the war.

[256] Gorkín, *El proceso de Moscú en Barcelona*, p. 234.

time as the judicial investigation for the trial of General Asensio and members of the Republican military high command for responsibilities in the collapse of Malaga in February 1937.[257]) But the POUM trial took place at a far more critical juncture for the Republic politically and militarily. In spite of this pressure, however, and the fact that the PCE had done its best to intimidate the defence council and to harden public opinion against the POUM, the trial followed constitutional procedures.[258] It was not in any sense a 'Moscow show trial' – in spite of the title of the memoirs published in 1974 by POUM defendant Julián Gorkin.[259] (The third and final Moscow trial had taken place in March 1938.) Moreover, given that the five judges in the POUM trial were state appointees (as decreed for the courts of espionage and high treason), we could deduce that the Republic's young constitutionalism was far healthier than might reasonably have been expected in the dreadful autumn of 1938.

The POUM leaders were found not guilty of treason or espionage. But some of them were convicted of rebellion against the Republican state.[260] It has been claimed that Negrín demanded that the court impose the death penalty – on the understanding that the cabinet would commute it. The prime minister would appear to have considered this option in October 1937.[261] Moroever, as we have noted before, it was consistent with his demand that the death penalty be applied to General Sanjurjo, who had led the military rebellion of August 1932 against the Republic. Of course, the POUM leaders had endorsed and joined an already occurring rebellion rather than planning or leading their own. But for Negrín there was also the added irritant of the party's perceived Catalanism (in spite of Andreu Nin's best efforts here). Most of all in Negrín's calculations, however, there was the acute military situation of late 1938. There is nevertheless something problematic in the speculation over Negrín's call for the death penalty: namely the manner in which it

[257] See chapter 3 above.

[258] The anti-stalinist left outside Spain had feared it would not – see, for example, the French left socialist Marceau Pivert's visit to Pascua on this matter: M. Pascua (in telegram) to J. Alvarez del Vayo, 13 July 1938, AHN/MP *caja* 1 (21). Pascua suggested publishing the trial proceedings to allay fears in France.

[259] *El proceso de Moscú en Barcelona* is in fact an expanded edition of Gorkin's earlier work, *Caníbales políticos* (Mexico: 1941). On Gorkín, see H. R. Southworth, 'Julián Gorkin, Burnett Bolloten and the Spanish Civil War', in Preston and Mackenzie, *The Republic Besieged*, pp. 261–310.

[260] The sentence is reproduced in Alba and Ardevol, *El Proceso del P.O.U.M.* and also in Suárez, *El proceso contra el POUM*, pp. 202–9.

[261] A. Elorza and M. Bizcarrondo cite the somewhat telegrammatic notes made by the PCE ministers of a cabinet meeting held in late October 1937, *Queridos camaradas*, p. 379.

is said to have occurred. The public prosecutor in the trial, José Gomis, was very close to the government. Yet he did not demand the death penalty for any of the POUM defendants. Instead, hearsay has Negrín attempting to intervene at the eleventh and three-quarter hour of the trial to influence the presiding judge.[262] The oddity of this does not, of course, prove that it never happened. It may be that finally Negrín, deprived of the support of his own party and much of his own government, had himself succumbed to the panic-induced siege mentality that was gradually taking over in the Republican zone.

The denunciation or persecution of those deemed to be 'enemies within' was now also fuelled by popular anxieties over the war. As the post-Ebro retreat of Republican forces began in the second half of November – and with it a huge movement of civilians – the vacuum of authority on the ground and the ensuing chaos led to many violent incidents.[263] Soldiers took food and intimidated or killed civilians who tried to stop them. Retreating soldiers were sometimes shot by other military personnel who saw them as deserters. Civilians too were at times caught up fatally in this maelstrom. Its most notorious victim was the belligerently pro-rebel Bishop of Teruel, Anselmo Polanco, who had been in Republican custody since the beginning of 1938. He would be killed in unclear circumstances in February 1939 en route to the French frontier.[264]

Among Republican security forces too – the SIM included – it was the war's cumulative influence that explains their *modus operandi*. The political culture of the Russian advisers in Republican Spain also had a strong component of siege mentality, of course – deriving in part from the extreme experience of the Russian Civil War and the subsequent international isolation of the Soviet Union. But they plugged into existing and well-founded Republican fears as much as they shaped them. This was as true in 1938 as it had been during the siege of Madrid in November and December 1936.[265] Comintern fears of the 'enemy within' in

---

[262] Bolloten, *SCW*, pp. 518–19.

[263] Juliá et al., *Víctimas de la guerra civil*, pp. 259–62 and see also pp. 252–3.

[264] Raguer, *La pólvora y el incienso*, pp. 237–9, 178. If indeed Polanco's killers knew who he was, then his quite bellicose political sidetaking is enough to account for what happened. To ascribe his death to a form of atavistic and visceral popular anti-clericalism seems otiose and, indeed, deeply misleading, Montero Moreno, *Historia de la persecución religiosa en España*, pp. 424–7.

[265] See Col. Sverchevsky ('General Walter') to Voroshilov, report of 2 Aug. 1938, in Radosh, Habek and Sevostianov, *Spain Betrayed. The Soviet Union in the Spanish Civil War*, pp. 477–87, which gives

war-torn Spain were doubtless fuelled throughout by the atmosphere given off by the Moscow trials. But this was never simply transferred 'neat' or unmediated to Republican Spain – as if the latter were simply a blank screen to be written on. Rather the real and increasing vulnerability of the Republic to fifth column sabotage blended with the fears, ambitions and sectarianism of a populist, massified PCE. This was magnified through the 'sound box' of the Comintern to become mutually reinforcing.

In the end, to focus criticism on the SIM specifically – and especially on a mythic, Sovietised one – is to miss the point that the SIM was symptomatic of a broader problem. The harshness of its policing activities was part of how the imperatives of war had led to the militarisation of the Republican home front in a desperate attempt to hold off the disintegration born of material inferiority and lack – simply to hold things together and discipline the war effort. Increasingly harsh police action and the erosion of constitutional and judicial norms were not evidence of communist, still less Soviet, influence. They were evidence that the *war* was consuming everything: individuals, parties (the PCE included) and the very fabric of Republican democracy.

For the Caballeristas and others with political grievances inside the socialist organisations, and for many anarchists and republicans as well, there now seemed no point in repressing their anger and dissent any longer. There was also a growing sense that no peace terms could be worse than what they were already enduring. Negrín, from a different vantage point, knew better. But although the logic of his resistance strategy was impeccable, it was soon to come up hard against the opinion of influential members of his military high command, in particular that of the chief of staff, General Rojo. Their belief that, after the massive destruction of the Republican Army at the Ebro, any resistance capacity was to be measured in months would give a tremendous boost to Negrín's political opponents. Precisely because of this, and given the disintegration inside the PSOE, Negrín looked increasingly to the PCE by the end of 1938 to bolster resistance, thus further alienating many socialists. It was Munich, then, which lit the long fuse on the time bomb primed

ample evidence of how the immense pressures of war against the odds were intensifying fears of the 'enemy within'. The language/categories employed in the report (by a Soviet officer to his political masters) are the monolithic ones of the purges. But we have to read their meanings in the light of the rising military crisis on the Ebro and the desperate war weariness of the Republican home front.

in centre-south Spain by hunger and demoralisation. It would explode some months later in the shape of the Casado coup.[266]

CONCLUSION

Isolated in Europe, the Republic was always dependent upon the full-scale political and economic mobilisation of its home front to sustain the war effort. Within the Popular Front it was the PCE that had come closest to appreciating the importance of strategic propaganda work and, thereby, went some considerable way to achieving mass home-front mobilisation. As a result, the reconstituted wartime Popular Front was able to go some distance over 1937 to articulating the political power and state infrastructure crucial to a sustained defence against the military rebels and Germany and Italy. But thereafter this would be undermined by lack of time and financial and human resources. The Republic was at full stretch simply administering the military and home fronts, as well as sustaining its 'war' on the diplomatic front. There was neither energy nor resources to devote to extending social reform (in health, welfare, education) beyond what Largo's October 1936 decrees had envisaged. Ultimately, then, the way the war had to be financed (since very limited credit was available from outside) prevented the Republic from building a social contract with those fighting and dying for it. How, in the face of increasing material shortage and cumulative military defeats, could the Republic believably enact or sustain a wide mobilisation in the name of a social order that did not yet exist?[267]

Precisely because of the overwhelming material lack of everything in Republican Spain by 1938 it is deeply problematic even to pose further questions about how far its political shortcomings 'explain' its collapse. The Popular Front certainly failed to develop sufficient multiple discourses and mobilising strategies. A more politically liberal, more materially inclusive Republican project (than that of 1931–3) remained unrealised. But how could even the most sophisticated or modern of political systems have sustained popular morale once it could not deliver

---

[266] See chapter 7 below.

[267] The national Republican community may, ironically, have been realised only in the army – through the work of political commissars, education and welfare facilities and through the solidarities forged under fire. This seems a reasonable working hypothesis for the period prior to the desperate mobilisations, shortages and (consequent) disciplinary brutality of 1938 that seriously eroded military morale. But as yet we lack any thoroughgoing study of the Republican army that might address such questions.

to its population the basic wherewithal of daily life? By 1938 many were actually starving. In the end, the political erosion of the Popular Front project always comes back to the long term impact of Non-Interventionist embargo. The 'common cause' of any war effort is always provisional, conditional and potentially fragile.[268] In the face of too great a material disadvantage, no amount of ideological mobilisation can ever be enough.[269]

---

[268] See Calder, *The Myth of the Blitz*, p. 90.
[269] See J. Barber and M. Harrison, *The Soviet Home Front 1941–1945* (Harlow: Longman, 1991), p. 177.

CHAPTER 7

The collapse of the Republican home front

To fight on because there was no other choice,
even if winning was not possible, then to salvage
what we could – and at the very least our self respect.

Why go on resisting? Quite simply because we
knew what capitulation would mean.

The angel would like to stay, awaken the dead,
and make whole that which has been smashed.
But a storm is blowing from Paradise . . .
This storm irresistibly propels him into the future
to which his back is turned, while the pile of debris
before him grows skyward.
This storm is what we call progress.[1]

At the meeting of the Republican parliament held at the beginning of
October 1938 in Sant Cugat del Vallès, Negrín requested and received an
unconditional vote of confidence from the assembled MPs. This meant
that a vote had been cast in favour of the prime minister's strategy of
defensive resistance – resistance, that is, until a peace could be achieved
which offered guarantees for the defeated. That Negrín obtained this
result in the Cortes, notwithstanding his vehement critics in both the
PSOE and republican ranks, highlights two crucial realities. The first
was that no one else was prepared to take political responsibility for
the Republic's fate. Second, this was so because no one had – or ever
would have – any alternative political strategy to substitute for Negrín's.[2]

---

[1] The first two quotations are from Negrín in the *Epistolario Prieto y Negrín*, p. 37 ('Seguir luchando, porque no había más remedio para, si no se podía ganar, salvar lo que se pudiera o, al menos, salvar el decoro') and p. 44 ('Resistir, ¿por qué? Pues sencillamente porque sabíamos cuál sería el final de la capitulación'), both in Negrín's letter of 23 June 1939. The third is from Walter Benjamin, *Theses on the Philosophy of History*, IX.

[2] Graham, *Socialism and War*, pp. 156–7; S. Juliá, 'La doble derrota de Juan Negrín', *El País*, 26 Feb. 1992.

It was precisely a tacit awareness of this that explains why none of the republican intrigues against Negrín ever solidified.[3]

But even if there was no alternative, except unconditional surrender by the Republic, unfortunately that did not mean that Negrín, even equipped with his vote of confidence, necessarily had the wherewithal to pursue his own policy. In the wake of the Ebro retreat, the prime minister would manage to negotiate further arms supplies on credit from the Soviet Union. In connection with this, the patrician communist and chief of the Republican Airforce, Ignacio Hidalgo de Cisneros, visited Moscow in early December.[4] A not insignificant amount of war material was dispatched – even though it fell short of Negrín's shopping list.[5] But vital as was the promise of Soviet supplies, the *domestic* requirements of Negrín's defensive resistance were just as important. And here the political backing of his PSOE-based government was vital. But Negrín could no longer rely on this.

In the middle of November the Ebro retreat had begun. By the 18th the last units of the Republican Army had withdrawn across the river to its north bank. Knowledge of the magnitude of this military reverse split wide open the political divisions inside the PSOE. At Azaña's invitation, Besteiro came from Madrid to Barcelona to talk about a peace government. But both men knew that they lacked the positive political backing – in the PSOE or beyond – to take such a step. Besteiro also attended the extraordinary meeting of the PSOE national executive committee on 15 November, called by general secretary Lamoneda in a last-ditch attempt to solder leadership unity in the face of the Republic's

---

[3] For this reason, it is somewhat problematic to refer to the opposition to Negrín as a 'party of peace' – as do Angel Bahamonde Magro and Javier Cervera Gil in their excellent study of the end of the war, *Así terminó la guerra de España* (Madrid: Marcial Pons, 1999).

[4] Cisneros' memoirs exaggerate the significance of his trip (see *Cambio de rumbo* (Vitoria-Gasteiz: Ikusager, 2001), pp. 543–49). As Marcelino Pascua, Republican ambassador in Moscow, indicated, previous Soviet credits had always been negotiated by Negrín personally through formal diplomatic channels, and there is no reason to suppose that it was any different in the last months of 1938, Pascua to A. Viñas, 13 Feb. 1977, AHN/MP *caja* 8 (13). Viñas agrees, *El oro de Moscú*, p. 419. Cisneros' trip was a way of underlining the urgency of Negrín's – independent – request. Conceivably, it was also intended to function as a kind of 'diplomatic semaphore' to Britain and France that the Republic intended to continue resisting. It may also have been designed to stay the PCE's diminishing belief in Negrín's own commitment to resistance. For the text of the letter from Negrín to Stalin carried by Cisneros, see *Guerra y revolución en España*, vol. 4, pp. 198–200.

[5] Howson, *Arms for Spain*, p. 243: Pascua to Viñas, 13 Feb. 1977, AHN/MP *caja* 8 (13). As Pascua indicates, we certainly cannot assume the accuracy of Hidalgo de Cisneros' claim that a one hundred million dollar loan was agreed, virtually over dinner (*Cambio de Rumbo*, p. 548). To date, however, we lack access to Negrín's own papers, where documentary evidence of the figure, and how and when it was agreed, may be located.

mounting military crisis. But Besteiro carefully insisted that his presence did not mean he accepted 'membership' of the party executive. Indeed, he used the occasion to make a blistering indictment of Negrín's war policy and its consequences for the PSOE. His hysterical denunciation of the communists replicated Francoist propaganda in both its vehemence and its naivety.[6] Virtually in the same breath, however, Besteiro admitted that there was no alternative to an alliance with the PCE if the Republic was to be kept alive. In short, he was acknowledging Negrín's dilemma as prime minister but, like Prieto before him, Besteiro refused to share the political responsibility which should logically have derived from his reasoning. All three veteran (*histórico*) socialist leaders – Largo Caballero as well as Besteiro and Prieto – used the November meeting to reiterate their withdrawal from party life – effective since the PSOE national committee of August. Henceforward, the *históricos* and some of their followers would actively be searching for a way to end the war. Besteiro, like Largo, seemed to be assuming that a Franco dictatorship would resemble that of Primo de Rivera in the 1920s, with its space for collaboration with 'responsible' socialists.[7] Besteiro and others – both inside and outside the socialist movement – were coming to believe, consciously or otherwise, that all that stood between them and peace was the blind will of the PCE as 'the party of war'. Indeed, Besteiro would seemingly be coming to believe the Francoist propaganda line that, by handing over the PCE, the Republicans could 'purify' themselves and establish a basis for post-war reconciliation 'between Spaniards' (although obviously not Spaniards who were communists). Otherwise, it is hard to make sense of the role Besteiro would later play in the rebellion against Negrín led by Colonel Segismundo Casado, the commander of the army of the Centre, in March 1939.

   Munich and the Ebro defeat had, then, radically destabilised Negrín's support base in the PSOE.[8] Precisely because of this, Negrín was obliged to look to the PCE for 'iron in the soul' – even though this inevitably further alienated many socialists. In early December Negrín vainly floated the idea of dissolving the political parties into a single political

---

[6] A verbatim account of Besteiro's tirade is to be found in the minutes of the 15 November meeting, Fundación Pablo Iglesias (Madrid), AH-20-5; Preston, *Comrades*, pp. 182–4.

[7] Besteiro would articulate this sentiment during the Casado events, Bahamonde Magro and Cervera Gil, *Así terminó la guerra de España*, pp. 407–8. Nor was this a sentiment confined to party leaders: see the preparations of the Ciudad Real PSOE in March 1939 to 're-establish the fabric and content' of their organisation, *Adelante*, 8, 9 March and *Avance* 14, 17 March 1939, cited in Graham, *Socialism and War*, p. 239.

[8] See Lamoneda's comment to Togliatti on 21 November 1938, cited in Elorza and Bizcarrondo, *Queridos camaradas*, p. 425.

coalition ('Frente Nacional' or 'National Front'). He saw it as a means of breaking the deadlock of factionalism and also freeing himself from the international accusation that he was an instrument of the PCE. But the Politburo was not keen.[9] At heart, most of the Spanish communist leaders were no happier than their socialist counterparts at the prospect of a diminished party-organisational identity. (The PSOE leadership, needless to say, opposed Frente Nacional root and branch.) The communists were also wary of Negrin's personal absorption of more and more executive authority. Indeed, relations were deteriorating between premier and party – not least because of the suspicion, shared by Togliatti, that Negrín's coalition idea was also inspired by his desire to break through to negotiations with opposition elements in the Francoist camp.[10]

However, it was not Negrín's agenda that constituted the heart of the PCE's dilemma, but the tenor of feeling deep inside the PSOE and the general war weariness beyond. Both had played their part in the fierce response to the dismissal on 10 November of a socialist political commissar, Fernando Piñuela, by the communist leader, Jesús Hernández, then head of the political commissariat for the centre-south army group.[11] Relations between the PCE and the PSOE were so bad on the ground that, to all intents and purposes, the Popular Front was extinct. That being the case, if defensive resistance was to be maximised, one could argue that it would have been in the best interests of the PCE as a party to abolish the fiction of the Popular Front and take up a much more visible level of governmental responsibility. But the fact was that the PCE was simply not powerful enough to do this on its own initiative – even in the absence of any other coherent Republican alliance or strategy. Nor, even if it had been, would the Soviet Union have had any interest in a communist 'coup'.

Maintaining Republican resistance for as long as possible went on being important for the Soviet Union after Munich because it was a means of staving off fascist aggression in the east that would be directed against itself. This was why Stalin agreed to send further aid to the Republic in late November – in spite of the Soviet Union having more pressing foreign-policy concerns than Spain by then, and in spite of the logistical problems of transportation and the risks of the arms falling into enemy hands. (This aid would reach the Republic by the second half of

[9] Togliatti, report of 21 May 1939, *Escritos sobre la guerra de España*, p. 237.
[10] Elorza and Bizcarrondo, *Queridos camaradas*, p. 426.
[11] Graham, *Socialism and War*, pp. 160–1, 227.

January 1939. But it was already too late to make any difference.[12])
In fact, the Soviet leadership never entirely gave up on the possibility
of prolonging Republican resistance until this was definitively capsized
by the rebellion against Negrín in March.[13] Nevertheless, Stalin knew
that Spanish resistance was time-limited. He was also contemplating
the potential of an anti-German alliance with Britain and France being
achieved – even *after* Republican defeat. For this strategy to remain feasible, however, there could be no departure in the interim from the Popular
Front line in Republican Spain. Hence the Comintern's vehement rejection of Negrín's Frente Nacional idea, which chimed with Togliatti's
own reservations and those of the Politburo.[14] Precisely because this was
the Comintern's logic, it makes little sense to interpret the POUM trial
of October 1938 as having been somehow imposed on the Republic by
external Soviet pressure.

The PCE thus continued trying to galvanise resistance from behind
the slogan of the Popular Front. But this was an immensely dangerous
strategy for the party. It meant that the PCE would inevitably be focusing
on itself all the intensifying political hatreds, frustrations and general war
weariness in the Republican zone without having any means of protecting itself against those animosities. Ironically, this scenario was obliquely
forecast by the PSOE executive during the conflict over Piñuela's dismissal. Indeed, it is a fear of what popular and populist 'anti-communism'
(i.e. a mixture of war weariness, the peculiar isolation-inspired anxiety
permeating the centre-south zone, political disillusion of diverse origins
and cypto-Francoism) would do *to the PSOE* if it were unleashed that
explains why the party executive backed down from its confrontation
with Negrín over Piñuela's reinstatement.[15] For the PCE, however, the
consequences of its increasing vulnerability would not be long in making
themselves felt.

[12] The Soviet Union was particularly worried by Franco's demand that France should hand over
the material to him. The Soviet Union insisted that the French government return the arms
since they had been sent on credit and were therefore still not paid for: Howson, *Arms for Spain*,
p. 243.
[13] Elorza and Bizcarrondo, *Queridos camaradas*, p. 433 cite a telegram sent from Moscow on
5 March 1939. It requested information on the state of Republican resistance and made clear that
continuing aid was still on offer if that resistance was holding and passage through France could
be assured. The fear of weaponry falling into enemy hands was now acute, hence Voroshilov's
earlier cautious response of 16 February 1939, cited in Radosh, Habek and Sevostianov, *Spain
Betrayed. The Soviet Union in the Spanish Civil War*, p. 512 (doc. 81).
[14] Comintern telegram to Togliatti of 10 December 1938, cited in Elorza and Bizcarrondo, *Queridos
camaradas*, p. 427.
[15] Graham, *Socialism and War*, p. 161.

Meanwhile, whatever the recommendations of Negrín's defensive resistance strategy, sustaining it required not only material aid from the
Soviet Union and internal support from the PCE (in lieu of a functioning Popular Front government) but also an army in fighting condition and an international power prepared to bring about mediation.
But mediation would always remain beyond the reach even of Negrín's
tremendous political will and intelligence. And in the wake of the Ebro
losses, it was far from certain whether the Republic's forces in Catalonia[16]
could withstand the coming enemy offensive – in terms of either material or morale. Once the Ebro retreat had begun, and in the light of
the shattering knowledge of Munich, the feeling was widespread that
the war was *in the process of ending*. General Rojo sought to implement a
series of diversionary actions on other Republican fronts in the centre-
south zone in order to pre-empt Franco's offensive and take the pressure
off Catalonia. But these were, for whatever reason, delayed by Miaja
and Matallana, the generals in charge of the army group of the centre.
Certainly the Ebro defeat had eroded Negrín's credibility in the eyes
of many professional army officers who were now beginning to reassess
the validity and viability of prolonging the resistance.[17] In the event, the
various diversionary actions came too late and were too small to serve
the purpose.[18] As a result, Franco's Catalan offensive, which had begun
on 23 December, accelerated rapidly from 3 January 1939 as the Republican forces rapidly ran out of reserves, both human and material. On
15 January, Tarragona fell to the rebels, thus opening up a direct route
to Barcelona. Franco's progress was facilitated by the fact that Madrid's
military intelligence was riddled with spies. His forces had known about
the diversionary strategies as soon as had those Republican military commanders charged with implementing them – and in some cases probably
ahead of those Republican commanders.

Republican forces in Catalonia continued to fight. But for the most
part they were fighting to delay Franco's advance as they themselves
retreated. Moreover, the bleakness of the international environment and
the chaos and panic of these times further hastened the collapse of civilian
morale in Catalonia. Since April 1938 urban Catalonia had been isolated

---

[16] Some 220,000 men, compared to c. 500,000 in the centre-south armies. But of the forces in
Catalonia, only just over half (c. 140,000) were encadred in the effective, mobile Mixed Brigades.
[17] Bahamonde Magro and Cervera Gil, *Así terminó la guerra de España*, pp. 350–1.
[18] M. Tagüeña Lacorte, *Testimonio de dos guerras* (Mexico: Ediciones Oasis, 1973; 2nd edn, 1974),
pp. 264–5, 274–5. The reduced scale of the operations also seems to have been at the insistence
of Miaja and Matallana.

from Valencian food. By the last quarter of 1938 it was facing what today's aid agencies would term a major humanitarian crisis. Starvation, homelessness and threatening epidemic disease – all fed the rising tide of war weariness and disillusion.

On the night of 21 January Rojo told Negrín that the Republican front was broken in crucial places *en route* to Barcelona. The fall of the capital was imminent. As the military crisis in Catalonia deepened, the prime minister ordered the evacuation of state and government apparatus which began its slow journey of stages to the French frontier, amid a great tide of soldiers and civilians. On 23 January, Negrín finally declared a state of war across Republican Spain. The evacuation of Barcelona marks the point at which, to all intents and purposes, central government and Republican state machinery ceased to exist as operational apparatuses of power – even if they certainly went on existing as legal entities. Republican forces covered their departure. But now there was no front, and nothing to stop the advance units of enemy troops – Navarrese, Italian and Moroccan – who entered the city unopposed on 26 Janury 1939.

The manner of Barcelona's fall has generated a range of accusatory myths and other suspiciously totalising 'explanations', in which the subject of blame ranges from Catalan nationalism through stalinist counter-revolution to the depredations of the central Republican state. Catalan nationalists' commitment to the war had certainly been eroded by Negrín's heavy-handed centralism. This had also produced debilitating tensions within the PSUC leadership between Catalanists and communists. So too the erosive daily struggle for material survival which sapped the will to resist across 1938–9 could have been internalised by CNT-related worker constituencies as the consequence of earlier revolutionary failure. But it is difficult to extrapolate from this to 'outcast' or even working-class Barcelona as a whole and impossible to know if even CNT-related sectors went on explaining things predominantly in these terms throughout the war. What we do know, however, is that Barcelona was a refugee-packed city blasted by bombs in 1938, starved of food, and then of hope by the 'bomb' that was Munich. By the end of 1938 Catalan industry was militarised to the teeth. But production could not be sustained – not least because of the power shortages that had followed Franco's conquest of important hydroelectric resources in the spring of 1938. Among troops as well as pro-Republican civilians the knowledge of a totally blocked international horizon weighed like lead. In short, the answer to why 'Madrid, November 1936' was not replicated in 'Barcelona, January 1939' lies in the intervening years of warfare and what they had cost both materially and psychologically.[19] Between 'Madrid' and 'Barcelona' lay a gulf of experience and knowledge. The Republic had done and given everything. But everything was clearly never going to be enough. Hence the growing sentiment: 'let it be over, however it ends, just let it be over now'.[20]

Nor would the inevitability of closure ever be far from Negrín's mind in these February days. At midnight on 1–2 February in the old castle at Figueras he summoned the remnants of the Republican Cortes to meet for the last time on Spanish soil. His three conditions for ending Republican resistance – a guarantee of Spain's territorial integrity, a national plebiscite to decide the country's political future, and a guarantee of no reprisals against the Republican population (with a right of evacuation for all those who felt themselves to be at serious risk) – had already in fact been reduced to the last of these three. But the third condition, as Negrín had already informed France and Britain, and as he would reiterate many times over subsequent days, was not negotiable. The diplomats were silent. But Franco's vindictive reply to Negrín would soon ring loud and clear in the scarifying terms of the Law of Political Responsibilities, published on 16 February.[21] Yet still France and Britain (and especially the latter) kept up the pressure for Negrín to capitulate. He was caught in an impossible situation. On the one side stood an implacable military and political enemy which would not cede what could be taken by force and, anyway, saw the purging and punishment of Republican Spain as integral to its new political project. On the other side, the British and French political establishments had not the least expectation of influencing Franco – and probably little concern to do so either.

When Negrín accompanied Azaña over the frontier to France on 5 February, the prime minister already knew from Rojo that what

[19] *Franco in Barcelona* (United Editorial: London, 1939), pp. 5, 13 (this was an eyewitness report of the fall of Barcelona, written by a Quaker relief worker, Muriel McDiarmid); R. Abella, *Finales de enero, 1939. Barcelona cambia de piel* (Barcelona: Planeta, 1992), *passim*, but especially pp. 85–6, 87–9, 134–7.

[20] The feeling was widespread – as recalled, for example, by Eduardo Pons Prades, interviewed in 'Victory and Defeat', the final programme of the Granada Television series *The Spanish Civil War* (first broadcast 1982).

[21] For Negrín's acute verdict on this, see his speech in the Palacio de Bellas Artes, Mexico, 1 August 1945: 'in a savage civil war without quarter, such as ours has been, either every crime is a "common crime" or none are' (referring to Franco's dubious claim to make a distinction under the law between political crimes and common crimes perpetrated during the war), *Documentos políticos para la historia de la República Española* (Mexico: Colección Málaga, 1945), pp. 25–6.

remained of Catalonia was falling.[22] (Franco had taken Girona on the 4th, and the island of Minorca was in the process of a British-brokered surrender.) Having signed the final orders for retreat on 8 February, Negrín, accompanied by Rojo and the cabinet ministers Julio Alvarez del Vayo, Vicente Uribe and Francisco Méndez Aspe,[23] saw the first Republican units march across into France. Most of the remainder would have crossed over by the 11th.[24] The end of Republican resistance in Catalonia vastly increased the anxiety of the Soviet Union that military aid dispatched to the Republic might fall into enemy hands before reaching the centre-south zone.[25] General Rojo, who on 29 January had confided to Azaña and Negrín that only minimal, short-term defensive resistance was possible, also signalled his effective withdrawal by remaining in France.[26] But Negrín, Alvarez del Vayo and Santiago Garcés, the head of the SIM, returned immediately to Spain on 8 February, flying from Toulouse to Alicante in the centre-south zone.

Negrín's January declaration of a state of war had effectively handed power in the centre-south zone to the military – and specifically to Miaja and Matallana as, respectively, chief of the centre-south army group and chief of the general staff. Negrín had had no choice if he wanted to keep the centre-south zone afloat. But in thus downgrading the authority of civil governors and other civilian agents of the central government in

---

[22] Azaña was acompanied by his old friend José Giral, first prime minister of the Republic at war and later foreign minister, and the Republican vice-president, Diego Martínez Barrio. The Basque and Catalan premiers, José Antonio Aguirre and Luis Companys, left later the same day.

[23] Once Negrín had taken over the defence portfolio from Prieto in April 1938, Méndez Aspe, Negrín's deputy in the treasury, effectively assumed ministerial responsibility.

[24] The bulk of the Republican units had come across by 11 February, covered by the 35th Division, under the command of the very young Lieutenant Colonel Pedro Mateo Merino: see his memoirs, *Por vuestra libertad y la nuestra. Andanzas y reflexiones de un combatiente republicano* (Madrid: Editorial Disenso, 1986). The Thirty-Fifth International Division, to give its full title, had encompassed the remainder of a number of International battalions, although by the time of the Ebro these were largely manned by Spanish soldiers.

[25] Even the Soviet aid that had arrived in the middle of January often remained in, or was returned to, France for fear that it would fall into enemy hands, Howson, *Arms For Spain*, p. 244. The planes that crossed the frontier in pieces were sent back because there were no longer functioning aerodromes in Catalonia where they could be rebuilt.

[26] Zugazagoitia, *Guerra y vicisitudes*, pp. 530–1. Zugazagoitia's criticisms of Rojo's refusal to obey Negrín's order to return to Spain were even harsher in private. Both he and Marcelino Pascua (who described Rojo as having a 'difficult' or 'prickly' personality ('espinoso carácter')) were appalled by what they saw as the evasion of personal responsibility, sustained by half-truths at best, evident in Rojo's book *¡Alerta los pueblos!* (1939), Zugazagoitia to Pascua, 12 Feb. 1940 and Pascua to Zugazagoitia, 27 March 1940, AHN/MP, *caja* 2 (bis) 16 (*exilio*). This, as well as the charged and hyper-personalist politics of exile, no doubt explain Rojo's notable hostility to Zugazagoitia and his lukewarm response to the appeal against Zugazagoitia's death sentence by the Francoist courts.

what remained of Republican territory, he was laying the structural basis for later military-led action, and ultimately rebellion, against himself. But why did Negrín return from France at all? Few, if any, of his military and political collaborators were expecting him too.[27] On 10 February Negrín met Miaja and Matallana, at the Peñón de Ifach, near Alicante. On the succeeding two days he held cabinet meetings near Valencia and then in Madrid. (All his ministers had followed him back to Spain, save the republicans (who included Giral and Méndez Aspe).[28]) It is virtually inconceivable by this stage that Negrín was still hoping against hope for a diplomatic – or other – explosion on the wider European scene to save the Republic.[29] Negrín was now focusing intently on one thing: how to make Franco publicly guarantee that he would take no reprisals against the defeated population. Prolonging resistance was about maintaining pressure to this end. All of this chimes with comments Negrín had made in 1938: '[n]egotiate? But . . . what about the poor soldier in Medellín?'[30] By which he meant what would happen to ordinary soldiers on the farthest edges of the Republican front who could not get out? Once Catalonia had fallen, prolonging centre-south zone resistance was supremely about creating the time and space to structure a staged retreat, maintaining Republican control of air facilities and, above all, of the key Mediterranean ports long enough to allow the evacuation of those personnel most at risk of reprisals. Such a strategy would also have allowed time to train and implant guerrilla units whose logic was also evident to a prime minister who believed that in the coming – and inescapable – European conflagration, the Republic would still have everything to play for.

It was precisely this strategic vision – in which the PCE would necessarily have a crucial role – that reinforced Negrín's *ethical* rejection of the one form of intra-organisational 'politics' now rising like scum to the surface of the becalmed centre-south zone. This was an anti-communism of diverse and contradictory origins that favoured 'sacrificing' the PCE

---

[27] For memoir assessments see Cordon, *Trayectoria*, p. 470; Vega Díaz, 'El último día de Negrín en España', pp. 61–3. Negrín himself commented in 1945, 'If I hadn't gone back at that point, I would have no self-respect today, I simply could not have lived with myself ('no hubiera podido sobrevivir al asco de mí mismo'), speech in the Palacio de Bellas Artes, Mexico, 1 August 1945, *Documentos políticos para la historia de la República Española*, p. 26.

[28] Zugazagoitia, *Guerra y vicisitudes*, pp. 542–4. The returnees: Uribe (PCE), Moix (PSUC), Tomás Bilbao (ANV), Gómez (PSOE), González Peña (PSOE/UGT), Segundo Blanco (CNT).

[29] Certainly this was the Politburo view, PCE archive microfilm XX, 238, frame 95.

[30] '¿Pactar? Pero . . . ¿y el pobre soldado de Medellín?', Vázquez Ocaña, *Pasión y muerte de la segunda República española*, p. 62. Medellín, in Extremadura, fell to the rebels at the end of July 1938, Chaves Palacio, *La guerra civil en Extremadura*, p. 250.

on the altar of a supposed reconciliation with Franco. Such an idea had already been crystallising in the autumn of 1938 when it was articulated by Besteiro to the PSOE executive. But it posed a far greater danger in the power vacuum of the centre-south zone in February 1939. For there was now nothing to contain either the explosive organisational rivalries between socialists and communists or the desire of some CNT leaders to avenge their post-1937 political marginalisation. These sentiments animated David Antona in Ciudad Real, while in the Madrid region Eduardo Val made an offer of unilateral support to Casado. The CNT's support for Casado can be traced back to its organisational rivalry with the PCE on the Madrid Defence Council in 1936–7.[31] More generally, these sectarian tendencies in 1939, as in autumn 1936, were symptomatic of the collapse of all political centres. But now such tendencies were also propitiated by the international environment, with the virtual disintegration of the French Popular Front alliance and the exclusion from it of the PCF. Nor, on the threshold of defeat, did many see any valid reason to hold off any longer from a brutal settling of political scores. Everywhere in the centre-south zone the opportunism characteristic of the old, ingrained clientelist politics exacerbated tensions and held up a mirror that reflected the image of defeat.

The widespread feeling that the war was almost over fuelled these sentiments in the centre-south zone. Morale there was – it is true – less uniformly poor than it had been in Catalonia after Munich and the Ebro retreat. The centre-south zone troops had not experienced the crushing defeat in their own flesh and blood. And some munitions and light arms could still be turned out in Valencia, Albacete, Alicante and Murcia. But there were no professional army officers – *not even those belonging to the PCE* – who still believed that sustained military resistance was possible.[32] The Ebro defeat, even at one remove, had corroded Negrín's credibility. Among the civilian population too, material privations had weighed increasingly heavily since April 1938, when the zone had been cut off from Catalonia – and thus the French frontier. And in this context of extreme political isolation, the most effective annihilator of civilian morale was the bombing raids: thus the population of the port cities of the Levante coast was now experiencing what Barcelona's had earlier in 1938.[33] In this environment, Falangists and other fifth columnists were growing in confidence and political daring. Some had established themselves as

[31] See chapter 3 above.   [32] Togliatti, *Escritos sobre la guerra de España*, pp. 269–70.
[33] Valencia, Gandía and Alicante. *De les bombes a l'exili* (exhibition catalogue) (Gandía: CEIC Alfons el Vell, 2001).

links between Franco's military intelligence and key military and political figures on the Republican side – most notably Julián Besteiro.[34]

Negrín sought to stem the rising tide of hostility to the PCE with a powerful and determined speech in Madrid on 12 February in which he spelled out the realities of the Republic's situation: in essence, 'all of us or none' will be saved.[35] But the power of conviction was all that remained to Negrín by way of a weapon to disarm his opponents. Lacking virtually any governmental or administrative support, by February 1939 Negrín was already a prime minister without the means of exercising power.

This governmental void did not, of itself, pose problems in terms of day-to-day survival. The declaration of a state of war had, as we have seen, formally transferred power to the military authorities. The real danger lay in the fact that, by mid February, there was no consensus over resistance policy among the Republic's operational military commanders. On 16 February Negrín met with them at the Los Llanos aerodrome near Albacete. Present at the meeting were Miaja and Matallana, along with the acting chiefs of the airforce (Camacho) and navy (Buiza), the head of the Cartagena naval base (Bernal) and the commanders of the armies of the Centre, Levante, Extremadura and Andalusia – respectively Casado, Menéndez, Escobar and Moriones. At this point only Casado and Matallana openly declared further resistance to be impossible. But most were pessimistic. Only Casado was so far an active political dissident.[36] (By 5 February he had established direct contact with the Madrid fifth column. On the 14th he had met with representatives of Izquierda Republicana to ask them to go to Paris to persuade Azaña to return and sack Negrín.) But Miaja, Matallana and Menéndez all knew of Casado's activities, and Moriones suspected. What made this situation particularly precarious was the fact that none of these officers could see the point of even attempting further military resistance. Indeed, Admiral Buiza's threats to withdraw the fleet if an end to the war had not been agreed by 4 March must surely have rung alarm bells for Negrín.[37] After all, a crucial part of his own *raison d'être* was an orderly

---

[34] For Besteiro's contacts with Madrid's fifth column and the capitulationist 'underground' in the capital, see Cervera, *Madrid en guerra. La ciudad clandestina 1936–1939*, chapters 7 and 12. These contacts dated back to 1938: for a summary, see Preston, *Comrades*, pp. 180–3.

[35] 'O todos nos salvamos, o todos nos hundimos en la exterminación y el oprobio', *El Socialista* (Madrid), 14 Feb. 1939.

[36] Bahamonde Magro and Cervera Gil, *Así terminó la guerra de España*, pp. 265–9, 314. Bernal had refused involvement in Cartagena, ibid., p. 430.

[37] The government had SIM intelligence on fifth column activity and the generally poor political environment/morale in Cartagena: Bahamonde Magro and Cervera Gil, *Así terminó la guerra de España*, pp. 427–9.

evacuation of at-risk groups – something which required access to the defensive capacity of the fleet.[38]

Negrín opted for one last-ditch attempt to convince the assembled military personnel of the absolute need to hold on until Franco agreed to take no reprisals against the defeated. In retrospect, one might be tempted to argue that Negrín should have taken the initiative after the Los Llanos meeting and promoted the PCE to all the key army and defence posts. The party's core, ideologically convinced commanders (men such as Juan Modesto and Enrique Líster) and the generation of PCE *mandos* who had come through militia school, were still committed to functional resistance – not least in order to organise a guerrilla force and the party apparatus for clandestinity. But Negrín did not do this – after Los Llanos *or ever*: even though he was aware of Casado's disloyalty, and of increasing fifth column activity in Madrid. Negrín stood by because – even leaving aside all other political objections – he knew that summoning the PCE would have been entirely counter-productive. By resorting to the one *military* holding action that might have bought him some time, Negrín would have provoked the very political collapse he was trying to stave off. Given the rising tide of anti-war feeling now manifesting itself as anti-communism, Negrín would have been opening the floodgates and sweeping away the very thing he was desperate to protect – the wherewithal to prolong resistance in order to ensure space and time for an orderly withdrawal and *evacuation*.

Negrín's apparent political paralysis in the crucial second half of February was, then, a function of the broader circumstances. He was forced to take a gamble that the loyalty of professional officers like Casado would outweigh their scepticism over his depiction of what was at stake in a peace 'without guarantees'. Negrín also had to deal, simultaneously, with escalating criticism from Azaña in Paris. The President's complaint that Negrín was not doing enough to obtain the humanitarian intervention of Britain and France seems particularly ill made. Britain was demanding a clear statement of rendition from the Republican government *before* it would even deign to raise the issue of guarantees and evacuation with Franco. But Negrín understood what virtually no one else seemed to – that once the Republic had liquidated the resistance, it would also have liquidated any chance of wresting guarantees from Franco.

---

[38] The remnants of the fleet – 3 cruisers, 12 destroyers and a submarine – did not have the capacity to carry out the evacuation – but they would be vital to protect evacuation boats against the rebel destroyers patrolling the access to the Republic's Mediterranean ports.

From his base in the Paris embassy, Azaña attempted to intervene personally with the British via the Republican ambassador in London, Pablo Azcárate.[39] But the British availed themselves of Negrín's understandable discretion to claim they that had no official interlocutor with whom to discuss such matters and thus washed their hands of the issue. Britain was increasingly reluctant to complicate its relations with Franco. In this it was no doubt influenced by the uncompromising tenor of the recently published Law of Political Responsibilities. Azaña was ever more disheartened. He made no secret of his desire to resign the presidency. But he held off – hoping against hope that Negrín would achieve a last-minute diplomatic breakthrough.

By the same token, however, Azaña refused to take the one action that Negrín knew was essential if there was to be any last-minute breakthrough – namely that, as titular head of the Republic, Azaña should return to the centre-south zone. Every day that Azaña remained away crucially strengthened the French and British arguments for the official recognition of Franco. But in spite of the frantic efforts of both Alvarez del Vayo and (an increasingly exasperated) Pascua (ambassador in Paris since June 1938), Azaña would refuse to move until the 26th, when he left not for Spain but for the south of France – to announce his resignation as Republican president the following day.[40]

Throughout the latter part of February Negrín remained sunk in a deep solitude. This was the consequence of the sheer weight of political responsibility that by now he was bearing virtually alone.[41] His insistence on maintaining strategic resistance had since December 1938 put such a strain on his relations with the republican groups and many in the PSOE that they had effectively withdrawn active and practical political support. But nor could the PCE make good the shortfall. For in spite of Negrín's speech of 12 February, his relationship with the Communist Party was also increasingly tense.

For the prime minister the PCE, like the PSOE before it, was a tool, to be used to the utmost as such without any thought for what that might

---

[39] Spanish sources for this are to be found in the Archivo de Negrín, in the archive of the foreign affairs ministry, Madrid – in particular Azcárate's own report and misc. correspondence 11 Jan. to 8 Mar. 1939, *caja* RE: 150 (14). Also Moradiellos, 'Una misión casi imposible: la embajada de Pablo de Azcárate en Londres 1936–1939', pp. 140. There are also French diplomatic reports in the Quai d'Orsay which I have not consulted: see Bahamonde Magro and Cervera Gil, *Así terminó la guerra de España*, p. 442.

[40] A critical account of Azaña's behaviour during this period is in Pascua's unpublished article, 'Azaña en la embajada de París', AHN/MP, *caja* 1 (9).

[41] On this point see, Vega Díaz, 'El último día de Negrín en España', pp. 61–3.

mean for the viability of the party. But the fall of Catalonia – which had concentrated Negrín's own mind on peace conditions – had also capsized the Spanish communists' carefully promoted image of 'strength', exposing its very real weaknesses. To make matters worse, while Togliatti was still in France – after the loss of Catalonia – elements in the party continued to issue intransigent public statements about iron resistance 'to the last'. These reflected a current of opinion, identified with the Comintern adviser Stepanov, but present in the Politburo and the wider party, which saw Negrín's declaration of a state of war as offering the chance to go for communist vanguardism and a 'Numantian resistance'.[42] Exalted speeches were made by the party's Madrid leadership at its provincial conference between 9 and 11 February.[43] In these one can glimpse the unresolved ideological debate of an earlier period: the united workers' front (*frente único*) versus the inter-class alliance of Popular Front.[44] For the partisans of 'Numantia' tended to be those, such as Pasionaria, who in 1938 had expressed disquiet at what they saw as the neutering of communism by the requirements of wartime Popular Front.

But it may well be that this exaltation had a strategic purpose too. In the mould of the PSOE left's own verbal radicalism of 1934–6, designed to stay the hand of the military and political right, the PCE's *exaltados* of February 1939 may have been trying to warn off the would-be conspirators whose plotting in Madrid was by this point an open secret. But as with the socialist left, so too with the PCE – its strategy was myopic and dangerous because it provoked an enemy which it had no effective means of countering. For even if it had been prepared to, the PCE was simply not in position to 'take power' in what remained of Republican Spain after the fall of Catalonia. Far from producing a nascent communist dictatorship, the military take-over of the centre-south zone had exposed the fragility of the PCE – on both the military and the home fronts.

The PCE had made Catalonia the focus of its efforts, and the Army of the Ebro had come to symbolise its resistance strategy. But the Ebro army had been defeated and Catalonia had fallen. At the same time, a great many of the PCE's wartime recruits, in both the military and civilian spheres, were present in party ranks for a range of broadly opportunistic reasons – whether economic defence, political protection or individual

---

[42] The fortress of Numantia, near Soria, was the scene of a desperate resistance of Spanish indigenous peoples to the Roman conquerors.

[43] Togliatti, *Escritos sobre la guerra de España*, p. 275

[44] Elorza and Bizcarrondo, *Queridos camaradas*, pp. 428–30.

career advancement. At the very best one can say that the PCE's burgeoning base had for a time reflected the general feeling that the party represented the Republic's best hope for winning the war. Precisely because this was the nature of a great deal of wartime 'communism' in Spain and because it had since become evident that the PCE could not secure military victory, the party's reputation was now mortally wounded in what remained of Republican territory. In the last analysis, the rhetorical 'Numantia' of some communist leaders in Madrid has thus to be read as an admission of weakness. It also further increased the PCE's isolation, as the party became a magnet for the anti-war sentiment of sectors of the political class and of the weary population at large.

Moreover, Negrín read the PCE's protestations of intransigent resistance as a declaration of *autonomous* party policy, and thus as a form of insubordination to himself. On 16 February an exasperated premier declared to the PCE's cabinet minister, Vicente Uribe, that he would 'shoot all the communists'.[45] Fortunately Togliatti's return from France to the centre-south zone the same day was able to reinforce less exalted opinion in the Politburo and thus succeeded in mending relations with the prime minister. Under Togliatti's influence, the PCE leadership introduced a crucial nuance into its manifesto of 26 February. For the first time the PCE publicly referred to the idea of 'ending the war'. The function of resistance was now delineated as a means of ensuring Negrín's three points for peace from the Figueras parliament – and most crucially a guarantee of no reprisals. Togliatti had brought the PCE back to a position of fully supporting Negrín.[46]

But this scarcely diminished the gravity of the situation facing Togliatti and the PCE leadership: how to respond to the evident conspiracy in the face of Negrín's own paralysis and the underlying weakness of the party's position? By late February even the ideological communists among the military command had come to realise that serious military resistance was feasible no longer – given the psychological environment which obtained. Togliatti repeatedly sought advice from Moscow. In his telegram of 27 February he identified Casado as the danger. But a reply never came – or at least was never received.[47] Although holding off Franco's entry into Madrid still coincided with Comintern interests, the Politburo was entirely on its own, as events accelerated. Moreover, the immense

---

[45] Ibid., p. 431.

[46] Indeed, Negrín himself made it clear to Togliatti what the PCE needed to say, ibid., pp. 432–3; Bolloten, *SCW*, p. 711.

[47] Elorza and Bizcarrondo, *Queridos camaradas*, p. 434.

pressures on the leaders, the increasing difficulties of communication inside the zone and the growing fears among rank-and-file members of becoming a sacrificial offering for Franco meant that party structures were themselves breaking up.

The PCE in Madrid was largely thrown back on its own resources. The growing hostility towards the party there awakened a keen sense of the need to implement measures of self-defence to defend party resources and indeed lives. These measures were also crucial to ensure that cadres could be prepared for clandestinity. There was also a growing awareness that the size of the party – that is, its post-18 July cohort – now posed a threat to its very survival. For many of these new communists were clearly not to be trusted in the crucial task of planning protective measures against the threat of an anti-Negrín rebellion. This is surely part of the reason why neither the PCE's central committee nor its Madrid provincial committee were, *as a whole*, apprised of the party's self-defence plans. Instead these were worked out by trusted individuals – such as Isidoro Diéguez and Domingo Girón of the Madrid party leadership, who liaised with hand-picked communist commanders and commissars among the Madrid forces.[48]

This caution also points up another crucial facet of the PCE's dilemma with 'new' communists. By this stage there was a feeling that the party could not afford to rely on the many professional army officers who had joined the party in early wartime in very different circumstances. This problem had its remote origins in the conclusions drawn by many of these officers after the April 1938 division of Republican territory. By February 1939 the PCE had no confidence that professional officers would follow instructions just because they held a party card.[49] Again, the PCE's supposed strength – or rather the *hybridity* that had once been its strength in different circumstances – was actually now a weakness. It makes no sense, then, to measure the PCE's strength by the number of party cardholders in Madrid's military command. The hesitations and prevarications of so many 'communist' commanders in the initial phase of the now imminent Casado rebellion reinforce this crucial point. In Madrid and the other key cities of the centre-south zone many communist-affiliated officers in positions of command would choose *not to oppose Casado*, while some would join him.[50] Nor was the PCE – from Politburo to provincial

[48] Bahamonde Magro and Cervera Gil, *Así terminó la guerra de España*, pp. 366–71.
[49] Togliatti, *Escritos sobre la guerra de España*, pp. 269–70.
[50] Bahamonde Magro and Cervera Gil, *Así terminó la guerra de España*, pp. 377–8, 383, 386–9, 412, 416–18, 420–1; Tagüeña, *Testimonio de dos guerras*, p. 321.

leaderships – anywhere in possession of decent intelligence about the *mechanics* of the Casado coup. This itself raises questions about the nature of 'communist' influence in the SIM. If the PCE had been even half as powerful in the armed forces as is frequently suggested in numerous memoirs, then Casado and his fellow conspirators would not have made it to the starting line. The fact that the story runs differently should long ago have alerted us to the need to re-examine the received wisdom about PCE 'control' of the Republican army.[51] All the more so, given that within the standard narrative of the Casado events, references to PCE 'hegemony' have always been accompanied, somewhat problematically, by descriptions of the party's 'paralysis'.

THE CASADO COUP

What finally triggered Casado's long-planned action, however, was the need to pre-empt Negrín. But what Casado was pre-empting when he announced the Madrid Defence Council late on the evening of 5 March was not, as the received wisdom long had it, a wholesale promotion of communist commanders. This only ever existed as a *post hoc* justification of Casado's own invention. What Casado had to act to forestall was Negrín's bid to remove him and other 'defeatist' officers from operational command by kicking them upstairs – out of harm's way – to the general staff.[52] This removal was the logical concomitant of their public declarations at the Los Llanos meeting that no further resistance was possible. The fact that only Matallana's reassignment was published in the official bulletin of the defence ministry for 3 March[53] may have been an attempt to stay Casado's hand. Negrín repeatedly insisted on

---

[51] Bolloten, *SCW*, p. 600. Azaña himself complained about this, *Obras completas*, vol. 4, p. 883. But as I have already suggested, he had no alternative policy with which to replace Negrín's. Complaining about the PCE was, ultimately, a means of expressing frustration about the cul-de-sac in which the Republic found itself.

[52] Bahamonde Magro and Cervera Gil, *Así terminó la guerra de España*, pp. 364–5 (see also pp. 338–47). As the authors point out, the infamous blanket of PCE promotions that Casado claimed had figured in the official bulletin of the defence ministry on 3 and 4 March 1939 *never in fact appeared*. Rather it was the bulletin's 3 March stipulations as they affected Matallana and Miaja that explain the timing of the coup (the dissolution of the Republican army group, reducing Miaja's post to a figurehead, and Matallana's appointment to the general staff, where he would effectively be sandwiched between loyal operational commanders and Negrín himself as defence minister). As Michael Alpert also indicates, Casado's claims for the scale of Negrín's 'communist coup' grew significantly between the first version of his memoirs, *The Last Days of Madrid* (London, 1939), and the second, *Así cayó Madrid* (Madrid, 1968) – Alpert, *El ejército republicano*, p. 290. Also Bolloten, *SCW*, pp. 713–16.

[53] Bolloten, *SCW*, pp. 713–14; Bahamonde Magro and Cervera Gil, *Así terminó la guerra de España*, p. 341.

4 March that Casado and Matallana should travel from Madrid to see him at his headquarters outside Alicante, in the village of Elda.[54] Casado declined. But once he had done so, he had no choice but to act. He almost certainly did so in the deluded belief that he was increasing the Republic's chances of achieving a negotiated settlement with Franco. The fifth column had been assiduous in spreading the rumour that Franco was prepared to treat with professional army officers on the Republican side. Casado and others like him may even at some level have seen this offer, perversely, as a recognition of their status, which they felt had been threatened by the rise during the civil war of a new kind of officer of militia origin.[55] Whatever the case, in the oxygen-deficient atmosphere of those times, Casado was convinced that his own military credentials plus his preparedness to sacrifice the PCE as the mythical 'author of the Republic's woes' would be sufficient to appease the enemy and guarantee some form of national reconciliation thereafter.

But before this, Casado also wanted to ensure an orderly military withdrawal and the evacuation of the most politically compromised sectors of Republican personnel. He was to be thwarted, however, by events at the Cartagena naval base. On the evening of 4 March, as Casado was in the final stages of preparing the defence council in Madrid, a confused double rebellion of pro-Casado and pro-Franco supporters exploded in the south-eastern port city.[56] The government had received SIM intelligence reports of the likelihood of trouble at Cartagena. But although Republican forces did eventually manage to regain control, in the initial panic of what was an immensely uncertain situation, Admiral Buiza ordered the fleet to put to sea. Whether because he believed that the pro-Franco forces were gaining control in the port or because he was looking for a way out of what he saw as an impossible situation, whoever ended up in control of Cartagena – Buiza ordered the fleet to set sail for

---

54 This was a country house, Villa Poblet, denominated in war code 'posición Yuste'.

55 A. Bahamonde Magro and Cervera Gil allude to this tension, *Así terminó la guerra de España*, pp. 351, 354. Also suggestive is the fact that in Madrid the most resolutely anti-Casado commander was Ascanio (a *Mayor de Milicias*), while Ortega and Barceló, as professional offficers who were also communists, demonstrated much more ambiguous attitudes. To my knowledge, however, there has been no systematic investigation of these latent 'class wars' in the Republican army between professional officers from the pre-war period and those who had risen to command positions through the wartime militia schools. It would be interesting to know how important this factor was in fuelling hostility between the CNT and PCE: see Paz, *Durruti en la revolución española*, pp. 726–7. On Ascanio, see Alpert, *El ejército republicano*, pp. 356, 361.

56 L. Romero, *Desastre en Cartagena* (Barcelona: Ariel, 1971), *passim*; Zugazagoitia, *Guerra y vicisitudes*, pp. 559–66; Bahamonde Magro and Cervera Gil, *Así terminó la guerra de España*, pp. 421–38.

Algiers. There it would be interned by the French at Bizerta and later delivered to Franco. (France, along with Britain, had recognised Franco's government on 27 February.) Without the fleet the Republic had no hope of implementing any real or effective evacuation.

Meanwhile in Madrid, Casado was assembling the civilian constituents of his defence council. However, it is important to realise that the real strength of Casado's position derived from Negrín's formal declaration of a state of war in January. After the fall of Catalonia the only articulated structures in the centre-south zone were, anyway, military ones. But, additionally, under the terms of the Republic's public-order legislation of 1933, a state of war also formally bestowed on the military supreme and undivided *political* authority. This legislation was even more favourable to the military than its predecessor of 1870, which had at least required civilian representatives to be included on the ruling council of war.[57] Casado's own inclusion of civilians in the Defence Council was part and parcel of his bid to anchor its legitimacy and appeal to Franco in the 'anti-communism' that united sectors of the military and civilian political leaderships in the centre-south zone, while also giving the council a ready message with which to address the zone's war-weary inhabitants.

REBELLION AND RESISTANCE IN MADRID (6–13 MARCH 1939)

The Madrid PCE's opposition to the Casado rebellion was made in the name of the legitimate Republican government under Juan Negrín. But it was the party's isolation and sense of being besieged in the city which explains why this took the form of an armed response.[58] The plans for this were sketchy, poorly laid and chiefly geared to self-protection. The objective was to create a bargaining position from which to negotiate terms with the Defence Council in such matters as guaranteeing the integrity of PCE organisations and lives. But the difficulties of resistance were immediately apparent. First, because of the swift detention by pro-Casado forces of Domingo Girón, the linch pin of the party's defence

---

[57] Ballbé, *Orden público y militarismo en la España constitucional*, pp. 361–2. By dint of this, however, Casado's actions cannot really be seen as directly mirroring those of the military rebels in July 1936. In the latter case it was the rebels themselves who declared the full state of war – albeit assisted by the Republic's public-order legislation, which contravened its own constitution: see Ballbé, p. 13.

[58] An up-to-date summary of the Madrid fighting (based on important internal PCE documentation) is in Bahamonde Magro and Cervera Gil, *Así terminó la guerra de España*, pp. 379–404. See also Graham, *Socialism and War*, pp. 231–44, which uses both PCE and PSOE reports.

plan. Even more crucially, many 'communist' military commanders now refused to take action against Casado. Three of the four Madrid army corps were headed by professional officers with party cards: Barceló (I), Bueno (II) and Ortega (III). But in spite of desperate exhortations from the provincial party leadership, all argued that they could respond only to the orders of their *military* superiors.[59] Under pressure, Bueno and Barceló would eventually participate reluctantly against Casado – but Barceló only because of the pragmatic case made to him by his fellow officer Ascanio, who pointed out the increasing untenability of Barceló's own position.

There was fierce fighting in Madrid on 6 and 8 March from which the PCE's forces appeared to emerge with the upper hand. But the illusory nature of this advantage is immediately apparent on contemplation of the wider military and political context in the centre-south zone. Inside the Madrid area the communists had already mobilised all their disposable resources, whereas Casado still had an ace to play: the so far unused IV army corps commanded by the CNT's Cipriano Mera.[60] The Madrid PCE was also isolated by the virtual absence of communist resistance elsewhere in the centre-south zone. But what really capsized the morale of the communists in the capital was the message received from the Politburo on 9 March that they should end the fighting and reach a *modus vivendi* with Casado because the priority now was to prepare party cadres for clandestinity.[61] The message came from Togliatti and Checa in Albacete – and it was very much their own message. The centre-south zone had been *incomunicado* since the rising.[62] Togliatti had remained behind (very much against earlier Comintern advice) to help

---

[59] This emerges clearly from internal PCE documentation: see Bahamonde Magro and Cervera Gil, *Así terminó la guerra de España*, pp. 379, 387, 417. See also Togliatti, report of 21 May 1939, *Escritos sobre la guerra de España*, p. 227.

[60] Mera's units were still on the outskirts of Madrid. It was thus socialist-commanded units that had been crucial to Casado in the first days of rebellion. Mera himself supported Casado, although the CNT had, somewhat unrealistically, discussed the formation of an all-anarcho-syndicalist Defence Council.

[61] Togliatti, report of 21 May 1939, in *Escritos sobre la guerra de España*, pp. 290–1; Elorza and Bizcarrondo, *Queridos camaradas*, p. 436; Bahamonde Magro and Cervera Gil, *Así terminó la guerra de España*, p. 392 (based on internal PCE report by Jacinto Barrios: see p. 367). The message came by emissary since telephone and telegraph were uncertain. One of the emissaries (there were two) was probably a Valencian communist called Fernando Montoliú, Togliatti, p. 297 and F. F. Montiel, *Un coronel llamado Casado* (Madrid: Criterio, 1998), pp. 224–5. Montiel was one of two high-profile *tránsfugas* from the PSOE to the PCE at the beginning of 1937 (the other being Margarita Nelken). During the war Montiel worked for government press relations. In 1939 he was in the PCE in Madrid – for a time in charge of radio communications, J. García Pradas, *Como terminó la guerra de España* (Buenos Aires: Editorial Imán, 1940), p. 31.

[62] Falcón, *Asalto a los cielos*, pp. 175–6; Elorza and Bizcarrondo, *Queridos camaradas*, p. 434.

Checa and Fernando Claudín.[63] The rest of the Politburo left Spain in the very early hours of 7 March, in the wake of the departure of Negrín and his government ministers, as Casado's forces were closing in on his headquarters in Elda.[64] The knowledge that Madrid's resistance was effectively at odds with party policy caused consternation among provincial leaders like Isidoro Diéguez. Moreover, Negrín's departure, which they also now learned of, immediately deprived the resistance of its larger political justification.

There is no doubt that Negrín's departure from Spain on 6 March was the act which collapsed the shell of Republican resistance – its legitimacy already undermined by Azaña's resignation of 27 February and the ensuing vacuum in the presidency.[65] But in the end Negrín had been presented with little choice – other than to go down with the ship. His Elda headquarters were, geographically, in a Casadista vice. Had he allowed himself to be taken prisoner, he might well not have survived. Much has been conjectured about Negrín's existential despair during his final hours in Spain after the Casado rebellion. Certainly Negrín was physically and emotionally exhausted.[66] But what has often been extrapolated from this seems unjustified. Given what we know of Negrín, there is no reason to suppose that he was psychologically intimidated by the prospect that he might not survive the war. When he had returned to Spain in February, it had been to negotiate a staged hand-over of power. He had also assumed that procuring guarantees for the Republican population would demand that he became the propitiatory victim of Francoist justice.[67] But for Negrín a sacrifice had to be an intelligent sacrifice – that is one that stood a chance of attaining its purpose. Self-immolation post-Casado in March 1939 would not have achieved

---

[63] Elorza and Bizcarrondo, *Queridos camaradas*, p. 434. Irene Falcón attributes it to his close emotional identification with the PCE as well as a hard-headed understanding of the need to plan for clandestinity, *Asalto a los cielos*, pp. 176–8.

[64] The balance of military power in the Levante army (discussed below) meant that no military defence was open to the PCE (as both Modesto and Líster recognised), Togliatti, *Escritos sobre la guerra de España*, p. 290. The PCE's HQ was a ramshackle country house – code-named 'posición Dakar' – in the village of Elda.

[65] W. Carrillo, *El último episodio de la guerra civil española* (Toulouse: n.p., 1945), p. 9. The formal recognition of Franco by Britain and France on 27 February finally precipitated Azaña, who resigned hours later. He should immediately have been replaced by the vice-president, Diego Martínez Barrio. But he refused to step in unless Negrín gave him full powers to end the war.

[66] Falcón, *Asalto a los cielos*, pp. 171–5; Vega Díaz, 'El último día de Negrín en España', pp. 61–2. The author sketches a compelling picture of how Negrín's immense capacity of will momentarily succumbed in exhaustion at Elda to the 'last straw' of Casado's game playing. Negrín is reported to have said that the Colonel was 'leading [him] like a torero with a bull' ('me está toreando').

[67] Zugazagoitia, *Guerra y vicisitudes*, p. 541 and cf. p. 383; Negrín in speech, 1 Aug. 1945, Palacio de Bellas Artes, Mexico, *Documentos políticos para la historia de la República Española*, p. 26.

a peace with guarantees; whereas, as Negrín read the political moment then, the Republic still had everything to play for in the European conflagration that loomed. So more than any personal concerns and, still less, cowardice, what made Negrín choose survival over self-sacrifice was his sense that there was still some purpose – a patriotic purpose – to his political leadership.

That Togliatti and the PCE did not see matters this way is, of course, also understandable. Even before the political agendas of the postwar period complicated communist assessments of Negrín, the PCE was scarcely likely to be enamoured of a premier who, while relying on party support on the Republican home front, retreated ever more into himself as, across the last six months of the war, he had pursued his secret diplomacy in search of a negotiated peace.[68] Moreover, there is also no doubt an element of truth in Togliatti's assessment that the Casado takeover, as a *fait accompli*, gave Negrín personally an honourable way out of an untenable situation, thus allowing him to move on to the next round of the confrontation in which the terrain of battle would be all Europe. For Togliatti, Negrín's departure was flight pure and simple and, moreover, one which left the cupola of the PCE high and dry.[69]

But back in Madrid even the knowledge that Negrín had left Spain and what that meant did not deter anti-Casado army officers like Ascanio, who, in Bueno's absence, was commanding the second army corps. They had come too far to turn back – especially as Casado was not offering terms but demanding capitulation. In spite of plummeting morale, then, the communist resistance in Madrid continued because many felt that they had no other choice. Gradually, between 9 and 12 March, Casado gained the upper hand. This happened partly because of Francoist action, clearly designed to assist him, on the westerly Casa de Campo front and partly because of the entry of new troops (including Mera's), which was also facilitated by Franco.[70] The Republican airforce, now under the control of the Casadista Antonio Camacho, also bombed the PCE's

---

[68] Falcón, *Asalto a los cielos*, pp. 171–2. Negrín nevertheless felt that he had contracted a debt of honour to the PCE which was manifest in the time and effort he spent in the hours after the Casado coup procuring (as far as precarious communications would allow) the release of detained communist leaders. See also Togliatti's comments, *Escritos sobre la guerra de España*, p. 288.

[69] Togliatti, *Escritos sobre la guerra de España*, pp. 289–90.

[70] Franco's plan was to allow Casado to 'clean up' in Madrid. The Generalísimo had no interest in using the internecine war as an opportunity to breach Madrid's defences. Nor, in any case, had the internal fighting unmanned the fronts. Both the PCE and Casado had called mainly on reserve troops. For more on Franco's strategy, see Bahamonde Magro and Cervera Gil, *Así terminó la guerra de España*, pp. 397–401.

strongholds.[71] The communist resisters effectively came to be besieged inside the capital.

The hostilities concluded on 13 March. But, predictably, Casado refused to treat with the PCE. Ostensibly this was because of the assassination of a number of hostages: three of Casado's military commanders and a socialist political commissar. In reprisal Casado ordered the executions of Colonel Barceló, whom he erroneously considered the architect of the PCE's resistance, and of the communist commissar, Conesa.[72] But the rising in Madrid had been a war, and *both* sides had killed and been killed.[73] Nor was Casado's decision here fundamentally determined by an impulse of revenge. Rather his whole policy of negotiating successfully with Franco was predicated on the basis of dismembering the PCE. This was to be the offering in return for which Franco would, so the calculation went, concede a peace with guarantees for the defeated.[74] Other civilian members of the Madrid Defence Council concurred in this tactic – most notably the veteran socialist leader Besteiro, with his chimerical belief in the resurgence of a 'responsible' labour movement under a patrician dictatorship.[75]

THE CASADO EVENTS IN THE REST OF
THE CENTRE-SOUTH ZONE

Elsewhere the PCE's position in the wake of the Casado take-over appeared relatively less vulnerable. While in some places communists had

---

[71] L. Romero, *El final de la guerra* (Barcelona: Ariel, 1976), p. 331. Camacho took over from Hidalgo de Cisneros, who left Spain on 7 March.

[72] Of the other three communist commanders in Madrid, Ascanio and Ortega (who had declared himself neutral and took no part in the Casado fighting) were both shot by Franco after the war. Bueno, who fought against Casado (in much the same circumstances as Barceló – see Bahamonde Magro and Cervera Gil, *Así terminó la guerra de España*, p. 386), was removed from his command (by Casado) but apparently survived the war and the aftermath of the war too: Alpert, *El ejército republicano*, pp. 363–4.

[73] Graham, *Socialism and War*, p. 240. There were some 20,000 deaths as a result of the fighting.

[74] For a brutal description of this gambit, see the comments made by the PSOE's Molina Conejero, cited in Graham, *Socialism and War*, p. 237. Doubtless the pressures of war and internal political antagonisms also saw a certain internalisation of Francoist propaganda among Republican sectors.

[75] 'Those of us who have responsibilities, especially in the Union [UGT], we have to stay. I'm sure that nothing much will happen. We'll have to see how things turn out, and maybe we'll be able to reconstruct a more moderate UGT – along the lines of the British trade unions', Besteiro's comments on 11 March 1939 to the civil governor of Murcia, Eustaquio Cañas, in the latter's (unpublished) memoir, 'Marzo de 1939. El último mes' (1948), p. 30 – copy in the Archivo de Ramón Lamoneda (ARLF-172-30) FPI.

been detained and party premises attacked, nowhere had there been sustained armed confrontations as in Madrid.[76] Moreover, the active or tacit support for Casado from many military commanders in the centre-south zone was not predicated so much on anti-communism as on the need for a mechanism to end the war and to deliver some kind of peace terms that Franco was manifestly refusing to negotiate with Negrín. Above all, these commanders were concerned to avoid a civil war within the Republican army. Precisely for this reason, the Casado take-over in Valencia had been implemented by the police. The army commander there, General Menéndez, held his troops aloof. He was determined to protect their *esprit de corps* and morale, which had been built up – irrespective of political affiliation – through the combat experience of 1938–9. And precisely because Menéndez's objective was a peace with guarantees, he was also keen to keep the Popular Front formally intact in order to bolster Casado in his dealings with Franco.

In all the major Republican centres – Valencia, Alicante and Albacete – provincial communist leaders sought an accommodation with Casado's forces. Once they knew of Negrín's departure there was, anyway, little political point in resisting the new order. But their decision was motivated chiefly by the desire to guarantee their own safety and adequate conditions for the future operation of their organisations. Each provincial organisation acted on its own initiative. No real communication was possible between the local party organisations in the first days after the coup. Nor were they able to communicate with Togliatti or Checa until 9 March, when the Politburo representatives were released from prison in Alicante. (They had been detained, together with Claudín, hours after the departure of the rest of the leadership in the early hours of 7 March.[77]) The line instinctively followed by the provincial communist parties was rapidly endorsed by Togliatti after the fact since it served to defuse the political tension somewhat – thus buying time to prepare the PCE for clandestinity.[78]

Unfortunately, however, neither the local party negotiations nor Togliatti's efforts nor the goodwill of some sectors of PSOE and UGT could gainsay the groundswell of popular anti-communism in the centre-south zone. The determination of various Republican military commanders

[76] The most up-to-date overview of events is in Bahamonde Magro and Cervera Gil, *Así terminó la guerra de España*, pp. 408–21.

[77] Togliatti, *Escritos sobre la guerra de España*, p. 291; Falcón, *Asalto a los cielos*, p. 177.

[78] This was Togliatti's main objective – hence his concern that Negrín should keep trying to reach an accord with Casado right to the bitter end – i.e. even as the Casadistas were closing in on Elda on 6 March. Falcón, *Asalto a los cielos*, p. 176.

to keep the peace meant that there was no repetition of the extremes of political violence seen in Madrid. (For example, military censorship was used to prevent incendiary articles appearing in the press – and in particular the anarcho-syndicalist press.) In some places it was even possible for communist party organisations to regain some semblance of a functioning life. But to speak of the 're-entry' of the PCE, or the normalisation of political life after Casado, is misleading.[79] The Popular Front was dead. Its epitaph was written in the brutal organisational dismemberment of both the UGT and the JSU spearheaded by the angry and vengeful supporters of the ex-prime minister, Francisco Largo Caballero, in the weeks following Casado's take-over.[80] There were socialist leaders who sought to prevent this unedifying settling of scores on the threshold of defeat – men such as the UGT's Rodríguez Vega or Antonio Pérez, the union's representative on the Casado Defence Council, who cast the only vote against the death sentences on Barceló and Conesa.[81] But sadly they failed. Moreover, if we deconstruct the 'anti-communism' now driving events across the zone, their failure is scarcely surprising.

It is important to understand that the apparently monolithic phenomenon of anti-communism was a language through which many different kinds of anger, frustration and despair were being mediated. In terms of organisational politics, as we have already seen, anti-communism was part of a clientelist struggle for members between the PCE on the one hand and republicans, socialists and the CNT on the other. This competition was given enormous impetus and urgency by the special conditions of the civil war, which had seen an accelerated mobilisation of the population. Nowhere was the competition more acute than between the ideologically similar socialist and communist movements. The outrage of the Caballerista socialists derived in part from their conviction that the socialist movement was predestined to inherit both the Spanish working classes and the state – *en route* reabsorbing the Communist Party, whose 'separateness' was a constant, painful reminder of the wayward and unwarranted split in Spanish socialist ranks in 1921–2. But the civil war had rewritten the script. The Caballeristas

---

[79] Bahamonde Magro and Cervera Gil, *Así terminó la guerra de España*, pp. 402, 415.
[80] This story is told (from PSOE primary sources and the press) in Graham, *Socialism and War*; see especially pp. 239–44. Details of PCE expulsions are in PCE archive microfilm XX, 238, frames 134–7 (Valencia); 141–3 (Alicante); 149–50 (Ciudad Real/centre-south). For the new PSOE appointments see F. Ferrándiz Alborz, *La bestia contra España* (Montevideo: n.p. 1951), pp. 72–3.
[81] Graham, *Socialism and War*, p. 242.

could not acccept that this had happened, however, and consequently went looking for what were superfluous conspiratorial explanations of their own marginalisation.

The choice of the PCE as a scapegoat in 1939 was not, of course, an arbitrary one. The party had been a pro-active participant in the bruising war of organisations behind the Republican lines and had shown itself more than a match for its opponents. There had been many feuds and it had many enemies. Worker constituencies were also now physically exhausted after bearing the brunt of over thirty months of war. Some worker sectors were also hostile to the Popular Frontist role the PCE had played in bolstering a liberal republican order based on capital and a respect for private property. Other – urban and rural middling – constituencies, who were once very happy with the PCE in this respect, now focused their anxiety and disappointment on the party because they believed it to be an obstacle to peace with Franco. This belief in the possibility of a peace in reconciliation was precisely what Casado tapped into and in turn reinforced, as had, independently and for its own reasons, the fifth column in Madrid and Valencia.

By the second half of 1938 popular anti-communism was thus becoming part of a generalised and deepening war weariness – the product both of a closed political horizon internationally and cumulative and worsening material hardship (bombardment as well as hunger and shortage intensified by the economic effects of Non-Interventionist blockade). The PCE was targeted especially for blame by different (and sometimes mutually politically antagonistic) sectors of a disappointed Republican populace precisely because it had identified itself so closely with the war effort – and more specifically with victory. The PCE had been projected, and had projected itself, as the symbol *par excellence* of inter-class hopes for Republican success. In 1936 the party had derived kudos from an intense but entirely unrealistic popular belief in the 'epic' power of the Soviet Union. By 1939 those hopes had been consumed in the unforgiving heat of a gruelling and messy war. The resulting 'anti-communism' had about it an elemental force (the casting out of a secular god?) which serves to remind us that a crucial part of the PCE's original popular appeal lay in what was effectively a redemptive myth.

What existed through and after Casado, then, was not a rational political front – still less a rational political front against 'communist dictatorship' as has sometimes been suggested. Rather it was a visceral and chaotic amalgam of political and social constituencies brought together by a desperate war weariness and by the desire for an act of collective psychological and political unburdening. Someone or something tangible had to be found to blame for the fact that the war was about to be lost after so much sacrifice and superhuman effort. In the end, the meaning of the Casado episode was that the PCE, like all other forces in Republican Spain, had ultimately been consumed by the war.

Once Casado was in full political and military control of the centre-south zone, as he was by the middle of March, he turned his attention to the peace negotiations that he saw as the *raison d'être* of his victory.[82] In the wake of this, there had been a significant level of desertion – especially from the Madrid front – by ordinary soldiers who felt that peace had already arrived. Nevertheless, the Republican military fronts and home front for the time being remained stable. But Casado knew that he had to move rapidly to gain an assurance of no reprisals from Franco. Otherwise he would not be able to guarantee public order in the zone. Casado had, by his own actions, brought an end to effective Republican resistance. But he still believed he had a certain margin for negotiation with Franco by dint of their common anti-communism and the service he had done the Generalísimo in 'cleansing' the party from the political life of the Republic. This, so Casado hoped, would open up the way to his favoured scenario: the reunification of Spain via a reconciliation of its military family. For whatever reasons, Casado chose to ignore the awkard detail that by ending the Republic's resistance he had also removed the only reason Franco might ever have had to concede a peace *with terms*.

Also resolutely ignoring this, Republican political organisations across the centre-south zone entered into a frenzy of reformation, making ready for a 'normality' that would never come.[83] The pro-Casado press fed this groundless mass optimism, which clearly originated in a mechanism of psychological self-preservation. Only the PCE was exempt from the collective delusion by reason of its particular political situation. This would be reinforced by the Defence Council's bringing to trial of sixteen front-rank communist military commanders and political leaders on 24 March. The run-up to this did at least have the positive effect of concentrating the party's efforts on evacuating its leading cadres. On the day of the communist trial, Togliatti left Totana (Cartagena) in a plane bound for Algiers. He was accompanied by a number of party leaders including Jesús Hernández, Pedro Checa, Isidoro Diéguez and

---

[82] What follows here is an analytical overview of events. For a detailed account see Bahamonde Magro and Cervera Gil, *Así terminó la guerra de España*, pp. 439–99.

[83] For example, on 24 March the Madrid press published details of the new PSOE executive elected in the city. This and other examples are in Graham, *Socialism and War*, pp. 239–43.

José Antonio Uribes.[84] Over the subsequent four days the PCE also managed to evacuate other leading cadres (in small boats and the few merchant vessels that would take refugees) from the main Republican ports of Cartagena, Valencia, Alicante and Almería. Precisely because the PCE had been made brutally aware of the necessity of such an evacuation earlier than any other Republican group, it managed the operation relatively better. But neither this nor the PCE's relatively superior preparations for clandestinity could prevent thousands of communists from being caught up, along with those of other political affiliations or none, in the grim last chapter of Republican defeat.

For Franco's own reasons for facilitating Casado's take-over were, of course, quite different from Casado's interpretation of them. Franco had previously let it be known (including via the fifth column) that he would only negotiate with fellow army officers. He had also issued a text on 5 February detailing certain written 'concessions' which, again, reached Casado via the fifth column.[85] But what neither Casado nor his civilian supporters seemed to grasp (in spite of the publication of the Law of Political Responsibilities) was that these concessions were being wielded as an instrument of war in order to accelerate the end of the conflict rather than offered as a basis for reconciliation between victors and vanquished.[86] From the start Franco would demand of Casado unconditional surrender. For this reason, Franco refused to treat with Casado himself or other officers of the Republican general staff, insisting that those delegated to attend the joint meeting requested by the Republicans should be of subordinate rank. As far as Franco was concerned, they were not attending as interlocutors but simply to receive practical instructions for handing over the Republic's troops and territory.

This message was brutally reinforced by Franco's representatives at the meeting, which took place on 23 March at the Gamonal air base in Burgos. They refused to enter into any discussion with their Republican counterparts[87] about either formal guarantees for the defeated or any

[84] Togliatti, *Escritos sobre la guerra de España*, p. 297. They had to combat Casado's forces to get into the aerodrome. Diéguez had escaped Casado by disguising himself as an ordinary soldier on the sierra front: Romero, *El final de la guerra*, pp. 367–8.

[85] These included the provision of safeconducts for those wishing to leave Spain and the statement that simple political support for the Republic would be excluded from the definition of what was 'criminal'.

[86] Note that these 'concessions', which Franco refused to discuss with Casado, would again be broadcast on the eve of the Republican surrender in order to encourage the compliance of officers and troops, Bahamonde Magro and Cervera Gil, *Así terminó la guerra de España*, p. 462.

[87] The Republican delegates were Lt Colonel Antonio Garijo Hernández and Major Leopoldo Ortega Nieto. Garijo was certainly very sympathetic to the opposing camp, if not actively an agent, as the PCE would subsequently claim.

modification of the terms of the surrender. Casado had dispatched his representatives in the hope that it would still be possible to agree a staggered hand-over of territory in order to allow a slow, staged retreat of the Republican armies. But it was clear that Franco would accept no delay.

The outcome of the meeting of 23 March made Casado fully aware of his powerlessness. He was also painfully cognisant of his total isolation in this predicament. Britain had looked favourably on his actions thus far.[88] But now that Franco had definitively won, courtesy of those actions, British policy makers were determined to do nothing that might offend Spain's new ruler. The key to Britain's inaction was a determination to protect its own position in the Mediterranean by ensuring Francoist Spain's neutrality in any future European war. But the political and social animosity felt by the British establishment towards the Spanish Republicans also played a part here. For this reason there was absolutely no possibility that the British government would respond to Casado's desperate plea that it exert meaningful pressure on Franco to offer, at this late stage, some guarantee of no reprisals against the civilian population. Nor would it allow the Royal Navy to assist in any evacuation. Britain's negative in both regards was made ringingly clear. The essentials of the position evinced when Britain had recognised Franco on 27 February basically held throughout March – even though by 5 March the Republic had lost its own navy. The British authorities would do nothing without Franco's *express* approval.[89] As reasons, they adduced the following. There was probably no need to engage in a mass evacuation anyway. The Royal Navy did not want to be involved.[90] There was nowhere for such a large number of refugees to go. (Britain was disposed to admit only a reduced number of the economically solvent.) In short, as Lord Halifax publicly claimed on 9 March, Britain's stance was eminently justifiable on the grounds of 'political realism'. But there was also an unspoken assumption here: that even if Franco were to carry out mass executions of Republicans, these would pose no danger to British commercial or political interests.

[88] There is no doubt that the British were by February 1939 already *au courant* regarding Casado's plans, Bahamonde Magro and Cervera Gil, *Así terminó la guerra de España*, pp. 468–9.

[89] Britain had recognised Franco unconditionally. Neither guarantees for the Republican population nor evacuation was raised.

[90] In the early weeks of the war the Royal Navy had, entirely on its own account, taken off affluent and powerful refugees threatened by the popular violence that had followed in the wake of Republican state collapse. But in 1939 it chose to argue that it had no remit to 'intervene'. The issue was clearly not 'intervention' *per se*, but the fact that the naval high command and officer corps felt detatched from, when not actively hostile to, the social and political complexion of those they were now being asked to save.

The British recognition of Franco and the ensuing Casado events also saw Stalin move further away from viewing collective security as a viable strategic defence of Soviet frontiers. In his speech to the XVIII Congress of the CPSU, inaugurated on 10 March, he had alluded publicly for the first time to the possibility of seeking a *modus vivendi* with Nazi Germany.[91]

Casado was caught, as Negrín had been before him, between the rock of international isolation and the hard place of Francoist intransigence. On 25 March, as the Republican representatives met again with their Francoist counterparts, Casado wrote a personal letter to Franco in one final attempt to secure a written guarantee of no reprisals. He appealed now for the sake of a victorious *Francoist* public order, arguing that without such a guarantee there was no certainty that the orders of the Republican military command would be obeyed – there might be desperate resistance in some places, with the zone descending into chaos. Franco's only response was to announce the commencement of his final military offensive simultaneously on all fronts. To all intents and purposes, the General had broken off contact with the Defence Council. At this point, Casado, knowing that he had failed, and fearful above all things of increasing disorder in the centre-south zone, had no choice but to see through to the bitter end what he had started. Speed was of the essence. On 26 March the Republican Airforce was hastily surrendered to Franco. On 28 March Casado issued the order to the Republican armies to surrender on all fronts.[92] In Madrid some soldiers took the metro home, others the road east towards the Mediterranean ports. In some places there was fraternisation between the troops. In the end, Madrid – capital of Republican resistance and, for a time, of world anti-fascism – did not have to be captured. Franco's troops walked in unopposed. Inside the city it was the extremely well-organised fifth column which oversaw the mechanics of the, largely orderly, hand-over of power. Indeed, the fact that the fifth column was so well prepared and ubiquitous (including in Casado's own staff, in the person of José Centaño de la Paz) further problematises the notion of 'communist military hegemony' in Republican Spain.[93]

But the relative peace of Madrid, as well as being a peace of exhaustion, was also in part a function of the maelstrom having moved

---

[91] In fact previous feelers had been put out by Soviet diplomats in Berlin – although so far to no avail.
[92] That is, in the south, centre and Levante. For a summary of Franco's southern advance, see Bahamonde Magro and Cervera Gil, *Así terminó la guerra de España*, pp. 488–9.
[93] Ibid., pp. 454, 463.

elsewhere. As the news of Franco's unconditional demands and looming final offensive became known, the strange becalmed days which in many places had followed Casado's take-over gave way to the eruption of mass panic as the illusion of a peace with guarantees vanished. On 27 March tens of thousands of desperate Spaniards, in a frantic and disordered surge of humankind, made for the Republic's remaining Mediterranean ports – Valencia, Gandía and Alicante. But they went in search of boats that would never arrive.[94] Negrín's resistance policy had for a long time logically precluded any open preparations for a mass evacuation. And although the fall of Catalonia changed that, it also provoked a simultaneous administrative meltdown in government which once again precluded much effective planning. Nor by this stage could funds readily be accessed or channelled.[95]

It was the British diplomatic staff in Valencia and Gandía who, intensely alarmed by the flood of refugees and aware that the Royal Navy would not intervene, sought to channel it to Alicante with vague promises that there merchant ships awaited. Among those said to be arriving were vessels chartered on behalf of the French-led International Coordinating Committee for Information and Assistance to Republican Spain. (Its French representatives were particularly active in these evacuation attempts and had chartered boats belonging to the French Communist Party's own company, France Navigation.) The British consular officials were far from happy at this threatened contravention of their own government's policy of no evacuation without the approval of Burgos. But at least it had the advantage of removing the refugees from their immediate vicinity. Moreover, it also allowed the discreet and orderly embarcation in Gandía of Casado and his immediate circle, for whom the British had intervened with the Generalísimo.[96] Franco had facilitated the colonel's

<hr />

94 Even before the crisis of 27 March, the few merchant vessels in Republican ports that were prepared to embark refugees were already demanding payment in currencies other than the Republican peseta (which was by this stage virtually worthless). But foreign exchange was beyond the reach of many refugees.

95 The battle between the Republic's two rival exile funding bodies, the Spanish Republican Evacuation Service (Servicio de Evacuación de Republicanos Españoles (SERE) and the Committee of Assistance to Spanish Republicans (Junta de Auxilio a los Republicanos Españoles (JARE)), would be the first of many bitter conflicts that would poison the political life of the Republican diaspora. Thomas, *Spanish Civil War*, pp. 920–1; P. W. Fagen, *Exiles and Citizens. Spanish Republicans in Mexico* (Austin: University of Texas, 1973), *passim* and L. Stein, *Beyond Death and Exile. The Spanish Republicans in France 1939–1955* (Cambridge, Mass.: Harvard University Press, 1979), pp. 87–91. On exile more broadly: J. Cuesta & B. Bermejo (eds.), *Emigración y exilio. Españoles en Francia 1936–1946* (Madrid: EUDEMA, 1996).

96 This episode is covered in detail in Bahamonde Magro and Cervera Gil, *Así terminó la guerra de España*, pp. 469–70, 472–3, 474, 475–87. As the authors point out, however, this agreement

departure from Madrid[97] and journey to the port, and – in spite of issuing a subsequent formal diplomatic protest – was clearly entirely in agreement that Casado should depart on a British naval vessel. (The fifth column in Valencia was more or less in control of the city by 29 March, yet allowed Casado to pass through unmolested.) Indeed, without Franco's approval it is clear that the British would not have taken him off from Gandía.[98] Only those so approved left the port on British vessels. Meanwhile, further down the coast, Alicante had become the territory of last resort for beleaguered Republicans.

Reduced to its essentials, the tragedy of Alicante was the result of three things. First, the fact that Franco did not want any of the refugees to leave Spain and was maintaining his naval blockade of the Mediterranean to ensure that they did not. Second, that the Republic no longer had a navy of its own. Third, that Britain would not risk Franco's displeasure by using the Royal Navy either to perform large-scale evacuations or to protect the various merchant ships that hovered on the outskirts of the port, outside Spanish territorial waters, intimidated by the Francoist warships.[99] Nor was the French government prepared to offer any protection for its own merchant vessels in Spanish waters, in spite of the desperate last-minute appeals from the French solidarity delegates who had chartered them. Had the Republic still had its own navy, it could have fulfilled this protective function. But in the absence of this, most of the merchant boats simply turned around and, sometimes in sight of the refugees, sailed away empty. Even if all these boats had got through, however, they could not have evacuated everyone who wanted to leave. For there were somewhere between 12,000 and 15,000 people crammed onto the quayside at Alicante. Had the boats got through, however, well

did not extend to other leading members of the Defence Council such as General Miaja or the anarcho-syndicalist leader Cipriano Mera.

[97] The Defence Junta (except Miaja, who had already left) made its last broadcast from Madrid – with the approval of the Francoist authorities – on the evening of 27 March. Casado appealed for calm and clemency.

[98] The British government argued that this was the logical result of its recognition of Franco's legitimacy on 27 February. But it was also an eery replication of the military rebels' own inversion of legality in July 1936 whereby the Republicans themselves became 'the insurgents': see British cabinet minutes cited in Bahamonde Magro and Cervera Gil, *Así terminó la guerra de España*, p. 479.

[99] The British-owned merchant ship the *Stanbrook* took off about 2,000 refugees on 28 March. (Higher figures (up to 3,200) are sometimes given. But these seem unlikely as the ship was less than 1,000 tons.) The exact circumstances in which these refugees were accepted remain unclear. Maybe the master was bribed; maybe he was sympathetic to the refugees' plight. But it is unlikely that he was following company policy. The British government assumed that Franco would overlook the activities of the occasional merchant ship.

over half could have been rescued. As it was, it has been estimated that in the entire month of March the total number of evacuations from the centre-south zone was between 7,000 and 7,500. But this figure includes the 3,200 naval officers and ratings who reached Bizerta.[100] So it seems unlikely that more than around 4,000 refugees managed to get out of Alicante port at the end.

The fifth column gained control in Alicante before the arrival of the first Francoist forces. These troops were Italians commanded by General Gambara. The committee representing the refugees in the port attempted to secure his agreement that the port area be considered a neutral zone under international (consular) protection until the evacuation could be effected.[101] But Franco, unsurprisingly, refused to accept this. The rapid arrival by boat of more Spanish troops saw the gradual evacuation of the port as many refugees left landwards. By the night of 31 March about 2,000 remained on the quayside. This was the night of the Spanish Republic's last stand. Some opted for suicide. For the rest the concentration camps awaited.[102]

THE WAR AFTER THE WAR

From the start Franco had demanded of Casado unconditional surrender. Indeed, the Generalísimo even choreographed the final stages to reinforce the symbolism of absolute victory. All contacts with the Defence Council were broken off on 25 March in order for Franco to initiate his final offensive. Yet there was no military necessity for this. In the event there was little Republican resistance. But even in risking further bloodshed (including on his own side) Franco was effectively making clear his subsequent political intentions.

---

[100] Bahamonde Magro and Cervera Gil, *Así terminó la guerra de España*, p. 499. I am grateful to Michael Alpert for providing figures on the Republican Navy.

[101] This committee included the socialists Carlos Rubiera and Gómez Ossorio, former and (in March 1939) current civil governors of Madrid respectively, and both members of the pro-Casado PSOE executive elected in Madrid during the last days. Both would be shot by Franco. Graham, *Socialism and War*, p. 242.

[102] There is a growing literature on both concentration camps and Francoist prisons. See, for example, F. Moreno Gómez, *Córdoba en la posguerra (la represión y la guerrilla, 1939–1950)* (Cordoba: Francisco Baena Editor, 1987); V. Gabarda, *Els afusellaments al País Valencià (1938–1956)* (Valencia: Edicions Alfons el Magnànim, 1993); M. Núñez Díaz-Balart and A. Rojas Friend, *Consejo de guerra. Los fusilamientos en el Madrid de la posguerra (1939–1945)* (Madrid: Compañía Literaria, 1997); T. Cuevas, *Prison of Women: Testimonies of War and Resistance in Spain 1939–1975* (Albany, N.Y.: SUNY, 1998); Richards, *A Time of Silence*; C. Mir, *Vivir es sobrevivir. Justicia, orden y marginación en la Cataluña rural de posguerra* (Lleida: Milenio, 2000); R. Vinyes, '"Nada os pertenece…" Las presas de Barcelona, 1939–1945', *Historia Social*, 39 (2001), 49–66.

By ending the war through military action rather than parley, Franco reinforced the point made by his consistent refusal to offer any remotely defined guarantees to the defeated.[103] The Republicans would not be collectively recognised in any way as a legitimate interlocutor since this could be perceived as giving them rights or claims. Unconditional victory, not reconciliation, was Franco's aim. The new Spain would be made in the image of the victors and only of the victors. But nor had Franco been prepared to let the defeated go. He had blocked all evacuation attempts – except in the specific case of Casado. If Franco would not recognise the defeated or let them leave, then clearly he can only have had in mind blanket punishment – or 'penitence', as it was termed in the regime's own discourse.[104] What this meant, however, is the beginning of another story, and one that locates 1940s Spain in a broader European context of ongoing civil war.

These European civil wars, as this book began by outlining, had erupted in the aftermath of the Great War of 1914–18 in the heat of unresolved tensions and anxieties stemming from the vast processes of industrialisation and urbanisation occurring in uneven fashion across the European continent. Exacerbated by the inter-war crises of economy, polity and socio-cultural identity, these civil wars would run on into the overarching conflict of 1939–45. In Spain too, there would be ongoing irregular warfare throughout the 1940s as Republican guerrillas opposed the regime in a conscious effort to merge with the broader struggle being fought across Europe against the Nazi new order.[105]

The 'resolution' of all these civil wars would exact a terrible price. For the reconstruction of society and polity and the remaking of European 'nations' would happen, in Spain and elsewhere, through large-scale executions and the mass imprisonment of compatriots. In short, the recasting of power across Europe occurred through the creation of categories of the anti-nation and of non-persons deprived of civil rights. Precisely how (and when) 'the other' was constituted would depend on the

---

[103] For all Negrín's aspirations, however, nor would a formal set of written guarantees have assured the rights of the defeated. In a very similar situation after the Greek Civil War, the conservative victors agreed an amnesty. But they then manipulated its conditions in order to criminalise virtually the entire political opposition. For the Greek case – which closely parallels the Spanish experience – see M. Mazower (ed.), *After the War was Over: Reconstructing the Family, Nation and State in Greece 1943–1960* (Princeton, N.J.: Princeton University Press, 2000).

[104] That this punishment was intended to be blanket rather than exemplary can also be inferred from Franco's lack of interest in Casado's attempts to seek the extradition of Negrín to Spain: Bahamonde Magro and Cervera Gil, *Así terminó la guerra de España*, p. 456.

[105] There is a massively expanding literature on the guerrilla. See most recently F. Moreno Gómez, *La resistencia armada contra Franco. Tragedia del maquis y la guerrilla* (Barcelona: Crítica, 2001).

specific historical and cultural location. But whether Jew, Slav, enemy of the people, communist, Republican, urban worker, or the all-embracing Francoist epithet, 'red', the function and effects would be the same. So when Franco issued his famous dispatch of 1 April 1939, declaring the war to be over,[106] in fact only one phase – that of conventional military conflict – had ended. The Spanish Civil War itself still had years, indeed decades, to run.[107]

---

[106] 'On this day, with the capture and disarming of the Red Army, the National troops have achieved their final military objectives. The war is over. Burgos, 1 April 1939 – Year of Victory.' ('En el día de hoy, cautivo y desarmado el Ejército rojo, han alcanzado las tropas nacionales sus últimos objetivos militares. La guerra ha terminado. Burgos 1 de abril de 1939 – Año de la Victoria.') Franco's final war dispatch, published in *A B C* (Seville), 2 April 1939 and reproduced in Díaz-Plaja, *La guerra de España en sus documentos*, p. 509.

[107] It is obviously highly problematic to extrapolate the nature of any post-victory Republican state, given that this moves us into the realm of counterfactual speculation. We do know that the Republic represented a set of liberal and constitutional political values – indeed an ethic – which opposed the principles and values of Francoist Spain. However imperfect Republican liberalism (as I have pointed out, Spanish democracy was in its infancy when it was forced to fight a *total* war), this ethic was real, not a 'façade'. Nevertheless, we cannot extrapolate an entire Republican practice from such ideals and values. Conservative commentators have long tended to suggest – either implicitly or explicitly – that the big question is how severe the Republic's 'inverse' repression of Spain's affluent classes and elite groups would have been. But the supposition that such repression would occur does not square with the judicial history of the wartime Republic. The Tribunal de Responsabilidades Civiles was also relatively inactive, and the Negrín government refused to dismiss state employees purely on grounds of their political opinions or past political affiliations (referred to in chapter 6 above). Moreover, as this account has implied, the violence of the wartime Republican state (in the form of imprisonment and work brigades, but also work/factory discipline) tended to be far more in evidence as an instrument in the reconstruction of political, economic, social and cultural hierarchies. It was directed at controlling the Republican masses – not elite groups or 'conservative Spaniards'. In this respect at least there were some common concerns with the Franco regime (as indicated, for example, in chapter 5 above, p. 283, n. 120) – even though Republican constitutionality always supposed a crucial qualitative difference. There is an interesting (anonymous) attempt to wrestle with these questions in the Azaña material lodged in the Archivo de Barcelona. It is entitled 'Utópico plan de gobierno' and is contained in an envelope marked 'particular y reservado para S.E. Divulgaciones de un loco' (n.d.) in Archivo Particular de Manuel Azaña (Apartado 7) *caja* 133, *carpeta* 16.

I think that the key question with regard to a post-war Republican state is rather different from the one usually posed. Although it is hard to answer, what we have to ask is how Republican post-war reconstruction policies would in practice have affected Spain's urban and rural popular classes and, in particular, working-class sectors. How much of the integral liberal project (or, to put it more basically, how much welfare spending) could have been afforded by the Republic? For without it (or with little of it) the highest material cost of reconstruction would have been borne, as it was under Franco, by the urban and rural working classes. This, in turn, raises the question of how popular belief in, or commitment to, a Republican social contract could have survived the harsh economic consequences of such a peace. In other words, while the Republic's survival as a democracy would have depended on its finding a means of mediating relatively harsh economic policies, the Franco regime never faced this problem. In overtly excluding huge numbers of urban and rural workers (as the 'defeated', the 'reds' or 'anti-Spain') from its definition of the national community, it acquired an ideological justification for their economic exploitation in the name of 'national rebirth'.

Glossary

Only terms used repeatedly in the text are included here. Others are explained when they arise, either in the main text or in the relevant footnote. An asterisk indicates that the term also features in the glossary.

Africanistas – the officers who commanded Spain's colonial troops in Morocco

ANV – Acción Nacionalista Vasca, a non-confessional and politically liberal minority that split off from the PNV* at the end of 1930

Association of Anti-fascist Women (AMA) – one of the mass Popular Frontist organisations promoted by the Spanish Communist Party (PCE*)

Bloc Obrer i Camperol (BOC) (Workers and Peasants Bloc) (*see also* POUM*) – a leninist party based in Catalonia and with a strong Catalan nationalist component

CADCI (Centre Autonomista de Dependents del Comerç i de la Industria) – Barcelona shop and office workers' union

Carabineros – customs and frontier police

Carlists – originally a rival monarchist faction in the early nineteenth century, Carlism was a brand of Catholic traditionalism attracting mainly rural Spaniards who wanted to abolish the dominant developments of the modern age which they saw as enshrined in the Second Republic. Based in Navarre, the Carlists opposed the Republic from the start and supported the military rising in July 1936, contributing militia fighters known as the *requetés**

CEDA (Confederación Española de Derechas Autónomas/Spanish Confederation of Right Wing Groups) – a nationwide mass Catholic party formed in 1933

426

cenetista – member of the CNT*

checa – a private prison. The different political groups (but especially PCE* and CNT*) set these up in the coup-induced aftermath of Republican state collapse in July 1936. As state power was reconstructed, so these were eradicated – although not completely until after the moments of high political tension in May 1937 when some private interrogation centres reappeared, usually under the auspices of the PCE*

CNT (Confederación Nacional del Trabajo) – anarcho-syndicalist labour union founded in 1910

Comintern – the Communist (or Third) International

Ertzaina – Basque police

españolista – adjective referring to a vehemently centralist Spanish nationalism exalting all things Castilian

Esquerra Republicana de Catalunya (ERC) – Catalan Republican Left (a coalition which included Estat Català* and the Rabassaires*)

Estat Català – radical Catalan nationalist party

FAI (Federación Anarquista Ibérica) – anarchist federation founded in 1927 with the ostensible aim of defending core anarchist principles in the CNT*

faísta – member of the FAI*

Falange – Spanish Fascist Party

fifth column – the name given to those engaging in pro-rebel activity (i.e. spying and various forms of sabotage) within the Republican zone

Fifth Regiment (Quinto Regimiento) – the military unit of the Spanish Communist Party (PCE*), which served as a training unit and model of militarised discipline for the Republican militia

FNTT – socialist landworkers' federation and a constituent union of the UGT*

FOUS – POUM* trade union that joined the UGT* in 1936

Generalitat – Catalan regional government established by the autonomy statute of 1932

GEPCI (Gremis i Entitats de Petits Comerciants i Industrials) – UGT-affiliated Federation of Small Traders and Manufacturers, founded by the PSUC* at the start of the war.

Gudari(s) – Basque soldier(s)

incontrolables – literally the 'uncontrollable ones' – a term coined to describe the perpetrators of killings and violent acts in the period of Republican state paralysis following the military coup. Implicit in the use of the term is the notion that 'revolutionary' violence was often a cover for all manner of less exalted motivations, including common crimes

Izquierda Comunista – the small, dissident Left Communist party led by Andreu Nin which amalgamated with the BOC* in September 1935 to form the POUM*

Izquierda Republicana – Left Republican party (led by Manuel Azaña)

Juventudes Libertarias (JJ LL) the anarcho-syndicalist youth organisation

Juventudes Socialistas Unificadas (JSU) – the united socialist-communist youth federation initiated in April 1936 and by November 1936 (with the siege of Madrid) entirely in the political orbit of the Spanish Communist Party (PCE*)

ley de fugas – extra-judicial murder carried out by the Spanish police against those in custody and particularly prevalent in Barcelona during 1920–2 when General Martínez Anido was Civil Governor. Prisoners would be 'released' and then shot while 'attempting to escape'

libertarian movement (libertarians) – alternative term used to describe the anarcho-syndicalist movement (CNT*, FAI* and JJ LL*)

mando único – single political-military command which the wartime Republican coalition wanted to achieve in emulation of the rebels the better to prosecute the war, but also as a reflection of certain political preferences which sought the reconstruction of the liberal state

MAOC (Milicias Antifascistas Obreras y Campesinas) – the pre-war militia of the Spanish Communist Party (PCE*). It constituted the nucleus of the Fifth Regiment*

miliciana – militiawoman

miliciano – militiaman

NKVD – Soviet intelligence service

oligarchy – state ruled (directly or indirectly) by a small, exclusive group, or, by derivation, this group itself. In Spain this elite was constituted by a senior partner – the large landowners – and by a junior one – the industrial bourgeoisie

ORGA – Galician nationalist and republican party
OVRA – political police/intelligence service of Fascist Italy

paseo – the extra-judicial killings carried out in the aftermath of the July 1936 coup (literally, the 'stroll' taken to death)
patria chica (literally, 'the little country') – village or neighbourhood, the lived unit of experience to which loyalty is primarily owed/felt
PCE – the official Spanish Communist Party, affiliated to the Communist International (Comintern*)
PNV – Basque Nationalist Party
POUM – dissident Communist Party formed in September 1935 by the merger of BOC* with the leninist groupuscule, Izquierda Comunista*. The POUM's base was overwhelmingly Catalan and constituted by BOC cadres
poumista – member of the POUM*
PSOE – Spanish Socialist Party, founded in 1879
PSUC – United Socialist Party of Catalonia, formed in July 1936 from the merger of four small parties of which the most important was the social democratic and Catalanist USC (Unió Socialista de Catalunya)

Rabassaires – Catalan tenant farmers' and smallholders' association incorporated into the Esquerra* and the special power base of Esquerra leader, Luis Companys
regulares – indigenous troops from Spanish Morocco, commanded by Spanish officers (the Africanistas*)
Republican(s) – denotes all those who supported the Republic during the civil war of 1936–9
republican(s) – denotes members of specifically republican parties and groups
requetés – Carlist* militia

saca – the removal from gaol and extra-judicial murder of prisoners
SIM (Servicio de Investigación Militar) – Republican military police/intelligence service established in August 1937
STV – Basque Nationalist trade union (recruiting from ethnic Basque urban workers)

Tercio de Extranjeros (tercios) – Spanish Foreign Legion
tránsfuga – someone who abandons one political organisation for another (more emotively, a political renegade)

treintismo/treintistas – moderate syndicalist sectors (from Catalonia and the Valencia region) which split from the CNT in 1931–2 because of opposition to what was seen as the damage being done to the organisation by the violent direct action of the FAI*

Tribunales Populares – the Popular Courts established by the Republic in August 1936 in order to curtail extra-judicial violence and as a stepping stone to the reconstruction of liberal juridical norms

ugetista – member of the UGT*

UGT (Unión General de Trabajadores) – socialist-led trade union founded in 1888, traditionally strongest in Madrid and in the Asturian mining and Basque industrial zones

Unión Republicana (Republican Union) – a centrist republican party formed in 1934 when the more liberal wing split from Lerroux's Radical Party over its collusion with the CEDA*

Workers' Alliance (Alianza Obrera) – a failed initiative (of the BOC*) in 1934 to create a nationwide alliance of trade unions and left political parties

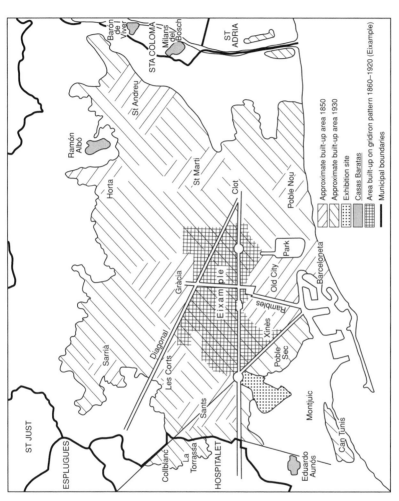

Map 3 Barcelona: urban development since 1850
(Plan drawn by Nick Rider and reproduced with his kind permission)

Legend:
- Approximate built-up area 1850
- Approximate built-up area 1930
- Exhibition site
- Casas Baratas
- Area built-up on gridiron pattern 1860–1920 (Eixample)
- Municipal boundaries

ST JUST
ESPLUGUES
Collblanc
La Torrassa
HOSPITALET
Eduardo Aunós
Can Tunis
Montjuic
Sarrià
Diagonal
Les Corts
Sants
Poble Sec
Xinès
Ramblas
Old City
Barceloneta
Park
Eixample
Gràcia
Horta
Ramón Albó
St Marti
Clot
Poble Nou
St Andreu
STA COLOMA
Barón de Viver
Milans del Bosch
ST ADRIA

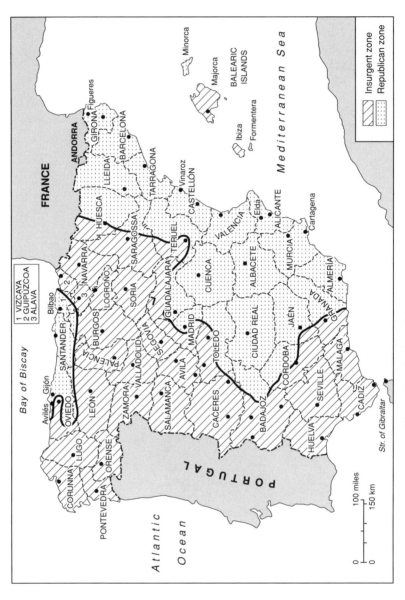

Map 4 The division of Spanish territory March 1937

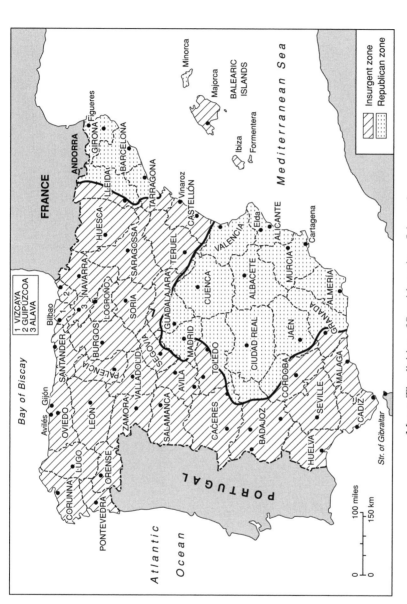

Map 5 The division of Spanish territory, July 1938

Bibliography

PRIMARY SOURCES

ARCHIVES

Archivo Histórico Nacional (Madrid) (archives of Marcelino Pascua and Luis
  Araquistain) (AHN/MP) (AHN/LA)
Archivo Histórico Nacional (Sección Guerra Civil) (Salamanca) (AHN-SGC)
Archivo del Ministerio de Asuntos Exteriores (Archivo de Barcelona) (AB)
Archivo del PCE
Fundación Pablo Iglesias (FPI) (Madrid) (Archivo Histórico de Moscú,
  (PSOE/UGT)) (AHM)
Public Records Office
Quaker Archive (Friends Service Council (Spain), Friends House, London)
  (FSC/R/Sp)

MICROFILMED ARCHIVAL MATERIAL

Southworth Collection (University of California)
Blodgett Collection

NEWSPAPERS

Adelante (Valencia)
Claridad (Madrid)
La Correspondencia de Valencia
Frente Rojo (Valencia/Barcelona)
Mundo Obrero (Madrid)
El Socialista (Madrid and Barcelona)
Solidaridad Obrera (Barcelona)
Spain and the World (London)
Treball (Barcelona)
La Vanguardia (Barcelona)

In facsimile

Milicia Popular (Diario del Quinto Regimiento) (fascsimile edition, Barcelona: Editorial Hacer, 1977) (comprises 151 issues from 26 July 1936 to 24 January 1937 when the Quinto Regimiento was incorporated in the new Republican Army under construction)

SECONDARY SOURCES

UNPUBLISHED DOCTORAL THESES

Ealham, C., 'Policing the Recession: Unemployment, Social Protest and Law-and-Order in Barcelona 1930–1936' (University of London, 1995)

Gómez, M. T., 'El largo viaje/The Long Journey: The Cultural Politics of the Communist Party of Spain 1920–1939' (McGill University, Montreal, 1999)

Montero, E., 'The Forging of the Second Spanish Republic: New Liberalism, the Republican Movement and the Quest for Modernisation 1898–1931' (University of London, 1989)

Schauff, F., 'Sowjetunion, Kommunistische Internationale und Spanischer Bürgerkrieg 1936–1939' (University of Cologne, 2000)

CONTEMPORARY PRINTED SOURCES/CONTEMPORARY MEMOIRS

Abad de Santillán, D., *Por qué perdimos la guerra*, Buenos Aires: Editorial Imán, 1940

Acier, M. (ed.), *From Spanish Trenches: Recent Letters from Spain*, London: The Cresset Press, 1937

Aguirre, J. A., *Veinte años de gestión del Gobierno Vasco (1936–1956)*, Paris, 1956

Alonso, B., *La flota republicana y la guerra civil de España. Memorias de su Comisario general*, Mexico: n.p., 1944

Alvarez del Vayo, J., *Freedom's Battle*, London: Heinemann, 1940

Bahamonde, A., *Un año con Queipo: memorias de un nacionalista*, Barcelona: Ediciones Españolas, n.d. [1938]

Bertrán Güell, F., *Preparación y desarrollo del alzamiento*, Valladolid: Librería Santarén, 1939

Buckley, H., *Life and Death of the Spanish Republic*, London: Hamish Hamilton, 1940

Bullejos, J., *Europa entre dos guerras 1918–1945*, Mexico: n.p., 1945

Canel, J. (pseud.), *Octubre rojo en Asturias*, Madrid: Agencia General de Librería y Artes Gráficas, 1935

Carrillo, W., *El último episodio de la guerra civil española*, Toulouse: Secretaría de Publicaciones JSE, 1945

'En torno al trágico fin de nuestra guerra', *Timón*, (Buenos Aires), Nov. 1939

Casado, S. *The Last Days of Madrid*, London: Peter Davies, 1939

Cowles, V., *Looking for Trouble*, London: Hamish Hamilton, 1941

Cox, G., *Defence of Madrid*, London: Victor Gollancz, 1937
Cuevas (Colonel), *Recuerdos de la Guerra de España*, Montauban: n.p., 1940
Delaprée, L., *Mort en Espagne*, Paris: Eds Pierre Tisné, 1937
Documentos políticos para la historia de la república española, Mexico City: Colección Málaga, 1945
Domínguez, E., *Los vencedores de Negrín*, Mexico: Nuestro Pueblo, 1940
Epistolario Prieto y Negrín. Puntos de vista sobre el desarrollo y consecuencias de la guerra civil española, Paris: Imprimerie Nouvelle, 1939
Fidalgo, P., *A Young Mother in Franco's Prisons*, London: United Editorial, 1939
Fischer, L., *Men and Politics*, London: Jonathan Cape, 1941
Foxa, A. de, *Madrid de corte a cheka*, San Sebastián: Librería Internacional, 1938
Franco in Barcelona, London: United Editorial, 1939 (the (anonymous) author was Muriel McDiarmid, a Quaker relief worker)
Galíndez, Jesús de, *Los vascos en el Madrid sitiado*, Buenos Aires: Ed. Ekin, 1945
García Pradas, J., *Cómo terminó la guerra de España*, Buenos Aires: Editorial Imán, 1940
Garrachón Cuesta, A., *De Africa a Cádiz y de Cádiz a la España Imperial*, Cadiz: n.p., 1938
Gerahty, C., *The Road to Madrid*, London: Hutchinson, 1937
Gorkín, J., *Caníbales políticos*, Mexico, 1941
Hanighen, F. C., *Nothing but Danger*, New York: NTC, 1939
Jellinek, F., *The Civil War in Spain*, London: Victor Gollancz, 1938
Jordan, P., *There Is No Return*, London: Cresset Press, 1938
Knickerbocker, H. R., *The Siege of the Alcazar*, London: Hutchinson, 1937
Knoblaugh, H. E., *Correspondent in Spain*, London/New York: Sheed & Ward, 1937
Koestler, A., *Spanish Testament*, London: Victor Gollancz, 1937
Largo Caballero, Francisco, *La UGT y la guerra. Discurso en el cine Pardiñas de Madrid*, Valencia, n.p., 1937
Lizarra, A. de, *Los vascos y la República española*, Buenos Aires: Ekin, 1944
Lojendio, L. M. de, *Operaciones militares de la guerra de España 1936–1939*, Barcelona: Montaner y Simón, 1940
López Fernández, A., *Defensa de Madrid*, Mexico: Editorial A. P. Márquez, 1945
Lunn, A., *Spanish Rehearsal*, London: Hutchinson, 1937
Martín Blázquez, J., *I Helped to Build an Army*, London: Secker and Warburg, 1939
Matthews, H. L., *Two Wars and More to Come*, New York, Carrick & Evans, 1938
Maurín, J., *Hacia la segunda revolución*, Barcelona: n.p., 1935
Mola, E., *Obras completas*, Valladolid: Librería Santarén, 1940
Mora, C. de la, *In Place of Splendor. The Autobiography of a Spanish Woman*, New York: Harcourt, Brace & Co., 1939
Morón, G., *Política de ayer y política de mañana*, Mexico: n.p., 1942
Núñez Morgado, A., *Los sucesos de España vistos por un diplomático*, Buenos Aires, 1941
Paul, E., *The Life and Death of a Spanish Town*, New York: Random House, 1937

Prieto, I., *Cómo y por qué salí del Ministerio de Defensa Nacional. Intrigas de los rusos en España*, Paris: n.p., 1939
Discursos en América, Mexico: Ediciones de la Federación de Juventudes Socialistas de España, n.d. [1944]
Ramón Laca, J. de, *Bajo la férula de Queipo: como fue gobernada Andalucía*, Seville: Imprenta del Diario Fe, 1939
Ruiz Vilaplana, A., *Doy fe... un año de actuación en la España nacionalista*, Paris: Editions Imprimerie Coopérative Etoile S.A., 1938
Sánchez del Arco, M., *El sur de España en la reconquista de Madrid*, Seville: Editorial Sevillana, 1937
Sanz, R., *Buenaventura Durruti*, Toulouse: Ediciones El Frente, 1945
Schlayer, F., *Diplomat in roten Madrid*, Berlin, 1938
Sheean, V., *Not Peace But a Sword*, New York: Doubleday, Doran & Co., 1939
Solano Palacio, F., *La tragedia del norte*, Barcelona, 1938
Somoza Silva, L., *El General Miaja. Biografía de un héroe*, Mexico: Editorial Tyris, 1944
Steer, G. L., *The Tree of Gernika*, London: Hodder and Stoughton, 1938
Torrent García, M., *¿Qué me dice Usted de los presos?*, Alcalá de Henares, Talleres Penitenciarios, 1942
Uribarri, M., *La quinta columna española*, vol. 1, Havana: n.p., 1943
El SIM de la República, Havana: n.p., 1943
Vázquez Ocaña, F., *Pasión y muerte de la segunda República española*, n.p.: Editorial Norte, 1940?
Whitaker, J. T., *We Cannot Escape History*, New York: Macmillan, 1943
'Prelude to World War: A Witness from Spain', *Foreign Affairs*, 21 (1) (October 1942)
Woolsey, G., *Death's Other Kingdom*, London: Longmans, Green & Co., 1939
Worsley, T. C., *Behind the Battle*, London: Robert Hale, 1939

BOOKS AND ARTICLES (INCLUDING PROTAGONISTS' MEMOIRS WRITTEN/PUBLISHED LATER)

AA.VV., *La iglesia católica y la guerra civil española. Cincuenta años después*, Madrid: Fundación Friedrich Ebert/Instituto Fe y Secularidad, 1990
Abella, R., *La vida cotidiana durante la guerra civil. La España republicana*, Barcelona: Planeta, 1975
Finales de enero 1939. Barcelona cambia de piel, Barcelona: Planeta, 1992
Abramson, P. and A., *Mosaico roto*, Madrid: Compañía Literaria, 1994
Aguilar, P., *Memoria y olvido de la guerra civil española*, Alianza, Madrid, 1996
Aguirre, J. A., *De Guernica a Nueva York pasando por Berlín*, Buenos Aires: Editorial Vasca Ekin, 1944
El informe del Presidente Aguirre al gobierno de la República (sobre los hechos que determinaron el derrumbamiento del frente del Norte), Bilbao: Editorial La Gran Enciclopedia Vasca, 1978
Diario de Aguirre, Navarre: Txalaparta, 1998

Alba, V., *Historia de la segunda república española*, Mexico: Libro Mex, 1960

El marxismo en España 1919–1939. Historia del B.O.C. y del P.O.U.M., 2 vols., Mexico: Costa-Amic, 1973

Dos revolucionarios: Joaquín Maurín, Andreu Nin, Madrid: Seminarios y Ediciones, 1975

La revolución española en la práctica. Documentos del POUM, Madrid: Ediciones Júcar, 1977

Alba, V. and Ardevol, M. (eds), *El proceso del P.O.U.M. Documentos judiciales y policiales*, Barcelona: Ediciones Lerna, 1989

Alba, V., Durgan A., Gabriel, P. *et al.*, *Andreu Nin i el socialisme*, Barcelona, 1998

Alba, V. and Schwartz, S., *Spanish Marxism Versus Soviet Communism: A History of the POUM*, New Brunswick/Oxford: Transaction Books, 1988

Alcaraz, R., *La Unió Socialista de Catalunya 1923–1936*, Barcelona: La Magrana, 1987

Alcofar Nassaes, J. L., *Los asesores soviéticos en la guerra civil española*, Barcelona: Dopesa, 1971

Alexander, M. S. and Graham, H. (eds), *The French and Spanish Popular Fronts. Comparative Perspectives*, Cambridge: Cambridge University Press, 1989

Alexander, R., *The Anarchists in the Spanish Civil War*, 2 vols., London: Janus, 1999

Alfaya, J. L., *Como un río de fuego. Madrid 1936*, Barcelona: Ediciones Internacionales Universitarias, 1998

Alía Miranda, F., *La guerra civil en la retaguardia, Ciudad Real (1936–1939)*, Ciudad Real: Diputación de Ciudad Real, 1994

Almendros, J., *Situaciones españolas: 1936/1939. Vivencias del que fue Secretario Militar del PSUC*, Barcelona: Dopesa, 1976

Alpert, M., *La reforma militar de Azaña (1931–1933)*, Madrid: Siglo XXI, 1982

La guerra civil español en el mar, Madrid: Siglo XXI, 1987

El ejército republicano en la guerra civil, 2nd edn, Madrid: Siglo XXI, 1989

A New International History of the Spanish Civil War, Basingstoke: Macmillan, 1994

'La diplomacia inglesa y el fin de la guerra civil española', *Revista de Política Internacional* (Madrid) (March–April 1975)

'Juan Negrín e Inglaterra', *Boletín Institución Libre de Enseñanza*, 24–5 (December 1996)

Altaffaylla Kultur Taldea, *Navarra 1936. De la esperanza al terror*, 2 vols., Tafalla: author-editor, 1992

Alted, A., Egido, A. and Mancebo, M. F. (eds), *Manuel Azaña: pensamiento y acción*, Madrid: Alianza, 1996

Alvarez, S., *Memorias II. La guerra civil de 1936/1939*, A Coruña: Ediciós do Castro, 1986

Osorio-Tafall. Su personalidad, su aportación a la historia, A Coruña: Ediciós do Castro, 1992

Juan Negrín. Personalidad histórica, 2 vols., Madrid: Ediciones de la Torre, 1994

Historia política y militar de las Brigadas Internacionales, Madrid: Compañía Literaria, 1996

Alvarez del Vayo, J., *The Last Optimist*, London: Putnam & Co., 1950

Alvarez Junco, J., *El emperador del Paralelo. Lerroux y la demagogia populista*, Madrid: Alianza, 1990

La ideología política del anarquismo español (1868–1910), 2nd edn, Madrid: Siglo XXI, 1991

Ambou, J., *Los comunistas en la resistencia nacional republicana. La guerra en Asturias, el País Vasco y Santander*, Madrid: Editorial Hispamerca, 1978

Andrade, J., *Apuntes para la historia del PCE*, Barcelona: Fontamara, 1979

La revolución española día a día, Barcelona: Nueva Era, 1979

Notas sobre la guerra civil. Actuación del POUM, Madrid: Ediciones Libertarias, 1986

Ansó, M., *Yo fui ministro de Negrín*, Barcelona: Planeta, 1976

Araquistain, L., *Sobre la guerra civil y en la emigración*, Madrid: Espasa-Calpe, 1983

Ardiaca, P., *La fundació del PSU de Catalunya*, Barcelona, 1986

Arenillas, J. M., *The Basque Country. The Nationalist Question and the Socialist Revolution*, Barcelona, 1937; reprinted by Leeds ILP, 1970

Arias Velasco, J., *La hacienda de la Generalitat 1931–1938*, Barcelona: Ariel, 1977

Arnaiz, A., *Retrato hablado de Luisa Julián*, Madrid: Compañía Literaria, 1996

Arnal, J., *Yo fui secretario de Durruti. Memorias de un cura aragonés en las filas anarquistas*, Zaragoza: Mira Editores, 1995

Arnau, R., *Marxisme català i qüestió nacional catalana, 1930–1936. Textos de dirigents i militants* (vol. 1); *Textos de moviments i partits polítics* (vol. 2), Paris: Edicions Catalanes de Paris, 1974

Aróstegui, J. (ed.), 'Violencia y política en España', *Ayer* (Madrid), 13 (1994)

Aróstegui, J., Calleja, E. G. and Souto, S., 'La violencia política en la España del siglo XX', *Cuadernos de Historia Contemporánea*, 22 (2000)

Aróstegui, J. and Martínez, J. A., *La Junta de Defensa de Madrid*, Madrid: Comunidad de Madrid, 1984

Avilés, Farré, J., *Pasión y farsa. Franceses y británicos ante la guerra civil española*, Madrid: Eudema, 1994

La fé que vino de Moscú. La revolución bolchevique y los españoles 1917–1931, Madrid: Biblioteca Nueva/UNED, 1999

'Francia y la guerra civil española: los límites de una política', in *Espacio, tiempo y forma*, Serie V, 5 (Madrid: UNED, 1992)

Aya, R., *Rethinking Revolutions and Collective Violence. Studies on Concept, Theory and Method*, Amsterdam: Het Spinhuis, 1990

Azaña, M., *Los españoles en guerra*, 3rd edn, Barcelona: Crítica, 1982

Causas de la guerra de España, Barcelona: Crítica, 1986

Apuntes de memoria y cartas, ed. Enrique Rivas, Valencia: Pre-Textos, 1990

Obras completas, vols. 3 and 4 (Madrid: Ediciones Giner, 1990)

Discursos Parlamentarios, ed. J. Paniagua Fuentes, Madrid, 1992

Azcárate, M., *Derrotas y esperanzas. La República, la guerra civil y la resistencia*, Barcelona: Tusquets Editores, 1994

Azcárate, P. de, *Mi embajada en Londres durante la guerra civil española*, Barcelona: Ariel, 1976

Azzuz Hakim, M. I., *La actitud de los moros ante el alzamiento. Marruecos 1936*, Malaga: Editorial Algazara, 1997

Bahamonde Magro, A. and Cervera Gil, J., *Así terminó la guerra de España*, Madrid: Marcial Pons, 1999

Balcells, A., *Crisis económica y agitación social en Cataluña de 1930 a 1936*, Barcelona: Ariel, 1971

Trabajo industrial y organización obrera en la Cataluña contemporánea 1900–1936, Barcelona: Laia, 1974

'El socialismo en Cataluña hasta la guerra civil', in S. Juliá (ed.), *El Socialismo en las nacionalidades y regiones*, Anales de Historia, vol. 3, Madrid: Fundación Pablo Iglesias, 1988

Balfour, S., *The End of the Spanish Empire 1898–1923*, Oxford: Clarendon Press, 1997

Balfour, S., and Preston, P. (eds), *Spain and the Great Powers*, London: Routledge, 1999

Ballbé, M., *Orden público y militarismo en la España constitucional (1812–1983)*, Madrid: Alianza, 1983

Ballester, R., *La batalla del Ebro*, Barcelona: Bruguera, 1974

Baquero Gil, G., *Laboratorio de retaguardia (Diario de la guerra en Madrid 1936–1939)*, Madrid, 1997

Bar, A., *La CNT en los años rojos. Del sindicalismo revolucionario al anarcosindicalismo (1910–1926)*, Madrid: Akal, 1981

Barber, J. and Harrison, M., *The Soviet Home Front 1941–1945*, Harlow: Longman, 1991

Barcelona any zero (1939) (història gràfica de l'ocupació de la ciutat), Barcelona: Proa, 1999

Bardavío, J., *Sábado Santo Rojo*, Madrid: Ediciones Uve, 1980

Barral, C., *Años de penitencia*, 1975; Barcelona: Tusquets, 1990

Barranquero Texeira, E., *Málaga entre la guerra y la posguerra*, Malaga: Editorial Arguval, 1994

Barrio Alonso, A., *Anarquismo y anarcosindicalismo en Asturias (1890–1936)*, Madrid: Siglo XXI, 1988

Barrull Pelegrí, J., *Violència popular i justícia revolucionària. El Tribunal Popular de Lleida (1936–1937)*, Lleida: Pagès editors, 1995

Bateman, D., *Joaquín Maurín 1893–1973. Life and Death of a Spanish Revolutionary*, Leeds: Leeds ILP, 1974

Bayo, A., *Mi desembarco en Mallorca*, 1944; Majorca: Miquel Font, 1987

Bedmar González, A., *Lucena: de la segunda república a la guerra civil*, Cordoba: n.p., 1998

República, guerra y represión. Lucena 1931–1939, Lucena: Ayuntamiento de Lucena, 2000

Ben-Ami, S., *The Origins of the Second Republic in Spain*, Oxford: Oxford University Press, 1978

Benavides, M. D., *Guerra y revolución en Cataluña*, Mexico: Ediciones Roca, 1978

Benet, J., *La mort del President Companys*, Barcelona: Edicions 62, 1998

Bengoechea, S., *Organització patronal i conflictivitat social a Catalunya. Tradició y corporativisme entre finals del segle i la dictadura de Primo de Rivera*, Barcelona: l'Abadia de Montserrat, 1994

Vuitanta-quatre dies de lock-out a Barcelona, 1919–20. Els precedents de la dictadura de Primo de Rivera, Barcelona: Curial: 1998

Beramendi, J. G. and Maíz, R. (eds), *Los nacionalismos en la España de la II República*, Madrid: Siglo XXI, 1991

Bernad, E. and Forcadell, C. (eds), *Historia de la Unión General de Trabajadores en Aragón. Un siglo de cultura sindical y socialista*, Zaragoza: Institución 'Fernando el Católico'/Diputación de Zaragoza, 2000

Bernecker, W. L., *Colectividades y revolución social. El anarquismo en la guerra civil española, 1936–1939*, Barcelona: Crítica, 1982

Berneri, C., *Guerra de clases en España 1936–1937*, Barcelona: Tusquets Editores, 1977

Biglino, P., *El socialismo español y la cuestión agraria 1890–1936*, Madrid: Ministerio de Trabajo y Seguridad Social, 1986

Bizcarrondo, M., 'Democracia y revolución en la estrategia socialista de la Segunda República', *Estudios de Historia Social*, 16–17 (1981)

Blanco Escolá, C., *Franco y Rojo. Dos generales para dos Españas*, Barcelona: Editorial Labor, 1993

Blanco Rodríguez, J. A., *El quinto regimiento en la política militar del P.C.E. en la guerra civil*, Madrid: UNED, 1993

Blinkhorn, M., *Carlism and Crisis in Spain 1931–1939*, Cambridge: Cambridge University Press, 1975

(ed.), *Spain in Conflict 1931–1939*, London: Sage, 1986

Bolloten, B., *The Spanish Civil War. Revolution and Counterrevolution*, Hemel Hempstead: Harvester/Wheatsheaf, 1991

(De les) bombes a l'exili (exhibition catalogue), Gandía: CEIC Alfons el Vell, 2001

Bonamusa, F., *El Bloc Obrer i Camperol (1930–1932)*, Barcelona: Curial, 1974

Andreu Nin y el movimiento comunista en España, Barcelona: Anagrama, 1977

Bookchin, M., *The Spanish Anarchists. The Heroic Years*, New York: Free Life Editions, 1977

Borja de Riquer, *El último Cambó 1936–1947*, Barcelona: Grijalbo, 1997

Borkenau, F., *The Spanish Cockpit*, London: Faber & Faber, 1937; London: Pluto Press, 1986

Borrás, J., *Aragón en la revolución española*, Barcelona: César Viguera, 1983

Bosch Sánchez, A., *Ugetistas y libertarios. Guerra civil y revolución en el País Valenciano, 1936–1939*, Valencia: Institució Alfons el Magnànim, 1983

Botti, A., *Cielo y dinero. El nacionalcatolicismo en España (1881–1975)*, Madrid: Alianza Universitaria, 1992

Bowers, C., *My Mission to Spain*, London: Victor Gollancz, 1954

Boyd, C., *Praetorian Politics in Liberal Spain*, Chapel Hill: University of North Carolina Press, 1979

Brademas, J., *Anarcosindicalismo y revolución en España (1930–1937)*, Barcelona: Ariel, 1974

Braojos Garrido, A., Alvarez Rey, L. and Espinosa Maestre, F., *Sevilla 36: sublevación fascista y represión*, Seville: Muñoz Moya y Montraveta, 1990

Brenan, G., *The Spanish Labyrinth*, 1943; Cambridge: Cambridge University Press, 1990

Personal Record 1920–1972, London, 1974; New York: Alfred A. Knopf, 1975

Bricall, J. M., *Política econòmica de la Generalitat (1936–1939)*, 2nd edn, Barcelona: Edicions 62, 1978

Broué, P., *Staline et la révolution. Le cas espagnol (1936–1939)*, n.p.: Editions Fayard, 1993

Broué, P., Fraser, R. and Vilar, P., *Metodología de la guerra y la revolución españolas*, Barcelona: Fontamara, 1982

Broué, P. and Témime, E., *The Revolution and the Civil War in Spain*, London: Faber & Faber, 1972

Buchanan, T., *The Spanish Civil War and the British Labour Movement*, Cambridge: Cambridge University Press, 1991

Britain and the Spanish Civil War, Cambridge: Cambridge University Press, 1997

Bueno Madurga, J. I., *Zaragoza 1917–1936. De la movilización popular y obrera a la reacción conservadora*, Zaragoza: Institución 'Fernando el Católico'/ Diputación de Zaragoza, 2000

Bueso, A., *Recuerdos de un cenetista*, 2 vols., Barcelona: Ariel, 1976, 1978

Bullejos, J., *La Comintern en España*, Mexico: n.p., 1972

Cabanellas, G., *La guerra de los mil días*, 2 vols., Buenos Aires: Grijalbo, 1973

Cabezas, J. A., *Asturias: catorce meses de guerra civil*, Madrid: G. del Toro, 1975

Cabrera, M., *La patronal ante la II República. Organizaciones y estrategia. 1931–1936*, Madrid: Siglo XXI, 1983

Calder, A., *The Myth of the Blitz*, London: Pimlico, 1991

Callahan, W. J., *Church, Politics and Society in Spain 1750–1874*, Cambridge, Mass.: Harvard University Press, 1984

Calleja, J. J., *Yagüe: un corazón al rojo*, Barcelona: Editorial Juventud, 1963

Caminal, M., *Joan Comorera. Catalanisme i socialisme, 1913–1936*, vol. 1, Barcelona: Empúries, 1984

Joan Comorera, Antología, ed. Miquel Caminal, Barcelona: La Magrana, 1987

Cañellas, C. et al., *Història de la presó Model de Barcelona*, Lleida: Pagès, 2000

Carabantes, A. and Cimorra, E., *Un mito llamado Pasionaria*, Barcelona: Planeta, 1982

Cárcel Orti, V., *La persecución religiosa en España durante la Segunda República (1931–1939)*, Madrid, 1990

Cardona, G., *El poder militar en la España contemporánea hasta la guerra civil*, Madrid: Siglo XXI, 1983

Carr, E.H., *The Twilight of the Comintern*, London: Macmillan, 1982

The Comintern and the Spanish Civil War, London: Macmillan, 1984

Carr, R., *The Civil War in Spain 1936–39*, London: Weidenfeld & Nicolson, 1986

Carrasquer, F., *Las colectividades de Aragón*, Barcelona: Laia, 1986

Carrillo, S., *Memorias*, Madrid: Planeta, 1993; 6th edn, 1994

La Segunda República. Recuerdos y reflexiones, Barcelona: Plaza & Janés, 1999

Carroll, P. N., *The Odyssey of the Abraham Lincoln Brigade. Americans in the Spanish Civil War*, Stanford, Calif.: Stanford University Press, 1994
Casado, S., *Así cayó Madrid*, 1968; repr. Madrid: Ediciones 99, 1977
Casanova, J., *Caspe 1936–1938. Conflictos políticos y transformaciones sociales durante la guerra civil*, Zaragoza: Institución Fernando el Católico, 1984
Anarquismo y revolución en la sociedad rural aragonesa 1936–1938, Madrid: Siglo XXI, 1985
De la calle al frente. El anarcosindicalismo en España (1931–1939), Barcelona: Crítica, 1997
'Anarchism and Revolution in the Spanish Civil War: The Case of Aragon', *European History Quarterly*, 17 (1987)
'Anarchism, Revolution and Civil War in Spain: The Challenge of Social History', *International Review of Social History*, 37 (1992)
'Guerra civil ¿lucha de clases?: el difícil ejercicio de reconstruir el pasado', *Historia Social*, 20 (1994)
'Civil Wars, Revolutions and Counterrevolutions in Finland, Spain and Greece (1918–1949): A Comparative Analysis', *International Journal of Politics, Culture and Society*, 13 (3) (2000)
(ed.), *El sueño igualitario. Campesinado y colectivizaciones en la España republicana 1936–1939*, Zaragoza: Institución Fernando el Católico, 1988
Casanova, J. et al., *El pasado oculto. Fascismo y violencia en Aragón 1936–1939*, 2nd edn, Zaragoza: Mira Editores, 1999
Casas de la Vega, R., *El terror: Madrid 1936*, Madrid: Editorial Fénix, 1994
Seis generales de la guerra civil. Vidas paralelas y desconocidas, Madrid: Editorial Fénix, 1998
Castell, E., Falcó, L., Hernàndez, X., Junqueras, O., Luque, J. C. and Santacana, J., *La batalla de l'Ebre. Història, paisatge, patrimoni*, Barcelona: Pòrtic, 1999
Castells, A., *Las brigadas internacionales de la guerra de España*, Barcelona: Ariel, 1974
Casterás, R., *Las JSUC: ante la guerra y la revolución (1936–1939)*, Barcelona: Nova Terra, 1977
Castilla del Pino, C., *Pretérito imperfecto. Autobiografía*, Barcelona: Tusquets Editores, 1997
Castro Delgado, E., *Mi fe se perdió en Moscú*, Barcelona: Luis de Caralt, 1964
Hombres made in Moscú, Barcelona: Luis de Caralt, 1965
Catalunya i la guerra civil (1936–1939), Barcelona: L'Abadia de Montserat, 1988 (various authors)
Cattell, D. T., *Soviet Diplomacy and the Spanish Civil War*, Berkeley, Calif.: University of California Press, 1957
Communism and the Spanish Civil War, New York: Russell and Russell, 1965
Caudet, F., *Las cenizas del Fénix. La cultura española en los años 30*, Madrid: Ediciones de la Torre, 1993
Cazorla Sánchez, A., *Las políticas de la victoria. La consolidación del Nuevo Estado franquista (1938–1953)*, Madrid: Marcial Pons, 2000
Cebrian, C., *Estimat PSUC*, Barcelona, 1997

Cenarro, A., *El fin de la esperanza. Fascismo y guerra civil en la provincia de Teruel 1936–1939*, Teruel: Diputación Provincial de Teruel, 1996
Cruzados y camisas azules. Los orígenes del franquismo en Aragón 1936–1945, Zaragoza: Prensas Universitarias de Zaragoza, 1997
Cervera, J., *Madrid en guerra. La ciudad clandestina 1936–1939*, Madrid: Alianza, 1998
Chamorro, V. *Historia de Extremadura* (6 vols., Madrid: Victor Chamorro, n.d., [1985])
Chaves Palacios, J., *La represión en la provincia de Cáceres durante la guerra civil (1936–1939)*, Cáceres: Universidad de Extremadura, 1995
La guerra civil en Extremadura, 2nd edn, Cáceres, 1997
Violencia política y conflictividad social en Extremadura. Cáceres en 1936, n.p.: Diputación de Badajoz/Diputación de Cáceres, 2000
Chiapuso, M., *El gobierno vasco y los anarquistas. Bilbao en guerra*, San Sebastián: Editorial Txertoa, 1978
Christie, S., *We, the anarchists! A Study of the Iberian Anarchist Federation (FAI) 1927–1937*, Hastings: The Meltzer Press/Jura Media, 2000
Cierva, R. de la, *1939. Agonía y victoria*, Barcelona: Planeta, 1989
Cifuentes Chueca, J. and Maluenda Pons, P., *El asalto a la República. Los orígenes del franquismo en Zaragoza (1936–1939)*, Zaragoza: Institución 'Fernando el Católico', 1995
Cimorra, E., *España en las trincheras*, Madrid: Editorial Nuestro Pueblo, 1938
Claudín, F., *The Communist Movement. From Comintern to Cominform*, Harmondsworth: Penguin, 1975
Santiago Carrillo: crónica de un secretario general, Barcelona: Planeta, 1983
Cobb, C., *Los milicianos de la cultura*, Bilbao: Universidad del País Vasco, 1994
'The Educational and Cultural Policy of the Popular Front Government in Spain 1936–9', in M. S. Alexander and H. Graham (eds), *The French and Spanish Popular Fronts. Comparative Perspectives*, Cambridge: Cambridge University Press, 1989
Cobo Romero, F., *La guerra civil y la represión franquista en la provincia de Jaén (1936–1950)*, Jaén: Diputación de Jaén, 1993
Conflicto rural y violencia política, Jaén: Universidad de Jaén/Universidad de Granada, 1998
'El voto campesino contra la II República. La derechización de los pequeños propietarios y arrendatarios agrícolas jiennenses 1931–1936', *Historia Social*, 37 (2000)
Coll, J. and Pané, J., *Josep Rovira. Una vida al servei de Catalunya i del socialisme*, Barcelona: Ariel, 1978
Collier, G. A., *Socialists of Rural Andalusia*, Stanford: Stanford University Press, 1987
Collins, L. and Lapierre D., *Or I'll Dress You in Mourning*, London: Weidenfeld & Nicolson, 1968
Comin Colomer, E., *Historia del Partido Comunista de España*, 3 vols., Madrid: Editora Nacional, 1967

Contreras, M., *El PSOE en la II República. Organización e ideología*, Madrid: CIS, 1981

Corbin, J. R., *The Anarchist Passion. Class Conflict in Southern Spain 1810–1965*, Newcastle upon Tyne: Avebury, 1993

Corbin, J., 'An Anthropological Perspective on Violence', *International Journal of Environmental Studies*, 10 (1977)

Cordón, A., *Trayectoria*, Paris: Colección Ebro, 1971

Cortada, J. W. (ed.), *A City in War: American Views on Barcelona and the Spanish Civil War 1936–1939*, Wilmington: Scholarly Resources, 1985

Costa Vidal, F., *Villena durante la guerra civil 1936–1939*, Alicante, 1998

Costello, J. and Tsarev, O., *Deadly Illusions*, London: Century, 1993

Crome, L., 'Walter (1897–1947): A Soldier in Spain', *History Workshop Journal*, 9 (Spring 1980)

Cruells, M., *Mayo sangriento. Barcelona 1937*, Barcelona: Editorial Juventud, 1970

L'expedició a Mallorca. Any 1936, Barcelona: Editorial Juventud, 1971

La societat catalana durant la guerra civil, Barcelona: Edhasa, 1978

Cruz, R., *El Partido Comunista de España en la II República*, Madrid: Alianza, 1987

Pasionaria, Madrid: Biblioteca Nueva, 1999

Cruz, R., '¡Luzbel vuelve al mundo! Las imágenes de la Rusia y la acción colectiva en España', in R. Cruz and M. Pérez Ledesma (eds.), *Cultura y movilización en la España contemporánea*, Madrid: Alianza, 1997

Cuadernos de la guerra civil, *Los sucesos de Mayo (1937)*, Madrid: Fundación Salvador Seguí, 1987

Las relaciones CNT-UGT, Madrid: Fundación Salvador Seguí, 1989

Las transformaciones colectivistas en la industria y los servicios de Barcelona (1936–1939), Madrid: Fundación Salvador Seguí, 1992

Cuadrat, X., *Socialismo y anarquismo en Cataluña 1890–1911*, Madrid: Revista del Trabajo, 1976

Cuesta, J. and Bermejo B. (eds), *Emigración y exilio. Españoles en Francia 1936–1946*, Madrid: Eudema, 1996

Cueva Merino, J. de la, 'El anticlericalismo en la Segunda República y la guerra civil', in E. la Parra and M. Suárez (eds), *El anticlericalismo español contemporáneo*, Madrid: Biblioteca Nueva, 1998

Cuevas, T., *Prison of Women: Testimonies of War and Resistance in Spain 1939–1975* Albany, N.Y.: SUNY, 1998

Dallin, A. and Firsov, F. I. (eds), *Dimitrov and Stalin 1934–1943. Letters from the Soviet Archives*, New Haven: Yale University Press, 2000

Déak, I., Gross, J. and Judt, T. (eds.) *The Politics of Retribution in Europe. World War II and its Aftermath* (Princeton: Princeton University Press, 2000)

Díaz, J., *Tres años de lucha*, Toulouse, 1947; 3 vols., Barcelona: Laia, 1978

Díaz Nosty, B., *La comuna asturiana. Revolución de octubre de 1934*, Madrid: Zero, 1974

Díaz-Plaja, F., *La guerra de España en sus documentos*, Barcelona: Ediciones GP, 1969

Los grandes procesos de la guerra civil española, Barcelona: Plaza & Janés, 1997

Dolgoff, S., *The Anarchist Collectives*, New York: Free Life Editions, 1974

Doña, J., *Desde la noche y la niebla. Mujeres en la cárceles franquistas*, Madrid, 1978; 2nd edn, 1993

Durgan, A. C., *B.O.C. 1930–1936. El Bloque Obrero y Campesino*, Barcelona: Laertes, 1996

Durgan, A., 'Trotsky, the POUM and the Spanish Revolution', *Journal of Trotsky Studies*, 2 (1994)

Durruti 1896–1936, Madrid: Fundación Anselmo Lorenzo, 1996

Ealham, C., 'Anarchism and Illegality in Barcelona, 1931–7', *Contemporary European History*, 4 (2) (1995)

'La lluita pel carrer, els vendedors ambulants durant la II República', *L'Avenç*, 230 (November 1998)

'"Revolutionary Gymnastics" and the Unemployed. The Limits of the Spanish Anarchist Utopia 1931–37', in K. Flett and D. Renton (eds), *The Twentieth Century: A Century of Wars and Revolutions?*, London: Rivers Oram, 2000

Egido León, A. (ed.), *Azaña y los otros*, Madrid: Biblioteca Nueva, 2001

Ehrenburg, I., *Memoirs 1921–1941*, New York: Grosset & Dunlap, 1966

Ellwood, S., 'Spanish Newsreels 1943–1975: The Image of the Franco Régime', *Historical Journal of Film, Radio and Television* 7 (3) (1987)

Elorza, A., *La utopía anarquista bajo la Segunda República*, Madrid: Ayuso, 1973

'La estrategia del POUM en la guerra civil', in *La II Repúblic. Una esperanza frustrada* (Actas del congreso Valencia Capital de la República), Valencia: Edicions Alfons el Magnànim, 1987

'Stalinisme et internationalisme en Espagne 1931–1939', in S. Wolikow and M. Cordillot (eds), *Prolétaires de tous les pays – unissez-vous? Les difficiles chemins de l'internationalisme 1848–1956*, Dijon, 1993

Elorza, A. and Bizcarrondo, M., *Queridos camaradas. La Internacional Comunista y España 1919–1939*, Barcelona: Planeta, 1999

Escobal, P. P., *Death Row. Spain 1936*, New York/Indianapolis: Bobbs-Merrill Co., 1968

Escofet, F., *Al servei de Catalunya i la República*, Paris, 1973

Espín, E., *Azaña en el poder. El partido de Acción Republicana*, Madrid: CIS, 1980

Espinosa Maestre, F., *La guerra civil en Huelva*, Huelva: Diputación Provincial de Huelva, 1996

La justicia de Queipo. (Violencia selectiva y terror fascista en la II División en 1936) Sevilla, Huelva, Cádiz, Córdoba, Málaga y Badajoz, Seville: Centro Andaluz del Libro, 2000

Estruch, J., *Historia del P.C.E. (1920–1939)*, vol. 1, Barcelona: El Viejo Topo, 1978

Historia oculta del PCE, Madrid: Temas de Hoy, 2000

Fagen, P. W., *Exiles and Citizens. Spanish Republicans in Mexico*, Austin: University of Texas Press, 1973

Falcón, I., *Asalto a los cielos. Mi vida junto con Pasionaria*, Madrid: Temas de Hoy, 1996

Febo, G. di, *Resistencia y movimiento de mujeres 1936–1976*, Barcelona: Icaria 1979

Febo, G. di and Natoli, C. (eds), *Spagna anni Trenta. Società, cultura, istituzioni*, Milan: FrancoAngeli, 1993

Fernández, C., *Paracuellos del Jarama: Carrillo culpable?*, Argos Vergara, 1983
Fernández Santander, C., *Alzamiento y guerra civil en Galicia (1936–1939)*, 2 vols., A Coruña: Edicios do Castro, 2000
Ferrándiz Alborz, F., *La bestia contra España. Reportaje de los últimos días de la guerra española y los primeros de la bestia triunfante*, Montevideo: n.p., 1951
Figueras, J. M., *El Consell de guerra a Lluis Companys*, Barcelona: Proa, 1997
Foltz, C., Jr, *The Masquerade in Spain*, Boston: Houghton Mifflin, 1948
Fontana, J. M., *Los catalanes en la guerra de España*, Barcelona: Ediciones Acervo, 1951
Forner Muñoz, S., *Industrialización y movimiento obrero. Alicante 1923–1936*, Valencia: Institució Alfons el Magnànim, 1982
Fraser, R., *In Hiding. The Life of Manuel Cortes*, London: Allen Lane, 1972
Blood of Spain. The Experience of Civil War 1936–1939, 1979; Harmondsworth: Penguin, 1981
Fyrth, J., *The Signal was Spain. The Aid Spain Movement in Britain 1936–39*, London: Lawrence and Wishart, 1986
Gabarda, V., *Els afusellaments al País Valencià, (1938–1956)*, Valencia: Edicions Alfons el Magnànim, 1993
Gabriel, P., 'Población obrera catalana', *Estudios de Historia Social*, 32–3 (1985)
'Sindicalismo en Cataluña 1888–1938', *Historia Social*, 8 (1990)
García, C. *Las cárceles de Soledad Real. Una vida*, Madrid, Ediciones Alfaguara, 1982
García, M., *Miguel García's Story*, ed. A. Meltzer, Orkney: Cienfuegos Press, 1982
García de Consuegra Muñoz, G., López López, A. and López López, F., *La represión en Pozoblanco*, Cordoba: Francisco Baena, Editor, 1989
García Delgado, J. L. (ed.), *El primer franquismo: España durante la segunda guerra mundial*, Madrid: Siglo XX, 1989
García Durán, J., *La guerra civil española: Fuentes*, Barcelona: Crítica, 1985
García García, C., 'Aproximación al estudio de la represión franquista en Asturias: "paseos" y ejecuciones en Oviedo (1936–1952)', *El Basilisco*, 2 (6) (1990)
García Oliver, J., *El eco de los pasos*, Paris: Ruedo Ibérico, 1978
García Pradas, J., *¡Teníamos que perder!*, Madrid: G. del Toro, 1974
Garitaonandía, C. and Granja, J. L. de la (eds), *La guerra civil en el País Vasco. 50 años después*, Bilbao: Universidad del País Vasco, 1987
Garrido González, L.,*Colectividades agrarias en Andalucía: Jaén (1931–1939)*, Madrid: Siglo XXI, 1979
Gazur, E. P., *Secret Assignment. The FBI's KGB General*, London: St Ermin's Press, 2001
Gerhard, C., *Comissari de la Generalitat a Montserrat (1936–1939)*, Barcelona, L'Abadia de Montserrat, 1982
Gibaja Velázquez, J. C., *Indalecio Prieto y el socialismo español*, Madrid: Fundación Pablo Iglesias, 1995
Gibson, I., *The Assassination of Federico García Lorca*, London: W. H. Allen, 1979
Paracuellos: cómo fue, Barcelona: Argos Vergara, 1983
Queipo de Llano: Sevilla, verano del 1936, Barcelona: Grijalbo, 1986
Lorca. A Biography, London: Faber & Faber, 1989

Gil Andrés, C., *Echarse a la calle. Amotinados, huelguistas y revolucionarios. La Rioja 1890–1936*, Zaragoza: Prensas Universitarias de Zaragoza, 2000

Gil Bracero, R., *Revolucionarios sin revolución. Marxistas y anarcosindicalistas en guerra. Granada-Baza 1936–1939*, Granada, 1998

Ginard i Féron, D., *Heriberto Quiñones y el movimiento comunista en España (1931–1942)*, Palma/Madrid: Edicions Documenta Balear/Compañía Literaria, 2000

Goldman, E., *Vision on Fire*, New York: Commonground Press, 1983

Gómez Casas, J., *Los anarquistas en el Gobierno 1936–39*, Barcelona: Bruguera 1977

Gómez Ortiz, J. M., *Los gobiernos republicanos. España 1936–1939*, Barcelona: Bruguera, 1977

González, V. ('El Campesino'), *Comunista en España y antiestalinista en la U.R.S.S.*, Mexico: Editorial Guarania, n.d.

González Calleja E. and Rey, F., *El Mauser y el sufragio. Orden público, subversión y violencia política en la crisis de la Restauración, 1917–31*, Madrid: CSIC, 1999

González Echegaray, R., *La marina mercante y el tráfico marítimo en la guerra civil*, Madrid: San Martín, 1977

González Egido, L., *Agonizar en Salamanca. Unamuno, julio–diciembre 1936*, Madrid: Alianza 1986

González Martínez, C., *Guerra civil en Murcia. Un análisis sobre el poder y los comportamientos colectivos*, Murcia: Universidad de Murcia, 1999

González Portilla, M. and Garmendía, J. M., *La guerra civil en el País Vasco. Política y economía*, Madrid: Siglo XXI, 1988

Goodway, D. (ed.), *For Anarchism. History, Theory, Practice*, London: Routledge, 1989

Gorkín, J., *España. Primer ensayo de democracia popular*, Buenos Aires: Asociación argentina por la libertad de la cultura, 1961

El proceso de Moscú en Barcelona, Barcelona: Ayma, 1974

Graham, H., *Socialism and War. The Spanish Socialist Party in Power and Crisis, 1936–1939*, Cambridge: Cambridge University Press, 1991

'The Socialist Youth in the JSU', in M. Blinkhorn (ed.), *Spain in Conflict 1931–1936*, London: Sage, 1986

'Community, Nation and State in Republican Spain 1931–1938', in C. Mar-Molinero, and A. Smith (eds), *Nationalism and the Nation in the Iberian Peninsula*, Oxford: Berg, 1996

'War, Modernity and Reform: The Premiership of Juan Negrín', in P. Preston and A. MacKenzie (eds), *The Republic Besieged. Civil War in Spain 1936–1939*, Edinburgh: Edinburgh University Press, 1996

'Spain 1936. Resistance and Revolution: The Flaws in the Front', in T. Kirk and A. McElligott (eds), *Opposing Fascism. Community, Authority and Resistance in Europe*, Cambridge: Cambridge University Press, 1999

Graham, H. and Labanyi, J. (eds), *Spanish Cultural Studies. An Introduction*, Oxford: Oxford University Press, 1995

Graham, H. and Preston, P. (eds), *The Popular Front in Europe*, Basingstoke: Macmillan, 1987

Grand, A. de, *In Stalin's Shadow. Angelo Tasca and the Crisis of the Left in Italy and France 1910–1945*, Northern Illinois University Press, 1986

Granja, J. L. de la, *Nacionalismo y II República en el País Vasco*, Madrid: Centro de Investigaciones Sociológicas/Siglo XXI, 1986

República y guerra civil en Euskadi. Del Pacto de San Sebastián al de Santoña, Oñati: HAEE/IVAP, 1990

Grossi Mier, M., *La insurrección de Asturias*, 1935; Madrid: Ediciones Júcar, 1978

Guarner, V., *Cataluña en la guerra de España*, Madrid: G. del Toro, 1975

L'aixecament militar i la guerra civil a Catalunya, Barcelona, 1980

Guerra y revolución en España 1936–39, 4 vols., Moscow: Editorial Progreso, 1966–77

Guillamón, A., *The Friends of Durruti: 1937–1939*, Edinburgh: AK Press, 1996

Gullón, R., 'Justice et guerre civile: souvenir d'un procureur', in C. Serrano (ed.), *Madrid 1936–1939*, Paris: Editions Autrement, 1991

Guzmán, E. de, *La muerte de la esperanza*, Madrid: G. del Toro, 1973

Año de la Victoria (Memorias de la guerra de España), Madrid: G. de Toro, 1974

Haro Tecglen, E., *Arde Madrid*, Madrid: Temas de Hoy, 2000

Haslam, J., *The Soviet Union and the Struggle for Collective Security in Europe 1933–1939*, London: Macmillan, 1984

Hermet, G., *The Communists in Spain*, Lexington, Mass.: Lexington Books, 1974

Hernández, J., *En el país de la gran mentira*, Madrid: G. del Toro, 1974

Yo fui un ministro de Stalin, Madrid: G. del Toro, 1974

Herrmann, G., 'The Hermetic Goddess: Dolores Ibárruri as Text', *Letras Peninsulares* (Spring 1998)

Heywood, P., *Marxism and the Failure of Organised Socialism in Spain 1879–1936*, Cambridge: Cambridge University Press, 1990

Hidalgo de Cisneros, I., *Cambio de Rumbo*, Vitoria-Gasteiz: Ikusager, 2001

Hills, G., *The Battle for Madrid*, London: Vantage Books, 1976

Hofmann, B., Joan i Tous, P. and Tietz, M. (eds), *El anarquismo español y sus tradiciones culturales*, Frankfurt-on-Main/Madrid: Vervuert-Iberoamericana, 1995

Hopkins, J. K., *Into the Heart of the Fire. The British in the Spanish Civil War*, Stanford, Calif.: Stanford University Press, 1998

Howson, G., *Aircraft of the Spanish Civil War*, London: Putnam Aeronautical Books, 1990

Arms for Spain, London: John Murray, 1998

Huertas Clavería, J. M., *Obrers a Catalunya*, Barcelona: Avenc, 1982

Ibárruri, D., *En la lucha. Palabras y hechos 1936–1939*, Moscow: Editorial Progreso, 1968

El único camino, Madrid: Editorial Castalia, 1992

Iglesias, I., *La fase final de la guerra civil*, Barcelona: Planeta, 1977

Iglesias, I., Cabo, F. de and Andrade, J., *A l'entorn del centenari d'Andreu Nin 1892–1992*, Barcelona: Fundació Andreu Nin, 1993

Imágenes en guerra. Memoria estampada en la España de los años 30, Colección de J. Diazi Prosper y J. Roca Boix, Valencia, 1998

International Solidarity with the Spanish Republic 1936–1939, Moscow: Progress Publishers, 1975

Irujo, M. de, *Un vasco en el ministerio de Justicia, Memorias*, 3 vols., Buenos Aires: Editorial Vasca Ekin, 1976–9

Iturralde, J. de, *El catolicismo y la cruzada de Franco*, Bayonne, 1955

Jackson, G., *The Spanish Republic and the Civil War 1931–1939*, Princeton, N.J.: Princeton University Press, 1965

Historian's Quest, New York: Alfred A. Knopf, 1969

Jiménez de Aberasturi, L. M., 'Guerra y movilización popular en el País Vasco', in J. Aróstegui (ed.), *Historia y memoria de la guerra civil. Encuentro en Castilla y León*, Valladolid, 1988

Juliá, S., *La izquierda del PSOE (1935–1936)*, Madrid: Siglo XXI, 1977

Orígenes del Frente Popular en España 1934–1936, Madrid: Siglo XXI, 1979

Madrid, 1931–1934. De la fiesta popular a la lucha de clases, Madrid: Siglo XXI, 1984

Historia del socialismo español 1931–39 (vol. 3 of M. Tuñón de Lara (ed.), *Historia del socialismo español*, Barcelona: Conjunto Editorial, 1989)

Manuel Azaña. Una biografía política, Madrid: Alianza, 1990

'Manuel Azaña: la razón, la palabra y el poder', in V. A. Serrano and J. M. San Luciano (eds), *Azaña*, Madrid: Edascal, 1980

'Sindicatos y poder político en España', *Sistema*, 97 (July 1990)

'La doble derrota de Juan Negrín', *El País*, 26 February 1992

'Presidente por última vez: Azaña en la crisis de mayo de 1937', in A. Alted, A. Egido and M. F. Mancebo (eds), *Manuel Azaña: pensamiento y acción*, Madrid: Alianza, 1996

(ed.) *Socialismo y guerra civil, Anales de Historia*, vol. 2, Madrid: Editorial Pablo Iglesias, 1987

(ed.) 'Política en la Segunda República', *Ayer* 20, 1995

Juliá, S. et al., *Víctimas de la guerra civil*, Madrid: Temas de Hoy, 1999

Justicia en guerra (Jornadas sobre la administración de justicia durante la guerra civil española: instituciones y fuentes documentales) (Salamanca, 26–8 November 1987), Madrid: Ministerio de Cultura, 1990

Kalyvas, S. N. *The Logic of Violence in Civil War*, Madrid: Fundación Juan March, 2000

Kaplan, T., *Red City, Blue Period. Social Movements in Picasso's Barcelona (1888–1937)*, Berkeley, Calif.: University of California Press, 1992

Kelsey, G., *Anarchosyndicalism, Libertarian Communism and the State. The CNT in Zaragoza and Aragon 1930–1937*, Amsterdam: Institute for Social History, 1991

'Anarchism in Aragon during the Second Republic: The Emergence of a Mass Movement', in M. Blinkhorn (ed.), *Spain in Conflict*, London: Sage, 1986

Kemp, P., *Mine Were of Trouble*, London: Cassell, 1957

Kern, R. W., *Red Years, Black Years. A Political History of Spanish Anarchism 1911–1937*, Philadelphia: ISHI, 1978

Kisch, R., *They Shall Not Pass. The Spanish People at War 1936–9*, London: Wayland Publishers, 1974

Klehr, H. and Haynes, J. E., *The Secret World of American Communism*, New Haven: Yale University Press, 1995

Koltsov, M., *Diario de la guerra española*, Madrid: Akal, 1978

Labanyi, J., 'Women, Asian Hordes and the Threat to the Self in Giménez Caballero's *Genio de España*', *Bulletin of Hispanic Studies*, 73 (1996)

Laboa, J. M., *Iglesia e intolerancia: la guerra civil*, Madrid: Atenas, 1987

Ladrón de Guevara, M. P., *La esperanza republicana. Reforma agraria y conflicto campesino en la provincia de Ciudad Real, (1931–1939)*, n.p.: Diputación de Ciudad Real, 1993

Lama, J. M., *Una biografía frente al olvido: José González Barrero, Alcalde de Zafra en la II República*, Badajoz: private edition, 2000

Lamoneda, R., *Ramon. Lamoneda. Posiciones políticas; documentos; correspondencia*, Mexico: Roca, 1976

Lannon, F., *Privilege, Persecution and Prophecy. The Catholic Church in Spain 1875–1975*, Oxford: Clarendon Press, 1987

Lannon, F. and Preston, P. (eds), *Elites and Power in Twentieth-Century Spain. Essays in Honour of Sir Raymond Carr*, Oxford: Clarendon Press, 1990

Largo Caballero, F., *Mis recuerdos*, 2nd edn, Mexico DF: Ediciones Unidas, 1976

Escritos de la República, with introduction and notes by S. Juliá, Madrid: Fundación Pablo Iglesias, 1985

Laruelo Roa, M., *Asturias, octubre del 37 ¡el Cervera a la vista!*, 2nd edn, Gijón: Imprenta la Industria, 1998

Leval, G., *Collectives in the Spanish Revolution*, London: Freedom Press, 1975

Lincoln, B., 'Revolutionary Exhumation in Spain, July 1936', *Comparative Studies in Society and History*, 27 (2) (1985)

Líster, E., *Nuestra guerra*, Paris: Colección Ebro, 1966

Memorias de un luchador, vol. 1, Madrid: G. del Toro, 1977

Little, D., *Malevolent Neutrality. The United States, Great Britain and the Origins of the Spanish Civil War*, Ithaca/London: Cornell University Press, 1985

Litvak, L., *Musa Libertaria. Arte, literatura y vida cultural del anarquismo español (1880–1913)*, Barcelona: Antoni Bosch, 1981

Llarch, J., *La Muerte de Durruti*, Barcelona: Ediciones Aura 1973

Cipriano Mera. Un anarquista en la guerra civil española, Barcelona: Producciones Editoriales, 1977

Negrín ¡Resistir es vencer!, Barcelona: Planeta, 1985

Lloyd D., and Thomas, P., *Culture and the State*, London, Routledge: 1998

López, J., *Una misión sin importancia. Memorias de un sindicalista*, Madrid: Editorial Nacional, 1972

López Fernández, A., *General Miaja, Defensor de Madrid*, Madrid: del Toro, 1975

Lorenzo, C. M., *Los anarquistas españoles y el poder 1868–1939*, Paris: Ruedo Ibérico, 1972

Low, M. and Breá, J., *Red Spanish Notebook*, 1937; San Francisco: City Lights Books, 1979

Lozano, J., *La Segunda República. Imágenes, cronología y documentos*, Barcelona: Ediciones Acervo, 1973

Lynam, S., *The Spirit and the Clay*, Boston, Mass.: Little, Brown & Co., n.d.

Macarro Vera, J. M., *La utopía revolucionaria. Sevilla en la Segunda República*, Seville: Monte de Piedad y Caja de Ahorros de Sevilla, 1985

Socialismo, República y revolución en Andalucía (1931–1936), Seville: Universidad de Sevilla, 2000

'Causas de la radicalización socialista en la II República', *Revista de Historia Contemporánea* (Seville), 1 (Dec. 1982)

'Economía y política en el Frente Popular', *Revista de Historia Contemporánea*, 7 (1996)

Madariaga, R. M. de, 'The Intervention of Moroccan Troops in the Spanish Civil War: A Reconsideration', *European History Quarterly*, 22 (January 1992)

Maddox, R., 'Revolutionary Anti-Clericalism and Hegemonic Processes in an Andalusian Town. August 1936', *American Ethnologist*, 22 (1) (1995)

Maisky, I., *Spanish Notebooks*, London: Hutchinson & Co., 1966

Majuelo, E., *Luchas de clases en Navarra (1931–1936)*, n.p.: Gobierno de Navarra, 1989

Malefakis, E., *Agrarian Reform and Peasant Revolution in Spain*, New Haven/London: Yale University Press, 1970

Malefakis, E. (ed.), *La guerra de España 1936–1939*, Madrid: Taurus, 1996

Manent i Segimon, A. and Raventós i Giralt, J., *L'Església clandestina a Catalunya durant la guerra civil (1936–1939). Els intents de restablir el culte públic*, Barcelona: L'Abadia Montserrat, 1984

Mangini, S., *Memories of Resistance. Women's Voices from the Spanish Civil War*, New Haven/London: Yale University Press, 1995

Marichal, J., *La vocación de Manuel Azaña*, Madrid: Cuadernos para el Diálogo, 1968

El intelectual y la política, Madrid: CSIC, 1990

Márquez Rodríguez, J. M. and Gallardo Romero, J. J., *Ortiz. General sin dios ni amo*, Barcelona: Hacer, 1999

Martí Gilabert, F., *Política religiosa de la Segunda República española*, Pamplona: Eunsa, 1998

Martí Gómez, J., *La España del estraperlo (1936–1952)*, Barcelona: Planeta, 1995

Martin, B., *The Agony of Modernisation. Labor and Industrialisation in Spain*, Ithaca, N.Y.: ILR Press, Cornell University, 1990

Martin, B. F., *The Hypocrisy of Justice in the Belle Epoque*, Louisiana State University Press, 1984

Martín Ramos, J. L., *Els orígenes del Partit Socialista Unificat de Catalunya (1930–1936)*, Barcelona: Curial, 1977

Martínez Amutio, J., *Chantaje a un pueblo*, Madrid: G. del Toro 1974

Martínez Bande, J. M., *Los cien últimos días de la República*, Barcelona: Luis Caralt, 1973

Martínez Barrio, D., *Memorias*, Barcelona: Planeta, 1983

Martínez Leal, J., *República y guerra civil en Cartagena (1931–1939)*, Murcia: Universidad de Murcia, 1993

Martínez Paricio, J. I., *Los papeles del general Rojo*, Madrid: Espasa-Calpe, 1989

Martínez Saura, S., *Memorias del secretario de Azaña*, Barcelona: Planeta, 1999

Martorell, M., *Jesús Monzón. El líder comunista olvidado por la historia*, Pamplona: Pamiela, 2000

Massot i Muntaner, J., *El desembarcament de Bayo a Mallorca. Agost–Setembre de 1936*, Barcelona: L'Abadia de Montserrat, 1987

La persecució religiosa de 1936 a Catalunya. Testimoniatges a cura de J. Massot i Muntaner, Barcelona: L'Abadia de Montserrat, 1987

El Cònsol Alan Hillgarth i les Illes Balears (1936–1939), Barcelona: L'Abadia de Montserrat, 1995

Mateo Merino, P., *Por vuestra libertad y la nuestra. Andanzas y reflexiones de un combatiente republicano*, Madrid: Editorial Disenso, 1986

Matthews, H. L., *Half of Spain Died*, New York: Charles Scribner's Sons, 1973

Maura, M., *Así cayó Alfonso XIII*, Barcelona: Ariel, 1995

Maurín, J., *La revolución española*, Barcelona: Anagrama, 1977

Maurín, J., *Cómo se salvó Joaquín Maurín. Recuerdos y testimonios*, Madrid: Júcar, 1980

Mazower, M., *Inside Hitler's Greece. The Experience of Occupation 1941–44*, New Haven/London: Yale University Press, 1993

Mazower, M. (ed.) *After the War was Over. Reconstructing, the Family, Nation and State in Greece 1943–1960*, Princeton, N.J.: Princeton University Press, 2000

Meaker, G. H., *The Revolutionary Left in Spain 1914–1923*, Stanford: Stanford University Press, 1974

Meer, F. de, *El Partido Nacionalista Vasco ante la guerra de España (1936–1937)*, Barañáin-Pamplona: Eunsa, 1992

Melossi, D., *The State of Social Control. A Sociological Study of the Concepts of State and Social Control in the Making of Democracy*, Cambridge: Polity Press, 1990

Méndez, R., *Caminos inversos: vivencias de ciencia y guerra*, Mexico: Fondo Cultura Económica, 1987

Mera, C., *Guerra, exilio y cárcel de un anarcosindicalista*, Paris: Ruedo Ibérico, 1976

Mercader, L. and Sánchez, G., *Ramón Mercader. Cincuenta años después*, Madrid: Espasa Calpe, 1990

Miliband, R., *The State in Capitalist Society. The Analysis of the Western System*, London: Quartet, 1973

Mintz, F., *La Autogestión en la España revolucionaria*, Madrid: Ediciones de la Piqueta, 1977

Mintz, F. and Peciña, M., *Los amigos de Durruti, los trotsquistas y los sucesos de mayo*, Madrid: Campo Abierto, 1978

Mintz, J. R., *The Anarchists of Casas Viejas*, Chicago: University of Chicago Press, 1982

Mir, C., *Vivir es sobrevivir. Justicia, orden y marginación en la Cataluña rural de posguerra*, Lleida: Milenio, 2000

Miralles, R., *El socialismo vasco durante la II República*, Bilbao: Universidad del País Vasco, 1988

'La gran huelga minera de 1890. Los orígenes del movimiento obrero en el País Vasco', *Historia Contemporánea*, 3 (1990)

'Juan Negrín: al frente de la política exterior de la República (1937–1939)', *Historia Contemporánea*, 15 (1996)

'Paz humanitaria y mediación internacional: Azaña en la guerra', in A. Alted, A. Egido and M. F. Mancebo (eds), *Manuel Azaña: pensamiento y acción*, Madrid: Alianza, 1996

Miravitlles, J., *Episodis de la guerra civil espanyola*, Barcelona: Editorial Pòrtic, 1972

Modesto, J., *Soy del Quinto Regimiento*, Barcelona: Laia, 1978

Molins i Fábrega, N., *UHP. La insurrección proletaria de Asturias*, Madrid: Ediciones Júcar, 1977

Monjo, A., 'Militantes y afiliados cenetistas en los años treinta', in M. Vilanova (ed.), *El poder en la sociedad*, Barcelona: Antoni Bosch, 1986

Monjo, A. and Vega, C., 'La clase obrera durante la guerra civil: una historia silenciada', *Historia y Fuente Oral* 3 (1990)

Monleón, J., *El mono azul. Teatro de urgencia de la guerra civil*, Madrid: Ayuso, 1979

Monreal, A., *El pensamiento político de Joaquín Maurín*, Barcelona: Ediciones Península, 1984

Montero Moreno, A., *Historia de la persecución religiosa en España 1936–1939*, 1961; Madrid: BAC, 1999

Montiel, F. F., *Un coronel llamado Casado. Mentiras y misterios de la guerra de Stalin en España*, Madrid: Criterio, 1998

Montoliú, P., *Madrid en la guerra civil*, Madrid: Sílex, 1998

Montseny, F., *Mis primeros cuarenta años*, Barcelona: Plaza y Janés, 1987

Moradiellos, E., *Neutralidad benévola. El gobierno británico y la insurrección militar española de 1936*, Oviedo: Pentalfa, 1990

La perfidia de Albión. El gobierno británico y la guerra civil española, Madrid: Siglo XXI, 1996

'The Origins of British Non-Intervention in the Spanish Civil War: Anglo-Spanish Relations in early 1936', *European History Quarterly*, 21 (1991)

'British Political Strategy in the Face of the Military rising of 1936 in Spain', *Contemporary European History*, 1 (2) (1992)

'Appeasement and Non-Intervention: British Policy during the Spanish Civil War', in P. Catterall and C. J. Morris (eds), *Britain and the Threat to Stability in Europe 1918–45*, Leicester: Leicester University Press, 1993

'Una misión casi imposible: la embajada de Pablo de Azcárate en Londres durante la Guerra Civil (1936–1939)', *Historia Contemporánea*, 15 (1996)

Moreno de Alborán y de Reyna, F. and S., *La guerra silenciosa y silenciada. Historia de la campaña naval durante la guerra de 1936–39*, 4 vols., Madrid: Gráficas Lormo, 1998

Moreno Gómez, F., *La guerra civil en Córdoba (1936–1939)*, Madrid: Alpuerto, 1985

La resistencia armada contra Franco. Tragedia del maquis y la guerrilla, Barcelona: Crítica, 2001

Morrow, F., *Revolution and Counter-Revolution in Spain*, 1938; London: New Park Publications, 1976

Mosher, J. R., *The Birth of Mass Politics in Spain: Lerrouxismo in Barcelona 1901–1909*, New York: Garland, 1991

Munis, G., *Jalones de derrota, promesa de victoria. Crítica y teoría de la revolución española (1930–1939)*, Madrid: Zero, 1977

Nadal, A., *Guerra civil en Málaga*, Malaga, Editorial Arguval, 1984

Nadal, J., *El fracaso de la revolución industrial en España, 1814–1913*, Barcelona: Ariel, 1975

Nash, M., *Defying Male Civilisation: Women in the Spanish Civil War*, Denver, Colo.: Arden Press, 1995

Nenni, P., *La guerra de España*, in Italian, 1958; 4th edn, Mexico: Ediciones Era, 1975

Neves, M., *La Matanza de Badajoz*, Badajoz: Editorial Regional de Extremadura, 1986

Nin, A., *Los problemas de la revolución española (1931–1937)*, n.p.: Ruedo Ibérico, 1971

Por la unificación marxista, Madrid: Castellote, 1978

Socialisme i nacionalisme, Barcelona, 1985

Núñez Díaz-Balart, M., *La prensa de guerra en la zona republicana durante la guerra civil española (1936–1939)*, 3 vols., Madrid: Ediciones de la Torre, 1992

Nuñez Díaz-Balart, M. and Rojas Friend, A., *Consejo de guerra. Los fusilamientos en el Madrid de la posguerra (1939–1945)*, Madrid: Compañía Literaria, 1997

Núñez Florencio, R., *Militarismo y antimilitarismo en España 1888–1906*, Madrid: CSIC, 1990

Octubre 1934 (various authors), Madrid: Siglo XXI, 1985

Olaya, F., *El oro de Negrín*, Madrid: Ediciones Madre Tierra, 1990

Ollivier, M. and Landau, K., *Espagne. Les Fossoyeurs de la révolution sociale*, Paris: Spartacus, 1975

Orlov, A., questionnaire response (1968), *Forum für osteuropäische Ideen und Zeitgeschichte*, 4 (2000)

Ors Montenegro, M., 'La represión de guerra y postguerra en Alicante', in *Violencia política i ruptura social a Espanya (1936–1945)*, Lleida, 1994

La represión de guerra y posguerra en Alicante (1936–1945), Alicante: Instituto de Cultura Juan Gil-Albert, 1995

Ortiz Heras, M., *Violencia política en la II República (Albacete 1936–1939)*, Madrid: Siglo XXI, 1996

Ortiz Villalba, J., *Sevilla 1936. Del golpe militar a la guerra civil*, Seville: Diputación Provincial de Sevilla, 1997

Ossorio y Gallardo, A., *Vida y sacrificio de Companys*, Buenos Aires, 1943; Barcelona: Nova Terra, 1976

Oyon, J. L. (ed.), *Vida obrera en la Barcelona de entreguerras*, Barcelona: n.p., 1998

Páez-Camino Arias, F., 'Juan Negrín en nuestra historia', *Zona Abierta*, 23 (1980)

Pagès, P., *Andreu Nin: Su evolución política 1911–1937*, Bilbao: Zero, 1975

El movimiento trotskista en España (1930–1935), Barcelona: Ediciones Península, 1977

Historia del partido comunista de España, Barcelona: Hacer, 1978

456 Bibliography

Pagès i Blanch, P., *La presó Model de Barcelona. Història d'un centre penitenciari en temps de guerra (1936–1939)*, Barcelona: L'Abadia de Montserat, 1996
La guerra civil espanyola a Catalunya (1936–1939), 2nd edn, Barcelona, 1997
Pàmies, T., *Cuando éramos capitanes. Memorias de aquella guerra*, Barcelona: Dopesa, 1974
Paniagua, X., *La sociedad libertaria. Agrarismo e industrialización en el anarquismo español*, Barcelona: Crítica, 1982
Parga, C., *Antes que sea tarde*, Madrid: Compañía Literaria, 1996
Pastor Petit, D., *Espionaje. España 1936–1939*, Barcelona: Bruguera, 1977
Payne, S., *The Spanish Revolution*, London: Weidenfeld & Nicolson, 1970
Basque Nationalism, Reno, University of Nevada Press, 1975
Spain's First Democracy. The Second Republic 1931–1936, Madison: University of Wisconsin Press, 1993
Fascism in Spain 1923–1977, Madison: University of Wisconsin Press, 1999
Paz, A., *Durruti. The People Armed*, New York: Free Life Editions, 1977
Durruti en la revolución española, Madrid: Fundacion Anselmo Lorenzo, 1996
Peirats, J., *La CNT en la revolución española*, 3 vols., Paris: Ruedo Ibérico, 1971
Peiró, J., *Escrits 1917–1939*, Barcelona, Edicions 62, 1975
Trayectoria de la CNT (Sindicalismo y anarquismo), Madrid: Ediciones Júcar, 1979
Pérez-Baró, A., *30 meses de colectivismo en Cataluña*, Barcelona: Ariel, 1974
Pérez Verdú, F., *Cuando Valencia fue capital de España*, Valencia: Generalitat Valenciana, 1993
Pérez Yruela, M., *La conflictividad campesina en la provincia de Córdoba 1931–1936*, Madrid: Ministry of Agriculture, 1979
Pernau, J., *Diario de la caída de Cataluña*, Barcelona: Ediciones B, 1989
Pestaña, A., *Lo que aprendí en la vida*, Madrid, 1972
Trayectoria sindicalista, ed. A. Elorza, Madrid: Tebas, 1974
Pike, D. W., *Vae Victis! Los republicanos españoles refugiados en Francia 1939–1944*, Paris: Ruedo Ibérico, 1969
Les Français et la guerre d'Espagne 1936–1939, Paris: Presses Universitaires de France, 1975
Ponamariova, L. V., *La formación del Partit Socialista Unificat de Catalunya*, Barcelona: Icaria, 1977
Pons, S., *Stalin e la guerra inevitable 1936–1941*, Turin, 1995
Pons i Porta, J. and Solé i Sabaté, J. M., *Anarquía y República a la Cerdanya (1936–1939). El 'Cojo de Málaga' i els fets de Bellver*, Barcelona: l'Abadia de Montserrat, 1991
Porte, P. La, *La atracción del imán. El desastre de Annual y sus repercusiones en la política europea (1921–1923)*, Madrid: Biblioteca Nueva, 2001
Prados de La Escosura, L., *De imperio a nación: crecimiento y atraso económico en España 1780–1930*, Madrid: Alianza, 1988
Preston, P., *The Politics of Revenge. Fascism and the Military in Twentieth-Century Spain*, London: Unwin Hyman, 1990
Franco. A Biography, London: HarperCollins, 1993

The Coming of the Spanish Civil War. Reform, Reaction and Revolution in the Second Republic, 2nd edn, London: Routledge, 1994

Comrades, London: HarperCollins, 1999

Doves of War. Four Women of Spain, London: HarperCollins, 2002

'The Great Civil War 1914–1945', in T. C. W. Blanning (ed.), *The Oxford History of Modern Europe*, Oxford: Oxford University Press, 2000

(ed.), *Revolution and War in Spain 1931–1939*, London: Methuen, 1984

Preston, P. and Mackenzie, A. (eds), *The Republic Besieged: Civil War in Spain 1936–1939*, Edinburgh: Edinburgh University Press, 1996

Prieto, H. M., *Posibilismo libertario*, Val-de-Marne, France: n.p., 1966

Prieto, I., *Palabras al Viento*, 1942; Mexico: Ediciones Oasis, 1969

Yo y Moscú, 2nd edn, ed. de Mauricio Carlavilla, Madrid: Nos, 1960

Convulsiones de España. Pequeños detalles de grandes sucesos, 3 vols., Mexico: Ediciones Oasis 1967–9

Discursos fundamentales, Madrid: Ediciones Turner, 1975

Textos escogidos, ed. R. Miralles, n.p.: Clásicos Asturianos del Pensamiento Político, 1999

Puelles Benítez, M. de, 'El sistema educativo republicano: un proyecto frustrado', *Historia Contemporánea*, 6 (1991)

Pugliese, S. G., *Carlo Rosselli: Socialist Heretic and Antifascist Exile*, Cambridge, Mass.: Harvard University Press, 1999

Quilis-Tauriz, F., *Revolución y guerra civil. Las colectividades obreras en la provincia de Alicante 1936–1939*, Alicante: Instituto de Cultura 'Juan Gil-Albert', 1992

Quirosa-Cheyrouze y Muñoz, R., *Política y guerra civil en Almería*, Almería: Cajal, 1986

Almería 1936–37. Sublevación militar y alteraciones en la retaguardia republicana, Almería: Universidad de Almería, 1997

Radcliff, P., *From Mobilisation to Civil War. The Politics of Polarisation in the Spanish City of Gijón 1900–1937*, Cambridge: Cambridge University Press, 1996

Radosh, R., Habek, M. R. and Sevostianov, G. (eds), *Spain Betrayed. The Soviet Union in the Spanish Civil War*, New Haven/London: Yale University Press, 2001

Ragsdale, H., 'Soviet Military Preparations and Policy in the Munich Crisis: New Evidence', *Jahrbücher für Geschichte Osteuropas*, 47 (1999)

Raguer, H., *La espada y la cruz. La iglesia 1936–1939*, Barcelona: Bruguera, 1977

Salvador Rial, Vicari del Cardenal de la Pau, Barcelona: l'Abadia de Montserrat, 1993

La pólvora y el incienso. La iglesia y la guerra civil española (1936–39), Barcelona: Ediciones Península, 2001

Rama, C., *Fascismo y anarquismo en la España contemporánea*, Barcelona: Bruguera, 1979

(ed.), *Camillo Berneri: Guerra de clases en España 1936–1937*, Barcelona: Tusquets, 1977

Ramos, V., *La guerra civil (1936–1939) en la provincia de Alicante*, 3 vols., Alicante: Biblioteca Alicantina, 1974

Ranzato, G., *Lucha de clases y lucha política en la guerra civil española*, Barcelona: Anagrama, 1977

Rees, T., 'The Highpoint of Comintern Influence? The Communist Party and the Civil War in Spain', in T. Rees and A. Thorpe (eds), *International Communism and the Communist International 1919–43*, Manchester: Manchester University Press, 1998

Regler, G., *The Owl of Minerva*, London: Rupert Hart-Davis, 1959

Reig Tapia, A., *Ideología e historia. Sobre la represión franquista y la guerra civil*, Madrid: Akal, 1986

Violencia y terror. Estudios sobre la guerra civil española, Madrid: Akal, 1990

Memoria de la guerra civil. Los mitos de la tribu, Madrid: Alianza, 1999

Rey, F., *Propietarios y patronos. La política de las organizaciones económicas en la España de la Restauración, 1914–23*, Madrid: Ministerio de Trabajo y Seguridad Social, 1992

'Capitalismo catalán y golpe de Primo', *Hispania*, 168 (1988)

Richards, M., *A Time of Silence. Civil War and the Culture of Repression in Franco's Spain, 1936–1945*, Cambridge: Cambridge University Press, 1998

'Civil War, Violence and the Construction of Francoism', in P. Preston and A. MacKenzie (eds), *The Republic Besieged. Civil War in Spain 1936–1939*, Edinburgh: University of Edinburgh Press, 1996

Richards, V., *Lessons of the Spanish Revolution*, 2nd edn, London: Freedom Press, 1972

Richardson, R. D., *Comintern Army. The International Brigades and the Spanish Civil War*, Lexington: The University Press of Kentucky, 1982

Ripa, Y., 'La tonte purificatrice des republicaines pendant la guerre civile espagnole', *Identités féminines et violences politiques (1936–1946). Les cahiers de l'Institut d'Histoire du temps présent*, 31 (October 1995)

Rittersporn, G. T., *Stalinist Simplifications and Soviet Complications. Social Tensions and Political Conflict in the USSR 1933–1953*, Chur, 1991

Rivas Cherif, C. de, *Retrato de un desconocido*, Barcelona: Grijalbo, 1979

Roberts, G., 'Soviet Foreign Policy and the Spanish Civil War 1936–1939', in C. Leitz and D. J. Dunthorn (eds), *Spain in an International Context 1936–1959*, Oxford/New York: Berghahn Books, 1999

Robinson, R. H., *The Origins of Franco's Spain. The Right, The Republic and Revolution 1931–1936*, Newton Abbott: David & Charles, 1970

Rodríguez, E., *Acotaciones para la historia del POUM*, Barcelona: Fundación Andreu Nin, 1989

Rodríguez Miaja, F., *Testimonios y remembranzas. Mis recuerdos de los últimos meses de la guerra de España (1936–1939)*, Mexico: n.p., 1997

Rojas, C., *La guerra en Catalunya*, Barcelona: Plaza & Janés, 1979

Rojo, V., *Alerta los pueblos!*, 1939; Barcelona: Ariel, 1974

España heroica. Diez bocetos de la guerra española, 1942; Barcelona: Ariel, 1975

Así fue la defensa de Madrid, 1967; Madrid: Comunidad de Madrid, 1987

(Rojo) Homenaje al General Vicente Rojo en el primer centenario de su nacimiento, Sagunto: Fundación Municipal de Cultura, 1998

Romero, F., *Spain 1914–1918. Between War and Revolution*, London: Routledge, 1999

Twentieth-Century Spain. Politics and Society 1898–1998, Basingstoke: Macmillan, 1999

'Spain and the First World War: The Structural Crisis of the Liberal Monarchy', *European History Quarterly*, 25 (1995)

Romero, L., *Tres días de julio*, Barcelona: Ariel, 1967

Desastre en Cartagena, Barcelona: Ariel, 1971

El final de la guerra, Barcelona: Ariel, 1976

Romero Maura, J., *'La Rosa del Fuego'. Republicanos y anarquistas: la política de los obreros barceloneses entre el desastre colonial y la Semana Trágica 1889–1909*, Barcelona: Grijalbo, 1989

Romeu Alfaro, F., *El silencio roto: mujeres contra el franquismo*, n.p.: n.p., 1994

Rosado, A., *Tierra y libertad. Memorias de un campesino anarcosindicalista andaluz*, Barcelona: Crítica, 1979

Rosal, Amaro del, *Historia de la UGT de España 1901–1939*, 2 vols., Barcelona: Grijalbo, 1977

Ruiz, D., *Insurrección defensiva y revolución obrera. El octubre español de 1934*, Barcelona: Labor, 1988

Ruiz-Castillo Basala, J., *Funcionario republicano de reforma agraria y otros testimonios*, Madrid: Biblioteca Nueva, 1983

Sabín, J. M., *Prisión y muerte en la España de la postguerra*, Madrid: 1996

Saborit, A., *Julián Besteiro*, Buenos Aires: Losada, 1967

Sacaluga, J. A., *La resistencia socialista en Asturias 1937–1962*, Madrid, 1986

Safón, A. and Simeón Riera, J. D., *Valencia 1936–7. Una ciudad en guerra*, Valencia: n.p., 1986

Sahlins, P., *Boundaries: The Making of France and Spain in the Pyrenees*, Berkeley: University of California Press, 1989

Saiz Valdivielso, A., *Indalecio Prieto. Crónica de un corazón*, Barcelona: Planeta, 1984

Salas, N., *Sevilla fue la clave: república, alzamiento, guerra civil (1931–1939)*, 2 vols., Seville: Castillejo, 1992

Salas Larrazábal, R., *Historia del ejército popular de la república*, 4 vols., Madrid: Editora Nacional, 1973

Sánchez, J. M., *The Spanish Civil War as a Religious Tragedy*, Notre Dame, Ind.: University of Notre Dame Press, 1987

Sánchez Albornoz, N. (ed.), *The economic modernisation of Spain 1830–1930*, New York: New York University Press, 1987

Sánchez Recio, G., *Justicia y guerra en España: Los Tribunales Populares (1936–1939)*, Alicante: Instituto de Cultura 'Juan Gil-Albert', 1991

La República contra los rebeldes y los desafectos. La represión económica durante la guerra civil, Alicante: Universidad de Alicante, 1991

Los que fuimos a Madrid, Toulouse: n.p., 1969

Savater, F., *Para la anarquía. Y otros enfrentamientos*, Barcelona: Orbis, 1984

Saz Campos, I., *Mussolini contra la II República: hostilidad, conspiraciones, intervención (1931–1936)*, Valencia: Edicions Alfons el Magnànim, 1986

Schauff, F., 'Company Choir of Terror: The Military Council of the 1930s – The Red Army between the XVII and XVIII Party Congresses', *Journal of Slavic Military Studies*, 12 (2) (June 1999)

Sedwick, F., *The Tragedy of Manuel Azaña and the Fate of the Spanish Republic*, n.p.: Ohio State University Press, 1963

Seidman, M., *Workers against Work. Labor in Paris and Barcelona during the Popular Fronts*, Berkeley: University of California Press, 1991

Semprún-Maura, C., *Revolución y contrarrevolución en Cataluña (1936–1937)*, Barcelona: Tusquets, 1978

Sender Barayón, R., *A Death in Zamora*, Albuquerque: University of New Mexico Press, 1989

Serrano, C., *Final del Imperio. España 1895–1898*, Madrid: Siglo XXI, 1984

L'Enjeu espagnol: PCF et guerre d'Espagne (Paris: Messidor, 1987)

Le Tour du Peuple. Crise nationale, mouvements populaires et populisme en Espagne (1890–1910), Madrid: Casa de Velázquez, 1987

(ed.), *Madrid 1936–1939. Un peuple en résistance ou l'épopée ambiguë*, Paris: Editions Autrement, 1991

Serrano, V. A. and San Luciano, J. M. (eds), *Azaña*, Alcalá de Henares: Fundación Colegio del Rey, 1991

Servicio Histórico Militar (Col. Martínez Bande, J. M.)

La marcha sobre Madrid, Madrid: Editorial San Martín, 1968

La lucha en torno a Madrid, Madrid: Editorial San Martín, 1968

La campaña de Andalucía, Madrid: Editorial San Martín, 1969

La guerra en el norte, Madrid: San Martín, 1969

La ofensiva sobre Segovia y la batalla de Brunete, Madrid: Editorial San Martín, 1972

Nueve meses de la guerra en el Norte, Madrid: Editorial San Martín, 1980

El final de la guerra, Madrid: Editorial San Martín, 1985

La batalla del Ebro, Madrid: Editorial San Martín, 1988

La Invasión de Aragón y el desembarco en Mallorca, Madrid: Editorial San Martín, 1989

Shubert, A., *The Road to Revolution in Spain. The Coal Miners of Asturias 1860–1934*, Urbana/Chicago: University of Illinois Press, 1987

A Social History of Modern Spain, London: Unwin-Hyman, 1990

Simeón Riera, J. D., *Entre la rebelió y la tradició (Lliria durante La República y la Guerra Civil. 1931–1939)*, Valencia: Diputació de València, 1993

Simpson, A. W. B., *In the Highest Degree Odious. Detention without Trial in Wartime Britain*, Oxford: Oxford University Press, 1994

Smith, A., 'Anarchism, the General Strike and the Barcelona Labour Movement 1899–1914', *European History Quarterly*, 27 (1) (1997)

Smyth, D., 'The Politics of Asylum. Juan Negrín in 1940', in R. Langhorne (ed.), *Diplomacy and Intelligence during the Second World War*, Cambridge: Cambridge University Press, 1985

Smyth, T. M., *La CNT al País Valencià 1936–1937*, Valencia: Eliseu Climent, 1977

Solà i Gussinyer, P., *Educació i Moviment Libertari a Catalunya (1901–1939)*, Barcelona: Edicions 62, 1980

Solé Sabaté, J. M. and Villarroya, J., *L'ocupació militar de Catalunya*, Barcelona: L'Avenç, 1987
Solé i Sabaté, J. M. and Villaroya i Font, J., *La repressió a la reraguarda de Catalunya (1936–1939)*, 2 vols., Barcelona: l'Abadia de Montserrat, 1989–90
Souchy, A., *With the Peasants of Aragón*, Orkney: Cienfuegos Press, 1982
Souchy, A. *et al.*, *The May Days*. Barcelona 1937, London: Freedom Press, 1987
Southworth, H. R., *Guernica! Guernica! A Study of Journalism, Diplomacy, Propaganda and History*, Berkeley, Calif.: California University Press, 1977
El mito de la cruzada de Franco, 2nd edn, Barcelona: Plaza & Janés, 1986
Spain 1936–1939. Social Revolution and Counter Revolution, London: Freedom Press, 1990
(The) 'Spanish Civil War. The View from the Left', *Revolutionary History*, 4 (1–2) (winter 1991–2)
Starinov, I. G., *Over the Abyss. My Life in Soviet Special Operations*, New York: Ivy Books, 1995
Stein, L., *Beyond Death and Exile. The Spanish Republicans in France 1939–1955*, Cambridge, Mass.: Harvard University Press, 1979
Stone, D., 'Ontology or Bureaucracy? Hannah Arendt's Early Interpretations of the Holocaust', *European Judaism*, 32 (2) (1999)
Suárez, A., *El proceso contra el POUM*, n.p.: Ruedo Ibérico, 1974
Sueiro, D., *La flota es roja*, Barcelona: Argos Vergara, 1983
Suero Roca, M. T., *Militares republicanos de la guerra de España*, Barcelona: Península, 1981
Suero Sánchez, L., *Memorias de un campesino andaluz en la revolución española*, Madrid: Queimada Ediciones, 1982
Tagüeña Lacorte, M., *Testimonio de dos guerras*, Mexico: Ediciones Oasis, 1974
Tavera, S., 'La premsa anarco-sindicalista (1868–1931)', *Recerques*, 8 (1977)
Tavera, S. and Ucelay da Cal, E., 'Grupos de afinidad, disciplina bélica y periodismo libertario, 1936–1938', *Historia Contemporánea*, 9 (1993)
Tavera, S. and Vega, E., 'La afiliació sindical a la CRT de Catalunya: entre l'eufòria revolucionària i l'ensulsiada confederal 1931–36', in (various authors) *Revolució i Socialisme*, vol. 2, Barcelona: Universitat de Barcelona, 1990
Thomas, H., *The Spanish Civil War*, Harmondsworth: Penguin, 1977
Togliatti, P., *Opere 1935–1944*, Rome: Editorial Riuniti, 1979
Escritos sobre la guerra de España (Barcelona: Crítica, 1980)
Tortela, G., *El desarrollo de la España contemporánea. Historia económica de los siglos XIX y XX*, Madrid: Alianza Universidad, 1994
Toryho, J., *No eramos tan malos*, Madrid: G. del Toro, 1975
Townson, N., *The Crisis of Democracy in Spain. Centrist Politics under the Second Republic 1931–1936*, Brighton/Portland: Sussex Academic Press, 2000
(ed.), *El republicanismo en España (1830–1977)*, Madrid: Alianza, 1994
Tuñón de Lara, M. (ed.), *Gernika: 50 años después (1937–1987). Nacionalismo, república, guerra civil*, San Sebastián: Universidad del País Vasco, 1987
(ed.), *Los orígenes culturales de la II República*, Madrid: Siglo XXI, 1993

Tuñón de Lara, M. *et al.*, *La guerra civil española. 50 años después*, Barcelona: Labor, 1985

Tuñón de Lara, M., Miralles, R. and Díaz Chico, B. N., *Juan Negrín López. El hombre necesario*, Las Palmas: Gobierno de Canarias, 1996

Ucelay da Cal, E., *La Catalunya populista. Imatge, cultura i política en l'etapa republicana (1931–1939)*, Barcelona: La Magrana, 1982

'Socialistas y comunistas en Cataluña durante la guerra civil: un ensayo de interpretación', in S. Juliá (ed.), *Socialismo y guerra civil. Anales de Historia*, vol. 2, Madrid: Editorial Pablo Iglesias, 1987

'Cataluña durante la guerra', in E. Malefakis (ed.), *La guerra de España 1936–1939*, Madrid: Taurus, 1996

Ugarte Tellería, J., *La nueva Covadonga insurgente. Orígenes sociales y culturales de la sublevación de 1936 en Navarra y el País Vasco*, Madrid: Biblioteca Nueva, 1998

Ullman, J. Connelly, *The Tragic Week: A Study of Anticlericalism in Spain 1875–1912*, Cambridge, Mass.: Harvard University Press, 1968

Vargas, B., *Rodolfo Llopis (1895–1983) Una biografía política*, Barcelona: Planeta, 1999

Vázquez M. and Valero, J., *La guerra civil en Madrid*, Madrid: Tebas, 1978

Vázquez Montalbán, M., *Barcelonas*, London: Verso, 1992

Pasionaria y los siete enanitos, Barcelona: Planeta, 1995

Vega, C., Monjo, A. and Vilanova, M., 'Socialización y hechos de mayo', *Historia y Fuente Oral*, 3 (1990)

Vega, E., *El trentisme a Catalunya. Divergències ideològiques en la CNT (1930–1933)*, Barcelona: Curial, 1980

Anarquistas y sindicalistas durante la Segunda república. La CNT y los Sindicatos de Oposición en el País Valenciano, Valencia: Institució Alfons el Magnànim, 1987

Vega Díaz, F., 'El último día de Negrín en España', *Claves de Razón Práctica*, 22 (May 1992)

Ventín Pereira, J. A., *La guerra de la radio (1936–1939)*, Barcelona: Editorial Mitre, 1986

Vidal, C., *Las Brigadas Internacionales*, Madrid: Espasa Calpe, 1998

Vidarte, J. S., *Todos fuimos culpables*, 2 vols., Barcelona: Grijalbo 1978

Vignaux, P., *Manuel de Irujo, Ministre de la République dans la guerre d'Espagne 1936–1939*, Paris: Beauchesne, 1986

Vila Izquierdo, J., *Extremadura: la guerra civil*, Badajoz: Universitas Editorial, 1983

Vilanova, M., *Las mayorías invisibles. Explotación fabril, revolución y represión*, Barcelona: Icaria, 1996

'Anarchism, Political Participation and Illiteracy in Barcelona between 1934 and 1936', *American Historical Review*, 97 (1) (1992)

Villarroya i Font, J., *Els bombardeigs de Barcelona durant la guerra civil (1936–1939)*, 1981; 2nd edn, Barcelona: L'Abadia de Montserrat, 1999

Viñas, A., *El oro español en la guerra civil*, Madrid: Instituto de Estudios Fiscales, 1976

El oro de Moscú. Alfa y omega de un mito franquista, Barcelona: Grijalbo, 1979
Guerra, dinero, dictadura. Ayuda fascista y autarquía en la España de Franco, Barcelona: Crítica, 1984
Franco, Hitler y el estallido de la guerra civil. Antecedentes y consecuencias, Madrid: Alianza Editorial, 2001
Viñas, A., 'Gold, the Soviet Union and the Spanish Civil War', *European Studies Review*, 9 (1) (Jan. 1979)
'The financing of the Spanish Civil War', in P. Preston (ed.), *Revolution and War in Spain 1931–1939*, London: Methuen, 1984
'Las relaciones hispano-francesas, el gobierno Daladier y la crisis de Munich', *Españoles y franceses en la primera mitad del siglo XX*, Madrid: CEH-CSIC, 1986
Viñas, R., *La formación de las Juventudes Socialistas Unificadas (1934–1936)*, Madrid: Siglo XXI, 1978
Vincent, M., *Catholicism in the Second Spanish Republic. Religion and Politics in Salamanca 1930–1936*, Oxford: Clarendon Press, 1996
'The Martyrs and the Saints: Masculinity and the Construction of the Francoist Crusade', *History Workshop Journal*, 47 (1999)
Vinyes, R., *La Catalunya Internacional. El frontpopulisme en l'exemple català*, Barcelona: Curial, 1983
' "Nada os pertenece..." Las presas de Barcelona, 1939–1945', *Historia Social*, 39 (2001)
Zafón Bayo, J., *El Consejo Revolucionario de Aragón*, Barcelona: Planeta, 1979
Zaragoza, C., *Ejército popular y militares de la República (1936–1939)*, Barcelona: Planeta, 1983
Zugazagoitia, J., *Guerra y vicisitudes de los españoles*, Buenos Aires, 1940; 3rd edn, Barcelona: Crítica, 1977

NOVELS

Barea, A., *La forja de un rebelde*, 3 vols., Madrid: Turner, 1984
Bates, R., *Lean Men*, Harmondsworth: Penguin, 1934
Lewis, N., *The Day of the Fox*, London, 1957 and reprints
Malraux, A., *Days of Hope*, 1938; Harmondsworth: Penguin, 1982
Olaizola, J. L., *La guerra del General Escobar*, Barcelona: Planeta, 1983
Vázquez Montalbán, M., *El pianista*, Barcelona: Seix Barral, 1985
Wolff, M., *Another Hill*, Urbana/Chicago: University of Illinois Press, 1994

Index